RUNES AND
RUNIC INSCRIPTIONS

COLLECTED ESSAYS ON
ANGLO-SAXON AND VIKING RUNES

RUNES AND
RUNIC INSCRIPTIONS

COLLECTED ESSAYS
ON ANGLO-SAXON AND VIKING RUNES

R. I. PAGE

EDITED BY
DAVID PARSONS

WITH A BIBLIOGRAPHY BY
CARL T. BERKHOUT

THE BOYDELL PRESS

First published 1995
The Boydell Press, Woodbridge
Reprinted in paperback 1998

ISBN 0 85115 387 9 hardback
ISBN 0 85115 599 5 paperback

The Boydell Press is an imprint of Boydell & Brewer Ltd
PO Box 9, Woodbridge, Suffolk IP12 3DF, UK
and of Boydell & Brewer Inc.
PO Box 41026, Rochester, NY 14604–4126, USA

A catalogue record for this book is available
from the British Library

Library of Congress Catalog Card Number: 95–5825

This publication is printed on acid-free paper

Printed in Great Britain by
St Edmundsbury Press Ltd, Bury St Edmunds, Suffolk

CONTENTS

FOREWORD

Dear Ray,

Many people have contributed to this book. Simon Keynes from your former Department of Anglo-Saxon, Norse and Celtic in the University of Cambridge first approached the publishers with a suggestion for reprinting your *Opuscula Runologica*. Carl Berkhout has been meticulous in producing a comprehensive bibliography of your works including frivolities which you forgot you had ever written, reviews which spoke the truth in love, articles which demonstrate the depth and breadth of your scholarship, books which show your willingness to bring that scholarship to the wider world of the general reader. David Parsons has re-typed your work with scholarly precision, taking an editor's role in re-shaping conventions originally dictated by variety of requirement in different journals, and imposing as far as possible consistency of presentation throughout. But the work remains your own. We are grateful to you not only for the original articles but for all the time and thought you have given this last year to updating them, bringing new finds to bear on earlier discussion and conclusion.

We know that you would not accept a festschrift. We approve both the decision and its rationale. But we hope that you will gain pleasure from this volume, not merely because of the quality and quantity of its scholarship, but also because it represents an international recognition of you as scholar, in one specific and significant field. We know your range has been wider than this, and we could equally have produced a collection of your work on glosses or on manuscripts. We know that you have had other roles, and that the help you have given to hundreds of scholars in your capacity as Librarian of the Parker Library, Corpus Christi College, has been given unstintingly in spite of the time taken from your own work. We simply single out here what seems to us one of your major contributions to Anglo-Saxon and Norse studies in the twentieth century and as we offer it to you we also thank you with warm appreciation for having, in the first place, given it to us.

I sign this as a representative of those friends, colleagues and Persons whose wish it was to give you this seventieth birthday present, no small token of their affection and esteem.

David M. Wilson

May 1995

PREFACE

Professor R. I. Page has been working on runes, though not exclusively on runes, for most of his academic life. He began the compilation of the corpus of Anglo-Saxon runic inscriptions for his Ph.D. thesis, and had already published the important 1958 and 1959 articles reproduced in this volume even before his thesis was presented. His books on runes, one in print, the other regrettably not, are two indispensable tools for anyone teaching Anglo-Saxon epigraphy. This volume will provide the third. The corpus which needs updating in view of the many recent finds, is a publication to which we confidently look forward as the fourth.

Most of the articles in this book deal with Anglo-Saxon runes, but Page, expert in Old Norse as well as Old English, in Norse runes as well as Anglo-Saxon ones, is also an authority on the Norse runes of the British Isles. Two of the articles in this volume (1980 and 1983) deal with Norse runes in the Isle of Man, and next year we anticipate the publication by Page, together with Professors Michael Barnes and Jan Ragnar Hagland, of the Dublin runes.

It is many years since Page described himself as a sceptical rather than a romantic runologist. The recent terrifying increase of fantasy writings and cults in which runes of power flourish like green bay trees has increased also the need for scholarship and teaching in genuine runic studies, if real knowledge of the real subject is not to disappear without trace in a world where educational management puts popularity of courses above academic value. Whether Page will be more fortunate than Cnut in turning back tides remains to be seen. It is also many years since D. M. Wilson (Sir David Wilson in private life) defined the first and second laws of runo-dynamics: the first that for every runic inscription there shall be as many interpretations as there are interpreters; the second that if you don't understand it it must be magic. Page's ability to look at evidence with a clear eye unclouded by presumptions and preju- dices, to demonstrate flaws in interpretations based on assumption rather than argument, are the qualities which have brought runic scholarship in the twentieth century out of disrepute and wild imaginings. His insistence on the importance of 'field runology', of examining and understanding relationships between artefact and text, has also significantly increased the rigour of a discipline, too easily confined to 'desk runology'.

The twenty-three articles printed here span thirty-seven years. The collection is introduced by a new paper from Professor Page where he brings us up-to-date news of runic finds and applies up-to-date wisdom in matters of recent controversy. The remaining articles follow in the chronological order of their original publication. One, '*Runeukyndige risteres skriblerier*: the English Evidence', appears here for the first time. Full details of the original publications of the others will be found in the list of Page's published writings at the end of the book. This list being a substantial one, the papers here reprinted are there signalled by an asterisk.

To most of these papers Page has appended a postscript discussing evidence that has come to light and/or opinion that has been expressed in the years since he first wrote them. In addition some few observations and references have been added in square brackets to the notes and, very occasionally, minor corrections have been silently introduced to the text. Some attempt has been made to impose consistency of layout and bibliographical reference on this collection where the original publications conformed, of course, to the varying requirements of various journals, but it has not been our aim totally to update the texts in every respect. Readers should note one deliberate 'inconsistency'. Until 1984 Page transliterated Anglo-Saxon runes according to the system devised by Bruce Dickins. In his article of that year 'On the Transliteration of English Runes' he defined a modified version of Dickins's system which he has subsequently used.

We have great pleasure in recording our debts to the various people who have supported this publication. Specifically we acknowledge permission to reprint and good wishes from:

The Society for Medieval Archaeology (three articles from *Medieval Archaeology*, 1959, 1968 and 1984);

Max Niemeyer Verlag (one article from *Anglia*, 1959);

The Society for the Study of Medieval Languages and Literature (two articles from *Medium Ævum*, 1961 and 1968);

The Institute of Archaeology (one article from the *Journal of the British Archaeological Association*, 1964);

The British Numismatic Society (one article from the *British Numismatic Journal*, 1965);

The Cambridge Bibliographical Society (one article from the *Transactions of the Cambridge Bibliographical Society*, 1972–6);

The Viking Society for Northern Research (one article from the *Saga-Book of the Viking Society*, 1980, and one from the Viking Congress Proceedings volume *The Viking Age in the Isle of Man*, 1983);

The editors of *Studia Neophilologica* (one article, 1958);

The editors of *Nottingham Medieval Studies* (one article, 1960);

The editors of *English Studies* (one article, 1962);

The editors of the *Journal of English and Germanic Philology* (one article, 1962);

The Athlone Press (contribution to *Medieval Literature and Civilization: Studies in Memory of G. N. Garmonsway*, 1969);

The Cambridge University Press (contribution to the Dorothy Whitelock festschrift, 1971);

Almqvist & Wiksell Förlag AB (paper from *Runor och runinskrifter*, 1987);

Seminarie voor Engelse en Oud-Germaanse Taalkunde (contribution to the René Derolez festschrift, 1987);

Boydell and Brewer (contribution to *St Cuthbert, his Cult and his Community to AD1200*, 1989);

John Benjamins Publishing Company (Amsterdam) (paper from the Fifth International Conference on Historical Linguistics, 1990).

A special thank you goes to emeritus Professor René Derolez, elder statesperson of Anglo-Saxon runology, in whose festschrift the article 'A Sixteenth-Century Runic Manuscript' first appeared. 'Where' asks Professor Derolez, but the question is rhetorical, 'would runic studies in the British Isles stand now if it had not been for Ray?'

We also wish to acknowledge the support of four funding bodies. Professor Page's first academic post was as lecturer in the Department of English Studies of the University of Nottingham, where he is now Special Professor, and we warmly acknowledge the generous grant to offset publication costs from the Research Publications Fund administered by the Board for Postgraduate Studies of that University's Senate. Subsequently, Professor Page moved to Cambridge where it is hard to know whether his fame as Parker Librarian for Corpus Christi College eclipsed his status as Professor and Head of the Department of Anglo-Saxon, Norse and Celtic or vice versa. The Master of Corpus Christi was delighted to donate on behalf of the College 'a small token of all that Ray has achieved during his time as Librarian'. The printing has also been made possible by a gift to the University of Cambridge in memory of Dorothea Coke, Skjæret, 1951, and we are grateful to the Managers of that Fund. Finally we acknowledge the munificence of the Persons from Porlock, without whom the preparation of this volume would have been a more solemn and sober undertaking.

The portrait of Ray Page as frontispiece is taken from one that hangs in the Senior Combination Room of his college. The perceptive artist is Andrew Festing. For permission to reproduce it we are once again indebted to the Master and Fellows of Corpus Christi College, Cambridge.

And of course we have great pleasure in acknowledging the constant courtesy and support of Richard Barber of Boydell and Brewer.

Carl Berkhout
David Parsons
David Wilson

REFERENCES AND ABBREVIATIONS

The following works are generally cited by short title:

Arntz, H. and H. Zeiss, *Die einheimischen Runendenkmäler des Festlandes* (Leipzig, 1939)

Bammesberger, A., ed., *Old English Runes and their Continental Background* (Heidelberg, 1991)

Bammesberger, A. and A. Wollmann, eds, *Britain 400–600: Language and History* (Heidelberg, 1990)

Brown, G. B., *The Arts in Early England* (London, 1903–37)

Brunner, K., *Altenglische Grammatik nach der Angelsächsischen Grammatik von Eduard Sievers neubearbeitet*, 2nd ed. (Halle/Saale, 1951)

Bugge, S. and M. Olsen, *Norges indskrifter med de ældre runer* (Christiania, 1891–1924)

Campbell, A., *Old English Grammar* (Oxford, 1959)

Dahl, I., *Substantival Inflexion in Early Old English: Vocalic Stems* (Lund, 1938)

Derolez, R., *Runica Manuscripta: the English Tradition* (Brugge, 1954)

Dickins, B., 'A System of Transliteration for Old English Runic Inscriptions', *Leeds Studies in English* 1 (1932), 15–19

Elliott, R. W. V., *Runes: an Introduction* (Manchester, 1959; 2nd ed. Manchester and New York, 1989) [References are to the first edition unless specified]

Jacobsen, L. and Moltke, E., *Danmarks runeindskrifter* (Copenhagen, 1941–2)

Keary, C. F., *A Catalogue of English Coins in the British Museum: Anglo-Saxon Series* I, ed. R. S. Poole (London, 1887)

Ker, N. R., *Catalogue of Manuscripts Containing Anglo-Saxon* (Oxford, 1957)

Krause, W. and H. Jankuhn, *Die Runeninschriften im älteren Futhark* (Göttingen, 1966)

Luick, K., *Historische Grammatik der englischen Sprache* I, part i (Leipzig, 1914–21)

Okasha, E., *Hand-List of Anglo-Saxon Non-Runic Inscriptions* (Cambridge, 1971)

Olsen, M. et al., *Norges innskrifter med de yngre runer* (Oslo, 1941–)

Redin, M., *Studies on Uncompounded Personal Names in Old English* (Uppsala, 1919)

Stephens, G., *The Old-Northern Runic Monuments of Scandinavia and England, Now First Collected and Deciphered* (London and Copenhagen, 1866–1901)

Stephens, G., *Handbook of the Old-Northern Runic Monuments . . .* (London and Copenhagen, 1884)

Ström, H., *Old English Personal Names in Bede's History: an Etymological-Phonological Investigation* (Lund, 1939).

In addition, works written or co-written by R. I. Page, but not reprinted here, are abbreviated by short-title and date. Full details of them will be found in the list of his published writings at the end of the volume.

The following abbreviations are used:

ANF	*Arkiv för nordisk filologi*
APS	*Acta philologica Scandinavica*
ASE	*Anglo-Saxon England*
ASNSL	*Archiv für das Studium der neueren Sprachen und Literaturen*
ASPR	*Anglo-Saxon Poetic Records*
ASSAH	*Anglo-Saxon Studies in Archaeology and History*
BAR	*British Archaeological Reports*
BGDSL	*Beiträge zur Geschichte der deutschen Sprache und Literatur*
BNJ	*British Numismatic Journal*
EEMF	*Early English Manuscripts in Facsimile*
EETS	*Early English Texts Society* [All references are to works in the Original Series]
EPNS	*English Place-Name Society*
JEGP	*Journal of English and Germanic Philology*
MLR	*Modern Language Review*
N&Q	*Notes and Queries*
NTS	*Norsk tidsskrift for sprogvidenskap*
PBA	*Proceedings of the British Academy*
PSAL	*Proceedings of the Society of Antiquaries of London*
PSAS	*Proceedings of the Society of Antiquaries of Scotland*
SBVS	*Saga-Book of the Viking Society*
TCWAAS	*Transactions of the Cumberland and Westmorland Antiquarian and Archaeological Society*
TPS	*Transactions of the Philological Society*
TRHS	*Transactions of the Royal Historical Society*
VCH	*Victoria County History*
ZDA	*Zeitschrift für deutsches Altertum*
ZDP	*Zeitschrift für deutsche Philologie*

1

(1994)

QUONDAM ET FUTURUS

The elderly Jonathan Swift, it is said, on reading a work of his youth was driven to exclaim, 'What a genius I had when I wrote that book!' I cannot claim Swift's genius, but I share his surprise at re-reading my first articles and finding how much I have forgotten in thirty years. Many of the earlier papers in this volume concentrate on philological assessment rather than epigraphical examination, and here I must admit that, though I think the material remains valid within its own terms, the approach has been superseded or rather marginalised. In later papers I take more note of matters like literacy, textual layout, Anglo-Saxon attitudes to runic script and its relationship to roman. No doubt there is more to be done within this pattern of thought, in great part because of the cogent questions posed by that most eminent of Anglo-Saxon runologists René Derolez.

Derolez has rightly stressed two aspects of the English runic corpus: (i) the tiny, random and indeed incalculable sample that survives out of what must have been written, and (ii) the importance of viewing the epigraphical and manuscript runes as aspects of the same tradition. Of the first there can be no doubt, and any discussion must consider what proper use can be made of the small amount of material that survives. On the whole Derolez has been pessimistic; indeed one of his latest articles ends gloomily *testis unus testis nullus*.[1] Whether our gloom need be inspissated is perhaps a matter of temperament. I can see some runic circumstances where a single testimony may legitimately provoke a striking conclusion. To take an example. It has been a commonplace that the south-west and the west Midlands have no epigraphical runes. This took a bit of a jolt when the Watchfield runes appeared, from West Saxon territory bordering on Mercia – if indeed those political terms are appropriate to the date of this inscription. However, since the Watchfield text is on a portable object that could (though need not) be a traveller, it need not shake our preconceptions. A short time ago I wrote a note that concluded that towards the end of the Anglo-Saxon period runes could have been written at Worcester, but that 'knowledge of the letter forms was limited and based on manuscript rather than epigraphical use'.[2] Which coincided adequately with our prejudices; and was all very well until a runic

---

[1] R. Derolez, 'Runic Literacy among the Anglo-Saxons', *Britain 400–600*, ed. Bammesberger and Wollmann, pp. 397–436, at 432.
[2] R. I. Page, 'Runes in Two Anglo-Saxon Manuscripts' (1993), p. 18.

1

inscription turned up at Worcester. Oddly enough it was cut in the glaze of a fragment of Roman Samian ware, which ought to encourage the sceptic to recall John Brent's joyous cry, 'Rejoice! Rejoice! I have got a small piece of Samian ware . . . inscribed with six Runes!', which turned out on further examination to be cursive roman.[3] However, these Worcester graphs do appear to be runes, and the archaeological report makes it likely they are genuine. There are two fragmentary lines of characters: '] s w i þ u' (or perhaps less likely '] s w i r') and '] d i s'. It is perhaps unlikely that a group of runes cut casually on a fragment of old dish would be a traveller. Here, then, we have *testis unus* of runes inscribed at Worcester, but nobody, I hope, would claim it is *testis nullus*. The nearest other epigraphical runes to this site are from a distance, perhaps those of Leek, Staffordshire, and Bakewell, Derbyshire (both on stones), and Llysfaen, Clwyd, and Wakerley, Northamptonshire (on portable objects). The archaeological evidence for the Worcester find is unfortunately not helpful – the fragment is from the infill of a pit – so no very close date can be given to the inscription (though it is likely to be later rather than earlier). Nevertheless, the appearance of this group of runes in Worcester should make us revise our distribution maps and possibly even our opinions. The *testis unus* may have important and even plural implications. A surprising number of Anglo-Saxon runic inscriptions have been discovered in recent times, and we may expect the history of runic usage to be modified in a number of ways in coming years. As, for instance, by another *testis unus*, the newly reported find of a coin of Alberht/Æthelberht of East Anglia, a king otherwise unknown in the numismatic record. Both its legends, royal and moneyer's names, are runic.[4]

Derolez's second point, the close link between epigraphical and manuscript runes, calls for sharper scrutiny. Derolez put forward his argument in a thought-provoking paper, 'Epigraphical versus Manuscript English Runes: One or Two Worlds?' He comes down against two worlds; and concludes:

A systematic contrasting of epigraphic and manuscript runes tends to obscure more issues than it will illuminate. Inscriptions on stones and other materials, and futhorcs in manuscripts, emanate from a common stock of runic lore, and may even occasionally have been the work of one and the same person. The difference between the two media of transmission . . . is due to their different *modus operandi*, not to their springing from different sources or to their being motivated by different conceptions of the runes.[5]

Derolez supports his case in part by citing some of the most exciting runic finds of recent years: the graffiti discovered in Italy, apparently cut by English travellers to holy places. In both Monte S. Angelo, Gargano, and Rome have been found Anglo-Saxon names cut in runes, evidence of 'Anglo-Saxons with a living

[3] Below, p. 161, n. 3.
[4] M. Archibald and V. Fenwick in *British Museum Magazine* 13 (1993), p. 19. The king is little known, and only from post-Conquest sources: E. N. Fryde *et al.*, *Handbook of British Chronology*, 3rd ed. (London, 1986), p. 9.
[5] *Academiae Analecta*, Mededelingen van de Koninklijke Academie voor Wetenschappen, Letteren en Schone Kunsten van België, Klasse der Letteren 45, 1 (1983), pp. 71–93, at 92.

knowledge and practice of runic writing' who 'left traces of their activity on the Continent'.[6] This type of knowledge Derolez links, perhaps somewhat obscurely, with the Continental *runica manuscripta* which give information on English runes. We might also link it, less obscurely, with a practice so far spotted in only a few Anglo-Saxon manuscripts, of runic names scratched or cut in margins; as for instance the pair *Eþelstan, Eþeldryþ* in the St Petersburg (Leningrad) Gospels and the name fragment 'a þ i l f' in MS Corpus Christi College, Cambridge 326. (There is something of a parallel in the name [h]auarþ in Norse runes in a margin of MS CCCC 57).[7] If we then regard this as evidence that some literate Englishmen were both able and prepared to shift from roman to runic as they pleased, we can add a number of other suggestive runic marginalia in English manuscripts. Below (pp. 124–5) I have put forward the theory that odd comments in MS CCCC 41 have implications for English runic literacy. From this it follows that we need to do a thorough check of the apparently casual use of runes in manuscripts, more thorough than Derolez was able to achieve in the fifth chapter of his *Runica Manuscripta*. The contexts of runic marginalia need more detailed description. We should also be alive to the implications of some new finds of runes. David Parsons has suggested that those cut into the recessed surface of the Blythburgh writing tablet might be evidence for runic usage in some scriptorium or schoolroom context; indeed that they imply that runes were scratched in the wax surface(s) that once covered the recess. Of course, this is interpretation rather than observation though it is plausible interpretation at that.[8]

It is no surprise to learn that there were Anglo-Saxons who could cut both runic and roman scripts. This has long been evident from the bi-alphabetical inscriptions of the Falstone and certain Lindisfarne stones, not to mention from the Franks Casket and the coffin of St Cuthbert.[9] In so far as this 'does not oblige us to set up an impenetrable partition between the world of carved runes and that of manuscripts',[10] we can accept Derolez's preference of one to two worlds. But it is a simplistic preference, for there must have been rune-masters who knew runic but not roman (even if only because they were in England in the early period, before Christianity and Romanisation, and when Germanic peoples in this country were unlikely to be close students of surviving Romano-British inscriptions). I see no reason why there

---

[6] Made readily available to English readers in R. Derolez and U. Schwab, 'The Runic Inscriptions of Monte S. Angelo (Gargano)', *Academiae Analecta*, Mededelingen van de Koninklijke Academie voor Wetenschappen, Letteren en Schone Kunsten van België, Klasse der Letteren 45, 1 (1983), pp. 95–130; and R. Derolez, 'Anglo-Saxons in Rome', *Nytt om Runer* 2 (1987), 14–15. The latest find in M. G. Arcamone, 'Una nuova iscrizione runica da Monte Sant' Angelo', *Vetera Christianorum* 29 (1992), pp. 405–10. We should also note graffiti with Anglo-Saxon names in roman script at these sites.

[7] Page, 'Runes in Two Anglo-Saxon Manuscripts', p. 19. Derolez records what might be Continental examples of runic signatures in *Runica Manuscripta*, pp. 406–13.

[8] In detail in his 'Anglo-Saxon Runes in Continental Manuscripts', *Runische Schriftkultur in kontinental-skandinavischer und -angelsächsischer Wechselbeziehung*, ed. K. Düwel (Berlin and New York, 1994), pp. 195–220, at 208–10.

[9] See below, pp. 322–3.

[10] Derolez, 'Epigraphical versus Manuscript Runes', p. 80.

should not have been rural craftsmen in later times who worked in an old tradition and without taking note of roman script forms. I see no reason why runes should not have been kept distinct, by some who were perfectly conversant with the roman script, as an esoteric form of writing, perhaps asserting their local and English tradition against that of Rome. Derolez's statement that 'inscriptions on stones and other materials, and futhorcs in manuscripts, emanate from a common stock of runic lore' comes hardly as a surprise. But, to quote a parallel, Elizabethan secretary hand and its contemporary roman type-face emanate from a common stock of roman scribal lore but that does not make them identical nor does the practice of one necessarily throw light on the other. 'The difference between the two media of [runic] transmission' are indeed likely to be 'due to their different *modus operandi*' but these in turn could lead to significant differences: a small cross is easier to cut than a small parallelogram and this could produce the specialisation that distinguished epigraphical 'j' (✳) from manuscript 'j' (✦). So I am inclined to object to Derolez's choice of one world rather than two, and suggest that both figures are an underestimate, that there may have been many different permutations of runic and roman knowledge. I wonder in fact if Derolez is not knocking down a coconut he has set up himself.

As Derolez presents things he disguises the problem. Nobody, so far as I know, denies the close links between runic and roman texts, or at any rate epigraphical texts, in the later Anglo-Saxon period. The question is rather, despite their common origin, do the *fuþorcs* and alphabets of the *runica manuscripta* as preserved to us and the runic inscriptions as preserved to us embody the same tradition; or are they stemma variants descending from a single source? If indeed we can talk of the inscriptions – or the *fuþorcs* – as a single group of texts. At this point we come upon a few obstinate facts not, as far as I know, in dispute:

(a) there is one epigraphical rune that is not recorded in any extant manuscript *fuþorc*. Admittedly it occurs in only one inscription, that of the Ruthwell Cross. For all that there is a distinctive graph in that inscription, transliterated 'k̄', which appears in no manuscript list of runes, from England or the Continent. So striking and rare is it that Christopher Ball would like to sweep it away, pretending it is a variant of the 'k' rune (though based on the form of 'ḡ') used elsewhere on this stone.[11] For an allograph that has no functional purpose it is a very complex form for anyone to invent and a difficult one to cut.

(b) manuscript *fuþorcs* and alphabets may contain a few letter-forms that have not hitherto been discovered in any epigraphical texts. I have called these 'pseudo-runes' much to the horror of critics who find the element 'pseudo-' disparaging. (I am not clear why this is, for I certainly would not be thought to refer to George Eliot disparagingly simply because I used her pseudonym.) Specifically, there are the runes that are conveniently transliterated 'q' (named *cweorþ*) and 'st' (*stan*). These certainly occur in only a few manuscript accounts of runes; but they have not yet

---

[11] C. J. E. Ball, 'Problems in Early Northumbrian Phonology', *Luick Revisited: Papers read at the Luick Symposium at Schloss Liechtenstein*, ed. D. Kastovsky and G. Bauer (Tübingen, 1988), pp. 109–17, at 115–16.

appeared in inscriptions (unless you consider the St Petersburg Gospels *Eþelstan* an inscription). There is of course no need for either of these symbols in practical phonological use – Ruthwell manages perfectly well without them in such words as 'k w [o] m u' and 'g i s t o d d u [n]'. But at least 'q' fits well with the roman alphabet and is needed if you are going to insist on presenting runes in alphabetical order, as, so far, only in manuscripts.[12]

(c) there are manuscript runes from areas/times for which we have no sign of epigraphical runes. Such a region is the south-west of England. So far there has been a resounding epigraphical silence from runic Wessex, the nearest inscriptions being the very occasional early coin that may have been minted in its eastern parts, and Watchfield, early and near the Mercian border. Yet the West Saxon kingdom was not unaware of the runic script, for runes are used, for instance, in tenth-/eleventh-century manuscripts from Exeter, as the *Exeter Book* and MS CCCC 41. Are there two traditions here, an epigraphical one that rejects runes and a manuscript one that finds their worth on occasions? Or is the lack of epigraphical runes a chance effect? Can we argue *ex silentio*? After all, if *testis unus* is *testis nullus*, how much is *testis nullus* worth?

I say these details are not in dispute. But I should add 'so far'. It is always possible that a new inscription, or a new runic manuscript, will supply evidence to disprove my assertion, and this is where a major problem of our limited sample lies. A small discovery may have important effects: *testis unus* may become *testes multi*. The newly-found Brandon pin provides part of a *fuþorc* – only the second epigraphical one from Anglo-Saxon England – which has an embarrassing use of the symbol ✢ for the twelfth rune, something that hitherto has only appeared in manuscripts.[13] What new finds lie in wait for the incautious runologist?

In discussing this general topic I move on to a runic graph that hitherto has received too little notice. It too may turn out to be 'pseudish', rather as Bruce Dickins suspected many years ago. I refer to the fifteenth rune, transliterated 'x', which Dickins defined as 'a fossil in Old English. In runic *alphabets*, it is sometimes used for *x* for which a separate character was not provided in the *fuþorc*'.[14] Dickins was writing before *Runica Manuscripta* revealed the occasional attribution of the value *x* to this letter in manuscript *fuþorcs*. He knew the rune in the sacred inscription 'i h s x p s' of St Cuthbert's coffin, but did not register an important example written in MS CCCC 41 and crudely recorded by M. R. James.[15] Beonna of East Anglia's pennies with the rune in the royal title *rex* had not yet appeared. There are now three distinct cases of this graph recorded (not counting those in *fuþorcs* and alphabets).

---

[12] I exclude here the Rome fragment, since its authenticity has still to be formally established. It is most recently published in G. Franzén, 'A Runic Inscription found in Rome', *Saga och Sed* (1986), 101–8. The piece has most of an alphabet, including a graph representing *q*, but the form used for it is the Norse **k**-rune.
[13] D. Parsons, 'New Runic Finds from Brandon, Suffolk', *Nytt om Runer* 6 (1991), 8–11, at 8.
[14] Dickins, 'System of Transliteration', p. 17.
[15] M. R. James, *A Descriptive Catalogue of the Manuscripts in the Library of Corpus Christi College Cambridge* (Cambridge, 1912) I, 82.

That on St Cuthbert's coffin, dated 698, is a visual equivalent only with no phonological value: it represents the form of the Greek graph χ, chî, interpreted as Latin X.[16] The context in MS CCCC 41 (the manuscript from the later eleventh century) is 'x i i . 7 . x x x', apparently a pair of numbers, 12 + 30. Again, there is no phonological use of the letter; it represents the Roman numeral *x*. The use of 'x' on the Beonna coins is different and debatable. The obverse legends of the Beonna coins, king's name and title, are sometimes in roman, sometimes in runes, and sometimes in a mixture of the two scripts – and of course in the cases of the letters B and R there will be uncertainty as to which script is intended.[17] The few (? two dies only) which have an interlace reverse and so have no moneyer's name(s) read '· b e o n n a r e x'. Otherwise the royal title is in roman, REX, save for a group of related coins of the moneyer Efe which have the mixed REss, and a group that have an arbitrary symbol apparently indicating the whole title. How we interpret the use of 'x' on the interlace coins is a considerable problem. If REss is an attempt at the sound of the title as it was locally pronounced, then 'r e x' is not.[18] In 'r e x' the runes will then be a transliteration of the roman version of the title; that is the rune 'x' is again used not as a phonetic, but as a visual symbol. The runes are secondary to the roman in the legend.

A value *x* for this graph is recorded in occasional manuscript *fuþorcs* and alphabets, though it is not the only value given and it is clear the letter caused scribes a deal of trouble. The Anglo-Saxon rune-name is *eolhx, ilx, ilix, ilcs*, hard to account for.[19] The sound-value of the graph in earliest runic times was apparently *z* found in word endings, and it became -*R* in Primitive Norse. There is no phonological progression from these earliest uses of this rune form to what it represented in the few Anglo-Saxon epigraphical instances or in MS CCCC 41. These examples do not present a natural development of the rune and its value in Old English. They look to be an adaptation, almost a recreation, to fill a recognised gap. Such a gap would not be significant for Old English texts but might be for Latin ones transliterated into runes. As David Parsons has pointed out to me, when the consonant cluster *x* was needed for an Old English inscription on the Brandon bone handle the rune-cutter wisely cut 'h s' in 'w o h s w i l d u m d e [o] r a͡ n'.[20] There is no need of a rune *x* for English, and indeed it seems to go against Derolez's theory of the 'perfect fit' of

---

[16] See below, p. 319.

[17] Full details of these coins and their legends in M. M. Archibald, 'The Coinage of Beonna in the Light of the Middle Harling Hoard', *BNJ* 55 (1985), 10–54. I am most grateful to Miss Archibald for discussing these coins with me and for giving me information on more recently found coins of Beonna.

[18] Examining all the Beonna coins with the REss type legend I am assured that the third letter is commonly 's', though there is perhaps a single case of 'i' as Blackburn has suggested: see below, p. 144. The group 'i s' in the word *rex* is presumably parallel to 'h s' on the Brandon bone handle, discussed below.

[19] Recent discussion of the various interpretations of this name in M. Halsall, *The Old English Rune Poem: a Critical Edition* (Toronto, 1981), pp. 129–31. Further in E. Seebold, 'Die Stellung der englischen Runen im Rahmen der Überlieferung des älteren Fuþark', *Old English Runes*, ed. Bammesberger, pp. 439–569, at 534–5.

[20] Parsons, 'Finds from Brandon', p. 10. I am not sure how significant this single example is. It looks like another *testis unus*. But see note 18 above.

English runes, 'one phoneme, one grapheme'.[21] So 'x' appears to be, not a fossil as Dickins saw it, but an old graph adapted to a new use. This adaptation has all the appearance of a learned one. Whether it penetrated 'demotic' runes, runes used for the vernacular language, is an interesting question, one on which we can say nothing without more evidence. There is some similarity here to the creation of the graph 'q' which again is not needed for Old English but would be convenient in writing Latin. It is possible we shall some day come upon 'q' used epigraphically for learned material but until then it remains, as even Derolez has admitted, a 'pseudo-rune'.

The Beonna coins offer a warning against facile generalisation about the relationship of runic to roman script. In an article written in 1985 (and already rendered partly out of date by more recent finds) Marion Archibald defined the coinage of this eighth-century king. Three moneyers' names are known from the reverses, Efe, Wilred and Werferth, and there is a small group with no moneyer's name but an interlace pattern on the reverse. Archibald puts the types in chronological order based on the progressive debasement of the metal: those of Werferth, then Efe, then interlace, the latter overlapping with the final group, the coins of Wilred.[22] Efe's name is always in roman save for an occasional use of the rune 'f', and on his coins the royal name and style are either fully roman, or part roman, part runic. The Werferth examples (only one in 1985, now three, all from the same die) have the royal name and style part roman, part runic; and the moneyer's name in runes. The interlace type has the royal name and style in runic.[23] Wilred's coinage uses only runes both on obverse and reverse. At a preliminary glance, then, there seems a progressive replacement of roman by runic, which is hardly what we might expect. Needless to say, this conclusion is simplistic. In the first place, the chronological order is not absolute and exclusive. At least one all-roman Efe coin is, from its silver content, later than the part-runic coins of Werferth. Again, Beonna's coins may not have been all minted in the same place, though all are East Anglian. There could be a distinction between earlier coins, perhaps from Thetford, and later, perhaps from Ipswich.[24] So a difference of script could be regional not chronological.

However, even these objections are naive. The Beonna coins were issued over a comparatively short period of time, and it is unlikely they evidence a general progression from one writing system to another. Issuing a coinage involved several individuals: (i) the issuing authority, (?) the king in council, in the case of the interlace coins (?) an ecclesiastical power,[25] (ii) the moneyer who was responsible for the quality and weight of the coins, (iii) the die-cutter who formed the designs of obverse and reverse, (iv) the customer who accepted coins as genuine. Perhaps others. Any or all of these might influence the final design of the coinage. How far the issuing authority oversaw the design of coins is unknown. The customer was important in

---

[21] Derolez, 'Epigraphical versus Manuscript Runes', p. 75.
[22] Archibald, 'Coinage of Beonna', p. 31.
[23] Except for a recent find, which has a nonce-formation in place of the word *rex* as do the Wilred pennies.
[24] Archibald, 'Coinage of Beonna', p. 31.
[25] *Ibid.* p. 30, n. 25.

that to be convincing to a tradesman a coin must look like a coin, must have characteristics the customer recognised,[26] and that could include one or more legends. Whether the customer need be able to read or understand the legend(s) is less certain – our own coins have enough examples of abbreviations and letter sequences that are not generally understood. What the chain of command was between issuing authority and die-cutter is again unknown. Who made the decision as to what form the legend(s) should take, and by what method was it passed to the die-cutter? In writing or by word of mouth? It is possible that the variants REss and 'r e x' represent two ways of conveying the information, the first in speech, the second in writing. Might it be significant that the coins of Wilred (? the same Wilred) issued in the name of Offa of Mercia had roman legends? There are so many uncertainties here that all that can be affirmed about the scripts on Beonna's coins is that they indicate a range of acceptable letter forms available in mid-eighth-century East Anglia; and that there was no obvious difference of status or acceptability between runic and roman.

It should be clear to English runologists that the coin evidence is of the first importance; also that the runologist cannot assess its significance without the skilled help of the numismatist. To take a simple example. From the die-cutter's point of view, a significant feature would be the number of individual dies of a particular coin-type cut. From the customer's point of view it might be the number of individual coins found to derive from each known die. And of course there are likely to be mixes of dies, obverse-reverse combinations changing in no sequence we can trace. The identification of individual dies, the significance of hoard evidence in contrast to that of individual finds, the scatter of find-spots, the silver content of individual specimens, all these are matters where the runologist must take advice. He must keep in touch with the numismatic record, for new specimens keep coming to light in these metal-detecting days. He must be aware of techniques of coin production – it is no use believing that the pointed bows of the initial B on the Beonna coins indicate that the runic form is intended if the die-cutter had no tools for forming a rounded bow. On the other hand, the exact forms of the letters B, R on obverses that have sequences in roman letters ought to be compared with their corresponding forms in runic surroundings, to see if die-cutters did make conscious distinctions of letter form here. Again, the numismatist can help the runologist by his experience.

Students of runes are fortunate that over the last thirty years a number of learned numismatists have been prepared to investigate the English runic coinages. Luckily too, the line has not come to an end. Of course, some of the complexities I have drawn attention to are not confined to *numismatic* evidence. Of the formal memorial inscriptions we could equally well ask who it was who gave shape to the text, what form did it reach the stone-cutter in? Though perhaps we should not stay for an answer. With all inscriptions we should keep practical problems in mind; how were the letters cut, what tools were available, what were the constraints on the carver? In

---

[26] Miss Archibald draws to my attention the immense variety of designs in the earlier *sceat* coinage. A customer might indeed find it hard to define what characteristics of a design made an official coin recognisable as such.

8

answering such questions we face again Derolez's first point, our small sample of evidence and the consequent difficulty of establishing general principles. It is only in respect of the coins that we are likely to see a dramatic increase in material.

This makes it the more important to use fully the data we have, and it is fairly clear we have not done so up to now. I have just pointed out the need to examine more carefully the forms certain runes take on the Beonna coins – can we properly distinguish their runic 'b', 'r' from their roman B, R? Hitherto I have not tried. Indeed, I am not sure how one would define the phrase 'in runic surroundings' that I used so glibly earlier. It is certain, however, that we need a more detailed inventory of English runic forms than we have; so that they can be compared with the range of forms from other runic regions. Only thus can we isolate graphs that are characteristic of Anglo-Saxon England or of the 'Anglo-Frisian' region. I made a plea for such careful study in a paper delivered at a conference in Eichstätt in 1989. That lecture was not published until 1991,[27] so it cannot be in response that Bengt Odenstedt produced his survey of early runic forms in 1990.[28] Odenstedt's study has attracted criticism,[29] and it is not my purpose to add to it here. Instead I want to point to some consequences of his approach.

Odenstedt's intent is to define the varying forms of runic letters from the earliest records up to 750 A.D.: Scandinavian, Continental Germanic, Frisian and English. The date 750 is chosen for the convenience of Scandinavians, for about then the older *fuþark* came to be replaced by the later one. There is no parallel change in the English *fuþorc*, but Odenstedt applies the same closing date to Anglo-Saxon material, because he wants 'to make typological comparisons between *contemporary* inscriptions'.[30] This sounds methodologically rigorous enough but leads him into a wilderness of dating problems. Dating Anglo-Saxon inscriptions is notoriously hard and the eighth century is not the easiest to divide in two. Odenstedt's English catalogue is Caistor-by-Norwich, Undley, Watchfield, Chessell Down I and II, Gilton, Loveden Hill, Welbeck Hill, Dover brooch, Sandwich, Ruthwell, Bewcastle, Auzon (Franks), Thames scramasax, Monkwearmouth II, Hartlepool I and II, Falstone, Mortain. Now there is only one Anglo-Saxon runic monument that can, I think, be dated with precision and that before 750: St Cuthbert's coffin. We may ask, why is this omitted? To it can be added a fair number of coins that numismatists put confidently before 750: the 'b e n u :+: t i d i' and related tremisses, the 'd e s a i o n a' (formerly read 'd e l a i o n a') group and the 'p a d a' coins, all these given the date range *c.* 625–75 by Blackburn: and the later, *c.* 675–750, coins with forms of the legends 'æ p a', 'e p a', 'æ þ i l i r æ d', 'w i g r æ d' and 't i l b e r h t'.[31] Again all omitted from

[27] 'Anglo-Saxon Runic Studies: the Way Ahead?' (1991).
[28] B. Odenstedt, *On the Origin and Early History of the Runic Script: Typology and Graphic Variation in the Older Futhark* (Uppsala, 1990).
[29] For example, by Klaus Düwel in *Göttingische Gelehrte Anzeigen* 244 (1992), 234–41; by Henrik Williams in *ANF* 107 (1992), 192–205; replies in B. Odenstedt, 'On Graphic Variation in the Older Futhark', *Umeå Papers in English* 16 (1993).
[30] *Origin and Early History*, p. 14.
[31] M. Blackburn, 'A Survey of Anglo-Saxon and Frisian Coins with Runic Inscriptions', *Old English Runes*, ed. Bammesberger, pp. 137–89, at 169–70.

Odenstedt's list. He tells us why: 'I have had to exclude some inscriptions in the older *futhark* [and that includes the coffin and the coin runes] because good photographs or drawings of them were not available to me',[32] which is a perfectly good explanation but not a good excuse. For St Cuthbert's coffin there are the recent excellent reproductions in the 1985 conservation report of J. M. Cronyn and C. V. Horie.[33] If that was unavailable, there is the detailed account of the coffin in the monograph on the relics of St Cuthbert of 1956.[34] Much the same applies to the early coins. There is no shortage of published reproductions of many of these – to mention at random C. H. V. Sutherland's 1948 corpus of gold coins; the Fitzwilliam Museum, Cambridge, catalogue of 1986; the plates in various volumes of the British Academy's Sylloge of English coins.[35] It is certainly unfortunate if a distinguished scholar must work without primary source material like this, but the question is apposite, can Odenstedt's subject be commanded with such inadequate resources?

It is important to note some of the effects of this. St Cuthbert's coffin has texts in runes, roman and mixtures of the two; among them is the sequence 'x p s' for the Christ title. As well as having the important example of 'x', this also gives a clear case of 'p', and a form of 's', Y, which is a rarish variant. 'p' also appears in the legends of the 'æ p a', 'e p a' and 'p a d a' coins. The matter is important because of Odenstedt's suspicion of this particular rune. He finds only one example in his Old English material, from Mortain, though he mentions *en passant* the examples on the Whitby comb as well as the 'p a d a' and 'e p a' coins, describing them as 'these late inscriptions'.[36] On this basis he can suggest that the use of 'p' is 'an English innovation', primarily so that he can then identify the clear 'w' form on Watchfield as a *p*-rune.[37] Lateness in an inscription is a matter of definition. Myself I would not describe an Old English inscription of *c.* 660–70, Blackburn's dating of the earliest *Pada* coins,[38] as particularly late. If 'p' had by then become so accepted that it could be used in a semi-official context like a moneyer's name on a coin, it must have been current for some time. The graph occurs in two *fuþarks*, those of Kylver and Grumpan, from the fifth or early sixth centuries, and there are closely similar, (?) derivative, graphs in the sixth-century Breza and Charnay *fuþarks*. In these cases, of

---

[32] *Origin and Early History*, p. 17.

[33] *St. Cuthbert's Coffin: the History, Technology & Conservation* (Durham, 1985), particularly foldouts 1a and 1b.

[34] *The Relics of Saint Cuthbert*, ed. C. F. Battiscombe (Oxford, 1956), plates VII and X.

[35] C. H. V. Sutherland, *Anglo-Saxon Gold Coinage in the Light of the Crondall Hoard* (Oxford, 1948), pls I, II and IV; P. Grierson and M. Blackburn, *Medieval European Coinage with a Catalogue of the Coins in the Fitzwilliam Museum, Cambridge: I The Early Middle Ages (5th–10th Centuries)* (Cambridge, 1986), pls 31 and 32; various volumes in the series, Sylloge of Coins of the British Isles, as I, *Fitzwilliam Museum Cambridge*, part I, by P. Grierson (London, 1958), pls VII and VIII; II, *Hunterian and Coats Collections University of Glasgow*, part I, by A. S. Robertson (London, 1961), pls I and II; IV, *Royal Collection of Coins and Medals National Museum Copenhagen*, part I, by G. Galster (London, 1964), pl. II.

[36] *Origin and Early History*, p. 81.

[37] But see something of a withdrawal of this interpretation in his contribution to C. Scull, 'Excavation and Survey at Watchfield, Oxfordshire, 1983–92', *Archaeological Journal* 149 (1992), 124–281, at 249.

[38] Blackburn, 'Survey', p. 145.

course, there is no way of determining the phonetic value of the graph, though Odenstedt does not question the usual identification as a *p*-rune.[39] I think it beyond the bounds of probability to assert that there is no continuity between the earliest use of this graph, its continued use into the sixth century in *fuþarks* outside England, and its appearance on the *Pada* coins and thereafter. But by marginalising the coin evidence and ignoring that of the Cuthbert coffin, Odenstedt is enabled to deny the likelihood that 'p' would be used in Watchfield. What slight evidence there is has been skewed to fit a hypothesis.

There are further methodological questions to ask of Odenstedt's Anglo-Saxon corpus. To the eighth century he ascribes the two Hartlepool rune-stones and the similar fragment from Monkwearmouth; but not the Lindisfarne grave-markers that look to be in the same tradition. For what it is worth Professor Cramp's corpus of sculptured stones dates the Hartlepool, Monkwearmouth and Lindisfarne pieces to 'mid seventh to mid eighth century'/'last quarter of seventh to first quarter of eighth century'/'eighth century' (Hartlepool and Monkwearmouth), 'mid seventh to mid eighth century'/'first half of eighth century'/'eighth century' (Lindisfarne).[40] If Hartlepool and Monkwearmouth are acceptable, Lindisfarne should be so too.

So much for exclusions, but there are inclusions too that warrant question. Odenstedt accepts the Falstone stone which Cramp puts rather later and therefore outside the bounds of his study: 'mid eighth to mid ninth century'.[41] The linguistic evidence is inconclusive but is consistent with either eighth or ninth century. Whether the stone's condition is good enough for us to guarantee the exact forms of the letters is doubtful. It is certainly unwise to rely overmuch on the idealised drawing that accompanies Stephens's account of the inscription, as Odenstedt does at second hand.[42]

The Thames scramasax *fuþorc* is certainly of primary importance to the Anglo-Saxon runologist and Odenstedt makes good use of it – for its unusual *j*-rune, its *p*-rune, its rarish form of 's', and so on. But on what grounds does the Thames *fuþorc* come within his dating limits? He puts it in the eighth century but gives no authority. Musset agrees with this dating ('VIIIe s. sans doute'[43]) but his freedom from doubt is not shared by D. M. Wilson whose authoritative catalogue of late ornamental metalwork ascribes the scramasax to the late ninth century.[44] Odenstedt also includes the Sandwich/Richborough stone, which he puts at *c.* 550–600. Again I know of no evidence to support the dating (which is admittedly less precise than Stephens's

---

[39] *Origin and Early History*, pp. 79–80.
[40] R. Cramp, *The British Academy Corpus of Anglo-Saxon Stone Sculpture, I: County Durham and Northumberland* (Oxford, 1984), pp. 98, 124 and 203–5.
[41] *Ibid.* p. 173.
[42] *Origin and Early History*, p. 22 refers to Elliott, *Runes: an Introduction*, pl. 32/fig. 32, which is Stephens, *Old-Northern Runic Monuments* I–II, 456. The Stephens drawing is said to have been taken from a cast. Luckily a very detailed drawing accompanies the first publication of this stone in *Archæologia Æliana* 1 (1822), 103–4, and this shows the stone in its present worn state.
[43] L. Musset and F. Mossé, *Introduction à la runologie* (Paris, 1965), p. 183.
[44] D. M. Wilson, *Anglo-Saxon Ornamental Metalwork 700–1100 in the British Museum* (London, 1964), p. 146.

'about A.D. 428–597'[45]). Since Stephens this rune-stone has been assumed to be pagan, and there is certainly no other quite like it in the English tradition. Stephens's argument for a date in the pagan period is based on three points: (a) it has no Christian symbols, (b) it was found in unconsecrated ground, (c) it bears remarkable similarity to the oldest Scandinavian rune-stones. (a) is true as far as it goes, but the stone surface is friable and its present condition poor, so we cannot be quite sure there was never, say, an incised cross on the surface, though none can now be seen. But then, neither Overchurch nor Kirkheaton bears Christian symbolism though nobody suggests they are pagan. As to (b), we know little about where the stone was discovered. The earliest report, 1844–5, put it simply as 'at Richborough'.[46] The next, in a letter from John Brent to Canon Robertson (Royal Library, Stockholm, dep. 189), defines the spot as 'in a field somewhere near Sandwich'. This is on the evidence of a local resident, Rolfe, who wrote in 1857, years after the discovery. Have we enough information here to determine whether the site had or had not been consecrated? In any case there is the warning example of the Falstone stone, undoubtedly Christian, which was found at a site not known to be consecrated. There is no doubt about (c), though Kent, unlike East Anglia, is not an obvious place for Scandinavian influence. Moreover the layout of Sandwich is paralleled by Viking Age Scandinavian material as well as earlier: compare, for example, the text of the Øster Løgum, Denmark, stone, with its personal name running vertically between framing lines.[47]

One further point about Odenstedt's citation of evidence. Even when we know of an inscription that was available and acceptable, we do not always know how much of it was used. There are some inscriptions that Odenstedt was 'able to read only in part', and this includes Bewcastle and Ruthwell.[48] To say that the texts here are only partly legible is of course sound. Bewcastle is severely weathered overall, and comparatively few of its runes can be read with certainty and delineated accurately. Ruthwell is different. Parts of its top stone, head and Visitation panel on the south face, have runes often badly worn, and it would not be surprising if Odenstedt omitted these from his survey. In so far as the lower stone survives, it has many well preserved runes. These Odenstedt should have recorded and identified. Sometimes he does not. For instance, in his account of the rune 'ŋ' he quotes the distinctive English form ᛝ ('curious and unique') but records only two examples, Thames scramasax and Bewcastle.[49] Yet Ruthwell has a clear form in '$\bar{k}$ y n i ŋ c' (and another less well preserved but recognisable in 'u ŋ $\bar{k}$ e t'). Did Odenstedt not have access to these bits

[45] Stephens, *Old-Northern Runic Monuments* I–II, 363.
[46] T. Wright, *The Archaeological Album* (London, 1845), p. 12.
[47] Jacobsen and Moltke, *Danmarks runeindskrifter*, no. 15. A philological case has also been argued for an early date for Sandwich, but the traditional reading of the stone upon which it depends is most uncertain. As with Falstone, an early drawing casts doubt on the later ones which Odenstedt accepts. David Parsons tells me he has recently written on this in 'Sandwich: the Oldest Scandinavian Rune-Stone in England?', *Proceedings of the Twelfth Viking Congress*, ed. B. Ambrosiani and H. Clarke (forthcoming).
[48] *Origin and Early History*, p. 14.
[49] *Ibid.* p. 111.

of Ruthwell? If not, we must ask why not? Pictures of the Ruthwell Cross are not hard to come by, and there is a clear depiction of one of its ŋ-runes in (to pick a text-book not too hard to get hold of) R. W. V. Elliott's *Runes: an Introduction* (pl. XVII). The drawings in G. Baldwin Brown's Ruthwell and Bewcastle volume of *The Arts in Early England* show both Ruthwell examples clearly. If Odenstedt could not include them, he was working from inadequate source material. But he may have omitted them in error. We have no means of knowing.

In distinguishing rune forms and practices we should be careful to note contextual features of the inscription that may affect them. For instance, the Thames scramasax has the 's' form ⊬. But this is a letter that the rune-cutter first missed out and then added in the space available.[50] He might have chosen his form of 's' because that was the only one that would fit in. Citing occasional doubled runes in early non-Anglo-Saxon inscriptions Odenstedt quotes **unnam** on the Reistad stone and **iddan** on the Charnay brooch.[51] The first is a genuine example: **iddan** not so. Though that is the form given in Krause's glossary, the inscription in fact reads **id | dan**, the two *d*-runes separated by the full width of the brooch head. Such an example is clearly to be distinguished from, say, Ruthwell 'g i | s t o | d d u | [*n*]' where doubling the *d*-rune in fact prevents the word from ending at its line end. Any summary account of runic usage or of rune forms which classifies the material and so takes the individual item out of its context is likely to mislead.

I have said it is not my intention to mount a criticism of Odenstedt's book. His subject is a major one in the field of runic studies, and we must applaud the attempt if not always the achievement. I want to use my misgivings about the book to produce positive suggestions for any future discussion of this subject. They are fairly simple ones but perhaps worth making: (i) to include all possible examples, seeking them out rather than accepting what is readily available, (ii) to study inscriptions from the originals if possible, (iii) to be aware of the constraints on carving the runic forms, (iv) to be wary of earlier drawings and interpretations, and to try to free ourselves from existing preconceptions, (v) to allow for the effect on rune forms of context – layout, spacing, etc., (vi) to try to make significant distinctions of form, identifying and subordinating accidentals.

Above all: (vii) to use the subjunctive more often. An indicative is perilous to runologists though it may be tempting, and many have yielded to temptation.[52] Our small sample of English runes and the way a new find may overturn our ideas is one reason against assertion. To take an example. Designating the known forms of the rune 's', Odenstedt noted: 'there are no examples with five, six or eight strokes in

---

[50] See, for instance, the reproduction and photograph in Wilson, *Ornamental Metalwork*, p. 144 and pl. XXII.

[51] *Origin and Early History*, p. 142.

[52] Cf. Michael Barnes's review of E. Moltke's methods of expression in 'On Types of Argumentation in Runic Studies', *Proceedings of the Third International Symposium on Runes and Runic Inscriptions at Grindaheim, Valdres, Norway 8–12 August 1990* (forthcoming). Cf. also R. I. Page, review (1987) of Moltke, *Runes and their Origin*.

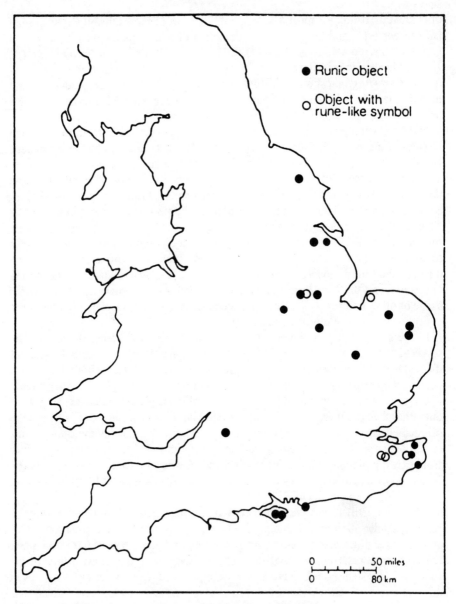

FIG. 1   Pre-650 runic monuments

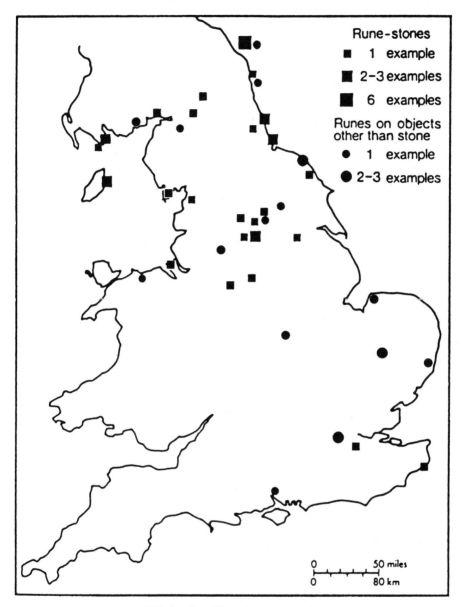

FIG. 2   Post-650 runic monuments

English inscriptions'.[53] He could not anticipate that, lurking in the undergrowth waiting to pounce, was the brooch from Harford Farm, Caistor-by-Norwich, Norfolk, with its five-staved 's' in 's i g i l æ'.[54]

Our archaeologists and metal detectors continue to find new inscriptions with high frequency. The tentative distribution maps I produced in 1973 showing inscriptions that could be clearly localised and dated before/after 650 were out of date by 1987 when 'New Runic Finds in England' (below, pp. 275–87) was published. That article is in turn outdated.[55] Bringing the two 1973 maps up to the present produces figs 1 and 2. The pre-650 map is most dramatically changed, with much fuller scatters of runes in East Anglia and the East Midlands and an outlier further north. East Anglia is also more prominent in the post-650 map than it was in 1973, and it is obvious that this region must be given more attention in any future discussion of English runes. What cannot be shown on any of these maps is the significance of the coin evidence, for I do not know how that could be presented. Suffice it to point to the increased weight that new discoveries have given to East Anglian and Kentish runic coins. Two considerations make the new maps no more definitive than their earlier versions. (i) the dividing date of 650 is, as I have said, one of convenience rather than principle. Above I give examples of problems of setting close dates to English runic monuments. 650 seems to work as a dividing line, but that is all that can be said for it. (ii) the maps remain tentative. For instance, I attribute three inscriptions to Brandon in my later map but only two, I think, can be put clearly post-650. The third, on a bone handle, is included by association. Again, I have not added the Worcester find to the later map though I suspect it properly belongs there. That might be established in a formal excavation report. It would be an intriguing addition.

The past few years have brought an upsurge of interest in Anglo-Saxon runic studies, in part because of the entry to the field of distinguished younger scholars. I hope the present collection helps by giving something of the background to English runic research. The papers have been reprinted without major changes. Occasional literals and indeed some minor errors have been corrected, but I must still take responsibility for any significant mistakes I have made in my runic career. Postscripts are added in most cases, but here I have not attempted scholarly completeness. They are my immediate reactions to aspects of the papers that need updating, or to criticisms that call for response. The original papers came out in a variety of journals, each with its own style; so references have been rationalised. I must thank David Parsons for the hard work he has put into making them as consistent as possible. He has also made them accord with modern practice by adding to the notes that high polish of pedantry required for any pretence to scholarship nowadays. I also acknowledge most warmly the care Carl Berkhout has put into preparing my bibliography, and the enthusiasm with which he has included items I would fain have omitted. I bow to his maturer judgment.

[53] *Origin and Early History*, p. 135. Odenstedt draws quite extensive conclusions from this type of evidence.
[54] J. Hines, 'A New Runic Inscription from Norfolk', *Nytt om Runer* 6 (1991), 6–7.
[55] See the postscript to it, below p. 287.

16

2

(1958)

NORTHUMBRIAN *ÆFTER*
(= IN MEMORY OF) + ACCUSATIVE

It may be important in the interpretation of an Old English inscription to know what case is governed by the preposition *æfter* in the sense of 'in memory of'. The subject has been briefly dealt with in Dahl's study of Old English substantival inflexion,[1] but a more extensive examination of the evidence is necessary. In its more usual senses *æfter* can govern three cases, the accusative, dative and instrumental. The instrumental is common in adverbial usages such as *æfter ðon, æfter ðisse*, but it is not often found elsewhere. Of the other two cases the dative is normally more common than the accusative. It is well-known, however, that the accusative usage is found quite frequently in certain Northumbrian texts. Unfortunately these texts are glosses, and gloss evidence is hard to assess. Glossators' methods often lead to the production of anomalous forms with, for example, noun and attributive adjective not agreeing.[2] Moreover *æfter* is used to translate Latin *post, secundum* or, occasionally, *iuxta* + accusative, and it is possible that, in using an accusative after the Old English preposition, the glossators are copying the Latin construction rather than following a genuine Northumbrian one. Little original Northumbrian remains, but there is one example of *æfter – æfter deothdæge Bede's Death Song* 5 – and here the dative is used.

The examples from the various Northumbrian glosses cannot be so easily divided into accusative and dative constructions as their editors appear to believe. Often it is impossible to decide which case is intended, since accusative and dative forms of a word may be identical, as for example in words ending in *-ung* or *-nis* and often in the pronoun form *me*, while in certain texts the accusative form is commonly used for the dative.[3]

The following evidence is afforded by the Northumbrian glosses:

---

[1] Dahl, *Substantival Inflexion*, p. 162.
[2] U. Lindelöf, *Rituale ecclesiae Dunelmensis: the Durham Collectar* (Durham, 1927), pp. lvi–lxi.
[3] A. S. C. Ross, *Studies in the Accidence of the Lindisfarne Gospels* (Leeds, 1937), p. 121.

(1)   *The Lindisfarne Gospels.*[4]

87 cases in the text of the Gospels themselves: 35 accusative, 20 dative and 32 ambiguous forms.

Accusative: mec Mt. 3, 11; 4, 19. Mk. 1, 7; 1, 17. L. 9, 23; 14, 27. J. 1, 15; 1, 27; 1, 30 *meh* Mt. 16, 23; 16, 24 *mech* Mk. 8, 34. *ðas* Mk. 16, 12. L. 5, 27; 6, 26; 10, 1; 12, 4; 17, 8; 17, 30; 18, 4. J. 3, 22; 5, 1; 6, 1; 7, 1; 11, 7; 19, 38 *ðæs* L. 6, 23. *ðas uutedlice dagas* L. 1, 24. *ðone hælend* L. 23, 26. *dagas* J. 4, 43. *ða* J. 13, 7; 19, 28; 21, 1. *þ'bread* J. 13, 27. *dagas æhtuo* J. 20, 26.

Dative: dagum sex Mt. 17, 1; Mk. 9, 2. *tuæm dogrum* Mt. 26, 2 *twæm dogrum* Mk. 14, 1. *ðrim dagum* Mt. 26, 61; 27, 63 *ðriim dagu* Mk. 8, 31. *dagum* Mk. 2, 1. J. 4, 43. *gecostung ðæræ* Mk. 13, 24. *word ðinum* L. 1, 38. *ðriim dogrum* L. 2, 46. *ðasum wordum* L. 9, 28. *menigum dagum* L. 15, 13. *him* L. 19, 14; 21, 8. J. 12, 19. *lytlum* L. 22, 58. *ðæm* J. 5, 14. *anum* J. 8, 9.

Ambiguous: ymbcerr Mt. 1, 12. *tid* Mt. 2, 16. J. 5, 4. *geleafa Iurre* Mt. 9, 29. *usig* Mt. 15, 23. *werc* Mt. 16, 27; 23, 3. *costunge* Mt. 24, 29. *mægn* Mt. 25, 15. *erest* Mt. 27, 53. *gesetnisse* Mk. 7, 5. *lytle huile* Mk. 14, 70. *gewuna* L. 1, 9; 2, 27; 2, 42; 22, 39 *ge-una* L. 4, 16. *ae* L. 2, 22; 2, 39. J. 19, 7 *æ* J. 18, 31. *þte* L. 2, 24; 22, 22. *word ðin* L. 2, 29. *willa* L. 12, 47. *bebod* L. 23, 56. *clænsunge* J. 2, 6. *ðis* J. 2, 12; 11, 11. *styrenise* J. 5, 4. *onsione* J. 7, 24. *lichoma* J. 8, 15.

Because of the accusative-dative syncretism found in this text many accusative singular forms have had to be put in the third section. It is clear that in many cases – *usig, word ðin, ðis*, for example – an accusative is much more likely than a dative. The number of accusative usages, as compared with dative, is probably higher than the figures above indicate.

(2)   *The Durham Ritual.*[5]

11 cases: 5 accusative, 2 dative and 4 ambiguous forms.

Accusative: micla miltheartnis' 24, 15. *gimett* 83, 1. *god* 92, 17. *firsto* 97, 22. *micle milsa* 167, 19.

Dative: onfoendvm smyltnisse 184, 15. Presumably the inflected infinitive *girædenne* 92, 19.

Ambiguous: monigfaldnise 20, 10 *monigfaldnis'* 125, 9. *willo* 27, 10. *giliornise vsa'* 124, 4.

(3)   *The Rushworth₂ Gloss.*[6]

54 cases: 7 accusative, 23 dative and 24 ambiguous forms.

---

4   Text in W. W. Skeat, *The Holy Gospels in Anglo-Saxon, Northumbrian and Old Mercian Versions* (Cambridge, 1871–87).
5   Lindelöf, *Rituale.*
6   Skeat, *Holy Gospels.*

Accusative: ðas wutudlice dagas L. 1, 24. ðas L. 10, 1; 12, 4; 17, 8. ða J. 7, 45; 13, 7. Probably *lytle hwyle* Mk. 14, 70.

Dative: ðrim dagum Mk. 8, 31; 14, 58. *dagum sexum* Mk. 9, 2. *twæm dagum* Mk. 14, 1. ðissum Mk. 16, 12. *worde ðinum* L. 1, 38; 2, 29. ðrim dogrum L. 2, 46. ðissum worde L. 9, 28. *monigum dagum* L. 15, 13. *him* L. 19, 14. J. 12, 19. ðæm L.21, 8. J. 1, 31. *lytlum hwile* L. 22, 58. ðæm hælend L. 23, 26. *bibode* L. 23, 56. ðassum J. 3, 22. *wutudlice twoege dagum* J. 4, 43. *tide* J. 5, 4. *anum* J. 8, 9. þ'æm breode J. 13, 27. *dæge æhtowum* J. 20, 26.

Ambiguous: gisetnisse Mk. 7, 5. *me* Mk. 8, 34. L. 9, 23; 14, 27. J. 1, 15; 1, 27; 1, 30. *costunge* Mk. 13, 24. *giwuna* L. 1, 9; 2, 27; 2, 42; 22, 39. *æ* L. 2, 22; 2, 39. J. 18, 31; 19, 7. ðætte L. 2, 24; 22, 22. *efne-giwuna* L. 4, 16. *willo* L. 12, 47. *clænsunge* J. 2, 6. *styrenisse* J. 5, 4. *onsione* J. 7, 24. *lichoma* J. 8, 15.

There is clearly a much higher number of accusative usages, as compared with dative, in (1) and (2) than in (3). This suggests a dialectal difference between North Northumbrian (*Lindisfarne Gospels* and *Durham Ritual*) and South Northumbrian (*Rushworth₂*). The evidence of Mercian glosses tends to confirm this. So:

(4)   *The Rushworth₁ Gloss.*[7]

25 cases: 2 accusative, 15 dative and 8 ambiguous forms.

Accusative: þas Mt. 8, 5. *þa* Mt. 21, 30.

Dative: babilonia fære Mt. 1, 12. *þære tide* Mt. 2, 16. *geleafan incrum* Mt. 9, 29. *weorcæ his* Mt. 16, 27. *dagum sex* Mt. 17, 1. *þonne wærcum heora* Mt. 23, 3. ðrycnissum Mt. 24, 29. *his mægene* Mt. 25, 15. *micclum fæce* Mt. 25, 19. *twæm dagum* Mt. 26, 2. ðrim dagum Mt. 26, 61 *þrim dagum* Mt. 27, 63. *his æristæ* Mt. 27, 53. *þæm gearwunga dæge* Mt. 27, 62. *dagum* Mk. 2, 1.

Ambiguous: me Mt. 3, 11; 4, 19; 16, 23; 16, 24; Mk. 1, 7; 1, 17. *us* Mt. 15, 23. *reste-dæg* Mt. 28, 1.

(5)   *Vespasian Psalter and Hymns.*[8]

48 cases: 2 accusative, 30 dative and 16 ambiguous forms.

Accusative: rehtwisnisse mine 17, 21. *synne ure* (*peccata nostra*, though formally dative singular is also possible) 102, 10.

Dative: rehtwisnisse minre 7, 9; 17, 25. *hehnisse ðinre* 11, 9. *heortan ðinre* 19, 5. *mildheortnisse ðinre* 24, 7; 34, 24; 118, 88, 124, 149 ðere miclan mildheortnisse ðinre 50, 3. *wercum* 27, 4. *niðum* 27, 4. *noman ðinum* 47, 11. *werce* 61, 13. *lustum* 80, 13. *werce ðinum* 85, 8. *dege* 94, 9. *word dinum* (*sic*) 118, 25 *worde ðinum* 118,

---

[7] *Ibid.*
[8] Text in H. Sweet, *The Oldest English Texts*, EETS 83 (London, 1885), pp. 183–420.

65, 107. *gesprece ðinum* 118, 41, 58, 76, 133, 169, 170. *dome* 118, 132 *dome ðinum* 118, 149, 156. *rime* Hy. 7, 15.

Ambiguous: mengu 5, 11; 9, 25; 50, 3; 68, 17; 93, 19; 105, 45; 150, 2. *unsceðfulnisse* 7, 9; 17, 21. *rehtwisnisse his* 7, 18. *ðe* 49, 17; 62, 9. *gelicnisse* 57, 5. *micelnisse* 78, 11. *heanisse* 102, 11. *endebyrdnisse* 109, 4.

The three texts from the Midlands and North Midlands show a strong preference for the dative over the accusative. In the North the *Lindisfarne Gospels* gloss uses accusative more often than dative. This could be a special case of the copying of the Latin usage in a single text, but it is supported by the usage of the *Durham Ritual*, though the number of examples from that text is small and probably not significant statistically. At least there must remain the possibility that within Northumbrian local dialects existed in which the accusative usage with *æfter* was common. In the special case of memorial inscriptions, where *æfter* = 'in memory of', we might expect that such a usage would be even further extended by analogy with Old Norse. On the Danish rune-stones the cognate forms *æft, æftir* always govern the accusative,[9] and this is also true of the Viking rune-stones found in the British Isles. There are unfortunately no early Anglian inscriptions giving evidence of the Old English usage in pre-Viking times. The preposition 'æft' has been traced on the early main inscription of Bewcastle, but the ending of the following name has an unusual rune or bind-rune form which has not yet been satisfactorily deciphered.

In the later Northumbrian inscriptions *æfter* (= in memory of) is found:

(a) with the dative. The Dewsbury (W. R. Yorks.) fragment A[E]FTER BEORNAE, Falstone (Northumberland) [AE]FT*AER* HROETHBERHTÆ and AEFTAER EO-MAE, and Great Urswick (Lancs.) 'æfter toroȝtredæ' and 'æfter his bæurnæ'.[10] There is also the Thornhill (W. R. Yorks.) III inscription 'æfte êateȝnne' with its shorter form of the preposition. The non-runic Thornhill inscription quoted by Dahl in this connection[11] cannot be used as evidence, since the endings are not certain. The fragments show the lower parts of AEFT, the letters OSBER directly below them, and then to the left and on the line below the fragments of serifs which could belong to TAE, though not enough remains to make the identification certain.

(b) with the accusative or dative. Thornhill II 'æft[.] berhtsuiþe', though here also the shorter form *æfte* was probably used. The name *Berhtsuiþe* could be either accusative or dative, and there is no formal reason for preferring either.

(c) (?) with the accusative. Three inscriptions may show an accusative construction:

(i) Thornhill I 'æfter eþelwini' and the lost Wycliffe (N. R. Yorks.) AEFTER

---

[9] Jacobsen and Moltke, *Danmarks runeindskrifter*, cols 743–4.
[10] Readings are based on personal examination unless otherwise stated. Runic texts are transliterated according to the method described in Dickins, 'System of Transliteration'.
[11] Dahl, *Substantival Inflexion*, p. 162.

BERCHTVINI.[12] The element *-wini* could clearly be accusative: it is less certain if it could be dative. There is little evidence for the early dative endings of *i*-stem masculine nouns. That produced by Dahl[13] indicates three forms, *-i*, *-æ*, and *-e*. Of these *-i* is the most rare. It is found certainly only in three related readings in the early Mercian glosses, *sume daeli Corpus* 1471, *Epinal* 731 and *sumae dœli Erfurt* 731. Another possible case is *cum antistite trumuini* in the Leningrad manuscript of Bede's *Ecclesiastical History* 114ʳ, though Anderson assumes this to be a nominative form.[14] *-æ* is found in the single example *Husmerae* in the 736 charter of Æðelbald, in the two *Epinal-Erfurt* examples *suicae* 692, *faengae* 727, possibly in the *Corpus* reading *maenoe* 49/887, and, in the south, in three examples *Bipplestydœ, Bipplestydę, Acustydę* in Kentish charters. *-e* is found in two examples in *Corpus suice* 1468, *fenge* 1630 and in a number of examples found in the various manuscripts of Bede's *Ecclesiastical History*.[15] So in the Moore manuscript there are five examples *Aeduine* 124, *Eduine* 354, *Uine* 195, *Trumuine* 272, *Goduine* (a Continental name) 295. Four of these are found in the Namur manuscript, three in Cotton Tiberius A. XIV, four in the Leningrad manuscript and four in Cotton Tiberius C. II. In addition, Cotton Tiberius A. XIV, Leningrad and Cotton Tiberius C. II have one further form *Eduine* 97. Such *-e* endings are unlikely at such an early date to be derived from *-i*, since *-i* still remains, certainly in Northumbrian, in the nominative-accusative of the *i*-stem masculines. *-e* is more likely, as Dahl suggests, to derive from earlier *-æ*, and this is also suggested by the correspondence between *Epinal-Erfurt suicae, faengae* and *Corpus suice, fenge*.

Because of the sparsity of evidence it is not possible to establish certainly the relative frequencies of *-i* and *-æ/-e* as dative endings of *i*-stem masculines in early Anglian. *-i* is clearly infrequent, but so are certain examples of *-æ*, and of *-æ* > *-e* outside the texts of the *Ecclesiastical History*. To establish the greater frequency of *-æ/-e* it is necessary to accept the *Ecclesiastical History* examples, and it is just these whose significance is doubtful. There is some doubt whether these *-e* endings are Old English. Dahl takes them as such, but Anderson argues[16] that they are more probably Latin third declension ablative endings, basing his argument on the fact that, if they are Old English endings, they show a far larger number of cases of *-æ* becoming *-e* than can be found in case endings which are undoubtedly Old English; in, for example, the genitival ending *-æs/-es*. Anderson's figures are certainly significant statistically, and his argument is hard to answer unless it is suggested that *æ* remained longer before *s* than when it was final. No evidence for this suggestion can be produced, if only because of the shortage of texts for Anglian dialects of the

---

[12] Text in Stephens, *Handbook*, p. 149. [The Wycliffe stone has been rediscovered. See Okasha, *Hand-List*, pp. 129–30].

[13] Dahl, *Substantival Inflexion*, pp. 161–3.

[14] O. S. Anderson, *Old English Material in the Leningrad Manuscript of Bede's Ecclesiastical History* (Lund, 1941), p. 109. The form *excepto illo uuini* (C. Plummer, *Venerabilis Baedae historiam ecclesiasticam gentis anglorum . . .* (Oxford, 1896) I, 195) is a misreading of the Cotton Tiberius C. II text. The correct reading is *uuine* (cf. Sweet, *Oldest English Texts*, p. 141).

[15] Text in Plummer, *Venerabilis Baedae*, I.

[16] Anderson, *Leningrad Bede*, pp. 110–13.

eighth century. On the other hand it can be cogently argued against Anderson that, while there is clear evidence of the Bede manuscripts latinising Old English masculine names into the Latin second declension (so, for example, in nominative *Uilfridus* 185, vocative *Ecgbercte* 193, accusative *Aeduinum* 98, genitive *Alduulfi* 253, dative *Aeduino* 98, ablative *Aeduino* 97, nominative plural *Heuualdi* 298: accusative, genitive, dative and ablative forms are all common), there are no certain examples of Old English masculine nouns taken into the Latin third declension. There are, for example, no accusatives in *-em* or genitives in *-is*. The possibility of the *Ecclesiastical History* examples representing OE *-æ* > *-e* must then remain.

This makes it doubtful whether *-i* can be accepted as a normal or common dative ending of *i*-stem masculines, and strengthens the case for regarding the Thornhill I and Wycliffe form *-wini* as accusative. One other possibility remains. The form *-wini* may represent the normal dative *-wine*, with *-e* replaced by non-etymological *-i* as an attempted archaism. False archaisms of this sort are perhaps found elsewhere in Northumbrian inscriptions.[17]

(ii) Yarm (N. R. Yorks.) AEFTER HIS BREODERA. Here again the noun form is hard to define. The stem vowel *eo* represents the *i*-mutation of *o*. *eo* is found occasionally in this capacity elsewhere in Anglian texts; so, for example, *Rushworth2* has *eofesta* (L. 19, 5) as well as the more usual *oefest*, *Erfurt* reads *geleod* 229 where *Epinal* has *gloed*, and *Lindisfarne* has such forms as *gebleodsad* (Mt. 21, 9), *gebeotes* (Mt. I. 14, 13), *geceola* (L. 16, 24) and *greofa* (J. 18, 33). *i*-mutation is usual in the dative singular of *brodor* and is the phonologically regular form of the nominative-accusative plural, though seldom appearing there in Old English. It appears regularly in Old Norse nominative-accusative plural *brœðr*, and there is a single Anglian example of it in *Rushworth1 broeþre*.[18] The Yarm *-a* ending is paralleled in the *Lindisfarne* nominative-accusative plural forms *broðra/broðera*. Yarm may clearly be another example of *æfter* + accusative. It is more doubtful if *breodera* could be a dative singular form, though the *i*-mutation suggests such a case. There is no evidence for an Anglian dative singular *-a* ending in this declension, and if the Yarm form is in fact dative, it must be analogical, representing perhaps the *Lindisfarne -e* with *-a/-e* variation, perhaps by analogy with the *n*-stem nouns.

The evidence given above does not certainly prove a Northumbrian use of *æfter* (= in memory of) + accusative. It does, however, suggest that the possibility of such a usage is too great to be rejected out of hand, and that in certain texts *æfter* should be glossed as 'with accusative or dative'.

---

[17] A. S. C. Ross, 'The Linguistic Evidence for the Date of the "Ruthwell Cross" ', *MLR* 28 (1933), 145–55, at 150–1 and 154–5.
[18] Brunner, *Altenglische Grammatik*, § 285 Anm. 3 (b).

AN EARLY DRAWING OF THE RUTHWELL CROSS

The Ruthwell Cross, probably the most important of the Anglo-Saxon sculptured stones which have come down to us, also bears the most extensive of the Old English runic inscriptions, the poetic text closely related to parts of the *Dream of the Rood* of the Vercelli book. It is well known that the cross as it now stands is a nineteenth-century rebuilding, made up of six fragments of the Anglo-Saxon monument with the shaft supplemented by a number of pieces of plain stone and a modern cross-beam added to the head. Originally the cross was built of two stones, an upper one forming the top of the shaft and the cross head, and a lower one comprising the base and the greater part of the shaft. The lower stone bore the *Dream of the Rood* text, cut in four sections: *a*, across the top and down the north border of the present east face; *b*, down the south border of the east face; *c*, across the top and down the south border of the west face; and *d*, down the north border of the west face.[1]

In the seventeenth century the two stones were thrown down and shattered, presumably as a result of the 'Act anent Idolatrous monuments in *Ruthwall*' known to have been passed by the General Assembly of the Church of Scotland in 1642.[2] Thereby the lower stone, the base of which had already been severely defaced, was broken into two, roughly at right angles to the shaft axis. The two fragments remained within the parish church of Ruthwell for over 140 years after the passing of the 1642 act. The base fragment seems at first to have been almost completely buried in the earth floor, for reports up to and including A. Gordon, *Itinerarium septentrionale: or, a Journey Thro' Most of the Counties of Scotland, and Those in the North of England* (London, 1727), pp. 160–1, describe only its south face. From the late seventeenth century onwards, however, antiquaries describe all four faces of the top fragment which must, therefore, have been more readily accessible and regularly examined. In 1794 the cross fragments were in the churchyard, and in 1802 they were erected in the form of a pillar, perhaps with the addition of some plain stone to make up for the missing pieces, in the manse garden. In 1823 the new cross-beam was added, cut by a local mason to the design of the minister, Henry Duncan. The cross

---

[1] Convenient for reference is the drawing of the inscription which forms the frontispiece to B. Dickins and A. S. C. Ross, *The Dream of the Rood* (London, 1934).

[2] Only the title of this act survives. It appears in the *Index of the principal acts of the Assembly holden at St. Andrews, 27. July, 1642, not printed*, added to the edition of *The Acts of the General Assemblies of the Church of Scotland, from the year 1638 to the year 1649, inclusive* of 1691.

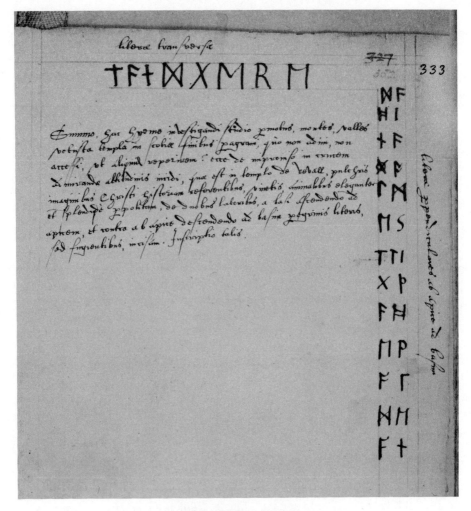

THE RUTHWELL CROSS
Reginald Bainbrigg's drawing of the Ruthwell runes,
MS Cotton Julius F. VI, fol. 352

then remained in the manse garden until 1887, when it was transferred to the specially-built cross-chamber in the church, where it now stands.

The stone on which this important runic text was inscribed had, then, been defaced, fractured, allowed to stand about in the church where one piece at least could be turned over for examination, put out into the churchyard, joined with cement, and left exposed to the elements for over eighty years, before it reached its present protected site. Not surprisingly, much of the inscription has been lost. Most of this lost material is probably gone for ever, but, by studying drawings of the stone made by early antiquaries, scholars have been able to recover some letters destroyed by exposure and handling in more recent times. The earliest illustration yet used for this purpose seems to be pl. iv of G. Hickes, *Linguarum vett. septentrionalium thesaurus grammatico-criticus et archæologicus. 3. Grammaticæ islandicæ rudimenta* (Oxford 1703), a figure based on the work of the antiquary William Nicolson of Carlisle, who examined the fragments in April, 1697.[3] Nicolson's drawing gives full texts for the four sides of the upper fragment of the lower stone, and is our only authority for some letters which were soon to disappear under the handling the stone received in the church, while of other runes which disappeared at a later date it is our earliest record. For all that, the drawing was made too late to be of the greatest use. It shows the state of the cross after it had been knocked down and broken, when a considerable amount of the text had already been destroyed.

Luckily there is an even earlier drawing (p. 24) of the Ruthwell Cross, made while it was still standing, presumably complete and undamaged, in the parish church. It is unfortunate that this record gives only a small part of the runic text, but this includes a few runes which had disappeared by the time Nicolson was working and which were presumably destroyed when the cross was attacked. This early drawing is part of a short note by Reginald Bainbrigg of Appleby, which now forms MS Cotton Julius F. VI, fol. 352. Though its existence was noted as early as 1911,[4] the drawing does not yet seem to have been published, nor has its material been used, even in the latest editions of the runic text of the Ruthwell Cross.[5]

Bainbrigg, a northerner by birth, returned to Appleby from one of the universities in 1580 to become headmaster of the grammar school there. He interested himself in local antiquities, and in 1599 and 1601 made journeys into the north to collect material for a new edition of Camden's *Britannia*. Probably the Ruthwell drawing was made for the same work, though Camden did not use it. Bainbrigg died in 1606. His drawing can, then, be dated *c.* 1600.

The drawing shows the beginning of section *a* of the *Dream of the Rood* text, giving the runes of the top border, with above them the words 'literæ transversæ', and the first fourteen lines of runes (line 5 accidentally omitted) of the north-east border, the words 'literæ perpendiculares ab apice ad basim' accompanying them down the right-hand edge of the leaf. Below is added:

'Summo, hac hyeme, investigandi studio permotus, montes, valles vetusta templa in scotiæ finibus peragraui, quo non adiui, non accessi, vt aliquid reperirem. ecce de improuiso in crucem admirandæ altitudinis incidi, quæ est in templo de Revall,[6] pulchris imaginibus Christi historiam referentibus, vinetis, animalibus eleganter et splendide perpolitam, de duobus lateribus, a

---

[3] Used in Brown, *The Arts in Early England* V, 206–11. It is not clear why Brown used the Hickes plate in preference to Nicolson's original drawings, some of which survive.

[4] F. Haverfield, 'Cotton Iulius F. VI: Notes on Reginald Bainbrigg of Appleby, on William Camden and on some Roman Inscriptions', *TCWAAS* n.s. 11 (1911), 343–78, at 373–4.

[5] See, for example, E. V. K. Dobbie, *The Anglo-Saxon Minor Poems*, ASPR 6 (London and New York, 1942), p. 204, where missing letters are supplied by conjecture only.

[6] A common early type of spelling for Ruthwell. Dickins and Ross (*Dream of the Rood*, p. 1) note a pronunciation [rivl], though a spelling pronunciation is now common locally.

basi ascendendo ad apicem, et contra ab apice descendendo ad basim p*er*egrinis literis, sed fugientibus, incisam. Inscriptio talis.'

In its present condition section *a* of the inscription begins:[7]

'[.] g e r e | d æ | h i | n æ | $\overline{g}$ o | d a | l m | e ʒ | t t i | g þ | a *h* | e w | a l | d e | o n
       5   10   15   20   25   30

| $\overline{g}$ a | l $\overline{g}$ | u g | i s t | i $\overline{g}$ a'
35   40   45

corresponding loosely to the Vercelli text:[8]

> Onʒyrede hine þa ʒeonʒ Hæleð,   (þæt wæs ʒod ælmihtiʒ),
> strang 7 stiðmod.   ʒestah he on ʒealʒan heanne . . .

Several letters are lost before rune 2, 'g'. The centre of this character is 5·3 inches from the left-hand edge of the stone, and to its left the surface is broken away and partly covered with a layer of cement, no traces of letters remaining. Bainbrigg gives runes 2–34 (omitting 14–15), and also shows the four lost characters that preceded 2. By Nicolson's time these four had already disappeared, and it is reasonable to assume that this top corner of the lower stone was broken away when the great cross was thrown down forty or so years after Bainbrigg's visit. Bainbrigg is thus our only authority for the beginning of the inscription at this point.

A comparison of the drawing with the runes that survive gives us some idea of Bainbrigg's accuracy. It turns out to be only fair. Apart from the complete omission of a line, there is a good deal of distortion of individual runic forms. So, 'ʒ' is made to look like S, 't' (20) like T, while 't' (21), 'l' (30) are also distorted. The Ruthwell 'd' form is the so-called younger form with the cross-staves touching the stems a good way from their ends. This is correctly reproduced in Bainbrigg's drawing of 31, but for 6 he gives the so-called older form in which the cross-staves meet the stems at their ends. For '$\overline{g}$' he draws a form similar to the usual manuscript variant of the rune, its two cross-staves having a circle surrounding their crossing. This treatment of 'd' and '$\overline{g}$' – replacing the forms on the stone by possible variants – might suggest that Bainbrigg had some knowledge of runes, but it is unlikely that he had, for, though he knew and drew the Bewcastle 'kyniburuḡ' text and the Bridekirk Font inscription, he did not recognize their runic nature. Moreover, he was unable to distinguish between the similar runes 'o', 'a' and 'æ'. He gives 'æ' for 'a' (25), 'o' for 'a' (29), and 'a' for 'o' (33), though the last is not a glaring mistake, for the outer stave of the lower arm of the rune is very faint, and it appears as 'a' in a number of later drawings. It is unlikely, then, that Bainbrigg's version was influenced by any

---

[7] This reading is the result of a number of examinations of the Ruthwell Cross between August, 1955, and July, 1958. Runes are transliterated according to the system described in Dickins, 'System of Transliteration', and further in Dickins and Ross, *Dream of the Rood*, p. 8, n. 2.
[8] Dickins and Ross, *Dream of the Rood*, p. 25.

previous knowledge of runes, and it can be looked upon as a rather fumbling attempt to represent what he actually saw.

Of the four characters indicated by Bainbrigg before 2, three can be readily identified. The first is a cross, the third 'n', the fourth 'd'. 'd' is here given the older form, but, as in the case of 6, this is probably a mistake. The second character cannot be identified with certainty. Formally it seems to be 'æ', but in view of Bainbrigg's difficulty with this type of letter it may have been 'o', 'a' or 'æ'. 'æ' is not possible in the context, but both 'o' and 'a' are. The text then began with '+ond' or '+and'. Either reading would fit into the space available on the stone.

The cross at the beginning is paralleled in a number of runic inscriptions – those, for example, of the Dover grave-stone, the Falstone 'hog-back' and the Great Urswick and Thornhill stones – while early drawings of section *c* of the Ruthwell *Dream of the Rood* text show that that too once began with a cross, which seems to have disappeared towards the end of the eighteenth century. The verbal prefix *and-* appears in Old English as a doublet of the *on-*, found in the *ongyrede* of the parallel Vercelli text. *And-* is properly a stressed form found in nominal and adjectival compounds, *on-* appearing as its unstressed equivalent proper to verbs. Confusion of use does, however, sometimes occur in Old English, with the result that *and-* is evidenced in verbal compounds.[9] *Ond-* is a common variant spelling of *and-*, produced by the partial rounding of earlier *a* before a nasal consonant. Both *o* and *a* are used as symbols for this sound in early Northumbrian texts, *o* spellings predominating.[10] Unfortunately the sound does not occur again in the Ruthwell texts, so we do not know how the Ruthwell rune-master represented it. The first word of section *a* of the *Dream of the Rood* text must, then, be transcribed '[+ₒ*nd*]geredæ', where the second character is either 'o' or 'a'.

One other point deserves mention in connexion with Bainbrigg's drawing. 0·4 inches to the right of the crossing of rune 23, 'g', and on the centre-line of the line of runes there now appears a small dot. This could be accidental, but section *b* of the text begins '[.] | icr | iicn | æk̄y | niŋ | c' (*ahof ic ricne Cyninʒ* in the Vercelli text), after the last letter of which there is also a small dot, this time less likely, judging from its appearance, to be intentional. Accidental pitting of the surface at this part of the stone is, however, rare, and the two dots appear each at the end of the first verse line of its text. They could then be punctuation points. The lack of punctuation elsewhere in the runic texts of Ruthwell is not a significant objection, for Old English punctuation is irregular, both in written and in epigraphical material. The accidental appearance of two dots in such positions would be something of a coincidence, and strong evidence would be needed to reject them. Nicolson did not show them, but this may have been because he did not notice them or did not regard them as important. The *a* dot is first given in pl. 57 of Gordon's *Itinerarium septentrionale*, but Gordon does not show the *b* dot, which is first recorded in A. de Cardonnel's pl. lv in *Vetusta*

---

9 Campbell, *Old English Grammar*, § 73 and n. 1.
10 *Ibid.* § 130, n. 2.

monumenta II (London, 1789). The fact that Bainbrigg does not show the point after rune 23 of the *a* text may be thought further evidence for the belief that these dots are accidental.

POSTSCRIPT

I am glad to note that this early drawing is now commonly taken into account in editions of the Dream of the Rood, even reaching Fred C. Robinson and E. G. Stanley, *Old English Verse Texts from Many Sources: a Comprehensive Collection*, EEMF 23 (Copenhagen, 1991), no. 44.1.2.2. In the matter of the 'Act anent Idolatrous monuments in *Ruthwall*', Dr Elisabeth Okasha traced the text of this act in the minutes of the General Assembly of the Church of Scotland, Scottish Record Office, CH 1/1/9, p. 15, and quotes 'the Assemblie finds that the monument therin mentioned is idolatrous, and therefore recommends to the Presbytrie that they careful[l]y urge the order prescrived be the act of Parliament anent the abolishing of these monuments, to be put to execution'.[11] The text is important as indicating there was only one such monument at Ruthwell, not more as some have hopefully urged. It is a curiosity of academic politics that Dr Okasha's priority in recording this find has been largely ignored, the most recent writer preferring to quote a less accurate text of the minute and to refer to Dr Paul Meyvaert's later publication of it in 1982: cf. B. Cassidy, 'The Later Life of the Ruthwell Cross: from the Seventeenth Century to the Present', *The Ruthwell Cross: Papers from the Colloquium Sponsored by the Index of Christian Art, Princeton University, 8 December 1989*, ed. B. Cassidy (Princeton, 1992), pp. 3–34, at 4.

[11] Okasha, *Hand-List*, p. 108, n. 6.

4
(1959)

LANGUAGE AND DATING IN OLD ENGLISH INSCRIPTIONS

In a discussion of the chronology of Anglo-Saxon sculptured stones the evidence of those with inscriptions in the vernacular might be expected to play an important part. The language of an inscription may show features which can be dated with some closeness, and so may suggest a date for the stone which bears it. For such a dating of a stone to be valid two conditions must be fulfilled: the cutting of the text must have been contemporary with the carving of the stone, and the language of the inscription must have been that of the time and place of inscribing. If either condition does not apply the linguistic dating may mislead us as to the date of the stone.

Unfortunately, it is usually hard to tell whether these conditions apply or not. Two very general suggestions can be made as to the application of the first of them. If an inscription is an important part of the design of a monument, particularly of a large or intricately carved monument, or if it is an artist's signature, stone and inscription may well be contemporaneous. To take examples: the Great Urswick rune-stone is a piece of work elaborate enough to have been specially designed to hold that particular text, so it is likely that text and pattern were cut at about the same time: the signature 'eoh:woro | htæ' on the Kirkheaton stone[1] is presumably that of the sculptor of the clumsy decoration. There are, however, other cases where we cannot be certain that stone and text are contemporary, where an existing stone could have been re-used, or where stones could perhaps have been mass-produced at quarries or in workshops, with texts added when they were sold as memorials. At Whithorn, Wigtownshire, was found a stone bearing the fragmentary runic text '[.]ferþs' (or '[.]ferþs-'), clearly containing the common Old English personal name element -ferþ. The stone is a thin slab, elaborately though crudely carved on face, back and edges, and designed as a head-stone. The text is cut down one of the edges, and the firm, bold lines of the runes contrast with the tentative, chipped lines of face and back patterns. Here an old stone could have been re-used with an added text, so the metathesised element form -ferþ does not necessarily give any information on the date of the sculpture of the stone itself. A similar case is that of the Chester-le-Street stone with its partly-runic inscription EADm | VnD. Here the characters are cut in two irregular lines across the upper part of the pattern of the face of the stone. Had the stone been

---

[1] Forms quoted from inscriptions are based on the author's own readings. Runes are transliterated according to the system described in Dickins, 'System of Transliteration'.

29

originally intended to hold this text we might have expected the sculptor to have provided a panel or at least a space in the design for the purpose, as for example on the 'tidfirþ' stone from Monkwearmouth. Again, the stone may be a re-used one. The Hartlepool and Lindisfarne name-stones could be examples of mass-produced works with their texts added later, and so could the generally alike and more elaborate Thornhill rune-stones. In the cases of the 'hilddigyþ' stone from Hartlepool and the three Thornhill rune-stones there is a contrast between the care and accuracy of the setting-out of the pattern on the stone and the carelessness of the spacing of the inscription. Carver and rune-master may have been different people, and there may have been a time lag, not necessarily very long, between the cutting of the stone and the adding of the text.

More important from the linguist's point of view, however, is the question of the application of the second condition. Is the language of the inscription characteristic of that used at the time when, and in the place where, the inscription was cut? Here the question of the linguistic validity of the text is introduced. The inscriber may for some reason have tried to reproduce the language forms of an earlier period (or of a different dialect area, though that is less likely) from the one in which he was working. He may have succeeded only partially, so that his text contained contemporary forms mixed with archaistic forms, and perhaps too with forms which have no etymological justification, but which were produced by false archaism. On the other hand, he may have succeeded completely, in which case a linguistic dating of the text will be misleading as to the date it was actually cut. If the inscriber successfully reproduced the language of an earlier date, the linguist alone would not be able to detect that the material was misleading. This would only become clear if the opinion of the philologist as to the date of the text came into conflict with the opinion of the art historian as to the date of the stone. Such a conflict should only arise if each could give a firm and close date to his material.

This question of the validity of linguistic dating of inscriptions has been raised by C. L. Wrenn in his important article 'The Value of Spelling as Evidence'.[2] There Professor Wrenn argues that the way words are spelt in a text is only part of the total evidence to be used in dating that text. The study of the spelling alone, 'when not sufficiently related to other kinds of evidence', may mislead. No-one will object to this general argument, but when Wrenn takes as an example the dating of the Ruthwell Cross he is on more debatable ground.

The argument here may be summed up in the following terms:

(i) The Ruthwell text of the *Dream of the Rood* generally preserves unstressed *i* and *æ* 'which were both replaced by *e* about the middle of the eighth century'. In view of this and of the appearance there of 'a number of apparently early forms' this text is dated 'early in the eighth century'.

(ii) From non-philological sources W. G. Collingwood, writing in *Northumbrian Crosses of the Pre-Norman Age* (London, 1927), produced 'almost overwhelming

---

[2] *Trans. of the Philological Soc.* (1943), 14–39, particularly 19–22.

evidence for a date at the very end of the eighth century'. He also gave a 'plausible historical background to his date for the inscription at the close of the century'.

(iii) The conflict between (i) and (ii) makes a further examination of the Ruthwell texts necessary.

(iv) There are a number of inconsistencies and unusual forms in the Ruthwell text. So, unstressed *æ*, while generally remaining, is occasionally replaced by *e*, as in 'wald*e*'. The form 'rodi' has the early instrumental ending -*i*, proper to nouns of the *a*-declension, but not to those of the *ō*-declension, while in the phrase '[*m*]iþ b*lodæ*' the -*i* ending appropriate to the *a*-stem instrumental has been replaced by -*æ* more suitable to an *ō*-stem noun. 'There is, besides, the doubtful form *(i)dægisgæf*, which, if considered as the remains of the sentence *wæpidæ giscæft* . . ., would be extraordinarily archaic'.

(v) Inscriptions for the dead tend to use archaic forms of language. In runic inscriptions one might compare the survival of the rune '3', which originally seems to have represented *hw*, as a spirant in the personal name form 'toro3tredæ' (= *Torhtredæ*) of the Great Urswick inscription. The Ruthwell Cross also preserves this symbol, with the same value, in 'alme3ttig'.

(vi) It is therefore suggested that the Ruthwell text of the *Dream of the Rood* 'was deliberately an attempt at the end of the eighth century to imitate the appearance of the language of the beginning of the century'. The inconsistencies and unusual forms are then explicable as errors of the archaizing rune-master.

(vii) 'The inscription was to be connected with the memory of the considerably earlier Northumbrian king Alcfrith, and hence the *deliberate* archaizing added to the natural tendency of most inscriptions to introduce older or obsolescent forms of language'.

In this argument Wrenn makes no attack on any particular work dealing with the date of the Ruthwell Cross, but his remarks on the forms 'rodi' and '[*m*]iþ b*lodæ*' rather suggest that he had in mind the linguistic discussion in B. Dickins and A. S. C. Ross, *The Dream of the Rood* (London, 1934), pp. 12–13. This in turn depends on the fuller article by A. S. C. Ross, 'The Linguistic Evidence for the Date of the "Ruthwell Cross" '.[3] Objection can certainly be made to individual points in the Dickins-Ross discussion. So, the stem vowel of 'men' is considered significant as a dating point, Ross declaring that Ruthwell's use of *e* for the *i*-mutation of PrOE *a/o* indicates that the language of the text 'can hardly be referred to a period much earlier than that of the glossaries and the earliest Northumbrian texts'.[4] This argument is based on the appearance in *Epinal, Erfurt* and, to a less extent, *Corpus* of forms where the *i*-mutation of *a/o* is represented by *æ*, this being regarded as an early stage from which Ruthwell's *e* has developed. In fact, there are virtually no *æ* forms (< *a/o* by *i*-mutation) in early Northumbrian texts. These consistently example *e*: so, *end:*

3 *MLR* 28 (1933), 145–55.
4 'Linguistic Evidence', p. 147.

Franks Casket (= *FC*), *end*: *Cædmon's Hymn* in the Moore manuscript (= *CHM*), *Penda*: *List of Northumbrian Kings* (= *LNK*), Hengist, Penda, Quentauic, *Rendlæsham* and perhaps *Denisesburna*: Bede's *Historia Ecclesiastica* in the Moore manuscript (= *HEM*), *Hengist, Middilengli, Penda, Rendlaesham, Denisaesbrunna*: *Historia Ecclesiastica* in the Leningrad manuscript (= *HEL*). There is also the Celtic *Pentæ HEM*, *Pentae HEL* (but *Paentae* in the Namur manuscript). The only exception in these texts is *Quæntauic HEL*, and that is a foreign name.

There is no reason to believe that the evidence of the early Mercian glossaries is relevant to Northumbrian. The appearance in the non-Northumbrian *Historia Ecclesiastica* of Cotton Tiberius C. II (= *HEC*)[5] of the forms *Haengest, Haengist, Middilęngli, -aengli, Raendlesham, Dęnises burnna, Paente* (but *Penda*) indicates the retention of *æ* in some Midland dialects at a time when *e* was established in Northumbrian, and the *æ* forms of the glossaries may only be further indications of this point.

Objection can also be made to the Dickins-Ross use of the pronominal form 'hiæ' and the unsyncopated 'hêafunæs' as dating points. But criticisms like these, made with reference to specific parts of the discussion, are not criticisms of the principle of dating on philological grounds implicitly accepted in the Dickins-Ross edition.[6] Wrenn, however, suggests that the language forms of an inscription may be largely irrelevant to its date, and so attacks the principle of dating inscribed stones on linguistic evidence. It is one thing to say generally that Anglo-Saxon inscriptions could have been archaistic, and quite another to assert that in a particular and important case the inscription *was* the work of an archaizer. If Wrenn is right, dates given on linguistic grounds to other Old English inscriptions must be under suspicion. His argument needs examination, and under examination proves weak. So:

(i) Wrenn's dating of the language of the Ruthwell texts is suspect. The date of the replacement by *e* of unstressed *i* and *æ* cannot be given with precision, for our knowledge of early Northumbrian is too slight. The Ruthwell texts: (a) retain PrOE unstressed *æ* in '[*æ*]þþilæ', 'b*l*odæ', 'dorstæ', 'fus[*æ*]', 'hêafunæs', 'hinæ', 'hinæ', 'hweþræ', 'limwœrignæ', 'riicnæ', '-geredæ' and probably '[*li*]cæs', but evidence *e* in 'walde'. The form 'æt[ḡ]ad[*re*]' (< *gaduræ)[7] can be added to these. Its *-e* ending, now lost, was still extant when William Nicolson of Carlisle was making his drawings of the cross in 1697 and 1704. Early drawings also enable us to restore '*mo*dig f[*ore*]', where the last four letters may represent the single word *fore* (< *foræ*) or may be *for* with the beginning of a following word. Finally there is the pronominal form 'hiæ', but this is not important for dating purposes, since it is not uncommon in texts from

5 It should be noted, however, that opinions differ as to the place of origin of this manuscript. E. A. Lowe (*Codices Latini antiquiores* II (Oxford, 1935), p. 21) and Dahl (*Substantival Inflexion*, pp. 25–6) argue that it is non-Northumbrian. C. Plummer (*Venerabilis Baedae historiam ecclesiasticam gentis anglorum . . .* (Oxford, 1896) I, xciii) and Ker (*Catalogue*, p. 261) suggest that the manuscript is from Northumbria. The linguistic evidence certainly favours a non-Northumbrian origin.
6 In 'Linguistic Evidence' Ross distinguishes (pp. 154–5) between the date the inscription was engraved and the date of the language of the inscription.
7 Dickins and Ross, *Dream of the Rood*, p. 27.

the tenth century. The Ruthwell texts: (b) retain PrOE *i* in 'almeȝttig', '[*æ*]þþilæ', 'bi[*h*](*êald*)', '[*b*]*i*smæræ[*d*]u', '*bist*[*e*]mi[*d*]', 'bi[.]', 'gi*d*ræ[*f.*]d', 'gistīga', 'gistoddu[*n*]', 'giwundad', '*k̄*yniŋc', 'limwœrignæ', '*mo*dig', '*ni*', 'rodi', though PrOE *i* has become *e* in 'uŋ*k̄*et', '-geredæ'. Several of these forms are not significant from the point of view of dating. The suffixes -*ig*, -*ing* remain through the Old English period. The -*il*- of '[*æ*]þþilæ' could be a tenth-century form with retention of unstressed *i* after a palatalised dental,[8] while the prefixes *bi*-, *gi*- are found in those forms in some tenth-century Northumbrian texts. There remain, then, three significant *i* forms '*bist*[*e*]mi[*d*]', '*ni*', 'rodi' to set against two *i* > *e* forms.

Of Northumbrian texts of any length only *FC* consistently preserves PrOE unstressed *æ*. *CHM* has *astelidæ, hefaenricaes, metudæs, moncynnæs, tiadæ*, but *haleg, heben, hrofe*. The Leningrad text of *Cædmon's Hymn* (= *CHL*) reads *hefen* (2x), but *hrofæ*, replaces *haleg* by *halig*, but otherwise agrees with the *M* text. The whole of the material of the early *HE* texts is not available. *HEM* is given in Plummer, *Venerabilis Baedae historiam ecclesiasticam gentis anglorum*, and there is a collection of the Old English material of *HEL* in O. S. Anderson, *Old English Material in the Leningrad Manuscript of Bede's Ecclesiastical History* (Lund, 1941). Variants from the Cotton Tiberius A. XIV text (= *HEB*) and the Namur text (= *HEN*) are given by Plummer, and there is also material from these manuscripts in H. Sweet, *The Oldest English Texts*, EETS 83 (London, 1885), pp. 132–47, but since there are lacunae in both manuscripts it is unsafe to argue from the silence of Plummer and Sweet. Some forms based on a new collation of *HEB* are given in Dahl, *Substantival Inflexion*. Finally, a few forms from MS Kassel, Landesbibliothek, Theol. Q 2 (= *HEK*) are given in G. Storms, 'The Weakening of O.E. Unstressed *i* to *e* and the Date of Cynewulf', *English Studies* 37 (1956), 104–10.[9]

The evidence of the texts of *HE* is confused by the fact that it is not always clear whether an ending is Old English or Latin.[10] However, *HEL* has twenty-six -*æ(s)* / -*e(s)* endings which are certainly Old English, and of these twenty-three are in *æ* and only three – *Cnobheresburg, Cynuisse, Medeshamstedi* – are in *e*.[11] In the same twenty-six endings *HEM* has seven *e* forms, *Clofeshoch, Cnobheresburg, Cynuise, Denisesburna, Hrofescæstir* (but *Hrofæscæstræ*), *Medeshamstedi, Streaneshalch* (but *Streanæs-* (3x) *Strenæs- Strenaes-*) as well as one form in *ę Uilfarędun*. The following forms are available for *HEB, HEN*:

HEB: Augustinaes, Berctae, Cerotaesei, Clofaeshooh, Cnobheraesburg, Earcongotae, Hrofaes caestrae, Hrofaescaestir, Idlae, Rendlaesham, Selaeseu, Streanaes- (2x) *Streonaes- Streunaes-, Uilfæraesdun*, but *Streanęs-*, and *Cynuisse, Medeshamstedi*.

HEN: Clofaeshooh, Denisaes brunna, Hrofaescaestir, Selaeseu, Streanaes- (2x),

---

8 K. D. Bülbring, *Altenglisches Elementarbuch* I (Heidelberg, 1902), §§ 416 (b) and 516.
9 [The Old English of this manuscript is now available in T. J. M. van Els, *The Kassel Manuscript of Bede's 'Historia ecclesiastica gentis anglorum' and its Old English Material* (Nijmegen, 1972).]
10 Anderson, *Leningrad Bede*, pp. 112–13.
11 *Ibid.* pp. 110–11.

Uilfaraesduun, but *Cynuise̩, Dorcicæstre̩*, and *Cnobheres burrug, Earcongote, Geuisse*.

The form *Medeshamstedi*, found in *HE(MLB)* and with no alternative noted for *HEN*, probably derives from the original text of *HE. Cynuis(s)e (HE(MLB)*, but *-e̩ HEN*) and *Cnobheres- (HE(MLN)*, but *-aes- HEB*) may also have been in Bede's original text, which otherwise had *æ* forms. This evidence suggests that as early as 731, the date of the completion of *HE*, occasional *e* forms were used in texts which had predominantly *æ*. By 737, the date of *HEM*, *e* forms were common enough to be substituted on occasion for *æ* in copied texts. This substitution may indicate local dialectal differences, the *M* scribe coming from an area where the change of *æ* to *e* took place earlier than in Bede's own speech. Equally well, the *M* scribe could be a man trained in a newer tradition, replacing an old-fashioned spelling by more up-to-date forms. In 746, the date of *HEL*,[12] it was still possible for the copyist of a text to produce mainly *æ* forms.

Little is known of conditions before 731. The original text of *HE* may have been a little old-fashioned in form when it was written down, for Bede was then a man in his late fifties, and may, moreover, have taken some archaic forms from his sources. *CHM, CHL* have a common original, presumably a manuscript deriving eventually from Cædmon's text. This original, written down between 660 and 737, probably had no *e* forms in its inflectional endings, for in the two texts derived from it there is only a single example, *hrofe CHM*, and that may well be a substitution by the *M* scribe (cf. *hrofæ CHL*). The forms *heben CHM, hefen CHL*, however, suggest that the original had *-en*, derived perhaps from earlier *-æn-* (cf. *hefaen- CHM*) < Gmc *-an-*. Such a shift, of unstressed *æ* to *e* before *n*, may have taken place earlier than the general change of unstressed *æ* to *e*.[13]

In its treatment of PrOE *æ* Ruthwell clearly compares with *HE* and could be contemporary with it. It could even be somewhat earlier, though not as early as 660, unless the change from *æ* to *e* in inflectional syllables began much sooner in the Ruthwell dialect than elsewhere.

The shift from *æ* to *e*, clearly begun by the first half of the eighth century, was complete by the tenth, for Northumbrian texts of that period use *æ* only as an occasional archaism. For the intermediate period there is little reliable evidence. *HEB, HEN*, as has been seen, keep a preponderance of *æ* forms. The *Liber Vitæ* of Durham (*LV*) has 5 *æ*, 2 *e̩*, 2 *e*, *Bede's Death Song (BDS)* 7 *æ*, 3 *e*, and the *Glossæ in Psalmos (GIPs)* 3 *æ*. In each of these cases, however, the text may not represent the usage of the time it was written down. *HEB, HEN* may derive some of their *æ* forms from their originals. *LV*, written down *c*. 840, is based at least in part on earlier

---

[12] This date, the evidence for which is summed up in O. Arngart, *The Leningrad Bede: an Eighth Century Manuscript . . . in the Public Library, Leningrad*, EEMF 2 (Copenhagen, 1952), pp. 16–18, is that usually given for *HEL*. E. A. Lowe has recently suggested ('A Key to Bede's Scriptorium', *Scriptorium* 12 (1958), 182–90, at 188–9) that the manuscript may well date from between 731 and 735 and have been produced in Jarrow itself.
[13] Luick, *Historische Grammatik*, § 301, 3; Anderson, *Leningrad Bede*, p. 133: but see also Bülbring, *Elementarbuch*, § 369, 1.

material, though Dahl argues that its language is roughly contemporary with its date of copying.[14] *BDS*, its earliest text from 850–900, must have been composed in 735, and its present form may indicate the linguistic situation of the first half of the eighth century. *GIPs* is considered an accurate ninth-century copy of an eighth-century text.

To sum up. From the point of view of its treatment of PrOE unstressed *æ* Ruthwell could clearly belong to the first half of the eighth century, though it could scarcely be much earlier. Certainly it could not be as late as the tenth century, as far as the textual evidence from that century goes. Whether it could be from the second half of the eighth century or the ninth cannot be decided, for we know very little of the linguistic situation of Northumbrian at that period.

The Ruthwell treatment of unstressed *i* gives no closer dating for the inscription. There are only five significant examples here, and no clear predominance of either *i* or *e*, so even at first glance it is unlikely that any accurate dating will arise from the evidence. PrOE *i* is, for example, found in tenth-century Northumbrian texts, but only as an occasional archaism. Nevertheless, it is conceivable that the present three cases of *i* out of five could appear in a tenth-century text, particularly if the change to *e* took place rather later in some areas than in others. Certainly parallels to all three cases can be adduced from tenth-century texts, for *ni* is an occasional form in the *Lindisfarne Gospels*, *-id* is sometimes found in *Rushworth₂*, *Lindisfarne* as a weak past participle ending, while *-i* is a rare dative-instrumental *a*-stem ending in these texts.

The earliest Northumbrian texts preserve PrOE *i* consistently, though the number of examples is small. *FC* has *ægili*, *drigiþ*, *romæcæstri* and perhaps *risci*. *CH* has *astelidæ* (*ML*), *aerist* (*M*) *ærist* (*L*), *dryctin* (2x) (*ML*), *eci* (2x) (*ML*), *maecti* (*M*) *mehti* (*L*), and *LNK Aeduini*, *Ælfuini*. The early texts of *HE* show occasional change of *i* to *e*. Apart from the case of *Bosel*, which may be a Celtic name,[15] the change only takes place in the name element *heri*,[16] and even there the early *HE* texts do not always agree. So, a comparison of the forms in *HEM*, *HEL* shows *M* reading *Heri-* in *Heribald* (Plummer 289), *Heriberct(o)* (3x) (274, 275), *Heriburg* (285), in all of which cases *L* reads *Here-*. *HEM*, *HEL* agree in reading *Herebald* (289), *Hereberct* (274). *HEM* has *Here-* in *Hereric(i)* (252, 255), *Heresuid* (253), where *L* reads *Heri-*. As a second element *HEM* uses *-heri* consistently, *HEL* agreeing except in the cases of *Sighere* (218) (*-here BK*), *Trumhere* (180) (*-here B*). In *Trumheri* (179) (*-here B*) *HEL* has *-here* with the last letter altered to *i* in the original hand. *HEN* has *Hlothere* (355), while *Cnobhere* (164) may be a nominative wrongly used for a genitive. *HEB* has *Forthere* (321) *[U]ulfhere* (141), *HEK Uulfhere* (207).

Unstressed *i* remains in the great majority of cases in *LV*, but *e* is found occasionally, and is consistently used in the first elements *Dene-*, *Here-* (but cf. the rather

---

[14] *Substantival Inflexion*, pp. 188 and 192.

[15] Redin, *Studies on Uncompounded Personal Names*, p. 141. Anderson (*Leningrad Bede*, pp. 101 and 106) treats it as a Germanic name.

[16] The prefix vowel of the tribal name *Geuissi*, *Geuissae* cannot be included, as it may be from Gmc *a*. Two forms from *HEK*, *stede*, *sebbe*, should, however, be mentioned here.

more common second element form *-heri*). First elements such as *Cyni-*, *Hildi-*, *Hysi-*, *Uini-* use only *i* as composition vowel.

The Northumbrian change of *i* to *e* was clearly only in its early stages when the first texts of *HE* were being copied. The fact that *HE* only evidences the change commonly in *Here-*, the *LV* evidence of the elements *Here-*, *Dene-*, both suggest that unstressed *i* became *e* first when medial and after *e* in the preceding syllable. This change, begun but incomplete at the time of *HE(ML)*, had been carried out by the time of the compilation of *LV* in the middle of the ninth century. The shift of *i* to *e* under other circumstances had scarcely begun when *HE* was written, while the linguistic stage represented by *LV* shows it by no means complete. The texts of Northumbrian coins indicate that the general change of unstressed *i* to *e* was commonly recorded in the second half of the ninth century.

Ruthwell has one example of the early shift of *i* to *e* in '-geredæ' and one of the later change in 'uŋk̄et'. It is, then, probably later than *HE(ML)*. A date in the tenth century is not beyond the bounds of possibility, but is unlikely. There remains the period from, say, 740 to the end of the ninth century.

It is clear that a Ruthwell dating 'early in the eighth century' cannot be proved by the sole evidence of the quality of unstressed vowels. Wrenn claims further 'a number of apparently early forms', but unfortunately does not specify them. There is, moreover, one respect in which Ruthwell shows a later linguistic stage than do the early *HE* texts and which may therefore suggest a date later than 750. The form 'hēafunæs' shows back-mutation. PrOE *e*, followed by *u* in the next syllable, is represented by the rune *ear*, which must indicate a diphthong, though its quality is uncertain. The rune-master of this text uses 'êa' for the stem vowel of '(bih)êa(l)[d]u' and for the fracture diphthong < PrOE *e* followed by *r* + consonant in 'fêarran'. If the rune-name *ear* is cognate with ON *aurr*,[17] 'êa' must also have represented for the Ruthwell rune-master the diphthong derived from Gmc *au*. The form 'hēafunæs' could clearly indicate the completion of back-mutation, with the common Anglian confusion of the *ea/eo* diphthongs, but it could also perhaps indicate that back-mutation had begun, but was not complete. 'êa' would then represent an intermediate diphthong, presumably with the second element *u*. *U*-mutation of *e* is not recorded at all in the forms available from the earliest Northumbrian texts. *CH(ML)* have *metudæs*, *HE(MLB)* several forms in *Herut-*, *Herud-* as well as the Celtic name *Cerotæs-*, *Cerotaes-*. The form *herutbeg GIPs* has been regarded as part of the evidence for an eighth-century original for that text. *LV* has four mutated forms, *Eoforhuaet*, *Eofuruulf*, *Hroeðgeofu*, *Osgeofu*. Ruthwell 'hēafunæs' is clearly at a later stage than the *CH*, *HE* forms, but need not be much later. The *CH*, *HE* spellings may have been taken over from earlier texts, and may have been archaic or old-fashioned when they were written down. But it is clearly possible that Ruthwell is later than *CH*, *HE*, and this may take us to a date at the middle of the eighth century or even later.

---

[17] B. Dickins, *Runic and Heroic Poems of the Old Teutonic Peoples* (Cambridge, 1915), p. 23.

Finally must be mentioned a number of facts which make such a precise dating as Wrenn's impossible. These are:

(1) our ignorance of the speed at which such sound changes as the shifting of unstressed vowels took place in Northumbrian. There are few Northumbrian texts from the ninth century and they are mainly based on earlier material. Whether early forms could still appear in considerable numbers in original ninth-century texts is not known.

(2) our limited knowledge of local dialectal divisions within Northumbrian. For the western part of Northumbria there are no certain texts, apart from inscriptions, before the very late Old English or early Middle English periods. Sound changes could well take place later in the west than in the areas which, perhaps, the *HE* texts represented.

(3) our uncertainty as to how long an elderly man, trained in his youth in an old spelling tradition, would retain the early forms after they had passed out of use among the younger generation. Coupled with this is our ignorance of whether the Ruthwell rune-master was old or young.

(4) our ignorance of the type of tradition the rune-master had to draw upon. In the case of the Ruthwell texts, for example, we do not know the extent to which he was literate in scripts other than runic, whether his spellings were traditional or phonetic, and whether we are justified in drawing the same conclusions from forms composed in runes as we would from their roman equivalents.

It is clear, then, that Wrenn's assertion that the Ruthwell texts are to be dated 'early in the eighth century' cannot be upheld. On the evidence available a date any time in the eighth century seems to be possible, so that even if Collingwood's date for the cross is accepted there need be no conflict between linguistic and artistic dating.

(ii) Collingwood certainly puts the Ruthwell Cross 'rather late in the eighth century',[18] but this date is rejected by many modern art historians who place the cross much earlier. The following are typical early datings: 'VII century' A. Kingsley Porter, *Spanish Romanesque Sculpture* (Florence, n.d.), p. 1; 'late seventh century' A. W. Clapham, *English Romanesque Architecture before the Conquest* (Oxford, 1930), p.138 n.; 'may well date from 700 or even earlier' O. E. Saunders, *A History of English Art in the Middle Ages* (Oxford, 1932), p. 16; before the Bewcastle Cross which is dated '*c.* 700' T. D. Kendrick, *Anglo-Saxon Art to A.D. 900* (London, 1938), pp. 128 and 133; 'a work of the last quarter of the 7th century' F. Saxl, 'The Ruthwell Cross', *Journal of the Warburg and Courtauld Institutes* 6 (1943), 1–19, at 19; 'de la seconde moitié du VIIe' H. Leclercq, 'Ruthwell', *Dictionnaire d'archéologie chrétienne et de liturgie* XV (Paris, 1949), col. 187; 'from 670 to 750' A. Gardner, *English Medieval Sculpture* (Cambridge, 1951), p. 21; 'some time between 675 and 685' L. Stone, *Sculpture in Britain: the Middle Ages* (Harmondsworth, 1955), p. 13.

[18] *Northumbrian Crosses*, p. 119.

A date between 700 and 750 could agree with the linguistic evidence. A date before 700 seems too early, though our knowledge of early Northumbrian is insufficient for us definitely to reject it. Further, we cannot be sure the text was cut at the same time the cross was carved. It could be a later addition.

(iii) There is thus no necessary conflict between the linguistic dating of the *Dream of the Rood* text and the art historian's date for the Ruthwell Cross, and so no need to suggest deliberate archaism in the inscription. Wrenn's argument must then rest on point (iv), the existence in the Ruthwell texts of forms only explicable as archaistic. Before this point is considered in detail, (v) and (vii) can be briefly dealt with.

(v) There is no evidence that the Ruthwell Cross was a memorial stone, for no commemorative text has yet been identified on it. A memorial inscription in a traditional formula might well contain archaic forms, but there is little reason to believe that such a text as the *Dream of the Rood* would. The Ruthwell use of the rune '3' needs a more detailed discussion than Wrenn gives it. In early times the symbol seems to have represented, not *hw* as Wrenn suggests, but a vowel of *i* or *e* quality,[19] and this value it retains in the Dover inscription '*j3slhêard*'. In the north of England, however, it does not have vowel quality, except perhaps in the Thornhill form 'êate3nne' (= *Eadþegne*) (cf. *Lindisfarne ðeign*), and here it could also be the palatal consonant. Perhaps '3' could be thought of as having some vowel quality in Ruthwell 'alme3ttig' (cf. *Lindisfarne reihtniss*), but since the velar consonantal quality in Great Urswick 'toro3tredæ' is certain it is reasonable to assume it in the Ruthwell word. There is then the group Thornhill, Great Urswick, Ruthwell, in which '3' is used as a consonant, palatal or velar. This group, with the inclusion of Bewcastle, is important in that it evidences the new rune *calc*, while Bewcastle and Ruthwell also use the new symbol *gar*, Great Urswick and Thornhill not offering scope for its use. It is clear that in the north, perhaps in the north-west, there is an area in which new runes are being developed, and perhaps here the superfluous vowel symbol '3' was re-used in a consonantal capacity. Far from indicating archaism, then, the Ruthwell use of '3' may be a sign of innovation in runic usage.

(vii) There is no reason at all to connect the Ruthwell Cross with the sub-king Alcfrith. The Ruthwell Cross is not certainly a memorial, and none of its inscriptions has been read as containing any name known to be connected with Alcfrith. The suggestion presumably arises from the often stated connection between Alcfrith and the Bewcastle Cross, but even this is, in the opinion of the present writer, doubtful.

Of the argument there remains only point (iv) in which Wrenn uses the idea of deliberate archaism to explain forms which seem to him inconsistent or anomalous. The rune-master might occasionally introduce a contemporary form, such as 'walde', into an otherwise archaistic text. If unstressed *æ* and *i* had fallen together in *e*, the

---

[19] O. v. Friesen, *Runorna* (Stockholm, 1933), p. 9, H. Arntz, *Handbuch der Runenkunde*, 2nd ed. (Halle/Saale, 1944), p. 72.

rune-master, faced with a contemporary *e*, might substitute for it the wrong earlier form, and so produce 'rodi' for 'rodæ', 'miþ blodæ' for 'miþ blodi'. This is certainly a possible explanation of these forms, and if the theory of deliberate archaism is rejected an alternative must be suggested. The form 'walde' presents no difficulty, for inconsistency of unstressed vowels is common in eighth-century Northumbrian texts. 'rodi' and '[*m*]iþ b*l*odæ' are more problematic, and to them may be added a third not discussed by Wrenn, the verbal form '[*b*]ismæræ[*d*]u'.

Dickins and Ross regard 'rodi' as illustrating the analogical introduction of the locative-instrumental -*i* ending of the *a*-stem nouns into the paradigm of the *ō*-stems, and quote *romæcæstri FC*, *maegsibbi* (= *affectui*) *Epinal* as further examples.[20] Wrenn argues against this working of analogy, rejecting the two parallels, for *maegsibbi* 'seems obviously to be a mere dittographing of the *i* of *affectui*', while the spellings of *FC* are 'evidently careless, inconsistent, or corrupt'. Wrenn's rejection of *maegsibbi* is too strongly put, for 'seems obviously' would be better expressed 'is possibly'. Some of the spellings of *FC* are certainly curious, but these are almost all confined to the *Bargello* side with its cryptic vowel runes. Forms on the British Museum fragments are normal though early, with the exception of the unusual 'giuþeasu', so Wrenn's rejection of 'romæcæstri' seems hasty. Moreover, other cases of an -*i* ending to a locative-instrumental of feminine nouns can be cited. Dahl quotes occasional examples in the *ungō*- and *ijō*-stems[21] and there is the late locative *on duni Lindisfarne* Mt. 26, 30, while the Collingham rune-stone reads 'æft[.]swiþi', presumably a form of the preposition *æfter* followed by a feminine instrumental in -*i*. There seems then no need to regard 'rodi' as a form produced by deliberate archaism.

'b*l*odæ' is a little harder to defend. It is presumably a dative form, not the instrumental we should expect. As Ross points out[22] there is little evidence for the Old English use of dative for instrumental, if only because in most texts the two case endings fell together for phonological reasons. However, Dahl quotes[23] occasional examples of -*æ* endings in *a*-stem nouns and in adjectives used in an instrumental sense, and dative is used for instrumental in Old Saxon and Old High German and so would not be unexpected in Old English.

The form '[*b*]ismæræ[*d*]u' has a curious penultimate vowel. The verb *bysmerian* takes the past tense form of either the first or the second class of weak verbs,[24] and the penultimate vowel of the plural past tense form should be either *i*, *e* or *a*, *o*, *u*. There is, however, an Old High German cognate *bismerēn* of the third weak class,[25] and the Old English verb may also have had a variant in this class. Old English (and Old Saxon) verbs of the third weak class add the dental of the past tense ending direct to the final stem consonant, without intermediate vowel. Old High German has the

[20] *Dream of the Rood*, p. 11; 'Linguistic Evidence', p. 150.
[21] *Substantival Inflexion*, pp. 123, 139–40 and 150.
[22] 'Linguistic Evidence', p. 149.
[23] *Substantival Inflexion*, p. 45.
[24] Ross, 'Linguistic Evidence', p. 149.
[25] J. Schatz, *Althochdeutsche Grammatik* (Göttingen, 1927), § 494.

intermediate vowel *e* and Gothic the diphthong *ai*, both of which could suggest an intermediate Old English vowel *æ*. The Old High German and Gothic forms have been explained as new formations within those languages,[26] and there may have been a similar new formation within Old English, existing side by side with the regular forms and only surviving in '[*b*]ismæræ[*d*]u'. But this is unlikely.

There are two other possible explanations of the form:

(1) that the penultimate *æ* is a sign of deliberate archaism, the rune-master reconstructing 'bismærædu' from the form, something like *bismæredu* (< **bismæridu*), which he used himself. If the rune-master's knowledge of the early language was as sketchy as this suggests, it is questionable if he could have reconstructed as many correct *æ* and *i* forms as Ruthwell contains.

(2) that the form 'bismærædu' was cut in error for 'bismæradu' or 'bismærodu', the error arising from the similarity of the runes 'æ', 'a', 'o', influenced by the presence of 'æ' in the stem syllable. This is certainly the most likely explanation of the form.

Finally, Wrenn's comments on *(i)dægisgæf* can be ignored, partly because the interpretation of this group of runes is uncertain, partly because there is no justification for the initial *(i)* of that group, and a reading *wæpdæ giscæft* would not be particularly archaic.

To sum up this discussion of Wrenn's case. Wrenn suggested that the language of the Ruthwell inscriptions was archaistic to explain (a) a discrepancy between linguistic dating and artistic dating, (b) the existence of anomalous forms, (c) the existence of an apparently archaic runic usage. But the discrepancy (a) cannot be proved to exist, nor can point (c). No evidence supports the additional assumptions that the Ruthwell texts were commemorative and that the Ruthwell cross was connected with Alcfrith. Alternative explanations can be given for the forms under (b), though sufficient evidence cannot be brought forward to support them in every case. Wrenn's case is clearly unproved. Yet it is not disproved, though in the opinion of the present writer the balance of probability is against it. However, this detailed discussion of Wrenn's article, though it has reached no conclusion in the case of the Ruthwell Cross, has thrown up a number of points of importance in the dating of these inscribed stones. It has indicated the disagreement that sometimes arises among art historians as to the dates of the ornament, etc., on the stones themselves, and pointed out again our need of a careful and comprehensive study of the sculptured stones of Anglo-Saxon England. It has shown how little we know of the chronology of some Old English sound changes, and how slight is the basis on which that chronology is built up. Here it is important to stress the lack of texts from certain areas of Anglo-Saxon Britain. In particular, from the whole of the north-west and the Isle of Man, that area which contains the rune-stones of St Ninian's Cave, Whithorn, Ruthwell, Bewcastle, Bridekirk, Great Urswick, Lancaster and Maughold and which reaches perhaps as far south as Overchurch in Cheshire, there are no known texts, and we may not be justified in applying to inscriptions from that area

---

[26] W. Streitberg, *Urgermanische Grammatik* (Heidelberg, 1896), p. 341.

chronologies of sound changes derived from texts from other parts of the country. To take again the case of the Ruthwell Cross. In its treatment of PrOE unstressed *æ* it compares with *HE*, is at about the same stage as *HEL* and seems to be slightly more archaic than *HEM*. Yet in its evidencing of back-mutation (though there is only a single example), it is more advanced than them all. Is this inconsistency due to incomplete archaizing, or is the chronology suggested by *HE* and *HE(ML)* invalid as far as Ruthwell is concerned? Again, Ruthwell shows the early change of medial unstressed *i* after *e* in the preceding syllable in '-geredæ', but not in '*b*ist[*e*]mi[*d*]', while it shows a later change of unstressed *i* in 'uŋk̄et'. Again there may be incomplete archaizing or there may not. A further example of this problem is found in the main inscription of the Great Urswick stone. This reads '+ tunwini setæ æfter toroʒtredæ bekun æfter his bæurnæ gebidæs þer saulæ', the consistent retention of the inflexional vowels *i*, *æ* suggesting an early date. The *-s* ending of the plural imperative 'gebidæs' is, however, unparalleled in Northumbrian texts before the tenth century. This inconsistency may again be due to incomplete archaizing, or the imperative plural *-s* ending may have appeared earlier in the west than elsewhere in Northumbrian, while in this particular case there is the further possibility that the absence of early Northumbrian *-s* endings may arise from the shortage of early texts evidencing verbal forms.

In the present state of our knowledge, then, the dating of inscribed stones by either art historian or linguist is seldom more than tentative,[27] and there should not be any clear conflict of opinion between the two types of expert. It is rare for us to be able to test the linguistic validity of an inscription by reference to external evidence, and there only remains the internal evidence on which Wrenn builds up point (iv) of his argument – the appearance in a text of inconsistencies or of etymologically impossible forms – to indicate whether it is archaistic or not. Inconsistencies there certainly are in Old English inscriptions, but so there are too in manuscript texts where there is no reason to expect archaizing. Etymologically unlikely, perhaps even impossible, forms also appear in inscriptions, but we cannot be certain they are the productions of archaizing inscribers. The form '[*b*]ismæræ[*d*]u', as has been seen, may be simply a mistake. Mistakes certainly occur in Old English inscriptions, perhaps partly because some of them at least were cut direct on the stone without any preliminary setting-out. So, Overchurch has 'fote' where the context clearly indicates 'fore'. A Hartlepool stone has 'hild | digyþ', with the 'd' doubled and the 'g' first omitted and then added above the line. The 'œ' of Ruthwell 'limwœrignæ' was first cut as 'g' and then altered to the correct form. Ruthwell 'rodi' and '[*m*]iþ b*l*odæ' could be the result of similar mistakes. Alternatively, 'rodi' and '[*m*]iþ b*l*odæ' could indicate local grammatical aberrations, for we know little of the extent to which illiterate or semi-literate usage followed the paradigms of the Old English grammars of today. Uncertainties of this sort prevent us using these forms as proofs of an archaizing inscriber.

---

[27] There are, of course, occasional examples of inscriptions which include the date of erection of a stone. The Kirkdale sundial is an obvious case in point.

To take another case, the Great Urswick 'bæurnæ' has an unusual diphthong. This word could be a form of *beorn* 'prince, nobleman, chief' or of *bearn* 'child, son' which in this dialect would fall together with it. The diphthong then arises from the fracture of either WGmc *e* or WGmc *a* before *r* + consonant. A fracture diphthong with the second element *u* is rare, though there is a probable example in the *HE* name *Eumer*, the first element of which has been identified as OE *eoh* 'war-horse'.[28] OE *ēo* (< WGmc *eu*) also occasionally has *u* as its second element in early texts: so, for example *greut FC, steupfaedaer Epinal* 1070, *Hreutford HE(ML), Streunœshalch HEL, Sceutuald* early in the *Nomina clericorum* of *LV*. A second element *u* in such a form as 'bæurnæ' may, then, indicate an early date. The first element *æ* is very rare in fracture diphthongs, but it is well known that the Old English long diphthong from WGmc *au* often appears in early Anglian texts as *œa/œo*: so, *Aeanfled (Ean-HE(LBN)) HEM, genaeot Corpus* 1117, *Aeostoruini* early in the *Nomina diaconorum* of *LV*.

The Great Urswick diphthong *œu* may then be an archaic form of *eo*, perhaps local to part of the Northumbrian area. The nearest parallel is perhaps the name *Ęuda* in the *Calendar of St Willibrord*, though there there may be influence from the Continental Germanic *Eudo*.[29] Equally well, however, the diphthong *œu* could be an archaistic form of *eo*, the first element archaized by analogy with the early spelling *œo* (< WGmc *au*), later *eo*, the second with *eu* (< WGmc *eu*), later *eo*. Evidence of this sort may be held to reinforce the suggestion of deliberate archaism which the appearance of a form 'gebidæs' in an otherwise apparently early text makes, but in the present state of our knowledge of early Northumbrian it cannot prove it.

There are a few more cases like these, where unusual epigraphical forms can be explained as the products of archaizing inscribers, but, in the opinion of the present writer, there is no case in which that explanation is the only possible one. It can even be admitted that in certain types of text some degree of archaism is likely. So, it is clear that traditional formulae were sometimes employed on memorial stones. The Great Urswick text uses the same formula as the Dewsbury fragment's -RHTAE BECUN A[*E*]FTER BEORNAE GIBIDDAD D[*A*]ER SA*U*LE, while the Falstone hogback's + EO[.]TA[.] *AEFTAER* HROETHBERHT*Æ* BECUN AEFTAER EO-MAE 3EBIDAED DER SAULE and '+ [.] æftær roe[.]tæ [*bec*]un æftær e[.] geb[.]æd þe[.] saule' and the Thornhill rune-stone's '+ jilsuiþ : arærde : æft[.] berhtsuiþe . bekun on bergi gebid/daþ *þær* : *saule*' are very similar. In such formulae word forms may have remained fixed over long periods of time, and spellings, once phonetic, may gradually have become traditional and archaic. Names added to such formulae may have retained their contemporary forms, or may have been archaized to give an appearance of consistency to the language of the inscription. These points are possible, but again have not been proved with respect to any specific example.

This article has largely been a negative one, concerned more with the destruction of some old theories than the putting forward of new. A discussion of Wrenn's article

28 H. Ström, *Old English Personal Names in Bede's History*, p. 94.
29 O. Arngart, 'The Calendar of St. Willibrord: a Little Used Source of Old English Personal Names', *Studia Neophilologica* 16 (1943–4), 128–34, at 131 and 133.

on the Ruthwell Cross was of course necessary before any further work on the linguistic dating of Old English memorials could be carried out, for it raised points of the greatest importance. This discussion has, it is hoped, shown how little reliance we can place on close dating of the Old English inscribed stones with our present knowledge, and how little we can say about the linguistic validity or otherwise of their texts. It is unlikely that we can get much further until basic work has been done in a number of fields. We obviously lack a comprehensive modern study of the Anglo-Saxon sculptured stones, preferably carried out by an art historian who has not been influenced by uncertain linguistic datings. There is room for a lot of detailed study of some of the early Old English texts, work of the nature, scope and quality of Anderson's study of the Leningrad Bede. The other early *Historia Ecclesiastica* texts and the *Liber Vitæ* of Durham are obvious subjects for such study. Finally, there is a clear need of a complete corpus of Old English inscriptions, runic and non-runic, so that the epigraphical material can be examined as a whole. Not until this basic work has been done, the materials from these various sources collected and ordered, will any serious work of collation be possible.

POSTSCRIPT

This article, as its wording makes clear, was written to contest arguments put forward by C. L. Wrenn: a junior lecturer at Nottingham taking issue with the Rawlinson and Bosworth Professor at Oxford. In those hierarchical days this was a feat of daring, but Professor Wrenn responded with graceful courtesy, thanking me for taking so seriously a few 'rather frivolous remarks' he had made in a lecture to the Philological Society. His sincerity in so describing them is attested by the fact that he republished them without alteration in his collected essays, *Word and Symbol: Studies in English Language* (London, 1967), pp. 132–5.

Certainly my article has an outdated air today since the display of philological minutiae is not particularly fashionable, even though it would be easy enough to achieve using electronic techniques of collecting and sorting. Yet it is not quite dead. Recently Professor E. G. Stanley has cogently reassessed this work and come to rather different conclusions. My own criticism of my earlier stance would take up two points: (a) whether it is proper to compare forms in two distinct writing systems, runic and roman, one epigraphical and one scribal, (b) whether the Ruthwell texts must be assumed to represent a local dialect or whether they could use an artificial form, developed for inscriptions and perhaps standing apart from contemporary spoken dialects.

Professor Stanley takes a different line.[30] He follows the suggestion I made and Dr Meyvaert took up that decoration and runic texts are not contemporaneous. Indeed

---

[30] 'The Ruthwell Cross Inscription: Some Linguistic and Literary Implications of Paul Meyvaert's Paper "An Apocalypse Panel on the Ruthwell Cross" ', in E. G. Stanley, *A Collection of Papers with Emphasis on Old English Literature* (Toronto, 1987), pp. 384–99.

Meyvaert argued that the lay-out of the runic text suggests it was added when the cross was already assembled and upright. Thus, continues Stanley, the date of the cross, even if that could be established with precision, is largely irrelevant to the date of the language of the inscription. Instead he asks the question: 'what is the linguistic evidence . . . setting an upper limit later than which the runic inscription cannot be dated?'

Stanley rejects the unstressed -*i* and -*œ* endings on which I laid such weight, postulating that they have no dating significance. This is not to cut the Gordian knot but to hew it in pieces, an activity liberating to the attacker but not helpful to the student of Gordian knots. Stanley rests his assertion on two theses: (i) the training of a rune-cutter may have made him aware of archaic forms in earlier inscriptions (compared to contemporary book spelling) and these he may have introduced into the Ruthwell texts, and (ii) cutting an inscription differs essentially from writing on parchment, taking longer and involving more physical effort. The runes 'i' and 'æ' were easier to cut than the two-stemmed 'e' (and took less space) and a rune-cutter might have preferred them to 'e' for that reason.

To these Stanley adds a further doubt founded on different considerations: whether in fact the form *blodæ* occurs on the Ruthwell Cross. This reservation he owes to an assertion by D. R. Howlett, 'the correct reading should be **miþ blodi**'.[31] Howlett noted early drawings that appeared to show an -*i* ending on this noun and could not himself find the distinctive 'æ' form. Indeed, Howlett retains *blodi* in his latest reading.[32] I do not accept his observation. On several occasions when I have looked to check the reading I have had no difficulty in seeing arms that distinguish 'æ' from 'i', faint but clear; as indeed Vietor had recorded them seventy years earlier.[33] In between they had been spotted by a number of scholars, among them G. Baldwin Brown and Bruce Dickins. Nor did Sir Christopher Ball nor Professor Swanton have trouble with this graph. I concede that with different lighting conditions these arms become less or more perceptible, and that one should properly admit there is an element of interpretation in the identification of a specific rune at this point. Indeed I now hesitate to assert so firmly what is 'the correct reading'.

On Stanley's two points of principle I observe:

(i) we know nothing of the training of the rune-cutter nor how literate he would be in roman. It is certainly possible he might consider an archaic set of forms appropriate to a church inscription or memorial, but if so he did not archaize consistently. Stanley's hypothesis is possible, but there is no means of proving it.

(ii) it is true that we should take into consideration the different techniques of engraving and writing. What is clear, however, is that the Ruthwell rune-cutter did

---

[31] 'Three Forms in the Ruthwell Text of *The Dream of the Rood*', *English Studies* 55 (1974), 1–5, at 4.

[32] 'Inscriptions and Design of the Ruthwell Cross', *The Ruthwell Cross: Papers from the Colloquium Sponsored by the Index of Christian Art, Princeton University, 8 December 1989*, ed. B. Cassidy (Princeton, 1992), pp. 71–93, at 87.

[33] 'Beistriche schwach': W. Vietor, *Die northumbrischen Runensteine. Beiträge zur Textkritik. Grammatik und Glossar* (Marburg in Hessen, 1895), p. 8.

not save either effort or space elsewhere in his inscription. He used two distinct forms of the g-rune when he could have used one (as the Mortain rune-cutter, for example, did for 'g o o d' and 'g e w a r a h t æ'); one of them is *gar*, not an easy letter to cut with its small bows at the intersections. Likewise he used three forms of the c-rune, including the distinctly complicated 'k̄' of 'k̄ y n i ŋ c' and 'u ŋ k̄ e t'. He sometimes doubled letters unnecessarily, as in 'a l m e i t t i g' and 'g i s t o d d u [n]'. It does not look as though the Ruthwell rune-master worried about 'the labour of cutting' or 'the space occupied'. Clinching here is the fact that he did not employ the obvious technique of saving labour and space, using bind-runes. The best way of representing 'd æ' economically would be to cut, not 'd i', but 'd͡ æ'.

In a pair of recent articles on the Ruthwell texts Sir Christopher Ball revealed to us how much we lost when he deserted runic studies for educational administration.[34] Both articles raise points that need detailed discussion elsewhere, but the second of them prompts a brief examination here in connection with my 1959 paper. In general (in his section 8) he accepts the approach I adopt to language forms, though he does not use it for dating purposes. He regards the spellings in 'æ' and 'i' of the unstressed vowels as 'graphic relics of a spelling tradition appropriate to an earlier state of the language'. Such forms as 'r o d i' and 'b i s m æ r æ d u' he defines as 'back-spellings', 'cases where -i or -æ . . . are used inappropriately'.[35] Of the two forms Ball comments: 'Although ingenious morphological explanations have been offered for these forms, it is preferable to assume that scribes, or inscribers, whose own pronunciation recognised a single unstressed vowel /e/, occasionally erred in the use of "traditional" spellings in -i or -æ'. He gives no reason for this preference, and I can only assume it is a natural Oxonian distrust of ingenuity. There follows a further speculation whose implications for the study of the Ruthwell texts are profound: 'the possibility that the runic text was itself transliterated from an original version in the Latin alphabet'. He suggests that other runic texts might be transliterations and adds the question: 'can we be sure that *any* runic text dated after about 650 is an "original" rather than transliterated?' The answer to this must be 'no', but if the question is reversed by substituting '*no*' for '*any*' the answer remains the same.

There is of course a major objection to the theory that the Ruthwell runes are transliterated from roman letters: Ruthwell distinguishes the two sets of dorsal consonants ('c', 'k', 'k̄' and 'g', 'ḡ') in a way no preserved text in roman graphs does. Of course Ball notes this and counters it in dashing manner: 'in spite of the absence of direct evidence, I am inclined to admit the possibility that there was for a time in Northumbria an alternative manuscript tradition, distinguishing the members of the two sets of dorsal consonants, from which the Ruthwell Cross usage is derived'. This is a well-known type of argument usually summed up as: 'I have made

---

[34] 'Problems in Early Northumbrian Phonology', *Luick Revisited: Papers read at the Luick Symposium at Schloss Liechtenstein*, ed. D. Kastovsky and G. Bauer (Tübingen, 1988), pp. 109–17; 'Inconsistencies in the Main Runic Inscriptions on the Ruthwell Cross', *Old English Runes*, ed. Bammesberger, pp. 107–23.

[35] Some years ago, agreeing for once with Howlett here, I rejected *bismærædu*, accepting the third vowel as a damaged 'a'. See below, p. 332, n. 20.

up my mind. Don't confuse me with facts'. Or we might ask Sir Christopher to apply his preferred standards of certainty here and to ask: 'can we be sure that *any* written text dated before about 900 consistently distinguishes the two sets of dorsal consonants?'

Roger Lass, no mean Gordian knot hewer himself, has taken up the problem of 'r o d i'.[36] As I understand him, he asserts that *rodi* need trouble no-one: it is an acceptable form, otherwise the Ruthwell rune-master would not have cut it. The difficulty philologists have with its ending is, he thinks, a signal of their reliance on outdated grammatical theory. It is certainly soothing to find someone who has such faith in a rune-cutter. Few runic epigraphers will share his trust.

[36] 'Of Data and "Datives": Ruthwell Cross *rodi* Again', *Neuphilologische Mitteilungen* 92 (1991), 395–403.

5

(1960)

THE BEWCASTLE CROSS

The Bewcastle Cross is generally agreed to be one of the most important of the Anglo-Saxon sculptured stones that have come down to us. Even as it now stands, a shaft some 14 feet 6 inches high, made from a single piece of stone, its shattered top cut out to fit the dowel of the lost head, it is an impressive piece of work. The carving is fine and its programme ambitious. The west face has three figure panels representing (from top to bottom) St John the Baptist bearing the Agnus Dei, Christ in majesty, His feet resting on two beasts, and St John the Evangelist, an eagle on his wrist. An inhabited vegetable scroll occupies the full length of the east face, while the north and south faces each have five decorative panels of interlace, vegetable scroll and chequers, one of the southern vegetable scroll panels enclosing a sun-dial.[1] Further, the Bewcastle Cross bears a number of runic inscriptions, and Old English rune-stones are rare enough indeed – only about thirty-five of them are known – for every one to be of importance.

But the Bewcastle Cross has a particular importance in the study of both Northumbrian sculpture and Old English epigraphy because of its apparent dateability. Two of the inscriptions have been found to refer to people who can be dated from other sources. The latest monograph written about the cross transcribes the main inscription (Text II on p. 49) as '+ þis sigbecn þun setton wætred woþgær olwowolþu æft alcfriþum an kuniŋ eac oswiuŋ + gebiddaþ [hine sauulo]', and one of the texts of the north side (Text IV on p. 52) as 'KYNIBURUG'.[2] The main inscription is translated: 'This slender victory sign set up Wætred, Wothgær, Olwowolthu in memory of Alcfrith, a King and son of Oswiu. + Pray for [his soul]', and the comment is made, 'sufficient of the main inscription is legible for us to identify Alcfrith, the son of Oswiu (or Oswy), King of Northumbria, who was made under-King of Deira about 655. He married Cyneburuh, daughter of Penda of Mercia . . . He probably died before Oswiu (who died in 671) for the histories would surely otherwise have explained how he came to be passed over in the succession'. The transcription and translation of this inscription by other scholars does not necessarily agree exactly

---

[1] For a more detailed description see Brown, *The Arts in Early England* V, 121–44.
[2] F. Willett, *The Ruthwell and Bewcastle Crosses* (Manchester, 1958), pp. 20–1.

with that quoted above, but it has been generally accepted in recent times that the names of Alcfrith and Cyniburg do appear on the Bewcastle Cross. Conclusions about its date have been drawn accordingly, and this great monument, so closely related to the equally important cross at Ruthwell, Dumfriesshire, has been seen as a fixed dating point on which a system of chronology for Anglo-Saxon sculptured stones can be based. So, R. H. Hodgkin[3] regards the Bewcastle Cross as 'probably erected to his [Alcfrith's] memory by Wilfrid or some member of Wilfrid's party', and dates it 'somewhere about 700', an opinion quoted with approval by T. D. Kendrick.[4] F. M. Stenton comments simply, 'A much weathered inscription seems to record that the Bewcastle cross commemorated Alhfrith son of Oswiu and his wife Cyneburg, Penda's daughter'.[5] Among recent art historians A. Gardner remarks that the Bewcastle inscription is 'said to contain the names of several persons known to have been living about the year 670',[6] while L. Stone argues that 'if the runes on the cross do actually refer to Alcfrith, Wilfrid's old patron at Whitby, the erection of the monument cannot possibly be subsequent to the latter's death in 709'.[7] The connexion between the Bewcastle Cross and Alcfrith and his queen is noted even by writers who reject the dating suggested by it. W. G. Collingwood, for example, finds it necessary to argue that the Bewcastle Cross, though established in memory of Alcfrith, was not set up until long after his death.[8] Clearly, then, a reconsideration of the Bewcastle Cross must begin with this point.

The first known mention of the Bewcastle Cross is that made by Reginald Bainbrigg in a collection of notes taken for a revised edition of Camden's *Britannia* during a tour of the North in 1601, the Bewcastle note now forming fol. 321 of MS Cotton Julius F. VI.[9] The cross was then where it now is, in the yard of the parish church of St Cuthbert, Bewcastle (National grid reference NY 566746). When William Nicolson, the Cumberland cleric and antiquary, visited the village in 1685 the main inscription was so badly weathered as to be virtually unreadable.[10] The cross had then been in the open air for a considerable period of time, and indeed there is no reason to doubt that, from the date of its first erection to the present day, the Bewcastle Cross has occupied the same exposed site, suffering there the impact of wind and weather. Weathering is not the only cause of damage to the cross. It may well have undergone deliberate attack, and has certainly suffered from the attempts of scholars of at least two centuries to clean, examine and record the texts engraved

[3] *A History of the Anglo-Saxons* (Oxford, 1935), pp. 300 and 363.
[4] *Anglo-Saxon Art to A.D. 900* (London, 1938), pp. 133–4.
[5] *Anglo-Saxon England*, 2nd ed. (Oxford, 1947), pp. 150–1.
[6] *English Medieval Sculpture* (Cambridge, 1951), p. 22.
[7] *Sculpture in Britain: the Middle Ages* (Harmondsworth, 1955), p. 10.
[8] *Northumbrian Crosses of the Pre-Norman Age* (London, 1927), pp. 116–17.
[9] Bainbrigg's account is recorded in F. Haverfield, 'Cotton Iulius F. VI: Notes on Reginald Bainbrigg of Appleby, on William Camden and on some Roman Inscriptions', *TCWAAS* n.s. 11 (1911), 343–78, at 355.
[10] W. Nicolson, 'A Letter . . . Concerning a Runic Inscription at Beaucastle', *Philosophical Trans. of the Royal Soc.* 15 (1685), 1287–91.

on it.[11] As a result, some parts of the inscriptions are illegible, others are uncertain. The following texts can now be identified on the stone:[12]

I.
      '[+] g [e] s s u s | k r i s t t u s'
       5   10   15

Rune height: from 2·1 (13) to 2·4 inches (9); width: 'e' = 1·3, 'r' = 0·8, 't' (13) = 0·8 inches.

Text I is cut in two lines in the space between the two top figure panels of the west face. This space, irregular because of the roughly rounded top of the Christ panel, is a minimum of 6 inches in height and *c.* 14·75 inches wide, no sign remaining of engraved side lines. The text is very faint, the cross-stave of 1 and the arms of 3 being quite lost, and the cross-staves of 4, 7, 11, 15 and the arms of 12 hard to distinguish. There is no reason, however, to doubt the usual reading +*gessus kristtus*.

II. This, the main inscription, is cut in nine lines in the space below the figure of Christ on the west face. It was set between engraved side lines, still partly traceable on the stone though clearer in photographs, which give a panel width of *c.* 14 inches. Panel height varies because of the rounded top of the figure panel below, but its minimum is 31·5 inches. The inscription is in a very bad state, but the following runes can be seen:

 '+ þ i s s i g b [.] c [.] | * [.] s e t t o/n h | w æ t r e d [. .] þ
   5   10   15   20   25

 | g æ r a [.] w [.] w o [.] | * [.] f t [.] l c f r i | * m [.] n ḡ u
  30   35   40   45   50

 [.] ŋ | [.] c b [. . . .] u/ŋ | [.] g e b i d [.] | [. .] s o [.] o'
  55   60   65   70   75

Rune height: from 2·6 (44) to 3·1 inches (22): width 'e' (15) = 1·3, 'æ' (30) = 0·6, 'w' (34) = 0·7, 't' (42) = 1·0 inches.

It is perhaps misleading to say that these runes can be seen. More accurately, depressions suggesting these runes can be seen, though some of them may have been made by accident or weather.[13] Besides this, incisions may have weathered away

---

[11] For specific cases of such damage see R. S. Ferguson, 'Report on Injury to the Bewcastle Obelisk', *TCWAAS* 12 (1893), 51–6; and W. S. Calverley, *Notes on the Early Sculptured Crosses, Shrines and Monuments in the Present Diocese of Carlisle*, ed. W. G. Collingwood (Kendal, 1899), p. 45.

[12] Runes are transliterated according to the method described in Dickins, 'System of Transliteration', and further in B. Dickins and A. S. C. Ross, *The Dream of the Rood* (London, 1934), p. 8. The asterisk is used to indicate characters of which the form is clearly visible but the value undetermined. The readings of the Bewcastle texts derive from a number of examinations of the cross between April 1956 and July 1958.

[13] A criticism that can be made of R. G. Collingwood's important drawing ('The Bewcastle Cross',

completely, leaving the remains of one rune looking much like another. So, 'æ' could be confused with 'a' or 'o', 'l' with 'æ' or 't', 'f' with 'o', 'u' with 'y', 'e' with 'm', 'ḡ' with 'k̄', and 'b' with 'w' or 'c'. An apparent 'i' form might be the remaining stem of a number of letters, and a number of forms could develop accidentally from 'i'. Finally, two stems, originally of separate runes, could be joined by accident into such two-stem letters as 'h', 'e', 'm', 'd'. Even the visible forms, then, must be received with caution.

Though these forms are visible, they are not always clear. The bows of 8, the arms of 15–18, 32, 75, the bow and tail of 47 are faint, while 52, 64 are altogether indistinct. The cross-staves of 25, 50, 70, the bow of 28, the centre of 53 are damaged. The surface has weathered away to the left of the incisions of 56 suggesting the possibility of the bind-rune 'i/ŋ' there.

Ambiguous fragments remain of some of the runes not yet accounted for. So, 27 is 'o', 'a' or, less likely, 'æ'; 33 is probably 'l', but 'æ', 'a' are not impossible; 35 is most likely 'o', but could be 'f'; 38 is 'æ' or 'l'; 40 'a' or 'æ'; 43 'o' or 'a'; 51 'æ', 'a' or 'l'; 57 'm' or 'e'; 60 'o', 'f' or, less likely, 'a'; 62 'm' or 'e'.

The forms which remain undescribed are:

9: two stems, called here S_1 and S_2, 1·3 inches apart, the surface between their tops worn away. From S_2 to the stem of 10 is 1·2 inches, unusually large if there were no arms or bows to the right of S_2. The surface here is much marked, most marks being due to accident or weather, but in some lights S_2 seems to have an arm as of 'l'.

11: a stem only, its lower half very faint, 1·5 inches from the stem of 10 and c. 1 inch from the side line.

13: a stem, its centre much worn, 0·9 inches from 12 and 1·2 inches from 14.

26: a very faint stem slightly to the left of mid-way between 25 and 27.

55: two faint stems, 1·4 inches apart, the first stem 0·8 inches from 54, the second 0·8 inches from 56.

61: two stems, 1 inch apart, with a cross-stave like that of H, but sloping down from right to left.

63: a faint and fragmentary stem 0·7 inches from 62 and c. 1 inch from 64.

65: a space, in which nothing can be traced, before the beginning of 66, 1·75 inches from the side line.

71: a space, in which nothing can be certainly seen, between 70 and the side-line 4·7 inches to its right.

72: two stems, 1·3 inches apart, with a cross-stave like that of H, but sloping down from left to right.

TCWAAS n.s. 35 (1935), 1–29, at 25) is that it makes too clear a distinction between incisions and accidental marks.

73: traces of stems 0·7, 1·3, 2·2, 3·3, 4·4 inches to the right of 72.

76: two 'u' forms, apparently joined by a cross-stave sloping down from left to right. 0·6 inches after the second 'u' is a faint stem, 1·3 inches from 77.

III.   '[.] s s u/s'
                        1 2 3 4

Rune height: from 4·25 (2) to 4·5 inches (4): width: 'u' = 1·0, 's' (2) = 0·9 inches.

Text III is a single line of runes taking up the full width of the north face at the shaft head. Like other texts on the cross it has suffered weathering, and as in other texts at the shaft head the weathering has been particularly severe. Rain, collecting on the broken top and running down the sides, has worn deep grooves down the topmost parts of all four faces. These grooves are not easily distinguishable from incisions, and in some cases may coincide with them.

FIG. 1

The top left-hand corner of the north face is broken away, and the first characters of III are too badly damaged to be legible. The first legible rune, 2, begins c. 7·25 inches from the face's original left-hand edge. About 0·5 inches to the left of 2 is a stem, before which, amid a number of weathering grooves, two more stems may be distinguished. Of the final letter complex the 'u' is clear, though its top is worn.

Bound to the 'u' is the cross-stave of 's' with its right-hand stem. This stem seems to be full-length, though the part above the cross-stave is fainter, and may have been produced by weathering. A left-hand stem of 's', rising above the curve of the 'u' may also be traceable in the weather damage at that point (fig. 1).

Text III presumably gives a form of the name *Jesus*.

IV.   'k y n i b u r * ḡ'
                            5

Rune height: from 1·65 (3) to 2·1 inches (1): width: 'k' = 1·2, 'b' = 0·6, 'n' = 0·5 inches.

Text IV is a single line of runes cut on the raised fillet, *c.* 2·4 x 13·8 inches, between the two lowest decorative panels of the north face. Engraved lines mark the sides of the runic panel. The fillet's top edge is fairly intact, its lower one damaged; in general, the runes seem to have been cut clear of the edges at top and bottom, though the top of 4 and the bases of 3, 4 and 6 probably ran out of the fillet. Though this face of the cross is sheltered by the church building, the stone surface has weathered, leaving, however, the runes quite legible. The very tops of 2 and 6 are lost, and the cross-stave of 3, the bows of 5 and the left-hand loop of 9 are faint. 4 is at a deeply eroded part of the surface, but the stem is clear, and there is no sign of a cross-stave of 'n', which has sometimes been read at this point.

V. Text V is a fragment of a single line of runes on the south face at the shaft head. The end of the text is broken away, and at the beginning it is hard to distinguish between incisions and weathering grooves. The following can be seen:

(i) a stem and arm as of 'l'. The arm, however, runs into a vertical groove, the top part of which could be an incision, forming the upper arm of 'o' or 'a'. Equally well, however, it could be a weathering groove, as its lower part almost certainly is. The reading 'li' is unlikely.

(ii) 'c'.

(iii) a stem, or groove, the base almost touching that of the arm of 'c'. To the right of this a much worn and grooved patch of surface.

VI.   '[.] g e [.]'
                            1 2 3 4

'e' is 1·75 inches high, 1·1 wide.

Text VI is a single line of runes cut on the raised fillet, *c.* 2·3 x 15·5 inches, between the two lowest decorative panels of the south face. So worn is the surface that only one complete rune remains, 3, which begins 11·5 inches from the left-hand edge of the panel. Immediately preceding it is the lower half of 'g', and immediately following a stem with an arm or bow at its top. 1·2 inches further to the right is a

(a)

(b)

(c)

(d)

(e)

(f)

(g)

(h)   (i)

PLATE I
BEWCASTLE INSCRIPTION IV
(a) as it is now; and as it appears in the drawings of (b) Bainbrigg, (c), (d) Nicolson,
(e) Smith, (f) Hutchinson, (g) Howard, and (h), (i) Maughan

second stem, 0·85 inches from the right-hand edge. This could be the stem of 'r', though the faint resemblance to that rune is more probably due to surface weathering.

No other texts can be seen on the cross, though the east and west faces of the shaft head have a number of weathering grooves, which may have originated in runic inscriptions similar to III and V. Texts identified by nineteenth-century investigators on other fillets of the north and south faces need not be taken seriously. Finally must be mentioned the recorded inscription of the lost cross head. This will be considered in detail later.

The ascription of the Bewcastle Cross to Alcfrith and Cyniburg is based on Texts II and IV, but each of these texts has a form, rune*, which is clearly visible but not readily identifiable, and which appears at the points where the names of Alcfrith and Cyniburg have been found. Rune* is the initial letter of lines 2, 5 and 6 of Text II (runes 12, 39, 49) and the penultimate letter of Text IV (rune 8). Its most clearly defined form, as well as its most clearly defined context, is in Text IV. This shows it to be formed as 'u', but with most of the space between the two lines of that rune filled by two rounded bows, one above and touching the other, projecting to the right of the vertical stem. The base of the lower bow is very slightly above the stem base: the top of the upper bow is below the stem top. Where the two ends of a bow meet the stem they tend to be overcut and to project slightly beyond it. Alternatively, the upper bow could perhaps be regarded as two horizontal incisions running across the width of the 'u', the bow effect resulting from weathering of the stone surface where they meet the curved stem. The upward curve of the bottom of the lower bow is, however, quite clear (fig. 2 and pl. I a).

The lines of this example are clearly cut, though the incisions forming the bows vary in depth. There is little doubt that their lines are deliberate. If the bows are not part of the original inscription, they are most readily explained as the result of some attempt at alteration or cleaning. They cannot be due to weathering, and are unlikely to be caused by accident. An unprejudiced observer of the stone in its present state could not fail to notice them, and in any case would not read the letter as 'u'.

The three examples in Text II are similar in form to that in IV, though there is less doubt as to the intentional shape of the upper bows. These runes are, however, severely weathered, and the bow incisions are particularly faint, so faint indeed as to suggest that they might have been formed accidentally – by numbers of students tracing with their fingers on Text II the form clearly found on IV. Certainly the loose stone surface could have been disturbed in such a way; but it should be noted that not until R. G. Collingwood's 1935 article was it recorded that there were three, *deliberately cut*, roughly horizontal incisions running across IV, 8, and by then the bows or cross-cuts were already noted on the three forms of the main inscription. The faintness of these marks is significant in that they might not be noticed by an observer who was not expecting to find them.

There are here, then, four cases of an unusual runic form, and any interpretation must fit all four contexts. If the form is genuine, it can be explained as:

(*a*) A special rune, probably invented in the north-west of the Anglo-Saxon area, and preserved only at Bewcastle. There are no other examples of unique Bewcastle

FIG. 2

runes, nor is this particular form found in non-epigraphical sources – in the various *fuþorcs* and runic alphabets found in manuscripts. Moreover, the Bewcastle Cross is less advanced in the development of new runes than is the Ruthwell Cross. Bewcastle and Ruthwell are the only rune-stones to have the late character 'ḡ' but Ruthwell also has a further rune, the voiceless back stop symbol 'k̄', which Bewcastle does not use. We would not expect to find on Bewcastle an additional rune not used on Ruthwell.

(*b*) A bind-rune. Bewcastle certainly uses bind-runes: so, 'u/s' in III, 'o/n', 'u/ŋ' and perhaps 'i/ŋ' in II. Such bind-runes are found at the end of a line ('u/s', 'u/ŋ', 'i/ŋ') so that a name or sentence ends at the line end, or where a combination can be made easily ('o/n').[14] The examples of rune* fit neither of these conditions. There is no need spatially to make the binds – the three examples in II begin lines rather than ending them – and the form, far from being easily made, is complicated and full of curves difficult to cut.

Nevertheless, the majority of modern interpretations of Bewcastle II assume rune* to be the bind-rune 'þ/u', and this possibility must be further examined. It was first suggested by J. Maughan, local antiquary and rector of Bewcastle, in *A Memoir on the Roman Station and Runic Cross at Bewcastle* (London, 1857). He was the first to record[15] a single, upper, bow to the right of the vertical stem of the rune. His illustrations show[16] the form Ꝥ for all four examples, and this is read as a bind of 'þ' and 'u'. For II he reads 'B[EA]CN [THU]N', 'ALWFWOL[THU]' and 'AL-CFRI[THU]', and for IV 'KYNNBUR(THU)G', making no attempt to explain the unusual form of the name's second element.

Maughan's reading has been followed substantially by most later students.

---

[14] This may have been a commonly used bind. It is evidenced, for example, on a rune-stone found at Kirk Maughold, Isle of Man, where the inscription, formerly read '-gmon', seems, in fact, to be '-gmo/n*'. The last symbol is a half-length stem, its top in line with the other stem tops; this may be a half-length 'i', or may be a punctuation dash ending the text.

[15] *Memoir*, pp. 17–18.

[16] *Ibid.* pp. 17 and 28.

PLATE II
BEWCASTLE INSCRIPTION II

(*a*) Stephens, *Old-Northern Runic Monuments* I–II, 398– from sketches, photographs and rubbings prepared by Maughan, and from an admittedly unsatisfactory cast of the main text. He has Ꝥ for all examples in II, and reads 'BECN ÞUN', 'OLWFWOLÞU' and 'ALCFRIÞU'. Text IV he reads 'KÜNNBURUG', admitting '*three* apparent bars or marks across the last U'.[17] These are shown on his general view of the cross, but not on the separate drawing of IV. The interpretation of IV, 8, as 'þ/u' is rejected on the grounds of the impossibility of a form 'KÜNNBURÞUG', and the marks across the penultimate letter are described as 'chips and flaws, of which there are many scattered up and down among the letters'.

Based on Stephens are the texts of H. Sweet, *The Oldest English Texts*, EETS 83 (London, 1885), p. 124, and G. F. Browne, *The Ancient Cross Shafts at Bewcastle and Ruthwell* (Cambridge, 1916), p. 16.

(*b*) W. Vietor's transliteration, *Die northumbrischen Runensteine. Beiträge zur Textkritik. Grammatik und Glossar* (Marburg in Hessen, 1895), pp. 13–16, is made with a prior knowledge of Maughan's and Stephens's texts, though Vietor views Maughan's readings with caution. He reads IV as " 'C'YNIBURUG' ", rune 8 being described as 'mehrfach quer verletztes U'.[18] II, 12, is read as 'U', II, 39 and 49, as '(U, mit Querstrichen)', while Victor regards Maughan's 'ALCFRIÞU' as 'sehr wahrscheinlich'.[19]

(*c*) The Calverley-Collingwood reading, *Notes on the Early Sculptured Crosses*, pp. 39–47, and W. G. Collingwood, 'Remains of the Pre-Norman Period', *VCH Cumberland* (London 1901–5) I, pp. 253–93, at 277–8, is that of Stephens, illustrated by a photograph of II with Maughan's letters painted in.

(*d*) There are three readings by G. Baldwin Brown: (1) in 'Kreuz von Bewcastle', *Reallexikon der germanischen Altertumskunde*, ed. J. Hoops (Strassburg, 1911–19) I, pp. 272–4. IV is transliterated 'CYNIBURYG', 8 being 'u' with a single line crossing it. Only part of II is given but that includes the reading 'ALCFRITHU', with the bind-rune 'þ/u'. (2) In 'Report on the Ruthwell Cross: with some references to that at Bewcastle in Cumberland', *The Royal Commission on Ancient and Historical Monuments and Constructions of Scotland: Seventh Report with Inventory of Monuments and Constructions in the County of Dumfries* (Edinburgh, 1920), pp. 219–86, at 241–2. Here Maughan's reading is generally accepted, with the readings '-becn thun' and 'æft Alcfrithum . . .', while fig. 163, p. 246, shows IV, transcribed 'KYNIBURU(Y?)G', and with 'u' with two transverse dotted lines for rune 8. (3) The same illustration of IV is given in *The Arts in Early England* V, pl. XXV, p. 201, and the comment is made (p. 260), 'The penultimate rune is a *u* much marked by transverse incisions, but without the vertical stroke of the *y* rune'. In II (fig. 18 (1), p. 247), the three examples are drawn as 'þ/u' and the readings 'becn þun', 'Olw.wolþu' and 'æft Alcfriþum' are given.

---

[17] *Old-Northern Runic Monuments* I–II, 404.
[18] *Die northumbrischen Runensteine*, p. 14.
[19] *Ibid*. p. 16.

Before R. G. Collingwood's 1935 article there is one exception to the general acceptance of Maughan's interpretation. In his article 'The Saxon Cross at Bewcastle', *Archæologia Æliana* n.s. 1 (1857), 149–95, at 152–4 and 192, and again in *The Conquest of Britain by the Saxons* (London, 1861), p. 37 and pl. II, D. H. Haigh reads runes II, 12, 39, and IV, 8, as 'u' and II, 49, as 'y'. His text has 'BECUN', 'FLWOLDU' (for *felwoldu*, conjecturally emendated to 'BOLDU' in the second version), 'YMB' and 'CYNIBURUG'. These readings, apparently in opposition to Maughan's, were, however, reached at least as early as, and perhaps rather earlier than, Maughan produced his 1857 text. In January 1856 E. Charlton read a paper 'On the Bewcastle Cross' at a meeting of the Society of Antiquaries of Newcastle upon Tyne. The paper was not published, but a report in the *Carlisle Journal* for 11 January 1856 indicates that it compared early Haigh and Maughan versions. We know something of the basis of Haigh's reading, though the evidence is that of the hostile witness Maughan, who devoted part of his *Memoir* to the subject.[20] Haigh had made drawings of the Bewcastle Cross as early as 1838, since when it had been extensively cleaned by Maughan. Haigh's 1857 interpretation, however, was to some extent reached on the basis of rubbings provided by Maughan.[21] Maughan claimed (*a*) that the rubbing of the main text was deliberately left unclear at certain points, and (*b*) that Haigh's final reading owed little to his subsequent visit 'limited to about two hours'.[22] A rubbing would be unlikely to reproduce the bows or cross-staves of the rune* forms of II. In the particular case of II, 12, Maughan records[23] that he drew Haigh's attention to the lines across that letter. Haigh's reply was *'they were merely accidental marks, and of no consequence at all'*. Haigh's reading of II, 12, 39, 49, then, may well have arisen from a study of the rubbings alone, not altered by the later examination of the original. It should be noted that in Text IV, of which he does not seem to have had a rubbing, he also reads the rune* form as 'u', but here he may have been influenced by the common form *burug*.

In general, Maughan's 1857 reading is closer to the stone as it now stands than Haigh's, which is only preferable if one assumes that the texts have been tampered with in more recent times. The continuous series of later readings agreeing with Maughan's makes this unlikely. There are few cases of later writers following Haigh's readings.[24]

In Maughan's reading of II and the later readings which agree with Maughan runes 12, 39, 49, have generally been read as 'þ/u' in an attempt to solve the problems that otherwise arise at these points. Vietor alone reads II, 12, as 'u', but gives no interpretation of that part of the text. Other scholars – and they knew the Bewcastle Cross from personal examination – had no hesitation in identifying the runes as binds of 'þ' and 'u'. But the treatment of IV shows how unsatisfactory is this identification.

[20] *Memoir*, pp. 31–8.
[21] Cf. 'The Saxon Cross at Bewcastle', p. 154.
[22] *Memoir*, p. 38.
[23] *Ibid*. p. 34.
[24] See, however, I. Taylor, 'Runes', *Chambers's Encyclopædia* IX (London, 1892), pp. 24–5, at 25, following Haigh's 1861 text.

IV, 8, is, as has been seen, identical in form with II, 12, 39, 49. Yet the reading 'þ/u' is manifestly impossible in IV, and hence the attempts to identify IV, 8, as 'u' or 'y', and to attribute the transverse marks to accident. Even in II the reading 'þ/u' is unsatisfactory. It necessitates the acceptance of readings 'þ/un', unusual formally and stylistically without parallel in these memorial inscriptions, and either 'alcfriþ/u' with its doubtful or very early ending or the Latin accusative 'alcfriþ/um', again unparalleled elsewhere in Old English memorial texts. Moreover, the form of rune* with its double bow cannot be traced back to a bind of 'þ' and 'u'. 'b/u' is more likely, but even such a form cannot be accepted. For the bows of rune* are fully rounded, while those elsewhere in the Bewcastle texts are made up of nearly straight lines, which curve only slightly inwards and meet nearly at a point. Further, the bows of rune* touch one another at the stem centre: those of the Bewcastle 'b' are separated by a length of stem.

The interpretation of rune* as 'þ/u' clearly causes difficulty. Fortunately, an examination of earlier records throws light on the form. Referring to II, 12, in his *Memoir*, Maughan talks of: 'The cross bars . . . having been noticed by me from the first'.[25] This is contradicted by his earlier accounts of the Bewcastle inscriptions. In 'The Maiden Way, section II. – the Branch Way and Roman Station at Bewcastle', *ArchJ* 11 (1854), 124–35, esp. 130–4, Maughan describes II, 12, as 'undoubtedly U', but this might stem from his desire to identify the name *Dunstano* in lines 1–2 of that text. A wood-cut shows II, 12, as 'u' with a cross-stave cutting the vertical stem at its centre and sloping down from right to left. II, 39, 49, are shown as 'u' forms. IV, 8, is 'u' with a dot at the centre of the vertical stem (pl. I, h), but it is described enigmatically as 'a compound of OU'.

A number of Maughan MSS cast further light on his readings. These are (*a*) MS 430A, Carlisle Public Library, dated 1852, *The Maiden Way*; (*b*) MS 427A, Carlisle Public Library, *The Runic Cross at Bewcastle, Cumberland. 1854*; and (*c*) a drawing, dated 1855, in Cumberland Brown Portfolio, Library of the Society of Antiquaries of London, p. 75. Documents (*b*), (*c*) give substantially the same account of the cross, (*a*) differs considerably, but agrees with the others as far as the forms of rune* are concerned. It is convenient, then, to quote from (*b*), the most complete record. II is given twice, on fols 22ʳ, 23ʳ, and IV on fol. 33ᵛ (pl. I, i). II, 12, IV, 8, are shown as 'u' forms with cross-staves, sloping down from right to left, cutting the vertical stems at their centres. II, 39, 49, are 'u' forms. No bows are shown on any of these runes. Of II, 12, Maughan comments: 'The next word is the compound word "Dunsetta", or perhaps Daunsetta or Dounsetta, as the second letter U seems to have a bar across it'.[26] Of IV he adds, 'I may also suggest that the word may be read "Kyneburoug" . . . the penultimate letter being the diphthong OU'.[27]

It is clear then that what Maughan first saw in the forms of rune* was neither the single bow which he later identified nor the double bow now visible. It is, of course, possible that the forms of the rune were obscured by dirt or lichen on the surface of

[25] *Memoir*, p. 18.
[26] MS 427A, 27ʳ.
[27] *Ibid*. 36ʳ.

the cross and were only clearly seen after Maughan's cleaning. On the other hand, it is possible that the inscriptions on the Bewcastle Cross were altered after his early readings and before his later one. It is important, therefore, to make some critical examination of earlier records of the Bewcastle Cross, and at this point it is convenient to refer only to IV, since that inscription is more easily legible, and should be more accurately recorded, than the others. The following records of Bewcastle IV were made before 1854:

(a) Reginald Bainbrigg's drawing in the account already mentioned gives a reading 'Ð+IBOROX·', clearly an attempt to read the runes as roman characters (pl. I, b). The rune 'y' is given by D with an I infix, 'n' by a cross, 'u' by O and 'ḡ' by X, the point of the right-hand loop being indicated by the following dot. Rune 8 is represented by O, suggesting that its form resembled that of 6. Bows or cross-staves were either absent or omitted by Bainbrigg, who regarded them as accidental blemishes on an O form.

(b) Nicholas Roscarrock's letter, dated 7 August 1607, to the antiquary, William Camden (MS Cotton Julius C. V, fol. 77), contains the following account:

'Yf you have any occasion to speake of the Crosse of Buechastell I assure my self the inscription of one syde ys Hubert de Vaux the rather for that the checky coate ys aboue yt on the same syde. & on the other the name of the ermitt that made yt. & I canne in no sorte be brought to thincke yt Eborax as I perceave you have beene advertised'.

The side with the 'checky coate' is the north side, decorated with a panel of chequers, and the reading 'Hubert de Vaux' is a transliteration of IV. Rune 7 ('r') could perhaps be read as A, while 9 ('ḡ') could easily be taken for X. 8 must then have been read as U or perhaps V, which are possible if there were no bows across the form. The rejected 'Eborax' was also presumably a reading of IV, though Roscarrock's statement is not clear on the point. 8 is then read as A, suggesting a form with one transverse line. It is possible, however, that 'Eborax' derives from Bainbrigg's reading.[28]

(c) William Nicolson's two accounts, the first in a letter, dated 2 November 1685, to Obadiah Walker, published in the Royal Society's *Philosophical Trans.* 15 (1685) 1287–91, the second, dated 30 July 1703, in his MS Visitation of the diocese of Carlisle in the library of the Dean and Chapter of Carlisle, published in *Miscellany Accounts of the Diocese of Carlisle*, ed. R. S. Ferguson (London, 1877), pp. 56–7. The first of these shows an inscription reading 'kunnburug', the runes being described as 'fairly legible' (pl. I, c). The second gives a similar reading, though 4 is less clearly 'n' (pl. I, d). The second element is certainly 'buruḡ' and the inscription is 'as fair & legible as it was at first'.

---

[28] A. S. Cook, *Some Accounts of the Bewcastle Cross between the Years 1607 and 1861* (New York, 1914), p. 148.

(*d*) George Smith's wood-cuts in the June and July issues of *Gentleman's Magazine* 12 (1742), pp. 318 and 369, show an inscription reading 'kyþiburug̅' (pl. I, e). The letters are described as 'fairly legible', and runes 5–8 are identified as 'BURU plain'.

(*e*) W. Hutchinson's *The History of the County of Cumberland* I (London, 1794) has an account of the cross (pp. 80–7). A wood-cut of IV is based on a reproduction produced 'by oiling the stone and pressing in wax, and then with printer's ink, taking upon paper the character'.[29] This non-selective process should have reproduced accurately the surface forms, but the wood-cut is clearly not always accurate. Distances – that from 'k' to 'n', for example – are not always truly represented, while forms such as 'b' and 'r' are distorted, possibly because their shapes resemble those of B and R known to the illustrator. The reproduction does, nevertheless, show clearly some aspects of the inscription's condition. It indicates some of the weathering – that round 'k', 'i' and 'g̅', for example – and shows, too, that the staves of 'y' can no longer be seen to meet at the top. There is no indication of bows or lines across 8: a simple 'u' is shown (pl. I, f).

(*f*) Henry Howard's original drawings for 'Observations on Bridekirk Font and on the Runic Column at Bewcastle, in Cumberland', *Archaeologia* 14 (1803) 113–18, pl. XXXIV, are preserved in Cumberland Red Portfolio, Library of the Society of Antiquaries of London, pp. 3 and 5. Howard gives the following account of his method:

> 'In taking the inscription I followed the same plan as at Bridekirk, working the paper in with the finger, and afterwards following the finger at the edges of every part of the letters with the pencil, so that, in the paper I send, you have all that can be either seen or felt of this inscription'.[30]

This suggests some selection. Howard's 'following the finger at the edges of every part of the letters' might imply that he thought he knew what shape characters he ought to find. The unevennesses of the stone are certainly not mechanically reproduced, for there are few signs of weathering in the drawing of IV, though some is shown to the right of 'i' and also around 'g̅'. On the other hand, Howard has not added to what he saw and felt, for his reproductions of both II and IV show no reconstruction of forms only partly visible, as in the case of 'g̅' (IV, 9) with its missing left-hand loop. Presumably Howard selected by sight and feel depressions which seemed to him to be deliberate incisions, and reproduced them, indicating only a minimum of other (weathering or accidental) depressions. Had the bows or lines across IV, 8, been clearly marked as they now are, Howard would surely have included them in his drawing. In fact, he shows a simple 'u' with a suggestion of weathering to the right of the stem and below its centre. This represents weathering still visible at or slightly below the present centre-point of the two bows (pl. I, g).

---

[29] *History of the County of Cumberland*, p. 85.
[30] 'Observations on Bridekirk Font', p. 118.

(g) The original drawings for D. and S. Lysons, *Magna Britannia; being a Concise Topographical Account of the Several Counties of Great Britain*, IV Cumberland (London, 1816), pp. cxcix–cci and pl. XXIII, are preserved in the British Library (Additional MS 9462, fols 109 and 113). IV is described by Lysons as 'a pretty perfect inscription in Runic characters'[31] and all drawings show the penultimate rune as 'u'. There is, however, some doubt about the extent to which the Lysons drawings are independent of Howard.[32]

The evidence can be summed up thus:

(1) There are six independent records of Bewcastle IV before Maughan's first text, those of Bainbrigg, Roscarrock, Nicolson, Smith, Hutchinson and Howard, and there are also the Lysons drawings. None shows any bow or group of transverse lines in rune 8. Five give the form 'u', while the other two interpret it as a roman character. Howard shows slight weathering to the right of the vertical stem, which may explain the A of Roscarrock's quoted *Eborax* as well as Maughan's 1852–5 forms.

(2) There is a difference between the form of IV, 8, shown on Maughan's early drawings and that of the 1857 *Memoir*.

(3) After 1857 all records indicate one or more bows or transverse lines across IV, 8. Haigh's texts, apparent exceptions to this, are based on rubbings and an examination carried out before 1857.

It is hard to doubt that the bows or cross lines of IV, 8, were either cut or opened out between, say, 1852 and 1857. If this is so, the validity not only of Bewcastle IV but of all the Bewcastle texts is called in question. IV, 8, could have been altered in two ways:

(*a*) By a mischievous tampering with the inscription. It is obviously unsatisfactory to explain an unusual form as a faked or altered one, but in the case of the Bewcastle Cross other evidence gives support to the suggestion. On several occasions Maughan was taken in by practical jokers living in the neighbourhood of Bewcastle, who faked antiquities and brought them to his notice. Two of these fakes were runic inscriptions, though the runes used in them were Scandinavian. These were the Barnspike inscription 'found' in 1864 and the text 'found' at Hessilgil Crag in 1872.[33] Both were reported to learned societies by Maughan. They were recognized as forgeries independently by Calverley-Collingwood[34] and R. S. Ferguson,[35] the latter claiming that it was common knowledge in the Bewcastle district that the inscriptions had

---

[31] *Magna Britannia* IV, cc.

[32] See below, p. 64.

[33] J. Maughan, 'The Runic Rock at Barnspike, Cumberland, England', *Mémoires de la société royale des antiquaires du nord* 5 (1866–71), 11–22, and 'A Runic Inscription on Hessilgil Crag: Murchie's Cairn', *TCWAAS* 1 (1883), 318–21.

[34] *Notes on the Early Sculptured Crosses*, pp. 48–53.

[35] *PSAL* 2nd ser., 18 (1899–1901), 88–91. A note in Ferguson's copy of Maughan's 'The Runic Rock' (Carlisle Public Library) reads 'Both the Barnspike and Hessilgill Runic Inscriptions are modern forgeries by a schoolmaster there'.

been faked. In a letter dated 11 December 1865 E. Charlton reported that the Barnspike runes had been 'freshly cut as on a tombstone of yesterday. The stone had been covered with black paint, and then each letter of the inscription had been cut out afresh with a sharp tool'.[36] Charlton, however, may have been a biased witness, for he backed Haigh against Maughan in the Bewcastle controversy. Maughan's reply, dated 3 February 1869, denied that re-cutting of the inscription had taken place: 'Mr. Little, the neighbouring farmer, who let me see the inscription, told me at the time that he and Watson had on different occasions scratched the letters to get the moss out of them, trying to find some letters which they could read. This I believe is all the fresh cutting which the letters have received'.[37] Later Charlton commented: 'it requires a keen eye to be certain that it is not a modern forgery'.[38] It is possible that what Charlton took for a re-cut inscription, and Maughan an old one newly cleaned of moss, was in fact a newly-cut fake. If this were so, a similar imposition could have been made upon Maughan when the various Bewcastle texts were cleaned.

(b) By a scholar cleaning the inscription of lichen and opening out faint and perhaps accidental marks on the stone. We know that during Maughan's rectorship a good deal of cleaning of the Bewcastle Cross took place.[39] Although Maughan professed great respect for the cross, venerating it 'as much as if it had been made from my own bones', he allowed the surface to suffer considerable attack. He himself, and such a visitor as Haigh, working under his surveillance, did not hesitate to scrape away at the stone with knives,[40] and this may account for scratches down the centre-lines of stems in Bewcastle II. Clearly, the marks across IV, 8, could have been made more distinct in this way, but in view of the appearance of identical forms in II it is unlikely that they would have been produced – cut for the first time – in this way. The mystery of the meaning of rune* then remains.

The result of the discussion so far has been to cast doubt on the validity of Bewcastle IV as it now stands. In turn this casts doubt on the validity of the other Bewcastle texts, in particular those texts easily accessible. Included among these is the main text, Bewcastle II, and this, too, must be compared with pre-1854 records. Unfortunately, these are few:[41]

(a) The wood-cut, presumably by Smith, in the March issue of *Gentleman's Magazine* 12 (1742), 132.

(b) Howard's drawing for his article in *Archaeologia* 14 (Cumberland Red Portfolio, Library of the Society of Antiquaries of London, p. 5). With this must be

---

[36] *Old-Northern Runic Monuments* I–II, 654.

[37] *Old-Northern Runic Monuments* III, 285.

[38] 'Runic Inscription on Baronspike', *Archæologia Æliana* n.s. 7 (1876), 82–5, at 83.

[39] *Memoir*, pp. 17–18 and 36.

[40] *Memoir*, pp. 12 and 36–8.

[41] The drawing sent by Nicolson to Thoresby (J. A. W. Bennett, 'The Beginnings of Runic Studies in England', *SBVS* 13 (1946–53), 269–83, at 277) seems to have been lost. [Since the present article went to press Nicolson's drawing of Bewcastle II has been traced in the library of the Yorkshire Archaeological Society. This drawing goes to confirm the conclusions of the present article.]

considered Lysons' drawing (B.L. Additional MS 9462, fol. 109), which is probably derived from the published version of Howard's drawing. Lysons knew of Howard's work,[42] and his text closely resembles Howard's, lines 2–5 being virtually identical, and 6, 9, very similar. Two readings confirm Lysons' debt to Howard: (i) the dot shown at the centre of the stem of II, 22, which derives from a blot of wash accidentally fallen on to Howard's original drawing and incorporated into his published text, and (ii) the part of the side framing line at the beginning of line 4 drawn by Howard and taken over by Lysons at this point.

(c) Maughan's 1852 text in Carlisle Public Library,

It is not surprising, in view of the fact that even in the seventeenth century Bewcastle II was in a very worn condition, that these versions differ considerably from one another. However, the following letters agree, more or less, in all three pre-1854 texts: 'wætr' (20–3), 'gær' (29–31), 'ri' (47–8), 'u' (54), while 'g' (7) is suggested in all. Further, (b) and (c) agree in reading 'is' (13–14). In all these cases the text of the cross as it now stands agrees with the early records. There are four discrepancies: 'li' (bc) for 'e' (24), H (ac) and 'æ' (bc) in uncertain contexts towards the end of line 6, and, most important, 'æ' (bc) where the text now reads 'o/n' (18). Obviously there is here no proof of tampering with the inscription, but the examples considered above comprise less than a quarter of the text. Equally important is the fact that none of the early records, not even that of the careful Howard, gives certain letter parts that are now comparatively clear on the stone: so, the arms or bows of 'c' (10), 'þ' (28), 'w' (34), 'l' or 'æ' (38) and 't' (42), and most of 'gebid' (66–70).

These facts, with what we know of the cross's history in the 1850s, suggest that that time may have seen some 'improvement' of the inscriptions. Investigators, clearing the stone surface, may have traced with knives or other implements forms they expected to find. Doubtful forms may thus have become clearer, and some forms even altered or produced. So, line 2, which now has 'setto/n', may earlier have had 'settæ', the singular verb agreeing with the first element of the compound subject and retaining PrOE unstressed -æ, (cf. the verbal forms 'setæ' on the Great Urswick rune-stone, GISETAE on the Yarm cross, and the retention of the early unstressed vowel in the 'ricæs dryhtnæs' of the lost Bewcastle head).

If, in fact, the Bewcastle inscriptions as they now stand are in part the product of such investigators, we would expect to find in them unusual runic or linguistic forms resulting from nineteenth-century misconceptions. We do find unusual runic and linguistic forms, but they cannot always be traced back to nineteenth-century readings. So, unusual forms of runes in Bewcastle II are:

(i) The 'i' (6), a half-length letter, its top in line with other tops, its base in line with stem centres. Brown identified a second 'i' of this type (69),[43] but it cannot now be found on the stone. All other 'i' forms on Bewcastle (I, 10, II, 3, 48, IV, 4) are of full size. The half-length 'i' is not certainly evidenced elsewhere, though there are three possible cases of it. The third Thornhill rune-stone has the name 'jilsuiþ', its

[42] *Magna Britannia* IV, cc.

second 'i' a half-length letter with its top in line with other stem tops, but the arrangement of the runes here suggests that the 'i' was first wrongly omitted and then added later, of a size to fit the available space. The second Thornhill rune-stone has the text '+êadred | seteæfte | êateȝnne' and below the left-hand stem of the 's' a short vertical incision which may be an 'i' converting the verb to 'isete' (= *gisette*) or which equally well may have been cut in error. Thirdly, there is the ambiguous example from Kirk Maughold.[44] There is no certain confirmation here of the existence of a half-length Old English 'i' rune. The Bewcastle example must then be considered unusual, perhaps erroneous.

(ii) The H-like forms (61, 72). 72, not given as this form in the early records, is read by Vietor as '(D oder H?)', by R. G. Collingwood as a damaged 'h' and by Willett as '[h]'. Vietor, Brown, Collingwood and Willett read 61 as 's', and, indeed, this identification is necessary if the patronymic *Oswiung* is to be found in the text. An 's' with both stems produced to full height in this way is not recorded elsewhere. All Bewcastle forms (I, 4, 5, 7, 11, 15, II, 4, 5, 14, 74, III, 2, 3) have the normal 's' form, save perhaps in 'u/s' (III, 4), where the apparent lengthening of the 's' stems is probably due to weathering.

Unusual linguistic forms are:

(iii) The name 'a[̥]w[̥]wo[̥]*', *Alwfwolþu* (Maughan), *Olwfwolþu* (Stephens), *Olw[̥]wolþu* (Brown), *Olwowol* / Alwowol** (Collingwood), *Olwowolþu* (Willett) bears little resemblance to known Old English name forms.

(iv) The preposition *æft* is not found elsewhere in Old English. Other runic texts have forms of the prepositions *æfter* (the Falstone 'hog-back', the Great Urswick stone, the first Thornhill stone), *æfte* (the second and perhaps the third Thornhill stones). A short form *aft*, *æft* is found on Scandinavian stones, but its origin is disputed.[45] If it derives from a short form in Germanic, the Bewcastle example could be cognate. If the short form is a development within Old Norse from an earlier *after*, a parallel development in Old English could produce the Bewcastle form. Bewcastle *æft* is, then, not inexplicable, but it remains unique.

The arguments presented above do not, of course, prove that Bewcastle II and IV have been altered. With the available evidence that would be difficult, probably impossible, to prove. But alteration of the texts may certainly have taken place.

To return, then, to the question of the dating of the Bewcastle Cross; those who would point to the names of Alcfrith and Cyniburg are faced with the following problems:

(*a*) That Bewcastle II and IV, in which these names are found, are of uncertain validity.

---

[43] *The Arts in Early England* V, 247–8.
[44] See above, p. 55, n. 14.
[45] Jacobsen and Moltke, *Danmarks runeindskrifter*, cols 741–2.

(*b*) That rune* cannot be derived formally from 'þ' (or even 'd' or 'th') essential for reading the name of Alcfrith.

(*c*) That if rune* is read as a bind of 'þ' and some other letter there are problematic readings in all four contexts, and particularly in Bewcastle IV.

Further, it must be noted that:

(*d*) The reading of the patronymic *Oswiung*, found on Bewcastle II from the time of Maughan's 1857 text, depends on the identification of a doubtful 's' form.

(*e*) The title given to Alcfrith on line 6 of Bewcastle II – *ean kyniŋ* (Maughan, Stephens), *an kyniŋ* (Brown), *an kuniŋ* (Collingwood, Willett) presents difficulties. The use in this context of *an* (? indefinite article, ? case ending) is, to say the least, unusual, while the facts that rune 53 is 'ḡ', not 'k̄' (which the Bewcastle Cross does not use) and 54 shows no sign of the inset 'i' which would turn 'u' into 'y' (for a form *kyning*) makes the form of the title a strange one indeed.

So far this discussion of the Bewcastle inscriptions has been destructive, an attack on the 'accepted' connexion between the cross and Alcfrith. It is hard to adopt a more positive attitude to the Bewcastle texts as they now stand. Texts I and III are probably valid even though there are no early drawings confirming them, for they are not readily accessible and are the less likely to have been tampered with. Unfortunately, being in Latin they are of little linguistic importance. Nothing can be made of the fragment VI, which is of little interest. Text IV, as has been seen, should read 'kyniburuḡ'. Text II remains a problem. Rejecting the text as it now stands, we are left with only the three early attempts at reproducing the worn and weathered inscription. Two of these, those of Smith and Maughan, are small drawings in which relative distances between staves are unlikely to be accurate. The Smith drawing, moreover, shows a very strange set of characters, while the Maughan text is incomplete and contains a large number of forms consisting of vertical stems alone. The Howard reproduction is a full-size tracing. Nearly all the staves it records are still visible on the stone, but there are many staves now to be seen which Howard does not show. Occasional runes can be identified with certainty on the Howard tracing, while in other cases readings can be tentatively reconstructed from the shapes given there. However, no fragment of text of any length can be recovered even from Howard's drawing. If, then, the reading of the stone is rejected, as owing much to re-touching and examination in modern times, the main Bewcastle inscription must be considered irrecoverable.

Finally must be examined the inscription of the lost head of the Bewcastle Cross. Part of the text of this fragment has survived in four versions. These are:

(*a*) MS Smith I, set after p. 644 of Camden's own copy of his *Britannia* in the Bodleian Library, Oxford. This gives a text 'ricæsdr*htnæs', rune* being ᚪ. Above the runes are written the values rinæs, then m with a dot above it and above that d, then r, a space above rune* and .h.tnæs. Beneath the text is written:

'I receaued this morning a ston from my lord of Arundell sent him from my lord William it was the head of a Cross at Bewcastell All the letters legable

66

ar thes in on Line And I hau sett to them such as I can gather out of my Alphabetts that lyk an .A. I can find in non But wether thes be only lettres or words I somwhatt dout . . . '.

The note is not signed or addressed, but it is believed to be from Sir Robert Cotton to Camden.[46]

(b) A letter, dated 1629, from Sir Henry Spelman to Palæmon Rosencrantz. The original is not known to survive, but its text is given in Olaus Worm, *Danicorum monumentorum libri sex* . . . (Hafniæ, 1643), pp. 159–62, reprinted as letter CCCCXXV in *Olai Wormii et ad eum doctorum virorum epistolæ* . . . (Havniæ, 1751). A text presumably one stage nearer the original survives in MS Gl. kgl. sml. 2370 4⁰, Royal Library, Copenhagen. This seems to be part of Worm's draft copy of his book, mainly in manuscript, most of which is in Worm's own hand, and with some printed pages interleaved and heavily annotated. The manuscript has no page numbering. Its text of the Spelman letter begins in a hand other than Worm's. Worm then wrote the descriptive passage immediately after the drawing of the Bewcastle inscription and added a number of unsuccessful attempts at interpretation, so it is likely that he made the drawing or at least checked its accuracy. The manuscript gives a text 'ricæsdr*htnæs', rune* having the same form as in MS Smith I. Below is the comment:

> 'Sculpta fuit hæc inscriptio epistÿlio crucis lapideæ, Bevcastri partib*us* Angliæ borealib*us* (ubi Dani plurimum versabantur) Cambdenoq̄ et mihi simul exhibita An. Dn. 1618, ab Antiqvitatum inter proceres Angliæ peritis-*simo* Dn. Gvilielmo Howard novissimi Ducis Norfolciæ filio'.

Worm's published text of the letter differs from this only in inessentials, but its drawing of the inscription shows rune* in the corrupt form ⋀, while the final 's' is followed by a point set above the line.

(c) MS Cotton Domitian XVIII, fol. 37ʳ gives a text 'ricæsdruhtnæs.', with the note:

> 'This Inscription was on the head of a crose found
> at Beucastell in   1615.
> The length of the stone.   bein the head of the Crosse – 16 inches
> The breadth at the vpper end – 12.ynches
> The Thicknes – 4.inches'

(d) MS Cotton Julius F. VI, fol. 313 has 'ricæsdruhtnæs' and adds:

> 'The length of the stone –
> beinge the head of a Crosse   16.ynches

---

[46] J. Wilson, 'The Runes on the Lost Head of Bewcastle Cross', *TCWAAS* n.s. 10 (1910), 503–7, at 504; and Brown, *The Arts in Early England* V, 114.

The b[. . .]dth at the vpper end – 12.ynches
The [. . . . .]nes ————————4 ynches'.

with the address 'Bucastle inscription For Mr Clarenceaulx'.

(c) and (d) have also been attributed to Cotton.[47] The hand of (c) certainly bears some resemblance to that of (a), so the two notes may be by the same writer. Manuscript (d) seems to be in a quite different hand, and Haverfield does not identify it.[48]

The history of the Bewcastle Cross head, as given in these accounts, is then as follows. The stone was 'found' in 1615. Lord William Howard of Naworth, a noted collector of Northern antiquities, had it in 1618, when he showed it to Spelman and Camden. Howard gave the stone to Arundel, from whom it passed, if the identification of the writer of (a) is correct, to Cotton. Camden saw the stone itself, and was twice informed of its text, once (as Mr Clarenceaulx) in (d), once, if the identification of the recipient of (a) is correct, by (a). There is no further record of the cross head.

The lost Bewcastle cross head undoubtedly held the text 'ricæsdryhtnæs', while Cotton's comment suggests that there were further, illegible, characters. The rune 'y' was probably blurred by weathering, with the result that it was read variously as 'u' and as Cotton and Spelman's rune*, from which derived Worm's printed form. The rest must have been surprisingly distinct, and this suggests that the inscription, like Bewcastle IV, was on the north face of the cross, and sheltered to some degree by the church building. (a) and (d) have no point at the end of the text. Manuscript (c) gives a point placed on the line, but this may have been added by the transcriber to indicate the text end. Worm's printed text of (b) shows a point set above the line, but the manuscript text shows none. It should be noted that no punctuation symbols of this sort have been found in the other Bewcastle inscriptions.

A fragmentary text *ricæs dryhtnæs* is ambiguous. *ricæs* can be the genitive singular of either the noun or the adjective *rice*, while *dryhtnæs* can refer to an earthly or a heavenly lord. Without the context the meaning cannot be determined.

In this essay I have indicated that there is good reason for rejecting the 'accepted' connexion between the Bewcastle Cross and the sub-king Alcfrith. The Cyniburg of Bewcastle IV can then no longer be identified, for the name is common enough in Old English for any identification to be doubtful. The only evidence for dating the cross on the basis of its inscriptions then becomes the evidence of the linguistic forms found in them. The inscription of the lost head and the Bewcastle IV text 'kyniburug' (together with the Latin inscriptions of Bewcastle I, III) are the only texts of the cross whose validity can be accepted, and so any dating of the cross on the linguistic evidence of its inscriptions must be based on these. Unfortunately, they are too slight for their evidence to be of any great use. The texts are later than *i*-mutation as the forms 'dryhtnæs', 'kyniburug' prove, and later than the Old English syncope of

---

[47] Bennett, 'The Beginnings of Runic Studies', p. 270.
[48] 'Cotton Iulius F. VI', p. 376.

vowels in middle syllables, as shown by the form 'dryhtnæs'. The condition of the unstressed vowels – PrOE æ retained in 'dryhtnæs', 'ricæs', and PrOE *i* in 'kynibu-rūg' – suggests quite an early date, though from only three examples all that can safely be deduced is that the Bewcastle inscriptions are not as late as the tenth century. Bewcastle compares with the Great Urswick and the third Thornhill rune-stones in its use of the rune 'k', and with the Ruthwell Cross in its use of 'k' and 'ḡ'. The most likely date – on linguistic grounds alone – for Great Urswick and Ruthwell is 750–850, while the third Thornhill stone seems to be rather later. The language of the Bewcastle inscriptions, as far as it survives, is at a similar stage to that of Great Urswick and Ruthwell, and a date 750–850 is therefore a possible one for the Bewcastle Cross. We do, however, know so little about the language of western Northumbria in Old English times that such a dating must be tentative in the extreme. It follows that the Bewcastle Cross loses some of its importance for the art historian, for it can no longer be regarded as a fixed dating point on which a system of chronology for Anglo-Saxon sculptured stones can be based.

POSTSCRIPT

When this paper came out colleagues criticised it for being 'negative', which showed unusual perceptivity on their part for that was what it was designed to be. However, I doubt if they intended the adjective to be complimentary; modern scholarship seems to judge it worthier to make an indicative statement, however inaccurate or unsupported by fact, than to utter a tentative subjunctive or to warn against relying on evidence that is untrustworthy or observation that is partial.

A brief account of the genesis of the article will illustrate what I was trying to do here. The story begins with Professor Richard Bailey (then a humble, well, a fairly humble, research student) and I sitting on the back row of a hall in Durham University listening to a lecture on the chronology of Anglo-Saxon stone sculpture. The lecturer was a most distinguished art/architectural historian/archaeologist, a Fellow of the British Academy no less. He named four stone monuments which could, he asserted, be dated from external sources. First he nominated the Bewcastle Cross, dateable from its references to King Alcfrith and Queen Cyniburg; at which my generous wrath was kindled. Bailey's ire became equally inflammable when the lecturer mentioned the other three 'fixed points'. Bailey and I determined to query the validity of this dating method in the period of question time afterwards, but we reckoned without the guile of a seasoned Fellow of the British Academy. His reply to the first naive question (put from the chair) took so long, roved over most of the history of early Christianity in Western Europe, and included so many personal reminiscences that there was no time for anything further. I resolved to put my objections into writing, and hence this paper. Its only purpose is to define the complexity of the problems involved in interpreting the inscriptions of this immensely important runic monument, and the danger of drawing firm conclusions from their uncertain wording. Luckily my doubts did not discourage Professor Cramp from constructing a context for the Bewcastle Cross on the basis that it was a memorial 'bearing the names of the royal family' of Northumbria and placing it in the first half of the eighth century.[49]

A few additions can now be made to what I said in this paper. I tentatively suggested there might be a case for identifying a half-length 'i' in English practice. Two more examples, this time manuscript, make the case slightly stronger. In the margin of Corpus Christi College, Cambridge, MS 41, p. 448 is written in runes the number 'x i i . 7 . x x x' with half-height 'i' forms. On fol. 7ᵛ of Munich, Bayerische Staatsbibliothek, Clm. 3731 is the marginal gloss 'm a i o r i', where the first 'i' is a small graph tucked beneath the upper arm of 'a'.[50]

On the pair of drawings of the lost head of the cross from the Cotton collection I have had the help of Mr Nigel Ramsay. He regards the Domitian XVIII report as a copy of Julius F. VI. The latter is 'perhaps in the hand of Lord William Howard', which would fit the suggestion that the note was prepared for a new edition of the *Britannia*.

---

[49] R. N. Bailey and R. Cramp, *The British Academy Corpus of Anglo-Saxon Stone Sculpture, II: Cumberland, Westmorland and Lancashire North-of-the-Sands* (Oxford and New York, 1988), pp. 12–22, and also p. 71.

[50] R. Derolez, 'Epigraphical Versus Manuscript English Runes: One or Two Worlds?', *Academiae Analecta*, Mededelingen van de Koninklijke Academie voor Wetenschappen, Letteren en Schone Kunsten van België, Klasse der Letteren 45, 1 (1983), pp. 71–93, at 91.

6

(1961)

THE OLD ENGLISH RUNE *EAR*

In recent years it has been usual to regard the Old English rune *ear* as a comparatively late development, the last of the four additional runes that go to make up the twenty-eight letter *fuþorc*. This theory is based on the non-appearance of 'êa'[1] in a number of early texts where it might reasonably be expected, the conclusion being drawn that such texts antedate the creation of the rune form. The argument appears in O. v. Friesen's article 'Runenschrift' in *Reallexicon der germanischen Altertumskunde*, ed. J. Hoops (Strassburg, 1911–19) IV, 5–51, at 25. It is stated in detail in M. Cahen and M. Olsen, *L'inscription runique du coffret de Mortain* (Paris, 1930), pp. 35–6 and 38, and the conclusions repeated in O. v. Friesen, *Runorna* (Stockholm, 1933), p. 60, W. Keller, 'Zur Chronologie der ae. Runen', *Anglia* 62 (1938), 24–32, at 25, Arntz and Zeiss, *Die einheimischen Runendenkmäler*, p. 441,[2] M. L. Samuels 'The Study of Old English Phonology', *TPS* (1952), 15–47, at 25, and, most recently, in Elliott, *Runes: an Introduction*, pp. 35–6.[3] Cahen-Olsen and Samuels ('Study of Old English Phonology', pp. 36–7) set out the material on which the argument is based.

The detailed statement of the case given by Cahen-Olsen can be summed up in the following terms. Two early Old English inscriptions evidence the use of 'a' for the sound which is later to appear as *ea*: these are the legends of the *skanomodu* solidus (the first element identified as Gmc **Skaun-*) and the *pada* coinage,[4] identified as that of *Peada* (assumed to represent *Pēada*) of Mercia (655–7). Rather later inscriptions give the sound by means of two runes, 'æa' in the 'æadan' of the Mortain Casket, 'ea' in 'giuþeasu' of the Franks Casket. The latest inscriptions of all use the single rune 'êa', and this appears also in the *fuþorc* of the so-called

---

[1] Runes are transliterated according to Dickins, 'System of Transliteration'. Note the use of the circumflex: 'êa' transliterates the single rune *ear*, 'ea' the two runes *eoh* and *ac*. Readings of inscriptions are based on personal examination, save in the cases of the Mortain Casket, known from the Cahen-Olsen account, and the Gilton sword pommel, known from photographs and the Stephens reproductions. The Bargello side of the Franks Casket is known from the British Museum cast.

[2] In 'Runen und Runennamen', *Anglia* 67–8 (1944), 172–250, at 248, Arntz produces a different argument, based on the rune-name *ear*, for a late dating of the creation of the rune. On this, see below, p. 73.

[3] [But cf. his different view in the 2nd edition, pp. 44–5.]

[4] There are, of course, a number of different coin types bearing the *pada* legend. It is convenient here to treat them as a single example.

Salzburg-Alcuin manuscript (= Vienna, Österreichische Nationalbibliothek, 795), the material of which, deriving from the period of Alcuin's youth, can be placed at the middle of the eighth century. The rune 'êa' was, then, created before that date, but after the middle of the seventh century, as the *pada* legend indicates. Most recently, Elliott has said of 'êa' that 'Its adoption cannot have taken place before the end of the seventh century, as there exist several Mercian coins, now in the British Museum, with the inscription . . . *pada*, mentioned by Bede as Peada, son of Penda, who flourished A.D. 655–7. Here the sound *ea* is still represented by the *a*-rune.'[5]

Such an argument seems to the present writer to be invalid. Its use of the examples of 'a' for *ea* (the *skanomodu* solidus and the *pada* coins) can be questioned; the latest writer on the Salzburg-Alcuin manuscript considers that 'Alcuin's authorship should not be considered as more than a bare possibility';[6] no attempt has been made to consider whether the biliteral spellings, 'æa' and 'ea', could exist, side by side with 'êa', as phonetic spellings, perhaps influenced by contemporary Old English practice in roman script. Further, the material set out by Cahen-Olsen and Samuels is incomplete, in part inaccurate or drawn from unreliable sources. A re-examination of the use of the rune 'êa' is, then, necessary, and this, in the opinion of the present writer, must lead to a new theory of the date and circumstances of formation of that rune.

The following evidence is relevant to the discussion:

1. The rune has the name *ear*, *eor* and the value *ea*, *eo* in the manuscript *fuþorcs*, with the unusual form *aer* and the value *z* in some of the *isruna* tracts. The meaning of the name can be deduced only from the verse in the *Runic Poem*:

> 'êa' byþ egle   eorla gehwylcun,
> ðonn fæstlice   flæsc onginneþ,
> hraw colian,   hrusan ceosan
> blac to gebeddan;   bleda gedreosaþ,
> wynna gewitaþ,   wera geswicaþ.[7]

where the usual interpretation 'grave, earth' is acceptable. A word *ear*, *eor* with this meaning is not recorded elsewhere, though a homonym with the meaning 'sea, ocean' is occasionally found.[8] Cognates to *ear* (= 'earth') may be ON *aurr* 'wet clay, loam,

---

[5] Elliott's view of the creation of 'êa' is, however, not clear. He apparently believes that the twenty-eight letter *fuþorc* evolved 'probably on Frisian soil' (*Runes*, p. 33), but gives no reason why the 'adoption' of 'êa' (? into general Old English use) should have been delayed until the late seventh century. Comments by v. Friesen (*Runorna*, p. 60) and Arntz (*Handbuch der Runenkunde*, 2nd ed. (Halle/Saale, 1944), pp. 123–4) suggest that they too noted this difficulty.

[6] Derolez, *Runica Manuscripta*, pp. 62–3.

[7] Derolez has pointed out (*Runica Manuscripta*, pp. 23–5) that the text of the *Runic Poem* from which Hickes made his transcript may have had no rune-name at the beginning of the verse. The name *car* (? = *ear*, ? *cur*) shown by Hickes to the right of the rune may have been added by him from a source not yet identified, or may have been in the original, but inserted by a later hand.

[8] The two words are usually assumed to be homonyms, though in fact there is no evidence from the manuscript forms of the rune-name for the length of its diphthong. There is further OE *ear* 'ear of corn', but for some reason this is not usually considered when the rune-name is discussed.

mud', *eyrr* 'gravelly bank near water', Gothic **aurahjons* 'tomb',[9] and if so 'êa' gives the reflex of Gmc *au*. This explanation of the rune and rune-name is certainly probable, but a number of alternatives must also be considered.

H. Arntz has suggested that *ear* is not an ordinary Old English word at all, but merely an arbitrary name, 'die gleiche Wiedergabe des Lautes *ēa*'.[10] He believes the name to be formed by analogy with *yr* and *ior, iar*, which were borrowed from Old Norse for use as rune-names only. Arntz gives no reason for his rejection of *ear* as an ordinary Old English word, and formation by analogy with *iar* is unlikely, since all the evidence suggests that *ear* is an earlier formation than *iar* – some manuscript *fuþorcs* containing *ear* do not have *iar* at all, whilst *ear* almost invariably precedes *iar* in others. Moreover, if the words *yr, iar* and *ear* have in Old English no meanings apart from the rune-names, we have to explain those attached to them in the *Runic Poem*. The verse dealing with *yr* suggests that it may have the meaning 'bow', and here we can point to the Old Norse rune-name *ýr* which, according to the Icelandic *Runic Poem*, means *bendr bogi*. The meaning given to *iar* in the Old English *Runic Poem*

> [*iar*] byþ eafix,   and ðeah a bruceþ
> fodres on foldan,   hafaþ fægerne eard,
> wætre beworpen,   ðær he wynnum leofaþ.[11]

seems to have no connection with the PrON **jāra*, from which Arntz would ultimately derive the name, while one is left to wonder under what circumstances a meaning 'grave, earth' became attached to the arbitrary formation *ear*. If the *Runic Poem* had any purpose at all – and the existence of similar poems in other Germanic languages shows that it was not an isolated composition – it was presumably mnemonic. This would lead us to believe that the meanings given to the various rune-names must have been generally accepted, or at least commonly recognizable. How the particular meanings given for *iar, ear* in the *Runic Poem* were arrived at Arntz does not explain. Further, if *ear* was in fact arbitrary and therefore in origin meaningless, one might expect it to take over the meaning of one of the homonyms (= 'sea' or 'ear of corn'), rather than be given a completely new one. However, the length of the diphthong of the rune-name may be significant in this connection.

K. R. Brooks,[12] following a suggestion by Joan Blomfield,[13] makes the following explanation of the attaching of the meaning 'grave, earth' to the name *ear*: 'the etymological methods of the author of the Runic Poem are often obscure, and it has been suggested with much probability that as the equivalent rune in most other *futharks* corresponds to *z*, the meaning may be simply "the end", which, if taken in

---

9   F. Holthausen, *Vergleichendes und etymologisches Wörterbuch des altwestnordischen* (Göttingen, 1948), S. Feist, *Vergleichendes Wörterbuch der gotischen Sprache*, 3rd ed. (Leiden, 1939), s.v.
10   'Runen und Runennamen', pp. 247–9.
11   The emended text given in E. V. K. Dobbie, *The Anglo-Saxon Minor Poems*, ASPR 6 (London and New York, 1942), p. 30.
12   'Old English *ÉA* and Related Words', *English and Germanic Stud.* 5 (1952–3), 15–66, at 47–8.
13   'Runes and the Gothic Alphabet', *SBVS* 12 (1937–45), 177–94 and 209–31, at 225.

the sense "death", would suit the OE Runic Poem admirably'. The development of a meaning 'the end' is thus seen as arising from an accepted correspondence between 'êa' and *z*, and from this came a secondary meaning 'death' (or presumably 'grave') as in the *Runic Poem*. However, that there was such a correspondence between 'êa' and *z* may be doubted. In the surviving manuscript *fuþorcs* (not the *fuþarks*, which, of course, would not include 'êa') the rune has the value *z* only in the *isruna* tracts, and can only be said to correspond to *z* in that it is the final letter of several *fuþorcs* as *z* is of the roman alphabet. But 'êa' is certainly not the only possible final letter of the *fuþorc*, for 'y', 'ḡ' and perhaps 'q' are all found in this capacity, while 'êa' is sometimes not the final letter in cases where the end of the *fuþorc* is lost. Finally, 'êa' is used for *z* in some runic alphabets – those of the *De inventione litterarum* group and that of MS Berne, Stadt- und Hochschulbibliothek, 207 – but other alphabets use 'h', 'y' and 'ḡ' for *z*, while 'êa' is used for *e* and *x*. There seems to be no manuscript of certainly English provenance in which 'êa' is explicitly related to *z*, so there is no reason to think that the name *ear* would be generally recognized as meaning 'the end', and even less as meaning 'death'.

Another theory has been put forward by R. W. V. Elliott.[14] According to him the rune-name *ear* had two meanings, 'earth, soil, gravel' and 'ocean, sea, wave'. The second was the usual meaning of the rune-name, the first being preserved only in the *Runic Poem*, where the alternative 'sea' is attached to the meaningless *iar*. However, no evidence is produced for a meaning 'sea' for the rune-name, save a speculative interpretation of the runes of *The Husband's Message*. Further, one is compelled to ask why the writer of the *Runic Poem* did not retain the supposedly common meaning 'sea' for *ear*, leaving the uncommon 'earth' for the meaningless *iar*. The poet could then close his work appropriately, if that indeed was his intention, with a stanza on 'earth, grave' by putting the runes 'êa', *iar* in that order, which is, after all, the order to be expected on the evidence of the other manuscript *fuþorcs*.

None of the arguments examined above is sufficiently convincing to make it necessary to reject the simple explanation of *ear* suggested by the existence of ON *aurr*, *eyrr* and Gothic *aurahjons. There is no reason why OE *ear*, cognate with these words and having the meaning 'earth', should not have survived only in the *Runic Poem*. A similar case is then that of the rune-name *os* (originally = 'god'), a word very rare in Old English, where, apart from its use as rune-name, it survives only as the personal name element *Ōs-* and uncertainly in two examples of a gen. pl. *esa*.[15] That rune-name is, however, identifiable by reference to its cognates, the common ON *áss* and the Gothic acc. pl. *ansis*.

2. The rune 'êa' is used epigraphically for:

(*a*) the reflex of Gmc *au* in 'êadred', 'êate3nne' (=*Eadþegne*) on the Thornhill III stone, and in 'bêagnoþ' on the Thames scramasax.

---

[14] 'The Runes in *The Husband's Message*', *JEGP* 54 (1955), 1–8, at 4–5.
[15] B. Dickins, *Runic and Heroic Poems of the Old Teutonic Peoples* (Cambridge, 1915), p. 13. See, however, W. Krause, 'Erta, ein anglischer Gott', *Die Sprache* 5 (1959), 46–54, at 48, n. 6.

(*b*) the stem diphthong, whatever its quality and origin, of '(*bih*)êa(*l*)[*d*]u' (=*beheol-don* in the Vercelli *Dream of the Rood* text, l. 64) in the main inscription of the Ruthwell Cross.

(*c*) two fracture diphthongs, (i) from Gmc *a* followed by *r* + consonant in 'jʒslhêard' on the Dover stone, and (ii) from Gmc *e* followed by *r* + consonant in 'fêarran' in the main Ruthwell inscription.

(*d*) the sound produced by *u*-mutation of PrOE *e* in 'hêafunæs' in the main Ruthwell inscription.

(*e*) the final rune of the Thames scramasax *fuþorc*.

'êa' may also be the first rune after the initial cross symbol on the Bingley font, though that inscription is too worn for any certainty to be possible. 'êa' is also found in the double inscription on the metal plate at the base of the Brunswick Casket. This inscription has not yet been satisfactorily read, and indeed, if the theory of A. Fink is correct, it may never be. Dr Fink came to the conclusion[16] that the runic plate is a modern copy, replacing an original in some precious metal. His argument depends on two facts: that the decoration of the runic plate is engraved, not cast as on the other metal plates of the casket, and that the plate was only stuck to the casket, whereas all the other plates are riveted. Holes still visible in the casket base indicate that a plate was once riveted there. An examination of the casket leaves little doubt of the correctness of Fink's contention that the present base-plate is not original, while the method of fixing it to the casket and the existence of a number of obviously corrupt forms in the inscription suggest a relatively late date for the present copy. The difficulties of interpreting the inscription are then partly to be explained as due to its being a version of a text which may have become badly worn, copied by someone with no runic knowledge. Certainly the contexts in which the 'êa' runes (two examples in the two identical halves of the inscription) are found give little help to the present discussion.[17]

3. There has been little discussion of the formal derivation of the rune 'êa'. Keller regards the rune as an adaptation of 'æ' (that is, the Germanic *a*-rune),[18] as are the Anglo-Frisian additions 'a' and 'o'. This is certainly very likely. The two arms – each made up of two staves – of 'êa' are of the same shape as the upper arms of 'a' and 'o', and have the same slight variations of form – their outer staves are sometimes

---

16 'Zum Gandersheimer Runenkästchen', *Karolingische und Ottonische Kunst*, ed. F. Geke *et al.* (Wiesbaden, 1957), pp. 277–81.

17 Since forms are still occasionally quoted from Stephens, *Old-Northern Runic Monuments*, it is worth noting a few cases of 'êa' recorded by him, but which are doubtful. On the Ruthwell Cross Stephens read '(H)EAF | (DU)M' (*heafdum* Vercelli, l. 63), and supplied 'BI(H) | (EA)L(D)' (*beheold* Vercelli, l. 58) and 'H(EA) | (FUN)' (*heofones* Vercelli, l. 64), EA in each case being represented by the 'êa' rune. In his reproduction of the Crowle stone he showed 'êa' in the context 'LICBÆCUN B(eAFTÆ)r . . .'. In each case the form cannot now be found on the stone, nor does it appear in early drawings. It is, then, likely to be a product of Stephens's fertile imagination. However, the remains of the Ruthwell text at the point suggest that the rune-master may have used 'êa' in *heafdum*.

18 'Zur Chronologie der ae. Runen', p. 25.

parallel to the stem, and sometimes they slope gently away from it; their tops are sometimes level with the stem top, sometimes rather higher.[19] The formal similarity between 'a', 'o' and 'êa' is, then, very striking, and 'êa' may have been derived from one or both of the other runes or have been created at about the same time as them.

4. 'êa' is the only single rune representing a diphthong. Another apparent example is the rune *iar*, *ior*, which is given the value *io* in MS Cotton Domitian IX. In no other manuscript, however, is such a value given, while the same form in epigraphical texts – 'j' – is used for palatalized Gmc *g* followed by *i* in a stressed syllable in 'jȝslhêard' (Dover stone), 'jilsuiþ' (Thornhill II stone), and **adujislu, jisuhldu** (Westeremden A weaving-slay). 'êa', then, is unique in epigraphical texts in representing a diphthong. What is immediately striking about this fact is that the creation of a new rune for this purpose would be quite unnecessary at that period of the seventh and eighth centuries in which the creation of 'êa' has been placed. The diphthong could perfectly well be given by two runes, 'æa' or 'ea', as on the Mortain and Franks Caskets. The rune-masters do not in general avoid using two runes for a diphthong, as the forms 'greut', 'reumwalus' (Franks Casket), 'bæurnæ' (Great Urswick stone), 'eoh' (Kirkheaton stone), 'þiiosne' (Mortain Casket) show, and we are left inquiring why a special rune should have been formed in this particular case.

An explanation of the origin of 'êa' must, then, show it representing the reflex of Gmc *au*, as 1 suggests, and is compatible with the material of 2, and explain 3, the rune's formal resemblance to 'a', 'o' and 4, the use of a single rune for the Old English diphthong. The 'traditional' explanation does not account for points 3, 4, and so a new one must be attempted.

There is little evidence for the course of the development of Gmc *au* to OE *ea*, and theories on the subject must necessarily be speculative. Two are of interest to the present discussion: (*a*) suggests an early lowering of the second element of the Germanic diphthong, OE *ea* being derived through an intermediate WGmc *ao*,[20] (*b*) a monophthongization of Gmc *au* similar to, though not necessarily contemporaneous with, that which produced Old Saxon *ô* and Old Frisian *ā*.[21] OE *ea* is then the result of a later re-diphthongization.

If (*a*) is correct, 'êa' could be regarded as a simplified bind of 'a' and 'o', and a

---

[19] The derivation suggested by M. Daunt's remark ('Old English Sound-Changes Reconsidered in Relation to Scribal Tradition and Practice', *TPS* (1939), 108–37, at 120) that 'êa' 'looks like the *e* rune balanced precariously on the stroke of the *a* rune' cannot be accepted. The stroke (presumably the stem) of the *a* rune cannot be distinguished in appearance from the stems of the other sixteen single-stem runes between 'f' and 'æ' in the *fuþorc*, while the usual proportions of the arms of 'êa' are quite different from those of an inverted 'e'.

[20] K. D. Bülbring, *Altenglisches Elementarbuch* I (Heidelberg, 1902), § 107, Anm. 2, Luick, *Historische Grammatik*, §§ 96 and 119. See also L. F. Brosnahan, *Some Old English Sound Changes: an Analysis in the Light of Modern Phonetics* (Cambridge, 1953), p. 51.

[21] R. Vleeskruyer, 'A. Campbell's Views on Inguaeonic', *Neophilologus* 32 (1948), 173–83, at 183. Campbell, *Old English Grammar*, § 3 notes the development of Gmc *au* to *ā* as a point by means of which 'Old English and Old Frisian are distinguished . . . from Old Saxon'. This suggestion does not tally with his treatment of the Old English development of Gmc *au* later in the same book.

parallel case may be that of 'a' itself, formed as a bind of the old *ansuz*-rune and 'i'. A number of objections can be brought against this suggestion. The need to postulate simplification of the bind-rune makes the explanation less satisfying than it would otherwise be. Moreover, bind-runes of this sort, one of the letters being reversed so that its arms do not interfere with those of the other, are not found elsewhere in Old English inscriptions. The same problem arose in the 'f/a' of the Bargello side of the Franks Casket, and here the arms of both letters were cut to the right of the stem, those of 'f' being above those of 'a'. Further, there is a chronological problem. If 'êa' originated in 'a/o', the creation of 'êa' must be later than that of 'a', which in turn presumably coincided with the fronting of Gmc *a*. If Gmc *au* > WGmc *ao* > *œo* by fronting > OE *ea*, the diphthong *ao* would not have been in existence at the date the rune 'a' was available to form the bind. This chronological objection may not be a serious one for little is known of the exact circumstances under which the Anglo-Frisian additional runes 'a' and 'o' were created, nor is it certain that fronting took place at the same time under all circumstances. If (*b*) is correct – and this seems likely to the present writer – 'êa' would originally indicate a monophthong, perhaps similar in quality to those given by 'a' and 'o' but distinct from them phonemically. The new rune would be created after 'a' and 'o', by analogy with them, and perhaps at a date when they were still remembered as new creations. The earliest non-runic Old English texts give a diphthong for the reflex of Gmc *au*, so the creation of 'êa' must precede the writing of these.

In either case the rune would, or at least could, have been in existence long before the mid-seventh century, and perhaps as early as the 'period of Anglo-Frisian unity'. The evidence which suggested a later date must then be re-examined. As has been seen, it divides into two groups of forms, (i) those using a single rune, not 'êa', and (ii) those using two runes, as 'æa', 'ea'.

Under (i) appear the traditional examples, the *skanomodu* solidus and the *pada* coinage, while Samuels also notes the forms 'ræȝhæn' (Caistor-by-Norwich astragalus), 'hærmbergæ' (Franks Casket),[22] and the name read as *ræhœbul* (Sandwich stone), these three regarded as cases of PrOE *æ* in circumstances where we would expect the fracture diphthong *ea*. The last three cases give rise to a further problem. The evidence given under 2 above shows that, in addition to its appearance for the reflex of Gmc *au*, 'êa' is found representing fracture and back-mutation diphthongs which (apart from the question of their length) fall together with that reflex in certain Old English dialects. However, we do not know whether, if 'êa' were an early formation for the reflex of Gmc *au*, it would necessarily be used for, say, a fracture diphthong as soon as such a diphthong appeared in the language. There may have been – and of this we know nothing – a tradition of runic spelling, and traditional spellings with a simple vowel rune may have been retained for some time after a diphthongal pronunciation had come into general use. Further, the appearance of a simple vowel rune in circumstances where we might expect, say, a fracture diphthong,

---

[22] The vowels on this side of the casket are in general not given by their usual rune forms, but by cryptic forms identifiable from the contexts in which they appear.

may merely indicate that the text in question antedates the onset of fracture, or that there was no fracture under these particular circumstances in the dialect represented. For these and other reasons the three Samuels examples cannot be accepted as evidence that the rune 'êa' had not been formed when they were cut. The two traditional pieces of evidence must, however, be considered in greater detail.[23]

(a) The *skanomodu* solidus, a gold coin or medal bearing the following Old English or Frisian runes: *sigel, cœn, ac, nead, œþel, man, œþel, dœg, ur*. The coin was first recorded in George III's collection, and is now in the British Museum. The find-place has not been traced, but the British Museum catalogue assumes an English provenance, quoting the great runologist L. F. A. Wimmer on the legend: 'That it is an Old English inscription is evident from the specially English rune "a" '.[24] When Wimmer wrote this, however, virtually nothing was known of Frisian runic inscriptions, and texts with the additional 'a' and 'o' were automatically assumed to be Old English. The finding in more recent times of several Frisian inscriptions evidencing forms of 'a' and 'o' has led modern runologists to regard these runes as Anglo-Frisian in origin rather than Old English, particularly since their formation is clearly connected with Anglo-Frisian sound-changes. Nevertheless, it is still possible for a runologist to say that 'on account of the shape of the *a*-rune I regard the Scanomodu coin as English and consequently as the oldest known English runic inscription.'[25] The reason for this is that two of the Frisian rune-inscribed objects – the wooden sword from Arum and the Westeremden A weaving-slay – bear a distinctive 'a' form not found in England, the distinctive feature being the shape of the upper arm. Some scholars, Elliott apparently among them, have accepted the Arum-Westeremden A 'a' as the typical Frisian form, the 'a' rune thus becoming a point of distinction between Old English and Frisian *fuþorcs*.[26] At the very outset one must stress the slenderness of the evidence for this assertion - only two examples of a rune form. Further, the so-called Old English 'a' appears on two runic finds (four examples of the rune) from Frisia, the Harlingen solidus and the Westeremden B staff, as well as on the 'Amay' comb, the find-place of which is uncertain, but which may be of Frisian origin.[27] If the Arum-Westeremden A 'a' is the only possible Frisian 'a' form (as Elliott's statement implies), these must presumably be imports from England. Linguistically, the inscriptions on the Harlingen solidus and the Amay comb could as well be Old English as Frisian, while no conclusion can be reached about that of Westeremden B since it has not yet been satisfactorily interpreted. Though the Harlingen solidus could well be such an import, there seems no reason for believing the Westeremden B staff to be, particularly as it comes from a district for which an accepted Frisian runic object is evidenced. There is, moreover, no reason to doubt

---

[23] Some points in the following discussion of the *skanomodu* and *pada* legends were made independently by Miss Janet M. Bately in her review of Elliott's *Runes* (*Medium Ævum* 30 (1961), 38–42).

[24] Keary, *Catalogue*, p. lxxxiv. See also, L. F. A. Wimmer, *Die Runenschrift* (Berlin, 1887), p. 87.

[25] Elliott, *Runes*, p. 77 [but cf. 2nd ed., p. 102].

[26] Arntz and Zeiss, *Die einheimischen Runendenkmäler*, pp. 440 and 117, n. 3.

[27] *Ibid.* pp. 438–9.

that the so-called Old English 'a' form would be known in Frisia. The Old English forms of the two early additional runes 'a' and 'o' are closely alike, both having the same shape of upper arm. The 'o' form on such an accepted Frisian find as the Arum sword is similar to the Old English forms, having the Old English type of upper arm. A parallel Frisian 'a' form would not be unexpected. The *skanomodu* solidus 'a' is, then, not sufficient evidence for an English rather than a Frisian origin of that coin. Formally, the other runes of the inscription point neither to England nor to Frisia. The *sigel*-rune is of a form not found in Frisia, but neither is it recorded in England, save perhaps in a single example on the Gilton sword hilt.[28] The *cœn*-rune is of a rare type found in Frisia in the Hantum inscription and in England on the Chessell Down plate. The other runes are of common form.

Linguistically, there is one point which suggests a place of origin for the *skano-modu* solidus. If the first element is in fact a form of Gmc *Skauni-*, *Skauno-* as is generally believed, rune 3 gives the reflex of Gmc *au*. This reflex, as has been seen, is recorded as *ea* in Old English, and *a* in Old Frisian. The rune 'a' represents the sound < Gmc *au* in **adujislu** on the Westeremden A weaving-slay. The *skanomodu* solidus may, then, well be Frisian. Numismatically, there is no objection to such an attribution.[29]

(*b*) The *pada* coins. The *sceattas* which bear the name 'pada' have long been associated with the Mercian king Peada, known from Bede's *Historia Ecclesiastica* to have flourished in the mid-seventh century. If the identification is correct there is apparently a case here of the *ea* diphthong of the name being represented by 'a'. Two points can be considered in this connection, the need to identify the 'pada' of the coins with the Mercian king Peada, and the need to read rune 2 of 'pada' as a diphthong *ea*.

The identification of 'pada' with Peada of Mercia is a long-standing one. It is put forward, for example, in the British Museum catalogue,[30] and in recent times has been accepted by the numismatist C. H. V. Sutherland[31] and by the runic scholar R. W. V. Elliott.[32] There is, however, a considerable body of modern numismatic opinion which would date the earliest of the *pada* coins at *c*. 700, a date far too late for the Mercian king.[33] Even if an earlier date for these coins is accepted there is no evidence

---

[28] I have not seen this inscription. Photographs do not show the 's' rune clearly, but Stephens's reproductions (*Old-Northern Runic Monuments* III, 164) indicate an 's' similar to the *skanomodu* example, and R. W. V. Elliott ('Two Neglected English Runic Inscriptions: Gildon [*sic*] and Over-church', *Mélanges de linguistique et de philologie: Fernand Mossé in memoriam* (Paris, 1959), pp. 140–7, at 141) describes it as 'a parallel to the equally archaic "s" of the sixth century Scanomodu coin'. However, the Gilton inscription shows a number of curious rune forms.

[29] The coin is given to Frisia in Arntz and Zeiss, *Die einheimischen Runendenkmäler*, pp. 258 and 117, n. 1. Mr R. H. M. Dolley of the Department of Coins and Medals, British Museum, has stated (orally to the author) that he could not discount the possibility of a Frisian origin for the coin.

[30] Keary, *Catalogue*, p. i.

[31] *Anglo-Saxon Gold Coinage in the Light of the Crondall Hoard* (London, 1948), p. 54.

[32] *Runes*, p. 78.

[33] See, for example, P. Grierson, *Sylloge of Coins of the British Isles: I. Fitzwilliam Museum Cambridge* I (London, 1958), no. 219. Mr R. H. M. Dolley and Dr J. P. C. Kent have both expressed

that the name 'pada' is a royal one, for the word *rex* never accompanies it. The name may be that of a moneyer, as on the closely related Merovingian coinage.[34]

'pada' could be read as a name *Pada* or perhaps *Padda*. It is often stated that single runes were used for double consonants in Anglo-Saxon England,[35] though the evidence for the assertion does not seem to have been examined in detail. However, it should be noted that, though there are a number of different patterns of coins with the legend *pada*, none with a double 'd' has yet been recorded. A name *Pada* is not found elsewhere in Old English, but there are two examples of *Padda*.[36]

(i) an early one in the *Historia Ecclesiastica* where Padda is named as one of the priests, of unknown origin, who helped Wilfrid in the conversion of the South Saxons in the seventh century. The name appears in that form in all early texts of the *Historia Ecclesiastica* and in all texts of the Old English Bede translation save that of Bodleian MS, Tanner 10, which has *Peadda*.[37]

(ii) a late example in *Domesday Book* (Suffolk).[38]

(i) has been accounted for as a lall-name,[39] and as a hypocoristic form of a longer name beginning with a labial consonant.[40] Feilitzen regards the *Domesday Book* name as distinct from the earlier one, being an original nick-name deriving from late OE *pad(d)e*, a word first recorded in the entry for 1137 in the *Peterborough Chronicle*, but probably available earlier in *Domesday Book* examples.[41] At the same time he quotes the Old English place-name *padde byrig* in a charter of 931 (the manuscript, however, *c*. 1200) (= W. de G. Birch, *Cartularium Saxonicum: a Collection of Charters Relating to Anglo-Saxon History* (London, 1885–93), no. 687), which may have the common noun (= 'toad') or, as W. W. Skeat believed, the earlier Old English personal name *Padda*.[42] There may here be a tenth-century

---

this view to the author. For a discussion of the question see the article by Dr Kent, 'From Roman Britain to Saxon England', *Anglo-Saxon Coins: Studies Presented to F. M. Stenton*, ed. R. H. M. Dolley (London, 1961), pp. 1–22.

[34] G. C. Brooke, *English Coins from the Seventh Century to the Present Day*, 3rd ed. (London, 1950), p. 7.

[35] Elliott, *Runes*, pp. 88 and 95. See also A. S. C. Ross, *N&Q* n.s. 7 (1960), 116 and ref.

[36] M. Redin, *Studies on Uncompounded Personal Names*, pp. 105–6. Redin notes (p. xxx) common interchange between single and double consonants in names of this sort.

[37] T. Miller, *The Old English Version of Bede's Ecclesiastical History of the English People*, EETS 95–6 and 110–11 (London, 1890–8) I, 302 and II, 350.

[38] O. v. Feilitzen, *The Pre-Conquest Personal Names of Domesday Book* (Uppsala, 1937), p. 343. The form here may give the name *Pada*, for v. Feilitzen notes occasional doubling of consonants as a characteristic feature of Anglo-Norman orthography (p. 123).

[39] H. Ström, *Old English Personal Names in Bede's History*, p. 74.

[40] O. S. Anderson, *Old English Material in the Leningrad Manuscript of Bede's Ecclesiastical History* (Lund, 1941), p. 71.

[41] A. H. Smith, *English Place-Name Elements*, EPNS 25–6 (Cambridge, 1956) II, s.v. **padde*. Professor R. M. Wilson draws my attention to the fact that *OED* gives no forms of the word with double *d* from before the fifteenth century.

[42] *The Place-Names of Berkshire* (Oxford, 1911), p. 107. [M. Gelling interprets the Berkshire *paddebyrig* as 'toad camp' (*The Place-Names of Berkshire*, EPNS 49–51 (1973–76) III, 688).]

example of the name *Padda*, or of the common noun which could give a nick-name *Padda* earlier than the *Domesday Book* example.

Padda, or perhaps *Pad(d)a*, is then a possible Old English name, at least as likely as *Peada*, which is rare.[43] *Pad(d)a*, *Peada* may have been separate names existing side by side through the Old English period, and they then form a pair of similar, but perhaps etymologically distinct, forms, as a parallel to which can be quoted the pair *Ad(d)a*, *Eada*. In the case of a similar pair, *Abba*, *Eabba*, Redin has noted[44] a possible confusion between two distinct names. A similar confusion may have led to the replacement of *Padda* by *Peadda* in the one Old English Bede text.

There is, then, no need to read 'pada' as *Peada*. Even if the identification 'pada' = Peada of Mercia is regarded as likely, there is no reason to believe that rune 2 represents a diphthong *ea*. The etymology of the name *Peada* is obscure,[45] but the diphthong may develop from the back-mutation of earlier *æ* < *a*.[46] This back-mutation is regarded as an eighth-century change,[47] and indeed no form of the name of Peada of Mercia exists in a pre-eighth-century text. Peada's own form of his name may conceivably have been *Pœda or even *Pada*.[48]

It is clear, then, that the *skanomodu* and *pada* inscriptions cannot be used to prove that, at their date, the rune 'êa' had not yet been created.

In section (ii), that of the forms where two runes are used for the type of diphthong under discussion, there are the following cases of the reflex of Gmc *au*: 'ædan' (Mortain Casket), and two examples, *eac* (Bewcastle Cross) and *eomæ* (Falstone 'hogback'), quoted by Samuels apparently from H. Sweet, *The Oldest English Texts*, EETS 83 (London, 1885), pp. 124 and 127, the Sweet texts deriving in turn from Stephens' readings. Examples where the dipththong involved is not the reflex of Gmc *au* are 'giuþeasu' (Franks Casket), 'bæurnæ' (Great Urswick stone), 'eoh' (Kirkheaton stone), and *gear* (Bewcastle Cross), *eomær* (Falstone 'hogback'), which again derive from Sweet. Finally must be mentioned the name *Beonna*, partly in runes, on a coin ascribed to Beorna of East Anglia.

Some of these examples can be rejected at once. The Bewcastle *gear* was identified by Stephens on the lowest fillet of the south face of the cross. It cannot now be read there, and the condition of the stone at this point makes it clear that the reading is an imaginative nineteenth-century reconstruction of the few fragmentary staves remaining.[49] In the same way, *eac*, read by Stephens at the beginning of line 7 of the main

---

[43] The county volumes of the English Place-Name Society give a number of place-names which may have *Peada* or *Pad(d)a* as elements: so, for example, *Padnall* (Essex), *Paddington* (Middlesex), *Padnell's Wood* (Oxford).

[44] Redin, *Uncompounded Personal Names*, p. 94.

[45] Campbell, *Old English Grammar*, § 207, n. 1.

[46] Redin, *Uncompounded Personal Names*, p. 105.

[47] Brunner, *Altenglische Grammatik*, § 108, 6.

[48] Cf., for example, the predominance of *a* forms in circumstances where back-mutation would later take place in the *Epinal Gloss* (Luick, *Historische Grammatik*, § 231, Anm. 3).

[49] See also R. G. Collingwood's comment on this text in 'The Bewcastle Cross', *TCWAAS* n.s. 35 (1935), 1–29, at 29.

Bewcastle inscription, can be rejected, for it is by no means certainly identifiable on the stone, while the validity of the main Bewcastle text as a whole must be considered in doubt.[50]

Of the *Beonna* coin Samuels writes, 'the first dateable occurrence of a diphthongization in a runic inscription is on the *Beonna* coin (*c.* 760), and here it is most significant that *b*, *n*, *n*, *a* are all in runes but *e*, *o* in roman. Does this show that the representation of these diphthongs was not usual in the earlier runic script?'[51] Samuels's description of the coin legend is, however, inadequate. The legend of the obverse is +*Beonna Rex*, while the reverse has the moneyer's name *Efe*. In the obverse legend the letters 'nna' are runic, EO and EX are roman, while *B* and *R* could be either runic or roman. The moneyer's name is in roman script. There is, then, no reason to believe that the use of roman script for the *eo* of *Beonna* was due to the lack of a runic symbol for the diphthong: the text is clearly an arbitrary mixture of runes and roman letters such as is found not infrequently on early coins. Confirmation of this is given by a second coin of the same king, now in the British Museum, though not in the printed catalogue.[52] This has the obverse legend +*Benna Ress*, with 'nna' in runes, the two E's in roman, *B* and *R* in either runes or roman, but with the *X* given by two 's' runes. The moneyer's name, again *Efe*, is in roman characters.

The Falstone 'hogback' must be considered in some detail. Here there are two texts, one in roman and one in runes. The stone is badly worn, as it was when it was first found,[53] but enough remains to show that the texts were virtually identical. Now visible are (*a*) +EO[.] | TA[.]*Æ*EFTAER | HROETHBERHT*Æ* | BECUNAEFTAER | EOMAE3EBIDAEDDERSAUL*E*, and (*b*) '+ [.] | æftærroe[.] | tæ[*bec*]unæftære[.] | geb[.]æ*d*þe[.]saule', the more complete texts of Sweet-Stephens being unacceptable. The forms *eomær*, *eomæ*, quoted by Samuels as examples of the diphthong expressed by two runes, cannot now be found on the stone, but what remains makes it likely that *eomæ*, or some form closely resembling it, was indeed once cut there. Here, then, is a probable example of two runes being used to represent the reflex of Gmc *au*. Since the carver of this inscription knew both roman and runic scripts, the possibility must arise that the runic representation of the diphthong has been influenced by the practice of roman script. Fortunately, there is in the Falstone (*b*) text one other case showing the undoubted effect of such influence. This is the (*b*) form 'roe[.]tæ' (= (*a*) HROETHBERHT*Æ*). Here the letters OE of the (*a*) form represent the sound developed by *i*-mutation of PrOE *ō*, a sound commonly given by *oe* in written Northumbrian texts. This sound is naturally represented in runes by 'œ', since that rune, by virtue of its name *oeþel*, *eþel* (< *ōþil), must indicate

[50] This point is discussed in the author's article 'The Bewcastle Cross', above pp. 63–5.

[51] 'Old English Phonology', pp. 36–7.

[52] See, however, G. C. Brooke, 'Anglo-Saxon Acquisitions of the British Museum', *Numismatic Chronicle* 5th ser., 3 (1923), 243–59, at 254.

[53] This is shown by the engraving accompanying the find report, J. Wood, 'Some Account of a Saxon Inscription, on a Stone found near Falstone, in the County of Northumberland', *Archæologia Æliana* 1 (1816), 103–4.

i-mutated *ō*. The use of the two runes 'oe' is then to be explained as due to influence from the (*a*) text, and the same could well apply to the use of 'eo' in *eomœ*.

Four cases remain in section (ii). Kirkheaton 'eoh' in 'eoh : woro | htæ' is presumably a personal name, and may be the same word as OE *eoh* 'war-horse'. 'eo' then represents the fracture diphthong derived from PrOE *e* followed by *h*.[54] Great Urswick 'bæurnæ' in '+tunwinisetæ | æftertoroʒ | tredæbeku | næfterhisb | æurnægebidæsþe | rs | au | læ' may be a form of *beorn* 'prince, nobleman, chief' or of *bearn* 'child, son', and 'æu' gives the reflex of either WGmc *e* or of WGmc *a* followed by *r* + consonant. As has been seen 'êa' is used for the fracture diphthong derived from earlier *e* in Ruthwell 'fêarran', but we cannot be sure that 'êa' is a suitable rune for such a diphthong in all parts of the Anglian dialect areas. 'giuþeasu' in the Franks Casket 'herfegtaþ | titusendgiuþeasu' is an anomalous form, the ending not readily explicable. 'æadan' in the Mortain Casket '+goodhelpe : æadan | þiiosneciismeelgewar | ahtæ' is the only one of the four containing the reflex of Gmc *au*, for the word is presumably an oblique form of the Old English personal name *Eada*.[55] Here we might well expect the rune 'êa' to have been used if it were in existence when the inscription was cut. The rune-masters of both Franks and Mortain Caskets were presumably acquainted with the roman alphabet: the Franks Casket has part of an inscription – the words HICFUGIANTHIERUSALIM – in roman characters, while the Mortain Casket has the roman inscriptions SCSMIH and SCSGAB. The possibility must arise, then, that the runic texts of these two caskets have been influenced by roman usage. There is no further evidence for such influence in the Mortain runic inscription. In the case of the Franks Casket can be noted the use of 'g' for the spirant in 'unneg', 'fegtaþ', a use unexampled elsewhere in Old English runic inscriptions, though the spirant is sometimes represented by *g* in early written texts.[56] Finally must be noted the possibility of a rune-master using two runes, such as 'ea', rather than an existent 'êa', even when uninfluenced by roman usage. Too few Old English runic inscriptions are available for us to know much of the type of spelling tradition the rune-master had to call upon. Faced with a diphthong he might well use two vowel symbols, rather than a single diphthong rune.

It is clear that we are not justified in concluding that the texts discussed above antedate the formation of the rune 'êa', and the present writer's suggestion of an early date of formation of that rune is not refuted. This suggestion can be expanded – speculatively – into the following theory. Gmc *au* was monophthongized in Anglo-Frisian, and a new rune, 'êa', was created to represent the monophthong, whatever its quality may have been. The form of the new rune was patterned on those of the Anglo-Frisian additional runes 'a', 'o'. 'êa' did not survive in Frisian inscriptions because in Old Frisian the monophthong developed further to *a*, and came to be represented by 'a'. In Old English the monophthong was diphthongized, the rune 'êa' being used for the diphthong thus developed, and then for other diphthongs which

---

[54] However, the Kirkheaton stone is mutilated, and it is possible that a lost rune once preceded the 'e' of 'eoh'. If 'eoh' is not the full name the origin of the diphthong is uncertain.

[55] Cahen and Olsen, *L'inscription runique*, p. 28.

[56] Campbell, *Old English Grammar*, § 57 (4).

fell in with it. These diphthongs were sometimes represented, more or less phonetically, by two vowel runes.

Such a theory explains more of the material available for the Old English rune *ear*
than that described at the beginning of this article. It also enables us to accept the
very early dating – *c*. 550–600 – recently suggested by B. Nerman for the Thames
scramasax.[57] However, there is one obvious objection to the theory which must be
countered. Most manuscript *fuþorcs* give the first four additional runes in the order
'a æ y êa', and this would commonly be taken as the order in which they were added
to the twenty-four letter *fuþark*. 'êa' would thus seem to be later than 'y'. 'y' is
developed as a result of the *i*-mutation of *u*, a sound change which has been attributed
to the sixth or seventh centuries,[58] and this seems to give an earliest possible date for
'êa'. It could be argued, however, that the chronological order of the additional runes
has been altered in the *fuþorcs* so that 'y' could be put among the other monophthong
runes. It is then interesting to note that the *fuþorc* of MS Vienna, Österreichische
Nationalbibliothek, 795 gives the rune order 'a æ êa y'.

POSTSCRIPT

Maureen Halsall has summed up a more recent state of discussion of this rune-name
in her edition *The Old English* Rune Poem: *a Critical Edition* (Toronto, 1981), pp.
160–2. Both of us missed (as Dorothy Whitelock did not when she read my article)
the use of *ear* as an English place-name element (Earith, Erith, Yarmouth, Isle of
Wight).[59]

More recent work on runes has clarified, or at least made more obscure, some
aspects of my arguments. We now know a little more about the **skanomodu** solidus
and its rune forms than we did (see below, pp. 159–60). There is little enthusiasm
nowadays for identifying coins with the legend 'p a d a' as issues of Peada of Mercia.
I seem to have been early among non-numismatists in publicising the theory that
Pada was moneyer, not king; and I pay thanks to the memory of Michael Dolley, who
instructed me in the beginnings of numismatic method here. Mark Blackburn writes
without qualification: 'Pada is now regarded as a moneyer, and the coinage is thought
to be Kentish'.[60] There is no need to regard 'p a d a' as a spelling of *Peada*.

Since this paper was written there has been a huge increase in the number of coins
of Beonna of East Anglia, and there is therefore a wider range of forms available for

---

[57] 'The Dating of the Runic-Inscribed Scramasax from the Thames at Battersea', *Antiquaries Journal*
39 (1959), 289–90. Nerman's date is not generally accepted. Mr D. M. Wilson of the Department of
British and Mediæval Antiquities, British Museum, ascribes the scramasax to the ninth century.

[58] Bülbring, *Elementarbuch* I, § 158, Luick, *Historische Grammatik*, § 201, R. Girvan, *Angelsaksisch
Handboek* (Haarlem, 1931), § 85.

[59] A. H. Smith, *English Place-Name Elements*, EPNS 25–6 (Cambridge, 1956) I, 143–4; E. Ekwall,
The Concise Oxford Dictionary of English Place-Names, 4th ed. (Oxford, 1960), s.n.

[60] 'A Survey of Anglo-Saxon and Frisian Coins with Runic Inscriptions', *Old English Runes*, ed.
Bammesberger, pp. 137–89, at 145.

the king's name and title: +BEONNAREX, +BEOnnaREX, BEnnaREss, 'b e o n n a r e x' together with a type with the royal title given by a monogram and the name '+ b e n + n a'.[61] What conclusion Samuels would have drawn from this range of forms about the use of the rune *ear* I do not know. For myself I would be more inclined than in 1961 to admit the likelihood of a strong influence from roman on some of the later runic inscriptions, and this certainly might affect those in mixtures in scripts, as often on the coinage. In view of that, the survival of the rune *ear* into the late period, as on the Dover stone, is notable.

I do not think there have been many new examples of the rune *ear* discovered since 1961, though it is worth drawing attention to a curious form on a coin of Offa of Mercia by the moneyer *Eadnoþ*, where the opening diphthong seems to be a bind of 'e' and an inverted 'ea'.[62] In contrast there is the almost equally interesting form from Rome, where the name *Eadbald*, a graffito on the fresco in the Cimitero di Commodilla, opens with a bind of the two runes, 'e͡ a'.[63] It is formally possible that the rune *ear* originated in such a bind-rune, simplified by dropping the first stem of 'e' and the lower arm of 'a'. This would remove the need to give an early date for the rune's creation, and explain why no *ear*-rune has been found in Frisia. Bright young scholars have begun to attack the early date given hitherto to the creation of the 'Anglo-Frisian' runes 'a' and 'o', and with regret I have to admit there is something in their arguments.

---

[61] M. M. Archibald, 'The Coinage of Beonna in the Light of the Middle Harling Hoard', *BNJ* 55 (1985), 10–54, at 19–21.

[62] C. E. Blunt and G. van der Meer, 'A New Type for Offa', *BNJ* 38 (1969), 182–3.

[63] R. Derolez, 'Anglo-Saxons in Rome', *Nytt om Runer* 2 (1987), 14–15.

7

(1962)

A NOTE ON THE TRANSLITERATION
OF OLD ENGLISH RUNIC INSCRIPTIONS

Old English runic inscriptions are commonly studied in transliterated versions. This is a matter of expediency. It is convenient to represent runes by letters readily obtainable for the typewriter. It is cheaper to print characters available in standard types, and because of this some editors of learned journals require their contributors to use Latin script only. Linguists who are not runologists usually find it easier to deal with transliterated texts than with the runic originals. For such reasons the runes of an inscription are often neglected, and the text is studied in transliteration according to one or other of the systems in use. In recent years that developed by Professor Bruce Dickins[1] has been much used.

However good such a system of transliteration may be it must be used with caution and commonsense. In particular, one must avoid the error of treating the transliterated text as if it were an original. This would seem an elementary point of method; yet the mistake is often made. An example is seen in the treatment by some scholars of the rune *œþel*, *eþel*, transliterated in the Dickins system by 'œ'. A. S. C. Ross, for example, notes the representation of the *i*-umlaut 'of Pr. Germ. *ō* by *œ* in 'gidrœ[fi]d,' 'limwœrignæ" as one of the features bearing 'upon the question of the geographical position occupied by the dialect of the *Ruthwell Cross*'.[2] The linguistic discussion of the Ruthwell Cross material in the Dickins-Ross edition of the *Dream of the Rood* contains the remark that 'PrGerm *ō* appears when mutated as *œ* in 'limwœrignæ', 'gidrœ[fi]d' (from the early ninth century an Anglian characteristic)'.[3] R. W. V. Elliott regards 'the characteristically Anglian use of *œ*' in 'twœgen', 'afœddæ' as a point of interest in the language of the Franks Casket inscriptions.[4] These scholars treat 'œ' (the single inverted commas indicate the transliteration of a rune) as though it were *œ*. The sound developed by *i*-mutation from WGmc *ō* is commonly represented by *oe* in written Anglian texts, but by *e* in those in West Saxon and Kentish. If the Ruthwell and Franks Casket texts had in fact *œ* for this reflex (the origin of the stem

---

[1] 'System of Transliteration'. This system is used in the present article.
[2] 'The Linguistic Evidence for the Date of the "Ruthwell Cross" ', *MLR* 28 (1933), 145–55, at 145–6.
[3] B. Dickins and A. S. C. Ross, *The Dream of the Rood* (London, 1934), p. 9. See also H. Bütow, *Das altenglische "Traumgesicht vom Kreuz"* (Heidelberg, 1935), p. 114.
[4] *Runes: an Introduction*, p. 103.

vowel of 'twœgen' is, however, obscure) there might be evidence of an Anglian dialect. But these texts use, not *æ*, but 'œ', the old *ō*-rune, which in Primitive Old English would have the name *ōþil*. After *i*-mutation this would be *oeþel* in the Anglian dialects, *eþel* in later West Saxon and Kentish.[5] By virtue of its name, then, the rune 'œ' represents the sounds developed by *i*-mutation of earlier *ō* in the various Old English dialects. 'œ' is a formal transliteration only, and the phonetic value of the rune in West Saxon and Kentish would be more accurately represented by *e*. There is no evidence that the use of the rune *oeþel* for the *i*-mutation of earlier *ō* is confined to Anglian inscriptions; indeed, there are no non-Anglian inscriptions in which, as far as we know, the sound is represented. The statements made by Ross, Dickens-Ross and Elliott result from a confusion of the transliterated text with an original in Latin script.

A similar error is found in Elliott's examination of the Chessell Down inscription. He reads the second word of this text as *sœri*, which he connects with OE *sorg* 'sorrow', remarking that '*œ* for *o* occurs in the corresponding verbal form *sœr(g)endi* in the mixed Mercian-Kentish Épinal glossary of about A.D. 700'.[6] This comment on the stem vowel may be irrelevant. Elliott does not date the Chessell Down sword, beyond ascribing it to a 'pagan Jutish cemetery'. Jutish colonies were established on the Isle of Wight in the early years of the sixth century.[7] According to Bede the Isle of Wight remained pagan until 685,[8] though at that date the civilisation may not have been Jutish. On the historical evidence the Chessell Down sword may be sixth or early seventh century. Archaeologists ascribe the sword to the sixth century. *i*-mutation has been placed in the first half of the sixth century,[9] so it is possible that the inscription antedates *i*-mutation and that the rune 'œ' or 'sœri' has its earlier value *o*, as it does, for example, on the *scanomodu* solidus.[10] The Chessell Down inscription would then contain two 'rival' symbols for the *o* sound, for it also has the *ōs*-rune.

Though these examples show error in method, yet the error has here no serious consequences. The Ruthwell and Franks Casket texts are certainly Anglian, while the reading *o* rather than *æ* in the Chessell Down inscription does not affect Elliott's interpretation. However, if the same error is made in the case of the rune *æsc* (transliterated 'æ') it may be seriously misleading. The Germanic form of this rune-name is usually given as **askiz*.[11] In some Old English dialects the initial vowel was fronted to *æ*, which remained unaffected by *i*-mutation.[12] In others – the 'second fronting' dialects – it was further fronted and raised (before *i*-mutation) to a sound

5 Runic manuscripts commonly give the Anglian form of the name, but *eþel*, *eðel* appear in Hickes's transcriptions of the Cotton Otho B. X (*Runic Poem*) and Galba A. II *fuþorcs*.

6 *Runes*, pp. 79–80. The *Epinal* form as given in H. Sweet, *The Oldest English Texts*, EETS 83 (London, 1885), p. 40 is *soer[g]endi*.

7 R. G. Collingwood and J. N. L. Myres, *Roman Britain and the English Settlements*, 2nd ed. (Oxford, 1937), p. 366. See also H. Kökeritz, *The Place-Names of the Isle of Wight* (Uppsala, 1940), pp. xxvi–xxxiii.

8 *Historia Ecclesiastica*, iv. 16.

9 Luick, *Historische Grammatik*, § 201.

10 This solidus may, however, be Frisian.

11 J. and E. M. Wright, *Old English Grammar*, 2nd ed. (Oxford, 1914), § 56. *OED* quotes, under *ash*, a Germanic form **ask-oz*. The acceptance of such a form would not affect the present argument.

12 Brunner, *Altenglische Grammatik*, § 96, 2.

represented in non-runic texts by *e*. This sound may or may not have been identical with the reflex of WGmc *e* in those dialects.[13] *i*-mutation had no apparent effect on the *e* produced by second fronting. The rune-name would thus be written *æsc* in West Saxon and Northumbrian, but *esc* in the 'second fronting' dialects. Runic manu-scripts give the form *æsc*, but there are occasional suggestions of *esc*. The rune-name of the *fuþorc* of MS Brussels, Koninklijke Bibliotheek, 9311–9319 began with *e*, the end of the name unfortunately being lost.[14] The rune 'æ' takes the place of *e* as fifth letter of the alphabet of the Rome bronze fragment,[15] while Derolez identifies an 'æ' form with the value *e* in MS Berne, Stadt- und Hochschulbibliothek, 207.[16]

In an area where second fronting caused WGmc *a* and *e* to fall together either completely or nearly so, the rune-master would be faced with a problem. He would have two runes, *esc* and *eh*, for *e*, but none for the *æ* which developed by second fronting from PrOE *a* or for the *ǣ* which may have survived from Gmc *ǣ* or have developed by *i*-mutation of earlier *ā*. He could solve this difficulty in a number of ways. He could, for example, use both *esc* and *eh* for *e*, and invent a completely new symbol for *æ* (cf. the use of the runes 'g' and 'j' for front *g* and the invention of the new character *gar* for back *g* in north-west Northumbria). He could use *eh* for the reflex of WGmc *e*, keeping *æsc* for that of WGmc *a* and also for *æ* produced by second fronting and *ǣ* (cf. the use of the rune 'g' for both front and back *g* in at least part of the Old English runic area). He could use *eh* for the reflexes of both WGmc *e* and *a* (> *e*), keeping the rune 'æ' for *ǣ* and retaining for it the rune-name form *æsc* which would thus be distinct from the common noun *esc*. I do not seek to prove that the rune-masters of the 'second fronting' areas adopted any one or other of these possibilities, but only to suggest that in dealing with runic texts from these areas we must think of the possibility of the rune 'æ' representing *e* as well as, perhaps instead of, *æ*. There is perhaps the further possibility of inverted spellings of 'e' for *æ*.

One of the Old English 'second fronting' dialects was Kentish, as Old and Middle English texts from that county prove. The other is the dialect called by modern scholars Mercian or West Mercian. Here A. Campbell regards second fronting as 'limited to a small part of the vast Midland area',[17] but a recent examination of the material by R. M. Wilson[18] has shown how little we know of the geographical distribution of the sound change. The 'Mercian' texts which evidence second fronting are the *Vespasian Psalter*, where it is practically universal, the *Royal Glosses* and the *Life of St Chad*, where it is common, and the *Epinal, Erfurt* and *Corpus Glossaries*, the *Lorica Glosses* and *Hymn*, where it is occasional. There are a few cases in other texts, notably in *Rushworth*₁, which also has spellings in *æ* for WGmc *e*. Of these

---

[13] Cf. Luick, *Historische Grammatik*, § 180, and R. M. Wilson, 'The Provenance of the Vespasian Psalter Gloss: the Linguistic Evidence', *The Anglo-Saxons: Studies . . . presented to Bruce Dickins*, ed. P. Clemoes (London, 1959), pp. 292–310, at 298.

[14] Derolez, *Runica Manuscripta*, pp. 68 and 72.

[15] C. D. Buck, 'An ABC Inscribed in Old English Runes', *Modern Philology* 17 (1919–20), 219–24.

[16] *Runica Manuscripta*, p. 189. See, however, the same writer's 'Ogam, "Egyptian", and "Gothic" Alphabets', *Scriptorium* 5 (1951), 3–19, at 12.

[17] *Old English Grammar*, § 168.

[18] 'Provenance of the Vespasian Psalter Gloss'.

texts only one is assigned by its scribe to a place of origin. *Rushworth₁* was written by one Farman *æt harawuda* usually identified with Harewood, near Leeds, though Harewood, Herefordshire, has also been suggested. The *Lorica Glosses* may be from Lichfield and the *Royal Glosses* from Worcester. The places of origin of the other texts are unknown.

Further evidence is provided by early Middle English texts in which the reflex of WGmc *a* is *e* rather than *a*. Some of these have been ascribed to the West Midlands, though again R. M. Wilson has shown how little evidence there is for such ascription. The *Worcester Glosses* and the early version of Lagamon's *Brut*, localised at Worcester and Areley Kings, Worcestershire, respectively,[19] have examples of *e* (as well as *a, æ*) for WGmc *a*, and this suggests that second fronting took place in the southern part of the West Midlands. Unfortunately this district is of no importance in the present discussion since no runic inscriptions have been found there. One would like to know how far north the area of second fronting extended, but here the Middle English literary texts fail us. Even in that part of the West Midlands where second fronting certainly took place, the *e* thus produced was replaced by *a* by 1300. Unfortunately there are very few pre-1300 texts known to have originated in the north West Midlands or the western half of the Northern area. For a West Midland area comprising Cheshire and parts of Shropshire, Staffordshire, Warwickshire, Leicestershire, Derbyshire, Yorkshire and Lancashire the editors of the *Middle English Dictionary* cite (without producing evidence for the localisation) only the Lambeth *Poema Morale*, which abounds in examples of *e* for WGmc *a*. The list of texts in S. Moore, S. B. Meech and H. Whitehall, 'Middle English Dialect Characteristics and Dialect Boundaries', *Essays and Stud. in Eng. and Comparative Lit.* 13 (1935), 51–7, includes the *Compassio Mariæ*, the manuscript though not the composition attributed to Chester 1250–1300. This has three examples of *wes* (which rhymes with *peas* (peace) and *endeles*) but also the rhyming pair *was, glas*.

Place-name evidence will give further information, but it must be set out in detail so that local and Chancery spellings can be distinguished, and so that we can be sure that individual *e* forms are not simply Anglo-Norman spellings for OE *æ*. So far only one relevant county, Derbyshire, has been examined in requisite detail. K. Cameron has made out a good case for a West Midland dialect in the western half of this county, one of its characteristics being second fronting.[20] Perhaps second fronting took place in the West Riding of Yorkshire just north of the Derbyshire border, and in Chester and perhaps south Lancashire to the west. More will be known of this when the place-name surveys of the West Riding and Cheshire are completed. E. Ekwall noted West Midland forms in Lancashire place-names south of the Ribble, though he does not specify second fronting as one of the characteristics.[21] There are runs of *e* forms for Ashton (Preston Parish) and Ashton Hall (Lancaster Parish), but these may be Chancery spellings. Occasional *e* forms appear elsewhere, including at least one from

[19] The composition of the text of Lagamon's *Brut* is localised, not the extant manuscripts.
[20] 'An Early Mercian Boundary in Derbyshire: the Place-Name Evidence', *The Anglo-Saxons*, ed. Clemoes, pp. 13–34.
[21] *The Place-Names of Lancashire* (Manchester, 1922), p. 228.

a local document, *Esseleye c.* 1250 *Chartulary of Cockersand Abbey* for Ashley (Kirkham Parish). WGmc *a* does not appear as *e* in the North Riding of Yorkshire.[22] Cumberland has occasional *e* forms, but it is unlikely that these indicate a 'second fronting' dialect in that county.

The area of second fronting certainly included western Derbyshire, and perhaps also the West Riding of Yorkshire as far north as Harewood, Cheshire and south Lancashire. In dealing with runic texts from these areas we must remember the possibility of the rune 'æ' being used for *e*. The same applies to inscriptions found in Derbyshire, Yorkshire and Lancashire but not more closely localised, and to those whose place of origin is quite unknown but which are identified as Anglian. A few examples will show the effect on our reading of inscriptions. The Overchurch (Cheshire) stone has the text 'folcæaraerdonbec- | [.]biddaþfoteæþelmu*n*-', 'fote' in the second line being clearly a mistake for 'fore'. It is likely that we should read *arerdon* and *Eþel-*. The fifth rune of line 1 has always presented difficulties. Professor Dickins has suggested that it was 'perhaps a blundered or damaged character abandoned by the carver',[23] but the letter is quite well cut and preserved. R. W. V. Elliott noted a possible northern plural in *-e*, but objected to the archaic nature of a form *folcæ*.[24] If we read *folce* the objection disappears. There is little evidence for the provenance of the Mortain casket, but it may be Mercian as I. Dahl has suggested on the basis of the form 'gewarahtæ'.[25] The text '+goodhelpe:æadan | þiiosneciis-meelgewar | ahtæ' should perhaps be read *+Good helpe:Eadan þiiosne ciismeel gewarahte*. The replacement of *æ* forms by *e* in *Eadan, gewarahte* will affect our estimate of the date of this inscription. Re-dating would also be necessary if the rune 'æ' could be read as *e* in the texts of the Franks Casket (where such a reading is possible, though there are objections) and the Lancaster and Great Urswick crosses (though there is little evidence to suggest that second fronting extended as far north into Lancashire as this). The Franks Casket would have the forms *Egili, þer, gibroþer, Romecestri* for 'ægili', 'þær', 'gibroþær', 'romæcæstri', and Great Urswick 'bæurnæ' would be replaced by the slightly more regular *beurne*. 'worohtæ' on the Kirkheaton (West Riding of Yorkshire, south of Harewood) stone should perhaps be read *worohte*, while æDRED, the name of the owner of the Lancashire gold ring, may be a spelling for *Edred*.

The same principle must be applied in the reading of the Kentish runic texts. The inscription of the Sandwich stone has commonly been read 'ræhæbul'.[26] The third rune is not certainly 'h'. No similar form with a value 'h' is found in the other Old English inscriptions, and it seems at least equally likely that this character is 's' (cf.

[22] A. H. Smith, *The Place-Names of the North Riding of Yorkshire*, EPNS 5 (Cambridge, 1928), p. xxxi.
[23] 'System of Transliteration', p. 19.
[24] 'Two Neglected English Runic Inscriptions: Gildon [*sic*] and Overchurch', *Mélanges de linguistique et de philologie: Fernand Mossé in memoriam* (Paris, 1959), pp. 140–7, at 145.
[25] *Substantival Inflexion*, p. 28.
[26] Recently, for example, in Elliott, *Runes*, p. 81 [but cf. 2nd ed., p. 106].

the similar, reversed, form in Franks Casket 'gisl') or a roman N. We may have to explain, not a word *ræhæbul*, but *rehebul, resebul* or *renebul*.

The *e* readings of the preceding paragraphs are possibilities, nothing more, but it should be remembered that the traditional *æ* readings are likewise only possibilities. Even if all the suggested *e* forms are rejected the methodological principle must remain, that runes should be treated as runes, and not simply transliterated and then neglected. Because the rune-name is in nearly every case a common noun in the language it is likely to have the same dialectal variants and undergo the same sound changes as other common nouns. The sound represented by a rune may vary according to dialect and date. Such variation is concealed when a formal system of transliteration is employed.

In a recent article I described some of the uncertainties encountered in any attempt to date Old English runic inscriptions on linguistic grounds.[27] The present note draws attention to a further field of uncertainty, and suggests that even the conclusions reached in that earlier article were too optimistic.

POSTSCRIPT

The principle of this article remains intact, though few seem to have noticed its existence. At any rate it is still possible for a phonologist like Anne King to assert that the Ruthwell use of 'œ' in 'g i *d* r œ [f .] d', 'l i m w œ r i g n æ' is 'a diatopic, rather than a diachronic feature', contrasting it with the unrounded *e*-forms to be expected in, say, West Saxon.[28]

Since this paper appeared there has been an immense amount of work done on the 'second fronting' dialects as they developed into Middle English. This would have to be taken into account in any revision of the paper, but it is too complex – and in some instances too controversial – to summarise in a postscript. There is debate as to whether the <e> produced by second fronting fell together phonemically with <e> from other sources. A good deal of place-name material has come into print, both in the publication of new volumes from the EPNS county survey and in the study of specific forms. Again, this is mostly inconclusive or disputed. For instance, the EPNS West Riding of Yorkshire volumes have now appeared, but all their editor, A. H. Smith, could say on the subject is 'OE *æ* normally appears as *a*, but in certain cases it also appears as *e*, as in p.ns. containing *æsc*'.[29] This looks promising for our purposes until Smith spoils it by adding, 'The variation in p.ns. containing *æsc* . . . may be due in part to the influence of ON *eski*'. The trouble is that it is theoretically possible that in certain dialects of Old English the pronunciation of the word for

---

[27] 'Language and Dating in OE Inscriptions', above pp. 29–43.

[28] 'The Ruthwell Cross – a Linguistic Monument (Runes as Evidence for Old English)', *Folia Linguistica Historica* 7 (1986), 43–79, at 71.

[29] *The Place-Names of the West Riding of Yorkshire*, EPNS 30–7 (Cambridge, 1961–3) VII, 77.

'ash-tree' was indeed affected by the Old Norse cognate, but whether that would affect the rune-name *æsc* > *esc* is another matter.[30] And whether my paper will ever encourage historical linguists to think in terms of the runic texts rather than their transliterations is even more doubtful.

---

[30] In another context R. Derolez writes, 'In view of the very rare instances of *esc* < *æsc*, the possibility of a value *e* is minimal, though perhaps not entirely excluded', 'Runic Literacy among the Anglo-Saxons', *Britain 400–600*, ed. Bammesberger and Wollmann, pp. 397–436, at 421.

8

(1962)

THE USE OF DOUBLE RUNES
IN OLD ENGLISH INSCRIPTIONS

That the early rune-masters did not use double runes, even to express long or repeated sounds, has become one of the commonplaces of runic study in recent times. It is, however, a commonplace which might well be questioned. There is, of course, no doubt that early Scandinavian rune-masters used double runes very rarely – so rarely indeed that when they did there is some reason to suspect magic or amuletic intent, or perhaps error in cutting. Some modern runologists, however, have not confined their acceptance of the principle to the field of Scandinavian inscriptions, but have suggested that the early rune-masters in general avoided double runes, and have sometimes interpreted non-Scandinavian inscriptions in the light of this claim. To take examples. H. Arntz states, 'in der Runenschrift werden Doppellaute grund-sätzlich einfach geschrieben', and again, 'In der Runenschrift gilt die Regel, daß überhaupt zwei aufeinanderfolgenden gleiche Laute in jedem Fall einfach geschrie-ben werden können'.[1] These remarks appear in the chapter 'Die altgermanische Runenreihe', though the illustrative examples quoted are all from Scandinavian inscriptions. R. W. V. Elliott writes, 'Double sounds, especially consonants, are not generally indicated as such in the older Germanic runic inscriptions, although there are some exceptions. This rule applies not only medially in words, but also when one word ends and the next word begins with the same sound'.[2] W. Krause has suggested that in the West Germanic inscription of the Freilaubersheim brooch a single rune was used for a double or long sound 'nach bekannter runischer Schreibregel', though he does not elaborate on this remark.[3] In the case of Old English runic inscriptions, with which the present article is particularly concerned, the principle has sometimes been invoked to explain unusual spellings. In an account of the Thornhill rune-stones R. W. V. Elliott remarks, 'The traditional runic practice of writing successive identical sounds once only persists in the shared *æ* of *settæfter* (*A*) and in the single *t* of *sete* (*B*)'. Of the double consonants in such Ruthwell Cross spellings as 'almeȝttig',

---

[1] H. Arntz, *Handbuch der Runenkunde*, 2nd ed. (Halle/Saale, 1944), pp. 78–9.
[2] Elliott, *Runes: an Introduction*, p. 20.
[3] W. Krause, *Runeninschriften im älteren Futhark* (Halle/Saale, 1937), p. 212. [In the second edition Krause reads the text differently! p. 284.] See also Arntz and Zeiss, *Die einheimischen Runendenk-mäler*, p. 229, n. 1.

'[æ]þþilæ' he comments, 'most probably the common runic rule of writing single consonants for double here operates *vice versa*',[4] a statement which Professor A. S. C. Ross has quoted with approval and a reference to his own study of the inscription.[5]

Some of the earlier runologists expressed themselves with more caution, or at least with more ambiguity, on the subject, for indeed it is sometimes hard to tell whether they refer to a postulated Germanic or to a Scandinavian practice. So, for example, L. F. A. Wimmer's comment, 'Doppelkonsonanten werden durch einfaches zeichen ausgedrückt', is made in a section referring to 'das alphabet von dem Vadstenaer brakteaten . . . und den ältesten inschriften', but it is not clear from his reference whether the latter are only the oldest Scandinavian inscriptions, or whether, as is less likely, he intends the phrase to include examples from outside that area.[6] S. Bugge remarks, 'Det betegnes i Regelen ikke, at en Konsonant udtales dobbelt eller lang', a reference apparently to the practice in inscriptions in 'den germanske Række paa 24 Tegn (med Undtagelse af den angelsaksiske)'.[7] But since Bugge gives no illustrative examples, it is not clear whether he thought the practice was evidenced in East and Continental West Germanic or not.

There is, as has been indicated above, no reason to doubt that such a practice of runic orthography can be deduced from the early Scandinavian inscriptions. But it could have been a principle peculiar to the Scandinavian rune-masters. Before we could be certain that it was followed by the engravers of 'the older Germanic runic inscriptions' we would like to find evidence for it also in inscriptions in either East or West Germanic dialects, or preferably both. There seems to have been no extensive examination of the East and West Germanic runic material from this standpoint, and the present article is therefore written as a first attempt at such an examination. It is particularly concerned with the Old English runic material, but first I must mention briefly the evidence to be derived from East and Continental West Germanic sources.

The evidence from East Germanic inscriptions seems inconclusive. There are few East Germanic runic texts, and their interpretations are uncertain. The Arntz-Zeiss corpus lists six *Denkmäler der Ostgermanen*: the spearheads of Dahmsdorf, Kowel and Rozwadów, the Pietroassa ring, and the Niesdrowitz and Sedschütz urns.[8] The Kowel spearhead and the Pietroassa ring do not survive, and the readings to be derived from extant reproductions are disputed. To one not a specialist in this particular field of runic study some, perhaps all, of the forms of the Niesdrowitz urn seem to be interpretable, not as runes, but as crude decorative patterns. The text of the Sedschütz urn is likewise uncertainly runic. It is not to be expected, then, that from this small and doubtful group of texts a significant number of certain cases of single for double runes will be derived. In fact there are two possible examples: **ranja**

4 Elliott, *Runes*, pp. 88 and 95 [The latter rephrased in the second edition, p. 122].
5 A. S. C. Ross, *N&Q* n.s. 7 (1960), 116 and ref.
6 L. F. A. Wimmer, *Die Runenschrift* (Berlin, 1887), p. 191.
7 Bugge and Olsen, *Norges indskrifter med de ældre runer* I, 12 and 14.
8 Arntz and Zeiss, *Die einheimischen Runendenkmäler*, pp. 453–55. C. J. S. Marstrander has identified a number of Gothic inscriptions on Scandinavian soil ('De gotiske runeminnesmerker', *NTS* 3 (1929), 25–157). Even if the identification is accepted, these inscriptions cannot be regarded as showing Gothic spelling practice uninfluenced by that of Scandinavia.

on the Dahmsdorf spearhead, connected by many scholars with Gothic *rannjan*, and **wihailag** on the Pietroassa ring, which has been interpreted as *wih hailag*. However, each of these interpretations has been questioned, and in the case of the Pietroassa ring even the reading has come under attack.

The Continental West Germanic inscriptions are more numerous, but unfortunately many of these, too, are uncertain of interpretation. Arntz-Zeiss list three cases of double consonants represented by single runes: **hada** on the Harlingen solidus, **ofilen** on the Osthofen brooch, and **atano** on the Soest brooch.[9] Of these, **ofilen** is a disputed reading and interpretation, while there is no reason to believe that the **d** of **hada** represents a double rather than a single consonant, as the Arntz-Zeiss discussion of the Harlingen legend shows. The Soest reading **atano** may have a single **t** for the double consonant, though even here Arntz-Zeiss quote as a parallel one non-runic form with a single *t*. Other cases noted by Arntz-Zeiss – **goda** for *godda* on the Freilaubersheim brooch, **wigiþonar** for *wigiþ þonar* on the Nordendorf A brooch, for example – depend on disputed readings or interpretations. On the other hand, the Charnay brooch has an example of a doubled rune. Its form **iddan** is commonly accepted as an oblique case of the personal name *Idda*. However, the two *d* runes are on different lines separated by the full width of the brooch, and this may account for the doubling.

Unless there is significant material not considered in the brief survey above, the East and Continental West Germanic inscriptions tell us nothing about whether their engravers avoided the use of double runes or not. The evidence of the Old English inscriptions then assumes a particular importance in the present discussion. Fortunately, these inscriptions are fairly numerous, and many of them can be read with certainty. The Old English material can be divided into three groups:

1. The use of double runes where, on the evidence of common practice in written texts, double letters are to be expected. There are the following examples of medial double runes: 'setto/n' Bewcastle Cross, '*iohann*[*i*]s' coffin of St Cuthbert, 'had/da' Derbyshire bone plate, 'afœddæ,' 'unneg' Franks Casket, '[.]*biddaþ*' Overchurch stone, 'fêarran' Ruthwell Cross, 'se*t*æfter' Thornhill I stone, 'gebid/da*þ*' Thornhill II stone, and the forms BEOnna (2x), BEnna on coins attributed to Beorna of East Anglia.[10] Double runes marking the end of one word and the beginning of the next are: 'þissigb[.]c[.]' Bewcastle, 'æftærroe[.]tæ' Falstone 'hogback', 'hossitæþ' Franks Casket, 'setæ æfter' Great Urswick stone, '[*b*]ismæræ[*d*]uu*ŋk̄*et' Ruthwell.

2. The use of single runes where, on the same evidence, double ones are to be expected: 'gebidæs', 'setæ' Great Urswick, 'gibidæþ' Lancaster cross, 'blagcmon' Maughold I stone, 'almeʒttig', 'men', '*men*' Ruthwell, 'êateʒnne', 'sete' Thornhill III stone. Here may be added the legend 'pada' found on a number of early *sceattas*, and perhaps the inscription on the Maughold II stone, which may read '-gmo/n'.[11]

[9] Arntz and Zeiss, *Die einheimischen Runendenkmäler*, p. 482.
[10] In these coin legends only 'nna' are certainly runes. E and O are roman letters, while B could be either runic or roman.
[11] This has formerly been read as '-gmon', but it is likely that the third rune is not 'o', but the bind

Falstone 'geb[.]æd' should almost certainly be supplemented 'geb[id]æd', for between 'b' and 'æ' are three stems in positions suitable for 'id', while the parallel roman text reads ЗEBIDAED. Finally there is the single example of a vowel rune common to consecutive words, 'settæfter' Thornhill I.[12]

3. The use of double runes where single runes are to be expected. Consonant runes are doubled in '[.]ssu/s', 'g[e]ssus kristtus' Bewcastle, 'hilddigyþ' Hartlepool II stone, 'almeзttig', '[æ]þþilæ', 'dominnæ', 'gistoddu[n]' Ruthwell, 'êateзnne' Thornhill III, vowel runes in 'good', 'þiiosne ciismeel' Mortain Casket, 'riicnæ' Ruthwell. In addition there is the case of the Brunswick Casket with its forms 'liin', 'þiis'. Dr Fink has suggested, and an examination of the casket tends to confirm, that its inscribed plate is not original, but may be a quite modern copy.[13] The inscription is certainly curious, yet its original may have contained a form of the demonstrative (surviving in 'þiis' or perhaps 'þii') and the word līn (appearing as 'liin') in some reference to the casket's function as a reliquary containing fragments of sacred material.

The examples in (1) cannot without further examination be taken as showing that the Old English rune-masters in general accepted the use of double runes. Here may be cases where runic usage has been influenced by the spellings of written texts or of non-runic inscriptions, the runes being, as it were, transliterations of roman characters. The carver of the Franks Casket, for instance, used both runic and roman scripts. His use of 'g' for the spirants of 'fegtaþ' and 'unneg' is not paralleled in other Old English runic inscriptions, though there are occasional parallels in early written texts.[14] On St Cuthbert's coffin runes are used in such a way as to suggest that they are transliterations of roman characters, that in fact runes were not commonly used by the monks of Lindisfarne, but survived perhaps only in archaistic usage on funeral monuments and furniture. There is, for example, the Christ symbol 'xps'. This derives from Latin XPS, in its turn a form of Greek ΧΡΙΣΤΟΣ. The Latin form replaces the Greek symbols with the roman characters nearest in shape, regardless of their phonetic value. If the runic form derived direct from the Christ name, it would appear either in the form 'gws' (or perhaps 'gwз') to approximate the appearance of the Greek, or as 'krs' (cf. Bewcastle 'kristtus') or 'crs' indicating the pronunciation. The form 'xps' must transliterate a written Latin form. In the same way 'iohann[i]s', using initial i in preference to 'g', 'gi' (cf. Bewcastle 'g[e]ssus', Franks Casket 'giuþeasu'), or perhaps 'j', may evidence a non-runic spelling tradition. The Falstone 'hogback' has a double inscription, one text in uncials and the other, almost identical, in runes. Both are badly worn, but enough remains of each to suggest the relationship

'o/n'. The fourth is a half-length stem, which may or may not have a cross-stave. It could then be 'n', 'i', or a dash indicating the end of the inscription.
[12] The reading 'setæfte' given for Thornhill III in Dickins, 'System of Transliteration', p. 19, and A. S. C. Ross, 'The Linguistic Evidence for the Date of the "Ruthwell Cross" ', *MLR* 28 (1933), 145–55, at 152, is incorrect. The stone shows quite clearly 'seteæfte'.
[13] A. Fink, 'Zum Gandersheimer Runenkästchen', *Karolingische und Ottonische Kunst*, ed. F. Geke *et al.* (Wiesbaden, 1957), pp. 277–81.
[14] Campbell, *Old English Grammar*, § 57 (4).

between them. Here again the roman text appears to be primary, the runic a transliteration. So, the roman text has HROETHBERHTÆ, the runic version being 'roe[.]tæ'. *oe* is a frequent Northumbrian scribal spelling of *i*-mutated *ō*. The natural way of representing this sound in runes would be to use, not the two characters 'oe', but the single one 'œ', which, by virtue of its name *oeþil* (< *ōþil*), must indicate *i*-mutated *ō*. The roman text reads 3EBIDAED DER SAUL*E*, the runic one 'geb[*id*]æd þe[.] saule'. The imperative ending in -*d* is unique in runic texts. In written texts, however, -*d* is found in this ending in the *Vespasian Psalter*, while examples of -*d* in the 3rd sg. pres. ind. are found in the *Rushworth*₁ and *Lindisfarne Gospels* glosses.[15] There is also GIBIDDAD in the non-runic Dewsbury inscription. These spellings in -*d* probably indicate a pronunciation in -*þ*.[16] We would expect, then, the Falstone runic text to have the verbal ending in 'þ' (cf. Lancaster 'gibidæþ', Overchurch '[.]þiddaþ', Thornhill II 'gebid/daþ'). These cases suggest the possibility of influence of non-runic orthography on the Falstone runic text. The *Beonna* coins, with legends in mixtures of runic and roman scripts, would be likely to employ a roman spelling technique. The Ruthwell Cross has inscriptions in both roman and runic characters, though no influence from the one on the other can be traced with certainty. Finally in this examination of the examples of section (1) it must be noted that the Bewcastle examples, taken from the main inscription of the cross, should be looked on with some suspicion, for that inscription is of uncertain validity.[17] However, even if we reject all the cases discussed in this paragraph there still remain the Derbyshire, Overchurch, and Thornhill examples of medial double runes, where there is no evidence to suggest influence from non-runic sources.

Section (2) comprises those cases where runic inscriptions use single letters, but where double letters are commonly used elsewhere. However, the runic spellings are, in nearly every case, not unparalleled in non-runic texts. Indeed there may be parallels enough outside the field of runic inscriptions to make it doubtful whether the examples in (2) can be taken as evidencing a specifically runic type of spelling.

Three of the cases are forms of the imperative pl. of *gebiddan*, 'gebidæs', 'gibidæþ', 'geb[*id*]æd'. The paradigm of this verb commonly shows a single consonant in the unsyncopated 2nd and 3rd sg. pres. ind. and imperative sg., but -*dd*- in all other forms derived from the infinitive stem. But analogical extension of the double consonant is sometimes found in *Rushworth*₁ and *Lindisfarne* (in the forms *biddeþ*, *biddes*),[18] and a similar extension of the single consonant appears in some Northumbrian texts: 2nd pl. pres. ind. *bidas*, inf. *gebida Lindisfarne*: 1st sg. pres. ind. *bido* (2x), the abbreviated form of the pl. pres. ind. appears commonly as *bid'* and only rarely as *bidd' Durham Ritual*: 1st sg. pres. ind. *bido*, pres. part. *bidende* (2x) *Rushworth*₂. It could be argued that these scribal spellings with single consonant

---

[15] Brunner, *Altenglische Grammatik*, §§ 357, Anm. 3 and 360, Anm. 1.
[16] R. Girvan, *Angelsaksisch Handboek* (Haarlem, 1931), § 396, Aanm.
[17] The evidence for this statement is examined in the author's article 'The Bewcastle Cross', above pp. 63–5.
[18] Campbell, *Old English Grammar*, § 752.

show the influence of runic orthography, but there seems to be no reason why they should.

As concerns the forms 'setæ', 'sete' Campbell has noted occasional simplification of -dd-, -tt- between vowels in the past tense forms of weak verbs of class I.[19] Parallel cases from non-runic texts are the past forms *aseton, asetun, geseton* (2x), *seton, togeseton* Lindisfarne: *gesetes, (gi)sete* (2x), *setun* (3x), *giseton* Rushworth₂, and *GISETAE* on the non-runic Yarm cross.

In the cases of 'blagcmon', '-gmo/n.', 'men', 'men' and the element *al-* of 'almeȝttig' there is simplification of the final or syllable-closing geminate (possibly only orthographic) as noted in K. D. Bülbring, *Altenglisches Elementarbuch* I (Heidelberg, 1902), § 554, and Brunner, *Altenglische Grammatik*, § 231. As the second element of a compound, *-man, -mon* is common, being found, for example, in the early texts of the *Historia Ecclesiastica*[20] and in the Durham *Liber Vitæ*.[21] A. S. C. Ross notes a simplified geminate in the *Lindisfarne Gospels*, occasionally in the simple word, and more commonly in forms of *-mon* in compound words,[22] while Rushworth₂ has roughly equal numbers of forms with single and double final consonant. If *al-* is indeed a form of *all-* (cf. *allmehtig, allmectig* in the Leningrad and Moore texts of *Cædmon's Hymn*), a parallel simplification is that commonly found in inflected forms of *all* where the ending begins with a consonant, as in *Lindisfarne, Rushworth₂, Durham Ritual alne, alra*, side by side with *allne, allra*. However, Ruthwell 'almeȝttig' may be a form of OE *ælmeahtig* (Old High German *alamahtig*), the vowel of the first element affected by Northumbrian *all*.[23] In any case there is a direct parallel in the quite common *Durham Ritual* abbreviation *alm'*.

The form 'êateȝnne' for *Eadþegne* shows consonant shortening after a long diphthong. Campbell suggests the following series of changes: $d + þ > t + þ$: $tþ > tt$: *tt* occasionally simplified to *t* after a stressed vowel.[24] His example *lād-þēow > lateow* shows a development exactly parallel to that of *Ēadþegne > Eategne*.

The coin-name 'pada' has been included in section (2) because the name is not recorded in this form elsewhere in Old English sources, though there are two examples of *Padda*.[25] However, names of this type commonly show interchange between single and double consonants,[26] and Redin lists the doublets *Badda / Bada, Eadda / Eada, Hadda / Hada*, so there is little reason to regard the 'd' of the coin legend as a runic spelling of *dd*.

---

[19] Campbell, *Old English Grammar*, § 751 (2).

[20] H. Ström, *Old English Personal Names in Bede's History*, p. 134; O. S. Anderson, *Old English Material in the Leningrad Manuscript of Bede's Ecclesiastical History* (Lund, 1941), p. 88.

[21] Ström, *Old English Personal Names*, p. 28.

[22] A. S. C. Ross, *Studies in the Accidence of the Lindisfarne Gospels* (Leeds, 1937), pp. 97–8.

[23] Anderson, *Old English Material*, p. 90.

[24] Campbell, *Old English Grammar*, §§ 480 (3), 481 (3) and 458.

[25] M. Redin, *Studies on Uncompounded Personal Names*, p. 105. One example is from *Domesday Book*, in which O. v. Feilitzen notes as a characteristic feature of Anglo-Norman orthography occasional doubling of consonants (*The Pre-Conquest Personal Names of Domesday Book* (Uppsala, 1937), p. 123). *Padda* here could stand for *Pada*.

[26] Redin, *Uncompounded Personal Names*, p. xxx.

There remains unexplained in section (2) only Thornhill I 'seṫæfter', which has been seen as a runic spelling of *settæ æfter*. Here, however, there may simply have been an error of cutting on the part of the rune-master, who omitted the final vowel of the verb or the initial one of the preposition. Such an error would be easy enough to commit if it involved a repeated symbol.

Clearly the material in (1) and (2) does not prove that the Old English rune-masters avoided double runes. Only (3) remains, the section where it could be argued that 'the common runic rule of writing single consonants for double . . . operates *vice versa*'. Some forms in (3) can be explained in other ways. Bewcastle '[.]ssu/s' (usually read as form of *Jesus*) and 'g[e]ssus', Ruthwell 'do*minnæ*' are Latin forms with doubled intervocalic *s* or *n*. The letter *s* is frequently, *n* much less frequently, doubled between vowels in Latin texts from Anglo-Saxon England. Such doublings are found, to take a few examples, in the Latin texts of the *Corpus* glossary,[27] the Moore and Leningrad manuscripts of the *Historia Ecclesiastica*,[28] and the *Durham Ritual*.[29]

The doubling in Ruthwell 'riicnæ', Brunswick 'liin' (if this is OE *līn*) can be explained as an indication of vowel length.[30] Parallels are then the forms *gediides*, *sgiiremonn*, *ōriim* in the *Lindisfarne Gospels*, *geciid*, *tiid*, *tiide* in the *Durham Ritual*.

The Hartlepool spelling 'hilddigyþ' is probably erroneous. A more accurate transcription is 'hild | digyþ', for the text is cut in two parts, one on each side of the shaft of the incised cross which occupies the face of the stone. The incised decoration is carefully set out, but the inscription is not. The base-line of the runes is not parallel to that of the incised border, and the first four characters are cramped over to the left-hand side of the face, leaving a considerable space between the last of them and the cross shaft. The poor layout of the inscription suggests that it was cut directly on the stone without an initial roughing-in in chalk.[31] The rune 'g' was originally left out, and added later above the line, a point between 'i' and 'y' indicating the insertion. This omission of 'g' suggests a carelessness on the part of the engraver which may also explain the doubling of 'd'. Alternatively, it may be suggested that the carver was illiterate or semiliterate, copying his text from an exemplar, written, say, on vellum, and that he misread 'ig' as the fairly similar 'di', being influenced by the preceding 'd' of 'hild'. 'g' would then have been added when the mistake was brought to his attention.

There remain 'kristtus', 'alme3ttig', '[æ]þþilæ', 'gistoddu[n]', 'êate3nne', 'good', 'þiiosne', 'ciismeel', and 'þiis' unexplained. To most of these, occasional parallels can be found in written texts: 'alme3ttig' can be compared to *Rushworth₂ mæhttes*,

---

[27] J. H. Hessels, *An Eighth-Century Latin-Anglo-Saxon Glossary, preserved in the Library of Corpus Christi College, Cambridge* (Cambridge, 1890), pp. xxxii and xxxv.

[28] C. Plummer, *Venerabilis Baedae historiam ecclesiasticam gentis anglorum . . .* (Oxford, 1896) I, xc; O. Arngart, *The Leningrad Bede: an Eighth Century Manuscript . . . in the Public Library, Leningrad*, EEMF 2 (Copenhagen, 1952), p. 27.

[29] U. Lindelöf, *Rituale ecclesiae Dunelmensis: the Durham Collectar* (Durham, 1927), pp. liv–lv.

[30] Campbell, *Old English Grammar*, § 26.

[31] It is not uncommon for the pattern of an Anglo-Saxon rune-stone to be carefully set out, and the inscription not. Other examples are the Thornhill I, II stones.

'gistoddu[n]' to *Lindisfarne biddendra* (*bīda*), *neddes* (*nēda*), 'êateȝnne' to *Rush-worth₂ ðegnnas*, while both *Lindisfarne* and *Rushworth₂* show occasional doubling of short vowels.[32] These anomalous written forms are commonly regarded as scribal errors. The nine unexplained runic examples could likewise be accounted for as rune-master's mistakes, but this explanation, though adequate to some of the cases, is not generally satisfying. Some of the forms are clearly not mistakes, or at any rate not mistakes of carelessness or lack of concentration. The doubling of four vowels of the Mortain text but none of its consonants suggests that the spelling is intended, not accidental. The doubling in Bewcastle 'kristtus' can hardly be disassociated from that in the word 'g[e]ssus' which immediately precedes it, and this doubling is confirmed by that in Bewcastle '[.]ssu/s', which presumably also gives the name *Jesus*. Spellings like these are only errors in the sense that they do not conform to the usual orthography of written texts. It could be suggested, however, that the Old English rune-masters worked within a less rigid, perhaps even a quite different, orthographical tradition from the Old English scribes, and so used spellings not acceptable to the latter. This would account for the quite large number of anomalous doublings detected in only a few short runic texts. Alternatively, we may accept S. T. R. O. d'Ardenne's explanation that the production of forms with doubled runes arose from the laborious and tedious nature of the process of cutting inscriptions.[33] Finally there is the possibility that the doubled runes in some of the cases under review resulted from a desire to set out the inscriptions more neatly on the stone. In 'kristtus' and 'êateȝnne' a rune may have been doubled towards the end of a word so that it might fill its line of the inscription panel more satisfactorily.

These explanations of the anomalous runic spellings are speculative and unprovable. Yet they are as likely to apply as Elliott's suggestion that the doubled runes were produced by the operation '*vice versa*' of 'the common runic rule of writing single consonants for double'. At the very least, Elliott's theory requires more precise statement. The existence of a rule that single runes only should be used for both short and long (or repeated) sounds scarcely explains why runes were sometimes doubled in the representation of short or single ones. Elliott's suggestion does make sense if there were no rigid rule, if in early times either single or double runes could be used for long or repeated sounds. This may have led to a confusion between the use of single and double runes, with resultant doubling where there was no need for it. Again, the inorganic doubling of runes could show the influence of scribal orthography on runic spelling. If the early rune-masters used only single runes for long or repeated sounds, later practitioners, becoming aware of the scribal use of double letters, may have tried to adopt the practice and have made occasional mistakes in doing so. In either case the irregular spellings discussed above do not prove the

---

[32] W. Stolz, *Der Vokalismus der betonten Silben in der altnordhumbrischen Interlinearversion der Lindisfarner Evangelien* (Bonn, 1908), p. 99; U. Lindelöf, *Die südnorthumbrische Mundart des 10. Jahrhunderts: die Sprache der sog. Glosse Rushworth²* (Bonn, 1901), p. 71.

[33] S. T. R. O. d'Ardenne, 'The Old English Inscription on the Brussels Cross', *English Studies* 21 (1939), 145–64 and 271–2, at 151, n. 32.

existence of an Old English runic rule of writing single symbols for double or repeated sounds.

To sum up. There is no reason to believe that the Old English rune-masters recognised a spelling rule that long or repeated sounds should be represented by single symbols, nor is the existence of such a rule confirmed by the material of the East Germanic and Continental West Germanic inscriptions as they are set out above. Consequently the existence of the rule outside the field of the Scandinavian inscriptions cannot be considered as more than a bare possibility. Of course, the East Germanic and Continental West Germanic inscriptions are of crucial importance to the present investigation. If such a spelling rule could be shown to have existed there, we might be more inclined to regard some of the Old English examples considered above as manifestations of the same principle. One would therefore like to see this aspect of the Continental runic inscriptions examined in detail by a scholar more knowledgeable and more competent to work in those fields than the present writer. Yet even if it could be proved that rune-masters outside Scandinavia avoided using double runes, it need not be assumed that the Old English rune-masters did so consistently and throughout the period in which runes were in epigraphical use. The rule should, therefore, be invoked with more caution than has perhaps been displayed in recent years. To take a specific case: it is likely that 'seꞔtæfter' in the Thornhill I text is not an illustration of this orthographical rule, but a rune-master's error, which should be amended to 'seꞔt<æ> æfter' or even 'seꞔt<e> æfter'. In favour of the second alternative is the fact that in Thornhill I 'æfter' PrOE *æ* in an unstressed syllable has been shifted to *e* (though indeed in such a word the shift may have taken place earlier than the general change from unstressed *æ* to *e*). Thornhill II and III are likely to be contemporary with stone I, and these have unstressed *e* < PrOE *æ* in 'arærde', 'berhtsuiþe', '*saule*', 'sete' and 'êateȝnne'.[34]

POSTSCRIPT

Of all the papers in this volume this is perhaps the one that most reveals its age. Indeed, when it was published it had already become outdated, as the final footnote shows – I produced it in the days when I was so innocent as not to realise that one of the best places for conducting fruitful excavation is the basement or storehouse of a major museum. Objects once thought to be lost survive for study. Completely new finds too will have some effect on the statistics to be quoted. For instance, the number of known coins (and, what is more important, coin dies) of Beonna of East

---

[34] Two articles, to which my attention has just been drawn, are relevant to the first part of this discussion. W. Krause reported the rediscovery of the Kowel spearhead during World War II, in 'Der Speer von Kowel, ein wiedergefundenes Runendenkmal', *Germanien* 13 (1941), 450–64. M. Is-basescu examined the Pietroassa ring recently in Bucharest ('Der goldene Halsring von Pietroassa und seine runische Inschrift', *BGDSL* (Halle), 82 (1960), 333–58) and confirmed a reading **gutani o wi hailag**. He takes the last two words as *wih hailag*.

Anglia continues to increase, but so far there has appeared no example with a single medial consonant, whether the name is given in roman, in runes or in a mixture of the two. In contrast we must adduce the verbal form 'g i b œ t æ', 'mended', on the recently found seventh-century brooch from Harford Farm, Caistor-by-Norwich, Norfolk.[35]

Sir Christopher Ball has taken me to task for including such an example as 'm e n' in my evidence, assuring us with his usual urbane certainty that 'at no stage in the known history of the English language is there reason to assume the phonological possibility of final long consonants'.[36] He adds that Campbell 'is misleading' on this point.[37] If Ball is correct, Campbell is not misleading, he is plain wrong; as is Bülbring, but not, I think, Brunner. But it would be helpful to have demonstration rather than assertion.

My present comment on this paper would put more stress on epigraphical rather than philological considerations. I suggest below (p. 333) that such forms as 'ea t e i n n e' on Thornhill II may have its doubled consonant because the carver wished to fit his word more gracefully into the space available, and needed another graph to do it. The same could apply to the Bewcastle spellings '[+] g [e] s s u s | k r i s t t u s' and the Ruthwell 'd o *m i n n* æ'. How far this argument can be taken I am not sure, partly because, in discussing manuscript spellings, the lay-out of the text on the page is also not usually allowed for; so we have no pattern of comparison. But there can be no obvious such explanation of the doubling in, for example, the Ruthwell 'a | l m | e i | t t i | g' or '[æ] | þ þ i l | æ', where using a single 't' or 'þ' would have allowed the carver to end his word at the line end. The whole subject needs further probing, and I am glad there are young scholars ready to do this.

[35] J. Hines, 'A New Runic Inscription from Norfolk', *Nytt om Runer* 6 (1991), 6–7.
[36] 'Inconsistencies in the Main Runic Inscriptions on the Ruthwell Cross', *Old English Runes*, ed. Bammesberger, pp. 107–23, at 115.
[37] *Ibid.* p. 115, n. 18. He cites Campbell, *Old English Grammar*, §§ 63 (? wrongly for 66) and 457.

9
(1964)

ANGLO-SAXON RUNES AND MAGIC[1]

Epigraphists are often tempted to interpret as magical the inscriptions of which they can make little straightforward sense. This is particularly true of runologists, since they may be influenced by the theory of rune-magic. The belief that there is an essential connexion between the characters of the runic alphabet and magical powers will affect one's approach to inscriptions whose meaning is difficult to determine, may modify one's interpretation of inscriptions whose meaning is tolerably clear, and is likely to influence one's preference if there are several interpretations all equally possible formally. If you believe, as many scholars do, that the Germanic peoples held that the runes were in some way magical, and that each rune either had its own magical power or could cause the release of such power simply by being cut or even named, you will tend to regard all early runic inscriptions as magical, no matter what their apparent meaning.

The tendency can be illustrated by a treatment of the runic text engraved on one of the gold horns from Gallehus, South Jutland. These great horns, which are known only from early engravings, are ascribed to the fifth century A.D. Their size, splendour, and the designs which covered their surfaces suggest that they were ceremonial, perhaps cult, objects. The inscribed one has a text commonly read (with modern division into separate words), **ek hlewagastiʀ holtijaʀ horna tawido**. The verb *tawido* is not certainly found elsewhere in early Norse, but is clearly cognate with West Germanic and East Germanic words, such as Gothic *taujan* (3rd sg. pret. ind. *tawida*), which have meanings connected with 'make, do, prepare'.[2] The readiest interpretation of the Gallehus text is 'I, Hlewagastiʀ holtijaʀ (personal name and byname), made this horn', which seems to be the craftsman's signature or the name of the man who commissioned the work. One of the editors of the collected edition of Danish runic inscriptions, E. Moltke, accepts this interpretation: the other, L. Jacobsen, feels obliged to modify it as a result of the belief that in Primitive Old Norse times runes were 'holy' – 'hellige' – in the sense that supernatural powers were attributed to them. Thus the inscription cannot be 'en profan håndværker-signatur',

---

[1] I wish to thank Professors Dorothy Whitelock and R. M. Wilson for valuable criticism of a preliminary draft of this paper, and Professor Bruce Dickins and Mr A. G. Woodhead for help on points of detail. The opinions expressed remain my own.
[2] Jacobsen and Moltke, *Danmarks runeindskrifter*, col. 723 and refs.

but must rather contain a 'religiøs-magiske jeg-formel, ved hvilken den handlende person tilkendegiver sig i al sin magtfuldkommenhed'.[3]

If the belief that runes were a magical or cult script affects the reading of texts in this way, it is obviously important that the validity of the theory be established. There are many more runic inscriptions in Scandinavia than in all other Germanic countries together. The Continental West Germanic and East Germanic inscriptions are few and for the most part of recent discovery. Those of Anglo-Saxon England are not plentiful, and are still uncollected and inadequately examined. As a result, conclusions about runic practice – and about rune-magic – have largely been drawn on the basis of the Scandinavian material. But even if rune-magic existed in Scandinavia, this does not necessarily mean that it must be taken into account in discussing inscriptions from outside that area. Rune-magic may have been a Germanic phenomenon which survived only in the north, dying out in the rest of Europe before the extant inscriptions were cut. Or it may have developed only in the North, after the division of Scandinavian runic traditions from those of the rest of Europe. Certainly so far as Anglo-Saxon England is concerned the existence of rune-magic has not been definitely demonstrated, though it has often been assumed.[4] This paper is largely an examination of the Anglo-Saxon evidence, but it must begin with some discussion of the reasons for modern belief in rune-magic outside England.

The evidence adduced for the existence of Scandinavian rune-magic is of four sorts, etymological, archaeological, runological, and literary.[5] The first involves a discussion of the semantics of *run* and its cognates in the Germanic languages, and in the Celtic languages which alone among Indo-European tongues certainly share the root.[6] Gothic *runa*, glossing Greek μυστήριον (and also occasionally βουλή), is commonly used of the divine mysteries, Gothic *garuni* means 'consultation, counsel', perhaps with the idea of secrecy. Old High German *runa*, *giruni* have similar meanings. The ON (pl.) *runar* sometimes means 'secret lore, mysteries'. There is a group of cognate verbal forms with the sense of 'whisper'. Old Irish *run* means 'secret', perhaps on occasion 'secret, cryptic text',[7] while Middle Welsh *rhin* means 'magic charm'. Finally, Finnish *runo*, 'song', perhaps originally 'incantation', is presumably an early borrowing from Germanic. From these the semantic series is postulated: 'secret', 'secret meeting', 'whisper', 'secret formula', 'incantation', 'charm', then perhaps by way of Germanic lot-casting in which runes may have been used, 'cryptic symbol', 'rune'. Clearly there is a possible, though not proven, connexion between *run*, rune, and magic.

By archaeological evidence I mean the appearance of runes in archaeological settings which suggest a connexion with magic. An example is the inscribed stone

---

[3] *Ibid.* cols 36–7. I find it hard to give precise meaning to these words.
[4] Recently in Elliott, *Runes: an Introduction*, pp. 41–2 and 67–72.
[5] I omit consideration of number-magic in runic texts, since this involves different principles from, and probably depends on the existence of, rune-magic proper.
[6] C. J. S. Marstrander, 'Om runene og runenavnenes oprindelse', *NTS* 1 (1928), 85–188, at 175.
[7] *Ibid.* p. 177.

of Kylver, Gotland. This bears the *fuþark*, the palindrome *sueus* which has no obvious meaning, and an engraved symbol which could be magical. It was found in connexion with a stone-lined grave of *c.* 400. Early accounts suggest that the runes faced the interior of the grave, though they may not be relevant since the burial was disturbed before it could be examined scientifically.[8] Those who reject the theory of rune-magic face the question: why was a meaningless *fuþark* cut at all, and how did it find its way to the grave? The proponents of the theory have a ready answer. The power of the runes has been invoked for some purpose connected with the dead, perhaps to ensure he rests undisturbed, or to prevent him walking again.

The runological evidence is plentiful, but of uncertain import. Under this heading are included the runic inscriptions – apparently or at least possibly magical formulae – on objects which may have had amuletic or sacral uses. So, the words **laukar, alu, agla** appear on bracteates, a ring, a skinning-knife, a fragment of stone, perhaps an arrow, and so on. *agla* is a well-known medieval magic word.[9] *alu* and *laukar* are known only from runic texts, where they are common, having apparently no practical meaning.[10] *alu* may be cognate with Gothic *alhs* 'temple' or OE *ealgian* 'protect', and so be a sacred or protection formula. *laukar* 'leek' may be connected with fertility.

In the final instance, however, the burden of proof is borne by the literary evidence, the long series of references to magical use of runes in Old Norse prose and poetry. A number are from the Eddic poems, central among them a passage from *Hávamál*:

> Veit ec, at ec hecc   vindgameiði á
>   nætr allar nío,
> geiri undaðr   oc gefinn Óðni,
>   siálfr siálfom mér,
> á þeim meiði,   er mangi veit,
>   hvers hann af rótom renn.
>
> Við hleifi mic sældo   né við hornigi
>   nýsta ec niðr:
> nam ec upp rúnar,   œpandi nam,
>   fell ec aptr þaðan.

'I know that I hung on the windswept tree for nine whole nights, pierced by the spear, given to Óðinn, myself given to myself, on that tree whose roots no man knows. They refreshed me neither with bread nor with drink from the horn. I peered down, I took up (? learnt) runes, howling I took them up, and then fell back'.[11] Here the great god apparently learns the runes as a result of a mystic sacrifice of himself. There follows a series of stanzas dealing with runes and magical spells. In *Sigrdrífumál* the different types of runes and their properties, victory runes, luck

8   W. Krause, *Runeninschriften im älteren Futhark* (Halle/Saale, 1937), p. 8.
9   Jacobsen and Moltke, *Danmarks runeindskrifter*, col. 627.
10 An element *ǫl-* in rare compounds (*ǫlrúnar, ǫltírr*) probably derives from PrON *alu*.
11 *Edda*, ed. G. Neckel, 3rd ed. rev. H. Kuhn (Heidelberg, 1962), vv. 138–9.

runes, protection runes, etc., are described in detail, while in *Skírnismál* Freyr's messenger, Skírnir, threatens the giantess Gerðr with a runic curse if she does not accede to the god's desires. And the poetry contains a number of other references to the powers the rune-master can control. The prose material too has frequent mention of rune-magic. It is convenient to take examples from a single work, *Egils saga*. Presented with a horn of poisoned drink by the servant of the wicked queen Gunnhildr, Egill cuts on it runes and colours them with his blood, whereupon the horn breaks asunder. On a journey to Vermaland Egill puts up at a farmhouse, where the *bóndi's* daughter lies ill. He asks if anything has been done to cure her, and the answer is that a neighbour has cut a runic charm which, however, has rather made her worse than better. After a brief look at the charm cut on a *tálkn* placed in the girl's bed-closet, Egill destroys it, speaking a verse which says that one should not meddle with runes if one does not understand them. He cuts a second runic charm and lays it under the girl's pillow. She recovers at once.

From evidence of the type illustrated has developed the theory, now almost an orthodoxy, which makes an essential connexion between runes and magical powers. Additional evidence, not decisive in itself, is then adduced to illustrate the theory. Tacitus mentions *notae* cut on sticks used by the Germani for divination. These have been identified as runes, though *nota* could mean any symbol used for identification purposes. Scholars have pointed to the formal similarity between some of the runes and certain symbols found in Bronze Age rock carvings, and suggested continuity of sacral use of the symbols. Imaginative, not to say speculative, interpretation of the rune-names has led to the building-up of a pattern of primitive Germanic pagan belief.

Though the theory of rune-magic has been widely accepted, it has not gone unchallenged. In an important book, *Målruner og troldruner: runemagiske studier* (Copenhagen, 1952), the Danish runologist, A. Bæksted, questioned the validity of much of the evidence cited by the proponents of the theory, suggesting alternative explanations of some of the examples. The etymological evidence, though connecting runes with mystery, does not relate them in essence and origin with magic. The equation, rune = magic, may be a secondary development, arising from the use of runes for magical formulae. Runes need be no more magical than roman characters, being used for early magical texts because they were the only script available to the Scandinavian peoples. The literary evidence is suspect on similar grounds, for texts usually leave it uncertain whether the runes are magical in themselves or because of the words they form. In the context of the present discussion one notes too the late date of the Old Norse literary material, for the Eddic poems are usually attributed to a period after 800 (though the reasons for fixing that date are obscure, and the poems may in any case preserve earlier material), while the prose texts are considerably later – *Egils saga* is a thirteenth-century work, though the incidents described above are supported by quoted verses which, if genuine, date from the tenth century. At the least this material is late for revealing the Germanic attitude to runes.

Despite Bæksted's scepticism about rune-magic, even he is obliged to admit its existence in a few cases. One is the inscription of the Lindholm (Skåne) amulet, one side of which has a text beginning **aaaaaaaaRRRnnn-**. This he says must be regarded as a row of letters used as magic symbols.[12] In some cases Bæksted's rejection of rune-magic is questionable. The Vadstena (Sweden) bracteate has the inscription **tuwatuwa** followed by the *fuþark*. Bæksted admits **tuwatuwa** to be magical, but not the *fuþark*, apparently explaining the latter as a meaningless text cut in imitation of the inscriptions of the imported Roman gold coins which were prototypes of the bracteates.[13] But it is hard to see why an inscription beginning with a magical charm should end with a meaningless sequence of letters. Bæksted's book must be taken, as it was intended, as a provisional expression of opinion, meant to make scholars rethink some of the principles of the rune-magic theory. It is a valuable warning against a too ready acceptance of the theory for a wide range of places and dates, against seeing rune-magic everywhere. That even a sceptic must admit evidence of the occasional magical use of runes in early Scandinavia is important to the present argument, for the Scandinavian material is needed to support the, in my opinion, weak evidence from Anglo-Saxon England.

The Anglo-Saxon evidence for rune-magic falls into the same groups as the Scandinavian: the etymological, or rather the semantic, the literary, the archaeological, and the runological. OE *run* has a range of meanings similar to that of the cognates already discussed. It translates *mysterium*, often used of religious mysteries, *halige rune* (*Elene* 333, 1168, *Juliana* 656).[14] Guthlac is described as *runwita* (*Guthlac* 1095) at a point in the story where Felix's life commonly refers to him as *vir Dei*; he is one wise in the mysteries of God. *Run* can also mean 'counsel, council' (*Elene* 411, 1161, *Juliana* 62), and forms with *ræd* an alliterating pair which persists into Middle English.[15] The semantic relationship between *run* and *ræd* is uncertain, for the words may be roughly synonymous, or may contrast, *run* implying private, confidential advice,[16] *ræd* open counsel. Hrothgar, in describing the dead Æschere as *min runwita ond min rædbora* (*Beowulf* 1325), may refer to two functions, 'privy counsellor' and 'public adviser' (or perhaps 'confidant' and 'adviser'), or one. In the line *Run bið gerecenod, ræd forð gæð* (*Exodus* 526), *gerecenod* may mean 'interpreted, explained', in which case *run* may mean 'secret', contrasting with *ræd*; or 'proclaimed, announced', when the second half-line repeats the matter of the first. That there is no sharp or necessary opposition between the meanings of the two words is suggested by:

> Monig oft gesæt
> rice to rune;   ræd eahtedon

---

[12] Bæksted, *Målruner*, p. 40.

[13] *Ibid.* pp. 124–31.

[14] Here too belongs the compound *searoruna gespon* (*Order of the World* 15). References are to texts in *The Anglo-Saxon Poetic Records* unless other editions are cited.

[15] See *OED* under *roun*, 4; also H. Marquardt, 'Kannte Layamon Runen?', *Indogermanica: Festschrift für Wolfgang Krause* (Heidelberg, 1960), pp. 114–20, at 115. Further discussion is needed of the Middle English meanings, both of the simplex and its derivatives, particularly those like *runisch*, *bokrune* not recorded in Old English.

[16] Cf. here *Judith* 54.

'Many a powerful man sat often in council. They debated their course of action' (*Beowulf* 171–2).

In some examples it is not the counselling, nor even the secrecy, that is stressed, but the isolation of the action. Men sit *sundor to rune* (*Andreas* 1161), *sundor æt rune* (*Wanderer* 111),[17] and Andreas is asked what wonders the Lord revealed when they *rune besæton* 'sat apart' (*Andreas* 627). A group of compounds, used with verbs of revealing, suggests a meaning 'secret, esoteric or private knowledge'. In *Elene* the wolf, sensing the approach of battle, *wælrune ne mað*, 'did not hide the slaughter-rune' (28), while Cyriacus *hygerune ne mað*, 'did not hide the secret of his heart' (1098). Juliana hears her enemies *eahtian inwitrune* 'declare wicked counsel' (*Juliana* 609–10), and Unferth *onband beadurune*, 'revealed a secret enmity' (*Beowulf* 501). In this group too should be included a passage from Exeter Book *Riddle 33*, if the emendation *heterune [on]bond* (7) is accepted.[18] The simplex is found in this sense in *Iobales runa* in a context describing the loss of the knowledge and experience of the biblical patriarchs,[19] and also relevant here is the passage in the Exeter *Gnomic Verses* which includes among a woman's duties that of *rune healdan* 'keeping counsel' (86).

Run is occasionally used in connexion with writing, though never certainly in Old English with the meaning 'runic character'.[20] In *Andreas* the Mermedonians record *on rune ond on rimcræfte* (equivalent to *per singula tabula scriptum/tabulas illas scripturas* in the parallel Latin text[21]) when their captives are due for slaughter (*Andreas* 134). The Exeter *Gnomic Verses* declare:

> Ræd sceal mon secgan,   rune writan,
> leoþ gesingan

'one must speak counsel, write *rune*, sing songs' (138–9), though the meaning of *run* here, and its connexion with *ræd* and *leoþ* is obscure. In *Daniel run* is used in a reference to the writing on the wall at Belshazzar's feast, where the prophet is asked

> þæt he him bocstafas
> arædde and arehte,   hwæt seo run bude

---

[17] Bosworth-Toller under *rún* notes a parallel case in Old Saxon. Cf. also *on synderlican runungum* (B. Assmann, *Angelsächsische Homilien und Heiligenleben* (Kassel, 1889), p. 79).

[18] P. J. Cosijn, 'Anglosaxonica IV', *BGDSL* 23 (1898), 109–30, at 129. The manuscript reading is retained by some editors and translators, though it involves taking *-rune* in the sense of 'spell, charm', which is doubtfully possible. See, for example, F. Tupper, *The Riddles of the Exeter Book* (Boston, 1910), p. 149; W. S. Mackie, *The Exeter Book, Part II*, EETS 194 (London, 1934), pp. 124–5; R. K. Gordon, *Anglo-Saxon Poetry*, 2nd ed. (London, 1954), p. 300.

[19] A. S. Napier, *Wulfstan: Sammlungen der ihm zugeschriebenen Homilien* (Berlin, 1883), p. 3. Professor Whitelock suggests that the description of Jubal as *pater canentium cithara et organo* (Gen. iv. 21) accounts for the use of *runa* here. *Iobales runa* is distinguished from *Adames gesyhð and sagu* and *Nôes and Abrahames and mœniges oðres word and weorc*.

[20] For *enge rune* (*Elene* 1261), see below, p. 112. On the Middle English evidence see Marquardt, 'Kannte Layamon Runen?'.

[21] F. Blatt, *Die lateinischen Bearbeitungen der Acta Andreae et Matthiae apud Anthropophagos* (Giessen, 1930), p. 37.

'that he should relate and explain the letters to him, what the *run* might portend' (739–40). Bosworth-Toller cite this as an example of the meaning, 'of that which is written, with the idea of mystery or magic', but the idea of writing may be distant here. The phrase *hwæt seo run bude*, which is also used in the same poem in Nebuchadnezzar's request to Daniel to interpret his dream of the lopped tree (541), probably means something as general as 'what the mysterious occurrence might portend'. The *runcræftige men* who could not interpret the *engles ærendbec* (*Daniel* 733–4) – the writing on the wall – may have been men skilled in mysteries, in esoteric lore, or perhaps even secret scripts.[22]

The cognate *(ge)ryne* has some of these meanings too. It is commonly used for 'religious mystery' (*Christ* 74, 95, 423, *Guthlac* 1121, occasionally in the Old English Bede and frequently in Ælfric's homilies), and glosses *secretis*, which in turn glosses *sacris .i. idolis*.[23] It can mean 'secret', glossing *arcana, secretum*,[24] and also 'secret, esoteric knowledge' (*Elene* 566, 589).[25] In the homilies *geryne* often means 'sacrament',[26] and indeed it glosses *sacramentum*.[27] Finally, it sometimes develops the meaning 'symbol, type', in such a phrase as *hwæt þæt geryne tacnaþ* 'what the symbol signifies'.[28] *Run* too may have had this sense: cf. the glosses *deglum runum* for *mystice*, and perhaps *runlic uel deoplice* for *misticæ*.[29]

Geryne, too, is used with reference to writing, though apparently always in combination with *word*: so,

> Sum biþ listhendig
> to awritanne wordgeryno

'one is skilled in writing (? or carving) words' (*Gifts of Men* 95–6).[30] The phrase *worda gerynu* is twice used in *Daniel* of the writing on the wall: once (746) referring

---

[22] Several Anglo-Saxon secret scripts are known but not interpreted; so, for example, the 'ogams' of the Hackness cross and the cryptic text on the band of silver riveted to the back of the Sutton, Isle of Ely, brooch. Code scripts, such as the *notae Bonifatii*, are quite common in Anglo-Saxon manuscripts.

[23] H. D. Meritt, *Old English Glosses* (New York, 1945), no. 28. 141.

[24] A. S. Napier, *Old English Glosses, Chiefly Unpublished* (Oxford, 1900), nos 1505 and 4216.

[25] A further example of this sense may be *þæra <stafena> gerena*, translated as 'the mysteries of the letters of the alphabet' (S. J. Crawford, *Byrhtferth's Manual*, EETS 177 (London, 1929), p. 194). But for a suggestion of an alternative identification of *gerena* see H. D. Meritt, *Fact and Lore about Old English Words* (Stanford, 1954), p. 203.

[26] R. Morris, *The Blickling Homilies of the Tenth Century*, EETS 73 (London, 1880), p. 83; B. Thorpe, *The Homilies of the Anglo-Saxon Church* (London, 1844–6) II, 270 and often in this homily.

[27] Napier, *Old English Glosses*, nos 1520, 2074 and 2141, T. Wright and R. P. Wülcker, *Anglo-Saxon and Old English Vocabularies*, 2nd ed. (London, 1884) I, col. 164.

[28] Morris, *Blickling Homilies*, p. 17. Cf. also such glosses as *typicum .i. mysticum, gerynelice, tropice .i. tipice, gery(nelice)* (Napier, *Old English Glosses*, nos 1083 and 5088), the translation *gerynelico word* for *mystica verba* (T. Miller, *The Old English Version of Bede's Ecclesiastical History of the English People*, EETS 95–6 and 110–111 (London, 1890–8) I, 94), and the contrast between *gerynelice* and *gesewenlice* (D. Bethurum, *The Homilies of Wulfstan* (Oxford, 1957), p. 173).

[29] W. W. Skeat, *The Holy Gospels in Anglo-Saxon, Northumbrian and Mercian Versions* (Cambridge, 1871–87), *John*, p. 4, *Mark*, p. 5.

[30] Cf. also *Elene* 289, where the poet seems to have in mind the scriptural records of the prophets' words.

to the content of the message, paralleling *orlæg* 'fate', once perhaps (722) to the actual characters since it parallels *baswe bocstafas* 'scarlet letters'.

The idea of secrecy is continued in the further cognate *geruna* 'confidant'. This glosses *sinmistes, uel consecretalis,* and *a secretis, uel principis consiliarius.*[31]

Finally, mention must be made of the possibility of *run* as a place-name element.[32] Rumwell (Somerset) and Runwell (Essex) may be *run-wella* 'wishing-well', which could be explained as 'secret' or 'magic well', or also as 'counsel well'. However, the first element of these place-names may be OE *hruna* 'tree trunk'.[33]

This is not an exhaustive survey of the semantic possibilities of *run* and *(ge)ryne*, but clearly their meanings centre on 'mystery' with the various modern English connotations of the word. The connexion with written or inscribed characters is tenuous. That with magic is even more so – the closest connexion seems to be a parallel between *ryne* and *galdorcwide* (the syntax of the sentence is, however, obscure) in Exeter Book *Riddle 48*, but since that is a Christian riddle it is likely that both words are to be taken in a Christian and religious, rather than a magical, sense. Neither *run* nor *(ge)ryne* is used specifically for 'runic character'. For that the common word is *runstæf*, and in Exeter Book *Riddle 42* there seems to be an opposition between the *rynemenn* 'those skilled in explaining mysteries', against whom the bonds of the riddle are locked, and the *runstafas* which reveal the answer *þam þe bec witan*. The opposition is not strong if the phrase *enge rune* (*Elene* 1261) both means 'oppressive secret' and forms a punning reference, 'narrow rune', to the *n*-rune which occurs in the preceding line.[34]

The elements *-run, -rune*, presumably related to the simplex, appear in compounds clearly connected with magic. Examples are mainly from glosses of learned words. *Burgrune, -runan* gloss *furiæ, parcas,*[35] *helrun pithonis*[36] and *hellerune* and the fem. adj. *helrynegu pythonissa.*[37] In a set of related glosses *hel(h)runan* is used for *p(h)itonissam, i.diuinatricem.*[38] *Hægtesse, wiccan* are quoted as alternatives to forms of *hellerune. Heahrun* also glosses *pithonissa*[39] in a reference to the 'damsel possessed with a spirit of divination' of Acts xvi. 16. Presumably related to it is the *heagorun* (given by Bosworth-Toller as a 'mystery in which magic is involved') of an account of the apocryphal magicians Iamnes and Mambres, the Old English freely translating a Latin text containing the word *nicromantia.*[40] In a less obviously learned context *helrunan* seems to mean 'demon' in *Beowulf* 163, and the appearance of the

31 Wright and Wülcker, *Vocabularies* I, cols 110 and 189.

32 A. H. Smith, *English Place-Name Elements*, EPNS 25–6 (Cambridge, 1956) II, under *run*.

33 P. H. Reaney, *The Place-Names of Essex*, EPNS 12 (Cambridge, 1935), p. 266.

34 P. O. E. Gradon, *Cynewulf's Elene* (London, 1958), p. 73.

35 Wright and Wülcker, *Vocabularies* I, cols 37, 245 and 410, Napier, *Old English Glosses*, no. 38. 2.

36 Wright and Wülcker, *Vocabularies* I, cols 343, 470 and 471.

37 *Ibid.* I, cols 188 and 472.

38 Napier, *Old English Glosses*, nos 1926, 2. 60, 7. 106 and 8. 106.

39 Wright and Wülcker, *Vocabularies* I, col. 493.

40 M. Förster, 'Das lateinisch-altenglische Fragment der Apokryphe von Jamnes und Mambres', *ASNSL* 108 (1902), 15–28, at 19. See also the reproduction of MS Cotton Tiberius B. V, fol. 87a in M. R. James, *Marvels of the East* (Oxford, 1929).

word in Old High German (*helliruna* 'necromantia') and Gothic[41] suggests that it was common Germanic. A further compound appears in the leechdoms *wiþ ælcre yfelre leodrunan and wið ælfsidenne*, where the last word means 'elfish magic' and *leodrunan* something similar, though whether the charmer or the charm is not clear.[42]

However, in all these cases the idea of 'magic' is probably in the first, rather than the second, element. -*run(e)* may be simply 'one skilled in mysteries': in the case of *hellerune* they are the mysteries of the dead or of hell, so the word means 'necromancer' or 'demon'. The first elements *heah-*, *heago-* may be related to those of *hægtesse* 'witch', *heagotho* 'manes'.[43] It is tempting to relate *leodrunan* to OE *leoð* 'song', whose Old Norse cognate *ljóð* occasionally has the meaning 'charm'. I know of no explanation of *burgrune*.[44]

The Anglo-Saxon literary evidence is slight compared with that from Scandinavia. Commonly quoted and highly valued is a story from Bede's *Historia Ecclesiastica*, iv. 20 (22). This tells of a young man, Imma, who had been taken prisoner after a battle between Northumbrians and Mercians, but who could not be fettered since chains always fell from him. The reason was that Imma's brother, Abbot Tunna, thought him dead and kept offering masses for his soul. At every celebration Imma's bonds were loosed. His captors, baffled by the occurrence, suspected him of sorcery, and their leader *interrogare coepit, quare ligari non posset, an forte litteras solutorias, de qualibus fabulae ferunt, apud se haberet, propter quas ligari non posset.* The Old English translation of this passage reads: *Ond hine ascode hwæðer he ða alysendlecan rune cuðe, and þa stafas mid him awritene hæfde, be swylcum men leas spel secgað and spreocað, þæt hine mon forþon gebindan ne meahte* 'and asked him whether he knew the releasing *rune* and had about him the *stafas* written out, such as men tell idle tales of, so that he could not be bound'.[45] R. W. V. Elliott translates the central passage, 'whether he knew loosening runes and had about him the letters written down', with the comment 'a clear testimony that the belief in the magical efficacy of runes was then still very much alive'.[46] Bede's story was used by Ælfric in a homily on the efficacy of the mass.[47] Ælfric gives the enemy leader's inquiry about Imma's magical abilities: *Þa axode se ealdorman þone hæftling, hwæðer he ðurh drycræft oðða ðurh runstafum his bendas tobræce* 'then the

---

[41] S. Feist, *Vergleichendes Wörterbuch der gotischen Sprache*, 3rd ed. (Leiden, 1939), under *haliurunnas*.

[42] O. Cockayne, *Leechdoms, Wortcunning, and Starcraft of Early England* (London, 1864–6) II, 139 translates the word 'rune lay' which he glosses as 'heathen charm'. G. Storms, *Anglo-Saxon Magic* (The Hague, 1948), p. 269 translates it 'witch'. The word persists into Middle English with a meaning 'charm': see R. Jente, *Die mythologischen Ausdrücke im altenglischen Wortschatz* (Heidelberg, 1921), p. 331.

[43] Förster, 'Fragment der Apokryphe', pp. 23–5.

[44] Professor Whitelock suggests ingeniously, 'When applied to the *parcae*, is it possible that by false etymology they connected this with "to spare"? This is one of the meanings of OE *beorgan*. But not as far as I know of *burg*, which never seems to have an abstract meaning.'

[45] Miller, *Old English Bede* I, 328.

[46] Elliott, *Runes*, p. 67 [but cf. 2nd ed., p. 81]. 'then' refers to the date of translation, not of Bede's original: cf. the same author's 'Runes, Yews, and Magic', *Speculum* 32 (1957), 250–61, at 250.

[47] Thorpe, *Homilies* II, 356–9.

ealdorman asked the captive whether he broke his bonds asunder by means of sorcery or *runstafum'*. Ælfric sometimes used the Old English Bede translation as well as the Latin original, but he does not seem to have done so at this point.

Before Elliott's assertion on this evidence can be accepted we must find out more clearly what Bede meant, and what his Old English translator and Ælfric thought he meant. Ælfric's case is clear. Theoretically his *runstafum* could be translated 'secret characters', but that would be perverse. Elsewhere *runstæf* means 'runic character', and presumably does so here. Ælfric's version of Bede's story is inaccurate: he gets important details wrong, including the sides on which captor and captive fought. Thus he gives no evidence for the period of Bede, but he does show that he himself, writing *c.* 1000, knew that runes and magic were connected, and expected his audience to understand without further explanation the phrase *ðurh drycræft oððe ðurh runstafum*. What Ælfric and his audience knew of rune-magic is unknown. Ælfric may have been recording an ancient or traditional belief, not vital in his own day, which he thought appropriate to an event taking place over three centuries earlier. Ælfric's Wessex is devoid of epigraphical runes: there is no evidence of a living runic tradition there, though runes appear quite often in manuscripts from that area.

Bede's *litteras* could be semantically either singular or plural: a letter or document, or characters or words. Thus it could refer either to a document with a formula for loosing bonds, or the actual words or letters of such a formula.[48] Here an Old English charm for obtaining favours is worth quoting. The instructions read:

> Gif þu wille gangan to þinum hlaforde oþþe to kyninge oþþe to oþrum menn oððe to gemote, þonne bær þu þas stafas; ælc þæra þonne biþ he þe liþa and bliδ:

'If you wish to go to your lord or to the king or to another man or to a meeting, then bear (or wear) these "staves". Each of them will then be gracious and kind to you.' The 'staves' to be carried, presumably on a slip of parchment or scratched on some portable object, consist partly of individual letters – *XX.h.d.e.o.e.o.o.e.e.e.* – partly of meaningful words and gibberish letter groups.[49] Bede's *litteras* could apply equally to these 'staves' or to a document containing the whole charm. There is no reason to believe that *litteras* is used here of runes, though it may be. Bede did not use the word *runa* which was available to him,[50] while at the date of the event, A.D. 679, roman characters might well be used.

The identification of Bede's *litteras* with runes may be thought to gain support from Old Norse literary evidence. In the list of magical abilities which Óðinn claims, following the runic passage of *Hávamál* quoted above, is the boast:

---

[48] Du Cange gives *literæ solutoriæ* as *characteres magici*, but quotes only the Bede example.

[49] Storms, *Anglo-Saxon Magic*, pp. 300–1.

[50] I do not know how common *runa* was in medieval Latin. It is used without explanation (though the context is suggestive) by Venantius Fortunatus (*Venanti Honori Clementiani Fortunati*, ed. F. Leo (Berlin, 1881), vii. 18) in the sixth century. This is the only example commonly quoted in the dictionaries, but R. Derolez notes several other cases, some with, some without explanation, in Old English runic manuscripts (*Runica Manuscripta*, pp. 120–2, where *runa* is sometimes treated as neut. pl., pp. 242 and 317).

Þat kann ec it fiórða,　ef mér fyrðar bera
　　bǫnd at boglimom:
svá ec gel,　at ec ganga má,
　　sprettr mér af fótom fiǫturr,
　　enn af hǫndom hapt.

'This fourth [skill] I know. If men put fetters on my limbs I chant such a charm as will let me escape. The fetter flies from my legs, the handcuff from my wrists.'[51] Even in *Hávamál*, however, no specific connexion is made between this skill and runes – the spell is oral, not written – so this gives no certain support to the theory.

There are two reasons for the difficulty of the Old English Bede version of the tale: *þa alysendlecan rune* could formally be either singular or plural: the translator may or may not use *rune* and *stafas* as synonyms. In the Old English Bede it is common for a single word of the original to be replaced by two. These are often synonymous – *compian and feohtan* for *pugnatura*, *latteowas and heretogan* for *duces*, *weaxan and myclian* for *grandescere*.[52] Less often, though still quite frequently, the words of the pair are not synonyms but are closely related within the context, one implying or including the other. So, *þæs þe he fulwihte and Cristes geleafan onfeng* 'from the time of receiving baptism and the faith of Christ' for *acceptae fidei*, *geðeode and gecyrre* 'attach and convert' for *societis*, *ge brohtan and us secgað* 'you have brought and say to us' for *adfertis*.[53] If *rune* is singular (cf. Miller's translation 'whether he knew the charm for loosing, and had the words with him written out') it can hardly mean 'runic character' or be synonymous with *stafas*. It could have Bosworth-Toller's meaning IV 'of that which is written, with the idea of mystery or magic', roughly equal to Miller's 'charm', though I am not sure that 'charm' is an accurate translation. 'Secret document' or 'esoteric practice' are at least equally possible, and it is noteworthy that the verb used with *rune* is *cuðe*, not *hæfde*. *Rune* then refers to the whole, *stafas* to its parts or appendages, and the relation between the nouns is similar to that in *Daniel* 739–40. If, as is perhaps less likely, *rune* is plural, it could mean 'characters, symbols', parallel to *stafas*, perhaps 'words, formulae', but not necessarily, I think, 'runic characters'. 'Secret characters' is perhaps the nearest one need get to 'runes' in the modern sense of the word.

It is hard to choose between these possibilities. If we take the Old English Bede's *rune* as 'runic characters', there is the difficulty that no other certain case of the word in that meaning exists.[54] If we take *rune* as *not* meaning 'runic characters' we face the unlikely situation of Ælfric using *runstafum* in that sense, the Old English Bede translator using *rune* and *stafas* in another.

---

[51] *Hávamál*, v. 149.
[52] Miller, *Old English Bede* I, 50 and 52.
[53] *Ibid.* I, 60 and 110.
[54] The Old Norse cognate *rún* means 'runic character' from early times. Professor Whitelock draws my attention to the fact that *run* is not used to mean 'mystery, counsel', etc. elsewhere in the Old English Bede, and suggests that this may be an archaic meaning preserved in poetry, glosses, and alliterative phrases. The Old English Bede could then be using *run* in a more modern sense of 'runic character'.

In the long run the interpretation of this passage depends on whether the interpreter is inclined to believe in rune-magic or not. Ælfric's reference to rune-magic is certain, Bede's at the best possible, that of the translator of the Old English Bede at the best probable. If Bede knew of rune-magic it was common knowledge, as his reference to the *fabulae* current about it shows.

A second piece of literary evidence is from the *First Poetical Dialogue of Solomon and Saturn*. Here Solomon, champion of Christian belief, expounds to his opponent Saturn the qualities of the *paternoster*. This he does figuratively by taking the letters which make up the prayer, in the order in which they appear in it, and describing how each attacks the devil. In the Corpus Christi College, Cambridge, 422 text of the poem each letter is preceded by its runic equivalent, and the editor, R. J. Menner, comments, 'It is significant that the warrior letters . . . are given their runic form, for the magic power of the rune was a deep-seated belief of the Germanic peoples'. The use of runes in the Christian *Solomon and Saturn* is 'the last vestige of an ancient pagan Germanic tradition, according to which the runes themselves possessed magic power'.[55] The objection to this interpretation, as K. Sisam has shown,[56] is that the runes were not originally part of the poem at all. The only other manuscript, Corpus Christi College, Cambridge, 41, does not have them. They are extra-metrical. The alliteration requires the letter-names *er, en, es, ef, em*, not the rune-names *rad, nyd, sigel, feoh, man*. The occasional descriptions of letter forms in the poem suggest roman characters rather than runic. Thus the runes are additions, possibly quite late and the product of literary antiquarianism. They may have been used to make the individual letters of the *paternoster* stand out from the written page, in which case they resemble the runic clues to some of the Old English riddles and the letters of Cynewulf's signatures.

Against this evidence in favour of a connexion between runes and magic must be put important negative evidence: the almost complete absence of runes in the Old English manuscript charms. Storms's collection gives eighty-six of these charms, mainly medical but also covering quite a wide field of everyday activity, catching a swarm of bees, improving the fertility of fields, ensuring protection on journeys, and against witches, elves, and other fiends, discovering thieves, obtaining favours, and so on. They preserve pagan material, naming Woden and others who have been identified, with more or less probability, as pagan Anglo-Saxon gods. Possibly if runes had been a major factor in pagan Anglo-Saxon magic, and certainly if they had been absorbed into Christian magic, we would expect them to appear in quantity in the charms. They do not. In a charm *wiþ lenctenadle* 'against (? typhoid) fever' in Bald's *Leechbook* there is a *godcund gebed* in which the words *In nomine dei summi sit benedictum* are followed by a group of twenty-one characters, some of which are

[55] R. J. Menner, *The Poetical Dialogues of Solomon and Saturn* (New York, 1941), pp. 48–9. The view is still occasionally expressed; see C. L. Wrenn, *Anglo-Saxon Poetry and the Amateur Archaeologist* (London, 1962), p. 14.
[56] Review of Menner, *Poetical Dialogues*, in *Medium Ævum* 13 (1944), 28–36, at 35. See also Derolez, *Runica Manuscripta*, p. 420.

formally identical with runes, others being blundered or clearly non-runic.[57] The group is unintelligible and may be magical gibberish. This charm has also a passage in Greek characters, part of which has a Christian reference though the rest remains uninterpreted, as well as a good deal of Latin, so the magical quality of the runes compared with other alphabets is not striking.[58] Otherwise runes are represented in these charms only by a single *d*-rune in a long gibberish passage in a charm (extant in two texts) for stanching blood.[59] This may be an example only of the common non-magical practice of using runes as abbreviation symbols. It appears in the sequence *Fil cron diw. d-*rune. *inro.cron.* The *d*-rune may be an error (one quite common in Old English manuscripts) for the closely similar *m*-rune used as an abbreviation for the rune-name *mon*, which would rhyme with the preceding and following *cron* and with syllables – *thonn, on(n)* – further away in the passage. The letter combinations *forrune, runice*, also in gibberish passages,[60] may bear reference to runes – *runice* could mean 'in runes', though it has also been explained as Old Irish *ru-n·ice* 'mayest thou heal us'.[61] Finally must be mentioned a passage in the *Nine Herbs Charm*:

> þa genam Woden VIIII wuldortanas,
> sloh ða þa næddran þæt heo on VIIII tofleah.

'Then Woden took nine glory-twigs, and struck then the serpent, that it flew into nine fragments.' Of *VIIII wuldortanas* Storms comments, 'nine glory-twigs, by which are meant nine runes, that is, nine twigs with the initial letters in runes of the plants representing the power inherent in them',[62] but this interpretation is speculative. It assumes the existence of rune-magic and cannot be used to demonstrate it.

Thus the runic content of the manuscript charms is minute. In one case the charm formula is specifically ordered to be written *greciscum stafum* 'in Greek letters',[63] but nothing is ever said of using runes for the purpose. The laws, penitentials, etc., which proscribe magical practices, never mention runes, though they may be included in the general prohibitions of heathen observances and witchcraft.

Finally, there is the evidence of the Old English runic inscriptions themselves. At first glance we are impressed by the practical purposes for which runes were used, but this initial impression may be misleading. Most of the extant inscriptions are quite late in date – from *c.* 700 onwards – and so from Christian times. Moreover, our first impression derives from the inscriptions interpretable with some certainty, and this is in general those of practical content or which can be paralleled in other

---

[57] Storms, *Anglo-Saxon Magic*, p. 270. See also the reproduction in C. E. Wright, *Bald's Leechbook*, EEMF 5 (Copenhagen, 1955), fol. 53*a*.
[58] J. H. G. Grattan and C. Singer, *Anglo-Saxon Magic and Medicine* (Oxford, 1952), p. 34, remark of the runic passage, 'The phrase . . . is in runic letters and so has special magic power'.
[59] Storms, *Anglo-Saxon Magic*, pp. 304–5.
[60] *Ibid.* pp. 304 and 315.
[61] H. Meroney, 'Irish in the Old English Charms', *Speculum* 20 (1945), 172–82, at 174.
[62] Storms, *Anglo-Saxon Magic*, p. 195.
[63] *Ibid.* p. 268.

scripts or cultures – coin legends, memorial inscriptions, owner's or artist's signatures, explanatory titles accompanying carvings, and so on. Yet a not inconsiderable number of Old English runic inscriptions – and this includes some of the earliest – have not yet been adequately explained. Some of these may be magic.

That runes and roman characters were used for the same purposes during at least part of the Old English period is undeniable. The names of the ninth-century Northumbrian moneyers, Brother and Wihtred, are found both in runes and roman letters, while a coin attributed to the eighth-century king Æthelberht of East Anglia has the moneyer's name 'lul' in runes but the royal name EÐIlBERH/T almost entirely in roman.[64] The Hartlepool runic memorial slabs, each inscribed only with the name of the deceased, 'hildiþryþ', 'hilddigyþ', are paralleled by the non-runic Wensley stones, which read DONFRI[D] and EATBEREHCT. The Great Urswick inscription:

> '+ tunwini setæ   æfter toroʒtredæ
> bekun æfter his bæurnæ   gebidæs þer saulæ'

'Tunwini raised this memorial to his lord (? son) Torhtred. Pray for his soul' uses the same verse formula as the Dewsbury fragment:

-RHTAE

BECUN A[E]FTER BEORNAE   GIBIDDAD D[A]ER SAULE

and there seems no reason to distinguish the runic signature of the Kirkheaton stone, 'eoh:worohtæ', from the non-runic one of the Pershore censer-cover, + GODRIC ME ÞVORHT<E>. Rings from Lancashire, now in the British Museum, and Llysfaen, now in the Victoria and Albert Museum, have legends using apparently arbitrary mixtures of runes and roman characters, while the inscription of the back of the Franks Casket begins and ends in runes, but has a central passage in roman letters.

One Christian memorial stone, the Falstone hogback, has almost identical parallel texts, one in uncials, the other in runes. The uncial text is primary, the runic one a transliteration of it.[65] R. W. V. Elliott has suggested that the use of runes in this case has a background of pagan magic, describing it as a 'sound insurance policy', presumably insuring that the dead man got the best of both other worlds, or that his body as well as his soul rested in peace.[66] This cannot be upheld. Double inscriptions are found elsewhere in the north-east, in Lindisfarne. Important are the texts on the coffin made by the monks of Lindisfarne for the body of St Cuthbert at its elevation in 698.[67] Here runes and roman characters are used side by side, roman for the names of archangels and apostles (save for an occasional runic 'm') and for the evangelist

---

[64] My own readings of inscriptions are given, unless otherwise stated. Runes are transliterated according to Dickins, 'System of Transliteration'. Non-runic inscriptions are in capitals. I divide all these texts into individual words.

[65] See above, pp. 82–3.

[66] Elliott, *Runes*, p. 71 [omitted in 2nd ed., pp. 94–5].

[67] B. Dickins, 'The Inscriptions upon the Coffin', *The Relics of Saint Cuthbert*, ed. C. F. Battiscombe (Oxford, 1956), pp. 305–7.

LVCAS, but runes for Matthew, Mark, and John: roman for Mary's name, but runes for the sacred name of Christ. There seems no differentiation of use of scripts. St Cuthbert can hardly have needed the help or control of pagan magic, nor is a script with strong pagan associations likely to have been picked out for Christ's name.[68] The texts of St Cuthbert's coffin presumably link with those of the small, incised memorial slabs from Lindisfarne, called pillow- or name-stones. These form a closer parallel to the Falstone hogback, for some of them have two inscriptions each, one in runes and one in roman lettering, giving one and the same personal name. In both coffin and name-stone texts there is some evidence that the runic inscriptions are secondary, transcriptions of roman characters commonly employed, and the question arises, why were runes used at all on these objects? A preliminary answer is that runes were a traditional script for grave furniture, at least in the north-east.

Out of the whole corpus of Old English runic inscriptions only a handful can be cited as possible evidence for the existence of rune-magic in this country. Undoubtedly magical are three related inscriptions on a group of amulet rings, one from Greymoor Hill, Cumberland, inscribed 'ærkriufltkriuriþonglæstæpon | tol', one from Yorkshire, commonly called the Bramham Moor ring, reading 'ærkriuflt | kriuriþon | glæstæpon/tol', and a third of unknown provenance early recorded in a Bristol collection, with the rather different but related 'ery.ri.uf.dol.yri.uri.þol.wles.te.pote.nol'.[69] Though these texts contain no identifiable Old English words they are not to be regarded as meaningless. B. Dickins observed that the letter group 'ærkriu' appears as *ærcrio, ær crio* in two versions of a charm for stanching blood,[70] and the same charms contain occasional other echoes of the ring texts, *thonn* (= 'þon'), *Fil* (= 'fl'), *leno* (= 'e.nol'). The rhyme pattern of the gibberish of the rings is the same as that often found in Old English manuscript charms, two syllables rhyming together followed by a third rhyming with a corresponding syllable of the next word. Thus the rings are amuletic, the inscriptions magical, whether heathen or Christian. This does not necessarily mean that the ring runes themselves are magical, since the magic may be supplied by the words only, not the characters of the inscriptions. One piece of evidence suggests that the individual letters are important. The Greymoor Hill ring has thirty runes, twenty-seven outside the hoop and three inside. The Bramham Moor ring has thirty also, divided by decorative symbols into three groups of nine, nine, and twelve. Three and its multiples are common magic numbers, amply evidenced in the Old English manuscript charms.[71] Thus part of the magical power of the amulet rings may reside in the individual runes cut on them, and there may be a link with Scandinavian runic number magic. Two points may be made in opposition.

[68] E. G. Stanley notes ('Hæthenra Hyht in *Beowulf*, *Studies in Old English Literature in Honor of Arthur G. Brodeur*, ed. S. B. Greenfield (Oregon, 1963), pp. 136–51, at 139–41) the opposition between Christian values and those of *das alte Germanenthum* in Old English poetry.
[69] For a more detailed account of these and the two following inscriptions see my Appendix A in D. M. Wilson, *Anglo-Saxon Ornamental Metalwork 700–1100 in the British Museum* (London, 1964), pp. 67–90.
[70] B. Dickins, 'Runic Rings and Old English Charms', *ASNSL* 167 (1935), 252. The charms are Storms, *Anglo-Saxon Magic*, pp. 304–5.
[71] Storms, *Anglo-Saxon Magic*, pp. 96–100.

The Bramham Moor text disguises its number of thirty runes by binding two of them, 'n/t', together. The Bristol ring engraver found no significance in three and its multiples. He cut thirty-two runes in eleven groups.

More clearly connected with rune-magic is the Thames scramasax. This is an elaborate and expensive weapon, with two texts and a decorative pattern cut along the length of the blade, the incised lines filled with metals of contrasting colours. The inscriptions give the twenty-eight letter Old English *fuþorc* and the masculine personal name 'bêagnoþ', which it is natural to take as that of the sword's owner. Early *fuþark* inscriptions are generally considered magical; otherwise, the pertinent question is asked, what is their purpose? Bæksted questions the magical interpretation, though his alternative explanations are not always convincing.[72] In the case of the Thames scramasax Bæksted tentatively suggests that the *fuþorc* is purely ornamental, but it is then odd that the rune-master, using runes practically in 'bêagnoþ', did not cut an inscription which was both practical and ornamental, as, for example, the owner-maker formula of the Sittingbourne scramasax, +S<I>GEBEREHT ME AH | + BIORHTELM ME ÞORTE. It is more likely that the Thames *fuþorc* has magical affinities, but of what sort? This *fuþorc* is anomalous. Three of the letters, 's', 'œ', 'y', show rare forms such as are more common in manuscript than epigraphical texts. One rune form 'd', is unique, and may be a rare example which has not survived elsewhere, a chance variant created by the difficulty the craftsman found in producing the standard 'd' in this medium, or a plain error. In favour of the last is the fact that the letter order of the Thames *fuþorc* is wrong, having 'eŋdlmœ' instead of the expected 'emlŋdœ' or 'emlŋœd'. If this *fuþorc* contains errors, it is suspect as magic. At least it was not cut by a competent magician.

A possible explanation is that the Thames *fuþorc* was cut at a time when there was no longer an extensive knowledge of runes in the area, or a living belief in their magical powers. The practice of inscribing runes, even magical *fuþorcs*, on weapons was an archaic one, known from earlier objects that had survived or descriptions of them. The smith who ornamented the Thames scramasax or the warrior who commissioned it wanted the practice to be followed, so the *fuþorc* was produced, inaccurately, perhaps from a hasty reading of a manuscript account of runes.

The amulet rings and the Thames scramasax are the two most convincing pieces of evidence for rune-magic among the Anglo-Saxons. Other examples are much more speculative. The silver object known vaguely as the Thames fitting, apparently a fragment of the ridge-piece of a gabled shrine, has the obscure and fragmentary inscription '-sbe/rædht3bcai | e/rh/ad/æbs'. This remains uninterpreted. Attempts to read it as plain language and Old English have failed.[73] I suggest no meaning for the text, but note the following curious points. The first seven characters of the inscription as it stands are repeated, with the addition of 'a', in the last eight. If the first seven runes are numbered 1–7 the repetition is in the order 347'a'6521, which does not look accidental. It corresponds with similar rearrangements of letters in Old

---

[72] Bæksted, *Målruner*, pp. 139–40.
[73] See the readings of Stephens, *Handbook*, p. 147; Bugge and Olsen, *Norges indskrifter med de ældre runer* I, 120–1; T. v. Grienberger, 'The Thames Fitting', *ZDP* 45 (1913), 47–55.

English code texts.[74] The Thames fitting inscription may be a cryptogram, perhaps anagrammatical. One small piece of evidence suggests that it is also magical. If its runes are replaced by the roman equivalents given them in Old English runic manuscripts, the following alphabetical groups are represented: *abcde* (which includes 'æ'): *hik* (which includes 'ȝ'): *rst*. This too does not look accidental. There may be a connexion with the alphabet magic which flourished in late Classical times and perhaps into the Middle Ages, though there is little other Anglo-Saxon evidence for alphabet magic.

In the Anglo-Saxon cemetery of Holborough, Kent, was found a spear-head with an inlaid symbol resembling an elaborated 't', or perhaps identifiable as the bind-rune 't/u' or even 't/i/u'.[75] The name of the rune 't' is *tir*, i.e. OE *Tīw*, ON *Týr*, the Germanic god who has pretensions to being a war-god. The rune would be an appropriate symbol to put on a spear for the magical purpose of strengthening its bearer or giving him protection or success in battle.[76] However, the Holborough symbol is not certainly runic. The seventh-century dating of the Holborough cemetery makes an invocation to the pagan god less likely, though the spear may have been an old one when buried, or a new one preserving an archaic pattern.

Among about thirty astragali found in a funeral urn in the Anglo-Saxon cemetery of Caistor-by-Norwich, Norfolk, was one with the incised runes 'ræȝhæn'. The inscription, probably the earliest extant in Old English, is dated from associated finds not later than the end of the fifth century. The sound represented by 'æ' – whether *æ* or *a* – is uncertain, as is the value of 'ȝ'. This inscription has been published in a detailed study by C. L. Wrenn.[77] Apparently starting from the premise that runes were essentially magical Professor Wrenn identifies the astragalus as a token used in a magical game or process of sortilege, supporting his theory by the evidence of the magical origins of such games as Old Norse *hneftafl*, the ancient practice of astragalomancy and the magical power of the number thirty.[78] He suggests two interpretations, the first that the runes form a word *rah(w)han*, cognate with ON *regin* 'gods', the first element of PrON *rAginArunAR*, *rAginoronoR* on the Björketorp and Stentoften (Blekinge) stones, and OE *regn-* in such a compound as *regnheard*: the second that the Caistor-by-Norwich runes represent their rune-names, words which form a picture of pagan Anglo-Saxon belief. Professor Wrenn accepts that these interpretations are not capable of proof.

---

[74] Cf., for example, *bprckpʃbn* for *bckprʃbn* (a cipher form of *aciorfan*), *weliogarn* for *wiolegran* in the Kentish Glosses (J. Zupitza, 'Kentische Glossen des neunten Jahrhunderts', *ZDA* 21 (1877), 1–59, at 26 and 44), and 'g', 'æro', 'hi' for *higoræ*, the answer to *Riddle 24* of the Exeter Book.

[75] V. I. Evison, 'An Anglo-Saxon Cemetery at Holborough, Kent', *Archæologia Cantiana* 70 (1956), 84–141, at 97–100 and pl. III.

[76] J. de Vries, *Altgermanische Religionsgeschichte*, 2nd ed. (Berlin, 1956–7) II, 21.

[77] C. L. Wrenn, 'Magic in an Anglo-Saxon Cemetery', *English and Medieval Studies Presented to J. R. R. Tolkien . . .*, ed. N. Davis and C. L. Wrenn (London, 1962), pp. 306–20.

[78] In his account of the finding of the inscribed bone Wrenn refers to 'some 30 sheep's astragali' ('Magic in an Anglo-Saxon Cemetery', p. 307), some of which were fragmentary. Presumably the exact number of astragali involved is unknown.

Finally, brief reference must be made to the recently discovered and yet unpublished cremation urns from Loveden Hill, Lincs.[79] Two have inscribed symbols on the sides, some of them formally identical with runes, others not. Presumably meaningful inscriptions are intended or at least imitated, though they are at present undeciphered. Another urn from the same cemetery has forms resembling 't' cut round the shoulder. These may be decorative, or may bear reference to the god Tiw. If the corpus of Anglo-Saxon urns were carefully examined more of these inscriptions might be recognized. I note only a single example of what T. C. Lethbridge called 'a magical inscription in bogus runes' on a sixth-century urn from Lackford, Suffolk.[80] This has forms resembling 'g' and either 'o' or 'h', followed by scribbled lines which were probably not meaningful. In these cases the suggestion of rune-magic arises from the context in which the runes appear. It is tempting to think of inscriptions on pagan funeral furniture as sacral or magical, perhaps connected with a cult of the dead, but again there is no proof.

Thus the Anglo-Saxon evidence for rune-magic, though not negligible, is slight. The only certain point is Ælfric's unambiguous reference. Without it the existence of rune-magic would hardly have been deduced from the English material alone. The other evidence, of Bede and his Old English translator and of the inscriptions, is not conclusive. Those who argue that Old English runes were commonly used for magical purposes must rely on supporting evidence from outside this country, in particular from Scandinavia. They should remember the differences in cultural development between Dark Age Scandinavia and Anglo-Saxon England, especially the early date of the conversion to Christianity and the introduction of roman script into this country. Admittedly the scepticism expressed in this paper leaves important questions unanswered, questions to which supporters of rune-magic would find ready replies. Why were runes introduced here at an early date by a people who had little need of a practical script? Why did runes become a traditional script for funeral furniture? Moreover, my method of putting forward the evidence is inimical to the theory of rune-magic. It does not allow the possibility that a script could have two simultaneous functions, that inscriptions which are practical may at the same time have magical efficacy.

To take examples from written texts. Beowulf slays Grendel's dam and beheads the dead Grendel with a wondrous sword, described as *sigeeadig bil, eald sweord eotenisc, giganta geweorc*, found in the underwater cave (*Beowulf* 1557–62). The hilt, which alone survives the encounter, is described later. It was rune-inscribed – *þurh runstafas rihte gemearcod* – the text telling *hwam þæt sweord geworht . . . ærest wære*, usually translated 'for whom the sword was originally made' (*Beowulf* 1694–8). This is a practical text, but the runes may have served the additional purpose

[79] I owe my knowledge of these to Mr K. R. Fennell. A brief account of one of them is given in C. L. Wrenn, *Anglo-Saxon Poetry*, p. 19. Photographs of two of them are reproduced in *Illustrated London News* for 31 Aug. 1963, pp. 320–1.
[80] T. C. Lethbridge, *A Cemetery at Lackford, Suffolk: Report of the Excavation of a Cemetery of the Pagan Anglo-Saxon Period in 1947* (Cambridge, 1951), p. 20 and fig. 27.

of extending the remarkable powers of this weapon. The runes of *The Husband's Message* have been read as a cipher message from man to wife or a reference to the elements which witnessed the faith pledged by one to the other.[81] At the same time the mystical powers of the runes may be invoked to help the keeping of the pledge.[82] Bede records a monument, surviving in his day, inscribed with the name of Horsa.[83] If it was contemporary with that chieftain's death its inscription must have been in runes, which could have served the secondary purpose of protecting the grave from desecration or the living from the dead man's ghost. The same arguments may apply to some extant Old English runic inscriptions. The Chessell Down scabbard-plate may record the name of the sword it held and the Gilton pommel inscription that of the sword's owner:[84] at the same time these runes may have helped the warriors in battle by their magical powers. The Christian prayers of the Whitby comb and the Mortain Casket may derive from a pagan use of runes as cult symbols, and the runes of Christian grave furniture from a pagan practice in the service of the dead.

Unfortunately these points cannot be proved, nor is there even a balance of probability in their favour. Old English runic inscriptions are still found from time to time, and future discoveries may add to our knowledge of Anglo-Saxon rune-magic. Meanwhile it is wise to hesitate before interpreting Old English runic texts as magical.

POSTSCRIPT

The subject is one of continued interest, partly because the modern world, in its search for the meaning of life, seems determined to abandon common sense and careful enquiry, preferring imprecision and mysticism. Hence the amateur nonsense often written about runes today. Professional runologists, particularly in Scandinavia, continue to stress the practical uses of the script, while accepting that it is sometimes found, as are other alphabets, in magical or cryptic texts.

Some of the targets attacked in this paper have long since been shot through. Nobody now, I hope, takes seriously Professor Wrenn's interpretation of the Caistor-by-Norwich astragalus inscription; an interpretation admirably suited to the achievement of the don in whose honour it was written. The Caistor text, which he should perhaps have represented **raihan**, is I think generally accepted now as a form or cognate of OE *raha*, 'roe-deer', the beast that supplied the astragalus. The Norwegian runologist Ingrid Sanness Johnsen and I reached this conclusion

---

[81] For some theories on these runes see R. F. Leslie, *Three Old English Elegies* (Manchester, 1961), pp. 15–17.
[82] Wrenn, *Anglo-Saxon Poetry*, pp. 14–15.
[83] *Historia Ecclesiastica*, i. 15.
[84] Elliott, *Runes*, p. 80, B. Dickins, 'The Sandwich Runic Inscription *Ræhæbul*', *Beiträge zur Runenkunde und nordischen Sprachwissenshaft*, ed. K. H. Schlottig (Leipzig, 1938), pp. 83–5, at 83.

independently;[85] and Professor Bammesberger has described it as 'the most widely accepted interpretation'.[86]

Other targets remain elusive. So far, in my opinion, there has been no adequate interpretation of the runes of the Loveden Hill urn inscription.[87] There are, however, a couple of new cases that must be brought under consideration. A group of cremation urns from Spong Hill, Norfolk, have a stamped pattern which Peter Pieper has interpreted, probably rightly, as the magical word **alu** (well-known from early Norse inscriptions) in doubled runes (*Spiegelrunen*). Runes on a silver bracteate from Welbeck Hill, Lincolnshire, may be an attempt at the magical word **laþu**.

Since this paper was written, younger and more daring scholars have cast more light, or perhaps darkness, on the general topic. There has been discussion both of the derivation of the word 'rune' and of the semantics of the element *run/run-* in Old English.[88] There remains a good deal more mileage in this subject. As an example, I draw attention to an aspect of the Old English translation of Bede's tale of Imma that seems to have escaped notice hitherto. The standard text of this passage has the sentence I quote in my paper: *ond hine ascode hwæðer he ða alysendlecan rune cuðe, and þa stafas mid him awritene hæfde, be swylcum men leas spel secgað and spreocað, þæt hine mon forþon gebindan ne meahte.* The version in Corpus Christi College, Cambridge, MS 41 (from eleventh-century Exeter) often differs quite extensively from the wording of other manuscripts, as it does for this passage. It reads instead (p. 304): *ongann wundrian and hine frinan and acsian hwæðer he þa alyfedlican rune cuðe and þa stanas mid him hæfde be swylcum* . . . Whatever *alyfedlican rune* means it is not 'loosening runes'. Presumably the clause here means 'whether he knew permitted secrets and had the stones with him, about which . . .' The omission of the past participle *awritene* shows the scribe had something rather different in mind from a spell written down, but whether this is a change he made with intent or by careless misreading is difficult to say. It is not that runes were unknown in Exeter at about this time since there are a couple of runic marginalia in this very manuscript. At the foot of p. 436 there is the beginning of a runic alphabet 'a b c d | ' which is presumably linked to the last words of the chapter that ends just above, *on leornunge úre stafa:* (book 5, chapter 14, *nostrarum lectione litterarum*). In the margin of p. 448 (part of book 5, chapter 19) is the word 's w i þ o r' which repeats the first word written on the adjoining line. It is preceded by a runic numeral 'x i i . 7 . x x x'. The word *þrittig* occurs on the line directly opposite on p. 449, but I cannot find a figure 12 anywhere in the neighbourhood. My suspicion is that it is an error for 10, and the pair refer to the ten and thirty hides of land that Wilfrid received at Stamford and Ripon according to this chapter. In late Anglo-Saxon Exeter,

---

[85] I. Sanness Johnsen, 'Den runologiske plassering av innskriften fra Caistor-by-Norwich', *ANF* 89 (1974), 30–43, at 42; Page, 'The Runic Inscription from N59' (1973), p. 117.

[86] A. Bammesberger, 'Ingvaeonic Sound Changes and the Anglo-Frisian Runes', *Old English Runes*, ed. Bammesberger, pp. 389–408, at 402.

[87] See here my comments in 'Anglo-Saxon Runic Studies: The Way Ahead?' (1991), p. 22.

[88] R. Morris, 'Northwest Germanic *rūn*- "Rune": a Case of Homonymy with Go. *runa* "Mystery" ', *BGDSL* 107 (1985), 344–58; C. E. Fell, 'Runes and Semantics', *Old English Runes*, ed. Bammesberger, pp. 195–229.

then, it seems that runes were known as an alternative script, and there was no thought that they were connected with magic. Nor that the word *rune* naturally brought the runic alphabet to the writer's mind. Instead it links with the word *stanas*, 'stones', but what these could be I know not.

10
(1965)

RALPH THORESBY'S RUNIC COINS

Numismatists and runologists have long known that among the early coins in the collection of the Leeds antiquary, Ralph Thoresby, was one with a runic inscription. This, one of Sveinn Estridsson's Lund coins by the moneyer Thorgot (Mø. 98 in Jacobsen and Moltke, *Danmarks runeindskrifter*: type 204 in E. Moltke, 'De danske runemønter og deres prægere', *Nordisk numismatisk årsskrift* (1950), 1–56, at 26), was identified as runic by William Nicolson, the celebrated antiquary, historian, collector and divine, then Archdeacon of Carlisle. On 17 April 1691 Thoresby seems to have written to Nicolson, suggesting that they should correspond, and asking him specific questions on antiquarian subjects, one of which suggested that he had a runic coin in his collection.[1] Thoresby's letter does not survive, but Nicolson's acknowledgment, dated 27 April, is among the Thoresby correspondence in the library of the Yorkshire Archaeological Society.[2] Nicolson writes:

> I never saw any coin with a *Runic* Inscription. Mr Walker (in his preface to K. Alfred's life) has given us the draught of three, which he once took to be of y^t nature; but he doubts they may be eastern coins; and he had good reason to do so. I have seen (in some Musæa in Germany) several pieces of Persian & other East-Countrey coins mistaken for Runic ones; and possibly some of yours may be of the like stamp.

Thoresby sent the Lund coin together with others to Nicolson in August 1691. They were returned the following month, as Nicolson reveals in a letter to Thoresby dated 9 September. He adds 'I have given you my thoughts of *your Coins*; which (especially on that with the *Runic Characters*) I hope will be grateful'. Nicolson's report on the coin does not accompany this letter, which is also in the keeping of the Yorkshire Archaeological Society,[3] but a holograph copy of it, made for a third person, perhaps George Hickes, is now MS Eng. Hist. b.2, fols 266–7 in the Bodleian

---

[1] In his review of his life (J. Hunter, *The Diary of Ralph Thoresby, F.R.S.* . . . (London, 1830) I, 196) Thoresby states that this correspondence began in 1690, a date which would include the first three months of 1691. Thoresby is probably in error here: his statement was made, or at least edited, after 1702 when Nicolson became Bishop of Carlisle.

[2] No. 154 n in H. W. Jones's unpublished handlist to the Thoresby correspondence in the library of the Yorkshire Archaeological Society.

[3] Jones 158, printed in W. T. Lancaster, *Letters addressed to Ralph Thoresby F.R.S.* (Leeds, 1912),

Library. Nicolson's report is headed 'Notes on a Runic coin in yᵉ possession of Mʳ Thoresby of Leeds, & communicated to W. N. Aug. 1691'. In it he comments:

> I much doubted whether the Inscription on this coin were truely Runic till I saw it. The Reason of my doubt was, because the best of the Danish Antiquaries are of opinion that no currant coin was ever minted in the Northern Kingdomes till the use of the Runic Character was laid aside.

Nicolson identifies the coin as an amulet, and the obverse figure as that of the 'antient God Thor . . . *Caput flammâ circumdatum* . . .' He gives a drawing of both sides of the coin, with the runic inscription accurately reproduced save that in place of the roman letter S added after the place name form *lunti* he draws the runic 's', and transliterates the runes: *Thur gut luetis. i.e. Thoronis Dei facies seu effigies*, with comment, 'I never yet saw any Runic Inscription so plain and Intelligible'. This note of Nicolson's is the basis of the first detailed published account of the coin, that in cols 814–15 of Gibson's revision of Camden's *Britannia*, which came out in 1695. Thoresby accepted Nicolson's reading. Among his manuscripts kept in a leather-bound volume in the library of Leeds Grammar School is 'A Catalogue of the Saxon Coines in my Collection'. The runic coin is no. 29, described as having 'a rude figure of the Idol Thor caput flamma circumdatum', the last five words added over an obliterated original. Thoresby originally continued, 'but yᵉ Letters are absolutely Ruinick (*sic*) as I conjecture', to which he later added with acknowledgment Nicolson's interpretation of the runes.

In 1693 Thoresby sent this coin and a number of others to Obadiah Walker (the Mr Walker of Nicolson's letter of April 1691), the ejected Master of University College, Oxford, who was then preparing his description of early British and English coinage for Gibson's *Britannia*. Thoresby spent part of 15 August 'taking account of the ancient coins and medals (above one hundred British, Roman, Runic, Saxon, &c.) sent to the editors of Camden', and two days later wrote to Walker about them.[4] Receipt of the coins was acknowledged later that month, and they were kept, apparently very carelessly, by Walker until May 1694, when those that remained were returned to their owner.[5] On this examination depend the reproduction of the Lund coin as no. 34 of Tabula II (*Nummi Britannici*) of Gibson's *Britannia* and Walker's brief reference to it in col. xcvi of that work.

The coin legend was further studied by Hickes early in the following century. Two letters, dated 14 August and 10 October 1701, from Hickes to Thoresby confirm Nicolson's transliteration but give an alternative explanation.[6] Hickes comments (adding a mass of philological explication):

---

pp. 22–3. Also in J. Nichols, *Letters on Various Subjects . . . to and from William Nicolson . . .* (London, 1809), no. 13, where it is wrongly headed 'To Mr. Gibson'.

[4] *Diary* I, 235. See also *Letters of Eminent Men, addressed to Ralph Thoresby, F.R.S.* (London, 1832) I, 139–40.

[5] *Letters addressed to Ralph Thoresby* I, 31–2.

[6] Jones 684 and 701, the first printed in *Letters addressed to Ralph Thoresby* I, 103–4. A further letter, Jones 697, dated 28 September, also mentions the runic coin without giving details.

I told you, y^t I thought *Þur gut Lüetis* written in Runic characters upon your Cimbric, or old Danish coin signified *Thor deus populi*, or *Thor nationis deus*, and not *Thori dei facies*, as the worthy, and learned Archdeacon explained the words.

In November 1703 Thoresby sent this coin to Hickes for examination. The Leeds Grammar School volume contains 'A list of my Saxon Coyns sent up to Sr Andrew Fountain & D^r. Hickes to be inserted in his work':[7] item 80 is 'the Amulet of ye God Thor Tab. II. 34 & p. 814 of ye new Brit^a.' Sir Andrew Fountaine's illustration of the coin and interpretation of its legend in *Numismata Anglo-Saxonica & Anglo-Danica breviter illustrata* (Oxford, 1705), p. 165, one of the parts of book I of Hickes's *Thesaurus*, derives from this examination. The study of this and related coins in the eighteenth century can be followed further in G. Galster, 'Runemøntforskning i det 18. aarhundrede', *Nordisk numismatisk årsskrift* (1941), 121–34.[8]

In Thoresby's *Musæum Thoresbyanum*, a catalogue of his collection printed in 1713 and appended to *Ducatus Leodiensis* (London, 1715), the Lund runic coin appears as no. 18 of the '*British, Runic, Saxon* and *Danish* Medals', with the following comment on Walker's identification of the runes, 'Mr. *O. W.* indeed miscalls all the unintelligible and *Exotic* Characters *Runic*. But this *single Medal* is the only one known to be in any *Musæum* in *Europe*, with the true *Runic* Letters upon it'. As Galster has shown, there were by 1713 Danish runic coins in other European collections, but the surprising thing about Thoresby's pronouncement is that it shows his ignorance of the fact that two more runic coins rested in his own cabinet. It is true that Walker's identification of runes was sometimes erratic, as when he found them on three probably Gaulish staters (nos 27, 28 and 29 of Gibson's Tabula II, presumably the same coins as Walker had chosen for Tabula VII of Spelman's *Ælfredi magni anglorum regis . . . vita . . .* (Oxford, 1678), to which Nicolson drew Thoresby's attention). These Walker had whimsically attributed to 'some of the kings of Cumberland, in which County are still extant some Runic Monuments'. But he was correct in identifying as runic the legends of two other coins in Thoresby's collection, nos 35 and 36 of Gibson's Tabula II, while being wrong in his belief that these runes were 'the writing of the *Visi*, or *Western Goths*', who 'acquired the Northern Parts of Britain, keeping (as it seemeth) their ancient Runic characters'. In fact the coins are Anglo-Saxon *sceattas*. No. 35 is one of the common *Epa* coins. No. 36 is a rare type, one of the *sceattas* with the reverse legend *Æþiliræd*, cut in two lines (divided at the end of the first element), boustrophedon, the second line inverted. I have records of nine of these coins. Seven have the reading 'æþili | ræd'. Two of these are in the Ashmolean Museum, one unprovenanced, the other, with a retrograde legend, from Canterbury (Evans Bequest 1941). A third example, found at Domburg on the island of Walcheren, Netherlands, was formerly

---

[7] In a letter to Lhuyd dated 25 November 1703 (Bodleian MS Ashmole 1817b, fol. 150) Thoresby refers to his dispatch of these coins 'a few days ago'. See also *Diary* I, 447.
[8] Reprinted as 'Research into Runic Coins in the 18th Century' in his *Coins and History* (Copenhagen, 1959), pp. 53–64.

in the de Man collection but its present whereabouts are unknown.[9] Two more were in the Grantley collection: sale catalogue no. 749 ex Montagu 174 and Shepherd 10, and no. 750, said to be ex Montagu ex Brice, now in the possession of Commander R. P. Mack. A sixth, of unknown provenance, is H. 31 in the Hunterian Collection, University of Glasgow, no. 49 in the Hunterian *Sylloge* volume. The British Museum has three specimens. One of them, Keary, *Catalogue*, p. 24, 4 which reads 'æþili | ræd', is almost certainly that found with other Anglo-Saxon coins at Reculver, Kent, in the first half of the eighteenth century.[10] This in turn may have been one of the five early Anglo-Saxon coins from Reculver listed as lot 17 in the William Gostling sale catalogue (1777) and bought by Young for 17s. 0d. The coin was in the Tyssen collection, and reached the British Museum in 1802. The second British Museum specimen (Keary, *Catalogue*, p. 24, 5) reads 'æþil. | ræd', the third (Keary, *Catalogue*, p. 24, 6) 'æ+ili | ræd' retrograde. Thoresby's *sceat* resembles the last of these in all respects – only these two have a cross or runic 'n' in place of the correct 'þ' – and it is presumably the same coin.

In *Musæum Thoresbyanum* the antiquary listed his *Æþiliræd* coin as no. 13 of the British, Runic, Saxon and Danish medals, while his description of no. 12 shows it to be almost certainly the *Epa* example. To these must be added Gibson's Tabula II no. 14 (= Thoresby no. 11). This is a *sceat* of the runic type, and, although no runes can be identified on Gibson's reproduction, Thoresby describes its obverse as 'a crowned Head with unknown Characters'. Gibson's Tabula II no. 38 was also an Anglo-Saxon *sceat*, with the suggestion of a legend, but without identifiable characters. In 1764 Thoresby's collections were sold by auction in London. The sale catalogue, also headed *Musæum Thoresbyanum*, lists the Lund coin, 'supposed to be the Figure of the God *Thor*', as part of lot 132, while the runic *sceattas* and Thoresby's no. 11, still regarded as British coins, form part of lot 130. The annotated copy of the Thoresby sale catalogue in the Department of Coins and Medals, British Museum, records that lot 130 was bought by Snelling for 15s. 6d. and lot 132 by Snelling for the Duke of Devonshire for £5 2 6d. Neither the Snelling (1774) nor the Devonshire (1844) sale catalogue lists these items as such. According to Galster the Lund coin was in the possession of John White of Newgate Street, London, in 1778, but he gives no evidence for the statement,[11] and the coin is not mentioned in the sale catalogue of White's collection (1788). Its present whereabouts are unknown, nor can the further history of Thoresby's *Epa sceat*, a common type, be traced. As has been seen Thoresby's *Æþiliræd* coin is now in the British Museum, but the date and

---

[9] M. de Man, 'Sceattas anglo-saxons inédits ou peu connus', *Tijdschrift van het nederlandsch Genootschap voor Munt- en Penningkunde* 3 (1895), 117–46, at 138–9 and pl. II, 17. A rather different drawing of the runes is given in the same author's 'Que sait-on de la plage de Dombourg? § II. Les monnaies', *TNGMP* 7 (1899), 85–116, at pl. VI, 4.

[10] There are pen drawings of these coins in British Library MS. Stowe 1049, fol. 26. The *Æþiliræd* coin is no. 4. The runes of the first element are badly reproduced, but 'ræd' is identifiable. Its forms of 'r' and 'd', which are irregular, correspond with those of Keary, *Catalogue* I, p. 24, 4. I owe this reference to Mrs J. S. Martin.

[11] 'Runemøntforskning i det 18. aarhundrede', p. 125.

circumstances of its acquisition are not recorded.[12] This suggests that it reached the national collection no later than 1838, for after that date acquisitions were commonly registered. However, in 1841 Hawkins, describing this coin type, remarked that 'the British and Hunterian Museums have each a specimen', clearly referring to Keary, *Catalogue*, p. 24, 4 as the illustration (pl. IV, 50) shows.[13] Thus Thoresby's coin reached the British Museum after 1840 unless Hawkins compiled this chapter some years earlier and failed to bring it up to date when he completed his work.[14] In 1868 Head recorded the *sceat* in the national collection.[15] Thus there is a gap of seventy-five to a hundred years in the coin's recorded history.

Thoresby's manuscripts and printed catalogues are unfortunately silent as to the ultimate provenances of his runic coins. The core of his collection was obtained by his father from the executors of the Lord General Fairfax. However, both Ralph Thoresby and his father made extensive additions, and it is unlikely that we shall now discover more about the early history of these coins.[16]

[12] A correction is necessary to R. H. M. Dolley and J. S. Strudwick, 'The Provenances of the Anglo-Saxon Coins Recorded in the Two Volumes of the British Museum Catalogue', *BNJ* 28 (1956), 26–59, at 27 where *Æþiliræd sceattas* nos 5 and 6 have been interchanged. The accessions register makes it clear that it is no. 5 which was presented by R. Hinde in 1867.

[13] E. Hawkins, *The Silver Coins of England . . .* (London, 1841), p. 19.

[14] The second edition (1876) states (p.v) that Hawkins wrote his book in 1840.

[15] B. V. Head, 'Anglo-Saxon Coins with Runic Legends', *Numismatic Chronicle* n.s. 8 (1868), 75–90, at 84–5.

[16] A number of scholars have helped me to compile this note. In particular I wish to thank Mrs J. S. Martin, Mr S. E. Rigold, Mr C. E. Blunt, Commander R. P. Mack, Mr P. Grierson, the Librarian of the Yorkshire Archaeological Society, the Headmaster of Leeds Grammar School, and members of the staffs of the Department of Coins and Medals, British Museum, the Heberden Coin Room, Ashmolean Museum, and the Fitzwilliam Museum.

THE OLD ENGLISH RUNE *EOH, ÍH,* 'YEW-TREE'

In a pair of interesting though controversial articles,[1] Professor C. L. Wrenn has presented a new and important runic inscription, that on one of a collection of sheeps' astragali found in a fifth-century urn in the mixed cremation and inhumation cemetery of Caistor-by-Norwich.[2] Though this cemetery was dug in the nineteen-thirties, circumstances have so far prevented its detailed publication, and the runic inscription was generally unknown until it was reproduced as pl. 43 of R. Rainbird Clarke's *East Anglia* (London, 1960). The significance of this inscription lies partly in its early date, for fifth-century runes are rare enough anywhere and particularly so in this country, where Caistor-by-Norwich is one of the oldest texts known. Indeed it may even be the oldest, for the only one to compete with it is that of the Loveden Hill, Lincs., urn 61/251 (A.11) which Professor Wrenn has also discussed and which has some relevance to this article. But the particular importance of Caistor-by-Norwich to my present purpose is that it gives a new example of a rare rune, that known variously as *eoh* and *ih*, a name meaning 'yew-tree'. In Professor B. Dickins's system (which is used elsewhere in this paper) this character is transliterated '3', but the sound it represented is the subject of some debate in view of the paucity of examples of the letter in texts where the meaning is clear.

Professor Wrenn's discussion of the Caistor-by-Norwich inscription involves the identification of '3', its third rune, as *hw*. He writes, 'The Old English manuscript rune-names *ēoh* and *īh*, as beside the prose word for the yew-tree *īw* (*ēow*) seem to look back clearly to the same Germanic root **eihwo*, whether we regard the consonant variation in the historical forms as due to grammatical change or to an ultimate difference in Indo-European suffix* (*Cf. J. Pokorny, *Indogermanisches*

---

[1] 'Magic in an Anglo-Saxon Cemetery', *English and Medieval Studies Presented to J. R. R. Tolkien . . .*, ed. N. Davis and C. L. Wrenn (London, 1962), pp. 306–20, and 'Some Earliest Anglo-Saxon Cult Symbols', *Medieval and Linguistic Studies in Honor of Francis Peabody Magoun, Jr.*, ed. J. B. Bessinger and R. P. Creed (London and New York, 1965), pp. 40–55.
[2] See also 'Saxons and Celts in South-West Britain', *Trans. of the Honourable Soc. of Cymmrodorion* (1959), 38–75, at 40–1, *Anglo-Saxon Poetry and the Amateur Archaeologist* (London, 1962), pp. 16–18. It is unfortunate that, in his two detailed articles on the inscription, Professor Wrenn has chosen to give, not a careful drawing of the letters, but a diagrammatic representation. This is misleading, particularly in giving the impression that the Caistor-by-Norwich runes are cut between framing lines, which they are not.

etymologisches Wörterbuch (Bern, 1948–59), under *ei-* Farbadjectiv, p. 297.): and the Old English variation between *īw* and *īh* <*īwu* and **īhu* . . . is most naturally explicable if we suppose the rune *īh ēoh* to have originally represented the Germanic sound *hw'*. He goes on to argue that this identification accounts for the use of the rune in Anglo-Saxon inscriptions where it seems to correspond sometimes with *h*, sometimes with a vowel (? derived from the initial of the rune-name), and concludes with an interpretation of the Caistor-by-Norwich text which assumes a value *hw* for its third rune.[3] I find the argument quoted in detail above obscure, though by this admission I lay myself open to the Johnsonian retort, 'Sir, I have found you an argument; but I am not obliged to find you an understanding'. Yet it seems that Wrenn professes, first, that the Indo-European words which lead to OE *īw* and *īh* respectively, even if formed by means of different suffixes, yet most probably develop together through Gmc **eihwo*. This may be true but it is unlikely, and it is odd that Wrenn quotes Pokorny in support of the assertion, since that scholar, as I read him, suggests for the two Old English forms *īw* and *īh* two distinct Indo-European forbears, **eiuo-*, **ei-ko-*, neither of which is the obvious precursor of Gmc **eihwo*. I take the point of the second part of Wrenn's statement to be that, whereas the common noun for 'yew-tree' in Old English is *ēow*, *īw* the rune-name preserves the otherwise obsolete *ēoh*, *īh*, which suggests that the rune represents a sound approaching *h* in quality. The difficulty here is the small amount of evidence and its lateness compared with Caistor-by-Norwich. I cite the material in detail below, but meanwhile it is worth noting that the distinction between common noun and rune-name may not be so striking as the limited evidence suggests.[4]

Wrenn's interpretation of '3' as *hw* is not one generally accepted, for the great majority of scholars have thought this rune to be a vowel: so, for example, Bugge in his classic exposition of the material as it was then known in *Norges indskrifter med de ældre runer* I, 117–48, C. J. S. Marstrander who defines it as 'lukket ē', O. v. Friesen who describes it as 'kort, öppet e', W. Krause and H. Arntz as a 'Zwischenlaut zwischen e und i', R. W. V. Elliott as 'a high front vowel lying between *e* and *i*, representing an earlier *ei*' and K. Schneider as perhaps '*ẹ̄* sehr geschlossener Qualität'.[5] For the identification Wrenn supports himself on B. Dickins whose suggestion that '3' originally gave *hw* was a tentative one only, with no cited evidence other than the fact that the Gothic alphabet represented this sound by a single

---

[3] 'Magic in an Anglo-Saxon Cemetery', p. 309.
[4] For **ig*, 'yew-tree' (presumably closely related to *ih*) in place-names see A. H. Smith, *English Place-Name Elements*, EPNS 25–6 (Cambridge, 1956) I, s.v. *īw*, and J. K. Wallenberg, *The Place-Names of Kent* (Uppsala, 1934), p. 100.
[5] C. J. S. Marstrander, 'Om runene og runenavnenes oprindelse', *NTS* 1 (1928), 85–188, at 157, O. v. Friesen, *Runorna* (Stockholm, 1933), p. 9, W. Krause, *Runeninschriften im älteren Futhark* (Halle/Saale, 1937), p. 4, H. Arntz, *Handbuch der Runenkunde*, 2nd ed. (Halle/Saale, 1944), p. 72, Elliott, *Runes: an Introduction*, p. 16, K. Schneider, *Die germanischen Runennamen* (Meisenheim, 1956), p. 284. L. Musset and F. Mossé, *Introduction à la runologie* (Paris, 1965), p. 96 contrives to get the best of both worlds: ' "3" représente sans doute une voyelle intermédiaire entre *ē* et *i*, héritée de *ei* plus ancien. A peut-être reçu dans le domaine anglais la valeur consonantique *h*'.

symbol.[6] For this character the Vienna Nationalbibliothek, 795 manuscript gives the Gothic name *uuær* which 'has no apparent contact with any letter-name'[7] and certainly bears no resemblance to the name of '$\mathfrak{z}$'. With the appearance of an important new inscription using the letter (and possibly a second on the Loveden Hill urn) and with the publication of the whole Anglo-Saxon manuscript material on runes in R. Derolez's monumental *Runica Manuscripta* a fresh statement of the evidence becomes desirable:

(a) The Old English rune-name is variously given as *eoh* and *íh*. Though this name is not recorded outside the Anglo-Saxon tradition some confirmation is provided by the name *ýr* which the Scandinavians attached, not to the rune '$\mathfrak{z}$', but to that representing the sound -*R*. *Ýr* is related to OE *eoh/íh* and has the same meaning, for the Norwegian runic poem defines it as *vetrgrønstr viða*, 'greenest of trees throughout the winter', while in the Icelandic version it has the developed idea of *bendr bogi*, 'bent bow', since bows were commonly made of yew. The Old English name for the *R*-rune (which has the Anglo-Saxon value 'x') is *eolhx*, a word of uncertain etymology and meaning. The relationship between the two forms which have the three names *eoh, eolhx* and *ýr* is obscure,[8] and it may be significant that the *fuþorcs* without rune-names of MSS Cotton Galba A. II (in Hickes's facsimile) and St John's College, Oxford, 17 confuse the two runes, giving '$\mathfrak{z}$' the value *x* and 'x' the value (? rune-name) *iu*.

(b) The etymology of the Old English name for the yew-tree is disputed, since there are different Old English forms of the word. Besides *eoh* (? found only in the *Runic Poem*) and *íh* (perhaps also **ig*), there are *eow, iw*, and Old High German has the same distinction between velar and labial spellings in *ígo, íwa*. In consequence many scholars, including here Wrenn, have postulated a primitive form with labio-velar consonant: the *Oxford Dictionary of English Etymology* gives **íχwaz, *ígwaz, *íχwō , *ígwō* and Kluge's *Etymologisches Wörterbuch der deutschen Sprache *íhwa, *ígwa*, Dickins **ihwiz*, Krause **íhwaʀ*, Arntz and Elliott **eihwaz*, Schneider **eiχuaz, *íχuaz, *eiguaz, *íguaz*, Wrenn variously **eihwo, *ixwō*.[9] There are, however, alternative etymologies which do not involve the labio-velar. Walde-Pokorny postulate the root *ōiuā*, whose *Schwundstufe* gives OHG *íwa*, OE *íw*, ON *ýr*, the g forms having a secondary guttural 'wie in Jugend'; and Holthausen and Jóhannesson seem to agree.[10] F.

---

6 Dickins, 'System of Transliteration', p. 16.
7 J. Blomfield, 'Runes and the Gothic Alphabet', *SBVS* 12 (1937–45), 177–94 and 209–31, at 231.
8 Miss Blomfield describes the *eoh/ýr* relationship as 'an old divergence in the Scandinavian and Anglo-Frisian adaptations of Germanic rune-names' ('Runes and the Gothic Alphabet', p. 217).
9 B. Dickins, *Runic and Heroic Poems of the Old Teutonic Peoples* (Cambridge, 1915), p. 16, Krause, *Runeninschriften*, p. 4 (but **iwaz* in the second edition (Göttingen, 1966), pp. 4–5), Arntz, *Handbuch*, p. 206, Elliott, *Runes*, p. 55, Schneider, *Runennamen*, p. 283, Wrenn, 'Magic in an Anglo-Saxon Cemetery', p. 309, 'Cult Symbols', p. 45.
10 A. Walde and J. Pokorny, *Vergleichendes Wörterbuch der indogermanischen Sprachen* (Berlin and Leipzig, 1927–32) I, 165, F. Holthausen, *Altenglisches etymologisches Wörterbuch* (Heidelberg, 1934), s.v. *íw*, A. Jóhannesson, *Isländisches etymologisches Wörterbuch* (Bern, 1956), pp. 80–1.

Specht suggests a root *ei-* taking variant suffixes in *-u-* and *-k-* to give the Germanic doublets in *w* and *g/h*: de Vries follows him, quoting *ī̆waz* as the primitive form of *ẏr*.[11] Pokorny I have already cited. To A. H. Smith OE *ig* involves the replacement of *-w-* by *-g-* as also in *nige/niwe*, 'new', *Tig/Tiw*, 'the god Tiw', etc., but he does not say if he thinks *ih* a late spelling of *ig*, or a doublet derived with *iw* from an earlier labio-velar form.[12]

(c) In the runic manuscripts belonging to the English tradition '3' is given (i) the value *eo* in hand A of MS Cotton Domitian IX, though hand B, confusing the rune with *sigel*, names it wrongly, (ii) the value *eo* (apparently taken from Domitian IX) in Hickes's transcript of the Runic Poem: the name *eoh* accompanies a variant form of the character, (iii) the name *eth*, (?) wrongly for *eoh*, in the *fuþorc* of Galba A. II, (iv) the value (? rune-name) *iu* in the *fuþorcs* without rune-names of Galba A. II and St John's College, Oxford, 17, though, owing to an error in the archetype from which both descend, this has been transferred to '*x*', whose value is ascribed to '3', (v) the name *ih* and the value *i & h* or *i & ch* in Vienna 795, (vi) the name *inc* corrected to *ih* in another hand in MS Brussels, Kon. Bibl., 9311–9319, (vii) the name *ih*, with the curious value *k* in four of the *isruna* tracts and *h* in the fifth, (viii) the values *e, i (i), k* in various runic alphabets and other writings.[13]

(d) Old English preserves twenty-four names which correspond to the runes of the early *fuþark*. Fourteen of these are confirmed more or less by later Scandinavian tradition, eight are not recorded in Scandinavia, and in the case of two, ON *þurs* and *ẏr*, OE *þorn* and *eolhx*, the names are substantially different. Of the Old English names (excluding for the present '3') all but two are acrophonetic: these are *Ing*, representing *ŋ*, and *eolhx*, the name of the rare English rune for the little-needed *x* whose Germanic precursor was used for *-z* whence the common Scandinavian *-R*. There is good reason why these two rune-names do not follow the acrophonetic principle of the others for Old English, Old Norse and Germanic had no words beginning with the appropriate sounds. Hence there had to be chosen for these two runes names containing the sounds represented, but not beginning with them. There was no shortage of words beginning with *hw*, and so no difficulty in finding a suitable acrophonetic name.

Walde-Pokorny's reference to a secondary guttural is curious since Bugge's article ('Zur altgerman-ischen Sprachgeschichte: germanisch *ug* aus *uw*', *BGDSL* 13 (1888), 504–15) to which they refer (p. 200) deals only with the change *-uw-* > *-ug-*. W. v. Helten suggests ('Zum germanischen Zahlwort', *Indogermanische Forschungen* 18 (1905–6, 84–126, at 101–2) the change of *w* > *g* in other circumstances, but the case is hardly proven for **iwa* > **iga*.

[11] F. Specht, *Der Ursprung der indogermanischen Deklination* (Göttingen, 1944), p. 63, J. de Vries, *Altnordisches etymologisches Wörterbuch* (Leiden, 1961), s.v. *ẏr*.

[12] Smith, *English Place-Name Elements* I, s.v. *īw*; II, s.v. *nīge* and refs.

[13] The material of this paragraph is taken from Derolez, *Runica Manuscripta*. It may also be relevant that Middle English uses the name *yogh* for a character which represents among other sounds the spirant *χ*. Miss A. C. Paues derived the name from the Old English rune-name *eoh* ('The Name of the Letter 3', *MLR* 6 (1911), 441–54) though H. Bradley thought it was formed from the noun *3o3oþ* (*MLR* 7 (1912), 520–1).

(e)   The Anglo-Saxon rune-masters used 'ᴣ' in 'ᵢᴣslhêard' (= *Gislheard*) on the Dover stone where it is a vowel rune, in 'almeᴣttig' on the Ruthwell Cross and 'toroᴣtredæ' (= *Torhtredæ*) on the Great Urswick stone where it represents a spirant, and in 'êateᴣnne' (= *Eadþegne*) on one of the Thornhill stones where it corresponds to palatalised *g*, the sound here perhaps approaching the vocalic.[14] The rune is also found in as yet unclarified contexts: in the sequences 'hᴣræ' and 'ælᴣjæliêa' on the Brunswick (Gandersheim) Casket, and in 'sbe/r/ædhtᴣbcai' on the silver fitting found in the Thames. In the two newly found inscriptions to be discussed briefly here, 'ᴣ' appears in 'ræᴣhæn' on the Caistor-by-Norwich astragalus and perhaps in 'sᴣþæbæd' or 'sᴣþæbld' on the Loveden Hill urn.

The material adduced presents a confused picture, perhaps because it comes from a wide range of places and times. One conclusion seems fairly clear to me, though it may not to others. If *eoh, ih* is the original rune-name it is unlikely that the character represented *hw*. This I conclude partly from the uncertainty as to whether the Germanic name for 'yew-tree' ever contained the sound *hw*; partly from the fact that *uuaer*, the name of the Gothic letter whose existence is held to support the identification 'ᴣ' = *hw*, is so clearly unrelated to *eoh, ih* though the great majority of Gothic letter names are quite closely connected with their runic equivalents; but principally from the fact that the inventor of the rune-names had no need to leave his general acrophonetic principle in devising a name for a character representing *hw*. It is true that many scholars believe in the close affinity between the Germanic rune-names and magical practices and beliefs, and they might argue that, since the yew-tree was held to possess magical powers, the inventor of the rune-names might wish to name one of his symbols after the charmed tree. Had he been determined on this, he could have called the 'i' rune *ih*, suppressed the name *is* and named his *hw* rune by a word beginning with that sound.

Equally well, however, it is hard to defend *eoh, ih* as the original name of the rune form for, unless the suggested etymologies of that name are totally wrong, the development of its initial vowel through Germanic into Primitive Old English differs in no way from that of *is*, the name of 'i'.[15] Thus either 'i' or 'ᴣ' would be otiose since both would represent the same sound. That 'i' had the precedence in this task is confirmed by its form and by its common use with the value *i* from the earliest runic times. I therefore suggest that *eoh, ih* does not derive from the primary rune-name but from a renaming brought about by the fact that either the letter's primary function had been superseded so that its form could be re-used with a new value, or the rune had retained its primary function which was no longer consistent with the rune-name, perhaps because that had undergone some sound change affecting its beginning. That

---

[14] K. D. Bülbring, *Altenglisches Elementarbuch* I (Heidelberg, 1902), p. 204, Brunner, *Altenglische Grammatik*, § 126 (2).

[15] See, however, W. Krause's distinction in 'Untersuchungen zu den Runennamen II', *Nachrichten der Akademie der Wissenschaften in Göttingen, philologisch-historische Klasse* (1948), 93–108, at 96 and below, p. 140.

runes were sometimes renamed (and sometimes simultaneously given a new value) can be readily demonstrated. Of the pair OE *þorn*, ON *þurs*, at least one must be an innovation, and it is reasonable to assume that the Christian Anglo-Saxons removed *þurs* because of its superstitious connotations. In England and perhaps in Frisia too the old *ansuz-rune was early given a new name *æsc* and a new fronted value.

If *eoh*, *ih* does not represent the original rune-name points (a) and (b) above are irrelevant, and the case for identifying 'ʒ' as *hw* is made even weaker. An explanation satisfying points (c) to (e) concerns the development of initial *c* to *h* in Primitive Germanic times. After this change the rune *hægel*, whose initial consonant was now the aspirate, may have been thought no longer suitable for the medial and final χ which remained. The old symbol 'ʒ' may have been revived for expressing this sound and given a new name. Since initial χ no longer existed (except in combination with *w*) the rune-name could not begin with the sound represented, but could contain it, as indeed *eoh*, *ih* does. This name may have been chosen out of all the words containing the spirant because it was sanctified by old usage, being the name of the old *z*-rune which had become *ýr* in Scandinavia and obsolete in England.[16] The revived rune would then have been used for the spirant as on the Ruthwell Cross and the Great Urswick stone, and as may be intended by the transliteration *h* in runic manuscripts.[17] The name and the prevalence of the acrophonetic system of naming runes may have led unskilful rune-masters into believing it could be used for the front vowel or the diphthong *eo*. Hence the Dover stone inscription and the transliterations *e*, *i*, *eo* in manuscripts. Hence perhaps too on the agate amulet ring in the British Museum the curious form ⟨ which resembles 'ʒ' and replaces the 'i' found in the other two examples of the magical formula.[18] The Vienna 795 value *i & h* (if it means that the rune can stand for both *i* and *h*)[19] may have been put in by a skilled runologist who knew in practice the character was used for both these sounds. The occasional value *k* in runic manuscripts is a plain error.

This explanation omits any discussion of the earlier value of the symbol 'ʒ' which had been abandoned at any rate quite early in the Anglo-Saxon period, and the question naturally arises whether Caistor-by-Norwich 'ræʒhæn' and Loveden Hill 's3þæbæd'/'s3þæbld' use 'ʒ' in its old or in its new value. The letter can hardly represent the spirant on Loveden Hill if the first group of runes of that inscription is a pronounceable word. The sequence 's3þ' points rather to a vowel value. If the

---

[16] In 'Om Runene', p. 157, Marstrander argues cogently that *ýr* cannot represent the original name of the old *z*-rune since *z* would not be essential in the word, but only a part of its nominative singular ending. He also accepts that *eoh*, *ih* cannot descend from the original name of 'ʒ' arguing that *eow*, *ýr* are both 'utviklinger, event. omformninger . . . av et oldgermansk runenavn, hvis første fonem var ę̄- og som i historisk tid feilagtig blev associeret med *īwa*- "barlind" '.

[17] There are a number of cases of 'h' used for the spirant, perhaps as a result of roman influence on runic usage: for example, 'eoh worohtæ' Kirkheaton, 'gewarahtæ' Mortain, 'berhtsuiþe' Thornhill, and 'wihtred', '+wihtrr', moneyers' names on Mercian and Northumbrian coins, as well as the unique 'g' in 'fegtaþ' Franks Casket. Some Northumbrian Wihtred coins have for the spirant a form resembling 'ʒ', but this is probably N for H, set askew, in an otherwise runic legend.

[18] D. M. Wilson, 'A Group of Anglo-Saxon Amulet Rings', *The Anglo-Saxons: Studies . . . presented to Bruce Dickins*, ed. P. Clemoes (London, 1959), pp. 159–70, at 167.

[19] See on this Derolez, *Runica Manuscripta*, pp. 59–60.

Caistor-by-Norwich text is a single word – and its general appearance on the bone suggests it is – '3' is unlikely to be a spirant since the 'h' which follows immediately upon it probably gives that sound. Thus in these two inscriptions '3' could either be the *i* recorded in the manuscripts, or the primary sound which the spirant superseded. In the Caistor-by-Norwich case one piece of evidence suggests the latter. The inscription's fourth rune is 'h', but of a form unexpected in an Old English text. The typical Anglo-Saxon, and indeed West Germanic, 'h' has two sloping cross-bars, Ⱨ; the 'h' of the North and East Germanic inscriptions (which is the type found on Caistor-by-Norwich) has only one, Ⱨ. As far as we can tell from extant material the formal distinction is significant. No North Germanic example has two cross-bars, save perhaps that on the Stenmagle, Sjælland, box, where the lines are nowhere near parallel, one being considerably shallower than any other part of the text, and probably accidental or incorrect.[20] Leaving aside Caistor-by-Norwich for the moment, no West Germanic text has one cross-bar, save the Hailfingen, Württemberg, sax where a pair of dubious examples accompany other curious and suspect forms, and the Sandwich stone which requires more detailed examination.[21] The border between areas using single- and double-barred forms cannot be plotted with precision. The single-barred 'h' occurs throughout Scandinavia from earliest times, with its most southerly examples at Torsbjerg, Angeln, and Gallehus, just north of the present Danish frontier. The double-barred 'h' is amply evidenced in Frisia as early as the sixth century when it appears on the Harlingen solidus, and in other West Germanic inscriptions from further south. A wide area in southern Schleswig-Holstein, Lower Saxony and Westphalia remains in which no runes have yet been found, and its 'h' type, if indeed the script was used there at all, is unknown. On this evidence Caistor-by-Norwich has closer affinities with North than with West Germanic inscriptions or indeed with other texts from Anglo-Saxon England. Archaeologically, the cemetery shows influence from Schleswig and North Holstein as well as from Frisia. It is clearly likely that the Caistor-by-Norwich value for '3' compares with that in the North Germanic material more closely than with that shown from Anglo-Saxon England, where it may have been affected by purely insular developments.

Inevitably Sophus Bugge's elaborate examination of the evidence for '3' in *Norges indskrifter med de ældre runer* is outdated. Bugge's texts from the Gilton pommel, the Thames fitting and the Thornhill 'êate3nne' stone are now quite indefensible, while the validity of some of his cited Scandinavian material is doubtful. Indeed it has been authoritatively stated that the only Scandinavian text which gives a useful

---

[20] A. Bæksted, 'The Stenmagle Rune Box and the Golden Horn Inscription', *Acta Archaeologica* 18 (1947), 202–10, at 204, fig. 2.
[21] For Hailfingen see Arntz and Zeiss, *Die einheimischen Runendenkmäler*, pp. 242–5. Sandwich has N which has traditionally been read 'h', though there seems no reason why it could not equally well be 's' (cf. the 's' of 'gisl' on the Franks Casket). This stone needs reconsideration in view of Miss V. I. Evison's criticism (*Antiquaries Journal* 40 (1960), 243–4) of the commonly accepted reading. A single-barred 'h' may have existed in MS Cotton Otho B. X, but this survives only in Hickes's transcript, and Hickes may have misread a double-barred form with one faded cross-stave. On these runes see Derolez, *Runica Manuscripta*, p. 24.

indication of the value of '3' is the Danneberg bracteate legend **gl3augiʀu 3urnʀ**.[22] This is usually read, expanded and divided *Gleaugiʀ weu r(u)n(o)ʀ* which Krause translates, '(Ich,) der Glanzäugige, weihe die Runen'.[23] *Gle-* is related to the Swedish dialectal *glia*, ON *gljá*, 'glitter', and *weu* to the early runic form *wiju* on the Kragehul spearshaft, and to ON *vígja* which appears on later Danish monuments in such contexts as **þur:uiki:runaʀ**, 'Thor hallow (these) runes' on the Sønder Kirkeby stone. On this evidence '3' represents a high front vowel in the region of *i*. Two Continental Germanic examples, those of the Freilaubersheim, Rheinhessen, and Nordendorf, Bavaria, A brooches, add little since their interpretations are uncertain. Freilaubersheim **þk:da[þ]3na go[d]a** (bracketed runes unclear) has been read *þ(i)k Daþena godda*, 'Dich beschenkte (?) Dathena'. Though there is disagreement over some details of both reading and translation, most scholars require a vowel (? *i* or *e*) for '3'.[24] Nordendorf's **awaleubwini∫**, the final symbol very crudely cut and not clearly recognisable, gives no information since the text could perfectly well do without '3' at the end (= *Awa Leubwini*, two personal names), and several scholars prefer to read the form as a closing punctuation mark.[25] Courageous attempts have been made to justify it as a rune, and to read, for example, *awa Leubwinie* (-*ie* for -*ii*), 'divine protection for Leubwini', though the ending is odd and it is hard to explain the use of '3' side by side with 'i' and 'e'.

From this brief and inadequate survey of the comparative material there seems some support for the belief that '3' was originally a vowel rune, no sign that it was ever used for *hw*. If there was an early high front vowel, the Anglo-Saxon examples of '3' = *i* are more likely to be survivals of it than the misconceptions of unskilled runologists taking the rune-name *eoh, íh* at its face value. The question naturally arises why the inventor(s) of runic script thought a high front vowel rune '3' was needed in addition to 'e' and 'i'. Krause argues for two *i*-phonemes in Primitive Germanic, one given by 'i' (= **eisaz/*eisan*) deriving from earlier *ei* and falling together in quality with the open sound of Germanic short *i*, the other given by '3' (= **īwaz*) deriving from IE *ī*. '3' he sees as a modified form of 'i'.[26] Some such explanation as this is likely, though Krause admits that the surviving runic inscriptions do not reflect this distinction accurately, while his theory puts the invention of runes back to at least the first century B.C., which is embarrassing in view of the fact that the earliest surviving examples are from some centuries later.

This paper has followed a speculative rather than a logical course, inevitably in view of the ambiguity of much of the cited material. I have tried to show that the reading of '3' as *hw* is based on conjecture largely unsanctioned by evidence, and that there is some case for taking '3' as a vowel rune in the region of *i*. The appearance

---

[22] Jacobsen and Moltke, *Danmarks runeindskrifter*, col. 952; Krause, 'Untersuchungen', p. 96; C. J. S. Marstrander, 'Om innskriften på sølvfibulaen fra Freilaubersheim', *NTS* 16 (1952), 355–64, at 362.

[23] Krause, *Runeninschriften*, pp. 56–7.

[24] *Ibid.* p. 212. See also Arntz and Zeiss, *Die einheimischen Runendenkmäler*, pp. 226–8 for the form *Daléna*, and Marstrander, 'Sølvfibulaen fra Freilaubersheim', pp. 362–3 for *Râdalîna*.

[25] See, for example, Krause, *Runeninschriften*, p. 204, Arntz and Zeiss, *Die einheimischen Runendenkmäler*, pp. 288–90.

[26] Krause, 'Untersuchungen', p. 96.

of the two new inscriptions of Caistor-by-Norwich and Loveden Hill enables us to test these two assertions. In runic studies destruction is easier and safer than creation, and I have already used the new texts to demonstrate the first. Checking the second is more difficult, principally because neither Caistor-by-Norwich nor Loveden Hill have known parallels elsewhere, so that we are at a loss as to the context in which to take these legends and the sense to expect.

Wrenn thinks Caistor-by-Norwich a magical inscription arguing (i) an interpretation of the legend as 'the deeply sacred and mysterious word' *rah(w)han*, 'divine power', related to ON *ragina-, ragino-* on rune-stones, ON *regin*, 'the gods', the Old Norse and Old English personal name elements *Ragn-, Rægen*, and OE *regn-* in compounds, (ii) simultaneously the interpretation of its runes, according to their names, as cult symbols invoking the world of the gods and of death, (iii) that the astragali found in the urn were used in some sort of magical game perhaps related to the astragalomancy of the ancients, or more clearly to the lot-casting or gambling of the Germani, (iv) the magical nature of the number 30, which is that of the astragali found in the urn, and of 33, which is the number of cylindrical (actually plano-convex) bone pieces, apparently belonging to some sort of board game, found with them. (i) is disposed of if we reject '3' as *hw* though it is perhaps also worth noting that in general scholars do not accept the derivation of ON *ragina-* etc. from an earlier form with labio-velar.[27] While (ii) is possible it is susceptible neither to proof nor to disproof, yet it is a strange coincidence that a group of runes which have a magical meaning by virtue of the sounds they represent, also carry a parallel meaning by virtue of the symbolism of their names. (iii) is possible. Indeed it is likely that these astragali were used in some game or other, for the shape and size of the bones are suited to counters, pieces, etc.[28] Van Hamel has suggested, but not proved, that some Germanic games were linked to magic,[29] but the Germani must surely have had non-magical games too if they were the great gamblers that Tacitus describes. The astragali could have been used in divination or lot casting, but is it not likely then that more than one of them would have a distinguishing mark? (iv) would be more convincing if we knew exactly how many astragali the Caistor-by-Norwich urn contained. Wrenn himself speaks of 'about thirty', 'the thirty astragali of the Caistor urn', 'one astragalus' together with 'some thirty others'.[30] In fact the exact number is unknown, for many are fragmentary, poorly preserved, and hard to distinguish from pieces of burnt bone from the cremated body.

So far I have argued against Professor Wrenn's reading of Caistor-by-Norwich, but have put nothing in its place. It is proper that I make at least a tentative suggestion, and accordingly I give the following, reading *raihan*. This word could be related to the root **rei-*, 'scratch, cut, tear', which, with the *-k(h)-* suffix gives such Germanic

---

[27] Walde and Pokorny, *Wörterbuch der indogermanischen Sprachen* I, 863, Jóhannesson, *Isländisches etymologisches Wörterbuch*, p. 716.

[28] Note the comment in P. V. Addyman *et al.*, 'A Dark-Age Settlement at Maxey, Northants.', *Medieval Archaeology* 8 (1964), 20–73, at 71: 'There is not a single example of a sheep astragalus, which may be fortuitous, but may also be due to the use of this bone for some purpose'.

[29] A. G. v. Hamel, 'The Game of the Gods', *ANF* 50 (1934), 218–42, esp. 229–33.

[30] 'twenty-four' in 'Celts and Saxons'!

words as OHG *riga*, 'line', *rīhan*, 'arrange in line', ON *rá*, *rámerki*, 'landmark, boundary', and, with suffix differentiation, OE *raw*, *ræw*, 'row'.[31] From this stem could be formed a *nomen agentis* **raiho*, acting either as a common noun, 'inscriber, (?) rune-master, (?) one who sets things out in rows', or subsequently as a personal name comparable with OE *Beta*, *Wealda*, *Hunta*, **Ridda*. *raihan* could be a Primitive Old Norse oblique form: cf. **wita(n)dahalaiban** on the Tune stone.[32] The text would then mean something like '(This belongs) to **Raiho*' or '(the property) of **Raiho*'. Possibly **raiho* could mean 'the object which marks' and apply to the bone itself, and the oblique case might then mean '(acting as) marker'. An alternative explanation of *raihan* would derive it from the root **rei-*, 'coloured, dappled' with *-ko-* suffix, and so relate it to OE *raha*, *ra*, 'roebuck', *ræge*, 'roe'.[33] A *nomen agentis* formed from this stem could perhaps mean 'stainer, colourer', which connects readily with the cutting of runic inscriptions since the Old Norse verb often used for this activity is *fá*, 'draw, paint', and some runic legends were certainly painted.[34] Thus **raiho* may mean 'painter, i.e. rune-master'. In his discussion of the place-name Teversall, Notts., E. Ekwall considers the element *tiefrere*, *tefrere* which he derives from OE *teafor*, 'raddle used as a pigment'. This word's cognates ON *taufr*, OHG *zoubur* mean 'magic', and Ekwall suggests that *tiefrere* might mean 'sorcerer'.[35] By a similar semantic process **raiho*, 'colourer', might develop the same meaning.

Professor Wrenn also records the runes of Loveden Hill urn 61/251, though he gives no detailed examination of the text. The first seven runes he reads *SIÞÆ*(or *A*)*BÆ*(or *A*)*G*, surely incorrectly.[36] Rune 2 is certainly not 'i'. It is probably 'ʒ', though slightly irregular in form being set too close to 's' and with its lower arm horizontal instead of sloping upwards away from the stem. It is thus tempting to reject the lower arm, cut more slightly than the rest of the letter, as an accidental gash, and to read 'l' (which would of course present the awkward sequence 'slþ'). However, the shape of this rune is more satisfactorily explained by considering the way it was cut in the clay. The rune-master made both first and second letters in three separate strokes, working from top to bottom. For 'ʒ' he cut (1) the upper arm, and being without the stem to guide him, made this too far to the left, (2) the stem, which is thus too near 's', (3) the lower arm, which he cut horizontal, perhaps in an attempt to avoid 's'. Rune 7 is certainly not 'g' but a clear 'd'. Rune 6 is something of a problem: a stem made from two parallel incisions has either one arm of two incisions

---

[31] Walde and Pokorny, *Wörterbuch der indogermanischen Sprachen* I, 857–8.

[32] Krause, *Runeninschriften*, p. 116.

[33] Walde and Pokorny, *Wörterbuch der indogermanischen Sprachen* I, 859.

[34] See, for example, the stones of Einang, Valdres (Krause, *Runeinschriften*, p. 77), and Valby, Vestfold (v. Friesen, *Runorna*, p. 85) and the Åsum bracteate (Jacobsen and Moltke, *Danmarks runeindskrifter*, cols 538–9). For literary references to painted runes see *Hávamál* v. 157, and *Guðrunarkviða* II, v. 22 (*Edda*, ed. G. Neckel, 3rd ed. rev. H. Kuhn (Heidelberg, 1962)), and the well-known line from Venantius Fortunatus *barbara fraxineis pingatur runa tabellis*. The Viking London stone (Jacobsen and Moltke, *Danmarks runeindskrifter*, cols 478–9) was certainly painted, and occasional Anglo-Saxon examples, Maughold, Isle of Man, and perhaps Collingham, show traces of red colouring.

[35] E. Ekwall, *The Concise Oxford Dictionary of English Place-Names*, 4th ed. (Oxford, 1960), s.n.

[36] In 'Cult Symbols', p. 51 Wrenn includes a photograph which shows up well the first part of this inscription.

or two arms of one each. Thus it is either 'æ' or 'l'. On the whole the appearance suggests the first. For this group of runes I read 's3(or 'l')þæbæ(or 'l')d' with the possibility that the 'æ' runes represent *a*. After this come two vertical cuts, probably dividing lines, followed by eight rune-like characters split into two groups of four by two further dividing lines. These seem to be 'þ(or 'w')icw(or 'þ') | hlæ[.]', the final form unclear. There are difficulties about both 'c' and 'h' while 'æ' has a double stem as in the earlier group, so that I do not propose to discuss this inscription in detail here. However, it is worth considering if a vowel value for '3' in the first word makes any obvious sense. We have to explain a form *siþabad/siþabld/siþæbæd/ siþæbld*. *siþabld* suggests a personal name *Siþabald* with omission of the vowel before *ld* as in Westeremden A **jisuhldu**. I know of no *Siþabald* in Anglo-Saxon records, but *-bald* is a common second element while *Siðe-* is a less frequent first one, combining with *-man*, *-red*, *-wine* and others.[37] *Siþa-*, or perhaps better *Siþæ-*, seems a possible early form of this element.

Of course these interpretations of the Caistor-by-Norwich and Loveden Hill runes are not intended to be final; they are tentative suggestions only, called forth by the need to replace Professor Wrenn's reading, which are also tentative and I think wrong. In particular I wish to show that his acceptance of '3' = *hw* is casual and inadequately documented, and to justify an alternative transliteration. I doubt if either of these inscriptions will ever be interpreted with certainty. In the much richer Scandinavian field there remain many early texts whose meaning is a matter of conjecture and of individual choice between several possibilities, each etymologically justifiable. The difficulty is that we have no idea what range of inscriptions a Dark Age people would put on grave-goods, funeral furniture, etc., nor do we know who the legends were addressed to or composed by.

---

[37] *Side-* may have been more fruitful in forming personal names than the recorded examples show. Occasional place-names suggest *Side-* names not otherwise known, as, for example, *Sidelac, Side-lakesham* 1213–28 in Eynsham, Oxon., and *Sidelufu*, Sidlow Mill (*Sideluue melne* late 12th), Surrey. Professor Whitelock draws my attention to a form with spirant, *Siðe-* in an Anglo-Saxon will which she hopes to publish. [This will, Sawyer 1497, now Princeton, Scheide Library, MS M140, was edited by Dorothy Whitelock *et al.*, *The Will of Æthelgifu: a Tenth Century Anglo-Saxon Manuscript* (Oxford, 1968). The name *siðemon* occurs on l. 57, pp. 14–15, but the letter *ð* is not as distinctive as one would like it. The will is also illustrated, as pl. 15 in *Facsimiles of Anglo-Saxon Charters*, ed. S. Keynes, Anglo-Saxon Charters, Supplementary Volume 1 (Oxford, 1991).]

POSTSCRIPT

After lying in lethargy for some years, this topic has been revived by discoveries reported in Mark Blackburn's preliminary discussion of the English runic coinage.[38] The earliest example he quotes is on a coin type from the second quarter of the eighth century bearing a form of the moneyer's name *Tilberht*. A newly-found specimen from Beechamwell, Norfolk, bears, he believes and probably rightly, the form 't i l b e r i t'.[39] Blackburn also identifies the 'i' rune on two ninth-century Northumbrian dies with the names *Dægberht* (in the form dEBeit) and *Wihtred* ('w i i t r e d').[40] The latter is an example I considered and rejected in 1968 (cf. my note 17), but on more mature thought I am inclined to accept it. These two examples parallel the use of the rune as a spirant in Ruthwell 'a l m e i t t i g'.

Blackburn quotes a further example, which I still remain sceptical of. He finds it on one of the mid eighth-century coins of Beonna of East Anglia, the die of the moneyer Werferþ. A royal title which I have presented as REss for *rex*, Blackburn would prefer to see as rEis (the first letter could be either roman or runic), with the statement that 'this character [i.e. 'i'] does appear to be a deliberate' *eoh/ih* rune.[41] While respecting Blackburn's experience in reading coin legends, I have to confess I am less certain of this identification, particularly in view of the undoubted form REss in other Beonna dies. Readers may make their own assessments.[42] I wonder what pronunciation a spelling 'rEis' would imply.

In these controversial days it is cheering to note that the interpretations I gave in 1968 to the Caistor-by-Norwich and Loveden Hill contexts of the *eoh/ih* rune seem to have been generally accepted.[43]

[38] 'A Survey of Anglo-Saxon and Frisian Coins with Runic Inscriptions', *Old English Runes*, ed. Bammesberger, pp. 137–89.
[39] *Ibid.* p. 155. I use here my more recent suggestion for transliteration of this rune, 'i': cf. p. 257 below.
[40] 'Anglo-Saxon and Frisian Coins', p. 156.
[41] *Ibid.* p. 159.
[42] *Old English Runes*, ed. Bammesberger, pl. 6, no. 28 (? rEis), no. 29 (REss). Cf. above, p. 6, n. 18.
[43] Cf. J. Hines, 'Some Observations on the Runic Inscriptions of Early Anglo-Saxon England', *Old English Runes*, ed. Bammesberger, pp. 61–83, at 79.

12

(1968)

THE RUNIC SOLIDUS OF SCHWEINDORF, OSTFRIESLAND, AND RELATED RUNIC SOLIDI

In one of the more important runological publications of recent years Dr Peter Berghaus and Professor Karl Schneider report on a new runic solidus, that of Schweindorf, Ostfriesland, discovered in 1948 and now in the Ostfriesisches Landesmuseum, Emden (pl. 1, a, b).[1] This solidus bears one of the distinctive Anglo-Frisian characters, the rune *ac*. It comes from a region where runes had not previously been found and which lies between the area of the 'Continental Anglo-Frisian' inscriptions[2] and that part of south-Denmark/Angeln which supplies several of the early North Germanic inscriptions. Moreover it links with two other runic solidi, both rather mysterious, the *hada* piece from Harlingen, Friesland (pl. 1, c, d), and the *skanomodu* solidus of unknown provenance, now in the British Museum (pl. 1, e–g).[3] In their monograph Berghaus and Schneider consider these three runic objects as a group, hoping thereby to cast light on the date of each, and on the meanings of their three legends. Though their paper is stimulating and publishes important new material, I think its form is in some ways unfortunate and I disagree with some of its conclusions. So I think it desirable, even at this early date, to act as *advocatus diaboli*, to examine the arguments the two scholars put forward and to define what I take to be their inaccuracies and weaknesses. Both numismatic and runic studies are specialized fields of work; there is always the danger that opinions expressed by experts in those fields on slender evidence will harden into an orthodoxy too readily accepted by people whose special knowledge lies elsewhere.

The monograph on the Schweindorf solidus divides into two parts, the first, by Berghaus, on the numismatic significance of the find, the second, by Schneider, on

---

[1] *Anglo-friesische Runensolidi im Lichte des Neufundes von Schweindorf (Ostfriesland)* (Cologne and Opladen, 1967).
[2] The phrase ' "Continental Anglo-Frisian" inscriptions' is deliberately vague. I avoid the question of the language of these texts, and refer only to their geographical distribution.
[3] The *skanomodu* solidus was part of George III's collection, given to the British Museum in 1825, but we do now know how it came into his possession, whether by inheritance or gift, from his English or Continental territories or farther afield. The manuscript catalogue, compiled in 1771 and checked up to 1814, gives no details of it, nor has any information been traced in the Queen's Archives, Windsor Castle. Professor A. Aspinall tells me that he has found no mention of the solidus in George III's correspondence.

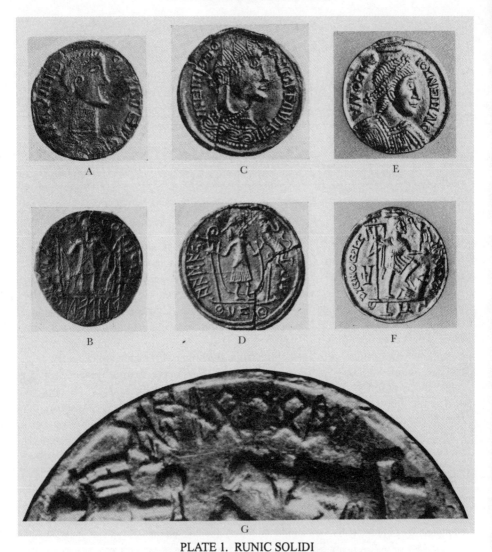

PLATE 1. RUNIC SOLIDI
A, B. Schweindorf, Ostfriesland. Sc. 3:2
C, D. Harlingen, Friesland. Sc. 3:2
E, F. Unprovenanced, now in the British Museum. Sc. 3:2
G. Enlargement of the *skanomodu* legend of the British Museum solidus. Sc. *c.* 6:1

its runological aspects and on religious considerations which he believes are bound up with them. These two parts are interlocking but each is to some degree independent, and this leads to structural weakness.

Dr Berghaus's section has two main themes. The first is a discussion of the relationships between the Schweindorf, Harlingen and *skanomodu* pieces, and between them and solidi from Uppsala and Wieuwerd, Friesland, and a number of coins of similar design. Berghaus establishes the dependence of the *skanomodu* piece upon late Roman coins, connecting the reverse specifically with a type from Ravenna. This gives him a *terminus post quem* of 402–3, the date of foundation of that mint. The reverses of Harlingen and Schweindorf derive from a similar design, though they are more remote. According to Berghaus the debased legend of their obverses links them to coins of Theodosius II (402–50). On typological grounds he puts the three runic solidi in order of fabrication, *skanomodu*, Harlingen, Schwein-dorf, and assigns them to the sixth century. Schweindorf must be somewhat earlier than the Wieuwerd hoard, buried 630–40, for that contains imitations of sixth-century gold coins, and a cast solidus, similar in many respects to Schweindorf, based on a later prototype. The runic solidi must be later than the two struck gold coins (from one pair of dies) from Kälder and Hovor, both in Gotland, ascribed on archaeological grounds to the fifth century, and they are fairly close in time to some of the Scandinavian gold bracteates. This gives Berghaus a date in the last decades of the sixth century for Schweindorf, in the third quarter of that century for Harlingen, and in its first quarter for *skanomodu*, which must be close to the similar Botes, Gotland, solidi, buried after 518.

It is hard for anyone who is not a numismatist to appreciate fully the validity of the arguments which an expert like Dr Berghaus puts forward. Inevitably, the specialist bases his work on a mass of material known generally to himself and his colleagues, and which therefore neither needs nor gets detailed exposition, though it may be unknown to the stranger in the field. I do not go beyond my knowledge in attacking Berghaus's arguments, but content myself with listing those points on which I personally would like more detailed comment. Specifically, I would enquire into the connexions of *skanomodu* with Ravenna, and Harlingen and Schweindorf with Theodosius II. The sole evidence quoted for the Ravenna link is the inverted 'A' to the left of the standing figure of the *skanomodu* piece. This Berghaus thinks 'ein missverstandener Überrest des R–V der Münzstättenangabe RaVenna'. From conversation with Dr Berghaus I understand that by this he means to derive the inverted 'A' from the Ravenna V, though the latter always appears to the right of the standing figure. To the novice in these matters it seems equally possible to regard inverted 'A' as a corruption of the initial M (to the figure's left) of MeDiolanum (Milan), and this could allow an earlier date for the prototype of *skanomodu*. Berghaus favours Ravenna partly because of the large numbers of coins issued by that mint, but Mediolanum also had a substantial output. Dr J. P. C. Kent draws my attention to two mints, active at about this time, whose mint-letters begin with A, Arles (A–R) and Aquileia (A–Q). Either of these could have provided the prototype for *skanomodu*, which would then invert the initial mint-letter, but their coins are rare and Mediolanum remains more likely. Though Berghaus links Harlingen (and Schweindorf) with Theodosius II, H. Zeiss thought the former derived from a coin of Theodosius I,[4] and certainly a specimen which J. W. E. Pearce ascribes to the first

---

[4] Arntz and Zeiss, *Die einheimischen Runendenkmäler*, p. 259.

Theodosius looks to a non-specialist an equally likely original for Harlingen.[5] Here again the size of the issue, larger for Theodosius II than for Theodosius I, is a relevant consideration, though not perhaps a decisive one.

These points of detail I regard of some importance, though they do not affect the main line of Berghaus's argument, since he nowhere uses them to determine the dates of his three solidi. At the most they reveal, perhaps, some lack of rigour in his argumentation. More important is a question involving method, and here I would ask: what degree of precision of dating does Berghaus claim for his group of three solidi (which show a good deal of individual variation) ordered on typological grounds between termini imprecisely established? Specifically, what limits would he set for the *skanomodu* solidus, dated with reference to two types (four specimens) found as far from the Anglo-Frisian area as Gotland?[6] Were his opinions on dating assisted or confirmed by Schneider's findings on the runological and linguistic evidence?

Berghaus's second theme is the nature and purpose of these solidi. He concludes that they were not coins but amulets, and cites the following evidence: (i) they are cast, not struck like the coins they derive from, (ii) they were fitted with loops for suspension, (iii) their inscriptions are appropriate to amulets, (iv) two of them, Schweindorf and Harlingen, have in the neighbourhood of their inscriptions pairs of circles with dots at their centres (*Punktringel*) which he calls *Augenpaare*, and which he thinks have 'zweifellos eine apotropäische Bedeutung'.[7] A tentative (v) is the relative position of obverse and reverse designs, the die-axes as they would be on struck coins. On the five related solidi in question, the three runic and the non-runic from Uppsala and Wieuwerd, these are either ↑↑ or ↑↓: 'Es ist nicht ausgeschlossen, dass den Münzen damit magische Eigenschaften gegeben werden sollten'.

Point (i) needs modification. I have not seen Schweindorf, nor have I looked at Harlingen with this consideration in mind, but Dr Berghaus has confirmed to me that he does not doubt that both were cast. The case of *skanomodu* is different. Several numismatists expressed doubt about Berghaus's judgement here, and the piece was sent to the British Museum Research Laboratory where it was examined by the X-ray diffraction back-reflection technique. The result showed that it was undoubtedly struck, not cast, so that it stands distinct in manufacturing method from Schweindorf and Harlingen. Even accepting Berghaus's submissions, his conclusions are not sustained by the evidence he cites. As he himself notes, (i) and (ii) suggest that the solidi were not coins, but do not prove them amulets. They could be decorative brooches, pendants or medalets. (iii) I want to discuss extensively in considering

5 J. W. E. Pearce, *The Roman Imperial Coinage* IX (London, 1951), p. 84 and pl. vi, 10.
6 Berghaus notes (*Anglo-friesische Runensolidi*, p. 20) the late survival in England of early types, though he draws no conclusion from the observation.
7 Schneider also regards the circles as important, but gives a different explanation (*Anglo-friesische Runensolidi*, p. 70). They are 'als Sternzeichen für Morgen- und Abendstern aufzufassen, und damit als Symbolzeichen für die beiden jugendlichen Götterbrüder, die im idg./germ. Glaubensbereich mit Morgen- und Abendstern zusammengebracht oder gar identifiziert wurden'. I am not clear how he regards one of these dotted circles when it appears alone.

Schneider's contribution to the monograph. Only (iv) and a tentative (v) remain for consideration at this point.

Before I go into (iv) in detail, a question of method presents itself. Out of the five solidi which Berghaus relates together, only two have *Augenpaare*, and it is reasonable to ask: even if *Augenpaare* were proved to have magical significance, would this necessarily imply that the three solidi without them were also amulets? Does the resemblance of design of the five pieces necessarily prove identity of function? I am not clear that it does, particularly as regards *skanomodu*, which is markedly closer to its prototype than the others. But in any case, are these particular *Augenpaare* magical, as Berghaus (iv) asserts? The circle with a dot at its centre is common enough in Germanic contexts where we might expect magic or an appeal to supernatural powers. Often it is connected with runes. There are several examples on the Kowel spear-head together with other symbols, including an elaborate swastika and a retrograde runic weapon-name. They appear on bracteates in company with such recognizably magical runic words as *laukaʀ* and *laþu*. The Hunstanton swastika-brooch with its rune-like forms has twenty. Berghaus himself does not cite strong evidence to show that his *Augenpaare* are magical, but is content with noting these dotted circles, sometimes singly, sometimes in pairs, on a number of sixth- and seventh-century coins from the Rhineland/Friesland area, concluding that these were 'Charonspfennig und Abwehrzauber zugleich'. He may be right, though this conclusion presumably derives from his assumption about the nature of *Augenpaare* and does not prove it. Moreover it is surely important to note that in these coins the dotted circles appear as individual characters in stylized copies of Roman legends, copies which are often nothing but collections of circles, semicircles and lines. They may represent roman letters, nothing more.

The question naturally arises whether the *Augenpaare* on the two runic solidi can derive from prototype Roman legends. In fact they can.[8] The reverses of these solidi copy at some remove an emperor facing right, holding a banner and the figure of Victory, and trampling upon a captive. Beneath this, in the exergue of the coin, the originals had the letters COMOB. This legend the Germanic copies reproduce in such blundered forms as COB on the Wieuwerd solidus and COIIO   on those from Botes (above p. 147). Two of the struck coins quoted by Berghaus (his pl. v, 20 and 21) have OIIO in the exergue, in one with dots in the circles, in one without, though Berghaus calls them *Augenpaare* in both. This so suggests the central part of COIIO that it, too, must surely derive from COMOB. The Harlingen solidus has its runic inscription, **hada**, cut radially, bases inwards, at the position where the radial legend of the prototype begins. Scattered round the edge are a few rough attempts at other letters of the roman original. In the exergue are the two circles of the *Augenpaar*, and between them formalized letters something like VC. I would have thought it probable

---

[8] I include the discussion which follows here for completeness. From conversation with Dr Berghaus I understand that he accepts that the *Augenpaare* of Harlingen and Schweindorf derive ultimately from the O forms of the prototype legend COMOB. It is worth noting as a comparative example the dotted circle, deriving from the second O of THEODOSIVS on the obverse of the unprovenanced solidus of his pl. v, 21.

that this group of symbols derives, like OIIO, from COMOB. The Schweindorf solidus has the *Augenpaar* set at the edges of the exergue, the two circles separated by the retrograde runic legend **þeladu** or **weladu**. According to the splendid Berghaus-Schneider photographs of this piece, the right-hand circle is poorly preserved, and neither has a very prominent dot at its centre. Perhaps these circles, too, could have their origins in the O forms of COMOB. However, a methodological difficulty arises here. The fact that these circles may derive from the prototype legend does not preclude their being interpreted as apotropaic by the copyist. In making an amulet he could have converted a roman letter into a significant magical symbol. Yet this argument can work in both directions. The presence of dotted circles on amulets and on objects whose effectiveness could be improved by invoking supernatural powers does not prove that the circles themselves always had magical significance. They could decline from magical to decorative symbols. The difficulty is in assessing the intention of the craftsman who cut the circles, and this we shall never know for certain.[9]

One more piece of evidence requires closer scrutiny than Berghaus gives it. He quotes several examples of Roman solidi being mounted with loops for suspension, presumably so that they could be used as ornaments by members of the different Germanic peoples. Unmounted solidi of the same types occur in large numbers in hoards and scattered finds in the various Germanic provinces, while some of the mounted examples (his pl. iv, 10 and 11, for example) are heavily worn, as in the course of trade. There is no reason to think that the barbarians did not recognize these solidi as coins, and it would then be absurd to imagine that they believed them amulets as soon as they were mounted. The most ready explanation of the runic solidi is that they were Germanic copies of mounted Roman solidi, and this would suggest that they, too, were simply ornaments. There would be reason to believe them amulets if the native goldsmiths had made drastic changes in design deliberately to introduce apotropaic motifs. In fact they reproduce the iconography of the originals with varying degrees of precision, replace Roman legends by those partly in the native runic character, and partly barbarize them, changing some letters into purely formal arrangements of lines, and perhaps others into Germanic decorative patterns such as the dotted circle.

Finally, if the runic solidi are simply copies of mounted Roman prototypes, the individual Germanic craftsmen may have copied with different intents. Because, say, the maker of the Schweindorf or of the Harlingen piece recreated his original as an amulet, this does not mean that the man who struck the *skanomodu* solidus (which is closest of the three to its original) intended the same. To give confidence, an amulet must surely look like an amulet. Even on Schweindorf and Harlingen the *Augenpaare* are not prominent in the design. They are absent from the other two cast solidi and from *skanomodu*, and are not replaced by any other magical symbols, despite the

---

[9] There is an interesting instance of a dotted circle on the tenth-century censer-cover from Pershore (D. M. Wilson, *Anglo-Saxon Ornamental Metalwork 700–1100 in the British Museum* (London, 1964), no. 56). This has the inscription +GODRICMEWVORHT (= + *Godric me wvorht(e)*), the first O with a dot at its centre, the second without. There is no likelihood of magical intent here.

fact that the Germanic peoples had quite a wide repertory of them, swastikas, crosses, triskeles, forms like several *t*-runes superimposed, all of which occur in the bracteates. Were there a very large sample of certain runic solidus amulets, we might conclude that a small group of similar objects which had no runes or apotropaic symbols were also amulets simply on the grounds of probability. But two, three or five are small samples to work with.

The mounted Roman coins may explain one more feature of the runic and the cast non-runic solidi which Berghaus (v) very tentatively suggests may have magical significance – the relative positions of obverse and reverse designs. His illustrated examples of these Roman pieces (his pl. iv, 10 and 11) show that they sometimes had die-axes ↑ ↑, sometimes ↑ ↓. Sometimes the Germanic craftsmen followed one exemplar, sometimes the other, but there is no reason to think that they attributed any significance to the different ways they set out their two designs.

As one not trained in numismatic disciplines, then, I feel that Berghaus's claim that the runic solidi are amulets is not substantiated by the numismatic evidence alone. His case requires more rigorous argument on that evidence, or alternatively needs the additional conviction to be gained from the epigraphy, and to this I now turn with much greater confidence in my ability to manage the material.

Schneider's part of the monograph divides into two sections. The first discusses in turn the runes of Schweindorf, Harlingen and *skanomodu*, with their interpretations, and dates them on linguistic and runological grounds. The second considers the further implications of these pieces for the history of Germanic paganism. Schneider, too, begins with the belief that the three solidi are amulets, and this he supports by two arguments, (i) they had loops for suspension, (ii) Berghaus has demonstrated the amulet character from the numismatic evidence: hence Schneider's reading of the three sets of runes as invocations of magical or religious powers. The weakness of the composite structure of the Berghaus-Schneider paper is here revealed, for this argument of Schneider's does not support Berghaus's, but merely repeats it. Berghaus appeals to Schneider and Schneider to Berghaus; the argument becomes circular. The thesis is valid only if (a) Berghaus's point (iv) satisfies, or (b) Schneider's interpretations of the legends are overwhelmingly convincing, or (c) the two together seem to have more strength than either singly.

At this stage it becomes important to consider how Schneider deals with the inscriptions themselves. Fortunately none of them presents problems of transliteration. In common with most scholars I read Harlingen as **hada**, though some have thought it **hama**.[10] The reading **skanomodu** has not been questioned, save by Dahl who believed, wrongly I think, that it was the Latinized **skanomodus**, the last letter set just within the exergue.[11] From the photographs there is no doubt that Schneider's readings **þeladu** or **weladu** for the retrograde Schweindorf runes are correct, though the last letter is fragmentary or notably undersized.

[10] See, e.g., Arntz and Zeiss, *Die einheimischen Runendenkmäler*, p. 260.
[11] Dahl, *Substantival Inflexion*, pp. xi–xii.

The word *hada* has always been read as a personal name in the nominative. Schneider argues against this, but so elliptically that his statement must be quoted in full:

> Da aber dieser Solidus, wie aus den verbliebenen Resten einer abge-brochenen Hängeöse zu folgern ist, genauso wie der Solidus von Schwein-dorf Amulettcharakter hatte, würde man erwarten, dass der Name, wäre er der Name des Münz- und Runenmeisters, etwa mit dem Zusatz "machte dies" oder "heisse ich" vorläge oder, sofern es sich um den Namen des Besitzers handle, dass dieser entweder im Dat.Sg. stünde, also *hadan* lautete – Bedeutung: "dem Hada (gehört dies)" – oder im Nom.Sg. mit dem Zusatz "besitzt dies" versehen wäre. Da aber all dies nicht der Fall ist, scheint es auf Grund des Amulettcharakters ratsamer und auch sinnvoller, in dem männlichen Namen einen Vokativ zu sehen und damit die Inschrift als *had(d)a*! aufzufassen.[12]

In his footnotes 30 and 31 Schneider quotes maker and owner formulae used on bracteates: *ik AkaR fahi*, 'I, AkaR, paint (the runes)' on the Åsum bracteate, *Auþa þit eih*, 'Auþa owns this' on that from Overhornbæk. But this is scarcely proof that makers or owners must use some such formulae if their names were to appear on imitated solidi. There is, after all, a long series of runic personal names in the nominative on inscribed objects of various dates from early to late times, and it is at least likely that some of them give owners' or makers' names: *Harja* on the Vimose comb, *Hariso* on the Himlingøje I and *WiduhudaR* on the Himlingøje II brooch, *Leþro* on the Strårup collar, *SigaduR* on the Svarteborg medalet, *Husibald* on the Steindorf sax. In Great Britain the Thames scramasax has the name 'bêagnoþ' and the Llysfaen ring the partly-runic ALHSTAn, and there is no need to imagine that either of these is in the vocative, while the existence of parallel non-runic examples in this country, the royal rings with +ETH/ELVVLFR/X and +EAÐELSVIÐREGNA and the ring with the expanded formula NOMEN CHLLAFIDINXPO, suggests that there was probably a common practice of adding owners' or donors' names to objects of value. The most persuasive of the examples from England is the later sixth-century Leudhard medalet from St Martin's, Canterbury, which has the obverse legend, LEV·DAR·DVS·EPS (= *Leudardus ep(iscopu)s*) retrograde.[13] In appearance, in date and in text type this is close to the Harlingen solidus, and, as P. Grierson has suggested, the craftsman who made it might have been used to the runic character.[14] The legend records a connexion between the medalet and one bishop Leudhard who may have been its owner or donor, or who may have used this type of medalet to honour the friends of the Christian church in Kent before the conversion. Need we believe that the personal name *Hada* had some quite different relationship to the

---

[12] *Anglo-friesische Runensolidi*, p. 50.
[13] C. H. V. Sutherland, *Anglo-Saxon Gold Coinage in the Light of the Crondall Hoard* (Oxford, 1948), no. 1. Leudardus is identified with the bishop Liudhardus who accompanied the Frankish princess Berchta to Kent on her marriage to King Ethelbert.
[14] P. Grierson, 'The Canterbury (St Martin's) Hoard of Frankish and Anglo-Saxon Coin Ornaments', *BNJ* 27 (1952–4), 39–51, at 41–2.

Harlingen solidus? Schneider, arguing that the name *Hada* is related to OE *heaþu-*, 'battle', and so means 'zum Kampf Gehöriger, Kämpfer', refers it to the figure portrayed on the reverse of the solidus. This figure, he thinks, was interpreted by the Germanic craftsman as a supernatural being who should be invoked for help or protection. Such a reading of the legend makes the prior assumption that the solidus is an amulet: it does nothing towards proving it.

Scholars have commonly interpreted the legend **skanomodu** as a personal name, but to this Schneider objects because of the 'namenmorphologischen und auch sprachhistorisch-runologischen Schwierigkeiten' it presents. He prefers to read three words, *scan o modu*, the first one 3rd sg. pret. ind. of *scinan*, 'shine, glitter', the second *o*, an emphatic form related to OE *a* (Gothic *aiw*), 'ever', the third instr. sg. of OE *mod*, 'courage, might': 'Er hat immer durch Mut (Macht) geglänzt'. As with the Harlingen legend this is referred to the reverse figure of the solidus, a god or other superior being. The comment 'he has always shone by virtue of his power (courage)' is made because the owner of the charm hoped that this coruscation would continue for his own benefit. This interpretation needs a good deal of justification. The form *o*, 'ever', Schneider compares with the Old Frisian emphatic negative *no*, 'never', but it is not clear if he regards the *skanomodu* example as an Old English equivalent otherwise unrecorded, or as essentially Frisian – he calls it *Urfries*. The instr. sing. *modu* he justifies by comparing the *-u* instr. sg. in Old Saxon, Old High German *o*-stems and the loc. sg. (doubtfully identified) of Westeremden B. The vowel symbol of *scan*, 'shone', derives from WGmc *ai* which should give OE *ā* and Old Frisian *ē*. Schneider argues that in *skanomodu* the rune *ac* may represent *æi* (in accordance with the derivation of the letter form from the old *a*-rune + **i**) and that this could be an intermediate stage between Gmc *ai* and the recorded Old English and Old Frisian vowels. This is, of course, possible, for we know little of how the new Anglo-Frisian runes were created, nor have we any evidence of the intermediate stages between the Germanic diphthongs and their equivalents in Old English and Old Frisian. Yet there does seem a lot of special pleading required by Schneider's interpretation of *skanomodu*.

I think, moreover, that a more effective general mode of attack is possible. Is it likely that, in a text intended to encourage a god's future favours, it would be enough to describe elliptically his past activity without mentioning the god's name or title at all? In Schneider's version the god appears only as '(he)', contained within the verb form itself. In the surviving (North Germanic) pagan literature there is no sign that divine names or titles were avoided as tabu, and Schneider himself argues that god-titles are used on a group of bracteate amulets.[15] Why be so cryptic on the *skanomodu* solidus? A clue ought to be given by other magical texts within a similar context or date range, for, if Schneider's interpretation is correct, one or other of these should bear a structure something like *scan o modu*. Unfortunately it is hard to assess a rune-master's intention and to determine which texts are magical and

---

[15] *Anglo-friesische Runensolidi*, p. 65. Schneider seems to be referring to some sort of tabu when he speaks of the 'wohl aus religiösen Erwägungen verschwiegene Subjekt' of the Schweindorf and *skanomodu* legends (*ibid.* p. 59).

which are not, save by applying the well-known epigraphical law that whatever is incomprehensible is magic.

Some runologists would suggest that the majority of runic texts are magical simply because runes were a magical script. Against this view I have argued in detail elsewhere.[16] However, there are a number of objects, roughly contemporary with these solidi, which are commonly accepted as having supernatural significance. These are the Lindholm amulet and the various runic bracteates.[17] The Lindholm amulet has two texts, the first announcing the name or title of the rune-master, *ek erilaʀ sa wilagaʀ hateka*, 'I, the erilaʀ, am called "wise in sorcery" ', the second a combination of runes incomprehensible to us, **aaaaaaaaʀʀʀnnn[.]bmuttt:alu:**. The last three letters comprise a magical word or rune sequence, for they are quite common on bracteates and elsewhere, as are other sequences of no obvious import, such as **laþu** and **laukaʀ**. Some bracteates have curious groups of runes, each sequence evidenced only once, which are probably magical because they are pronounceable, not meaningful to us, and seem the right sort of words for magic: **luwatuwa, salusalu, tantulu**. There is an occasional pregnant phrase, *gibu auja*, '(I) give luck'. On some bracteates are rune sequences which have been taken as personal names, *Frohila, Niuwila, Houaʀ*. Some have formulae naming the rune-master or the craftsman: *Hariuha haitika: farauisa*, 'I am called Hariuha, wise in danger', *Uuigaʀ eerilaʀ fahidu uuilald*, 'Uigar, the erilaʀ, inscribed (this) work of skill (? magic)', *wurte runoʀ an walhakurne . . . Heldaʀ Kunimudiu . . .*, 'Heldaʀ made runes for Kunimu(n)d on the bracteate'. There are the *fuþarks*, always assumed to be magical, and a lot of jumbled and often blundered letter groups whose significance will probably never be known. And there are combinations of the various types of inscription listed above. But there is nowhere, to my knowledge, anything like 'he has always shone by virtue of his power'.

On the other hand, if we take *hada* and *skanomodu* as personal names in the nominative, no contextual problems arise. If the solidi are not amulets, the names may simply be those of the owners, makers or donors. If they are amulets, *hada* and *skanomodu* could still be owner or rune-master names as *Frohila* and *Niuwila* on the bracteates, and they may, though personally I am sceptical about this, add the magic of the runic script to the might of the bracteate. There is no need to demonstrate the point in the case of *hada*, which, it is generally agreed, could be a nominative personal name. In the case of *skanomodu*, as Schneider implies, we must resort to hard arguing which looks uncommonly like special pleading. Presumably the first identification of this legend as a personal name derives from the belief that the solidus was a coin, for Anglo-Saxon coins commonly had the name of king and/or moneyer, and the runic specimens record 'pada', 'æþiliræd', 'lul', 'broþer', 'botred', 'wihtred' and others. Theoretically, at least, this could still apply, for the solidus could be a coin, being struck and of an appropriate weight (4·35 g.) and material. At first glance *skanomodu* seems a likely dithematic name with a second element *-mod*, but there

---

16 'Anglo-Saxon Runes and Magic', above pp. 105–23.
17 The texts cited are to be found in Krause and Jankuhn, *Runeninschriften im älteren Futhark*. There are occasional difficulties of reading, but none affects the present discussion.

is difficulty about the quality of the unstressed vowels. The first element could be cognate with OE *Scen-*, recorded only in *Scenuulf* in the Durham *Liber Vitæ*, and with Old High German *Scauni-*. There is also a simplex *Sc(i)ene*, related to Old High German *Scónea* and to the Old English adjective *scene*, 'beautiful', and this has been identified in such place-names as Shingay, Cambs. (*Sceningeie* 1086), Shingham, Norfolk (*Siengham* 1198), Shinfield, Berks. (*Soanesfelt* DB, *Schiningefeld* 1167) and in the lost *Scynes weorþ*, BCS 820. The mutated vowel of *scen-*, the form of *scauni-* and the declension of the Gothic cognate **skauns* or **skauneis* (preserved only in *skaunjai* and *-skaunjamma*) point to an *i-* or *ja-*stem which is hard to reconcile with the unstressed vowel of *skano-*. There may, however, have been an Old English parallel unsusceptible to *i-*mutation: cf. OE *scean-* in the occasional compound *sceanfeld*. A similar form may be the Old Norse place-name *Skaun* which Magnus Olsen regards as 'nær beslektet med gotisk *skauns*'.[18] An *a-*stem adjective used as a name element could give *skano-* with unstressed *o* (perhaps Indo-European *o*) retained to a late date.[19] O. v. Friesen's alternative is that the unstressed *-o-* wrongly anticipates the main vowel of *-modu*, which is possible, though it is methodologically weak to explain a difficulty away as an error.[20] The final vowel of *-modu* is a problem too, and one I cannot confidently solve. In OE *-mod* is not a *u-*stem, though v. Friesen, noting the Old Norse genitive *-móðar*, suggests that it may have been in this example. This is not a very satisfactory explanation. An alternative, also weak, is to point to a number of cases of aberrant final *-u* in Anglo-Saxon runic texts – Franks Casket 'flodu', 'giuþeasu' are the most cogent examples – and to suggest that this vowel rune was occasionally used in early times as a space filler.

So far I have discussed *skanomodu* as though it were an Old English legend, despite the lack of any confirmatory provenance. The use of the *a-*rune to represent Gmc *au* in *skano-* (if that is cognate with Old High German *Scauni-*) suggests that the text is in fact Frisian. Final *-u* could then be an indefinite unstressed vowel, as it seems to be in **adugislu** and **gisuhldu** on the Westeremden weaving-slay.[21] In this case *skanomodu* could simply be an oblique form of the personal name, perhaps with the meaning 'for Skanomod' as in the more explicit formula embodying the name *Kunimudiu* on the Tjurkö bracteate I (Jacobsen and Moltke, *Danmarks rune-indskrifter*, cols 547–9, br. 75). Such a legend would be more appropriate to a unique piece cast from a mould than to one of a group struck from dies. The interpretation seems unlikely if the *skanomodu* solidus is a coin.

The words *hada* clearly, and *skanomodu* much less clearly, could be personal names recording people connected with these solidi. The Schweindorf solidus is a different case. From the photographs I would take its inscription as **weladu**, though **þeladu** is certainly possible. Schneider reads *we ladu*, 'Wir (haben dies gemacht).

---

[18] M. Olsen, *Stedsnavn* (Stockholm, 1939), p. 52.

[19] C. T. Carr, *Nominal Compounds in Germanic* (Oxford, 1939), pp. 271–2.

[20] O. v. Friesen, *Runorna* (Stockholm, 1933), p. 50.

[21] Arntz and Zeiss, *Die einheimischen Runendenkmäler*, pp. 386–7. This weaving-slay is, however, ascribed to the eighth or ninth century (*ibid.* p. 382), so its linguistic relevance to *skanomodu* is uncertain.

(Es ist, bzw. dieser ist) Unterstützung, Hilfe, Verteidigung', or, *þe ladu*, 'Für dich bzw. dir (ist dies, oder: ist dieser) Unterstützung, Hilfe, Verteidigung'. He takes *ladu* as an early form of OE *lad*, 'leading, support, maintenance, sustenance, way, journey'. I would like a more detailed semantic examination at this point, for, though *lad* could clearly mean 'leading, maintenance, sustenance, way, journey' and 'defence' in the specific sense of 'legal defence, exoneration', I am not clear from the authorities cited, Bosworth-Toller's and Clark Hall's dictionaries, that it could imply 'support, defence' in a general sense, or 'help'. Schneider rejects *we ladu* on the grounds that it uses the regal 'we', whereas rune-masters elsewhere modestly use the singular form, but a stronger objection is surely the unhelpful nature of such a legend. That a craftsman or rune-master should sign his name is likely enough, but that he should be content with recording himself simply as 'we' is improbable in the extreme. Schneider's alternative suffers from a similar weakness. On a variety of objects rune-masters name themselves and the person for whom the object was made. That they should record such a person as 'you' is unlikely too.

It is, however, hard to provide a convincing alternative. Examining the bracteate texts with their many obscurities, I am struck by the number of times they contain **l** and **a** in combination with **u**, **w**, and/or **þ**, sometimes with other letters too: **alu**, **laukaʀ**, **alawin**, **jalawid**, **lalgwu**, **laþu**, **lþdul(u)**, **uldaul**. **þeladu** or **weladu** fits well into such a list. Most interesting of the bracteates in this connexion is that from Tønder, south Jutland (Jacobsen and Moltke, *Danmarks runeindskrifter*, cols 493–4, br. 4). This has a standing figure facing right and bearing a bow. Around it are various other, much smaller, stylized figures, some perhaps men, others animals. Radially and at the left edge is a retrograde runic text, **uldaul**, and radially below the figure where the exergue of a coin would be, a second retrograde legend, **lþdul(u)**, the last letter uncertain. Though this bracteate is not strikingly like any of the runic solidi, it bears a general resemblance in design, and it is interesting to remember that the standing figure on the non-runic Uppsala solidus also has a bow, though he handles it differently from the more competent archer of Tønder. The similarity of appearance is emphasized by some similarity of legends, Schweindorf's **þeladu/weladu** against Tønder's **lþdul(u)**. These two uses of a limited range of letters are striking and perhaps significant. Jacobsen and Moltke wisely left the Tønder bracteate text uninterpreted, and I am inclined to do the same with Schweindorf.

Some may feel that, in admitting to the discussion the resemblance between the Schweindorf solidus and the Tønder bracteate, I have tacitly accepted the likelihood that Schweindorf is an amulet, for the bracteates are often connected with religion or the supernatural, and many of their legends, particularly those containing **alu** or rearrangements of those three letters, are thought magical. This may be so, and I would not deny the possibility of Schweindorf being an amulet, but I would not hold it proven, nor do I even think it necessary to believe that Tønder is an amulet. Many of the bracteate inscriptions may be traditional groups of letters or combinations of rune-like forms no longer meaningful at the time they were stamped. Certainly, many bracteates have curious symbols which, though they point to an origin in the script, are no longer runes. Schweindorf could represent a similar decline from a meaningful to a meaningless group of characters. In any case, there is no reason to accept

Schneider's interpretations of *hada* and *skanomodu*, nor to admit that these two runic solidi were amulets.

The final part of Schneider's contribution need not concern us here. It is a speculative discussion of the place of the cast solidi in the history of Germanic religion. Schneider argues that the rune-masters responsible for the pieces looked upon their reverse figures as those of gods, and so added appropriate legends. He then suggests that the gods in question were the two youthful brothers whom Tacitus records as worshipped by the Naharvali, and whom he equates with Castor and Pollux. This thesis is argued with persistence and a wealth of comparative detail, but it is in a sense irrelevant to the rest of the article. It is an extension of Schneider's interpretation of the runic legends, but not a necessary one.

Finally, I must consider briefly the linguistic evidence for dating the three solidi. Schneider puts forward the following criteria for determining the *terminus ante quem*:

(i) The retention of *-u* after a long syllable in *ladu* and *-modu*. On Luick's authority this puts Schweindorf and *skanomodu* before 600.

(ii) The use of the rune *oeþil* for *o* unaffected by *i*-mutation in *skanomodu*. This puts the solidus no later than *c*. 525, for Luick ascribes *i*-mutation to the first half of the sixth century, while the Franks Casket, which Schneider dates *c*. 540/80, uses the rune for a mutated vowel.

The *terminus post quem* is *c*. 450 since:

(iii) The provenance of Schweindorf suggests a date after the migration of Anglo-Saxon units to Friesland, parts of which they occupied as a staging-post on their way to England.

(iv) The form of the rune *cen* in **skanomodu** is an Anglo-Frisian intermediary between the equivalent Germanic rune and the common Anglo-Saxon type.

Objections can be brought against each of these. In (i) and (ii) Schneider fails to distinguish between Old English and Old Frisian sound-changes, and assumes that the chronology appropriate to the one necessarily applies to the other. But Luick's dates may not apply if these solidi are Frisian. Moreover, Luick prefaced his dating of the Old English sound-changes (as opposed to his placing of them in chronological order) by a strong warning of the weakness of the evidence, and the uncertainty of its application in the same way to different local dialects.[22] (i) depends on Schneider's interpretations of the two inscriptions. If we reject *ladu* as an early form of OE *lad*, we need not believe its main vowel long, and so need not assume early loss of *-u*. If *þeladu/weladu* is a magical or arbitrary word, it may not undergo the same sound-changes as common words. The ending of *-modu* is a problem, and I would hesitate to use it as a dating criterion. (ii) ignores the possibility of a conservative spelling tradition, retaining the rune *oeþil* for the unmutated vowel after *i*-mutation had taken place or at least begun. We do not know how the rune-masters learned spelling

---

[22] Luick, *Historische Grammatik*, § 291.

methods, or how tenaciously they stuck to them. Few people would put the Franks Casket as early as 540/80. To me it is clearly no earlier than the seventh century, and late in the century at that.[23] Despite this, (ii) may contain a valid point. The Chessell Down scabbard-plate has the text 'æco: ᛿œri', seemingly using *oeþil* where the vowel is liable to *i*-mutation, but *os* where it is not. This inscription was probably cut *c*. 550. Its spelling practice might confirm an early date for *skanomodu* if the two rune-masters used the same runic conventions. Unfortunately we do not even know if they belonged to the same race. (iii) may be right, though we know less than we would like about the relationship between Anglo-Saxon and Frisian runes, and the routes by which the script came both to this country and to Frisia. The weakness of (iv) is our ignorance of the forms in which the various runic characters were introduced into these two countries. England has three 'c' types, < on the Loveden Hill urn 61/251 (and also on the 'Bateman' brooch, British Museum 93, 6–18, 32, which may have been inscribed on the Continent), ᚲ commonly, and the intermediate ᚴ of Chessell Down, which is also the *skanomodu* shape. This last Schneider takes as Anglo-Frisian, presumably because it also occurs on the Hantum, Frisia, bone plate. But a similar, though smaller, type appears quite often in Denmark, in such early inscriptions as the Kragehul spear-shaft, the Vimose plane and the Lindholm amulet, and very recently a full-length form, exactly equivalent to Chessell Down and *skanomodu*, has turned up in Norway, on the Eikeland, Rogaland, brooch.[24] This makes it uncertain whether the *skanomodu* 'c' type is specifically Anglo-Frisian. It could be a common Germanic variant whence derived the orthodox Anglo-Saxon type.

Summing up, I think there is reason to believe that the *skanomodu* text is early because of its similarities with Chessell Down (and its archaic 's' rune, otherwise found in England only on the Ash (Gilton) pommel, is an additional piece of evidence),[25] but on the linguistic and runological material I would hesitate to ascribe it to so precise a period as the first quarter of the sixth century. In my opinion Harlingen and Schweindorf have no runological and linguistic features which enable us to date them with any closeness at all. The dates suggested by Berghaus may be correct, but they must be reached on numismatic grounds alone.

In this 'review article' I have tried to give the grounds on which I hold unproven

---

[23] Opinions have differed as to the date of this object, but many scholars accept *c*. 700. To me such a date seems likely on the linguistic and runological evidence, while R. L. S. Bruce-Mitford has reached a similar conclusion on the evidence of art history.

[24] A. Liestøl, 'Runeinnskrifta på Eikelandspenna', *Frá haug ok heiðni* (1965), 155–8. It is fair to admit that the base of the rune seems to be damaged, so there is perhaps some doubt as to its exact form.

[25] For the runes of the Ash (Gilton) pommel see S. C. Hawkes and R. I. Page, 'Swords and Runes in South-East England' (1967), pp. 3–4, 11 and pl. i, and V. I. Evison, 'The Dover Ring-Sword and Other Sword-Rings and Beads', *Archaeologia* 101 (1967), 63–118, at 70, 88 and fig. 10*a*, with a detailed account of the inscription and a discussion by J. M. Bately, pp. 97–102. Schneider is surely wrong in saying (*Anglo-friesische Runensolidi*, p. 57) that the 's' of **skanomodu** is a three-stroke form ᛉ, as indeed Berghaus transcribes it (*ibid.* p. 23). The coins shows clearly ᛉ, with the lower stroke almost certainly intended as part of the rune (pl. ii, g). Four-stroke *s*-forms occur elsewhere in early inscriptions.

Dr Berghaus's contention that these three runic solidi are amulets. I have given reasons why I am sceptical over the interpretations which Professor Schneider gives to their legends, and over the dates he supplies. Of course, in dealing with small samples of material or small numbers of objects, we cannot get statistical or absolute proof, and must be content with a weight of evidence for or against a thesis. I do not think that weight has been demonstrated in the present case.

ACKNOWLEDGEMENTS

For help with this article I wish to thank Miss M. M. Archibald and Dr J. P. C. Kent of the Department of Coins and Medals, British Museum, and Mr Christopher Blunt, all of whom gave me numismatic information, and the keeper and staff of the British Museum Research Laboratory who subjected the *skanomodu* solidus to scientific test. Dr Berghaus was so kind as to discuss a number of the points I have brought forward here, and I thank him for his courtesy. I should add that in a recent letter, dated 9 December 1968, Dr Berghaus tells me that he is advised that the British Museum tests on the *skanomodu* solidus are not conclusive. I leave this matter to the scientific experts, and merely repeat here that, after visual examination of the solidus, several numismatists concluded that it was struck, not cast.

POSTSCRIPT

I have little to add to this piece, largely because I have thought little about the subject since 1968. In his 'A Survey of Anglo-Saxon and Frisian Coins with Runic Inscriptions',[26] Mark Blackburn gives the latest numismatic opinion on the three solidi discussed in the Berghaus-Schneider paper of 1967. The **skanomodu** solidus is, he claims, struck not cast, though it is perhaps disturbing to note that the only authority he quotes for his assertion is this article from 1968. The **hada** and **weladu/þeladu** specimens are 'casts probably from moulds that have had their designs scratched directly into the clay(?) surfaces, and the effect is one of much rougher workmanship than the 'skanomodu' coin, which was struck from dies prepared by a combination of engraving and sinking with punches'. Blackburn is sceptical about Berghaus's fairly close dating sequence for the three pieces, preferring to say that 'it would be more reasonable to suggest that the 'weladu' and 'hada' solidi are likely to be late sixth- or early seventh-century, while the 'skanomodu' coin, produced by different techniques, has to be considered quite separately. Its fineness (89% silver) implies that it was probably produced before *c.* 610'.

On the mint-places of these solidi Blackburn is less informative, accepting **skanomodu** as possibly English, possibly Frisian, and the other two pieces probably Frisian. Which leaves us much where we were. He refers to all three pieces as 'coins', but whether these were coins in the sense of currency is less clear. 'The earliest coins to be struck in England . . . were spasmodic and used mainly as personal jewellery

---

[26] *Old English Runes*, ed. Bammesberger, pp. 137–89, at 140–4.

or ornaments', he says. This raises a question of how to place these three solidi in context. From the second half of the seventh century onwards there is a clear tradition of a coinage inscribed in runes (sometimes mixed with roman) in eastern England. There is no such continuity in Frisia, and it would be proper to question whether the cast **hada** and **weladu** specimens should be defined as coins, or rather considered as cast ornaments; that is, whether strictly they are to be grouped with **skanomodu**, whether the three form a sequence. Or whether the natural successors of **skanomodu** are the **æniwulufu** tremisses.

Recent discussion of the **skanomodu** solidus inscription[27] suggests, not surprisingly, that the coin may be either Frisian or English with the balance in favour of the first of these, while the other two solidi are commonly accepted as convincingly Frisian, largely on the evidence of their findspots. Which leaves us much where we were. Arendt Quak, however, firmly asserts a Frisian origin for **skanomodu** on the grounds of the vowel quality in *skān-* and the ending *-u*; and includes it in his corpus of Frisian runic inscriptions.[28]

The text of the Schweindorf legend has been read as **wela<n>du**, an early Frisian form of the personal name better known in its Old English cognate *Weland*.[29] This is a possibility to be considered, though it requires us to assume that the rune-master omitted **n** before the homorganic consonant *d*, however that is to be explained in terms of phonetic theory. Such an omission would be readily accepted in early Norse (and some other) inscriptions. I would like to see the evidence for this epigraphical practice within the 'Anglo-Frisian' runic world,[30] and with particular respect to its occurrence within Anglo-Saxon practice, but that is something that has not yet been attempted or even thought necessary. It is possible to find examples where 'n' is not omitted before 'd' in English inscriptions: Ruthwell 'g i w u n d a d', Overchurch 'æ þ e l m u *n* [*d*]' are cases in point.

The unusual 'c' rune of the **skanomodu** piece exercises us less since the discovery of another case of the same form (three examples) in the second Chessell Down inscription (below, p. 285), and for further instruction there is probably yet another, related but distinct, variant 'c' on the Watchfield purse mount.[31] The multi-staved 's' of **skanomodu** which caused Bammesberger such concern[32] is now perhaps illuminated by the even more multi-staved 's' of the back-of-a-brooch inscription from Harford Farm, Caistor-by-Norwich.[33]

---

27 As A. Bammesberger, 'SKANOMODU: Linguistic Issues', *Britain 400–600*, ed. Bammesberger and Wollmann, pp. 457–66.
28 'Runica Frisica', *Aspects of Old Frisian Philology* (= *Amsterdamer Beiträge zur älteren Germanistik* 31–2 / *Estrikken* 69 (1990)), 357–70, at 359 and 361.
29 K. Düwel and W.-D. Tempel, 'Knochenkämme mit Runeninschriften aus Friesland: mit einer Zusammenstellung aller bekannten Runenkämme und einem Beitrag zu den friesischen Runeninschriften', *Palaeohistoria* 14 (1968 [1970]), 353–91, at 381–2.
30 Düwel and Tempel adduce the cases of **kabu, kobu**, 'comb' on a couple of eighth-/ninth-century bone combs found in Frisia, 'Knochenkämme', pp. 365 and 369.
31 J. Hines, 'The Runic Inscriptions of Early Anglo-Saxon England', *Britain 400–600*, ed. Bammesberger and Wollmann, pp. 437–55, at 437 and 439.
32 'SKANOMODU: Linguistic Issues', p. 458.
33 J. Hines, 'A New Runic Inscription from Norfolk', *Nytt om Runer* 6 (1991), 6–7.

13
(1969)

RUNES AND NON-RUNES[1]

The study of Anglo-Saxon runes has long been bedevilled by the admission to the corpus of doubtful and even clearly non-runic inscriptions and incised objects. There are good semantic and historical reasons for this. Since their first appearance in the language in the seventeenth century, the words 'rune' and 'runic' have acquired wide ranges of meaning, and the adjective has been applied to things on which there are no runes, or even inscriptions at all, as, for example, the Sandbach and Blackwell crosses.[2] The more emotive meanings of the words have attracted mystics, muddlers and cranks, who have enthusiastically discovered runes where none exist,[3] while the epigraphical examples of the Laird of Monkbarns and Mr Pickwick have been earnestly followed in the runic field. Some artefacts on which runes might be expected are so poorly preserved that chance surface marks have been seen as runic letters, letters indeed whose very forms make them easily confused with scratches, plough-marks, damaged decorative motifs and the like.[4] There seems to be a primary

---

[1] Many scholars have helped with this paper, and I should like to express thanks to Mr C. E. Blunt, Rev. I. H. Bowman, Mr R. S. L. Bruce-Mitford, Dr J. C. Corson, Mr P. Grierson, Mr D. Hamer, Mr H. Hargreaves, Dr E. Okasha, Mr P. S. Peberdy, Mr P. K. Roberts-Wray, the late Professor A. H. Smith and Dr D. M. Waterman; and to the staffs of the National Museum of Ireland, the Birmingham and Brighton Public Libraries, the library of the Society of Antiquaries of London, and the Royal Library, Stockholm, from whose collection of Stephens papers (dep. 189) all quotations from unpublished letters to that scholar are taken.
[2] F. H. Crossley, *Cheshire* (London, 1949), p. 228; W. Stephenson, 'Blackwell, and its Sculptured Cross', *Journal of the Derbyshire Archæological and Natural History Soc.* 39 (1917), 75–80, at 79. These two examples are of unequal value. No inscription has ever been recorded on the Blackwell cross. Of Sandbach, the Elizabethan antiquary, William Smith, writing before the crosses were thrown down and damaged in the Civil War, reported, 'In the market place do stand hard together two square *Crosses* of *Stone*, on steps, with certain Images and Writings thereon graven; which, as they say, a man cannot read, except he be holden with his head downwards' (W. Smith and W. Webb, *The Vale-Royall of England* . . . (London, 1656), part i, p. 46).
[3] Witness here C. Roach Smith's ready identification of a lost 'helmet with letters upon it which nobody could read' as 'probably a bronze dish inscribed with runes' (*Collectanea antiqua* (London, 1857) IV, appendix, p. 34), and, in two letters, dated 12 February and 15 April 1868, to G. Stephens, J. Brent's jubilant cry, 'Rejoice! Rejoice! I have got a small piece of Samian Ware . . . inscribed with six Runes!' followed by the crestfallen admission that they had proved 'cursive Roman'.
[4] See, for example, D. M. Wilson's comment on possible runes on a silver plate associated with an Anglo-Saxon sword from Långtora, Uppland, Sweden ('Some Neglected Late Anglo-Saxon Swords', *Medieval Archaeology* 9 (1965), 32–54, at 38).

epigraphical law by which characters which cannot be identified as anything else are called runes.

The present paper has two aims: to prune the corpus of some texts which have been wrongly or doubtfully listed as runic, and tentatively to suggest a few additions. Professor H. Marquardt's invaluable *Bibliographie der Runeninschriften nach Fundorten* (Göttingen, 1961) has done much towards the first of these, and my study is intended rather as a development than as a criticism of that distinguished scholar's work. The *Bibliographie* is not ruthless enough. Though she listed inscriptions 'die in der Literatur als "runisch" gedeutet worden sind, deren runischer Charakter aber zweifelhaft ist', Professor Marquardt failed to show just how doubtfully runic some of them were, or how slight the basis of identification. In dealing with the lost stones from Amesbury, for example, she queries 'Mit Runen?' The Amesbury stones owe their inclusion in the bibliography to G. Stephens's citation of them in the introduction to the English section of *Old-Northern Runic Monuments* I–II, 360. Stephens derives his material from R. C. Hoare, *The Ancient History of South Wiltshire* (London, 1812), p. 198, and Hoare in turn quotes John Aubrey, who is thus our sole authority, and one not noted for scholarly precision. Even Aubrey only says, ''Tis said here there were some letters on these stones, but what they were I cannot learne', so the evidence for Amesbury runes is slight indeed. An example of different treatment in the *Bibliographie* is the golden armlet found at Aspatria, Cumberland, in 1828, on which Marquardt records '5 Zeichen, von W. Hamper als Runen gelesen'. This is true as far as it goes, though we note that Hamper's interpretation (*Archæologia Æliana* 2 (1832), 267–8) and its accompanying illustration derive, not from the armlet, but from a drawing of it. The seven relevant *Bibliographie* entries which follow Hamper's all either ignore the runes or dispute their existence. The armlet is still extant, in the British Museum (inv. no. 1904, 11–12, 1), and is neither runic nor Anglo-Saxon.

A key figure in the present discussion is inevitably George Stephens, whose four monumental, enthusiastic and extravagant volumes contain the nearest thing to a corpus of Anglo-Saxon runic inscriptions that we yet possess. Four groups of objects in Stephens's collection require notice.

(1) Those which Stephens never thought to be runic, since he included them only as parallel illustrative examples: the Aldborough sundial, the memorial stone fragments from Dewsbury, Yarm, Wycliffe (then lost but since recovered), and Thornhill, Yorks (W. R.) (not to be confused with the rune-stones from the same church), and the Cuxton disc-brooch with its owner formula *Ælfgivv me ah*. Of these Dewsbury and Yarm contrive to get into the *Bibliographie*, but only because they were wrongly listed among the English rune-stones by H. Arntz in his *Die Runenschrift* (Halle, 1938), p. 89 and elsewhere.

(2) Four inscriptions which Stephens, in some cases in common with other scholars, wrongly called runic; the Brough-under-Stainmoor stone, correctly identified as Greek by A. H. Sayce and G. F. Browne independently;[5] the Chertsey bowl,

<hr/>

[5] See the story as told by G. F. Browne in *The Recollections of a Bishop* (London, 1915), p. 204.

which Stephens, following the great J. M. Kemble, thought to be in 'mixt Runes and decorated Uncials', though he subsequently reported that it had been read as modern Greek ('this piece therefore *goes out*'); the St Andrews ring, which is probably late medieval and certainly not runic; and the Roman pig of lead from Truro on which Stephens found the runic letter *stan*.

The inscriptions in these two groups can be easily disposed of, as can some others of the same sort not in Stephens but in the *Bibliographie*: the Beckermet stone, with its virtually unreadable but certainly not runic text, and the Great Edstone sundial whose Old English inscription, + *Loðan me wrohtea*, contains, contrary to Marquardt's statement, no runes other than *wynn*.

The last two groups, however, need detailed examination.

(3) Inscriptions found on objects which are still known, but which now have no visible texts; one of the two Sandwich stones (*Sandwich B* in the *Bibliographie*), the Kirkdale slab and the Irton cross: perhaps too the Bingley font. Further, Stephens records more extensive texts than can now be read on a number of other objects, such as the Bewcastle cross, the Falstone 'hogback' and the Gilton pommel.

(4) Inscribed objects now lost, and known only from early references, sometimes supported by drawings:[6] the Hoddam and Leeds stones, the brooch from a collection in the north of England, listed by Stephens under Northumbria, the so-called pocket sundial from Cleobury Mortimer, the 'owi'[7] ring of unknown provenance. Here also may be included the coin found at Wijk-bij-Duurstede, Netherlands, which could, from Stephens's reproduction of the runic forms, be either Anglo-Saxon or Frisian.

From group 3 the Sandwich B stone can be removed at once, for nobody has yet read runes on it though both D. H. Haigh and Stephens list it among the runic monuments, and Stephens argues that a pagan inscription was cut away from its surface in Christian times. The other items in the group call for a discussion of the runic work of Haigh, who is a key witness in every case. That of the Kirkdale inscription is confused by the existence of a double find report. Two versions, referring to the one stone, have been listed as separate items: they are given in Stephens, *Old-Northern Runic Monuments* III, 184 and 214. The first records Haigh and J. T. Fowler's examination of 'part of a coffin-slab . . . on which was cut a Latin Cross Quadrate. . . .. On the 4 ends of this Cross were Old-English runes, slightly carved.' Haigh read 'k̄yni | ŋœþi | lwal | dæg', which Fowler could not support, for though he agreed that 'runes *were* there', he 'could not make anything out of them'. Stephens adds that deterioration of the stone had now left 'not one distinct stave'.

Announcing Sayce's identification to Stephens in a letter dated 27 June 1884, J. T. Fowler commented, 'the wonder to me now is that anyone could ever suppose it to be anything else' and added the warning which all runologists would do well to remember, 'My good friend, doth not much O.N. learning make you see everything through O.N. spectacles?'

6 I omit here the Bewcastle Cross head which Stephens mentioned (*Old-Northern Runic Monuments* I–II, 398) and reproduced without knowing what it was (*The Runes, Whence Came They?* (London, 1894), pp. 58–9, listed under 'England, Northumbria'). On this fragment see above, pp. 66–8.

7 Runes are transliterated according to Dickins, 'System of Transliteration'.

The second report also derives from Haigh and Fowler, describing how they took casts of a 'ruined *Runic Cross* at Kirkdale' in or about 1870. Fowler stated, 'The staves are I fear hopelessly gone, only just enough is left to see that there *were* runes; one is ᛝ ['ŋ']'.[8] These are certainly two versions of the same record of the cross-inscribed flat stone known as 'King Ethelwald's grave-slab', still preserved inside Kirkdale church.[9] Stephens thought of two stones, a cross and a slab, and recorded them as such in his *Handbook* and in *The Runes, Whence Came They?* Such later writers as W. Vietor and W. G. Collingwood followed him, and Marquardt lists two in her *Bibliographie*. Apart from Haigh, the only investigator to have read an extensive runic inscription on the Kirkdale slab was G. F. Browne. In 1885 he commented, 'Now only one rune can be seen, though others are detected in a careful rubbing'.[10] His illustration to the Disney lectures given in 1888, nos 1–2, fig. 11, shows a clear 'k̄uni | ŋœþi | lwal | dæg', which seems to be an imaginative reading of a rubbing, helped by memories of Haigh's interpretation, though Browne's runes are set, not at the four ends of the cross, but above and below its horizontal arms. Otherwise, as has been seen, Fowler as early as 1870, and several writers since, have found little or nothing legible on the Kirkdale slab.[11] Even Fowler's 'ŋ' is suspect, for this form could easily be part of a decorative interlace or other pattern misread as a rune, as has happened, for example, on some of the *Wigrœd* sceattas.[12]

For the Irton cross inscription too, we are reliant upon Haigh, who reported, in a panel on its west side, three lines of letters, very much worn, but with several runes preserved, notably 'ḡ', 'þ', 'f', 'm' and 'æ'. These he first reconstructed as *gibidæþ forœ . . . (g = gar)*, but later, in a paper presented in 1870, completed the text '+ḡebiddæþ | forægodm | undæssawle', marking the first twelve characters as distinct.[13] This inscription has not been remarked by anyone else, neither by earlier recorders of the cross, such as the Lysons brothers (1816) and Jefferson (1842), nor by a later investigator such as J. Romilly Allen who reported in 1880 that there was *'absolutely no trace of letters of any kind'*.[14] Vietor thought he saw fragments of 'b'

---

8 The original letter, dated 21 June 1870, survives, showing Stephens to be a fairly inaccurate copyist.
9 This is shown by Fowler's extant letters. Stephens was worried by the Kirkdale material for he asked Fowler about it several times. Three of Fowler's replies survive, from 1870 (quoted above), from 1880 and from 1891. It is sufficiently clear from them that Haigh and Fowler made only a single common visit to Kirkdale. In 1870 Fowler said the runes were on a cross, in 1880 on a cross on a coffin-slab and in 1891 on a cross-shaft.
10 ' "Scandinavian" or "Danish" Sculptured Stones Found in London . . .', *Archaeological Journal* 42 (1885), 251–9, at 256. Yet in a letter to Stephens, dated 2 January 1884, Browne remarked that a rubbing of the slab 'does not shew the slightest trace of letters'.
11 See, for example, W. Vietor, *Die northumbrischen Runensteine. Beiträge zur Textkritik. Grammatik und Glossar* (Marburg in Hessen, 1895), p. 19; W. G. Collingwood, 'Anglian and Anglo-Danish Sculpture in the North Riding of Yorkshire', *Yorkshire Archæological Journal* 19 (1907), 267–413, at 278.
12 P. Grierson, *Sylloge of Coins of the British Isles: I. Fitzwilliam Museum Cambridge* I (London, 1958), nos 235–6.
13 Stephens, *Old-Northern Runic Monuments* I–II, 469; D. H. Haigh, 'The Runic Monuments of Northumbria', *Proc. of the Geological and Polytechnic Soc. of the West Riding of Yorkshire* 5 (1870), 178–217, at 217 and fig.
14 D. and S. Lysons, *Magna Britannia; being a Concise Topographical Account of the Several*

where Haigh read 'þ', but otherwise only horizontal incisions to mark a three-line text.[15]

Haigh's runic work is, like so much of the same date, idiosyncratic. It is uneven in quality, occasionally recording with apparent accuracy data of importance.[16] But in general it shows the same tendency towards extensive reading of faint and weathered texts as do the examples already discussed. On the Collingham stone where only the remains of two words, 'æft[.] | [.]swiþi', can now be seen, Haigh read an elaborate memorial text containing several odd Old English forms, *Œonblœd this settœ œfter gisibœ ymb Auswini cyning gicegœth thœr sawle*, this being a version, amended and completed from the study of casts and rubbings, of an earlier attempt.[17] On the Bewcastle Cross, Haigh, in company with several of his contemporaries, read a number of lines of runes certainly not there now, and we have an admittedly unfriendly account by the rival antiquary, J. Maughan, of Haigh's methods of obtaining and treating his evidence.[18] The Bingley font inscription, now completely illegible except for a very few scattered and doubtfully identifiable runes, received a long and elaborate interpretation, based partly on photographs, casts and rubbings,[19] while on a part of the Alnmouth cross where now only V, E, and H can be read Haigh confidently found [HL]VDWYG·MEH·FEG[DE].[20]

In two cases Haigh's results can be checked fairly closely, the Gilton sword-pommel and the Falstone 'hogback'. In 1872 Haigh reported runes on both sides of the pommel, reading ICU IK SIGI MUARNUM IK WISA on that where a confused text is still clear, and DAGMUND (i. e. *Dœgmund*) 'nearly effaced' on the other, where no traces now remain.[21] No runes are shown on the earliest drawings of this side in T. Wright, *The Archaeological Album* (London, 1845), p. 204, or J. Y. Akerman, *Remains of Pagan Saxondom* (London, 1854), pl. xxiv, while Haigh's earliest published account of the pommel, in 1861, also ignores them.[22] From the date it was first recorded until the present the Gilton pommel has been in various antiquarian collections, and there is no reason to believe that its condition has deteriorated since

Counties of Great Britain, IV Cumberland (London, 1816), p. cci; S. Jefferson, *The History and Antiquities of Cumberland* II (Carlisle, 1842), p. 207 and fig.; Stephens, *Old-Northern Runic Monuments* III, 200.

[15] *Die northumbrischen Runensteine*, p. 16.

[16] As, for example, in his drawing of the badly-damaged runic face of the Hackness cross ('The Monasteries of S. Heiu and S. Hild', *Yorkshire Archœological and Topographical Journal* 3 (1875), 349–91, at pl. 3 no. 4).

[17] 'Runic Monuments of Northumbria', pp. 199–202.

[18] D. H. Haigh, 'The Saxon Cross at Bewcastle', *Archœologia Æliana* n.s. 1 (1857), 149–95, at 152–4 and figs 3–13; J. Maughan, *A Memoir on the Roman Station and Runic Cross at Bewcastle* (London, 1857), pp. 31–8.

[19] 'Runic Monuments of Northumbria', p. 206. See the variant reading in 'Yorkshire Runic Monuments', *Yorkshire Archœological and Topographical Journal* 2 (1871–2), 252–88, at 254.

[20] 'Saxon Cross at Bewcastle', p. 186 and fig. 18; but cf. J. Stuart's drawing in *The Sculptured Stones of Scotland* (Aberdeen and Edinburgh, 1856–67) II, pl. cxvii, which shows the stone in much its present condition.

[21] 'Notes in Illustration of the Runic Monuments of Kent', *Archœologia Cantiana* 8 (1872), 164–270, at 259–60.

[22] *The Conquest of Britain by the Saxons* (London, 1861), pp. 51–2.

1872, or indeed that the runes of one side have been lost and those of the other preserved. Of the Falstone 'hogback' a very detailed and convincing drawing accompanies the find-report of 1822.[23] This makes it clear that the condition of the stone has altered little since the early years of the nineteenth century. Yet in 1857 Haigh published a transcript of the texts showing them to be considerably more complete than now.[24] Almost identical readings were given by Stephens, *Old-Northern Runic Monuments* I–II, 456, on the basis of a cast in the National Museum, Copenhagen. This cast still survives, and gives the runes in very much their present state.

From this discussion of Haigh's runic work it is clear that the Irton inscription was a figment of Haigh's fertile imagination, and Kirkdale may be the same, though Fowler's evidence gives some, if very little, support to that text. Fowler was a careful epigraphist as his treatment of the sadly deteriorated runes of the Crowle stone shows.[25]

Of the inscriptions in group 4 pictures exist of the Leeds, Cleobury Mortimer, 'owi' and Wijk inscriptions. The Leeds rune-stone was one of a number of early carved stones found when the old parish church was demolished in 1837–8. A year or two later the architect responsible, R. D. Chantrell, lectured on his finds to the Institute of British Architects and the Leeds Philosophical and Literary Society, though I know of no record of this discourse. At about the same time, according to G. F. Browne in a letter to Stephens on 9 November 1882, he made full-scale drawings of the material, but there was no publication until 1856,[26] and we do not know where the rune-stone was then. The fragments of the great Anglo-Saxon cross now in Leeds parish church were removed by Chantrell and ultimately put in his garden at Rottingdean, Sussex, not being returned until the 1870s. The rune-stone may have gone south with them, though it is then surprising that it did not return with the great cross. More probably it was among the mass of ancient material taken by Leeds citizens from the site of the old church, as its historian, R. W. Moore, tells.[27] Thus the 1856 publication may have been based on a sketch made nearly twenty years before. Other pictures of this monument derive from Chantrell's early drawing. The most prolific and influential writer on the subject, once again D. H. Haigh, worked only from the architect's version, and did not see the original himself,[28] nor is there sign that the Leeds stone was examined by later writers. According to Chantrell it was fragmentary, with parts of two lines of runes, 'cuni-' (? 'cunl-') and 'onlaf'. Though Haigh's interpretation of this as *cyning Onlaf*, 'king Olaf', can be rejected

---

[23] J. Wood, 'Some Account of a Saxon Inscription, on a Stone Found Near Falstone . . .', *Archæologia Æliana* 1 (1822), 103–4.

[24] 'Saxon Cross at Bewcastle', p. 155 and fig. 15.

[25] *PSAL* 2nd ser., 4 (1867–70), 187–90.

[26] D. H. Haigh, 'On the Fragments of Crosses Discovered at Leeds in 1838', *Proc. of the Geological and Polytechnic Soc. of the West Riding of Yorkshire* 3 (1856–7), 502–33.

[27] *A History of the Parish Church of Leeds* . . . (Leeds, 1877), p. 56. See also Chantrell's remarks, *Proc. of the Geological and Polytechnic Soc. of the West Riding of Yorkshire* 3 (1856–7), 537.

[28] This is indicated by Haigh's 'When the fragment can be examined by an experienced eye, I suspect that the second character will prove to be Y', 'Runic Monuments of Northumbria', p. 214.

out of hand, there is nothing improbable in either the letter forms illustrated or their sequence. Indeed, 'cun' could be part of the word *becun*, 'cross, monument', often found in memorial inscriptions, while 'onlaf' may be the Old English personal name *Onlaf* (*becun æfter Onlafe*, 'memorial for Onlaf', with the first letter of the preposition fragmentary), or could contain the common noun *laf*, 'relict, widow' or perhaps 'remains, corpse'. It is likely, then, that Chantrell drew an accurate picture of a genuine runic find.

The Cleobury Mortimer 'pocket sundial' and its two accompanying stone discs were found in 1816 but not published until 1868, when the 'dial' was accurately described as an 'uncertain stone implement'.[29] It was last recorded in the collection of a Dr E. Whitcombe of Birmingham – presumably the Edmund Bancks Whitcombe, native of Cleobury Mortimer, who died in Birmingham in 1911 – towards the end of the nineteenth century. A drawing of one side of the 'dial' accompanied the find-report, and was repeated in (?) 1869 when the well-known antiquary Albert Way first publicized du Noyer's identification of it as a sundial.[30] In 1879 Haigh produced new drawings of both 'dial' and discs, recording runes on the latter.[31] On one he shows a retrograde, roughly radial inscription in which 'l', 'a', 'æ', 'i' and 'w' are clear and the early 'c' form   and a damaged 'œ' are possible. On the other Haigh found 'æo', worn and only faintly traceable. No other drawings of these characters are known, so that, until the 'sundial' is rediscovered, Haigh remains our only authority for them, which is unfortunate in view of the speciousness of his other work in the field. However, there is nothing fundamentally unlikely about the runes Haigh drew, except perhaps for the archaic 'c'. South Shropshire is rather an unusual place to find runes though there are occasional West Midlands examples, and, since the uncertain stone object is also a portable one, the place of discovery may be far from the place where the inscription was cut.

The only drawing of the 'owi' ring seems to be that given in W. Jones, *Finger-Ring Lore* (London, 1877), p. 421, whence derives the illustration in Stephens, *Old-Northern Runic Monuments* III, 213. Though the runes shown certainly read 'owi', the ring is suspect, and was, for example, intentionally omitted from D. M. Wilson's handlist of material outside the British Museum in his catalogue, *Anglo-Saxon Ornamental Metalwork 700–1100 in the British Museum* (London, 1964). Jones's book gave no details of the ring at all, apart from a title to the illustration, which, as we shall see, is suspect too. According to Stephens, 'The engraving was lent to Mr Jones . . . by one of the English learned societies. But unhappily no note was made of it, and he cannot say whence it came or where it is publisht and described'. This seems a delicate rewording of Jones's more forthright account in a pair of letters

---

[29] J. W(ilson), 'Uncertain Stone Implement', *Archæologia Cambrensis* 3rd ser., 14 (1868), 446–8. The identification as a sundial was suggested in G. V. du Noyer, 'Uncertain Stone Implement Explained', *Archæologia Cambrensis* 3rd ser., 15 (1869), 87–8.
[30] 'Ancient Sun-Dials', *Archaeological Journal* 25 (1868), 207–23, at 222–3. There is a dating discrepancy here. Way's article was published after, though it is dated before, du Noyer's, which derives from a letter written in December 1868.
[31] 'Yorkshire Dials', *Yorkshire Archæological and Topographical Journal* 5 (1879), 134–222, at 201–3.

written to Stephens in May 1877. Jones investigated the source of the illustration which had, at the publishers' request, been hastily added to make the book ready for the season. 'The cut you particularly mention . . . was . . . merely inscribed "A new Year's ring", though why and wherefore I cannot tell . . .' 'The artist engaged upon that work informs me that he does not remember whence the copy was taken', though Jones thought that the source was probably the *Archaeological Journal* where, however, I have been unable to find it. Jones added the opinion of a friend, an expert on rings, who dated this example to the early modern period. Unless Stephens had further information, which does not survive, from Jones, he was, to say the least, disingenuous in his treatment of the story of this illustration. The picture shows a slim ring with an oval or circular bezel which bears a fairly convincing 'owi', though the shape of 'o' is slightly irregular and the other two symbols are not exclusively runic. The general effect is not unlike one of the fifteenth-and sixteenth-century signet rings with merchants' marks which survive in quite large numbers,[32] and it may have been one of these that the original artist copied.

The silver coin found at Wijk in 1836 is recorded in Stephens, *Old-Northern Runic Monuments* I–II, 563–4, and also in D. H. Haigh, 'Miscellaneous Notes on the Old English Coinage', *Numismatic Chronicle* n.s. 9 (1869), 171–96, at 192 and pl. v, which presumably derives from Stephens. The original is lost, apparently destroyed in the German advance on Louvain in August 1914. Stephens's picture was taken from a copy of a copy (by the careful van der Chijs) of an original whose silver was 'in very poor condition', so there is likely to be error in it, particularly since it hardly indicates the state of the coin. Stephens shows a radial legend of runes and rune-like forms, mostly with bases towards the centre, and with no indication of the beginning. The sequence 'x' (or 'k' inverted), 'l' (inverted), (?) 'u', 'læ', 'n' or 'g', 'au' and an obscure form (?) 's' can be seen. The reverse has a monogram which Stephens identified as *Ecgberht*. As illustrated, the coin does not fit into any known Anglo-Saxon series. Its weight as given by Stephens is aberrant. The use of the monogram is a non-English feature and Stephens's confident reading of it is dubious. The forms of the runes – if they are correctly drawn – are not characteristically Anglo-Saxon (unless one is in fact 'k'), nor does their sequence give any Anglo-Saxon word. Unless another coin of this type appears we can never know (a) whether the legend has been accurately copied, and was in fact runic, (b) whether the coin was Anglo-Saxon or Continental Germanic.

Of the Northumbrian brooch we have no drawings, only a transcript of the runes in Stephens, *Old-Northern Runic Monuments* I–II, 386–7. This reproduces the inscription from a letter written by J. M. Kemble to J. J. A. Worsaae in 1847. Kemble had not seen the text, but Worsaae, to whom the piece had been shown by 'a gentleman in Northern England', had sent him details for his opinion on them. The brooch has never been traced despite a certain amount of nineteenth-century publicity, nor do I know of either Kemble's or Worsaae's original letter. Stephens's version is in two lines and divided into individual words, though this may be Kemble's

---

[32] See, for example, O. M. Dalton, *British Museum: Franks Bequest: Catalogue of the Finger Rings* . . . (London, 1912), nos 356, 423 and 559.

arrangement. The runes he gives are 'judrd mec worh[t] | e ælchfrith mec a[h]', 'c' being   throughout. Kemble added the two bracketed runes. He interpreted the text as a maker and owner formula similar to those on the Sittingbourne scramasax and the Lancashire ring, 'Guthrid made me. Ælchfrith owns me'. There are, however, formidable runological problems. The Scandinavian type 'c' is suspect. 'j' is not elsewhere used for OE back g. A vowel must be supplied in *Guthrid*, which is presumably a form of *Guðred*. The spirant spellings in 'd', 'th' and 'ch' are unusual in Anglo-Saxon runic usage.

Finally, in the case of the Hoddam stone we have no extant reproduction, only a description by a single authority, C. K. Sharp, who reported that 'in the ancient church of Hoddam, a sculptured stone, which was built into the wall, bore an inscription of some length, in Runic characters'.[33] The old church was demolished in 1815, and the stone has not been noted since. There are three difficulties here. We do not know what Sharp meant by 'Runic', for he may, as will be seen later, have used the term loosely to mean something like 'archaic', 'mysterious'.[34] If he used the word precisely, to mean 'drawn from the runic alphabet', his identification of the characters may or may not have been correct. If his identification was correct, the runes may have been either Scandinavian or Anglo-Saxon. Hoddam is, of course, within the Anglo-Saxon runic area, situated not far from Ruthwell and Bewcastle. It is also in the coastal region of north-west England and south-west Scotland where Scandinavian runes were used, as on the Hunterston brooch, the Bridekirk font and the wall of Carlisle cathedral.

Thus of the nine inscriptions in groups 3 and 4, one, Leeds, is probably genuinely runic: two, Cleobury Mortimer and Wijk, may be: five, Sandwich B, Kirkdale, Irton, Northumbria, and 'owi' are strongly suspect: and of one, Hoddam, there is inadequate evidence. Marquardt lists Leeds, Sandwich B, Irton, Northumbria, and 'owi' as 'Inschriften in angelsächsischen (anglischen) Runen', Cleobury Mortimer and Hoddam as 'Inschriften mit runenähnlichen Zeichen'. Kirkdale appears twice, once (A) in the first list, once (B) in the second. Wijk is intentionally omitted.

Before leaving Stephens's work I must consider two inscriptions whose interpretations are still in doubt; the cryptic text of the Sutton, Isle of Ely, brooch, and the 'æniwulufu' legend of a coin in the British Museum. When Stephens wrote on the Sutton brooch it was known only from Hickes's engraving.[35] In 1951, however, the piece came to light again after an interval of two and a half centuries, and it was then possible to establish the high degree of accuracy of the *Thesaurus* picture. Scratched round the rim of the brooch back is an Old English text, comparatively easy to interpret, in roman characters. A strip of metal is riveted to the back of the brooch,

[33] D. Wilson, *The Archæology and Prehistoric Annals of Scotland* (Edinburgh, 1851), p. 550.
[34] Wilson himself warns against the unclear use of 'runic' (*Archæology and Prehistoric Annals*, pp. 542–3). He also notes a stone in Anwoth parish, Kircudbrightshire, with marks which some antiquaries 'suppose to be Runic inscriptions'.
[35] A. Fountaine, *Numismata Anglo-Saxonica & Anglo-Danica breviter illustrata* (Oxford, 1705), p. 186, in Hickes's *Thesaurus*.

and on this is inscribed a second text, this time not in roman letters. Stephens thought they were 'stave-runes, several runes on the same stave',[36] here following Hickes who had called them '*Runæ* sive potius *Runarum* jugationes'. In fact, as I have noted elsewhere, these symbols bear only a slight similarity to Anglo-Saxon, or indeed any other, runes. They are probably a cryptic script, perhaps contrived for magical use. What they say I have no idea.

In the case of the 'æniwulufu' coin (listed by Marquardt as *England B*) there is doubt both as to the correct identification of the characters and as to the authenticity of the specimen. This gold coin, of the module of a tremissis, has an obverse legend +C ᴨᎩᴨ1ᴨᐸΙᛏᛱ LIO and a reverse VENA with scattered letters elsewhere in the field. For the obverse Haigh suggested the reading 'æniwulufu', retrograde and set within another legend, CLIO, which he explained variously as *gliw*, 'wise', and *hleo*, 'protector'. This reading of the runes has been commonly followed, save by Stephens who read *Æniwulu ku(nung)* (= Anwulf king) and Hempl who preferred the absurd *æniþu lufu*, 'unity (and) love'.[37] The legend certainly resembles 'æniwulufu', with two, though unimportant, epigraphical difficulties. The fourth character, ᛉ, could be read with Hempl 'þ', though 'w' is probably equally possible. The penultimate, ᚠ, is only 'f' if it is a blundered form omitting the lower arm of that rune. Otherwise it should be 's', as on St Cuthbert's coffin and the Greymoor Hill amulet ring. It is tempting to take, with Haigh, the legend as the common Old English personal name *Eanwulf*, though the final 'u' is as embarrassing as it is in other runic inscriptions – the *skanomodu* solidus text and the words 'flodu', 'giuþeasu' on the Franks Casket. A first element *Æni-* could be paralleled in the occasional form *Ænheri* of the Moore and Leningrad manuscripts of Bede's *Historia Ecclesiastica*, where it is presumably related to the Continental Gmc *Auni-*, having early *æ* for the reflex of WGmc *au* . . . *i*.[38] Unless the coin is very early, the medial *-i-* could hardly be the original unstressed vowel, but must be an intrusive one, perhaps due to the simplex *Eni* and influenced by such common variant pairs as *Cyn-/Cyni-*, *Sig-/Sige-*. *-wuluf* would show an intrusive vowel of the common type which developed between *l* and a following consonant, as in the Whitby comb 'h/e/lipæ'.

There are, however, difficulties over identifying this coin as runic. It was given to the British Museum by Count de Salis, who bought it in 1856 and was told it was found in England early in the nineteenth century. But there is doubt if this specimen is genuine. The compilers of the British Museum catalogue of Anglo-Saxon coins intentionally omitted it, and Sutherland rejects it.[39] It may in fact be a cast, as casts of this or similar coins are known to have circulated in the early nineteenth century. The reverse type, with its two figures holding up grotesquely large hands, is unusual,

---

36 *Old-Northern Runic Monuments* I–II, 292.

37 D. H. Haigh, 'Miscellaneous Notes on the Old English Coinage', *Numismatic Chronicle* n.s. 9 (1869), 171–96, at 172–3; Stephens, *Old-Northern Runic Monuments* III, 236–41; G. Hempl, 'Old-English Runic *æniþu lufu*', *Trans. of the American Philological Association* 27 (1896), lxiv–vi.

38 Ström, *Old English Personal Names in Bede's History*, p. 114; O. S. Anderson, *Old English Material in the Leningrad Manuscript of Bede's Ecclesiastical History* (Lund, 1941), p. 104.

39 C. H. V. Sutherland, *Anglo-Saxon Gold Coinage in the Light of the Crondall Hoard* (Oxford, 1948), p. 49, n. 4 and refs.

but appears on two related coins, probably genuine. The first, in the Royal Coin Cabinet. The Hague, which can be traced back to the collection of J. L. Kuijt of Leiden, has a similar reverse with the legend ꟼEN F-SI/// and an obverse with the text +CORNILIO, clearly related to the C. . . .LIO of the British Museum example.[40] The second, in the collection of Mr P. Grierson of Cambridge, has the reverse legend VEN/TA and other scattered letters, and on the obverse +CΛÞΛINDI+FILIO. This is the specimen illustrated in A. de Belfort, *Description générale des monnaies mérovingiennes* (Paris, 1892–5) III, no. 4731, where it is ascribed to Winchester, and by Ponton d'Amécourt in 1883, and it can be traced back to the Norblin collection in the 1830s.[41] A further coin, or perhaps the British Museum specimen, was found at Folkestone and exhibited to the Society of Antiquaries of London on 24 February 1736–7.[42] Its legend is recorded in the minute book as +CꟼꟼꟼꟼꟼꟼDI+ ꟼLIO, which is remarkably like that of the British Museum example, though the exhibitor's transcript, +CUÞUÞUDI CHRISTI FILIO, shows distinctive resemblances to the Grierson coin. Clearly the legends of the British Museum and Grierson pieces are closely related, deriving from a common original. On the whole it is likely that this original was in roman characters. The resemblance to a retrograde 'æniwulufu' is then chance, but it is so striking as to suggest that the die-cutter knew runes and was experienced in cutting them.

Five stone inscriptions, unnoticed by Stephens, are listed in the *Bibliographie*, three fragments from Whitby, and the sundials of Darlington and Old Byland. The three Whitby stones are now in the British Museum. One is part of a cross-head whose inscription was first cautiously recorded by W. G. Collingwood: 'the lettering, incised in a frame . . . has the look of runes; one might even imagine "[Ky]niswith." ' [43] The text is repeated, queried, in the same writer's catalogue of Anglo-Saxon inscriptions in Yorkshire, while the *Victoria County History* lists it as a 'worn inscription'.[44] Baldwin Brown is positive: 'A plain strip runs across the face of the transom with an inscription in runes, but nothing can be made of the few surviving characters'.[45] In 1943, however, C. A. R. Radford rejected this 'inscription' in terms which certainly now apply to the stone. 'The parallel lines . . . have been thought to contain a Runic inscription. I can find no trace of this. The lines are not horizontal and I consider that they represent damage at a later date'.[46] In the same article Radford himself published two inscribed stones and identified them as runic:

[40] Stephens, *Old-Northern Runic Monuments* III, 241–2.

[41] See *BNJ* 31 (1962), 171–2 and refs.

[42] See D. M. Metcalf, 'Eighteenth-Century Finds of Medieval Coins from the Records of the Society of Antiquaries', *Numismatic Chronicle* 6th ser., 18 (1958), 73–96, at 87–8.

[43] 'Anglian and Anglo-Danish Sculpture in the East Riding, with addenda to the North Riding', *Yorkshire Archaeological Journal* 21 (1911), 267–413, at 302; also 'Anglian and Anglo-Danish Sculpture in the West Riding . . .', *Yorkshire Archæological Journal* 23 (1915), 129–299, at 290.

[44] R. A. Smith and W. G. Collingwood, 'Anglo-Saxon Remains', *VCH Yorkshire* (London, 1907–25) II, 73–131, at 128.

[45] Brown, *The Arts in Early England* VI part ii, 100.

[46] Sir Charles Peers and C. A. R. Radford, 'The Saxon Monastery of Whitby', *Archaeologia* 89 (1943), 27–88, at 37. Similar parallel grooves run obliquely across another Whitby fragment, Radford no. 15 (= W. 11).

no. 14 (= W. 6 in the British Museum), with an 'Illegible Runic inscription', and no. 21 (= W. 8) with a 'Runic inscription with an initial cross'. The characters on stone 14, though much weathered, do not resemble runes in the least. They are much more like one of the minuscule scripts, perhaps even post-Conquest, in which case the stone has been reused at a later date. Only a fragment of the beginning of stone 21 inscription remains, the bases of most letters lost. Some of the characters look like runes: the first (after the clear initial +) could be a seriffed 'u', the second 'w' or 'þ' (though these two are not confined to runic alphabets), and the fourth 'l'. Other letters, however, are clearly non-runic, being made up of curling lines which rune-masters usually avoid. Too little of this stone remains for us to be able to make any constructive comment on its text.

Fowler was the first to notice, in 1863, the early double-sided sundial at Darlington. He sent a rubbing to Haigh who included an account and a drawing of one side in his article on Yorkshire sundials, apparently without having seen the original himself.[47] Haigh showed unusual caution in describing a mark 'almost effaced, something like the rune **Dæg** ... indicating the **dægmæl** point'. His drawing shows a clear form, indeed rather like a widened 'd', set radially between two of the rays. Unfortunately Haigh's hesitancy was fruitless, for in the *Victoria County History* Hodges, who was confused about the two sides of the dial, spoke firmly about 'the rune',[48] and Marquardt listed the stone, 'Mit D-Rune zur Bezeichnung des "dægmæl-point" (?), heute nicht mehr sichtbar'. This comment is ambiguous, suggesting at least the possibility that a genuine rune had deteriorated and become lost, so it is worth recording what can actually be seen on the Darlington stone. Its two dials are cut on the two faces of a flat slab which is broken at one edge. One has eight concentric circles, the other six, in each case divided into sectors by the rays. Both sides of the slab are weathered and abraded, the eight-circle side the more so, and on it no runes are visible nor (despite Hodges) have any ever been found there. On the six-circle side, at the point where Haigh saw the rune-like form, the surface is damaged and there are two fairly straight lines crossing. These are almost certainly accidental, and are only remotely like 'd'. As Marquardt noticed, a shape like the rune 'd' is shown in a similar, though not identical position, on Haigh's drawing of the Anglo-Saxon sundial at Old Byland.[49] Accordingly she listed this 'Mit D-Rune?' though no previous scholar had made the identification. The Old Byland sundial is both difficult of access and badly weathered. It is doubtful if in fact the letter 'd' is there.

A mixed group of objects remains to be disposed of. The weight from Ahlheden, Jutland, now in the National Museum, Copenhagen, on which F. Magnussen identified 'œui', was rejected even by the eclectic Stephens: 'It is not sure that the strokes are runes at all'.[50] The brooch from the Bateman collection (British Museum 93, 6–18, 32), traditionally associated on slender grounds with Kent, has an undoubted

---

[47] 'Yorkshire Dials', pp. 154–5.
[48] C. C. Hodges, 'Anglo-Saxon Remains', *VCH Durham* (London, 1905–28) I, 211–40, at 240.
[49] 'Yorkshire Dials', p. 141, taken from a cast, though Haigh saw the original himself.
[50] *Old-Northern Runic Monuments* I–II, 160.

but uninterpreted runic inscription which could be either Anglo-Saxon or Continental Germanic. Two urns, one from Lackford and one from Loveden Hill, have rune-like symbols, which may show an inadequate knowledge of runes on the part of their cutter.[51] D. M. Wilson has pointed out a group of fakes, copies of the amulet ring from Kingmoor, now in the British Museum (see *England D* in the *Bibliographie*).[52] Finally in this section we must note that there are modern inscriptions in Anglo-Saxon runes which will never – it is to be hoped – get into the runic corpus. Two examples serve to illustrate. In the church at Great Ormside, Westmorland, is a lectern, apparently local work from or after the restoration of 1885, on whose pedestal are cut the runes 'i·s·x·'. I do not know the explanation of these: the sequence suggests an attempt at the name of Christ (cf. 'ihs xps' on St Cuthbert's coffin), but the use of points may indicate initials, perhaps those of J. S. Twigge, the early twentieth-century antiquarian parson, with 'x' in error for the similar 't'. In the garden at Grove Place, Nursling, Hampshire, stand two statues, probably eighteenth- or nineteenth-century, each with a runic title on the plinth. These read 'þunr' and 'wodn'. From the context – the figures are crowned, one sceptred as Jove, the other armed as Mars – these are obviously *Þunor* and *Woden*, the first confirmed by a symbol containing 'thunder-flashes' above the name.

On the positive side there are a number of new inscriptions, recently found or published, to be added to Marquardt's catalogue: the Monkwearmouth, Orpington and Lindisfarne rune-stones, the Leningrad Gospels, the Loveden Hill urns, the Dover brooch, the Welbeck Hill bracteate and the Sarre pommel, together with rune-like characters on the Hunstanton brooch and on pommels from Faversham and Gilton.[53]

Not included in the *Bibliographie* and indeed not generally known, though details of them have long been published, are the inscriptions of York and Hamwih, Southampton. The first of these is on a wooden spoon, now in the Yorkshire Museum (register no. C 628), which was recorded first in J. Raine, *Yorkshire Museum: Handbook to the Antiquities* (1891), p. 218, and then in D. M. Waterman, 'Late Saxon, Viking, and Early Medieval Finds from York', *Archaeologia* 97 (1959), 59–105, at 85–6, where the runes are accurately delineated. According to Raine the spoon was discovered, with a large number of other objects, 'in 1884 in Clifford street whilst rebuilding the place of worship, etc., belonging to the Quakers'. He included it in a group of 'Scandinavian curiosities'. Waterman expresses no opinion as to whether the spoon is Scandinavian or English, though he dates it later than the Danish occupation of the city – to the tenth or eleventh century. The runes are ᚲᚣ,

[51] T. C. Lethbridge, *A Cemetery at Lackford, Suffolk: Report of the Excavation of a Cemetery of the Pagan Anglo-Saxon Period in 1947* (Cambridge, 1951), p. 20 and fig. 27; *Illustrated London News* for 31 August 1963, pp. 320–1.
[52] 'A Group of Anglo-Saxon Amulet Rings', *The Anglo-Saxons: Studies . . . presented to Bruce Dickins*, ed. P. Clemoes (Cambridge, 1959), pp. 159–70, at 168–70.
[53] For details of these finds see S. C. Hawkes and R. I. Page, 'Swords and Runes in South-East England' (1967).

almost certainly to be read that way up: they are presumably the Anglo-Saxon 'cx', though they could perhaps be Scandinavian **um**.

The Hamwih inscription, the runes 'catæ' scratched on the foot-bone of a cow, was discovered during the 1951 excavations of the storage pits related to the Anglo-Saxon settlement site of Southampton. It was in pit 66A, in Grove Street. The related finds have not been analysed in detail, and only a provisional report of the runes has yet appeared, in *The Archaeological News Letter* 4 (1951–3), 62. The bone is preserved, with the other Hamwih material, in the City Museums, Southampton.

The only other commonly unknown object for which we have some positive runic evidence is the lost Anglo-Saxon stone fragment from Norham, Northumberland. This was still in existence in 1776 when Hutchinson recorded its inscriptions, which seem to have been in roman characters save for a runic 'm' in an uncertain context.[54] By 1852 the stone had been lost and has not since been seen, so we must rely on Hutchinson's illustration, reluctantly since it gives a most un-Anglo-Saxon impression. It is likely that the letter in question was a damaged or weathered roman M, but the north-east occasionally evidences mixed inscriptions of runic and roman forms, such as the Alnmouth cross and the Chester-le-Street stone. Moreover, 'm' is one of the runes which sometimes intrudes into non-runic texts, as in the archangel's name [R]VmIA[EL] on St Cuthbert's coffin, in the Chester-le-Street name EADmVnD, and in a number of coin legends.[55]

A painting of a rune-stone otherwise unknown forms part of the portrait of Humfrey Wanley now in the library of the Society of Antiquaries of London, a picture which dates from 1711.[56] This shows the scholar surrounded by the treasures of the Harley collection of which he was keeper. In the foreground is an antique vase which elsewhere appears in a portrait of Edward Harley, and on the table rests the Guthlac roll, while Wanley holds up a Greek manuscript of St Matthew's gospel, wrongly described by the Society's historian as 'a book with Anglo-Saxon runes'.[57] In the left foreground stands a rune-stone, shown as a sort of pillar, square in cross-section and with a rather rounded top on which marks which may be runes can just be traced. On one face of the pillar is a panel formed in incised lines, framing an inscription of six runes, upside down, the first two retrograde. The runes are 'þrxfds', the letters clearly cut and well preserved. Since other objects in the picture are genuine, this stone should be genuine too, though it resembles none now known and the only rune-stones to be connected with Wanley reached Harley's collection in 1721, as will

---

[54] W. Hutchinson, *A View of Northumberland* . . . (Newcastle, 1778) II, 25. See also J. Raine, *The History and Antiquities of North Durham* (London, 1852), p. 259.

[55] For example, in the royal name, abbreviations of *moneta(rius)* and *me fecit* on coins of Eadmund of East Anglia and on his memorial coinage, Keary, *Catalogue*, p. 92, 68; p. 102, 178; p. 112, 327; p. 115, 381; p. 119, 426.

[56] The back of the picture bears a note giving the date 1711, but this is a copy of an earlier document, and it has been suggested that 1711 is an error for 1717, since the painter, Thomas Hill, made other portraits of Wanley in 1716 and 1717.

[57] J. Evans, *A History of the Society of Antiquaries* (Oxford, 1956), pl. iv. Unfortunately this plate cuts out the corner with the rune-stone. The picture is no. LI in G. Scharf, *A Catalogue of the Pictures Belonging to the Society of Antiquaries* . . . (Bungay, 1865), which contains a detailed account with the rune-stone described as 'An oriental inscribed stone of the cushion form'.

be seen below. In fact, however, this is unlikely to be a picture of a real stone in view of the inverted and (in some cases) retrograde setting of the characters, and in view of the sequence of the runes. The picture is probably imaginary, designed to illustrate one further aspect of Wanley's antiquarian interests.

When a reference to a runic object is unsupported by any drawing we are faced with the difficulties I have mentioned in discussing the Hoddam stone, primarily the problem of the meanings to ascribe to the words 'runic' and 'rune'. *OED* gives the following relevant meanings and dates: for 'runic', A. I, consisting of runes (as in 'runic characters'), 1662; Ib, carved or written in runes, 1685; Ic, inscribed with runes, 1728; 2, of poetry, etc., such as might be written in runes, especially ancient Scandinavian or Icelandic, 1690; 3, belonging to ancient Scandinavia or the ancient North, 1665; 3b, of ornament, of the interlacing type which is characteristic of rune-bearing monuments, 1838: for 'rune', I, a letter of the earliest Teutonic alphabet, 1685/90; 2a, an incantation or charm denoted by magic signs, 1796. This is useful as an indication of the danger of accepting early uses of the words at their face value, though the *OED* articles on these words are by no means complete and in most of the references can be readily antedated. For example, the editors of the dictionary made no use of the endearingly eccentric work, *Britannia antiqua illustrata* by the seventeenth-century Cambridge antiquary, Aylett Sammes, who used 'rune' in sense I ('the Ancient *Getes* or *Saxons* nam'd their Characters, *Runes*') and 'runic' in sense Ib ('their *Runick* or Magical Writings'),[58] while some years earlier still, in 1668, Junius used 'runic' in sense Ib and probably Ic ('the Runike inscription left with him', 'manie Runike monuments').[59] Sammes often connects 'runic' with 'magical', explaining that the 'Character [*sic*] . . . called *Runick* . . . were made use of by *Woden*, not only for Inscriptions, but Magical Charms and Imprecations'. There is clearly here a connection with meaning 2a of 'rune' which can thus hardly be as late as 1796.[60] Certainly 'runic' was in use as one of the Gothick words of the eighteenth and early nineteenth centuries, contrasting with the staider 'Roman' and having such connotations as 'magical', 'mysterious', 'sinister', 'eerie'. It is thus that Scott overworked the word in *The Pirate*. At the same time the history of runic studies in England explains the intimate association of the word 'runic' with 'Scandinavian'.

[58] *Britannia antiqua illustrata* (London, 1676), pp. 440 and 434. Those who delight in antedating *OED* will rejoice in Sammes's book which contains such examples as: *Berserker* (*OED* 1822), 'this sort of furious Onset was called Berserker', p. 438; *Edda* (*OED* 1771), 'To begin then with this EDDA, concerning the Expedition of WODEN out of *Asia*', p. 431; *Skald* (*OED* 1763), 'the Founder of that Tribe called Scalders, which . . . made it their business to set forth in Verses' (elsewhere *Skaldi*, *Skaldri*), p. 438.
[59] W. Hamper, *The Life, Diary, and Correspondence of Sir William Dugdale, Knight* (London, 1827), pp. 384–5.
[60] *Britannia antiqua illustrata*, p. 439. Sammes may, in fact, use 'rune' in sense 2a in 'These Runes our Ancestours set up against the Enemies', p. 442, though it is just possible that he refers here to the letters rather than the import of the text. See also W. Nicolson, *The English Historical Library* (London, 1696–9) I, 132: 'The Characters themselves were first . . . call'd *Runer*; tho afterwards that word came to acquire some new significations: As, I. *Enchantments* . . .' For further discussion of 'rune', 'runic' see H-G. Goetz, *Geschichte des Wortes 'rūn (rune)' und seiner Ableitungen im Englischen* (Göttingen, 1964), pp. 72–114.

Probably the most important stimulus to the development of runic scholarship in this country was the work of the Dane, Ole Worm, whose books *Runer, seu Danica literatura antiquissima* (Copenhagen, 1636), *Danicorum monumentorum libri sex* (Copenhagen, 1643) and *Specimen lexici runici* (Copenhagen, 1650) were avidly read here and often quoted. Worm's *Monumenta* is abundantly illustrated with woodcuts of rune-inscribed monuments from Norway, Sweden and Denmark. His *Specimen* is an Old Norse-Latin dictionary, the catch-words given in both runic and roman script. Not surprisingly 'runic' came to be used of both the epigraphical script of the monuments and the medieval Scandinavian language of Worm's lexicon and the literature written in it. The preponderance of Scandinavian runic remains over those of other countries and in other tongues, and the eagerness with which runic studies were pursued in the North, has resulted in the word being associated with Scandinavia down to the present day, and the confusion between script and language lasted at any rate into the nineteenth century, despite the attempts of scholars like Hickes to make a clear distinction between the two. Thus right from the seventeenth century, when they first appeared in English, 'rune' and 'runic' were used with a wide range of meanings, so that any reference to a runic monument must be regarded with suspicion. Just as writers have sometimes been baffled by the form of 'runic' – witness Thoresby's 'Ruinick'[61] – so they have often been ignorant of any proper meaning for it, and the alert reader will often spot such absurdities as 'The vignette represents a Runic or Buddhist cross near Ramsey Bay, Isle of Man' or such misrepresentations as 'stones inscribed with the runic alphabet known as Ogham'.[62]

A very early and undoubted allusion to a lost rune-stone, though there is no way of knowing what sort of runes it displayed, is the unidentified Westmorland place-name *Runcrosbanc* 1286.[63] Most references are much later, from or after that great period of learning in the late seventeenth century when amateurs up and down the country were on the look-out for Anglo-Saxon antiquities. From these more modern times come a number of accounts of runic objects now lost or unidentifiable, but only when a reference is given by a scholar skilled in the script and precise in his language can we think it likely that the object actually was inscribed in runic characters. Such a scholar was Wanley who mentions four examples, all of which he had seen himself. In his journal which lists his dealings on Harley's behalf (Lansdowne MS 771, in the British Museum) Wanley notes for 16 February 1720/1, 'My Lord [Harley] sent in an antient Gold Ring found at Newbury in Berkshire, which the Lord Bathurst gave him yesterday. There are some Runic Letters discernable upon it'. His entry for 25 November 1721 records 'two stones with Runic Letters, and another with the Armes of Courtney, found by Mr Auditor Harley in the Church of [*blank space*] in Northamptonshire, in an heap of Rubbish'.[64] Presumably

[61] See above, p. 128.
[62] E. Forbes, *A History of British Starfishes, and Other Animals of the Class Echinodermata* (London, 1841), p. 230; J. M. White, 'Tristan and Isolt', *Myth or Legend?* (London, 1955), p. 73.
[63] A. H. Smith, *The Place-Names of Westmorland*, EPNS 42–3 (Cambridge, 1967) II, 187.
[64] C. E. and R. C. Wright, *The Diary of Humfrey Wanley 1715–1726* (London, 1966) I, 87 and 123. The latter are presumably among the 'divers pieces of Antiquity' which Wanley proposed to send to

all three came from Northamptonshire, though Wanley may mean only that the heraldic stone did. Neither Berkshire nor Northamptonshire is a known runic area. Wanley's fourth reference to a runic monument is in Bodley H.9.5 Art., a copy of the second edition of W. Nicolson's *The English Historical Library* (London, 1714) with manuscript annotations. Apropos of a note on runes Wanley wrote: 'When Sir Andrew Fountain was in Ireland, he met with and bought [*sic*] to London a Wooden Hand or Scepter of an Irish or Danish King with many Runic Letters on it'. This must be the 'old Irish Hand, Scepter, or Mace, which I borrowed of him [Fountaine]' mentioned in Wanley's journal for 10 September 1720, though without reference to any runes.[65] It could be – though the dates make this rather doubtful – the object commented on by William Nicolson, bishop of Carlisle, in a letter to Lhuyd (Bodleian MS Ashmole 1816, fol. 515, undated, but *c.* 1701), 'your Irish Inscription (which, tho' it seems somew^t to counterfeit a Runic Motto, I take to be no more than a casual and insignificant flourish)'. It may also, though this is even more doubtful, be intended by Stephens's obscure entry, 'Dublin Museum, Ireland. The *later* runes. On a wooden Cavel. Apparently only a scribble. Cannot be further dated',[66] though this again could be the 'little stick' which, according to a letter in the Royal Library, Stockholm, G. M. Atkinson sent to Stephens on 21 June 1872 with the remark, 'This is the only relick of the Rune staff I have seen in Ireland'. None of these can be traced further. The 'sceptre' is not listed in the Fountaine sale catalogue (1889). The National Museum of Ireland knows nothing of Stephens's cavel.

There is no point in listing in detail the poorly authenticated references to runic objects. A pair of examples will stress the difficulties. Lot 87 in the sale catalogue of the collection of John White of Newgate Street (1778) is described as 'An antient Runic ring, found near the Picts Wall, 1773', with the tantalizing addition '*See the account with it*'. This lot was sold to Tyssen for £1 13s. 0d., though it does not appear in the Tyssen sale catalogue (1802). Besides the usual problems of identification here there is a further cause for suspicion. White was a well-known dealer in antiquaries, which he sometimes made himself. This ring could well be a fake, and Tyssen an innocent dupe. The account of the Abbotsford stone, given in Mrs Hughes's *Letters and Recollections of Sir Walter Scott* (ed. H. G. Hutchinson, London, n.d.), p. 100, makes specific mention of a runic inscription, yet probably wrongly. The entry for 5 May 1824 begins, 'Walked again to the stone in memory of Kerr of Cessford and looked at the large stone with a Runic inscription which is in the adjoining plantation'. The stone examined by Mrs Hughes can only be identified with a Pictish cross slab, uninscribed, now in the National Museum of Antiquities of Scotland, Edinburgh. This elaborately sculptured stone was discovered in the old castle of Woodray, Aberlemno, Forfarshire, and was presented to Scott who put it up on his estate.[67] The

---

Wimpole on 1 December 1721 (*ibid.* II, 434). No rune-stones are mentioned in the Harley sale catalogue (1742).

[65] Wright, *Diary of Humfrey Wanley* I, 68.

[66] *The Runes, Whence Came They?*, p. 58.

[67] Stuart, *Sculptured Stones of Scotland* I, 31 and plates xcviii and xcix.

stone is runic in sense 3b only, and it is curious that this lady, so well-informed and under Sir Walter's tutelage, should have referred so explicitly to an inscription.

I have tried in this paper to define some difficulties of establishing the Anglo-Saxon runic corpus. Inevitably a few hard cases remain for extended discussion elsewhere – the Bury St Edmunds lead plate, with its quotation from Ælfric following a (?) runic title; the Rome bronze fragment, with its Anglo-Saxon runic alphabet which, however, uses a Scandinavian 'c'; the Coquet Island ring, which has now collapsed into a greyish powder; a dubiously Anglo-Saxon sword of unknown provenance with (?) runes engraved on its tang and perhaps inlaid in its blade;[68] the Gandersheim (Brunswick) Casket, of walrus ivory, with a metal plate inscribed with runes stuck to its base – a genuine casket with a suspect inscription;[69] a number of urns which have rune-like symbols of uncertain interpretation; sceattas with blundered legends which may derive from genuine runic ones which have not survived incorrupt. Inevitably, too, this study can only present a provisional statement. We may confidently expect fresh runic inscriptions in the coming years while lost ones may be rediscovered, and further material recovered from early records newly identified or studied.

POSTSCRIPT

The title of this piece, written when the donnishly jocular discussion about 'U and non-U' English was still raging, indicates its age. Much of it remains valid, particularly its destructive part. Several of its mysteries remain mysterious. Some of its entries need emendation or updating.

Despite the obscurities of the Stephens reproduction H. E. Pagan managed to identify the silver coin from Wijk as a type of Beonna of East Anglia, and later scholars have upheld the identification.[70] It is salutary to observe how distant from the facts is my 1969 reading of the runes of this coin as illustrated by Stephens.

The **æniwulufu** coin has gained a new lease of life. The British Museum specimen seems to be an eighteenth- or nineteenth-century copy of a coin found at Folkestone, recorded in 1732 and 1737 and then lost.[71] A new specimen, apparently from the same dies, has now emerged in the Hunterian Collection, University of Glasgow. Unfortunately its find-spot is unrecorded. John Insley identified the legend as a personal name in a diagnostically Frisian form on the basis of the final unstressed

---

[68] R. E. Oakeshott, *The Sword in the Age of Chivalry* (London, 1965), p. 32 and pl. 4A.

[69] A. Fink, 'Zum Gandersheimer Runenkästchen', *Karolingische und Ottonische Kunst*, ed. F. Geke *et al.* (Wiesbaden, 1957), pp. 277–81.

[70] H. E. Pagan, 'A New Type for Beonna', *BNJ* 37 (1968), 10–15; cf. M. M. Archibald, 'The Coinage of Beonna in the Light of the Middle Harling Hoard', *BNJ* 55 (1985), 10–54, at 10 and 35.

[71] Philip Grierson and Mark Blackburn give a detailed account of this and related pieces in *Medieval European Coinage with a Catalogue of the Coins in the Fitzwilliam Museum, Cambridge: I The Early Middle Ages (5th–10th Centuries)* (Cambridge, 1986), pp. 640–3: the Grierson coin is there identified as a modern derivative of the **æniwulufu** piece.

-*u*; and if that is in fact a significant feature (which I am a little less sure of than is Dr Insley) this coin is an important addition to the corpus of Frisian runic monuments.[72]

To the additions listed on pp. 173–4, there must now be supplied those recorded in my later paper 'New Runic Finds in England' and its postscript, pp. 275–87 below.

An occasional flash of light illumines a pair of modern runic monuments described towards the end of my paper. The two Nursling statues are part of a set of seven carved by the sculptor Rysbrack to represent the days of the week. These were commissioned for the park at Stowe in Kent but are now dispersed. The amiable folly of introducing runic inscriptions into the modern landscape flourishes yet. The most recent one I know is the text 'm o t a n · e a l l e · w e o d a · n u · w y r t u m · a s p r i n g a n' in a mosaic set in the floor of a new conservatory built on to the lodge of Slingsby Hall, York.

---

[72] M. Blackburn, 'A Survey of Anglo-Saxon and Frisian Coins with Runic Inscriptions', *Old English Runes*, ed. Bammesberger, pp. 137–89, at 143–4, and appendix 2 by J. Insley, pp. 172–4.

14

(1971)

HOW LONG DID THE SCANDINAVIAN LANGUAGE SURVIVE IN ENGLAND? THE EPIGRAPHICAL EVIDENCE[1]

It is forty years since Professor Eilert Ekwall published his 'How Long did the Scandinavian Language Survive in England?', the substance of a lecture given three years earlier.[2] In answering his question Ekwall used three types of evidence: inscriptions, place-names, loan-words. The last two I do not consider here: several English Place-Name Society Danelaw volumes have come out since Ekwall wrote, adding to his a wealth of material for careful sifting, while Dietrich Hofmann has re-examined the loan-words in *Nordisch-englische Lehnbeziehungen der Wikingerzeit* (Copenhagen, 1955). Only very recently, however, has the work of collecting and evaluating the country's early English and Norse inscriptions been taken in hand, and already it is clear that we need more precise description and analysis of the epigraphical material than Ekwall gave in 1930.

Ekwall used epigraphical evidence in two ways. He took three Old English inscriptions, all from Yorkshire, and argued that Scandinavians had commissioned them: the Kirkdale and Aldbrough sundials and the St Mary Castlegate, York, foundation stone. These he claimed showed Scandinavians leaving their native tongue for English. He then examined five inscriptions in Scandinavian which showed native speakers keeping to that tongue. In order of decreasing importance these are the Pennington, Lancashire, tympanum and the Carlisle graffito, both of which Ekwall studied in detail, and the Skelton in Cleveland, Thornaby on Tees and Harrogate stones which he mentioned only briefly. He listed also, but rejected as irrelevant, the Lincoln comb ('there is nothing to prove that the comb was made in

---

[1] In this paper I use lower-case bold for inscriptions in Norse runes, lower-case roman between single inverted commas for Anglo-Saxon runes, and upper-case roman for texts in roman characters. I use my own readings for runic texts. I have also examined some of those in roman characters, but here I rely too on the work of Dr Elisabeth Okasha, acknowledged in greater detail below. In a general account like this I cannot give such precise transcripts as would be expected in an epigraphical study, so that in minor points my transliterations may be incorrect or may differ from Dr Okasha's rigorous ones. For convenience I have adopted the practice of dividing texts into their individual words even if they are undivided in the original. For help on archaeological matters I wish to thank Mr D. M. Wilson.
[2] *A Grammatical Miscellany Offered to Otto Jespersen on his Seventieth Birthday*, ed. N. Bøgholm *et al.* (London and Copenhagen, 1930), pp. 17–30.

England') and the St Paul's, London, stone ('purely Scandinavian . . . probably commemorates some Dane who came over with Cnut'). It is a thin collection, and Ekwall felt obliged to apologize for it, comparing England's poverty with Manx plenty. 'I am inclined to believe . . . that the rare occurrence of Scandinavian runic stones in England is partly due to the quality of the stone used', for it is 'soft . . . easy to work but does not offer strong resistance to the effects of time and weather'.[3]

Ekwall's list of Scandinavian runic monuments in England was incomplete when he published it. The late Professor Hertha Marquardt's *Bibliographie der Runenin-schriften nach Fundorten* (Göttingen, 1961) adds Bridekirk (known since about 1600), Conishead (found 1928, recorded the following year) and Dearham (published in the nineteenth century), all from north-west England. It misses the York spoon, which the Yorkshire Museum catalogued in 1891, and which has two runes, possibly Norse but rather more likely to be English.[4] Also absent is the Settle slate, found in 1870 but not published until 1962.[5] One further fragment has appeared more recently, a small piece of magnesian limestone discovered under York Minster, having traces of two runes so slight that we cannot tell which type they belong to.[6]

Even with these additions it is a small field, so right at the beginning it is worth facing Ekwall's argument that many Scandinavian rune-stones failed to survive in this country because they were cut on poor quality material. Ekwall cites in contrast the plentiful Viking rune-stones of the Isle of Man, but I doubt if this is a valid comparison. L. Musset's summary of the rune-stones (up to the year 1300) in the various northern lands gives 2,400 to Sweden, rather more than 300 to Denmark and the neighbouring coastal areas, fifty to Norway and ninety to the Norwegian colonies overseas, a figure which includes the forty-seven Icelandic ones which do not belong to this period at all.[7] Publishing the newly found Kirk Maughold, Man, stone, A. M. Cubbon listed the inscriptions in the British Isles: thirty-one in the Isle of Man, forty-two in the Orkneys and Shetlands, eleven in the Western Isles, four in mainland Scotland, nine in England and Wales and three in Ireland.[8] Of course, not all these

3 *Ibid.* p. 23.
4 J. Raine, *Yorkshire Museum: Handbook to the Antiquities* (1891), pp. 216–18, republished in D. M. Waterman, 'Late Saxon, Viking, and Early Medieval Finds from York', *Archaeologia* 97 (1959), 59–105, at 85–6.
5 A. H. Smith, *The Place-Names of the West Riding of Yorkshire*, EPNS 30–7 (Cambridge, 1961–3) VII, 62.
6 I thank Dr B. Hope-Taylor for telling me of this find. So far (August 1969) all other inscriptions from this site have been non-runic and in either Latin or Old English. For completeness I note here a few more inscriptions to be rejected out of hand. Smith, *Place-Names of the West Riding* VII, 62, records 'the name "kuni Onlaf" on a stone at Leeds', but these runes are Anglo-Saxon and the name *Onlaf* not at all certain. Marquardt's *Bibliographie* lists two Swedish stones at Oxford which are modern imports. There is a second stone from St Paul's, London, on which G. Stephens, following G. F. Browne, identified runes; certainly there is a rough mark on its edge which looks like **k**, but the identification is doubtful. For other uncertain references to rune-stones see my 'Runes and Non-Runes', above pp. 161–78.
7 L. Musset and F. Mossé, *Introduction à la Runologie* (Paris, 1965), p. 241.
8 A. M. Cubbon, 'Viking Runes: Outstanding New Discovery at Maughold', *Journal of the Manx Museum* 7 (1966), 23–6, at 25–6. It is hard to arrive at exact figures in the absence of an adequate corpus of these inscriptions. M. Olsen gives slightly different statistics in 'Runic Inscriptions in Great

are from the Viking Age. Only 170–180 of the Danish examples come from that period.[9] Few runic inscriptions of any kind occur in early Viking Age Norway, and it seems that Norwegian Viking Age rune-stones are generally rare, though there are two groups of some size, those from Jæren which link to the Manx examples, and those in the Ringerike style which date from the last century of Viking activity. Surprising is the dearth of inscriptions in areas of intensive Scandinavian settlement. Iceland has no Viking Age runic monuments. Normandy has no runes at all. There are only three examples from the Faroe Islands. The Vikings who travelled *i austrveg* cut, as far as yet we know, only the *Aldeigjuborg* rune-inscribed stick, the Berezanj stone and the carving on the Piraeus/Venice lion. Greenland has as many as fifteen inscriptions, but all relatively late and several on wood which survived there in the frozen ground. The three Irish specimens apparently include the Nendrum, Co. Down, stone which is doubtfully runic and doubtfully Scandinavian. Otherwise the only Irish rune-stone is the runic-ogham cross from Killaloe, Co. Clare.

Compared with these numbers the English corpus does not look inadequate, which suggests that it has not suffered excessively from loss or decay through the years. On the contrary, it is the plenty of Manx inscriptions which needs accounting for, rather than the dearth of English ones. In any case, it is unlikely on practical grounds that Viking rune-stones have suffered more from poor quality material in England than elsewhere. The north of England is rich enough in stone, easy to obtain and cut, yet resistant to weathering, as the surviving Anglo-Saxon monuments show. Dr Elisabeth Okasha's *Hand-List of Anglo-Saxon Non-Runic Inscriptions* (Cambridge, 1971) gives over eighty inscribed stones in Old English or Latin in the northern part of the Danelaw, and of the thirty-seven Anglo-Saxon rune-stones thirty-four come from a region north of the Dee-Wash line. There must be thousands of fragments of carved, uninscribed Dark Age stones from the same area.

A preliminary corpus of Scandinavian inscriptions in England thus consists of five stones in the north-west coastal area (Carlisle, Bridekirk, Dearham, Conishead and Pennington), two from near the north-east coast (Thornaby on Tees and Skelton in Cleveland), two in the Pennines (Settle and Harrogate),[10] the London stone and the Lincoln comb. The two York inscriptions I exclude from the start since neither is clearly Scandinavian. Two of those provisionally accepted also look doubtful, Thornaby on Tees and Harrogate.

Stephens was the first to publish the Thornaby stone, and it is worth reproducing in full his rather naive account: 'Thornaby, Yorkshire, England. Slightly scribbled in, below a small stone Sundial in the wall of the Church, which is of early Norman date. Carvd about A.D. 1100. It was communicated to me by M. Fallow, Esq. In spite of many accidental-scratches, we can read: IT BISTR IS AN BI-UIK. *This is the best at Bi-wik.* Where BI-WIK is, I do not know. It is not in Philip's Atlas of the counties

---

Britain, Ireland and the Isle of Man', *Viking Antiquities in Great Britain and Ireland*, ed. H. Shetelig (Oslo, 1940–54) VI, 151–233, at 153. Cf. also K. Düwel, *Runenkunde* (Stuttgart, 1968), pp. 86–7.
[9] Jacobsen and Moltke, *Danmarks runeindskrifter*, col. 1020.
[10] To be precise, six miles south-west of Harrogate.

of England'.[11] I do not know if Fallow's drawing, from which Stephens worked still exists. Fallow's own description appeared posthumously, in 1911, and is vaguer about the textual details: the stone 'appears to have been inscribed with a sentence in runes, as well as some other marks'.[12] Certainly, Stephens's reading is convincing neither as Old Norse nor as a useful comment to cut on a stone. W. G. Collingwood also saw the Thornaby runes: at least he published a drawing of them in 1907, claiming to read BISTR with traces of letters on either side, but without room for the whole sentence that Stephens found. His picture shows B and, less clearly, R, either runic or roman, either English or Norse. There is a possible runic 's', either Anglo-Saxon or Danish, but no other identifiable letters.[13] Collingwood's accounts of the stone present a further problem. Fallow, whose description is the most detailed, reported that the stone was 'near the ground at the east end of the south wall'. Collingwood said it was 'under E. window outside', which sounds like a different place, unless Collingwood was misreading his notes.[14] Could there have been two faintly marked stones, on one of which Collingwood identified runes as a consequence of reading Stephens's account of the other? Collingwood said that the inscription had been lost since 1904, the date the church was restored, and it is certainly not to be found now. If there were runes they were very faint, and we cannot be sure they were Scandinavian. But can we even be sure there were runes?

The Harrogate case is quite different. This stone survives for examination, in the Pump Room Museum, Harrogate. Though it is sometimes called a hogback, it is an untypical specimen, for it looks like a plain boulder broken away at the back and one end. On the face where the 'runes' are, I can see no signs of tool-marks, of shaping or decoration. The 'runes' are a group of deep, coarse scores, somewhat weathered but quite distinct. W. J. Kaye found and published the stone, and there is an excellent photograph and a more detailed find-report, based on Kaye's evidence, in G. Baldwin Brown, *The Arts in Early England* VI, 265–7. Brown noted that the stone had deteriorated in condition since it was discovered, and that early photographs did not show the deep scar which now runs obliquely across the face below the last two 'letters'. Kaye sent photographs of his find to Fowler and Kermode who identified the 'runes', and the identification has persisted. The marks on the stone were, and still are, 'ᚾᛏ. Kermode suggested SUNA, a form of ON *sunr*, 'son' (Brown agreeing), but he was unsure of the second letter, and so gave the alternative STNA, an abbreviated form of *steinn*, 'stone', perhaps as a personal name element.[15] Neither of these fragments of text is helpful as it stands, for each needs a fair amount supplied to give a useful meaning, and the present size, shape and state of the stone preclude

[11] G. Stephens, *The Runes, Whence Came They?* (London and Copenhagen, 1894), p. 15. It may be significant that Professor S. O. M. Söderberg did not include the Thornaby runes in the fourth volume of *Old-Northern Runic Monuments* which appeared after Stephens's death.
[12] 'The Fallow Papers', *Yorkshire Archæological Journal* 21 (1911), 225–53, at 238.
[13] W. G. Collingwood, 'Anglian and Anglo-Danish Sculpture in the North Riding of Yorkshire', *Yorkshire Archæological Journal* 19 (1907), 267–413, at 402–3.
[14] R. A. Smith and W. G. Collingwood, 'Anglo-Saxon Remains', *VCH Yorkshire* (London, 1907–25) II, 73–131, at 127.
[15] *PSAL* 2nd ser., 19 (1901–3), 55.

much addition, while the rough marks on the battered back of the boulder are not likely to be the remains of an inscription. Clearly the 'runes' need re-examination. They are unlike any other Scandinavian runes in this country, being large (no. 3, for example, is 21 cm. high), rough, widely spaced and ill-disciplined, and the lines which form them are not markedly different from the modern score across the face. The first is a half-length vertical which could be Swedo-Norwegian **s**. Brown even claimed that it ended with a terminal dot, but this I cannot confirm. To me it looks as though the shortness of the stroke is due to the lower part of the stone face breaking away. The second 'rune' may have lost its left-hand base in the same way, though I am less sure of that. It now looks little like **t** and less like **u**. Its top is a wide curve such as rune-masters usually avoid, certainly in these two letters. The third could be Swedo-Norwegian **n** and the fourth Danish **a**, though each is simply two lines meeting or crossing at an acute angle. As a group the marks on this stone do not much resemble runes, though equally they do not seem accidental marks cut into the surface and then damaged by breaking.

Kaye's find-report shows that the stone, 'runes' uppermost, lay near a long barrow, and could have rolled from its top. There was no chance of a careful examination of the site, but a number of artefacts are somehow linked to the discovery: glazed pottery, remains of oak beams, an iron axe-head and two small horseshoes, a saw blade, flints and bones. Brown thought the axe-head, badly corroded as it was, to be Viking, and suggested that the Harrogate stone marked an intrusive Viking burial in the long barrow. If this were true it would tend to confirm the identification of the marks on the stone as Viking runes, but modern archaeologists have ignored this find and confirmation is lacking. For the moment we must suspend judgment. These do not look like Scandinavian runes to me. Even if they are, they are too fragmentary to tell us what language they record.

This last point may seem a quibble, for most people would assume that Scandinavian runes give a text in a Scandinavian tongue. The Bridekirk font shows this to be a false assumption. Reginald Bainbrigg, the sixteenth-century Appleby antiquary, reported that this font came from the neighbouring site of Papcastle, Cumberland, but throughout modern times the parish church of Bridekirk has sheltered it, and hence it survives in excellent condition, its surface lightly plastered and recently painted. It is a single block of stone with elaborate carving, which art historians date to the twelfth century. Across its east face a curling ribbon runs between two capitals, and here is cut a text in mixed runes and bookhand characters, for the most part intelligible: + **ricarþ : he : mē : iwrocte : 7 : to þis : me : rÐ : 3er : [..] : mē : brocte**, '+ Ricarth he made me, and . . . brought me to this splendour', the obscure sequence **3er[..]** perhaps representing a second personal name.[16] The runes are Scandinavian, supplemented by *eth*, *yogh* and *wynn* and the nota for *and*. The language is late Old English or early Middle English, its form fitting admirably the art historians' twelfth-century dating of the decoration. There is no clear sign of Norse influence on the language, and the name form *Ricarþ* could equally well be

---

[16] There are excellent pictures of the font in M. D. Forbes and B. Dickins, 'The Inscriptions of the Ruthwell and Bewcastle Crosses and the Bridekirk Font', *Burlington Magazine* 25 (1914), 24–9.

ON *Ríkarðr* or Continental Germanic *Ricard* which appeared in England as early as the mid-eleventh century.[17]

Since the Bridekirk font shows that Norse runes do not necessarily record a Norse legend, it follows that, where we cannot interpret a group of these runes, we can draw no conclusions about the language their rune-master spoke. The point is significant with regard to the Dearham stone, from a site some four miles from Bridekirk. This is an elaborately carved grave slab, ascribed by art historians to the twelfth century.[18] It records the name ADAM in decorative roman capitals. A plain border surrounds the design, and across its lower part (at the opposite end to the name and probably added to the finished stone) runs a line of runes, rather roughly cut and damaged at the beginning. The clearly readable part of the legend is · ⵝⵀⵉⵕⵖ, ·**hniarm** or ·**hniærm**, with three staves or lines preceding the point. This group has no obvious meaning, and a sequence **hn** is suspect at this date, since in all Norse dialects but Icelandic initial *hn* became *n* before the twelfth century. It is worth noting that the second *ætt* of the later *fuþark* begins with the group **hnia**, so the Dearham runes may preserve a casual memory of the *fuþark* scratched in the stone by some chance visitor to the grave.

The rest of the west coast inscriptions are meaningful, at any rate in part. The twelfth-century tympanum at Pennington on which Ekwall relied so heavily is poorly preserved. Part of its surface looks chiselled away, perhaps when later medieval masons re-used it as building material. For about a century after the new church was built in 1826 the stone was set into the wall of an outhouse, attacked by the weather. Only part of its text can be made out, some of this disputed. Ekwall's reading, '. . .kial (*or* mial) seti þesa kirk. Hubert masun uan m.', seems, from the two aberrant forms given for the first word and from the reading *þesa*, to derive from W. G. Collingwood's early attempts.[19] Independent is Bruce Dickins's 'KML : SETE : ThES : KIRK : HUBIRT : MASUN : UAN : M. . . .', 'Gamal built this church. Hubert the mason carved. . .', with *Gamal* taken as the name of the later twelfth-century lord of Pennington.[20] I read: -**kml : [.]et[.] : þe[.] : kirk : hub[.]rt : m[.]sun : u[.]n : m-**. Initial **k** is suspect for it is much bigger than other runes and is different in quality. Moreover there could have been up to two letters preceding it, now lost with the stone surface. The second word seems to begin with **l** not **s**, as indeed Collingwood showed. Certainly it could not have the **s**-form, ⵂ, used later in the text. The ending of the third word is damaged, but looks to me like two vertical staves with lines between them, perhaps **na**. Of **hub[.]rt** the fourth rune has a vertical set rather far from **b**, and in some lights this letter looks like ⵋ, **o**. A sloping gash cuts across the vertical which forms the second letter of **m[.]sun**. Collingwood, who examined the

[17] T. Forssner, *Continental Germanic Personal Names in England* (Uppsala, 1916), pp. 213–14.
[18] This date, which Collingwood suggested ('Remains of the Pre-Norman Period', *VCH Cumberland* (London, 1901–5) I, 253–93, at 281) is confirmed in a private communication by Mr R. Bailey of the University of Newcastle upon Tyne.
[19] See, e.g., 'Runic Tympanum at Pennington, Furness', *SBVS* 3 (1903), 139–41.
[20] A. Fell, *A Furness Manor: Pennington and its Church* (Ulverston, 1929), pp. 217–19.

inscription when it was in the open air, thought this mark accidental, and he may well be right.

It is worthwhile here summing up the objections to the earlier readings of this legend. Certainly **kml** could represent *Gamal*, with **k** used for a voiced stop and the vowels omitted in the personal name,[21] but such abbreviation is odd if the purpose of the inscription was to commemorate the church's founder, and, as we have seen, **kml** may not be a correct, or at least a complete, reading. *Seti* or *sete*, 'established, set up', is meaningful, but no other Old Norse inscription uses *setja* for 'found (a church)', *gera* being preferred. In any case, *sete* could be as well Old English as Old Norse. ON *setja*, OE *settan* are often found for 'set up (stones, memorials)', and the Old English St Mary Castlegate stone has *settan* in the context 'set up (this minster)'. Unfortunately I cannot find *seti/sete* on the Pennington tympanum, and the alternative *leti/lete* makes no sense. The demonstrative looks like *þena* which is acceptable as a masculine acc. sg. form, but not as the feminine which ON *kirkja* would require. We could here assume confusion of grammatical gender, just as we must assume loss of the distinctively Old Norse inflexional ending in *kirk*. Further, in such a sentence as this a word order *þena kirk* would be unusual for Old Norse where commonly the demonstrative follows its noun.[22] Some form of a personal name *Hubert* is probably acceptable, but a title *masun* would be strange at this early date, and a spelling with medial -*s*- also seems anachronistic. Perhaps we should accept here Ekwall's suggestion that this word is the patronymic *Másson*.

In this uncertainty it is hard to define the language of the Pennington inscription. Suggestive of Old Norse are (i) the runes, (ii) (?) the name *Gamal* and the (?) patronymic *Masun* and (iii) the word *kirk*. Characteristic of Old English are (iv) the word order *þena kirk* and (v) (?) the use of *seti/sete*. Neither specifically Old Norse nor Old English are (vi) the form of the verb *seti/sete*, (vii) the grammatical forms of *þena kirk*, (viii) the personal name *Hubert* and (ix) (?) the verb *uan*. (i) is, as I have shown, inconclusive, while I argue below that (ii) the possession of an Old Norse name does not stamp a man as of Scandinavian stock nor need he use a Scandinavian tongue. (iii), *kirk*, is interchangeable with English *cirice* in place-name forms probably as early as the twelfth century. Though Anglo-Norman spellings are ambiguous since scribes use *ch* for front and back stop alike, it looks as though a name like Whitkirk, Yorkshire -*Witechirche* 1154–66, *Withekirke* 1185, with runs of -*church(e)* and -*kirk(e)* forms down to modern times – shows the two elements used side by side through the Middle English period. If the Pennington legend is Old Norse, it is markedly corrupt Old Norse, presumably influenced by English. If it is Old English or Middle English it has been much affected by Old Norse. From it I would hesitate to argue what language the people of the area spoke in the twelfth century.

The Carlisle graffito has a few unusual features, but the find-report, recording its

---

[21] Cf. such Danish parallels as **þurlf** for *þorulf*, **askl** for *Askil* (Jacobsen and Moltke, *Danmarks runeindskrifter*, col. 1010).
[22] *Ibid.* col. 887. See also K. M. Nielsen, 'The Position of the Attribute in Danish Runic Inscriptions', *APS* 16 (1942–3), 212–32, at 227–9.

discovery 'on removing the plaster and white-wash from the interior of the south transept' of the cathedral, is convincing enough to guarantee its authenticity.[23] Nor, despite some points which need more detailed attention, is there reason to dispute the general tenor of the transcription, **tolfin : urait þasĩ runr a þisĩ s͡tain**, 'Dolfinn engraved these runes on this stone'. Such features as the retention of the diphthong in *urait* and *stain*, and of the labial before *r* in *urait* link the text tentatively with southern Norway. But Dolfinn is a name comparatively rare in Scandinavia yet widespread in this country and well recorded in Cumberland in post-Conquest times,[24] so the carver may be a local man or at least a man from the British Isles. The word order *þasi runr*, with the demonstrative preceding its noun, also suggests this.[25] The runes are quite carefully, though freely scratched on the stone, presumably by someone who visited the church after the block was laid or who was in the mason's shop after it was dressed. Carlisle cathedral was begun in the last years of the eleventh century, which gives the earliest possible date for the inscription.

From Conishead priory comes a stone which formed part of a thirteenth-century altar.[26] It has incised symbols, presumably mason's marks, and the runic text **dotbrt** on an inner face where it would be invisible when the structure was assembled. **d** is ᛏ, a late type which occurs first on Svein Estridsson's coins of *c.* 1065–75 and rather later on rune-stones where it is rare. This rune links the inscription specifically with Denmark, rather than Norway, Sweden or the other rune-using areas of the British Isles. *Dotbrt* seems to be a personal name with the second element *-bert*, its vowel omitted. The name is not in G. Knudsen and M. Kristensen, *Danmarks gamle personnavne* (Copenhagen, 1936–64). There are the simplex forms *Dota, Dot*, the latter occurring in Domesday Book where von Feilitzen regards it as likely to be of Norse origin.[27]

The other two northern stones give little information, though they seem to have held Scandinavian legends. In 1870 excavators at Victoria Cave, Settle, Yorkshire, found an irregular fragment of slate, very roughly 8·5 cm. square, bearing a group of Norse runes. This is now kept in the Pig Yard Club Museum, Settle, together with the manuscript journal of Joseph Jackson, director of the dig, which preserves the only find-report. The entry for 23 April runs, '3 Men at work all day at the Cave. found a flat stone (slate) with grooves scored upon it in various directions. under datum line 12 Inches deep in cave earth'. There were no associated finds, and the cave yielded material from widely differing dates, so there are no external dating features. The rune staves are quite clear and in the main unambiguous, though the tops of all letters are broken away with the slate edge. They read **a͡fra͡lfr**, or perhaps, though less likely, **a͡fra͡ufr** or **a͡fra͡ulfr**. This looks like a personal name with a second

---

[23] E. Charlton, 'On an Inscription in Runic Letters in Carlisle Cathedral', *Archæologia Æliana* n.s. 3 (1859), 65–8, at 66.

[24] A. M. Armstrong *et al.*, *The Place-Names of Cumberland*, EPNS 20–2 (Cambridge, 1950–2) I, 191.

[25] It is worth recording a similar word order in [I]**uan·brist·raisti·þisir·runur**, '[I]óan the priest cut these runes', on the Maughold, Man, I stone: see Olsen, 'Runic Inscriptions in Great Britain', p. 202.

[26] P. V. Kelly, 'Excavations at Conishead Priory', *TCWAAS* n.s. 30 (1930), 149–68, at 156–7.

[27] O. v. Feilitzen, *The Pre-Conquest Personal Names of Domesday Book* (Uppsala, 1945), p. 226.

element -*álfr* (which is rare) or -*úlfr*, perhaps with the spelling -*aulfr* for -*ólfr*. *Farúlfr*, recorded in Sweden though not in West Norse, would fit.[28] The retention of inflexional -*r* in the Settle form suggests that the language is still Old Norse, uninfluenced on this point by English.

Little of the Skelton in Cleveland sundial survives: part of the dial itself, with, below it, the ends of four lines in roman capitals, and to their right part of a vertical line of runes with a tiny fragment of a second. The roman text is -S·[.]T· | -NA ·G[.]ERA | -C·HWA | -A·COMA; the runic line reads -**iebel·ok**.[29] I cannot make much of this, though the individual word *ok* shows the text to be Scandinavian, and this may be confirmed by such words as *g[.]era* (could this be *giera* for ON *gera*?) and *coma* (? = ON *koma*).

To sum up. Of the seven northern stones admitted to the corpus, four seem to preserve casual graffiti, which, being casual and so personal, may be in a language untypical of the place and time in which they were cut: these are Carlisle (Scandinavian, though perhaps by a native of the British Isles), Settle (probably Scandinavian), Conishead (probably Scandinavian) and Dearham (as yet undeciphered). Foreign workmen or perhaps visiting tourists or worshippers could have cut Conishead and Carlisle. Settle is not from a settlement site and may be the work of a passer-by camping out in the cave above the town. Three, Bridekirk, Pennington and Skelton in Cleveland, are major monuments, using runes in formal inscriptions. Here we must assume their language is in some way representative of the region where they are found. Bridekirk is in English, Pennington in a mixed English and Scandinavian, and Skelton in Cleveland perhaps in Scandinavian though there is little to go upon.

Of these seven stones two are undated. The other five, Carlisle, Conishead, Dearham, Bridekirk and Pennington, are post-Conquest. I doubt if such western texts represent a continuity of Scandinavian usage from pre-Conquest and Viking times: they are more likely to show a new influx of Scandinavian speakers from areas such as Man where the language persisted at least until the twelfth century. The Bridekirk and Conishead rune-masters certainly had contacts with the Scandinavian runic world outside, for from there they must have got their late rune types ᛨ for **e** and ᚠ for **d**.

Ekwall's assessment of the last two examples, the gravestone from St Paul's churchyard, London, and the Lincoln comb or rather comb-case, is adequate. Unlike the monuments treated so far, these two are included in Jacobsen and Moltke's splendid corpus of Danish runes.[30] The design of the London stone links it firmly to Scandinavian, perhaps even Swedish, work of the first half of the eleventh century, and its text, **k[i]na:let:lekia:st | in:þensi:auk:tuki**, 'Ginna and Toki had this stone laid', fits such a date and provenance. The Lincoln comb has a legend in good Scandinavian: **kamb:koþan:kiari:þorfastr**, 'Thorfastr made a good comb', with

---

[28] G. Fellows Jensen, *Scandinavian Personal Names in Lincolnshire and Yorkshire* (Copenhagen, 1968), s.n.

[29] There is a good drawing of the dial, showing slightly more of the text than is now visible, in Stephens, *Old-Northern Runic Monuments* IV, 50.

[30] Jacobsen and Moltke, *Danmarks runeindskrifter*, cols 476–80 and 488, nos 412 and 418.

rune-forms of the Danish type. Jacobsen and Moltke date it to 1050–1150. As Ekwall pointed out, this is a portable object which may have strayed far from its place of manufacture.[31] Both these pieces suggest that the Scandinavian tongue was known in this country, but not necessarily used by its permanent inhabitants.

On this showing the Scandinavian runic inscriptions in England tell us little of the continued use of the Norse tongue in the lands the Vikings settled. They may, as Ekwall claimed, 'offer the utmost interest', but it is an interest aroused more by their ambiguity and scarcity than by their evidential value. They contrast with the other vernacular inscriptions of northern and eastern England during the Viking Age, which show a clear continuity of English used in formal style from the eighth century to the eleventh. The Anglo-Saxon runic examples are well listed in Marquardt's *Bibliographie*, but the non-runic ones are less well known, and in what follows I lean heavily on, without quoting precisely from, Dr Okasha's Cambridge dissertation, 'Anglo-Saxon Non-Runic Inscriptions', and the material of her published hand-list. I ignore a large group of texts which are probably pre-Viking Age but which cannot be precisely dated, as the Carlisle, Dewsbury, Gainford, Hexham, Thornhill, Wycliffe and Yarm stones, and the Aberford and Lancashire rings, and I also omit several from the later Anglo-Saxon period whose texts are obscure or uncertain. This leaves a collection of legends containing clearly identifiable material, and securely dated to the tenth, eleventh or perhaps the twelfth century on linguistic, artistic or historical grounds. In the roman character are the legends of the Aldbrough, Great Edstone and Kirkdale sundials, all in Yorkshire, the Ipswich stone, the St Mary-le-Wigford, Lincoln, and the St Mary Castlegate, York, dedication stones, the All Hallows, Barking, cross and the Sutton, Isle of Ely, brooch.[32] The Alnmouth and Chester-le-Street stones mix runic and roman scripts. From the Anglo-Saxon runic corpus I include here the Monkwearmouth 'tidfirþ', the Overchurch, Cheshire, the Crowle, Lincolnshire, and the Collingham, Yorkshire, stones.

Some show not the least sign of Scandinavian linguistic influence. Among these are the two name-stones, Chester-le-Street with EADmVnD and Monkwearmouth with 'tidfirþ'. The Ipswich carved slab has a simple title: HER:S͞C͞E MIHAEL:FEHT WIÐ ÐANE:DRACA (or perhaps DRAC͞A for *dracan*), 'Here St Michael fights with the dragon', which again is fairly consistent Old English. The Alnmouth cross has the fragmentary maker signature MYREDaH·MEH·wO-, and the genitive name form EADVLFES. The Overchurch stone reads 'folcæ arærdon bec-| [.]biddaþ fote æþelmun-', which, despite its two errors, must be Old English for 'The people set

[31] I correct the Jacobsen and Moltke entry which describes the comb as 'fra en samling i Lincoln; nøjere oplysninger om dens herkomst savnes'. The comb was found in Lincoln in 1851: see *PSAL* 2nd ser., 3 (1864–7), 382.

[32] On the Old Byland, Yorkshire, sundial D. H. Haigh read SVMARLEÐAN HVSCARL ME FECIT, with the Scandinavian name *Sumarliði*, and the name or title *huskarl* ('Yorkshire Dials', *Yorkshire Archæological and Topographical Journal* 5 (1879), 134–222, at 141). The inscription has long been illegible (cf. J. Romilly Allen's rubbing, now BM Add. 37581. 31 and 32, which shows traces of SVMAR-, perhaps -AN, and very little else). Haigh was an unreliable reader of Old English inscriptions, and in this case was working from a cast, though indeed with the help of J. T. Fowler, a more sober scholar in the field.

up a monument: pray for Æthelmund'. Perhaps most significant of this group is the Sutton, Isle of Ely, brooch, whose design is so influenced by Norse style that D. M. Wilson describes it as 'pseudo-Viking'.[33] The extensive text on the brooch back runs: +ÆDVWEN ME AG AGE HYO DRIHTEN DRIHTEN HINE AWERIE ÐE ME HIRE ÆTFERIE BVTON HYO ME SELLE HIRE AGENES WILLES, '+ Ædwen owns me, may the Lord own her. May the Lord curse the man who takes me from her unless she give me of her own free will'. Despite its strong stylistic influence from Scandinavia, there is no corresponding effect on the language. The Crowle and Collingham stones present similar, though less striking, examples. On Crowle the rune-master set out his text on a curving ribbon of stone in the Norse manner. Little of the legend survives, but one word, 'licbæcun' is readable. Though this word does not occur elsewhere, its two elements lic- and -bæcun are common in Old English, and the compound, with the meaning 'gravestone', is a plausible one. The Collingham inscription is likewise fragmentary. Only 'æft[.] | [.]swiþi' remains, presumably a memorial formula with the preposition æfter followed by a name with the second element -swiþ. The runes are Anglo-Saxon and the surviving text Old English despite the fact that the decoration of the stone shows strong Scandinavian influence.[34]

A small number of stones have Old English inscriptions incorporating names of a Norse type. One of these is the dedication stone of St Mary-le-Wigford, Lincoln, which has stood outside the church, affixed to its west tower, at least since the eighteenth century. Comparing its present condition with drawings and a photograph taken earlier this century Dr Okasha notes considerable modern deterioration. The versions of J. Wordsworth (1879) and R. G. Collingwood (1923), together with Bruce Dickins's report of 1946, enable us to restore the text: +EIRTIG ME LET WIRCE[A]N·7 FIOS GODIAN CRISTE TO LOFE 7 SCE MARIE, '+ Eirtig had me made and endowed with property in honour of Christ and St Mary'.[35] There are two points of difficulty. A construction godian + genitive of the thing given seems otherwise unrecorded in English, but neither is its equivalent found in Old Norse and it may be simply an individual or local peculiarity. Earlier readers of the legend record the builder's name as Eirtig though it is no longer clear on the stone. There is no such name in Old English. Bruce Dickins suggested it was a Norse name with an ending -ig representing ON -i, as in Tostig, Pallig etc.[36] It could perhaps be a form of the rare Eitri which has been identified in the lost village name Eterstorp, Yorkshire.[37]

The Great Edstone sundial has two texts, one the Latin ORLOGIV[M VIA]TORIS (or [VIA]TORVM as commonly read in the past).[38] The other is ill-arranged and probably incomplete, +LOÐAN ME WROHTEA; perhaps it was to have been a

[33] D. M. Wilson, Anglo-Saxon Ornamental Metalwork 700–1100 in the British Museum (London, 1964), pp. 50 and 86–8.
[34] Brown, The Arts in Early England VI part ii, pp. 154–7.
[35] R. G. Collingwood and R. P. Wright, The Roman Inscriptions of Britain I (Oxford, 1965), no. 262, where there is an excellent drawing and an extensive bibliography.
[36] B. Dickins, 'The Dedication Stone of St. Mary-le-Wigford, Lincoln', Archaeological Journal 103 (1946), 163–5.
[37] Fellows Jensen, Scandinavian Personal Names, p. 76.
[38] A. R. Green, 'Anglo-Saxon Sundials', Antiquaries Journal 8 (1928), 489–516, at 510.

double makers' signature, +*Loðan me wrohte a*(*nd* + a second name). The legend is
Old English, but the name *Loðan* Scandinavian, ON *Loðinn*, Old Danish *Lothæn*.
The St Mary Castlegate, York, stone is fragmentary, with a good part of the text
remaining. It begins in Old English, continues in Latin, and may revert to Old English
in a damaged ending. Dr Okasha reads [.]:M[*I*]N*S*TER SE*T*[.]*A*RD 7 GRIM 7 ÆSE:
O[.]*MAN* DRIHTNES HÆ[.], continuing in Latin.[39] The original was presumably
something like *þis minster setton . . .ard and Grim and Æse on naman drihtnes
hælendes*, '. . .ard and Grim and Æse established this church in the name of Our Lord
and Saviour'. Accepting a tenth-century date for the church Ekwall argued that 'in
York the Scandinavian language was given up early, for the persons mentioned in the
inscription were clearly Scandinavians'. *Grim* is indeed a common Scandinavian
name. *Æse* may be an Anglicization of the Scandinavian *Ási, Esi*,[40] but it could also
be a native Old English name, perhaps related to the recorded *Æsica*. In any case
Ekwall's comment begs an important question. He assumes that people with Scandinavian names need necessarily be Scandinavian, though this is palpably untrue,
and it is hard to see quite what 'Scandinavian' need mean in such a context. To take
an example, the Englishman Earl Godwine had by his Danish wife a number of
children, some of whom had Scandinavian names, as Swein, Tostig and Harold, and
others of whom had English names, as Leofwine and Wulfnoth. By his English wife
Harold Godwineson had sons whose names were Godwine, Edmund, Magnus, Ulf
and Harold. Despite their names Magnus and Ulf could hardly be thought Scandinavians. Even in the highly Scandinavianized York, people with Norse names need
not be of Norse descent. Surviving English inhabitants may have given their children
fashionable Norse names in imitation of a Norse dominant class.

   There remain three inscriptions where the language may be affected by Norse
usage. In the case of the All Hallows, Barking, cross the effect is minimal and
uncertain. The legend, being badly damaged, is obscure, but it seems to contain a
formula naming the man who put up the cross and the deceased it commemorated:
NN let settan ofer Here-.[41] The word *ofer* is incomplete but likely. Its use rather than
æfter in such a formula is unparalleled in Old English, but there are a few cases of
yfir in similar contexts on Danish and Norwegian rune-stones, and in the British Isles
on the newly found Iona specimen. Thus All Hallows shows possible influence from
Old Norse.

   The Aldbrough sundial is a more important case. The text is quite well preserved
and reads: +VLF LET (? *H*ET) AR*Œ*RAN CYRICE FOR H*A*NVM 7 FOR
GVNWARA SAVLA, usually translated, '+Ulf had this church built for his own sake
and for Gunnvǫr's soul'.[42] There is some trace of late Anglo-Saxon work in Aldbrough church, and certainly the inscription contains corresponding late linguistic

[39] Illustrated in A. G. Dickens, 'Anglo-Scandinavian Antiquities', *VCH York* (London, 1961), pp.
332–6, facing p. 333.
[40] Fellows Jensen, *Scandinavian Personal Names*, p. 24.
[41] E. Okasha, 'An Anglo-Saxon Inscription from All Hallows, Barking-by-the-Tower', *Medieval
Archaeology* 11 (1967), 249–51.
[42] There is an excellent photograph of this dial in A. L. Binns, *East Yorkshire in the Sagas* (York,
1966), p. 20.

forms, seen in the collapse of the classical Old English inflexional system. So, *cyrice* for acc. sg. *cirican* shows loss of final *-n* and has confusion of the unstressed vowel as does *savla* for *saule*. *Gvnwara* is presumably genitive. The Old Norse form should be *Gunnwarar* but the Aldbrough name may be Anglicized, its second element a borrowing of OE *-waru* which should have the genitive *-ware*. Loss of definition in the vowel ending is common in late Anglian texts and shows a breakdown of the Old English inflexional system which is not necessarily a result of Old Norse admixture. Aldbrough has also the difficult form *hanvm*, which is usually taken as dat. sg. of the 3rd personal pronoun, since attempts to derive it from OE *hean*, 'poor, desolate', seem semantically misguided. *hanum* is certainly the Old Norse dat. sg. of such a pronoun, but of course Old Norse would use the reflexive *sér* in this context. The Old English equivalent is *him*, and Old English has no reflexive. It looks as though the Aldbrough dialect has a pronominal system influenced but not superseded by the Old Norse one. Both *Vlf* and *Gvnwara* represent Scandinavian names, one with loss of inflexional *-r* (which suggests English affection), the other with a second element probably Anglicized. Whether these people spoke a Scandinavian dialect is impossible to say, for the evidence of the inscription is inconclusive, and we cannot identify them from other sources. According to Domesday Book one Ulf owned land at Aldbrough in Edward the Confessor's reign, and this could be the man named on the dial. But Ulf is one of the commonest of Scandinavian names in this country, and any identification is perilous.[43]

Finally there is one of the longest and most famous of early English inscriptions, that which accompanies the Kirkdale sundial, excellently preserved within the porch and above the south doorway of that church.[44] The main text reads: +ORM·GA-MAL·SVNA·BOHTE:SCS GREGORIVS·MINSTER ÐONNE HIT WES ÆL:TO-BROCAN·7 TOFALAN·7 HĒ HIT LET MACAN NEWAN·FROM GRVNDE XPE:7 SCS GREGORIVS·IN EADWARD:DAGVM·CNG 7N TOSTI:DAGVM ·EORL+, '+ Orm Gamal's son bought St Gregory's church when it was quite broken down and ruined, and he had it built anew from the foundations in honour of Christ and St Gregory in the days of King Edward and of Earl Tosti'. There are two others, the double maker formula, +7 HAWARÐ·ME WROHTE·7 BRAND PRS, and the comment on the dial itself, +ÞIS IS DÆGES SOLMERCA + ÆT ILCVM TIDE+, 'This is the day's sun-marker at every hour'. The references to King Edward and Earl Tosti allow us to date the inscription 1055–65, and so to identify Orm with the man who held *Chirchebi*, apparently Kirkdale, in Edward the Confessor's reign. Again the texts are recognizably English, but not classical Old English. They show typical late features, as the weakening of unstressed vowels in *svna*, *tobrocan*, *tofalan*, the loss of the distinctive 2nd weak conjugation infinitive ending in *macan* and of the inflexional endings in *Gamal svna*, *Eadward . . . cng*, *Tosti . . . eorl*, and the

---

[43] Binns, *ibid.* p. 21, confidently identifies him with Ulf Thorvaldsson who gave his estates to York Minster. This seems to be one of the few men called Ulf who it cannot be, for the Domesday survey shows Aldbrough owned, not by St Peter's, York, but by Drogo de Bevrere.

[44] There is an excellent picture in P. Hunter Blair, *An Introduction to Anglo-Saxon England* (Cambridge, 1956), pl. XII.

imprecision in the use of grammatical gender in the concord *ilcvm tide*. But again these are not the effects of a Norse admixture. Scholars have traditionally pointed to three specifically Norse features of the texts: (i) the admittedly Scandinavian names *Orm, Gamal, Haward* and *Brand* where however there is Anglicization in the loss of the nominative *-r*, (ii) the patronymic type *Gamal svna* and (iii) the use of the word *solmerca*. As I have shown above, (i) is an invalid criterion. Nor is (ii) acceptable since Tengvik pointed to English patronymics of this type from parts of England and from times in which Norse influence is unlikely.[45] (iii) is less clear than commonly supposed. *Solmerca* occurs nowhere else in Old English, whereas there is an ON *sólmerki*, apparently rare, having the sense 'sign of the zodiac'. The difficulty is the meaning of *solmerca* in the Kirkdale context. Scholars have usually glossed it 'sundial', presumably taking this part of the inscription as equivalent to the explanatory ORLOGIV[*M VIA*]TORIS of Great Edstone, or the fragmentary word on the broken Orpington, Kent, dial which should probably be supplied OR[*ALOGI*]VM.[46] The second element of ON *sólmerki* is presumably *merki*, 'a mark', where *solmerca*, 'sundial', needs a second element meaning 'marker, something which marks (the position of the sun)'. *-merca* would then be a *-jan*-stem nomen agentis related to the verb *mearcian* (cf. *dema*, 'judge' or *brytta*, 'distributor'), and could be a native Old English word. There seems to be a parallel in *inmerca, onmerca* which the Lindisfarne and Rushworth scribes use to gloss *inscriptio*, 'superscription, legend which marks a coin as belonging to a particular emperor'. Since *sol*, 'sun', is very rare in Old English but common in Old Norse, we must then assume *solmerca* to be a hybrid compound. The alternative, possible but less likely, is to translate the Kirkdale sentence as 'This is the mark of the sun for each hour', referring, not to the dial as a whole, but to the rays which give the times of the canonical hours. In this case *solmerca* could be a loan of the Old Norse word, with a weakening of the unstressed ending.

In this paper I have dealt with inscriptions only from the Danelaw, assuming it unlikely that those from the south and west show Scandinavian influence on the language. As a generalization this is acceptable, but there is an exception, a coped memorial stone found recently at Winchester.[47] This has an inscription reading +HER LIÐ GV[*N*]NI EORLES FEOLAGA, '+ Here lies Gunni, earl's (or possibly, with a personal name, Eorl's) comrade'. OE *feolaga* (< ON *félagi*, but with Anglicization of the first element) is not otherwise recorded before the eleventh century, and the 'here lies' formula is unusual in Anglo-Saxon contexts but common enough after the Conquest, which also suggests a late date for this text. *Gvnni* is a Scandinavian name recorded elsewhere in England, and the use of *eorl* as a title (if that is the correct interpretation) derives from Old Norse practice. It is likely that the Winchester slab dates from the late period of Danish control in English, and shows its linguistic effect even in Wessex.

The extant epigraphical evidence for my subject is slight. What survives shows

---

[45] G. Tengvik, *Old English Bynames* (Uppsala, 1938), pp. 147–66.
[46] H. M. and J. Taylor, *Anglo-Saxon Architecture* (Cambridge, 1965), pp. 476–7.
[47] M. Biddle, 'Excavations at Winchester, 1965', *Antiquaries Journal* 46 (1966), 308–32, at 325.

little use of the Scandinavian tongues, and a small effect on English epigraphical practice, facts to be noted in discussing the size and importance of Viking settlements in this country. Yet we cannot assume that because there are few Norse-influenced inscriptions there were few Norse speakers. It is easy enough to suggest other reasons for this epigraphical dearth: the Norse settlers may have belonged in the main to social classes with no tradition of setting up memorial stones, or the English church to which so many inscriptions are linked may have exerted influence against the use of an alien tongue and in favour of the language traditionally employed for vernacular texts. The inscriptions, like the Old English written sources, show surprisingly little Old Norse admixture compared with the Middle English material from many areas. They suggest a number of lines of investigation which might prove fruitful: the possible importance of Middle English epigraphy, of which we know practically nothing: the contrast between the situation in the Isle of Man where Old Norse inscriptions are plentiful, and that in related regions of England: continuing links between parts of England and the Viking North in post-Conquest times. In turn, these may add their quota of evidence to the debate about the nature, size and significance of the Viking influx into northern and eastern England.

POSTSCRIPT

Inevitably this piece is out of date for much has been found since 1971, both within the British Isles and elsewhere. To take examples related to the statistics on pp. 182–3, the ending of the cold war has defrozen a number of runic inscriptions in the former Soviet Union,[48] while recent excavations in Greenland have produced more runic pieces there.[49] Within the British Isles the Manx corpus has been increased by two new stones (below, pp. 223–4). The Irish material (the three examples in the 1971 list should be Killaloe, Beginish and Greenmount, the latter an inscribed belt-fitting) has been expanded by the discoveries in the Dublin excavations of the 1970s and 1980s. They produced some twelve portable pieces with runic (or rune-like) inscriptions, which suggest a more demotic, or perhaps democratic, use of the script. In addition, a rune-inscribed comb turned up in an independent excavation at Dublin Castle, and there is a single rune on a base silver bracelet from Roosky, Donegal. All these will appear in a corpus of Irish runes now prepared for publication, by Michael Barnes, Jan Ragnar Hagland and myself. There are new inscriptions from Orkney,

[48] For English accounts see, for instance, E. Melnikova, 'New Finds of Scandinavian Runic Inscriptions from the USSR', *Runor och runinskrifter: föredrag vid Riksantikvarieämbetets och Vitterhetsakademiens symposium 8–11 september 1985* (Stockholm, 1987), pp. 163–73; E. A. Melnikova and E. N. Nosov, 'Amulets with Runic Inscriptions from Gorodische near Novgorod', *Nytt om Runer* 4 (1989), 34.
[49] M. Stoklund, 'Objects with Runic Inscriptions from Narsarsuaq' in C. L. Vebæk, *The Church Topography of the Eastern Settlement and the Excavation of the Benedictine Convent (at Narsarsuaq) in (the) Uunartoq Fjord* (Copenhagen, 1991), pp. 63–5; *eadem*, 'Objects with Runic Inscriptions from Ø 17a' in C. L. Vebæk, *Narsaq – a Norse Landnáma Farm* (Copenhagen, 1993), pp. 47–52.

Shetland, Iona and the mainland of Scotland. Indeed, the known corpus of Norse runes in Great Britain (excluding the graffiti in Maeshowe, Orkney, which Michael Barnes regards as essentially Norwegian) now comprises six in Shetland, and fifteen each in Orkney, the rest of Scotland and England.

Within England several runic inscriptions have surfaced since this article was written. One rune-stone fragment, from Winchester, suggests a late use of runes and the Norse language there for traditional commemorative purposes.[50] From St Albans are a couple of bones, not yet published, with runic graffiti in Norse upon them, again implying a more wide-spread employment of the script than simply on memorials. They were found in a secondary context, material probably discarded in the later eleventh or earlier twelfth century. From near Penrith, Cumbria, comes a ninth- or tenth-century silver penannular brooch with a short-twig *fuþark* upon it, and, retrograde, the opening of a second one **fu**,[51] though strictly speaking this gives no indication of language as opposed to script. There are stone fragments tentatively identified as runic recorded from Canterbury and Rochester, but they are so slight as to be insignificant. And most recently has been spotted a Norse name fragment]**auarþ** cut or scratched in long-branch runes in the margin of Corpus Christi College, Cambridge, MS 57, an eleventh-century manuscript from Abingdon, a monastery known to have had a connection with Norway in its early Christian period.[52] One possible correction to the readings given in my 1971 paper. The Dearham inscription may well read **hnirm**. The line crossing **r** (which I read as a vowel **a** or **æ** bound with it) may well be accidental, as indeed Anders Bæksted declared it in his manuscript notes on this inscription.

Thanks to the two supplements to Elisabeth Okasha's *Hand-List of Anglo-Saxon Non-Runic Inscriptions* we now have better control over the non-runic epigraphy,[53] and can add the occasional example to those discussed in the present article, as for example her York IX, an ivory seal-die recording the Norse name *Snarri*.

My 1971 paper posed one question, rather tentatively, which I would now want to probe more carefully: how far do these inscriptions represent survival of Norse (as indeed Ekwall's paper implied), how far its reintroduction? My reading of the Manx stones shows that the use of runes in that island was a complex business, involving more than one tradition (see below, pp. 233–5). The Orkney runic corpus demonstrates the script (and language) used by inhabitants, but also, at a rather later date, by visitors (as in the Maeshowe graffiti). Whether England has as yet a large enough corpus of inscribed objects for us to distinguish clearly between different uses of the Scandinavian languages I do not know. The suggestions are there, as my paper shows. Perhaps now is time for reassessment.

---

[50] B. Kjølbye-Biddle and R. I. Page, 'A Scandinavian Rune-Stone from Winchester' (1975).

[51] R. I. Page, 'A New Find from Cumbria' (1990).

[52] R. I. Page, 'Runes in Two Anglo-Saxon Manuscripts' (1993), p. 19.

[53] In *ASE* 11 (1983), 83–117, and *ASE* 21 (1992), 37–85.

15
(1973)

ANGLO-SAXON TEXTS IN EARLY MODERN TRANSCRIPTS
1. THE ANGLO-SAXON *RUNIC POEM**

Cotton MS Otho B. X, a manuscript severely damaged in the 1731 fire, contained the only known text of the Anglo-Saxon *Runic Poem*. The fire destroyed the folio bearing this poem, which survives as far as we know only in the transcript in Hickes's *Thesaurus*.[1] George Hempl made the classic examination of the integrity of the *Thesaurus* material in his article, 'Hickes's additions to the Runic Poem'.[2] Professor René Derolez refined the form and corrected the detail of the attack, and N. R. Ker accepted the conclusions without comment in the Rune Poem entry of his catalogue.[3]

At first glance Hempl's case looks strong, yet nagging doubts remain, and it is worth expressing them since the integrity of Hickes's transcripts where the originals are lost is a matter of some importance to Anglo-Saxon studies. Hickes used two techniques in printing the *Runic Poem* (see fig. 1). The body of the text, a group of twenty-nine stanzas expounding the rune-names, he set in the Junian type which the Oxford University Press lent to his enterprise. For the rune forms themselves and some other prefatory and extraneous material, Hickes had two copper plates engraved, one running vertically down the inner margin of the page, the other across its foot. The second of these is of lesser importance to this discussion but requires brief description. It gives the pseudo-rune 's̄t' with its name *stan* and values *st* and *z*, and below it the rune 'g' with name *gar* and value *g*.[4] Divided from these by a vertical line is the remark: 'Hos characteres 'oldwnxfog' ad alia sestinans [with long *s* for correct *f*] studioso lectori interpretanda relinquo'. None of this material is formally linked to the *Runic Poem*.

The first copper plate is more important. Its material is threefold. At the left is a column of roman equivalents to the runes, with occasional rune-names: central is a

* [This is one part of a paper that illustrated three examples of early transcripts of Old English texts, and their importance to modern scholarship. The other two examples are not runic and so are not included here.]
1 G. Hickes, *Linguarum vett. septentrionalium thesaurus grammatico-criticus et archaeologicus. 1. Institutiones grammaticæ Anglo-Saxonicæ, & Mæso-Gothicæ* (Oxford, 1703), p. 135.
2 *Modern Philology* 1 (1903–4), 135–41.
3 Derolez, *Runica Manuscripta*, pp. 19–25; Ker, *Catalogue*, no. 179.
4 I transliterate runes according to Dickins, 'Transliteration', with the additional styles 's̄t' for *stan*, 'ı̂o' for *ior*, and 'q' for *cweorð*.

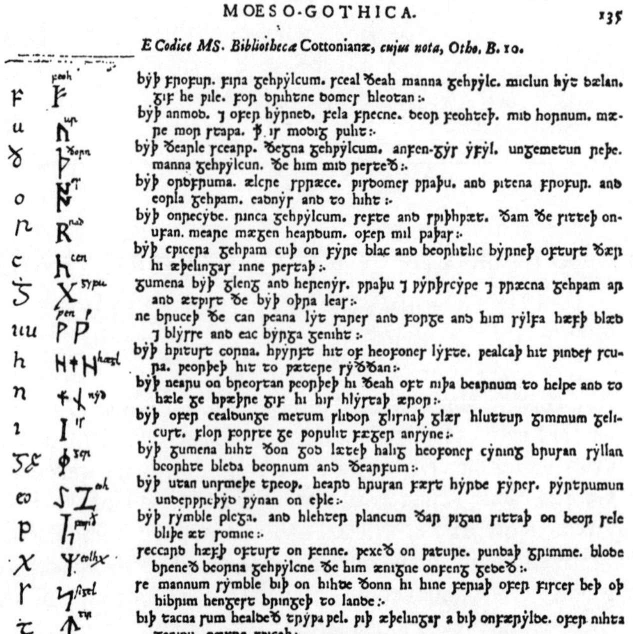

MOESO-GOTHICA.   135

E Codice MS. Bibliothecæ Cottonianæ, cujus nota, Otho, B. 10.

byþ fnoxup. fna zehpýlcum. rceal ðeah manna zehpýlc. miclun hýt bælan.
  zif he pile. fon bnihtne bomer bleotan:.
byþ anmob. 7 oren hýnneb. fela fnecne. beon feohteþ. mib honnum. mæne mon rtapa. þ ir mobiz puht:.
byþ ðeaple rceapp. ðezna zehpýlcum. anfen-zýr ýfýl. unzemetun neþe.
  manna zehpýlcun. ðe him mib nerteð:.
byþ onbýrnuma. ælcne rppæce. pirbomer pnaþu. anb pitena fnofup. anb
  eonla zehpam. eabnýr anb to hiht:.
byþ onpecýbe. nunca zehpýlcum. rerte anb rpiþhæt. ðam ðe ritteþ on-
  ufan. meane mæzen heapbum. oren mil paþar:.
byþ epicena zehpam cuþ on fýne blac anb beophtlic býnneþ orturt ðæn
  hi þelinzar inne nertaþ:.
zumena byþ zlenz anb henenýr. pnaþu 7 pýnþrcýpe 7 pnæcna zehpam an
  anb ætpirt ðe býþ oþna lear:.
ne bnuceþ ðe can peana lýt raper anb ronze anb him rýlfa hæþ blæb
  7 blýrre anb eac býnza zeniht:.
byþ hpiturt conna. hpynjt hit or heoroner lýrte. pealcaþ hit pinbeþ rcu-
  na. peoþheþ hit to pætene rýððan:.
byþ neapu on bneortan peoþheþ hi ðeah ort niþa beannum to helpe anb to
  hæle ze hpæþne zif hi hir hlýrtaþ ænon:.
byþ oren cealbunze metum rlibon zlirnaþ zlær hluttun zimmum zeli-
  curt. flon fonrte ze populit fæzen anryne:.
byþ zumena hiht ðon zob læteþ haliz heoroner cýninz hnuran rýllan
  beophte bleba beonnum anb ðeanrum:.
byþ utan unrmeþe tpeop. heapb hnuran fært hýnbe fýner. pýntpumun
  unbeppncþýb pýnan on eþle:.
byþ rýmble plega. anb hlehten plancum ðan pizan rittaþ on beon rele
  bliþe æt romne:.
reccanþ hæþ orturt on fenne. pexeð on patune. punbaþ znimme. blobe
  bneneð beonna zehpýlcne ðe him ænizne onfenz zebeð:.
re mannum rýmble biþ on bihte ðonn hi hine reniaþ oren fircer beþ oþ
  hibnim henzert bninzeþ to lanbe:.
biþ tacna rum healbeð tpýpa pel. piþ þelinzar a biþ onfæpýlbe. oren nihta
  zenipu. næfne rpiceþ:.
byþ bleba lear. beneþ efne rpa ðeah tanaz butan tubbep. biþ on telzum pli-
  tiz. þeah on helme hpýrteb fæzene. zeloben leafum lýfte zetenze:.
byþ fon eonlum æþelinza pýn. bonr hozum planc. ðæn him hæleþe ýmb. pe-
  leze on piczum ppixlaþ rppæce. 7 biþ unrtýllum æfne fnofup:.
byþ on mýnzþe hir mazan leof. rceal ðeah anna zehpýlc oðnum rpican.
  fon ðam bnýhten pýle bome rine þ eanme flærc eonþan betæcan:.
byþ leobum lanzrum zehuht zif hi rculun neþun on nacan tealtum. 7 hi
  ræ ýþa rpýþe bnezaþ. anb re bnim henzert bnibler ne zým.:.
þær zpert mib eart benum. ze repen reczun. oþ he rið ðan ert. oren pæz
  zepát pæn æften nan. ður heapbinzar ðone hæle nembun:.
byþ oren leof. æzhpýlcum men. zif he mot ðæn. pihten anb zenýrena
  on bnucan on blobe bleabum orturt:.
byþ bnihtner ronb. beone mannum. mæne metober leoht, mýnzþ anb
  to hiht eabzum anb eanmum. eallum bnice:.
byþ on eonþan. elba beannum. flærcer robon feneþ zelome oren zanoter
  bæþ zapreczz ranbaþ. hpæþep ac hæbbe æþele tpeope:.
biþ oren heah. elbum býne. rtiþ on rtaþule. rteþe nihte hýlt. ðeah him
  feohtan on finar monize:.
byþ æþelinza 7 eonla zehpær. pýn anb pýnþmýnb. býþ on picze fæzen. fært-
  lic on fæpelbe. fýnþ zeacepa rum:.
byþ ea fixa. anb ðeah abnuceð. robner onfalban. haraþ fæzenne eanb.
  pætne beponpen. ðæn he pýnnum leoraþ:.
byþ ezle eonla zehpýlcun. ðonn færtlice flærc onzinneþ. hnapcolian hnuran
  ceoran blac to zebebban bleba zebpeoraþ. pýnna zepitaþ pena zerpicaþ:.

Hos characteres ᚠᚢᚦᛟᚱᚳᚷ *ad alia festinans*
Studioso lectori interpretanda relinquo.

LI 2   Erat

FIG. 1   The *Runic Poem* in Hickes's *Thesaurus*

198

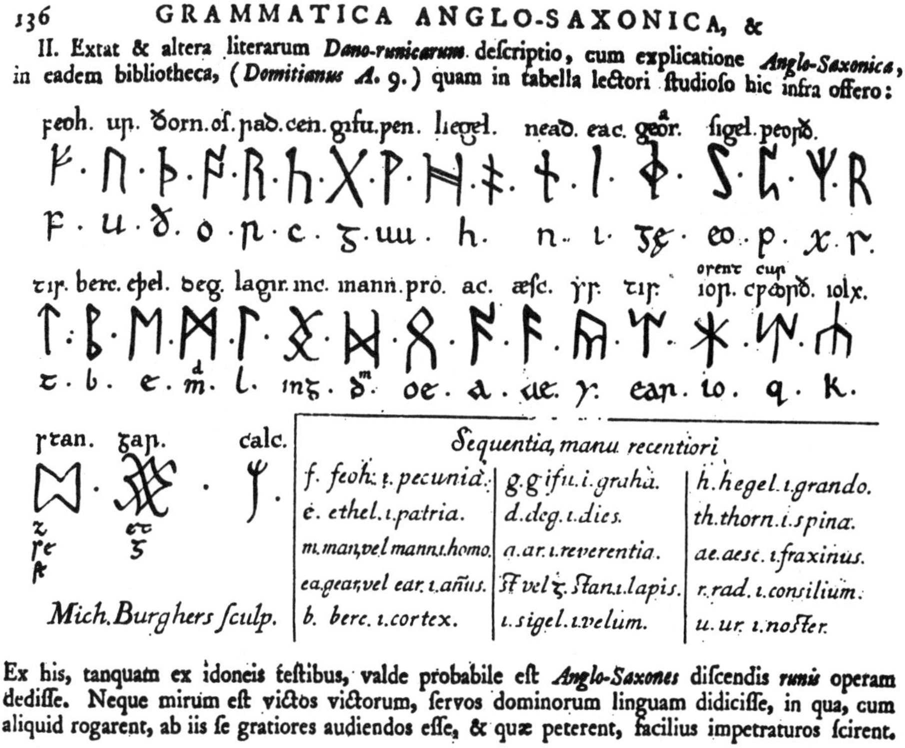

136   **GRAMMATICA ANGLO-SAXONICA, &**

II. Extat & altera literarum *Dano-runicarum* defcriptio, cum explicatione *Anglo-Saxonica*, in eadem bibliotheca, (*Domitianus A.* 9.) quam in tabella lectori ftudiofo hic infra offero:

feoh. un. ðorn. os. naд. cen. gifu. pen.   liegel.   neað. eac. geor.   figel. peoрð.

[runic characters]

f . u . ð . o . n . c . g . uu .   h .   n . i . ᴣᵹ . eo . p . x . r .

tiр. bere. eрel. ðeg. lagir. mc. mann. pro.   ac. æfc. yr. tiр.   ioн. cрðрð. iolx.

[runic characters]

t . b . e . m̃ . l . inᴣ . d̃ . oe . a . ae . y . ean. io. q. k.

			Sequentia, manu recentiori		
[rune]	[rune]	[rune]	f. feoh. i. pecunia.	g. gifu. i. gruha.	h. hegel. i. grando.
z	eſ	calc.	e. ethel. i. patria.	d. deg. i. dies.	th. thorn. i. spina.
re	ᴣ		m. man, vel mann. i. homo.	a. ar. i. reverentia.	ae. aefc. i. fraxinus.
ᵳ			ea. gear, vel ear. i. añus.	ſf vel ᴣ. ſtan. i. lapis.	r. rad. i. consilium.
Mich. Burghers fculp.			b. bere. i. cortex.	i. sigel. i. velum.	u. ur. i. noſter.

Ex his, tanquam ex idoneis teftibus, valde probabile eft *Anglo-Saxones* difcendis *runis* operam dediffe. Neque mirum eft victos victorum, fervos dominorum linguam didiciffe, in qua, cum aliquid rogarent, ab iis fe gratiores audiendos effe, & quæ peterent, facilius impetraturos fcirent.

FIG. 2   The Runes of Domitian IX in Hickes's *Thesaurus*

column of runes, a few with variant forms: generally above and to the right of each rune is a rune-name. This plate's runes mate pretty well with the lines of the *Runic Poem*,[5] but whereas there are twenty-nine stanzas, there are thirty-one runes. Two at the foot of the column have no corresponding verses, the pseudo-rune 'q', supplied with the name *cweorð*, and the genuine rune 'k', given neither roman equivalent nor rune-name.

Hempl contended that only part of the material of this first copper plate was in Otho B. X. He argued that (i) the equivalents and rune-names of the left-hand column Hickes took from a runic page in another Cottonian manuscript, Domitian IX, fol. 11ᵛ; (ii) from the same source he copied the variant rune forms of 'w' (and its accompanying name *wen*), 'h', 'n', 'ʒ', 'ŋ' and the 'extra runes below' which from the context should mean *cweorð* and 'k', but among which Hempl seems later to include *stan* and *gar*; (iii) the main series of rune-names was not an original part of the *Runic Poem*. Hempl hesitated over whether they were Hickes's additions, or those of a scribe who supplied them to the *Runic Poem* before Hickes's day. At any rate he did not identify the source from which the names were taken. Professor Derolez, with his unrivalled knowledge of *runica manuscripta*, has not found it either; nor have I.

There is no doubt that Hempl was right in contending that the material of column 1, equivalents and rune-names, and the variants of column 2 derive from Domitian IX. Three individual hands (at least) compiled that manuscript's runic page, and the *Thesaurus Runic Poem* page reproduces them all. Its debt is most clearly seen in its account of the similar runes 'm' and 'd'. Hand 1 of Domitian IX drew these letters and gave their correct values below. The second scribe confused the two, giving 'm' the name *deg*, and 'd' the name *mann*. A third (probably) added 'corrected' equivalents *d* and *m* above the original values. Such composite entries can only have arisen in Domitian IX itself, and the fact that the *Thesaurus* page repeats them is ample proof of provenance.

Less certain is Hempl's thesis that it was Hickes who added the Domitian IX material to the *Runic Poem*. His article, which at first sight seems to contain so assured an argument, in fact relies on inaccurate observation and contains a logical fallacy. Hempl begins by assuming that the layout of the *Runic Poem* in Otho B. X was dissimilar to that of Hickes's edition. 'Hickes arranged the poem so that the account of each rune begins a new line, and he placed the runes in a column in the left margin, so that each rune stands opposite the line in which it is treated of'. Hempl thought this inconsistent with the practice of other Old English poetical manuscripts, overlooking the fact that the *Runic Poem* differs from most Anglo-Saxon poems in being stanzaic. In the Exeter Book *Deor*, where again the poem is stanzaic, each stanza begins a new line, with the initial letter large and set out into the margin. If the *Runic Poem* manuscript had a similar arrangement there would be ample space

---

[5] Individual issues of the sheet differ slightly from one another in register. The runes of the vertical plate are rather more closely spaced than the lines of type they link to. Some copies of the *Thesaurus* seem to have used a single, L-shaped, plate, which must have broken early in the printing into vertical and horizontal pieces.

for additions of rune values, names or variant letter forms. Hempl continues with his logical fallacy. 'As for the phonological values, the variant runes, and the extra runes below, it is easy to show that all this was not in the manuscript of the Runic Poem, but was taken from the manuscript *Cottoniana Domit., A 9'.* I do not see why Hempl thought that the second of these precluded the first. True, he added, 'and that by Hickes himself', but he did nothing to demonstrate that Hickes did take Domitian IX material into the *Runic Poem*, contenting himself with showing that Hickes could have done so, since he knew that manuscript. In the event it is unlikely that Hickes took over the material, since it was the young Humfrey Wanley who had responsibility for producing and checking transcripts such as this, and Wanley certainly claimed that Otho B. X contained '*Alphabetum Runicum cum explicatione Poetica, Saxonicè, quod non ita pridem descripsi rogatu Cl. D. Hickesii'.*[6] But I want to go beyond such a pedantic objection to explore the likelihood that, when Hickes and Wanley saw it, Otho B. X already had additional material which an earlier scholar copied there from Domitian IX. There are three ways of approaching this: from what Hickes gives of the *Runic Poem* and of other runes; from what we know of the methods of producing these transcripts for the *Thesaurus*; from the inherent likelihood or unlikelihood of an earlier scholar's tampering with Otho B. X.

A first glance at the way Hickes presented his Otho B. X page and his transcript of Domitian IX, fol. 11ᵛ (on p. 136 of the *Thesaurus*) suggests that he thought them two independent pieces of evidence on Anglo-Danish runes. Unfortunately, Hickes's own comment on the subject, though long, is not as clear as it might be, so it must be quoted here *in extenso*. Hickes argued that runes were essentially Danish, but that in Cnut's reign the English learned them so as to ingratiate themselves with their conquerors. He continues:

> Hoc ut credam faciunt *runarum Danicarum*, tam simplicium, quam duplicium descriptio quædam poetica, *Anglo-Saxonice* explicata; quæ in bibliotheca *Cott.* extat, *Otho* B. 10. p. 165. quamque vix antea & ne vix observatam, nedum publici juris factam, plane quasi ab omnibus doctis spectatu dignam, hic cum *runis* ære incisis, operæ & sumptûs pretium exhibere judicamus, *Latinis* additis ex adverso elementis, ad ostendendam *runarum* potestatem, una cum iis nominibus quibus appellantur ipsæ *runæ*.

Then follows the facsimile page, headed '*E Codice MS. Bibliothecæ* Cottonianæ, *cujus nota, Otho, B. 10.*', and on the next (p. 136) the transcript of the Domitian IX runes with the note, 'Extat & altera literarum *Dano-runicarum* descriptio, cum explicatione *Anglo-Saxonica*, in eadem bibliotheca (*Domitianus A. 9.*) quam in tabella lectori studioso hic infra offero: . . . Ex his, tanquam ex idoneis testibus, valde probabile est *Anglo-Saxones* discendis *runis* operam dedisse' (see fig. 2).

The phrase *altera . . . descriptio, cum explicatione Anglo-Saxonica, . . . quam in tabella lectori studioso hic infra offero* surely implies a second and discrete piece of

---

[6]   H. Wanley, *Librorum vett. septentrionalium, qui in Angliæ bibliothecis extant . . .* (= book 2 of the *Thesaurus*) (Oxford, 1705), p. 192.

evidence, and since Hickes was arguing that the two documents show the Anglo-Saxons learning a Danish script, to suggest that he supplied Anglo-Saxon names or values to Otho B. X is virtually to accuse him of tampering with the sources.

C. L. Wrenn took Hickes's statement *Latinis additis - ipsæ runæ* to be an admission that he had put in 'the marginal rune-names and rune-values deliberately for the better carrying out of his purpose, which was, of course, primarily philological'.[7] This is a proper interpretation of the words, but I wonder if it is the only possible one. Could *Latinis additis . . . elementis* mean that the rune-values and rune-names were added in the manuscript, but by an earlier modern hand? In any case it is worth noting that the most that Hickes admitted to was adding rune-names and values, not variant rune-forms. The meaning of *runarum Danicarum, tam simplicium, quam duplicium descriptio* I find baffling unless it refers to the fact that, by Hickes's day, some stanzas of the Otho B. X text were prefixed by one rune form, some by two.

In fact, close examination of the variant or added runes – 'w', 'h', 'n', '3', 'ŋ' – of the *Runic Poem* page supports the argument that it was not Hickes or Wanley who supplied them. There is no doubt that they derive from Domitian IX, but whoever added them to the *Runic Poem* did so more casually and less consistently than Wanley or Hickes are likely to have done. The main runes of the poem have a lapidary quality, strongly and neatly formed and nearly all with pronounced serifs: it is reasonable to assume that this is the quality of the original hand of Otho B. X. The variant runes, made of thin strokes and unseriffed, differ from the corresponding letters of Domitian IX, which also are firmly written and often seriffed as the *Thesaurus* reproduction of that page shows. Thus these variant runes look less as though they were copied with Wanleian care, and more as if they were rather tentative marginalia already in Otho B. X when Wanley came to look at it. In their casual effect they resemble the nine characters 'oldwnxfog' of the lower copper plate, which Derolez suggests are a *probatio pennae* taken from the margin of the Otho B. X page.

Two variants are particularly embarrassing to Hempl's theory, 'n' and 'w'. The variant 'n' form has the cross-stave unusually returned to cut the main stem again near its top. Hempl thought this derived from a crease in the parchment of Domitian IX, but Wrenn denied it. In fact, Domitian IX has a faint scar across the page roughly at this point, and it could be this scar which the curious 'n' form reproduces. Significantly, Wanley did not note the line when he came to make his copy of Domitian IX for p. 136 of the *Thesaurus*, where he gives a normal 'n', so it is unlikely that he was responsible for the returned cross-stave in the *Runic Poem*. I do not think it can be an engraver's error because it is repeated in the Otho B. X material of a set of comparative runic alphabets later in the *Thesaurus*,[8] and, more cogently, because without the returned stroke the *Runic Poem* page would have two more or less

---

[7]   C. L. Wrenn, 'Late Old English Rune-Names', *Medium Ævum* 1 (1932), 24–34, at 26.

[8]   *Linguarum vett. . . . thesaurus . . . 3. Grammaticæ Islandicæ rudimenta* (Oxford, 1703), tabella II, 2. I am not sure of the status of the alphabets of this plate. They could derive from the earlier *Thesaurus* plates, and so not present independent evidence. On the other hand, Wanley was greatly interested in comparative letter forms (as, for example, his exquisitely written early book of alphabets, Bodleian Gough 33184 shows), and should have given these figures close attention.

identical 'n' runes. The implication is that someone else copied this variant into Otho B. X.

The variant 'w' differs from the original Otho B. X 'w' in having a pointed bow instead of a rounded one. Derolez properly asked 'why Hickes added a pointed variant of the *w*-rune, and not the pointed forms for **r, j, x, b** and **œ** as well [and could have added of *yr* too], which could also be borrowed from Domitian A 9'. Again the evidence suggests a less methodical copyist than Wanley or Hickes. An argument from omission points in the same direction. The *Runic Poem*, if the *Thesaurus* plate is to be believed, had a unique 'p' type without that rune's usual top arm. If it were Wanley trying to complete the runic material of the poem, surely he would have added the standard 'p' form, which Domitian IX shows.

We can get some idea of Wanley's accuracy at this stage of his career by comparing the runic page of Domitian IX with the *Thesaurus* reproduction of it on p. 136 (pl. V). The *Thesaurus* copy is good, but by no means an exact replica. Wanley altered the layout of letters, putting 'ío', 'q' and 'k' on the second line instead of at the beginning of the third. He missed details of pointing. He reversed the positions of names and values of the last five characters, 'ío', 'q', 'k', 'st' and 'g' so that values come below the symbols, rune-names above, consistent with preceding practice. He made minor copying errors in the names: *hegel* for *Hegel*, *eac* for an indeterminate (?) *inc*, *lagir* for *lagu*: and he left out the underpointed name *calc*. He put the unusual variant 'h' form on instead of above the general rune line, and omitted a rare, also superscript, *eþel*-rune. The most important of his deviations affects the last character of line 1. Domitian IX has the rather uncommon *sigel*-rune ᚴ with its value, insular *s*, below it, and above, the more common rune form with some letters which Derolez tentatively reads *sig*, but which are quite indistinct. The manuscript has darkened somewhat at this point, but the runic forms and the value are clear enough. Surprisingly, the *Thesaurus* puts instead the common runic 'r', and gives its value by insular *r* which, of course, bears a close resemblance to *s*. I do not know why Wanley made this change, but it was apparently intentional, not a slip. In the main the *Thesaurus* plate reproduces well both the runic and roman material of the manuscript, with a fair approximation to the letter forms of the original.

The *Runic Poem* page gives only a little of the Domitian IX material, and it is perhaps a rather less precise copy than p. 136, at least as regards the script letter forms: cf., for example, *a, y, deg, ear, cweorð*.[9] For the *sigel*-rune, however, column 1 has the correct equivalent *s*, and it would be strange if Wanley, failing or refusing to recognize this when he drew the copy for p. 136, nevertheless added it correctly to the *Runic Poem*.

Yet the case against Wanley's (or Hickes's) responsibility for the *Runic Poem* additions rests less upon the quality of scholarship they show than upon the confusion of purpose they suggest. What would Wanley have achieved by including on the *Runic Poem* page extraneous material from a manuscript whose runes he was going

---

[9] On the horizontal copper plate the words *stan* and *gar* are so unlike those on Domitian IX as to suggest that the engraver was not trying to imitate the letter forms.

to print overleaf in any case? An argument could be adduced for Wanley adding, to an incomplete collection of runic material in Otho B. X, such information from other manuscripts as would supplement, correct or clarify it. But this is just what the added material does not do. It supplies variants when they are not needed – 'w' and perhaps 'n' – and fails to put them in where they would be helpful – 'p' and probably the rare *eþel* type. It confuses the reader by giving him the conflicting *m* and *d* values and names – Wanley was a collector of alphabets and I suspect he knew that the 'corrections' made to Domitian IX at these points were wrong,[10] while his knowledge of Old English would have told him that the incorrect *deg* and *mann* fitted neither the sense nor the alliteration of the stanzas they had become attached to. If Wanley were seeking completeness, it is odd that he missed out the names *orent* and *cur* (unless he rejected them as spurious) and the value *k* and the name *calc*.[11] At the same time he did retain one bit of runic material which seems quite insignificant, the group of characters 'oldwnxfog' at the foot of the page, whose purpose remains unestablished. If, as Derolez maintains, they were a casual scribble in the manuscript margin, their inclusion on the *Runic Poem* page is evidence that Wanley was trying to reproduce his exemplar as closely as possible.

It might perhaps be argued that the confusions and inconsistencies I have defined above arose with the engraver of the copper plates, that Wanley gave him imprecise directions or inadequate copy, with imprecise or inadequate results. However, this would hardly square with what we know of Wanley's responsibility for overseeing the sheets of the *Thesaurus*. The letters that passed between Hickes and Wanley in the years when the book was in preparation and production show the confidence Hickes put in his younger colleague, and the care with which the latter held his trust. Wanley is commended for his skill in runic alphabets, his 'incomparable inimitable hand' in copying, his readiness 'to correct the sculptor's faults in the plates of Alphabets'.[12] In fact he seems to have kept close control over checking the sheets as they came out, and it is most unlikely that he would pass anything which fell short of his exacting requirements.

There remains to be explored the possibility that some scholar before Wanley put the Domitian IX runic material into Otho B. X, and added a runic scribble in the lower margin, and that Hickes simply reproduced the *Runic Poem* page *e codice . . . Otho, B. 10* as he claimed. There is a pointer to what may have happened on Domitian IX, fol. 11ᵛ, itself. The early Tudor antiquary Robert Talbot once owned this page,

[10] I am not certain of this, since some of the alphabets of tabella II (see note 8 above) confuse 'm' and 'd' runes.

[11] The treatment of 'k' may be a further significant distinction between p. 136 and the *Runic Poem* page. In Domitian IX *calc* is underpointed and *k* faintly crossed out, Derolez thinks by hand 2. On p. 136 Wanley noted the underpointing but not the stroke through *k*. Whoever added rune 'k' to the *Runic Poem* page presumably recognized that both name and value were cancelled in Domitian IX, since he omitted both.

[12] A number of letters in British Library, MS Harley 3779 show Hickes's debt to Wanley. For Wanley's control over engraving of plates in 1701, see *The Manuscripts of . . . the Duke of Portland* (HMC, 15, Report, App. IV) IV (London, 1897), p. 16. C. E. Wright gives Wanley's own view of Hickes's debt to him in 'Humfrey Wanley: Saxonist and Library Keeper', *PBA* 46 (1960), 99–129, at 104–5.

or at least took the liberty of annotating it. Derolez has shown that it was he who added to the page the list of Latin equivalents of Old English rune-names which Hickes reproduced under the heading, 'Sequentia, manu recentiori'. Below his list Talbot wrote, 'ther ys souch an other alphabet [. . .] in ye end off [m]y old saxonice be[de] de historia ecclesie gentis Anglorum y^t [is] w^t owt bordes in [y^e] last leaff off y^t bo[ke]'. Talbot was much interested in runes, particularly in their names and values. He once owned St John's College Oxford MS 17, which contains a page of cryptic letters and alphabetical codes, including runes both English and Scandinavian.[13] From it he seems to have copied into one of his notebooks, now Corpus Christi College Cambridge MS 379, an *Alphabetum anglicum*, which is a list of English and Norse rune-names, with their Latin translations, in alphabetical order. Talbot was an eager annotator of texts. N. R. Ker notes eight other Anglo-Saxon manuscripts which show his hand, and he certainly knew something of the language and its script.[14] His 'old saxonice bede' is untraced, but Ker suggests tentatively that the *Runic Poem* leaf of Otho B. X (which once belonged to some other manuscript) is the 'souch an other alphabet' referred to.[15]

I do not hold it proven that it was Talbot who added the Domitian IX material to Otho B. X, but it seems a good probability. Two pieces of evidence argue against him. Neither is conclusive, but both must be faced. The first is Hickes's *Latinis additis . . . elementis* which, as we have seen, Wrenn took as an admission that Hickes added the Latin equivalents. Classics assure me that this is the most natural way of taking the sentence, though they do not preclude its meaning that an earlier scholar made the additions. Hickes's Latin is not always classical and not always precise, and here he may have been guilty of ambiguity. The second is a piece of evidence from Wanley's annotated copy of Smith's Cottonian library catalogue, now Bodleian Gough London 54. Wanley defines the *Runic Poem* as 'Litteræ antiqæ Runicæ, numero plane viginti & nouem [he originally wrote 'triginta' but amended it apparently some time afterwards] cum obseruatt. Saxonicis', correcting Smith's 'numero tantum decem'. If in fact the *Runic Poem* page held only twenty-nine runes when Wanley wrote this, then Hempl was right, and all after *ear* are additions made in the *Thesaurus* plates. I contend that Wanley could have meant that the original poem – the runes with their Anglo-Saxon commentary – accounted for twenty-nine letters. He was not concerned with modern additions.

POSTSCRIPT

This paper was one part of a discussion of the contributions of early modern scholars to Anglo-Saxon studies, a subject that has achieved wider interest in more recent years. The relationship between Wanley and Hickes is now better known through the

[13] Derolez, *Runica Manuscripta*, p. 26.
[14] Ker, *Catalogue*, p. 1.
[15] Ker, *Catalogue*, p. 189.

publication of Wanley's correspondence.[16] Specifically his supervision of the plates of Hickes's *Thesaurus* is confirmed in a letter dated 9 November 1698: 'Mr Burghers [the engraver to Oxford University Press] ha's engraven the Saxon Alphabets which I drew, but so rudely, that I think the Prints will not be fit to appear, unless I may have the Liberty to correct the faulty places'.[17]

On Robert Talbot Mr Tim Graham has suggested that the 'old saxonice bede de historia ecclesie gentis Anglor*um*' was Cambridge University Library, MS Kk.3.18, a book that was one of Matthew Parker's gifts to that library in 1574. Graham finds traces of Talbot's distinctive hand in the manuscript.[18] According to his note in Cotton Domitian IX, Talbot's copy was disbound or at least without boards. Presumably, then, Parker had it rebound, removing a superfluous final leaf in the process. The present binding is twentieth-century, its flyleaves late sixteenth-/early seventeenth-century, apparently added by Parker when he had the book rebound in connection with his gift. There is no final page missing from the last quire of the manuscript, so if this was Talbot's Old English Bede, the 'last leaff off y^t book' is likely to have been an added (?) flyleaf which Parker's binders discarded.

16 *Letters of Humfrey Wanley: Palaeographer, Anglo-Saxonist, Librarian 1672–1726*, ed. P. L. Heyworth (Oxford, 1989).

17 *Ibid.* p. 107.

18 T. Graham, 'Robert Talbot's "Old Saxonice Bede" ', *Cambridge Bibliographical Society Newsletter* (Spring 1994), 6–7.

16

(1980)

SOME THOUGHTS ON MANX RUNES*

The Isle of Man is a place to attract Vikings of all sorts. To the zoological Viking, for instance, it is of interest because of its distinctive fauna; for it is the home of the tail-less cat, the three-legged coat of arms, the kippered herring and the Director of the British Museum. The constitutional Viking will visit the island this year to celebrate the millennium of Tynwald, of what the commemorative emblem calls 'A thousand years of unbroken parliamentary government', for which it surely deserves our admiration, not to say sympathy. But to the literate Viking it is important because it has over thirty rune-stones, and it is this aspect that I would like to discuss before an assembly of literate Vikings. Magnus Olsen gave a detailed account of the Manx runes in 1954, though he based it on a journey made as far back as 1911 and so did not deal at first hand with inscriptions found later.[1] More recently Ingrid Sanness Johnsen included most of the Manx runes in her book *Stuttruner i vikingtidens innskrifter* (Oslo, 1968). Before Olsen a long series of distinguished Norse scholars had worked on the inscriptions: Munch in the 1840s and 1850s, Guðbrandur Vigfússon in 1887, Sophus Bugge in 1899, Brate in 1907, while Marstrander used runic material in his studies of the Scandinavians on Man.[2] Anyone who makes pretensions to taking yet another look at these texts will have to put forward some justification, and the present paper is something of a progress report and apologia, presenting part of my preliminary thinking on the subject.

The present corpus consists of thirty-one rune-stones, of which two are tiny fragments that contribute only points on a distribution map, and another is so worn that it is little more. Two of the Manx stones, those which Olsen numbers Maughold I and II, he places in the later twelfth century, but the rest of his twenty-nine examples he regards as Viking though there are not always adequate dating criteria. Two more stones have appeared since Olsen's 1954 study. A total of nearly thirty Viking Age

* [This paper formed the Presidential Address to the Viking Society for Northern Research, delivered in May 1979.]

[1] Magnus Olsen, 'Runic Inscriptions in Great Britain, Ireland and The Isle of Man', *Viking Antiquities in Great Britain and Ireland*, ed. H. Shetelig (Oslo, 1940–54) VI, 151–233, especially 182–232. Note that in his introduction (p. 153) Olsen wrongly lists the late stones Maughold I and II as Marown I and II.

[2] There is a detailed bibliography in H. Marquardt, *Bibliographie der Runeninschriften nach Fundorten. I Die Runeninschriften der Britischen Inseln* (Göttingen, 1961), pp. 55–82.

rune-stones is impressive compared with Viking rune-stones elsewhere.[3] In Denmark itself there are probably fewer than 200 rune-stones from the Viking Age, and remarkably few in the Danish colonies overseas: none in Normandy and only two or three in the Danelaw. In Norway there are some 40 Viking rune-stones, and again the numbers in the colonies are few: three or so in Ireland, a couple in the Faroes, a handful in north-west England and none in Iceland. The numbers in the British Isles are hard to assess. Olsen's 1954 list shows four fragments of rune-stones from the Shetlands, five from the Orkneys, six from mainland Scotland and the Hebrides; and though there are now some additions, the order of numbers remains unchanged.[4] Thirty or so from an island as tiny as Man looks significant, and should make us wonder what is so special about Man that it should produce so many.

There is perhaps another thing to wonder at. In Man the only runic finds hitherto have been on stone. This is unusual. The Irish finds, for example, include the rune-inscribed sword-fitting from Greenmount as well as the newly discovered runic bone and wooden pieces from Dublin; the Scots ones include the Hunterston brooch, a Celtic jewel with a Norse text; the Orkneys and Shetlands can show runes on a steatite whorl and disc; the Danelaw those on the Lincoln comb-case. The question obviously arises whether the known Manx runes are on stones only because archaeological work on Man up to now has not been intensive or skilled enough to produce finds of other rune-inscribed objects. I do not think this is the answer, but in this matter, to quote some of my friends, only archaeologists can reveal the truth.[5] There may too be the question of suitability of materials. Are there Manx runic crosses because there was, on Man, a ready supply of easily worked stone? Certainly the island has plentiful blue slate that forms natural slabs and cuts fairly readily with a heavy knife, but again I do not think this is the reason, or at any rate the only reason, for the plenty of Manx rune-stones. After all, the Anglo-Saxons found in England stone suitable for their inscriptions, but for all that the Vikings do not seem to have emulated them there. There must, I think, be some other reason.

Anyone who has prepared a distribution map of archaeological finds will be uncomfortably aware that what he is plotting may be not the distribution of deposits of a particular kind of object, but the distribution of activity of people looking for it. This could be the case with the Manx rune-stones; perhaps we know so many on the Isle of Man because there has been so energetic a search for them. Because of this possibility it is worth taking a short look at the history of runic studies in Man.

The earliest pictures of Manx rune-stones that I know appear in Edmund Gibson's

---

[3] The number of Manx Viking stones must remain approximate here because of the uncertainty of some of the dating. There are, moreover, special cases such as that of the Onchan stone which is pre-Viking but with runes added in more than one hand, as well as a number of stones that have runic graffiti added.

[4] A. M. Cubbon gives more up-to-date details of numbers in 'Viking Runes: Outstanding New Discovery at Maughold', *Journal of the Manx Museum* 7, no. 82 (1966), 23–6, though his figures include post-Viking monuments.

[5] The acid soils of the Isle of Man do not preserve wood and bone, and there are few finds of precious metals on which runes might remain. Non-precious metals discovered are usually in so poor a state that any runes they may have held are now illegible.

adaptation of Camden's *Britannia*, the second edition published in 1722. They show
– and I use here and hereafter Magnus Olsen's numbering of the stones[6] – Andreas
II, Braddan IV and Kirk Michael III and V. They derive, as does the account of the
island in that volume, from Thomas Wilson, Bishop of Sodor and Man from 1697
to 1755 and an energetic recorder of Man's peculiarities.[7] Gibson's four stones were
the only ones known to Richard Gough when he published his revised Camden in
1789.[8] He printed what he thought of as 'correct copies of the four Runic inscriptions
communicated to bishop Gibson', though far from being correct they are in some
ways less accurate than the earlier versions. These four seem to be the only Manx
runic crosses published by the beginning of the nineteenth century, though others
may be recorded in unpublished texts. For instance, probably ultimately from Wilson
is a group of drawings preserved among Humfrey Wanley's papers. These are British
Library Loan 29/259 no. 17, which gives rough representations of the runes of
Andreas II and Kirk Michael V, together with another Andreas example which is
either a now lost cross or is Andreas IV in a much more complete state than the
present fragment.

In a group of related discourses published by the Society of Antiquaries of
Scotland in 1823,[9] H. R. Oswald, surgeon to the household of the Duke of Atholl,
recorded again Braddan IV and Kirk Michael V, but of Wilson's other two stones he
said in 1817: 'I know not whether these stones are still preserved, not having seen
or heard of them while I was in the island'. In a later communication in the same
group of notes, Oswald recorded also Andreas II, with detailed and important
drawings of his three runic monuments: the originals of the pictures, by G. W.
Carrington, are in the library of the Manx Museum. The rapid development of Manx
runic studies in the nineteenth century can be demonstrated roughly by charting the
work of William Kinnebrook, J. G. Cumming and P. M. C. Kermode, though these
are only three of a strong field of scholars working on the subject. Kinnebrook's
Etchings of the Runic Monuments in The Isle of Man (London, 1841) recorded nine
inscriptions, those of Andreas I and II, Braddan II and IV, Kirk Michael II, III, V and
VI, and Onchan. All these were fairly well known about this time, for, at a date
variously given as 1839 and 1841, a craftsman called W. Bally of Manchester made
casts of them all, which came into the possession of Sir Henry Dryden of Canons

---

[6] Unfortunately there are several different methods of numbering the Manx carved stones. Two
principal ones derive from (i) P. M. C. Kermode's corpus *Manx Crosses* (London, 1907), and (ii) the
Manx Museum catalogue. In addition Olsen uses Brate's numbering. Olsen's own order is alphabetical
according to parish name (save for Balleigh which is listed under its find-spot), and he numbers the
various rune-stones from the same parish in a haphazard order that pays no attention to the date either
of the carving or of the discovery. There are too many numbering systems already to make it desirable
to add another, so I follow Olsen, though I differ slightly in some name forms. For instance, I follow
the Ordnance Survey map in distinguishing Kirk Michael from Michael, and in calling Conchan
Onchan.
[7] *Camden's Britannia*, ed. E. Gibson (London, 1722), pp. 1458–9.
[8] *Camden's Britannia*, ed. R. Gough (London, 1789) III, 704.
[9] 'Account of a Stone with a Runic Inscription . . . and of Some Other Inscriptions of the Same Kind
in The Isle of Man', *Archaeologia Scotica or Transactions of The Society of Antiquaries of Scotland*
2, ii (1823), 491–4.

Ashby, Northants.[10] Kinnebrook also noted a text, almost defaced, on Kirk Michael IV, as well as showing views of the crosses of Ballaugh and Kirk Michael I without mentioning their runes, and one of Braddan III when it was still embedded in the wall of the church tower, its inscription invisible. Cumming's account of 1854 included ten stones acknowledged as runic.[11] Surprisingly he omitted Andreas I and Braddan II but gave the rest of Kinnebrook's corpus together with the runes of Kirk Michael I and IV, and added a completely new stone, German (St John's) I. His later list in the book *The Runic and Other Monumental Remains of The Isle of Man* (London, 1857) added further the runes of Ballaugh and Braddan III, and included two new stones, German (Peel) II and Jurby, making sixteen altogether. A second group of casts was made in 1854 or 1855 covering the Cumming material, and some of these subsequently came to the Manx Museum. In 1866 he recorded Braddan I.[12] Kermode's first *Catalogue of the Manks Crosses with the Runic Inscriptions* . . . appeared in 1887, and supplied to the corpus Andreas III, IV and V, and Bride, together with Marown (Rhyne) which he listed under Braddan. The second edition of 1892 added Maughold II. Kermode's great work of 1907, *Manx Crosses*, included two more inscribed stones, Maughold I and Kirk Michael VII. Thus, within seventy years of Kinnebrook's pioneer work the number of known Manx rune-stones had nearly trebled. Thereafter, Kirk Michael VIII was found in 1911, Maughold IV in 1913, and Braddan V and Maughold V both in 1965. This completes the corpus known so far, save for two fragments, Balleigh and Maughold III, on which there are tiny fragments of staves that were probably (and in the case of Balleigh certainly) runes, but which are inadequate for interpretation. This survey shows that the second half of the nineteenth century was indeed a key period for the discovery, recording and preservation of the Manx rune-stones, and does something to support the view that Man has so many rune-stones known because the search for them was so intensive. But it is not the only answer.

The order in which the Manx runic crosses were recorded is in general unsurprising. In commenting on Man Wilson remarked:

> Here are more *Runick Inscriptions* to be met with in this Island, than perhaps in any other Nation; most of them upon Funeral Monuments. They are, generally, on a long, flat, ragg Stone, with Crosses on one or both sides, and little embellishments of Men on horseback, or in Arms, Stags, Dogs, Birds, or other Devices; probably the Atchievements of some notable person. The Inscriptions are generally on one edge, to be read from the Bottom upwards. Most of them, after so many ages, are very entire, and writ in the old Norwegian Language . . . One of the largest of these stands in the

---

[10] There are varying accounts of these casts and of the later ones that Cumming had made. Sir Henry Dryden's version, which ought to have some authority, is given in a letter to *The Academy* 31 (Jan.–June 1887), 202–3.

[11] J. G. Cumming, 'On the Inscribed Stones of The Isle of Man', *Proc. of the Royal Irish Academy* 6 (1853–7, delivered 1854), 73–7.

[12] J. G. Cumming, 'On Some More Recently Discovered Scandinavian Crosses in The Isle of Man', *Archæologia Cambrensis* 3rd ser., 12 (1866), 460–2.

High-way, near the Church of St. *Michael*, erected in memory of *Thurulf*, or *Thrulf*, as the name is now pronounc'd in *Norway*.[13]

Unless this is the language of hyperbole, Wilson knew more rune-stones than the four he supplied to Gibson's Camden, even if we add to that the second Andreas stone of BL Loan 29/259. Nor would this be surprising. Wilson's home was at Bishopscourt, a few miles from Kirk Michael (where incidentally he is buried), so naturally he knew the impressive standing cross Kirk Michael V, as well as Kirk Michael III which was re-used as a lintel over a church window. It is, I suppose, possible that he knew some of the other rune-stones now at this church, though they may have only come to light on the demolition of the old church in the 1830s. I would expect him to know the Ballaugh cross which Kinnebrook recorded in the yard of the Old Church, though he may not have noted its runes any more than Kinnebrook did. At any rate Wilson rebuilt this church, and it probably stands on the site of an old burial ground so the Ballaugh cross may occupy its original place (though that is not at all certain as I shall show later). Since he knew Andreas II (in the churchyard) he would presumably also have seen Andreas I which, in 1841, was standing on the green nearby (though there is a difficulty about this too).

On the other hand, it is curious that though there are many journals of travels in the Isle of Man and accounts of that island dating from the later eighteenth and the early nineteenth centuries, none of them, so far as I know, illustrate rune-stones other than those recorded by Gibson; and very few of them mention other rune-stones. For example, Richard Townley's journal published in 1791 reports two rune-stones at Kirk Michael, one certainly Michael V and the other presumably Michael III though Townley refers to it only as 'some Danish characters upon one grave-stone'.[14] He spent some time in the churchyard at Kirk Braddan deciphering inscriptions on grave-stones, but made no mention of any runic crosses.[15] John Feltham, who toured the island in 1797 and 1798, noted Andreas II, Braddan IV and Kirk Michael III and V (that is to say Gibson's four stones), with a drawing of the latter that looks directly and faithfully derived from Gibson; but he reported no other rune-stones.[16] Thorkelin visited Man in 1790, claiming to come to examine the runes 'by the express order of his Danish Majesty', but departed after two days apparently little wiser than when he arrived.[17] I know of no notes he made on Manx runes. On the other hand, Townley, who seems to have been more enterprising than other visitors to the island, did make some discoveries to suggest that there were rune-stones to be spotted easily by anyone who would take the trouble. At Kirk Michael, for instance, he searched 'some rubbish places on the outside' of the churchyard, and there found a carved stone that he thought was Viking though he does not speak of an inscription. He took it with him

[13] *Camden's Britannia* (1722), p. 1455.
[14] R. Townley, *A Journal Kept in The Isle of Man . . .* (Whitehaven, 1791) I, 82. There is a detailed bibliography of the early guidebooks and journals in W. Cubbon, *A Bibliographical Account of Works Relating to The Isle of Man* (London, 1933).
[15] Townley, *Journal* I, 47–9.
[16] J. Feltham, *A Tour through The Island of Mann, in 1797 and 1798* (Bath, 1798), especially p. 202.
[17] Townley, *Journal* I, 156–8.

to Douglas, and its subsequent history is unknown.[18] Recording a visit to Onchan he says: 'In going into Kirk Onchan church-yard, this morning, I noticed a rude carving upon the highest step; the figure of a Danish warrior, in complete armour, with a number of Runic characters on one side of the stone'.[19] This is not the Onchan stone now known, nor indeed any known rune-stone, but of course Townley's identification of the marks on the (?) edge as runes may be wrong.

On the whole, however, working through the guidebooks, histories and journals of visits to Man from the late eighteenth and early nineteenth centuries is a depressing experience. They promise so much information but deliver so little, at any rate on the rune-stones. This is partly because there is such a lot of plagiarism and copying in them, so that we cannot take as directly known any statement that we find. A writer may record a stone at a particular site not because he saw it there, but because an earlier writer said it was there. He may have failed to record a prominent stone because nobody had yet reported it. Moreover these writers used the word 'runic' imprecisely, without reference to script. It may mean 'Dark Age' or 'Viking', or even just 'so badly preserved as to be unreadable'. This is sadly misleading when you are seeking references to rune-stones, and is particularly irritating when used of sites from which we now know rune-stones to exist. When, for instance, William Kneale, one of the more responsible guidebook writers, says of Onchan: 'Scattered about the churchyard are several Runic crosses', how exactly is he using the word?[20] Kneale could recognise runes. There is one rune-inscribed cross now known at Onchan, and if Townley was right a second recorded in the eighteenth century and now lost. How many Onchan crosses with runes on them did Kneale know in 1860? In these guidebooks too there is often grotesque confusion because their writers either could not read their notes or could not plagiarise others' work accurately. For instance, in G. Woods's *An Account of the Past and Present State of the Isle of Man* (London, 1811) is a description of a stone which must be Andreas II, but Woods claims it was in Bride churchyard.[21] The two distinct and complementary texts on Kirk Michael III are sometimes ascribed to two separate stones. Indeed, the second was often reported lost by writers who transcribed the first, while Thwaites and Kneale, writing in the 1860s, referred it to Onchan.[22] This sort of confusion may lead us to undervalue what may be genuine information. As an example, J. Welch's *A Six Days' Tour through the Isle of Man* (Douglas, 1836) mentions a rune-stone which must be Braddan IV since that is the only one consistently described as being in that churchyard from early times. At the same time he speaks of 'the remnant of another forming the stile'.[23] This we might ignore if it was not confirmed by another guidebook of the same date, which writes with such precision and freshness as to constitute a corroborative statement. *The Illustrated Guide and Visitor's Companion through the Isle of Man*

---

18 Townley, *Journal* I, 173 and 175–6.
19 Townley, *Journal* II, 166.
20 W. Kneale, *Guide to The Isle of Man* (Douglas, n.d., *c.* 1860), p. 108.
21 Woods, *Account*, p. 168.
22 W. Thwaites, *Isle of Man* (Sheffield, [1863]), p. 396; Kneale, *Guide*, p. 108.
23 Welch, *Tour*, p. 56.

by 'a Resident' (Douglas, 1836) speaks of 'leaving the church-yard, in the opposite direction to which we entered, over a stone slab which appears to have been formerly a memorial to departed greatness, as one side of it contains many runic characters'.[24] There are now five rune-stones known from Braddan. The stile stone cannot be Braddan IV for Carrington's drawings confirm that that was standing upright in the churchyard, nor can it be Braddan III which was still serving as a lintel in the church tower. Braddan II and V are too fragmentary to act as a stile, so it cannot be them unless they were severely damaged before being refound. It looks then as though this must be Braddan I, but that is otherwise always recorded as forming 'a door-step in the church'.[25] Must we question that account of Braddan I, or is the stile stone one that has since been lost? The answer is probably supplied by Kinnebrook. He shows a stone which 'forms the stile at the upper end of the Church-yard' at Braddan.[26] This, however, is a known cross which is non-runic, and which Kermode hesitatingly put in the pre-Viking period.[27] If, as seems likely, this is the stile stone referred to in the two 1836 accounts, they were independently in error in calling it runic.

What I have said raises the question of whether many Manx runic crosses were lost in comparatively recent times, before their runes were recorded. In the first half and indeed into the later nineteenth century there was little general care for the Manx rune-stones. As early as 1731 G. Waldron had pointed to one general source of damage. 'Having mentioned that there is no church-yard without a cross, I cannot forbear taking notice, that there is none which serves not also for a common to the parson's cattle; all his horses, his cows, and sheep, grazing there perpetually'.[28] When Kinnebrook came to look for the monuments for his 1841 volume, he claimed that the task of recording them became 'a tedious undertaking, from the absence of any complete guide to their situations, and the difficulty of obtaining information from the peasantry about things, in several instances, in their immediate neighbour-hoods',[29] and this complaint confirms Oswald's remark that he had not seen or heard of two of Wilson's stones. Worse than this neglect was wanton destruction. 'Within the last few months', laments Kinnebrook, 'two very richly carved crosses, one if not both, with Runic inscriptions upon them, were broken in pieces to form a part of Kirk Michael Church wall, upon the top of which, the fragments may be seen imbedded in mortar'.[30] In 1845 Train reported another way in which these crosses were lost to the island. At the orders of the Duke of Atholl, 'many runic stones were shipped for Scotland, which may, perhaps, account for many of the crosses mentioned by Waldron, being now nowhere to be found'.[31] Perhaps it would be worth while

[24] *Illustrated Guide*, p. 72.
[25] Cumming, 'More Recently Discovered Scandinavian Crosses', p. 460.
[26] Kinnebrook, *Etchings*, p. 14 and no. 24.
[27] Kermode, *Manx Crosses*, pp. 130–1. To add to the confusion, J. Train describes Braddan IV as 'forming a stile' at the churchyard entrance, while at the same time recording it in the centre of the churchyard (*An Historical and Statistical Account of The Isle of Man* (Douglas, c. 1845) II, 32).
[28] G. Waldron, *A Description of The Isle of Man*, ed. W. Harrison (Douglas, 1865), p. 61.
[29] Kinnebrook, *Etchings*, preface.
[30] Kinnebrook, *Etchings*, p. 9.
[31] Train, *Historical and Statistical Account* II, 31.

searching the precincts of Blair Atholl. We know that one cross, Braddan II, was certainly shipped away, for it spent part of the nineteenth century in a private museum at Distington, Cumberland.[32] As late as the end of that century, some of these crosses were subjected to unfortunate familiarities – Andreas I was used to post bills on, while photographs of Kirk Michael V show its base used as a place of rest for the aged and of play for the young. From another point of view, as early as 1887 Sir Henry Dryden pointed out that the island had an invasion of 150,000 tourists a year, and there was fear that unprotected stones would suffer from them.[33]

For a new examination of the Manx rune-stones, then, it will be important to scrutinise the corpus. We shall want to know what evidence there is of stones being lost or inscriptions broken away in modern times. Parallel to this we shall want to search for early drawings or casts of stones to see if they can supply lost material.

From what I have said so far it is clear that a vigorous interest in these Manx antiquities began in the 1830s when Bally made his casts. Thereafter people like Kinnebrook and Cumming assiduously recorded well-known and new pieces, and towards the end of the century the immensely active Kermode brought all the finds together into a coherent corpus and supplemented them by new discoveries, often of fragments that had been re-used as building material. Though I have mentioned chiefly these three important investigators, there were other scholars and amateurs who hold an honourable place in this study. For instance, the English writer George Borrow, a man with a magpie knowledge of languages, visited Man in 1855. When he was at Braddan he managed to persuade the church authorities to let him remove Braddan III from the wall of the church tower. So he revealed the inscription, and made not a bad attempt at transliterating and interpreting it.[34] To this extent the plenty of Manx rune-stones represents the vigour of those who looked for them. There is a related consideration, the effect on the statistics of the fact that a high proportion of Manx parish churches were rebuilt in the late eighteenth and nineteenth centuries: Braddan in 1773, Andreas in 1821, Jurby in 1829, Onchan in 1833, Michael in 1835, St John's chapel in 1849 and Bride in 1870, while there was an extensive remodelling of Maughold at the end of the century. Several of the rune-stones, we know, came to light during these works.

Before the 1830s there was a more desultory interest in these runes, but even from the earlier dates there may survive occasional useful drawings. For example, the Gibson and Gough depictions of Braddan IV apparently show the stone before it was

---

[32] J. G. Cumming, *The Runic and Other Monumental Remains of The Isle of Man* (London, 1857), p. 24.

[33] *The Academy* 31 (Jan.–June 1887), p. 203.

[34] Braddan III's runes are first illustrated in 'Ancient Runic Stone, Recently Found in The Isle of Man', *Illustrated London News* (8 December 1855), p. 685, which presumably derives from Borrow. There may be further details in Borrow's Isle of Man journal whose manuscript survives in the Library of the Hispanic Society of America, where, however, it is not generally available. There are quotations from it in W. I. Knapp, *Life, Writings, and Correspondence of George Borrow* (London, 1899) II, 144. See also Borrow's 'An Expedition to The Isle of Man', published in C. K. Shorter's edition of the complete works (London, 1923–4), *Miscellanies II* (vol. 16), pp. 454–500, and Shorter's book *George Borrow and his Circle* (London, 1913), pp. 296–303.

shattered across the shaft, damage that occurred before Carrington's drawing. From them can be supplied a couple of characters damaged with the break, and they settle an interesting if minor problem of punctuation. However, the only early drawing of real importance that I have found so far is that of the mysterious Andreas runes of BL Loan 29/259. The description that precedes these runes says simply: 'On the Edge of another stone in the same Churchyard [i.e. Andreas], toward the South, is the following Inscription, somewhat defaced at the Top; as are also the Animals Engraven on the other parts of the same'. I do not know whether the runic transcript that follows represents the complete inscription or only its first part. Whoever copied the runes was only middling successful. Fortunately, the same hand recorded two inscriptions that still survive, so we can judge his accuracy and find out what sort of mistakes he made. He produced a quite careful drawing of Kirk Michael V, and a rather less successful one of Andreas II. From them it is clear that he had difficulty with the minor staves of letters, missing out a number of those that convert a plain vertical stave into something else. Thus he draws | when he may mean ᚼ, ᚠ or ᛁ; similarly he puts || for ᚿ, and ᚱ for ᚴ. Again, the two runes **u** and **r** are not properly differentiated in some parts of these sketches. Taking these features into consideration it is possible to suggest a fairly complete reading for the (?) new Andreas text.

```
.   .  b a n  : s u  n : m . . . . . n s : .  a . : s . : .   .  . s : þ . . . a :
.   .  b a n  : s u  n : m . . . . . n s :  r  a i s t i : k r  u s : þ a i n a :
```

```
.  f t  . r  : . u f u : k u . . u : s . n  . : . r : . . . .  . : u f . . :
.  i f t i r : t u f  u : k u i n u : s i n a : . . : . . . .  . : u f a k :
```

I redraw it in the accompanying figure. My reconstructed text shows a number of letters that are not clearly recorded, but which can be guessed at from the context. After *krus* is a form of the article, and since it has four verticals after þ it is presumably *þaina* as on Andreas IV. Thereafter follows some spelling of the word *aftir*, though the vowels must remain uncertain. The appearance of the transcribed runes just about suggests the verb *raisti* and this fits the context perfectly, but this word was not one of the draughtsman's better efforts and there should remain some doubt. The commemorated woman has a name ending in **ufu**, and it is convenient to suggest *Tofa* (cf. the oblique form tufu on the Gunderup, Jylland, stone I).[35] The sense of the text, as far as *kuinu sina*, fits in well with other Manx inscriptions, and validates the

---

[35] Jacobsen and Moltke, *Danmarks runeindskrifter*, col. 180. *Tofa* is comparatively rare and late in West Norse, and it might be desirable to seek another, and more likely, name to fit the Andreas context.

accuracy of the drawing. Andreas IV, now just a fragment, reads . . . .r]ais(t)i (k)rus þaina aftiʀ. . . . in Olsen's transcript, which coincides nearly with the Wanley drawing, and despite some difficulty I am inclined to think that BL Loan 29/259 records an earlier and more complete form of that inscription. Strongly in favour is the deictic form *þaina* which is otherwise unparalleled in Man, other spellings of the word having only two or three vertical staves after þ. Against is the final letter of *aftir*, which the manuscript shows clearly as r, while the stone has ı, which seems to be the complete letter, not a fragment of it. The section after *sina* is hard to reconstruct, partly because we do not know if it is complete. Parallel examples in Man and elsewhere in Scandinavian territory suggest that any addition to the simple memorial formula is either (a) a phrase or clause describing the deceased, or (b) a completely new sentence, perhaps defining the dead, perhaps speaking of the maker or carver of the monument.

A new examination of the Manx runic material should also lead us to question the traditional accounts of the find-spots of these monuments. Several of the stones were still standing when they were first recorded, though it would be incautious to assume that they had always occupied the sites they were found on. This group consists of Andreas I, II and V, Ballaugh, Braddan IV and Kirk Michael V. Kirk Michael VII was certainly standing, but it had been re-used as a headstone and dated 1699, and its runes were noticed only late. Another group of stones had been used as building material, and were dug out of walls or found when churches were demolished or repaired. This includes Braddan III, Bride, German (St John's) I, Maughold I and Kirk Michael III, all found in their respective churches, as well as Braddan I which, if not part of a stile, was a threshold slab at Braddan Old Church. There is a piquancy in some of these finds. The old chapel at St John's from whose walls the rune-stone came was rebuilt under Bishop Wilson's patronage in 1699–1704,[36] so even while he was recording the significance of the crosses, Wilson was allowing them to be walled up in new structures; 1699, the date of the re-use of Kirk Michael VII, was during Wilson's episcopate and so when he was living in nearby Bishopscourt. It looks from this that Wilson was a less fervent preserver of Manx antiquities than has sometimes been said. Andreas III came from a churchyard wall, as did Braddan V, discovered in an accidental fall of stones. German (Peel) II was used as infilling in an arch in the ruined cathedral of Peel, which suggests that it was turned into building stone no earlier than the eighteenth century when that church fell into disrepair. Unfortunately, the early reports do not agree about where this stone was, for several mid-nineteenth-century writers record it in the south wall of the nave of the cathedral, while Kermode had it removed from the east wall of the north transept.[37] Maybe this stone was used several times for patching up the fabric before Kermode rescued it, and it may have suffered a good deal of damage in the process. Andreas IV was pulled out of the wall of the rectory stable at Andreas, built after the destructive storm of

---

[36] W. Harrison, *Records of the Tynwald and Saint John's Chapels in The Isle of Man* (Douglas, 1871), p. 50.
[37] J. L. Petit, 'Ecclesiastical Antiquities of The Isle of Man. Cathedral of St. German, in Peel Castle', *Archaeological Journal* 3 (1846), 58; Kneale, *Guide*, p. 171; Kermode, *Manx Crosses*, p. 209.

1839[38] (though if this is the same as the stone drawn in BL Loan 29/259 it stood before that in the churchyard), and Maughold V until recently formed a flooring slab in a cottage in that village. Four Michael stones, I, II, IV and VI were built into the churchyard wall apparently in the first half of the nineteenth century; in 1845 Braddan II is said to have been lying at the base of Braddan IV; but where all these were before we do not know. Three stones were retrieved from gardens: Jurby at or near the vicarage, Kirk Michael VIII next door to the church, and Onchan in a village cottage garden. These could have been brought in from anywhere, though Onchan is said to have come from the belfry of the old church of the place.[39] The Marown (Rhyne) stone was picked up from a stackyard of a farm, and its finder suggested that it came from a nearby chapel that had been levelled. Balleigh came from an ancient burial ground. Finally there are three Maughold stones. Maughold IV certainly came from that churchyard, from a controlled excavation near the north keeil. Maughold II was a casual find in the Corna valley, and the finder, S. N. Harrison, thought it came from the ruined chapel of Keeil Woirrey, which is some distance from Maughold church. Maughold III is from Ballagilley, over a mile from Maughold, where there is also a ruined chapel.

From this it is clear that the present method of naming stones by the parish they come from is misleading, since it lumps together stones from quite different sites. To prevent confusion or difficulty in reference I propose we keep the traditional names, but add in brackets the precise site of the find if it is known. Thus we have the following corpus of Manx Norse runes:

1 Andreas I	standing, outside churchyard
2 Andreas II	standing, churchyard
3 Andreas III	building stone, ? churchyard wall
4 Andreas IV	? standing/building stone in rectory
5 Andreas V	standing, churchyard
6 Ballaugh	standing, churchyard
7 Balleigh	burial ground, ? foundations of chapel
8 Braddan I	church doorstep
9 Braddan II	? churchyard
10 Braddan III	building stone, church tower
11 Braddan IV	standing, churchyard
12 Braddan V	building stone, churchyard wall
13 Bride	building stone, church
14 German (St John's) I	building stone, church
15 German (Peel) II	building stone, cathedral
16 Jurby	vicarage garden
17 Kirk Michael I	? building stone, church/churchyard wall
18 Kirk Michael II	building stone, church

[38] J. B. Laughton, *A New Historical, Topographical, and Parochial Guide to The Isle of Mann* (Douglas, 1842), p. 91.
[39] Thwaites, *Isle of Man*, pp. 396–7.

19 Kirk Michael III	building stone, church
20 Kirk Michael IV	churchyard wall
21 Kirk Michael V	standing, outside churchyard
22 Kirk Michael VI	churchyard wall
23 Kirk Michael VII	re-used as headstone of grave
24 Kirk Michael VIII	garden next door to church
25 Marown (Rhyne)	farmyard, ? from nearby chapel
26 Maughold I	building stone, church
27 Maughold (Corna valley) II	casual find, ? from chapel
28 Maughold (Ballagilley) III	keeil and burial ground
29 Maughold IV	churchyard, ? standing on secondary site
30 Maughold V	building stone, cottage
31 Onchan	cottage garden, ? building stone, church belfry

From this list it is clear that there is a close connection between the rune-stones and churchyards; and this is reasonable enough if you assume that the stones are (in almost every case) grave-stones. Many have assumed that, but is it necessary to? In Scandinavia there are certainly many rune-stones that cannot be grave-stones since they record the death (and sometimes even the burial) of a man far from home. These are memorial stones but not grave-stones. Other Scandinavian examples are put up by a man in his own honour, erected while he was still alive (and there is some parallel to these in Kirk Michael II, set up to secure the man's own soul). Further, there are numbers of Viking Age stones in Scandinavia that do not stand on burials, but are placed at other strategic sites, by a roadside, at a bridge-point, or at a legal meeting-place. The stone stands somewhere that people pass regularly, so the dead man's memory is kept green. Kermode records similar finds of incised (non-runic) stones in Man. It would therefore be as well to examine the runic list to see what justification there is for placing so many of the Manx stones in or near burial sites. As far as I know there is no established case of a Manx rune-stone being found in clear connection with its burial. Maughold IV was discovered at a grave and during proper excavation, but from Kermode's slightly confused account it looks as though this was a secondary use of the stone.[40] Of the six stones first recorded as standing, four were in churchyards: Andreas II, Andreas V, Ballaugh and Braddan IV (as well as the stone of BL Loan 29/259). Two were not in churchyards: Andreas I on the village green and Kirk Michael V on the roadside in the middle of the village. So far our first accounts go, though here it is important to stress the danger of trusting early accounts if they are not adequately supported. Of Kirk Michael V, H. I. Jenkinson's *Practical Guide to The Isle of Man* (London, 1874) says that it was 'found many years ago about a foot below the surface of the ground, in what is called the Chapel Field, or the Vicar's Glebe', and several other guides of the same period tell the same tale, putting the find-date 'about a century ago'.[41] Yet an entry in the *Gentleman's*

[40] P. M. C. Kermode, 'Further Discoveries of Cross-Slabs in The Isle of Man', *PSAS* 50 (1915–16), 55–6.
[41] Jenkinson, *Practical Guide*, p. 109; Thwaites, *Isle of Man*, p. 375.

Magazine for 1798 says that it had 'been removed from a field, where it formerly stood, near the Bishop's court'.[42] These stories of the moving of Kirk Michael V would be more convincing had we not got a series of records of this stone, beginning with Wanley and Bishop Wilson and continuing until the end of the nineteenth century showing that it stood by the roadside. On the opposite side we must note that in 1841 Kinnebrook saw the Andreas I stone on a prominent site 'on the green, near the entrance to the Church-yard'.[43] It is surely curious that Oswald, *c.* 1820, recording Andreas II, failed to notice Andreas I if it then occupied so distinctive a position. Nor, as far as I have found, did any earlier writer see the stone on the green. We must reckon with the possibility that Andreas I was put there at a comparatively late date. There is a similar uncertainty in the case of the Ballaugh stone. Kinnebrook found it 'in Ballaugh old Church-yard, on the south side of the Church',[44] but an unattributed newspaper cutting among Kermode's papers speaks of an ancient cross that 'used to stand on a mound outside the old Churchyard', but which had been moved inside it, while Feltham also spoke of an early cross outside the churchyard, though he saw it on a mount, not a mound.[45] There is no certainty that this was the rune-stone, but it may have been. Clearly, early find-reports need scrutiny. However, as far as we can tell, of the six or seven standing stones, two were not obviously over burials. Of the rest of the crosses, we can have no clear information of Jurby or Kirk Michael VIII, found in gardens; Onchan, also found in a garden, is reported to come from a church belfry but on no great authority. Maughold V can have come from anywhere in a job lot of paving stone. Balleigh was discovered 'loose in the foundations of what may have been a chapel' connected with an early Christian burial place. I wonder if the foundations were identified as a chapel because a rune-stone (assumed to be a grave-stone) was found in them. The other stones from this early Christian burial place are much earlier – by several centuries – than the Balleigh rune-stone, so there may be no continuity of use of the site.[46] There is at least the possibility that the foundations were of a later secular building, and that the runic fragment was brought as building stone from somewhere quite different. The Marown (Rhyne) stone was discovered in a farm stackyard, and it is guesswork only that links it to the nearby chapel and graveyard 'which had been completely razed'.[47] Maughold (Corna valley) II is a casual find by the river. Its text links it to the valley, but its discoverer recorded the tradition 'that it had been carried down from an old burial ground some distance away . . . called Cabbal Keeil Woirey'.[48] This, however, is a stone that is not a grave-stone (nor, as for that, Viking Age), and the name of the rune-master (as far as it can be read) connects it to the Maughold I stone from the fabric of the church at Maughold. Finally, the connection between Maughold III and the ruined chapel at

---

[42] *Gentleman's Magazine* 68 (1798), 749.
[43] Kinnebrook, *Etchings*, p. 11.
[44] *Ibid.*
[45] Feltham, *Tour*, p. 188.
[46] P. M. C. Kermode, 'More Cross-Slabs from The Isle of Man', *PSAS* 63 (1928–9), 357–60.
[47] Jenkinson, *Practical Guide*, p. 37.
[48] S. N. Harrison in *Yn Lioar Manninagh* 1, ii (1888–9), 140.

Ballagilley needs examination to see if this stone was not, in fact, simply a roadside cross, for Ballagilley stands on one of the roads from Ramsey to Laxey.

My purpose in looking critically at the early reports of these stones is only to draw attention to the fact that any distribution diagram of them can only be an approximate one, and that it will not be possible to draw too precise conclusions from it. There are a number of nineteenth-century reports – which perhaps we should not take too seriously – of sculptured stones being moved from one site in Man to another, and the earliest recorded whereabouts of the rune-stones may be misleading.

At this stage it is worth looking outside Man to the country, Norway, whose rune-stones are nearest in type to the Manx ones. A look at the Norwegian material produces interesting parallel information that ought to be taken note of.

(i) Though these stones, as in Man, are commemorative stones, they are not necessarily grave-stones, and so do not have to be linked to a church or a burial ground. An instructive example is the monument from Dynna, Hadeland. Like many of the Manx crosses this is a slim slab with the inscription cut up one edge. Like many of them it has a Christian reference on the face – on Dynna it is an Epiphany scene – but there is no Christianity in the text. Though it is a commemorative stone, it was not found in a churchyard: it is first recorded on a mound of unknown date close to the farm buildings at Nordre Dynna.[49] Presumably since it is a Christian monument, the remains of the girl it commemorates can hardly have been in the mound. Of the four runic crosses recorded from Viking Age Norway, two were found near churches – Njærheim I and Svanøy. Two seem to come from secular sites – Stavanger III on a hill near the highroad, and Tangerhaug from the farm at Sele. Such find-spots, a major farm or a position by the highroad, are not uncommon in Norway, and of course *Hávamál* v. 72 records the second:

> sialdan bautarsteinar   standa brauto nær,
> nema reisi niðr at nið.

(ii) Runic studies flourished earlier in Norway than in Man. In consequence there are detailed accounts of the Norwegian rune-stones from the seventeenth and eighteenth centuries. These reveal how many important stones vanished in comparatively recent years. Of the four runic crosses I have just mentioned, two are now lost. Bishop Wegner recorded Njærheim I in 1639. It was in pieces by 1712 and had gone altogether by 1745. Wegner also recorded the Tangerhaug stone, but by 1745 only a couple of bits of it survived, and these have since disappeared. Stones seem regularly to have been lost in the eighteenth and nineteenth centuries despite both a general and an official interest in them. One at Gran church in Oppland (Gran II) was preserved by being built into the church wall where it was seen as early as 1627. It was still there in the 1820s but is now lost; it is intriguing to speculate how you can lose a stone out of a church wall. The Sørbø I stone, Rogaland, was reported by Wegner but lost by 1745. Galteland also appears in Wegner's records, and was still

---

[49] Details of the Norwegian rune-stones are taken from their entries in Olsen *et al.*, *Norges innskrifter med de yngre runer*.

standing in 1821. Shortly after that it fell down (when an antiquary was examining it, having dug out the base to see it more clearly) and it broke, though without destroying the runes nor the antiquary neither. Later the bits were used as building material, and now the stone exists in seven fragments, with some of the inscription gone. The volumes of *Norges innskrifter med de yngre runer* give many a sad tale of vandalism, for the Norwegian workman was quite happy to break up rune-stones so that they could be used in foundations of buildings or of roads. There is no reason to think the Manx workman of recent centuries was more considerate, but we lack early reports and cannot trace losses. The case of Andreas IV (if that is what BL Loan 29/259 represents) looks a parallel example. According to Kinnebrook some of the Kirk Michael stones are others. As well as destruction there is the neglect that many Norwegian stones suffered over the years. For example, the Alstad stone. For centuries it stood amidst the farm at Alstad. At one time it was used for target practice, as shown by numerous pittings of the surface made by iron-headed bolts. At others the stone served as a whetstone for knives, axes and scythes. During building work nearby a beam lowered from the roof struck the stone and knocked it in two. The find-histories of the Norwegian stones are very like those of the Manx ones. Besides standing stones, rune-stones come from a variety of sources, re-used as building material in church and secular buildings, as steps or threshold stones to churches, dug up in churchyards and elsewhere, used in walls. It seems likely, then, that we can use the better recorded Norwegian experience to cast light on the Manx.

(iii) The Norwegian accounts show several authenticated cases of rune-stones travelling about in modern times, apart that is from their removal to museums. Few people, I would have thought, would want to lug a heavy stone about, but some obviously did. The Stangeland stone, for instance, stood for a long time by the highway on Stangeland farm. Then it served for many years as a bridge-stone over the river, and thereafter was set by the fence near the roadside, its rune side down. Subsequently the stone was raised up again, on the same spot as it had originally occupied. Helland II once stood on a mound near the farm. By 1745 it had been put in the middle of the farm yard. By 1902 it was back on its former site. Obviously we must be cautious in assuming that the first recorded place of a stone represents its original position. On the other hand, *Norges innskrifter med de yngre runer* cites several cases of folk traditions about the transport of rune-stones from one place to another which turn out to be completely false. Apparently in this matter the Norwegian evidence advises us to suspend both belief and disbelief.

Applying Norwegian experience to Man, I conclude that:

(a) Wilson's comment that there 'are more *Runick Inscriptions* to be met with in this Island, than perhaps in any other Nation' needs following up. We have probably lost a good number of inscriptions in the last three centuries, and some of them may turn up when buildings are demolished. Of the forty or so rune-stones from Viking Norway, some ten are lost. The Isle of Man may have lost as many in recent centuries.

(b) damage to the extant rune-stones may be comparatively recent, and early drawings may help to reconstruct their texts. One important aspect of any new study will involve a search for early references and sketches, and a critical assessment of their worth. Even the casts may yield information despite the savage criticisms that Guðbrandur Vigfússon brought against them.[50] Some of Cumming's rubbings and sketches survive, and they deserve attention.[51]

This discussion has gone far from the original question: why were there so many Manx rune-stones? I would like now to return to that by a circuitous route. Several scholars have looked at the Manx inscriptions to see what influence Celtic may have had upon their language. To take two examples. In his 1954 corpus Magnus Olsen noted certain traits of word order that he thought the effect of Celtic patterns of speech, and observed the number of Celtic personal names in the texts, and the inflexional confusion that he felt likely to arise in a bilingual society.[52] In 1937 Marstrander had denied that there was much Celtic influence in the inscriptions, though he detected one case, as he thought, of the effect of Celtic ecclesiastical phraseology, and remarked in Maughold II (a twelfth-century stone) Celtic modification of the Norse phonetic system.[53]

The new Andreas text (from BL Loan 29/259) may add a little here. We have already become accustomed to families celebrated in Manx inscriptions, some of whose members had Celtic names and some Norse. Braddan IV records one Fiak whose father was called Þorleifr and uncle Hafr. Kirk Michael III mentions a family with Celtic names whose daughter married one Aðísl. Braddan I has a man called Krínán whose son was Ófeigr. The new Andreas example supplies one more case to this list, but with a difference. For the wife commemorated on the stone it is easy to fit a Norse name, as *Tofa*, while no Celtic name suits the context. The men's names are not so accommodating. The only Scandinavian name that fits the genitive *m. . . .ns* (with the third rune either **u** or **r**) seems to be some spelling of *Marteinn*, and that is post-Viking Age in both Norway and Iceland. On the other hand, Old Irish could supply such names as *Marcán, Martan, Mercán, Mercón*. The first masculine name of the inscription, *..ban*, could also be Irish, for *-án* is a common diminutive ending, as in *Dubán*. A Welsh name may also be possible in the Manx context, perhaps some spelling of Old Welsh *Mermin*, a name recorded early on Man. The son's name could then be Old Welsh *Urban*.[54] Name does not clearly indicate race, but there is here the possibility, perhaps likelihood, of a Norse woman marrying a Celtic man, where hitherto we have had Norse-named men marrying Celtic-named women. This implication of a very close contact between the two races needs more examination, for it may be the key to the problem of the large number of Manx rune-stones.

In general the Manx runic crosses stick closely to the common Norse memorial

[50] *The Academy* 31 (Jan.–June 1887), p. 168.
[51] The Cumming material is MS Top. Man a 1, a manuscript not easily traceable in the Bodleian Library.
[52] Olsen in Shetelig, *Viking Antiquities* VI, 224–7.
[53] C. J. S. Marstrander, 'Om sproget i de manske runeinnskrifter', *NTS* 8 (1937), 247 and 254–5.
[54] I am grateful to Patrick Sims-Williams for help in identifying possible Celtic names for the Andreas inscription.

formula, but there is one important difference. Whereas the Scandinavian examples speak of raising a stone, the Manx ones raise a cross, **krus**. Even where the Scandinavian stones are in fact cross-shaped or strongly decorated with a cross motif, the word used on them is nevertheless *steinn*. Of the four Norwegian runic crosses, the three that can be clearly read have *steinn*, even Stavanger III which was erected by a priest. Only on Svanøy has Aslak Liestøl proposed that the formula incuded the word *kross*, though the state of the inscription suggests that this is guesswork rather than certainty. Otherwise, if the index of *Norges innskrifter med de yngre runer* is any guide, *kross* is late and rare in Norwegian epigraphy. Denmark also avoids the word. The Manx usage is then local and virtually unique (there are examples on Inchmarnock, Buteshire, and the Killaloe, Co. Clare, crosses, as well as **kurs** on the Kilbar, Barra, cross), and probably represents the influence of Latin or Celtic usage. A tentative theory is that the Manx rune-stones indicate the conflation of two cultures, the indigenous Celtic and the incoming Norse. The Manx people had a long tradition of erecting stones of various designs, but often with a cross prominent in their decoration. They are usually without inscription. The Norse had a tradition, not rich but adequate, of putting up memorial stones with inscriptions. When the two nations came together, the Norse tradition was enriched by the Celtic, or the Celtic modified by the Norse, and hence the Manx runic memorial cross with its typical memorial formula.[55]

POSTSCRIPT

This paper should be read as an introduction to the following one which surveys the texts of the Manx rune-stones. The history of runic study in the Isle of Man continues with the finding of two further pieces. In November 1991 workmen restoring Braddan Old Church came upon a fragment of a rune-stone (provisionally numbered Manx Museum 200) that had been used, in the eighteenth-century rebuilding, to prop up a floor-beam beneath the communion table. It turned out to contain the remains of a maker's signature, where the verb **kirþi**, *gerði*, 'made', could be clearly identified.[56] Another, minor, discovery has only an anecdotal find-report. Some time apparently in the early 1970s there was brought in a bit of a decorated stone slab (now Manx Museum 193) which had a few staves, apparently of runes, on its edge, though not enough remains for us to identify individual letters. It came from Larivane Cottage, Andreas, and had been used more than once, apparently as a gate post and

[55] I would like to thank Mr. A. M. Cubbon, Director of the Manx Museum, and Miss A. Harrison, Librarian of that institution, for their splendid guidance on some of the problems discussed here. Also I thank the British Academy for the generous grant that enabled me to carry out this work.
[56] R. I. Page, 'New Runic Fragment from the Isle of Man' (1992).

then as building material. These two finds confirm, if confirmation is needed, the conditions of survival of Manx runes into modern times that my 1980 paper records, and they offer the hope that we shall find more monuments, by such chance methods, in future years.

I should perhaps draw attention again to the finds of runic graffiti on existing rune-stones that I reported in my article 'More Thoughts on Manx Runes' (1981), pp. 132–4.

17

(1983)

THE MANX RUNE-STONES

In an elegant article in the *New Yorker*, the American writer Calvin Trillin began, 'There are no trained runologists in Maine . . .'. He continued more tactfully, 'A lack of runologists is nothing for a state to be ashamed of; there aren't many anywhere'. Much the same applies to the Isle of Man, and indeed to Great Britain, and this is perhaps the reason why there is still no adequate study of the Manx runes. Among archaeologists and other non-literate scientists there is the belief that if you can read one rune you can read them all, and that someone who can write on English runes should have no difficulties with Norse ones. I have rebutted this view myself (though arguing in the opposite direction) for I have from time to time rebuked northern runologists for thinking that their expertise in Scandinavian runes gave them author- ity to discuss Anglo-Saxon ones. No doubt this paper will give some of them a chance to get their own back, but I would like cunningly to draw their teeth by admitting that what follows is an amateur Viking runologist's account of the material. Indeed, I deliberately omit from it the two Manx rune-stones that I can speak of with some authority – the Anglo-Saxon incised slabs with English runes at Maughold.[1]

The standard edition of the Scandinavian runic inscriptions of Man must still be that of Magnus Olsen,[2] though it leaves a lot of room for improvement. It was published in 1954, but in using it we must bear in mind that the work derives from the collections made during a visit as far back as 1911, and that thereafter the inscriptions were studied only through the medium of squeezes, tracings and photographs. To the material gathered on the 1911 journey was added whatever came from new finds, which were therefore known only at second hand. So much Olsen tells us in his introduction or in the course of his text. Being human, Olsen was capable of error; being distant from his primary sources, he was liable to fall into it. Hence there are mistakes of detail in his descriptions of the Manx inscriptions;

---

[1] P. M. C. Kermode, *Manx Crosses* (London, 1907), pp. 110–11 and 217–8; see also Page, *Introduction* (1973), pp. 142 and 146.
[2] M. Olsen, 'Runic Inscriptions in Great Britain, Ireland and the Isle of Man', *Viking Antiquities in Great Britain and Ireland*, ed. H. Shetelig (Oslo, 1940–54) VI, 153–233, at 182–232. In the present article I use Olsen's naming and numbering of the crosses for the convenience of runologists, but I also add, for completeness of reference, the catalogue number given by the Manx Museum and National Trust (in the style MM 136) and the number in Kermode, *Manx Crosses* (in the style Kermode 109). On the naming see also above, pp. 209, 217–18, where I modify Olsen's style slightly.

particularly in minor and not easily distinguishable things like punctuation crosses and points, but also occasionally in the exact shapes of the runic letters themselves.[3] Because Olsen does not give consistent close descriptions of his texts, there is the problem of how he treats damaged or weathered letters where the detail is no longer clear (and to this can be added the problem that there is still no consistent or consistently applied system of transliteration of runes, nor one that would enable the reader readily to judge just how much is visible and how much conjectural).[4] In such points it is as well to be on one's guard against taking Olsen's account as final. He does not give any extensive consideration of the known history of his inscribed stones. Occasionally he refers to early pictures of damaged or worn stones which can be used to provide details no longer clear or certain. This is an important problem that needs thorough examination – the value of early drawings, rubbings and photographs for establishing the Manx runic corpus (and photographs will, of course, have a different value from drawings here, while there are also the casts to explore). In three cases, Braddan III (MM 136, Kermode 109), Andreas III (MM 128, Kermode 102) and Jurby (MM 127, Kermode 99), the stones have been badly damaged since they were first recorded; here it is clear that certain early reproductions are valuable. But there are many other cases where early students of the crosses recorded minor details that are no longer to be made out (the sort of thing that enables us to distinguish one runic form from another – the small staves that mark **a** or **n** from **i**) and here we should check the competence and accuracy of the earlier student to determine his ability to record what he saw rather than what he wanted to see. This sort of work has never been systematically done, and is only now in progress.

Clearly I have some, on the whole minor, reservations about Olsen's account of the Manx corpus. Similar reservations apply to Ingrid Sanness Johnsen's collection of the material which forms part of her book *Stuttruner i vikingtidens innskrifter* (Oslo, 1968). In her case, moreover, I echo Aslak Liestøl's uncertainty, which he expressed in his very detailed, not to say crushing, review of her book, as to whether Dr Johnsen had in all cases seen the inscription she transcribed, to what extent she relied on earlier scholars for her readings.[5] Valuable though both studies are, they fall some way short of a definitive account of the Manx runes. I certainly have not achieved one; in what follows I confine my discussion to a general view of the corpus,

---

[3] Punctuation is a problem, particularly in poorly preserved inscriptions, but for examples of Olsen's inaccuracy where he is clearly wrong cf. with mine his transcriptions of Maughold I (MM 145, Kermode 115) and Maughold II (MM 144, Kermode 114). Occasionally he gives an inaccurate letter form as in, for instance, his transcripts of Maughold IV (MM 142) and Kirk Michael III (MM 130, Kermode 104). Further on this see R. I. Page, 'More Thoughts on Manx Runes' (1981).

[4] Problems of transcribing runes are discussed in C. W. Thompson, 'On Transcribing Runic Inscriptions', *Michigan Germanic Stud.* 7 (1981), 89–97 and the subsequent debate. There is still room for experiment as new methods of type-setting and reproduction are developed. In the present article I am not consistent, for I use a more rigorous style in my transcripts in Appendix I below than I do in my citations of inscription forms in the course of my text. My remarks at the beginning of Appendix I should also be kept in mind.

[5] *NTS* 23 (1969), 171–80, esp. 173.

and suggest a few conclusions that are important for the wider context of Norse civilisation on the Isle of Man.[6]

One problem of the Manx corpus I have already drawn attention to: the reason for the large number of rune-stones on the island, considering its tiny size. There are, may I remind you, at least thirty-one rune-stones in the Manx corpus, not all crosses. Two of them Olsen dates to the post-Viking Age, and there is probably another late stone as well.[7] Two are only tiny fragments which yield nothing of importance either philologically or runologically. That still leaves twenty-six or so substantial rune-stones surviving, and to this we can probably add one that was recorded *c.* 1700 and which does not, apparently, survive.[8] There are also one or two stones with runic graffiti on them to be added to the corpus, though graffiti are always hard to date, and I shall return to these later.[9] Let us stick at the moment to the figure of twenty-six, and compare this with the Viking Age rune-stones elsewhere. For Norway, the most closely related area runologically to Man, exact numbers are hard to establish because of the problems of dating, but *Norges innskrifter med de yngre runer* gives, say, forty Viking Age rune-stones for the whole of Norway, of which some seven are known only from early drawings since they apparently no longer exist. They are recorded only from the fairly plentiful early reports wherein Norway is richer than the Isle of Man. Thus there are, say, thirty-three extant Viking Age rune-stones in Norway compared with, say, twenty-six in the Isle of Man; a staggering comparison.

Johnsen's list in *Stuttruner* provides a different sort of statistic, but one equally surprising. She includes twenty-two stones and fragments from Sweden, twenty-four from Norway, seven from a great *Vesterhavsområde* which includes Greenland, the Faroes, the Scots islands and Ireland, and twenty-five from the Isle of Man. Even using crude sampling methods like these the Manx numbers look significant. Elsewhere I have tentatively suggested that the plenty of Manx stones arises from local conditions, from the fact that they combine two energetic traditions. There is a local Celtic one of raising crosses, and an incoming Norse one of raising runic

---

[6] Provisional texts of the inscriptions are in Appendix I below.

[7] Olsen's late rune-stones are Maughold I and II, though he lists them wrongly as Marown I and II ('Runic Inscriptions in Great Britain', p. 153). The more recently found Maughold V stone (MM 175) may also be late: see A. M. Cubbon, 'Viking Runes: Outstanding New Discovery at Maughold', *Journal of the Manx Museum* 7 (1966), 23–6, at 25. Onchan also presents problems. Olsen, 'Runic Inscriptions in Great Britain', p. 194, says that it 'is an old Celtic cross . . . which has later been inscribed with runes'. D. M. Wilson tells me that he disagrees. More than one hand cut the runes on this cross, but the roughly carved decoration could, I think, be by the same hand as some of the roughly cut characters.

[8] See 'Some Thoughts on Manx Runes', above pp. 207–23. In that article I suggested that this early drawing represented the now fragmentary Andreas IV (MM 113, Kermode 87), but I now think I was wrong. The difficulties of equating the two are (a) Andreas IV's rune R in **aftiR** compared with, apparently, **aftir** in the drawing, (b) the mention, in the brief early description, of 'Animals Engraven on the other parts of the same [cross]', whereas Andreas IV now shows no sign of having had animal ornament.

[9] See p. 224. The discovery of some of these graffiti has led to a more intensive examination of the surfaces of known Manx crosses, and we may expect more examples to be announced in the future. On the other hand, it is not always easy to distinguish graffiti runes from casual scratches on the stone surface.

memorials.[10] In Man this combined practice, deriving from the intimate contact of the two peoples, is fruitful in the numbers of runic crosses it produces. To this theory I might add a refinement that the Church, with its stress on the written record, rendered the runic tradition more fruitful than it might otherwise be; that far from banning runic as a pagan type of script (as has sometimes been thought), the Church welcomed any method of recording for Christian purposes. There is a similar development in the Anglo-Saxon runic tradition of northern England.[11] Yet however one may refine the idea, it remains a naive one, a simple explanation of a more complex phenomenon. It may have some truth in it, but the material needs further examination.

As the numbers I have quoted show, most Manx inscriptions are in the type of runes that Johnsen calls *stuttruner*, which are also called *kortkvistruner*, short-twig runes. Some have wished to identify a variant of this type which is common to Man and the southwest of Norway, a variant they call for convenience the Man-Jær runes. This is less a type than a particular selection of items from the total number of rune forms available, a particular choice of the forms for **b, h, m** and **a̧**; and I again agree with Liestøl in finding it hard to identify a specific selection of rune forms in short or damaged inscriptions which may retain no examples of certain significant letters.[12] Hence it is convenient to think of these inscriptions simply as *kortkvistruner/ stuttruner* without any further qualification.[13]

One aspect of the Manx inscriptions encourages us to treat them as a coherent group. A core of inscriptions has the common commemoration formula, *N ... reisti kross þenna ept(ir) M ...*, 'N ... put this cross up in memory of M ...'. The person who raised the monument and the dead one commemorated may be further defined by adding the relationship to some other person (wife, son, nephew, daughter), or by giving a nickname (*hnakki, inn svarti*). To this primary commemoration text may be put a second one giving more information about one of these people, or adding the name of the man who made the monument or cut the runes. Of the Manx stones at least sixteen have inscriptions that fit this matrix exactly or are fragments that are fully compatible with it. To this number may be added one or two remains on fragmentary stones that look like the second, additional, texts of similar memorials; and there are a couple of variants, one (Kirk Michael II, MM 101, Kermode 74) telling that the stone was put up for the raiser's own benefit, and a second (Maughold V, MM 175) that has a commemorative formula in rather different terms but of the same general effect. So it may be said that most of the Manx rune-stones show a fairly common runic formula of an accepted pattern. The formula used is similar to that on many Norwegian rune-stones of the Viking Age, the only difference being that there the rune-masters use the word *steinn* 'stone', rather than *kross* 'cross'. This is not surprising in that for much of the Viking Age the Norwegians were pagan and

[10] Above, p. 223. Perhaps we should also consider the possibility of influence from an English runic tradition, from which only the two Maughold stones survive on Man.
[11] Page, *Introduction*, pp. 34–5.
[12] *NTS* 23 (1969), p. 175.
[13] Appendix II has a brief account of the different types of runes used in the Manx inscriptions.

would not need to refer to crosses, but it is worthy of note that even Norwegian runic crosses of the late Viking Age continue to use *steinn* and to avoid *kross*. So, as for that, do the Danish ones. The word *kross* seems typical of the Viking rune-stones of the west. Outside Man it is found in the two Scots inscriptions from Inchmarnock, Buteshire, and Kilbar, Barra, as well as on the Irish stone at Killaloe, Co. Clare (and indeed, the use of *kross* could have spread from Man to these other places). It is reasonable, therefore, to take it as a Celticism introduced into Norse usage, and so it gives coherence to the Manx examples – they apply a common Norse formula of commemoration, with a common Celtic variation of wording.

It is perhaps worth noting that in some minor characteristics too – the sort of detail that might well be taught by a school of rune-masters – Manx agrees with Norwegian usage. I am thinking here of the way the Manx rune-carvers employ punctuation points, using within the same inscription single, double and no points at all, or sometimes dividing off syntactically linked groups of words by their punctuation system. A word too on the lay-out of the runes on the Manx stones. Sixteen of the Manx corpus have their texts cut along the edge of a slab, that is to say on the very narrow side of a comparatively slim stone. In thirteen cases the inscription runs from the base upwards, in one from the top down; in two others the stone is too fragmentary for us to be sure which. Thus there is a common pattern for a memorial inscription running up (much less often down) one side (fig. 1). This general pattern is also found in Scandinavia. It is virtually never used in Denmark, only if the narrow side of a slab holds part of a longer inscription which also occupies part of the face,[14] but it is quite common in Norway, in the western provinces of Vest-Agder and Rogaland as well as in the more inland and easterly areas of Opland and Buskerud. In Norway, I think, the inscription always runs upwards.

In this aspect of design we could well see the practice of the home-land repeated, but repeated with variation. However, the Manx crosses have a second common pattern of lay-out of the inscription. This time it is set on the face of the slab. In this type the rectangular slab has a sculptured cross in relief on its face, together with other ornamentation. The inscription is also on the face, running upwards and filling the space to one side of the stem of the relief cross (fig. 2). There are six examples of this general design on Man, and it is a type not to be found in Norway (or again Denmark) in the Viking Age. Where an inscription does run up the face on a Norwegian stone, the arrangement is different. I do not know what modern ideas of this second general design of cross (and inscription) are, but Shetelig, writing in 1954 though expressing arguments formulated years earlier, suggested that it was the Vikings who brought to Man the sculptured relief cross on the face of a slab, and that they got the idea from Scotland where similar memorial stones are to be found.[15]

---

[14] Though one might note as an exception the Lund I stone: Jacobsen and Moltke, *Danmarks runeindskrifter*, no. 314 and plates 723–8.

[15] H. Shetelig, 'The Norse Style of Ornamentation in the Viking Settlements', *Viking Antiquities in Great Britain and Ireland*, ed. H. Shetelig (Oslo, 1940–54) VI, 113–50, at 123–5. The Gran Kirke IV stone has a text cut along the left-hand edge of its face, and this could, I suppose, supply a tentative Norwegian model for the Manx crosses, though there are problems of chronology (Olsen *et al.*, *Norges innskrifter med de yngre runer* I, 187).

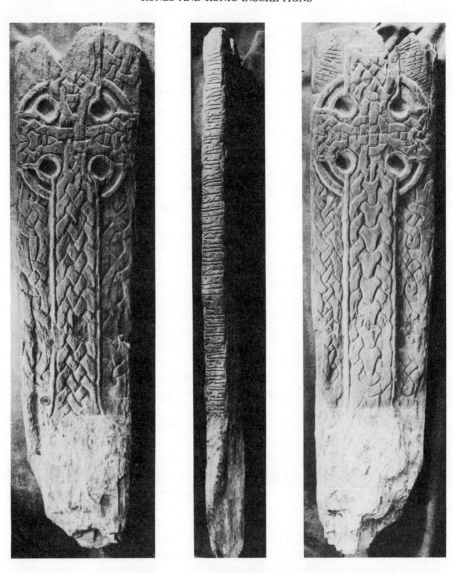

FIG. 1   Gautr's cross, Kirk Michael II (MM 101, Kermode 74). *Manx National Heritage*

I note that in his conference paper D. M. Wilson is more cautious, and speaks only of influences 'from the regions round the Irish Sea'.[16] At any rate it is clear, from this brief examination of the runic crosses, that they show both tradition and innovation in their inscriptions.

Among the inscriptions there are, side by side with those clearly derived from Norse exemplars with a Celtic element added, others which are quite different in a number of ways, and which show that the Scandinavian occupation of Man was anything but a simple affair. Among the earliest specimens of the Manx runic crosses is usually claimed to be Kirk Michael II whose memorial formula has the added clause **kaut×kirþi:þanạ:auk ala:imaun×** 'Gautr made this and all in Man'. It is argued, presumably by scholars who believe all they hear in television commercials, that if Gautr claimed to have made all the runic crosses in Man, there could at any rate not be a lot of others standing about made by earlier sculptors. Hence this must be one of the first generation of runic crosses.[17]

A man Gautr is named on a second cross, Andreas I (MM 99, Kermode 73), **kautr:kar[þ]i:sunr:biarnar fra:kuli[:]** 'Gautr made me, son of Bjǫrn of Kollr' (wherever Kollr may have been).[18] These two men are usually equated and I think rightly, and in that case we have two contemporary inscriptions, cut on crosses made by the same man (though I note that the inscriptions are not said to be by the same man). Looking at the two inscriptions in full, we find there are already varieties of form.

Kirk Michael II: **×mail:brikti:sunr:aþakans:smiþ:raisti:krus:þanạ:fur:salu: sina:sin:brukuin:kaut×kirþi:þanạ:auk ala:imaun×**

Andreas I: the inscription is unfortunately badly weathered and partly unrecoverable: **[ ]þ[an]a:[aft]ufaik:fauþur:sin:in:kautr:kar[þ]i: sunr:biarnar fra:kuli[:]**

There are already a few variations in rune usage and spelling, in accidence, in the forms of letters and in the style of the inscriptions. As examples of spelling variations I quote Kirk Michael II *þanạ* against Andreas I *þana*: Kirk Michael II has *kirþi*; Olsen, and I provisionally, read Andreas I *karþi* but I am not certain about the vowel **a** here, and would wish to reconsider the reading carefully. As for accidence, Andreas I has *kautr* but Kirk Michael II loses the nominative singular ending in *kaut* (and also some ending, nominative or genitive singular, in *smiþ*); both retain the ending of *sunr*. As to rune forms, Kirk Michael II has the form ᛏ **a**, save for two examples

---

[16] D. M. Wilson, 'The Art of the Manx Crosses of the Viking Age', *The Viking Age in the Isle of Man*, ed. C. Fell *et al.* (London, 1983), pp. 175–87, at 178.

[17] *Ibid.* pp. 178–82

[18] C. J. S. Marstrander had varying opinions on the subject, each expressed with his usual certainty. In 'Killaloekorset og de norske kolonier i Irland', *NTS* 4 (1930), 378–400, at 379, he argued from the place-name that Gautr 'var hjemmehørende på øen' (was a native of the island); some years later, in 'Suderøyingen Gaut Bjørnson', *NTS* 10 (1938), 375–83, at 381, he asserted that Gautr was 'sikkert suderøying' (clearly a Hebridean) from the island of Coll.

FIG. 2   Ballaugh (MM 106, Kermode 77), *Manx National Heritage*

of ᛏ in significant parts of the inscription, the name forms *mailbrikti* and *kaut*;[19] Andreas I has only ᛐ, except for a possible case of ᛏ in *karþi*. There is one small comment to make on the style of the characters in the two inscriptions: Kirk Michael II has straight lines for the arms of letters like **f, k,** ᚠ, ᚴ; Andreas I seems to have curved lines, ᚠ, ᚴ though it is hard to be sure because of the poor state of preservation of that stone. Here is another case where a thorough examination of the forms is needed. The two texts look to be by different rune-carvers, but that is a very subjective comment.

There are other runic crosses, as Kirk Michael I (MM 102, Kermode 75) and Braddan I (MM 112, Kermode 86) which have been ascribed to Gautr on stylistic grounds,[20] and their texts would add a little to the suggestion of diversity I have noted here. However, it is best not to use them to develop the point since not everyone is so convinced by stylistic arguments. Let us stick instead to the evidence of Kirk Michael II and Andreas I. We should not expect too much consistency on the part of any rune-master. Yet I would suggest that these two monuments, by their variant styles, indicate that in the earliest recorded runic times for the island there was a runic tradition that was not a simple one. There was more than one rune-master involved. Several different usages combine. Here it is important to look again at Gautr's claim. He does not say he made all the Manx runic monuments of his time, only that he made all the crosses. Behind the monuments that survive there may be a more extensive, but fugitive, runic tradition.[21] From the statistics I have quoted, it seems to have been one mainly of the use of *kortkvistruner*, short-twig runes, and this set of traditions certainly continued fruitful in Man, at least into the twelfth century. However, short-twig runes are not the only type of Scandinavian runes on the island, and when we look at a later cross, Maughold IV (MM 142), we find the tradition more complex than before, for that cross has a different set of runes and a variant formula. In fact it has several inscriptions on it, but here I am concerned with the two major ones only, since they, presumably, are contemporary with the carving of the cross, while the others, being more casual, are probably later additions:

1. **heþin:seti:krus:þinạ:eftir:tutur:sinạ** 'Heðinn put up this cross in memory of his daughter'
2. **arni:risti:runar:þisar** 'Arni cut these runes'.

In these inscriptions the runes are not the Norse *kortkvistruner* but are from (or perhaps it is better to say are strongly influenced by) the common or normal Danish rune types. In making this remark I am commenting on the forms only, not on their provenance, since Danish rune forms occur in Norway too, on such prestigious monuments as the Dynna stone, where they are mixed with *kortkvistruner*, and the

---

[19] Cf. the mixture of rune-forms on the Norwegian Dynna stone: Olsen *et al.*, *Norges innskrifter* I, 198.
[20] Wilson, 'The Art of the Manx Crosses', p. 180.
[21] See M. Cubbon, 'The Archaeology of the Vikings in the Isle of Man', *The Viking Age in the Isle of Man*, ed. C. Fell *et al.* (London, 1983), pp. 13–26, at 16, for the Ballateare 'memorial post'.

Alstad I stone.[22] Thus Maughold IV's runes are clearly distinguishable from the Manx rune forms dealt with hitherto, notably with their **a** and **n** forms, ↑, ↟, and their **t**-rune ↑. On the other hand the Maughold IV rune-master used the *kortkvistrune* form of **s** ↑. And he introduced the dotted form ╁ for **e**. The latter is important as a dating point, since it seems to have entered Danish usage *c.* 1000,[23] and Norwegian somewhat later.[24] So here we have an apparently up-to-date rune-master using new forms as well as those from a different runic tradition. Another significant variation on this stone is in the commemorative formula. The word for putting up the cross is not 'raised', *reisti*, but 'set', *setti*. The verb is very rare in Norwegian formulae, but relatively common in Viking Age Denmark and Sweden (and as for that in Anglo-Saxon England). Probably significant too is the verb that Arni used for 'carved', *risti*, from the weak verb *rista* rather than the strong verb *rísta*. This verb occurs on one of the inscriptions from Knestang, Buskerud, which is provisionally dated to *c.* 1190. Otherwise, says *Norges innskrifter med de yngre runer*, it is 'yderst svakt bevidnet i gammelnorsk, og først i langt senere tid enn 12te årh.' (it occurs very rarely in Old Norse, and then not till a long time after the twelfth century),[25] though the couple of other Norwegian epigraphical examples are not easily datable. On the other hand it is common in medieval Sweden and Denmark, in Swedish inscriptions from the eleventh century onwards, while there is a solitary early Danish example, Tillitse, Lolland, which *Danmarks runeindskrifter* puts in the period 1050–1150.[26] The Maughold IV inscriptions are obviously exotic in the Manx setting, suggesting perhaps Danish influence. Yet these are not pure Danish runes, as is shown by a possible single **a**-form ↑,[27] but more certainly by the **s**-form ↑. The commemorative text uses the Manx-Norse word *kross*, and the lay-out of the text is that common in Man but rare elsewhere, the runes running upwards on one side of the stem of a relief cross on the slab face. Again there seems here a mixture of tradition and innovation, though it is a new one.

More exotic still in its rune-forms is the Kirk Michael III (MM 130, Kermode 104) stone with its pair of inscriptions:

1. **mal:lymkun:raisti:krus:þena:efter:mal:mury:fustra :sine: totortufkals:kona :is:aþisl:ati+**
2. **[b]etra :es:laifa:fustra:kuþan:þan:son:ilan+**

These texts are long enough to have several significant letter forms, including **a**,

[22] Olsen *et al.*, *Norges innskrifter* I, 139–44.
[23] Jacobsen and Moltke, *Danmarks runeindskrifter*, col. 951. There is, of course, always the possibility that this development reached Man from Scandinavian England; the dotted e occurs, for example, on the Skelton in Cleveland sundial: see above, p. 189 and ref.
[24] Olsen *et al.*, *Norges innskrifter* V, 243.
[25] Olsen *et al.*, *Norges innskrifter* II, 88.
[26] Jacobsen and Moltke, *Danmarks runeindskrifter*, col. 699.
[27] Olsen, 'Runic Inscriptions in Great Britain', p. 207, reads this **a**-rune in the name **arni**, but I rather think it is a badly formed ↑. Of course, Olsen never saw the Maughold IV inscription and had to rely on published reports.

n, t and **s**. They also show the dotted **e**, and, what is a little disturbing, a dotted rune which I transcribe, without prejudice, as **y**. At least, I identify the latter, though Olsen doesn't, but then his account of this stone is not his best work, which is surprising since it is one of the better preserved of the Manx texts.[28]

The second of these texts presents no problems of understanding: 'it is better to leave a good foster-son than a bad son', apparently a proverb, but at any rate an undeniable truth. The first is more difficult because, frankly, this is rotten Old Norse. It begins all right, 'Mallymkun raised this cross in memory of Malmury (whatever the final vowel of this name form is)', but then founders on the grammar. The names *Mallymkun* and *Malmury* are troublesome because we do not know the sex of these characters. The names could be either male or female since the first element is the Celtic word for 'servant', and a servant could be of either sex. The Celtic sources that supply us with examples of personal names are sex-biased, having more male than female citations. *Mallymkun* has baffled Celtic scholars to whom I have submitted it, though earlier commentators chiefly produced, for its second element, the name form *Lomchon*.[29] *Malmury* means 'servant of Mary', and here one might possibly prefer a female identification. So we get a reading 'N (male?) put this cross up in memory of M (female?)' after which the grammatical trouble begins. It would be natural to take *fustra sine* as in apposition to *Malmury*. The ending of *sine* is, however, impossible, whatever sex *fustra* is. If *fustra* is accusative, as it should be in this interpretation, its form is that of a masculine and it must mean 'foster-son' as in the second inscription. In that case *Malmury* would be masculine (which is possible from the name citations in Celtic records but would require us to reconsider the tentative interpretation of the text). The text then continues *totor tufkals* 'daughter of Dufgal', with the word *totor* in the accusative, which adds a further confusion. The text ends *kona is aþisl ati*, 'the wife whom Aþisl married', with the word *kona*, 'wife' in the nominative. Thus we could perhaps re-order the text and give the reading, 'Mallymkun, daughter of Dufgal, the wife whom Aþisl married, set up this cross in memory of Malmury her foster-son'. This reading involves (1) the clear error in *sine*; (2) taking the whole phrase *totor tufkals kona is aþisl ati* as defining *Mallymkun* rather than the immediately preceding *Malmury* (which is possible if a bit unlikely); (3) having an embarrassing accusative *totor* (as I read it) instead of a nominative. The relationship to the second text is also embarrassing, since that inscription implies that the dead have left a living foster-son, whereas on this reading the commemorative wording implies it is the foster-mother who survived. The alternative is to follow Olsen, who read, 'M. erected this cross after his foster-mother, M., Dufgal's daughter, the wife whom Adils married'. Here you must assume (1) the same clear error in *sine*, and (2) that *fustra* and *kona*, in apposition to the accusative *Malmury*, are in the

---

[28] For instance, Olsen, 'Runic Inscriptions in Great Britain', p. 216, shows the **n**-rune ᚼ in the name **mallymkun**, though ᚾ is quite clear on the inscription. I differ significantly in reading, for Olsen's **totir**: the group **totor**; see here Page, 'More Thoughts', p. 132.

[29] I am indebted to David Dumville here. *Lomchon* could be the genitive of a name *Lomchu* (*Lommchú*), recorded as that of a disciple of St Patrick: J. O'Hanlon, *Lives of the Irish Saints* (London, 1875–) I, 151.

nominative instead of the expected accusative, but that *totor*, agreeing with them, is nevertheless correctly declined.

Whatever we do we are faced with grammatical problems, and we must finally admit that whoever framed the text for this stone was a poor writer of classical Old Norse. There was, as I have shown, grammatical imprecision on early Manx stones, as early indeed as Gautr's, whose name sometimes has the classical nominative ending -*r* and sometimes not; and one of whose stones has the endingless form *smiþ* whose function in the sentence is thus rendered uncertain. It may be that (as some have assumed) this gives evidence of a breakdown, even as early as the tenth century, of the strict system of accidence in Old Norse such as might be expected if that language were being used in a community of mixed Norse-Celtic speakers. On this argument Kirk Michael III would be showing progressive development of a demotic Norse, with more marked decline in the inflexional pattern.[30] There is a further implication, of some importance: that though this is an inscription by a rune-master trained in techniques untypical of Man,[31] he used his script to record a distinctively Manx speech. His text has the local word *kross*. Yet again there is the combination of tradition and innovation.

Finally, I make a jump to the latest Manx runic texts. Maughold I (MM 145, Kermode 115) and II (MM 144, Kermode 114) are linked together by their content, though their find-spots are some miles apart. Maughold (Corna valley) II names Christ and three Celtic saints, Malachi, Patrick and Adamnan. The latest of these is Malachi if he is correctly identified with the archbishop of Armagh who died in 1148. What time it took for a cult of him with the other two saints to develop I do not know, nor how it reached Man, direct from Ireland or from the west coast of Scotland where Malachi was popular. But in any case it can presumably not be before the mid-twelfth century, which is thus the earliest date for these two stones. For so late a date they show an archaic group of runes, with a *fuþąrk* which is a pure example of short-twig runes (with the omission of the otiose symbol for palatal *R*); there is no sign of the later runic developments that begin to show themselves *c*. 1000 – the use of the dotted **e** or the rather later dotted **y**, the even later dotted **k** and **b** runes, or the use of the character ᛏ for the open *æ* sound. In other words, if the rune-master Iuan of these inscriptions is using runes current in Man in the twelfth century (and not merely demonstrating his skill in an archaic script along with ogam), his characters descend directly from the earliest Manx runes and are uninfluenced by most later developments on the mainland of Norway. They even show no influence from the rune types of Maughold IV and Kirk Michael III.

We might support this theory – that the later Manx runes in general show relatively little development – on two types of evidence:

1. The Manx rune-stones that I have not examined here are based on the short-twig *fuþąrk* with little change. A couple show the dotted **e** (German (Peel) II, MM 140,

---

[30] Appendix III below discusses the grammatical problems in more detail.
[31] It is perhaps worth remarking that the lay-out of inscriptions on the Kirk Michael III stone is not characteristic of the Manx runic crosses.

Kermode 112 and Onchan, MM 141, Kermode 113), and the latter may also evidence the use of æ though the reading is not clear. A few of the inscriptions have the *ansuʀ* rune for the vowel *o*, displacing here the rune **u** in that function. Apart from these they show nothing of the considerable development of rune use that is characteristic of post-millennium medieval runology in Norway or indeed Denmark. In other words, there is no clear sign that, after the period 1000–1050, there was much runic contact between Man and the Viking homelands.

2. Some Manx stones have runic graffiti. They are often faint and confused. Most have been discovered only in recent years, and so have not been properly studied. There are probably more to be found by careful search.[32] Inevitably graffiti are undatable, or at best only to be dated with difficulty. Hence they have limited use as evidence, but for all that they should not be ignored. In some ways the most intriguing of the graffiti are those on the Maughold IV and German (St John's) I (MM 107, Kermode 81) stones. In these it looks as though someone tried to make copies of the main inscriptions – this is clearer in the Maughold case than in St John's. It is possible that some of the later Manx inscriptions were cut by men who had learned their runes in this way, from observing how the script was used in earlier times, rather than by men who had been taught by visiting Vikings or who had trained in Norway itself.

The material I have taken here from the Manx runes is slight, and it would be absurd to draw from it any very general conclusions. Moreover, I am acutely aware that much work remains to be done on the chronology of the Manx rune-stones, viewing them both as artefacts and linguistic records. The relationship between Manx runic traditions and those of mainland Scandinavia needs reconsideration; here I have assumed that new runic styles developed in Scandinavia and moved then to Man, but it may have been the other way round. Nevertheless, it is worth summing up the material I have presented to see what it amounts to, and to offer it to the archaeologists and historians to find out how well it fits their theories of the Viking presence in Man.

(a) The earliest surviving runes, from the tenth century, show a clear connection with Norway, as has long been recognised. At the same time they show Norsemen accommodating to a western tradition which has strong Celtic elements. Within the runic usage there is already some diversity of practice, showing that the introduction of the script was not a simple one.

(b) *c*. 1000 the runic tradition is affected by new techniques, suggesting incoming rune-using groups trained in different, perhaps newer, ways of using the script. These in turn adapt to some degree to the western tradition.

(c) Perhaps the mainstream of runic tradition on the island flows from (a) through the twelfth century, showing no strong influence from (b) or from new runic usages developing in Norway.

---

[32] Page, 'More Thoughts', pp. 132–4.

Can we see from this a general pattern of Viking settlement, vigorous and strong, with close links to western Norway but accommodating itself to Celtic manners; a settlement which responds to different Viking stimuli for some period *c.* 1000, but then continues in some isolation?

Appendix I. The Manx runic inscriptions

The following are provisional transcripts only. It is not possible, in such simple transcriptions, to indicate clearly how much is certain, how much likely from the verbal context, how much to be supplied from the fragmentary remains on the stone, how much derives from dependable early reproductions, and so on. Punctuation is particularly precarious. Final transcripts will differ in matters of detail like these, and will have to be accompanied by careful description. Meanwhile these are presented for the guidance of readers.

Andreas I (MM 99, Kermode 73): [ ]þ[an]a̱:[aft]uf̱aik:fauþur:sin:in: kautr:kar[þ]i:sunr:biarnar fṟa:ḵuḷi[:]

Andreas II (MM 131, Kermode 103): sa̱nt:ulf:hin:suarti:raisti:krus: þa̱na:aftir:arin:biaurk.kuinu:sina + the graffito u̱[.]k:au[.]: a̱ks (or bks)

Andreas III (MM 128, Kermode 102): þurualtr:̣ṛ[aisti]ḵṛu̱ṣ:þ̱[ ]

Andreas IV (MM 113, Kermode 87): [ai]s[t]i[k]rus:þaina:aftiʀ[ ]

Ballaugh (MM 106, Kermode 77): a̱ulaibr:̣liuṭuḷbsunr:r[ai]ṣ[tik]rs. þlna:aif̱ṯir.[ ] | b:sun[s]in

Braddan I (MM 112, Kermode 86): þu̱ṛ[ ]:raisti:krus:þa̱na̱:ift:ufaak: sun: krinais

Braddan II (MM 138, Kermode 110): [ ]ṇroskitil:uilti:i:triku: | aiþsoara :siin

Braddan III (MM 136, Kermode 109): utr:risti:krus:þa̱na̱:aft:fra̱[k]a̱ [:f] a̱ḇ[ursin:in:]þ̱[urbiaurn:]

Braddan IV (MM 135, Kermode 108): þurlibr:nhaki:risti:krus:þa̱na̱: aft [:]fiak:su̱[n]ṣin:ḇruþur:sun:habrs×IHSVS

Bride (MM 118, Kermode 92): [t]ruian:sur[t]uf̱kals:raistikrsþina:af̱ [t]aþmiu[.]:kunusi[n]

German (St John's) I (MM 107, Kermode 81): [ ]ina̱ṣru̱ḇṛ:raist:runar: þsar ×[ ] + graffito

German (Peel) II (MM 140, Kermode 112): [ ]u̱s:þense.efter.asriþi:kunu sina.ṯu̱tur.ut[ ]

Jurby (MM 127, Kermode 99): [un.si]n:in:a̱na̱n:raiti | [aftirþurb]

Kirk Michael I (MM 102, Kermode 75): [kru]ṣ:þna:af[tir:]

Kirk Michael II (MM 101, Kermode 74): ×mail:brikti:sunr:aþakans: smiþ:raisti:krus:þanạ:fur:salu:sina:sin:brukuin:kaut × | kirþi :þanạ:auk | ala:imaun×

Kirk Michael III (MM 130, Kermode 104): 1. mal:lymkun:raisti:krus: þena:efter:mal:mury:fustra:siṇe:totọrtufkals:kona:is: aþisl: ati+ 2. [.]etra:es:laifa:fustra:kuþan:þan:son:ilan+

Kirk Michael IV (MM 126, Kermode 100): [k]riṃ:risti:krus:þna:ift: rumụ[ ]

Kirk Michael V (MM 132, Kermode 105): +iualfir:sunr:þurulfs:hins: rauþa:risṭi:krus:þanạ:aft:friþu:muþur: sinạ+

Kirk Michael VI (MM 129, Kermode 101): [ ]ḳrims:ins:suarta×

Kirk Michael VIII (MM 123): [ ]:[ai]ftiṛ.mụ[.].ụ[ ]

Marown (Rhyne) (MM 139, Kermode 111): þurbiaurn:risti:krus:þạ[ ]

Maughold I (MM 145, Kermode 115): 1. [ ]iụan+brist+raisti+þasir +runur+ 2. [f]uḅạrḳḥniastbml+

Maughold (Corna Valley) II (MM 144, Kermode 114): +krisþ:malaki:ok baþrik:aþaṇman ⋇|·ˑ[nal].sauþ.a[.]:iuan.brist.ikurnaþal.

Maughold IV (MM 142): 1. heþin:seti:krus:þinạ:eftir:tutur:sinạ[ ] 1a. li[ ]
2. arni:risti:runar:þisar
3. sikuþr
4. lifilt + graffiti

Maughold V (MM 175): kuansunr×mailb[ ]ak[ ]+kirþi+lik+tin niftir+ | +kuinasina+

Onchan (MM 141, Kermode 113): 1. [ ]asunr×raisti×ift[k]ụ[i]ṇụsiṇa× | murkialu×m[ ]
2. þuriþ×raist×rune[.]×
3. kru[ ]
4. ×isukrist
5. ×ukikat×aukraþikr[.]t
6. An uncertain group that has been read, perhaps correctly, al͡æns

Omitted from this list are: the cryptic text Andreas V (MM 111, Kermode 84); the fragments Balleigh (MM 159), Braddan V (MM 176), Kirk Michael VII (MM 110, Kermode 85), Maughold (Ballagilley) III (MM 133, Kermode 106).

There are also ogam inscriptions on Kirk Michael III and Maughold I.

Appendix II. Manx fuþarks, and significant variants

1. *Kortkvistruner* (*stuttruner*, short-twig runes): Andreas I, II, III, IV, Ballaugh, Braddan I, II, III, IV, Bride, German (St John's) I, German (Peel) II, Jurby, Kirk Michael I, II, IV, V, VI, Marown (Rhyne), Maughold I, II (Corna valley), V, Onchan.

f u þ a̜/o r k h n i a s t b m l R

ᚠ ᚁ ᚦ ᚡ ᚱ ᚣ ᚼ ᚽ ᛁ ᚿ ' ᛁ ᚼ ᛦ ᚽ ᛁ

German (Peel) II and Onchan also have ᛁ **e** (with no examples of **h**), while Onchan may have one example of ᛏ **æ**. Of course, not all inscriptions have examples of all significant forms, and some characters, as **h, m**, are fairly rare; there is only a single example of ᛁ **R**, and that in a badly damaged part of a text.

2. Mixed runes: Maughold IV.

f u þ a r k h n i a s t b m l R
ᚠ ᚁ ᚦ ᚭ ᚱ ᚣ ᚼ ᛁ ᚿ ᛁ ᛏ ' ᛏ   ᚱ

The inscription has also ᛁ **e**.

3. Danish (common, normal) runes: Kirk Michael III.

f u þ o r k h n i a s t b m l R
ᚠ ᚁ ᚦ ᚠ ᚱ ᚣ   ᛏ ᛁ ᛏ ᚾᛏ   ᛣ ᚱ

This inscription has also ᛁ **e**, and, I think, ᚺ (?)**y**.

4. Indeterminate or too fragmentary: Balleigh, Braddan V, Kirk Michael VII, VIII, Maughold (Ballagilley) III.

5. Cryptic runes: Andreas V.

Appendix III. A note on the grammar of the Manx rune-stones

The irregular grammar of Kirk Michael III must be seen in the context of other non-classical forms in Manx inscriptions. These are:

(i) The nominative of strong masculine nouns has lost its *-r* inflexion in *sǫntulf* Andreas II, *kaut* Kirk Michael II, *[k]rim* Kirk Michael IV. Perhaps appropriate here is the loss of *-r* in the feminine (?) *þuriþ* Onchan, and there is also the form of uncertain status *lifilt* Maughold IV. Onchan has the endingless *krist*, but a Norse form was probably not intended there because preceding it is the Old Irish form *isu* (Jesus). A different development is the glide vowel that has, apparently, formed between stem and ending in *iualfr* Kirk Michael V, if that is a form of *Ióálfr* as Lind assumes.[33]

---

[33] I omit from consideration in this section Maughold I and II (Corna valley), which are generally considered late. Also I ignore some uncertain readings and interpretations as, for example, Maughold

(ii) The genitive singular of a strong masculine noun has lost its -*s* ending in *smiþ* Kirk Michael II if, as seems likely from the word order, that word agrees with *aþakans* rather than with the nominative *mailbrikti*. If it is in apposition to *mailbrikti*, *smiþ* should appear as a further example under (i) above.

(iii) The oblique form of the weak feminine noun is not signalled in *kuina sina* Maughold V.

(iv) The vowel of the ending of *rune[.]* (for *runar*) Onchan is imprecise.

In general, however, the Manx rune-masters get their grammar right in these sorts of cases. For instance:

(i) Inflexional -*r* is retained in *kautr*, *sunr* Andreas I, *þurualtr* Andreas III, *qulaibr*, *liutulbsunr* Ballaugh, *utr* Braddan III, *þurlibr* Braddan IV, *su(n)r* Bride, *qsruþr* German (St John's) I, *sunr* (contrast *kaut*) Kirk Michael II, *sunr* Kirk Michael V, *sikuþr* Maughold IV, *sunr* Maughold V, *sunr* Onchan.

(ii) Correct -*s* genitive forms occur in *habrs* Braddan IV, *þurulfs hins rauþa* Kirk Michael V, *krims ins suarta* Kirk Michael VI; and in the Celtic names *krinais* (?) Braddan I, *[t]ufkals* Bride, *aþakans* (contrast *smiþ*) Kirk Michael II, *tufkals* Kirk Michael III.

(iii) Correct oblique feminine forms occur in *kuinu sina* Andreas II, *kunu* Bride, *kunu sina* German (Peel) II, *salu sina* Kirk Michael II, *friþu* Kirk Michael V, *[k]u[i]nu sina* Onchan.

(iv) The correct plural *runar* occurs in German (St John's) I, Maughold IV.

Indeed, on the whole the grammar of the Manx stones is quite good, with correct, or at least adequate, forms given for nouns, adjectives and demonstratives. Apart from the forms quoted above, only *triku* Braddan II has been called in question. This word, if it is *tryggvar*, a word normally found only in the plural, should have the ending -*um*.

Magnus Olsen tentatively attributed the appearance of non-classical forms to Celtic influence.[34] The Norse and the Celts, he argued, formed a bilingual community, but the two languages had differing inflexional systems. Consequently, the strict Norse inflexional pattern was disturbed. In contrast, D. A. Seip drew attention to a parallel break-down of inflexional patternings that is recorded in the early Norwegian written texts.[35] Inflexional -*r*, he noted, is lost in the common assimilation to *l* and *n*

V's *liktinniftir* which A. M. Cubbon and Aslak Liestøl take to be a form of *leg þenna aftir*, 'this grave-stone to the memory of . . .' (Cubbon, 'Viking Runes', pp. 24–5). I am not sure that *leg* can mean 'grave-stone' rather than 'grave', and a grave would not be in memory of anyone, rather it would contain someone. The interpretation *tinn(a)* as *þenna* involves an unusual *t* for *þ*, and a disturbing doubling of *n*. *Leg* is a neuter word, so if we take the Cubbon-Liestøl reading, here is another case of grammatical confusion. I also leave out of consideration the endingless accusative of the feminine noun *arinbiaurk*, Andreas II, partly because the ending of *Arinbiǫrgu* is of uncertain status.

[34] Originally in 'Om sproget i de manske runeindskrifter', *Forhandlinger i Videnskabsselskabet i Christiania* 1 (1909).

[35] 'Norske paralleller til de uregelmessige fleksjonsformer i manske og irske runeinnskrifter', *NTS* 4 (1930), 401–4.

(as indeed in *roskitil* Braddan II, *þurbiaurn* Marown (Rhyne)), and there are less regular assimilations as in *son*, *sæl* for the common *sonr*, *sælr*. *-r* is lost, in written texts *c*. 1200, when there is another *r* in the neighbourhood, as in *burð*, *styrc*, *prest*; and also in some loanwords, as *biscup*. In the fourteenth century there is more widespread evidence of loss of *-r*, though a strong scribal tradition helps its retention. Again, the earliest Norwegian and Icelandic manuscript texts show occasional loss of *-s* in the genitive of nouns whose stem ends in *ð*, as genitives *guð*, *œið*. Variations between *-a* and *-u/-o* forms in feminine nouns is shown by such accusatives as *kirkia*, *kona*, *tunga*, and such nominatives as *þionasto*, *sálo*. Hence, Seip implies (though it is left to C. J. S. Marstrander to say it firmly)[36] the non-classical Manx forms are probably not caused by Celtic influence; they show the early appearance in Man of Norse forms that are to occur in the later written texts of the mainland of Norway.

Seip did not use as evidence the Viking Age runic texts of Norway, nor could he, for there was no support in them. Thus he quoted no forms before the beginning of the twelfth century, the earliest date of his manuscript material. The evidence of the Norwegian language as recorded in the Viking Age runes of Norway is interesting. As presented in *Norges innskrifter med de yngre runer* these inscriptions do not show the inflexional decline recorded in Man. Most important, the *-r* ending is always given to appropriate masculine nominatives. Particularly interesting in this connection is a text on Njærheim I which reads **in:ulfrikr: | srkþukrk**, interpreted as *en Úlfrekr sorgþungr g(erði)* 'and Ulfrekr, heavy with grief, made (this cross)'.[37] Though the rune-master had to shorten his text because of lack of space, he nevertheless included the *-r* ending of *sorgþungr*; if *-r* had been optional at this date, he might well have omitted it. There are, I think, no Norwegian epigraphical cases to parallel the genitive *smiþ*. Oblique weak feminines have the proper endings, though there are few examples on the Norwegian Viking Age stones. The plural *runar* only occurs, though again examples are rare.[38] Thus it seems that some of the Manx crosses show a rather different grammatical tradition from that of the Norwegian monuments.

In reassessing his position in 1954, Olsen pointed out that 'in the Norse settlements from Greenland to Orkney the nominative *-r*, and inflexion of women's names, were not affected by such disintegrating influences until far out into the Middle Ages. These settlements, however, had been seized and occupied by Norsemen only'.[39] Hence he reasserted his belief that the Manx break-down of inflexions was the effect of mixing with Celtic speakers. He added the support of the Killaloe cross in Ireland, which has the endingless nominative *þurkrim*, and presumably also shows Celtic

---

[36] Marstrander, 'Killaloekorset', pp. 385–7.
[37] Olsen *et al.*, *Norges innskrifter* III, 146.
[38] The Danish runic evidence seems to support the Norwegian on these points. According to the *formlære* section of Jacobsen and Moltke, *Danmarks runeindskrifter*: (a) inflexional *-r* usually remains, save in loan-words, nouns ending in *-l*, *-r*, *-n*, and moneyers' names where there may be English influence; (b) the genitive singular inflexional *-s* remains, except in an odd case where the following noun begins with *s*; (c) the oblique weak feminine ending is *-u* or *-o*, with a possible late exception in the form *mæss(æ)*; (d) the accusative plural *runar* is usual.
[39] Olsen, 'Runic Inscriptions in Great Britain', p. 224.

influence since it has a second inscription in Irish and in ogam. The material from the Western Isles is a less sure support, for the relationship between Celt and Norsemen in these areas is less easy to define.[40] Such runic inscriptions as survive from them seem to retain inflexional -*r*.

Where Olsen argued for the influence of 'a dominant bilingual population', Marstrander seems to believe that the sloppiness of some Manx grammar shows only that the Manx rune-masters had a less secure tradition of spelling. Either of these is, of course, a perfectly possible explanation.

To the decline of grammatical precision in the inflexional endings a parallel may be found in certain inscriptions from Anglo-Scandinavian England, notably that of the Pennington, Lancashire, tympanum, whose bastard Norse shows loss of inflexion and confusion of grammatical gender.[41] The specific case of the loss of nominative -*r* in Manx texts we could explain as interference from Celtic morphology, since Celtic does not signal the difference between nominative and accusative in its *o*-stem nouns. However, if names are anything to go by – and they are an uncertain guide – the decline in grammatical precision does not link specifically to a Celtic population. Andreas II, with its nominative *sạntulf*, has only Norse names, and so, as far as can be seen, has Kirk Michael IV with its nominative *[k]rim*. Kirk Michael II has the correct *sunr* in the Celtic group *mailbrikti sunr aþakans*, but omits the ending from the Norse *kaut*. Bride on the other hand seems to have only Celtic names, but gets the grammatical forms *su(n)r* and *kunu* right, while Maughold V also has *sunr* in a Celtic name context. Olsen's thesis is not clearly upheld.

There is objection also to Marstrander's view that the Manx rune-masters, in their formal texts, were readier to represent aspects of spoken Norse than their Norwegian contemporaries working in a firmer spelling tradition. From Seip's material it seems that, where the stem of a noun ended in *n* there was likelihood of early loss of -*r*. Yet *sunr* always retains its inflexional ending where it occurs in Manx inscriptions, even on Kirk Michael II where *kaut* loses -*r*. Indeed, whereas *[k]rim* Kirk Michael IV and *þuriþ* Onchan might be excused as examples of early loss of -*r* caused by a neighbouring *r* in the word, there seems no reason why either *kaut* or *sạntulf* should have lost their inflexions early.

There is of course no necessary conflict between the Olsen and Marstrander positions. The Celtic presence could have speeded up the inflexional decline of Manx Norse just as, in the opinion of some, the Scandinavian occupation of much of north, midland and eastern England led to a loss of the Old English inflexions earlier there than in the south and west. At the same time, the Manx rune-masters may have had a less formal training, or have developed a freer tradition, or simply had a more varied

---

[40] Compare, for instance, the situation in Skye as assessed by A. Small, 'Norse Settlement in Skye', *Les Vikings et leur Civilisation*, ed. R. Boyer (Paris and The Hague, 1976), pp. 29–37, where he argues for co-existence of Vikings and Celts, with that described on the archaeological evidence of the Udal, N. Uist, where I. A. Crawford deduces a complete destruction of Celtic culture and its replacement by Norse, 'War or Peace – Viking Colonisation in the Northern and Western Isles of Scotland Reviewed', *Proceedings of the Eighth Viking Congress*, ed. H. Bekker-Nielsen *et al.* (Odense, 1981), pp. 259–69.
[41] See above, p. 187.

background of runic practice than those of mainland Norway. The two factors combined could have led to the peculiarities of grammar in the Manx inscriptions.

How then do the grammatical peculiarities of Kirk Michael III look in the light of this discussion?

1. The Kirk Michael rune-master uses a different runic *fuþark* from the other Manx inscriptions, and moreover one that has the late rune **y**. He presumably adapted his text to fit local practices, but only to a limited degree – the lay-out of his text is quite un-Manx. Thus he may not have had a detailed knowledge of the runic tradition common in Man, and it is all the more remarkable that his language shares grammatical irregularities with other Manx inscriptions.

2. He commemorates a family with Celtic names, though he uses some version of the Norse tongue, and even quotes a Norse proverb. One member of the family was married to a man with a Norse name.

3. The forms *fustra* and *kona* can be defended as feminine accusatives on the analogy of *kuina* on Maughold V, an inscription that uses short-twig runes but does not employ the common Manx memorial formula. Maughold V also records Celtic names. The Kirk Michael III accusative singular *sine* cannot be defended, though perhaps it shows the same confusion of unstressed *e* for *a* as does *rune[.]* for *runar* Onchan.

4. Though the grammatical and/or phonological irregularities of Kirk Michael III can be paralleled elsewhere in Manx texts, yet the incidence of irregularity in the Kirk Michael text is marginally higher than elsewhere. The rune-master may have been a stranger to Manx dialect, and misunderstood some of its peculiarities.[42]

[42] I would like to thank the British Academy for its generous grant from the Small Grants Research Fund in the Humanities which enabled me to carry out the field work for this paper.

18
(1984)

ON THE TRANSLITERATION OF ENGLISH RUNES

For practical reasons it is convenient to transliterate runic inscriptions into some form of the Latin alphabet. Anglo-Saxon scholars have often followed the system put forward by Bruce Dickins in Leeds Studies in English *1 (1932), 15–19. Recently there has been criticism of the Dickins system, and the argument adduced that it is desirable to use, for the English version of the runic script, one closer to that commonly employed for Scandinavian runes. The present article puts the case for differentiating between English and non-English runes by using distinctive transcription methods for each, and suggests some modifications to the Dickins system for English use. The matter is of some immediate importance in view of the publication of the British Academy's* Corpus of Anglo-Saxon Stone Sculpture, *which requires transliterations of English runic texts.*

VARIETIES OF RUNIC TRANSCRIPTION

Runologists have long recognized the difficulties involved in presenting runic texts to the world; in particular in presenting them to interested readers who are not themselves runic scholars. There is the specific problem of how to transliterate runic symbols into non-runic letters, usually some form of the roman alphabet. Ideally, perhaps, there should be no such transcription, since transcription may lead to careless thinking and that to inaccurate conclusion.[1] Ideally scholars should be encouraged to approach these texts in runic terms, without seeking the easy way out of transliterating them into more familiar characters. Unfortunately this is not practicable since the material of the inscriptions is relevant to a range of external studies, philological, archaeological and historical, and the practitioners of those disciplines deserve some consideration. They can hardly be expected to control the complexities and confusions of the various runic alphabets in addition to taking note of the content of the inscriptions themselves. They want a more easily accessible text, one that is presented clearly, precisely and without ambiguity. They wish to be sure how much is certainty, how much reasonable conjecture and how much guesswork.

It is inconvenient that over the years scholars of different countries and traditions

---

[1] For examples of this see my 'A Note on the Transliteration of Old English Runic Inscriptions', above pp. 87–92.

have created different transcription systems for their runes. Even within the same tradition there can be individual variation, depending perhaps upon personal preference or upon typographical feasibility. These variations were pointed out in a discussion held at the First International Symposium on Runes and Runic Inscriptions, held at Ann Arbor, Michigan, in 1980. In his paper introducing the topic C. W. Thompson made a plea for a standard 'set of conventional symbols with which an editor reproduces a runic inscription so that the reader is reliably and consistently informed of its condition and of the limits to reading and interpreting it'.[2] He added that such a system should 'not become overly complicated by trying to indicate too much. The finer the distinctions it tries to make, the more graphically complex the reproduced text becomes, increasing the reader's burden. Since it is clear that a system of notation can never reproduce all the details of the original (often it merely serves to alert the reader to uncertainties and send the serious student back to the original), it is best to keep it relatively simple'.

As it happens Thompson's paper is more concerned with the accidentals than with the essentials of runic inscriptions. Thus, he deliberately avoids such a basic and thorny question as 'agreeing on appropriate Latin letter equivalents for the runic symbols themselves'. So he sidesteps such problems as how to deal with different forms of the same runic letter, and – one which will present major difficulties later in this paper – what to do with those runes whose significance changes over the centuries they are in use. On the first of these points Thompson shows himself rather imperceptive by a comment he adds in an endnote: 'I can see no point in printing the inscription first in runic symbols, as is done in *Niyr*. The rune forms are normalized and tell us little more about the actual shapes than a transliteration would do'.[3] These are the words of a man who has limited experience of runes. Anyone who has worked within, say, the Norwegian field will know that in Viking Age Norway there existed variant patterns of rune form – rune-masters made different choices from the distinctive letter forms available in the different *fuþarks*, the Danish/normal runes (*danske runer*), the short-twig runes (*kortkvistruner, stuttruner*), and mixtures of the two (*blandingsruner*) as well as the Man-Jær runes. Here it is convenient to have even a normalized representation of the rune forms of an inscription printed above the transcript; it shows at a glance what selection of letter forms an inscription employs, and whether it is consistent throughout in its usage. To say this tells us 'little more about the actual shapes than a transliteration would do' is nonsense.

The difficulty transliteration has in coping with sound-changes affecting the values of runes is highlighted by the treatment of the fourth rune, *áss*, in the standard Norwegian corpus, *Norges innskrifter med de yngre runer*. This rune-name, in its Primitive Old Norse form, is **ansuR*, and in the course of development to medieval Norwegian the initial vowel underwent lengthening and nasalization, and then rounding. In the *fuþarks* listed in the summary 'Norsk runeskrift i middelalderen',[4]

---

[2] C. W. Thompson, 'On Transcribing Runic Inscriptions', *Michigan Germanic Stud.* 7 (1981), 89–95, at 90.

[3] *Ibid.* 95, n. 6. *Niyr* = M. Olsen *et al.*, *Norges innskrifter med de yngre runer*.

[4] Olsen *et al.*, *Norges innskrifter* V, 238–45.

áss is given the value **a** in the tenth-century series, it varies between **a** and **o** in the first half of the eleventh century, and thereafter appears as **o**. To transliterate by **o** in the tenth century, or to continue to use **a** in the late eleventh would be phonologically misleading or tendencious, and here editors prefer phonetic approximation to consistency of representation. On the other hand, for the earlier period when the Norwegian rune-series has no specific symbol for *o*, the rune-masters often use **u** instead, as in the Manx forms **utr** (*Oddr*) Braddan III, **fustra kuþan** (*fóstra góðan*) Kirk Michael III.[5] Here runologists retain the transliteration **u**, preferring consistency of representation to phonetic approximation. In cases like this the editor is in a dilemma and has to make an arbitrary choice of what to do. The decision is pragmatic rather than logical, and in such circumstances it might be a help if the rune form were printed above the transcript.

However, Thompson deliberately refrains from discussing such major points of transcription. Instead he considers what type-face should be use to represent runic text in transliteration (he suggests bold-face or, for typewritten material, spaced text); how to represent linguistic normalization (by italic); reconstructions or conjectural restorations (between square brackets); bind-runes, that is, two runes ligatured as one (by a superscript curve joining the two letters); the end of a line of inscriptions (a single vertical stroke); damaged letters (subscript dots); missing beginnings, middles, ends (square brackets); countable missing letters (dots). All this is sensible enough, though by no means unexceptionable. For instance, if a text indicates word-division consistently or irregularly by a single dot (as German (Peel) I, Isle of Man), it will be misleading to use dots for missing letters. Thompson's system (which he suggests calling 'Ann Arbor') presents practical problems, as anyone who has tried using some of its conventions for printed work will confirm. Not all printers have bold-face with the full range of runic equivalents – a bold-face *thorn/thurs* is a particular case. Subscript dots are a difficulty. They have to be inserted into the original typescript, and they are easy to miss out or put under the wrong letters. Typesetters – or whoever is responsible for camera-ready copy – do not like them. When they are faced with a text occasional letters of which have subscripts, they tend to scatter the subscripts arbitrarily about, and proof-reading becomes tedious, correction expensive and error likely.[6] Damaged letters and conjectural restorations

---

[5] The Manx runic corpus is published in M. Olsen, 'Runic Inscriptions in Great Britain, Ireland and the Isle of Man', *Viking Antiquities in Great Britain and Ireland*, ed. H. Shetelig (Oslo, 1940–54) VI, 153–233, corrected and brought up-to-date in 'The Manx Rune-Stones', above pp. 207–23. For this form of naming and numbering the Manx stones see above, pp. 209, 217–18.

[6] I speak here after the bitter experience of correcting proofs of an article where Norse inscriptions were quoted in 'Ann Arbor', but I note that E. Moltke, in the discussion that followed Thompson's paper, *Michigan Germanic Stud.* 7 (1981), p. 97, also found difficulties with subscript dots. The objection raised by A. G. Woodhead, *The Study of Greek Inscriptions* (Cambridge, 1959), p. 121, n. 7, and repeated as late as 2nd ed. (1981), p. 126 ('Unless cast in one piece with the letter below which they stand, they must be set in separately, and the centrifugal force of the rotary printing process may cause them to fly out of place') is presumably irrelevant to new work as virtually all printing is now done from lithographic plates. However, even modern printing methods do not render subscript dots generally acceptable: in most cases someone who is not the author has to add them correctly to camera-ready copy. Not all founts are so designed as to allow tidy subscripts to be added: in one recent

are always something of a problem, for the personal element enters extensively into them. No two scholars, probably, will agree as to how damaged a letter has to be before the damage is signalled in the transcript; no two scholars, probably, will agree as to when a badly damaged letter can be signalled as damaged, when it must be regarded as conjectural restoration.[7] Obviously in many of these cases the transcript should 'send the serious student back to the original', but that only helps if the serious student is an epigrapher. Should he be a medieval philologist or an archaeologist or an art historian, his reluctant return to the original may not prove fruitful.

Thompson chose bold-face for runic transcriptions because that convention is already widely established. Indeed, it is the common form for transliterating Scandinavian runic texts, as in the great corpora of Norwegian, Swedish and Danish (but not Icelandic) inscriptions. Even then it is not universal even among Scandinavian runologists. The veteran Danish epigrapher, Erik Moltke, has turned away from it in his recent work, since he regards bold-face as intrusive and unattractive on the page. Instead he uses roman, not distinctive from the rest of his text.[8] In her *Stuttruner i vikingtidens innskrifter* (Oslo, 1968), the Norwegian Ingrid Sanness Johnsen used spaced roman, presumably for typographical reasons since her book is composed on the typewriter; transcripts of single runes are underlined. Bold-face has also often been used for Continental German inscriptions and for Frisian ones.[9] For his seminal work on Anglo-Saxon manuscript runes René Derolez transcribed into bold-face.[10] Despite this, bold-face has not been commonly used in the English tradition.[11] Thompson argued for a 'unified system of notation', hoping that this would include the use of bold-face for transcripts or, if that were not possible because of printing requirements, spaced roman. I would like to challenge the desirability of a unified system, one that would link more closely the English and Scandinavian methods of notation.

---

case, the standard letter *thorn* (þ) has a lowered bow which makes it quite impossible to add a subscript dot which is in line with dots under other letters.

[7] Note, for example, the differences between Bruce Dickins's transcription of the Dover and Thornhill II stone inscriptions and mine: Dickins, 'System of Transliteration', pp. 18–19, and Page, *Introduction* (1973), pp. 141 and 156. I number the Thornhill II and III stones differently from Dickins, giving them in order of finding rather than arbitrarily. My *Introduction* gives details of the various runic texts from England discussed in this article, and should also be consulted for the meanings of the various technical runic terms used.

[8] E. Moltke, *Runerne i Danmark og deres oprindelse* (Copenhagen, 1976); see also *Michigan Germanic Stud.* 7 (1981), p. 97.

[9] As in Krause and Jankuhn, *Runeninschriften im älteren Futhark*; W. Krause, *Runen* (Berlin, 1970); K. Düwel and W.-D. Tempel, 'Knochenkämme mit Runeninschriften aus Friesland: mit einer Zusammenstellung aller bekannten Runenkämme und einem Beitrag zu den friesischen Runeninschriften', *Palaeohistoria* 14 (1968 [1970]), 353–91. Interestingly enough, bold-face was avoided in Arntz and Zeiss, *Die einheimischen Runendenkmäler des Festlandes* which was to form the first volume of a prestigious *Gesamtausgabe der älteren Runendenkmäler*. Arntz and Zeiss use italic, supported by a lavish use of runic type.

[10] Derolez, *Runica Manuscripta*.

[11] In the case of my *Introduction*, the printers simply changed all my bold-face texts (used for Norse and occasional other non-English inscriptions) into italic, presumably on aesthetic grounds; to save expense and reduce risk of error I let the italic stand, to the generous indignation of reviewers. For my corpus of Manx runic inscriptions in 'The Manx Rune-Stones' the original editor replaced bold-face

DICKINS'S SYSTEM OF TRANSLITERATING ENGLISH RUNES

In 1931 Bruce Dickins, the leading English runic scholar, published his system of transliteration for English inscriptions.[12] It was one he had tried out over the years for classroom use, to present English runic texts to his students in philology. It was designed for the only method of cheap reproduction then available, cyclostyling from stencils cut on a standard (though slightly adapted) typewriter. It could use only one type-face, and that for convenience was roman. In later publications Dickins confirmed the convention of placing runic transcripts within single inverted commas to distinguish them clearly from other textual matter.[13] Damaged characters were given in italic (underlined in typescript); italic/underlined within square brackets represented lost letters 'which can reasonably be inferred'. (Dickins did not say on what

1	2	3	4	5	6	7	8:		9	10	11	12	13	14	15	16:
ᚠ	ᚢ	ᚦ	ᚩ	ᚱ	ᚳ	ᚷ	ᚹ:		ᚻ	ᚾ	ᛁ	ᛄ	ᛇ	ᛈ	ᛉ	ᛋ
f	u	þ	o	r	c	g	w:		h	n	i	j	ȝ	p	(x)	s :

17	18	19	20	21	22	23	24:	25	26	27	28	29	30	31.
ᛏ	ᛒ	ᛖ	ᛗ	ᛚ	ᛝ	ᛟ	ᛞ:	ᚪ	ᚫ	ᚣ	ᛠ	ᛣ	ᛢ	ᚸ
t	b	e	m	l	ŋ	œ	d :	a	æ	y	êa	k	k̄	ḡ .

FIG. 1   The Anglo-Saxon *fuþork* with the Dickins system of transliteration

he based his inference – whether on the space available, the fragmentary marks remaining, the likely content of the inscription, or early drawings.) All these, then, could be readily produced by an adapted typewriter, as could two other conventions that he suggested, one controversial, one not. Uncontroversial was the use of a vertical stroke to indicate line-end. Less acceptable was the slash that showed a bind-rune, as 'd/d' to give two *d*-runes bound together in 'gebid/daþ' Thornhill III. Finally Dickins implied conventions for material completely lost from inscriptions. These are not defined, nor are they clearly thought out. For instance, at the end of the [Great] Urswick inscription (Great Urswick ii in my edition)[14] Dickins transcribed the sequence 'lylþi | swo...'. This text must be a maker's signature *Lyl þis wo[rhtæ]*, 'Lyl made this', but it lost its ending when the Great Urswick slab was trimmed to fit a window-splay. Presumably Dickins did not want to commit himself to the end of this text – he may have been worried about the exact form of the verb, *worhtæ* or

by roman. English printers' and editors' obvious reluctance to use bold-face is a good pragmatic reason for having an alternative transliteration system.

[12] Dickins, 'System of Transliteration'.

[13] This is not formally stated in Dickins's 'System of Transliteration', but is used there in continuous prose, and also used in A. S. C. Ross, 'The Linguistic Evidence for the Date of the "Ruthwell Cross" ', *MLR* 28 (1933), 145–55, for whose benefit Dickins published his system, and popularized in B. Dickins and A. S. C. Ross, *The Dream of the Rood* (London, 1934).

[14] Page, *Introduction*, pp. 37 and 153.

worohtæ, or even remembered the Pershore censer-cover where the word was not completed at all[15] – so he left it open. His text of the Lancaster cross inscription is 'gebidæþfo | ræcunibal | þcuþbere*h*. . . .' ('cunibalþ' should read 'cynibalþ'). On this stone the end of the third line is worn away and it is not clear whether or not there was space for many more runes than can now be read. Here the dots must represent sheer uncertainty as to how the inscription went on. In the case of the Overchurch stone Dickins reads: 'folcæaræardonbec[. . | . .]biddaþforeæþelmun[. .]'. Presumably the dots within brackets show how many runes Dickins thinks were lost, though it is hard to see how he judged that there were just two missing at the end of each of the lines. For the Ruthwell Cross Dickins worked in a rather different manner, for he divided the text into its individual words (as also with inscriptions on the Franks Casket), presumably to make the poetry more accessible to the student. Thus he produces a verse line '[*m*]o*d*ig f[. . . . . . .] men' where he must assume seven letters missing; there are in fact two lines of runes destroyed here, and the carver was fitting in three runes to the line. Later in this text he transcribes 'gistoddu*n* him . . . . . *lic*æs [*hêa*]f[*du*]m' where the five dots, this time without brackets, also represent the loss of two lines of letters. One corner of the east face of the Ruthwell Cross was knocked away, and with it the opening of two sections of the text, so that Dickins reads '. .geredæ hinæ' and '. . . .ic riicnæ kyniŋc', where again the unbracketed dots seem to represent Dickins's calculation of the number of runes lost.[16] Finally, a red herring. In one line of the Thornhill III stone (= Dickins Thornhill II) is the sequence 'berhtsuiþe.bekun', where the dot simply represents a punctuation point on the stone. These examples do not exhaust the Dickins system of transliteration, but they are enough to be going on with. They seem to show that, though much of the system suits its purpose excellently, it is defective in minor and accidental details. Indeed, Dickins must have been aware of this himself for, when a couple of years later he published with A. S. C. Ross his edition of *The Dream of the Rood*, he modified his system: 'A missing letter for which there is quite certainly a space on the stone is indicated by [₀]; when there is a break but it is impossible to decide from the stone how many letters are missing, dots are placed in the text'.[17]

Clearly Dickins's system of transliteration is not so perfect that, in piety, we need to retain it for all time. In my own work I have ventured to challenge some of its details, making minor changes and, I hope, improvements, while keeping its main characteristics.[18] In this paper I want to discuss more drastic change: whether, in the interests of a single system of runic notation for all texts, it is desirable to approach Thompson's, even for Old English purposes. Particularly, in view of Derolez's example, whether to use bold-face for English runes. Dickins's system, occasionally

---

[15] D. M. Wilson, *Anglo-Saxon Ornamental Metalwork 700–1100 in the British Museum* (London, 1964), p. 84; cf. also the Alnmouth cross, Page, *Introduction*, p. 153, where the formula MYRE-DaH.MEH.wO may have been finished elsewhere on the stone or may have been left unfinished.

[16] We now know that the group 'geredæ' was preceded by a cross and three runes, though Dickins was unaware of the early drawing that showed this: see 'An Early Drawing of the Ruthwell Cross' above, especially p. 24 and plate.

[17] Dickins and Ross, *Dream of the Rood*, p. 8.

[18] As in my *Introduction*, particularly chapters 3 and 4.

modified, has lasted for some decades and achieved a degree of recognition, so it should not be changed without good cause. There are, as I have suggested, several objections to the use of bold-face, primarily practical ones. Moltke's, that the type is ugly and obtrusive, is sound enough, although I doubt if an aesthetic judgement should prevail in a scholarly matter. Certainly there is likely to be confusion, as Thompson ably demonstrated in discussion, if Moltke's alternative should prevail – that runic transcripts use the same type-face, without differentiation, as the rest of a book or article. At present, however, printers do not always make a good job of mixing bold-face into a work that is for the most part in plain roman. Their bold-face types may be limited and may lack some of the special letter forms that runic transcripts require. At present many typewriters cannot produce bold-face. But these must be temporary objections. Daisy-wheel or golfball typewriters can, I assume, be fitted with bold-face, while new techniques of printing will make a fuller range of bold-face types generally available.

There is, however, an objection of a different nature to producing a unified system of transliteration of runes. It is partly a chauvinistic one, but it depends on what Thompson calls the 'otherness' of English runes. Nearly 150 years ago the great J. M. Kemble spoke of this in an article whose good sense and ironic detachment can still raise pleasure:

> The [runic] characters of the Norwegians, Swedes, Danes and Icelanders are not less distinct from those of the Goths, High and Low Germans, and Anglo-Saxons, than the languages of the several nations which they represented. Unquestionably both the alphabets and the languages are, in the widest philosophical generalization, identical: but exclusive knowledge of the Anglo-Saxon or German Runes would as little enable us to decypher Old Norse inscriptions, as exclusive knowledge of the language of the Edda would enable us to read the Old German Krist, the Old Saxon Hêljand, or the Anglo-Saxon Beôwulf . . . These preliminary remarks will not be without service in assisting to explain why my interpretations of certain Anglo-Saxon Runic monuments differ *toto cœlo* from those of the learned Danes, who have been so obliging as to attempt to decypher them for us; and to save them this trouble in future, is partly the intention of this paper; especially as there seems to have been a sort of tacit understanding in this country, that the labour and the honour might just as well be left to them; in the propriety of which view it is difficult to concur.[19]

Kemble's argument – then needed even more than now – that there was nothing Scandinavian about Old English runes so that Scandinavians had no privileged insight into them, is significant to the present discussion. Of course, Scandinavian runic inscriptions outnumber English ones many times over; inevitably runic studies will flourish more freely there than here so that bold-face transcripts of runes will be more familiar to the general scholar. Yet if we accept the 'otherness' of English runes, it is surely sensible to signal that 'otherness' by a distinctive system of

---

[19] J. M. Kemble, 'On Anglo-Saxon Runes', *Archaeologia* 28 (1840), 327–72, at 327.

transliteration. It warns the Norse scholar against taking too lightly the differences between these writing systems and languages. In turn it warns the Anglo-Saxon student not to take liberties in using parallel material from Scandinavia.[20]

THE 'OTHERNESS' OF ENGLISH RUNES

To justify the case it becomes important to define the 'otherness' of English runes. This lies in:

(i) a distinctive expansion of the Germanic *fuþark*. In large part this is connected with sound developments variously known as Anglo-Frisian, Inguaeonic and *Nordseegermanisch*. The most important of these developments is that which affects the **ansuz* rune (no. 4 of the Germanic rune-row, fig. 2). Gmc **ans-* became, via nasalization and lengthening of the initial vowel, OE *ōs*; *a* sounds remain in other contexts; in yet other contexts *a* became fronted to varying degrees represented in English dialects by the graphs *e*, and *ę*, *æ*.[21] Thus three runic symbols were needed where one was adequate before, and this resulted in the Anglo-Frisian development of new forms and rune-names, *os*, *ac* and *æsc* (nos 4, 25, 26 of the English rune-row, fig. 1). A second group of changes, whose full importance will be dealt with in a later section, affected the stops *k*, *g* in palatal contexts; palatal allophones developed, which in Old English eventually became distinctive enough to be represented separately in the rune-row. Hence the appearance, side by side with the runes *cen* and *gyfu* (nos 6 and 7, which represent the Germanic runes), of the new formations *calc* and *gar* (nos 29 and 31). The palatalization of *g* also allows the *j*-rune (no. 12) to be used instead of *g* in such a context as 'jʒslhêard' (= *Gisl-*) on the Dover stone or 'jilsuiþ' on Thornhill III. Finally – as far as our evidence goes at present – there are the distinctively Anglo-Saxon runes *yr* and *ear* (nos 27 and 28) which represent English sound developments.

(ii) Anglo-Saxon rune forms (sometimes found elsewhere in Continental Germania) which contrast with Norse ones. Examples are the two-barred *h*-rune (no. 9) as against the single-barred rune of the North, and the distinctive *cen*-rune (no. 6). Less commonly evidenced but possibly also significant is the English form of the *ŋ*-rune (no. 22).

---

[20] As I point out in 'The Manx Rune-Stones', above p. 225. My objection is not strictly chauvinistic. English scholars who are experts on Scandinavian runes are no more competent thereby to judge Anglo-Saxon ones than their Scandinavian colleagues: cf. the review by M. Barnes of my *Introduction* (*Medieval Scandinavia* 9 (1976), 246–54).

[21] I do not attempt here any detailed or precise description of these sound changes. My account is incomplete since it takes no note of vowel length nor does it allow for such a change as that of *a* to *a/o* before nasals, since that is not reflected in runic developments. Moreover, I avoid phonetic or phonemic description, which would present problems in matters of dating and dialect. Instead, I give a rather old-fashioned philological account, which is not, I hope, misleading in the context of this article.

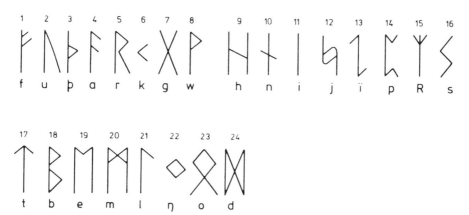

FIG. 2   The Germanic *fuþark*. There is no standard form of the *fuþark* and the version given is conflated from several sources

(iii) the Anglo-Saxons became Christian several centuries before the Scandinavians; and earlier than some (? all) of the Continental Germanic peoples who used runes.[22] From the seventh century there are Christian runic inscriptions in England, as on St Cuthbert's coffin, a monument that also uses the roman character. In consequence there is likely to be influence from roman-Christian on Anglo-Saxon runic. The same pattern of memorial formulae can be found on both runic and non-runic stones. There are some clear cases where runic spelling seems affected by non-runic/roman usage, as when the two runes 'oe' rather than the single 'œ', appear for the reflex of *o. . .i* in 'roe[.]tæ' (HROETHBERHTÆ in the parallel roman text) on the Falstone stone. The re-use of the rune *eolhx* (no. 15) with the value 'x' is another case in point. This symbol originally represented the *z*-sound found in inflexional endings, but as this did not survive in Old English, the rune was left free to be used for another purpose, giving *x* (not generally needed in Old English) in Latin texts, as the royal 'beonnarex' on some coins of Beonna of East Anglia.[23] Two other practices may reflect influence from non-runic tradition. It is usually said that early runic texts outside England – and this is certainly true of Viking Age Scandinavian inscriptions – (a) avoid using double consonants, and (b) omit a nasal before a homorganic stop. England has no such inhibitions, and produces such forms as (a) 'setto/n' Bewcastle Cross, 'had/da' Derbyshire bone plate, 'afœddæ', '*unneg*' Franks Casket,[24] and (b) EADmVnD Chester-le-Street stone (contrast **kuþumut** Helnæs, Denmark, stone), and '*k̄yniŋc*' Ruthwell Cross (contrast the common **kunukr, kunukʀ** in Scandinavian

[22] A recent interpretation of the sixth-century Nordendorf I brooch inscriptions suggests that runes were used for Christian purposes in southern Germany at that date: K. Düwel, 'Runen und interpretatio christiana: zur religiongeschichtlichen Stellung der Bügelfibel von Nordendorf I', *Tradition als historische Kraft: Interdisziplinäre Forschungen zur Geschichte des früheren Mittelalters*, ed. N. Kamp and J. Wollasch (Berlin, 1982), pp. 78–86.
[23] M. M. Archibald, 'The Coinage of Beonna in the Light of the Middle Harling Hoard', *BNJ* 55 (1985), 10–54.
[24] See 'The Use of Double Runes in Old English Inscriptions', above pp. 95–103.

inscriptions). Finally, the not infrequent mixing of runic and roman scripts in England is perhaps relevant here: as EADmVnD Chester-le-Street stone, +æDRED MEC AH EAnRED MEC agROf Lancashire (Manchester) ring, +BEOnnaREX on coins of the East Anglian king Beonna.

(iv) much written Old English is from the same date range as the bulk of Anglo-Saxon runic inscriptions, say 700–1100. At least two runic monuments, the Franks Casket and the Ruthwell Cross, contain important literary material, while many others illuminate philological developments of Old English dialects.[25] Any system of transliterating Anglo-Saxon runes should make this material as readily available as possible to the literary or linguistic scholar who is not a runologist. Old English had certain clear conventions of orthography, and runic transcripts should, if possible, coincide with them. An obvious case in point is the treatment of the *cen*-rune (contrasting here with the Norse *kaun*). In most Old English manuscript texts the graph *c* covered a group of sounds which included palatal and velar variants; the group *sc* represents the earlier [sk] palatalized and assibilated. Since the *cen*-rune has the same range of uses, Dickins rightly transliterated it 'c'. For Old Norse, where no such distinctions developed, the *kaun*-rune is transcribed **k**. To use parallel systems of transliteration for the two rune-rows would produce Old English forms like *kynibalþ* Lancaster cross, *likbækun* Crowle stone, *fisk* Franks Casket, repellent to the reader of non-runic Old English. For that part of the Old English area where a new rune *calc* was invented to mark the distinction between velar and palatal *c*, a new transcription symbol would be need to accommodate, for instance, both 'krist' and 'riicnæ' in Dickins's transliteration of the Ruthwell Cross.

The 'otherness' of the English runic tradition as I define it here is particularly significant in its contradistinction to the Scandinavian. Of course, the majority of Norse inscriptions are from the Viking Age or later, and so use either one of the restricted sixteen-letter *fuþarks* or one of the expanded runic alphabets that developed from them. These inscriptions are markedly different from the English in script and usage as well as language. Even in the earlier period, however, there are important differences between the two traditions, some of which I have implied above, while others depend on early developments within Norse – as, for example, the change in values of the **jāra-* and **ansuR*-runes.[26] The English tradition diverges from that of central Germania partly because of distinctive Anglo-Frisian changes, and partly because, as far as present evidence goes, the English used runes more extensively, for a wider range of texts, than did the Continentals. From its closest neighbour, the Frisian, the English tradition divides by its greater elaboration of the *fuþorc* which requires more symbols to represent it, while the Frisian runic material is slighter in content and more restricted in range than the English.

[25] Hence the inclusion of the Ruthwell Cross and Franks Casket poems in the Anglo-Saxon poetic records, E. V. K. Dobbie, *The Anglo-Saxon Minor Poems*, ASPR 6 (London and New York, 1942), pp. 115–16, and of several runic texts in H. Sweet, *A Second Anglo-Saxon Reader: Archaic and Dialectal*, 2nd ed. rev. T. F. Hoad (Oxford, 1978), pp. 102–4.
[26] D. A. Seip, *Norwegische Sprachgeschichte*, 2nd ed. rev. L. Saltveit (Berlin, 1971), p. 19; E. Moltke, *Runerne i Danmark*, p. 108.

Because of this distinctive nature of the Anglo-Saxon runic tradition it is unnecessary to use for it a system of transliteration that closely parallels those used for Old Norse, early Frisian and Continental Germanic. Indeed, there is a certain absurdity in the idea. It is no more sensible to insist on the same transliteration system for Norse and English than it would be to require the same pattern of editing for an Old English text and a piece of thirteenth-century Old Norse, with its own script, spelling tradition, extensive use of abbreviation and accepted practices of normalization. Further, as I have argued above, there is much to be said for stressing the differences of the traditions by employing different transcription methods. For Old English the Dickins system has been in use for over fifty years, and has been popularized in many publications, notably in the Methuen's Old English Library edition of *The Dream of the Rood* which generations of students have toiled over. Insofar as the Dickins system works, it seems pointless to change it. But it has a few weaknesses.

DICKINS'S SYSTEM MODIFIED

A system of transliteration for Old English runes should have the following characteristics, as far as possible: (a) it should be precise in its indication of what is visible, what is damaged but legible, what conjectured or restored; (b) it should produce one-to-one transcription, one rune represented by one transcription symbol; (c) it should be able to accommodate the range of symbols, other than runes, that occur in runic texts; for instance, punctuation symbols like + opening an inscription, or numbers of points, single or in vertical line, used as word dividers; (d) transcription should not be phonetically misleading, even if it cannot be precise; (e) it should not confuse the unpractised reader; it should not employ symbols in ways that conflict with their use in other well-known writing systems; (f) it should produce texts that look like Old English to the Anglo-Saxonist who is not a runologist.

Dickins's system (fig. 1) is successful in some, not all, of these. Misleading is Dickins's use of brackets in his transcription, '(x)', of the rune *eolhx* (no. 15, cf. also his presentation of the *fuþorc* of the Thames scramasax), since brackets suggest some sort of hesitation of reading, or perhaps imply that the letter supplements a lacuna in the text, makes a correction or expands an abbreviation. Presumably Dickins put the transcription of *eolhx* in brackets because he did not really believe in the rune. It was, he thought, 'a fossil in Old English. In runic *alphabets*, it is sometimes used for *x* for which a separate character was not provided in the *fuþorc*'.[27] It is an odd statement, since *x* appears as the value of this rune in the written *fuþorcs* of British Library, Cotton Domitian IX and Vienna, Österreichische Nationalbibliothek, 795, as Derolez has shown.[28] Moreover, the rune occurs at least twice in inscriptions. One is as a symbol only, in the sacred monogram 'x̄p̄s' on St Cuthbert's coffin, where it is a direct transliteration, with no phonetic value, of Latin *x* (ultimately Greek χ). The second is the royal title 'rex' on the interlace reverse coins of the East Anglian

---

[27] Dickins, 'System of Transliteration', p. 17.
[28] Derolez, *Runica Manuscripta*, pp. 9, 11 and 59–60.

king Beonna. It therefore seems absurd to pretend that the rune did not exist; we should simply transliterate it 'x', as indeed Dickins himself did in his publication of the St Cuthbert's coffin runes.[29]

Also liable to mislead, in my opinion, is the use of the slash for bind-runes, as 'd/d'. In common English practice the slash tends to divide rather than to combine, as in such a usage as and/or. I prefer to follow Thompson's advice (and common Scandinavian convention) here and use the superscript curve, 'd͡d', even though this has the disadvantage of having to be added by hand to a typescript. It is to be remembered that the Anglo-Saxon rune-masters sometimes bound more than two letters together, as on the Whitby comb where 'h', 'e' and 'l' are combined. Here we must presumably write 'h͡el' rather than 'he͡l'.

Dickins sustains the principle of one-to-one transliteration save in one case, that of the rune *ear*, a character which is used epigraphically to represent the reflex of Gmc *au*, together with fracture and *u*-mutation diphthongs that roughly fall in with it.[30] Dickins renders *ear* as 'êa', the circumflex indicating that the two letters represent one rune. I find this unsatisfactory, and have experimented with the superscript curve, 'e͡a'.[31] This certainly makes it clearer that the two letters of the transcript are intimately linked. Now, however, I want to reserve this convention for bind-runes, and an alternative must be found. Two occur to me. One is to use a superscript horizontal over both letters, as 'e̅a̅' (but this might lead to confusion in rare cases like the St Cuthbert's coffin 'ihs x̅p̅s̅' where the superscript horizontal is in the inscription itself). The other is to space the transcript, save for these two letters, so that, for instance, the Thornhill II stone has the name 'ea d r e d' and the Ruthwell Cross evidences such forms as 'h *ea* f u n æ s' and 'f e a r r a n'. On the whole I think the latter more attractive. The lack of a space in 'ea' shows that these represent a single graph, and so satisfies condition (b) above. This method has the further advantage that the unusual spacing draws immediate attention to the fact that the text is a transcript, rather as the Scandinavian use of bold-face does. There may, however, be typographical disadvantages – as, for instance, the problem of dividing a word at a line-end. Clearly experiment is needed here.

For phonetic correspondence the Dickins system is, with perhaps one exception, satisfactory. Of course, any close phonetic representation is out of the question, and there will be the same sort of inexactitudes as are encountered in Anglo-Saxon manuscript spelling. For instance, Dickins uses 'êa' to give two fracture diphthongs, the reflexes of Gmc *a* + *r* + consonant ('*j*ʒslhêard' on the Dover stone) and Gmc *e* + *r* + consonant ('fêarran' on the Ruthwell cross). Whether either element of these diphthongs is precisely rendered by 'êa' is doubtful, but the transcription is not seriously misleading. The real problem in this section is the rune whose name is *eoh* or *ih* (no. 13). Dickins renders this 'ʒ', but that is admittedly a compromise. I have

[29] B. Dickins, 'The Inscriptions upon the Coffin', *The Relics of Saint Cuthbert*, ed. C. F. Battiscombe (Durham, 1956), pp. 305–7.

[30] See above, pp. 74–5.

[31] Page, *Introduction*, p. 40.

discussed this problematic rune elsewhere;[32] here all that is important is its range of uses in English epigraphy. It represents (i) a pair of spirants in 'almeʒttig' on the Ruthwell Cross and 'toroʒtredæ' on the Great Urswick stone, (ii) a sound perhaps the second element of a diphthong in 'êateʒnne' (= *Eadþegne*) on the Thornhill II stone, where it corresponds to palatalized *g*, (iii) the vowel *i* in 'jʒslhêard' on the Dover stone, (iv) apparently the second element of a diphthong in 'ræʒhæn' on the Caistor-by-Norwich astragalus, where 'æʒ' may give the reflex of Gmc *ai*, (v) apparently a vowel in the unclear sequence 's3þæbæd'/'s3þæbld' on the Loveden Hill urn. No single symbol can cover this range, and it is inevitable that, whatever is chosen, there will be a difficulty with this rune. Most of the English uses suggest a vowel, and non-English runologists confirm this in their various transcription attempts at this rune, ė, ï, ᴇ.[33] It may well be that the consonantal examples of Ruthwell and Great Urswick represent a late recasting of the rune akin to the development that led to the invention of new runes *calc* and *gar*. On this line of thinking I would prefer to represent *eoh*, *ih* by a vowel symbol. Since Dickins has already borrowed the character 'ŋ' from the International Phonetic Alphabet to indicate the rune *Ing*, the same alphabet could be plundered to produce a vowel symbol in the high front range to render *eoh*. I would suggest 'ɨ', which has the advantage that it can be created on the typewriter.

Before leaving the essentials of Dickins's system, I would draw attention to inconsistencies in his presentation. The first is in his treatment of variant rune forms. In the main his transcriptions do not distinguish between different forms of a rune, between, say, the mirror image variants of the letter 's' (both of which occur on the Great Urswick stone) or the similar pairs of 'n' and 'ʒ': nor does he have special symbols for the rare variants of 'j', 'd', 'œ' and 'y' of the Thames scramasax.[34] Moreover, this scramasax has a variant *s*-rune ⨍. In the publication of his system in 1932 Dickins transliterated this variant simply as 's'. When in 1956 he published his texts of the St Cuthbert's coffin inscriptions where the same variant *s*-rune occurs, he used a special transcription symbol 'ʃ', arguing that on the coffin 'the Runic "s" is uniformly replaced by "ʃ", which is in origin an insular minuscule',[35] and comparing the Thames scramasax example. Thus he reads such texts as 'ihʃ x̄pʃ', '*m*/at/heuʃ', '*m*/arcuʃ' and 'iohann[i]ʃʃ'. I think this is a mistake, partly because I am doubtful about Dickins's derivation of the St Cuthbert's coffin 's' from a manuscript minuscule form – it is just as possible to derive it from the common *s*-rune (as in fig. 3).

Dickins's second inconsistency lies in his treatment of mixed runic and roman texts. This was not part of the 1932 article, but when, in 1940, Dickins and A. S. C. Ross published the material of the Alnmouth cross, they had to come to terms with

---

[32] Above, pp. 133–43.

[33] See, for example, H. Arntz, *Handbuch der Runenkunde*, 2nd ed. (Halle/Saale, 1944), p. 65; L. Musset and F. Mossé, *Introduction à la runologie* (Paris, 1965), p. 21; Krause and Jankuhn, *Runeninschriften im älteren Futhark*, p. 2.

[34] Dickins, 'System of Transliteration', pp. 17 and 19.

[35] Dickins, 'Inscriptions upon the Coffin', p. 306.

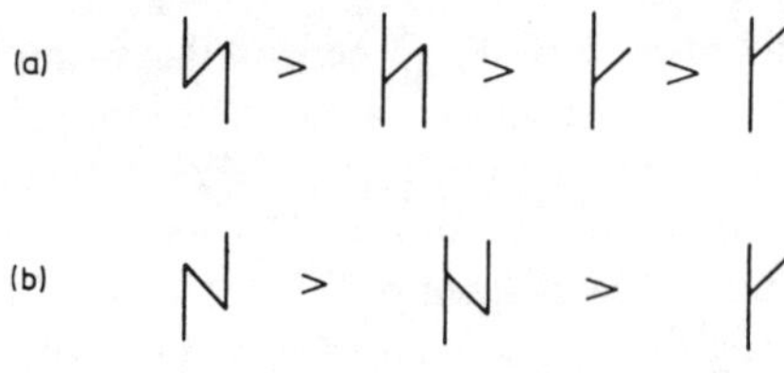

FIG. 3   Possible stages of development of
the Thames scramasax s-rune

mixed inscriptions. They decided to use capitals for roman/Latin letters, lower case for runes, putting the latter between single inverted commas 'save in inscriptions with mixed runic and Latin characters where this convention would be inconvenient'.[36] This was eminently sensible, and led to such a transcribed name form as MYREDaH, where only 'a' was a rune. In 1956, however, Dickins again revoked a decision and put single inverted commas in the middle of a word to indicate the change from roman to runic and back; the result is the absurd looking legend SCS [R]V'm'IA[EL] on St Cuthbert's coffin.[37]

To turn now to the accidentals of the system of transliteration, by which I mean those conventions which, rather than identifying the runes used, define their condition, indicate damage or lacunae, show how the inscription is divided among several lines of text or is subdivided by bands of ornament or structural features of the object inscribed, point to letters omitted by the carver or put in by mistake, etc. Though I call them 'accidentals', they are nevertheless of great importance in any system of transliteration since it is through them that 'the reader is reliably and consistently informed of [an inscription's] condition and of the limits to reading and interpreting it'.[38] They present problems since they often call upon an editor's discretion – how much damage should be signalled, can we be sure that a letter is put in by mistake? Dickins, as I have shown, was not clear about his practices.[39]

For the accidentals Thompson derived great comfort from the Leiden system of transliteration, one originally developed for other languages and scripts.[40] He suggested that runologists should employ conventions closely allied to those of Leiden, and there is a lot to be said for this idea since much that is true about epigraphical

[36] B. Dickins and A. S. C. Ross, 'The Alnmouth Cross', *JEGP* 39 (1940), 169–78, at 171.
[37] Dickins, 'Inscriptions upon the Coffin', p. 305.
[38] See above, p. 246.
[39] See above, pp. 249–50. There are other cases where Dickins's readings can be criticized in this respect. For instance, on the left side of the Franks Casket several runes were shattered when the box was torn apart, but the transcript signals none of this damage. Nor is there indication that only the top halves remain of the runes on the bottom line of Thornhill III (II in Dickins's numbering). The same stone has a letter lost at the end of line 1, but there is no indication of this in Dickins's text; it was presumably 'e', giving the prepositional form *æfte*.
[40] Thompson, 'On Transcribing Runic Inscriptions', 92–3; for the Leiden system, see B. A. van Groningen, 'De signis criticis in edendo adhibendis', *Mnemosyne* n.s. 59 (1932), 362–5; *Chronique d'Égypte* 13–14 (1932), 285–7; and, adapted to Greek epigraphy, Woodhead, *Study of Greek Inscriptions*, pp. 6–11. However, Leiden is not such a 'unified system of editing' inscriptions as Thompson implies; there is a good deal of room for personal idiosyncracy.

texts elsewhere will apply to the runic. Not all, however. For instance, the Leiden system allows for the expansion of abbreviations, added letters being enclosed within round brackets ( ). Classical inscriptions, and, as for that, Christian Latin texts in roman characters from the Anglo-Saxon period, need this convention, but I can think of no Anglo-Saxon runic text that uses a clear abbreviation system. For English runes the convention is unnecessary, and these useful brackets can be reserved for some other function.[41] The Leiden system of using a dot to represent a lost letter is, as I have shown, confusing for inscriptions that use the dot as an occasional word divider. Clearly the Leiden system needs some adaptation before it can be applied to Anglo-Saxon runes.

English runic texts need the following conventions:

1. For damaged runes which nevertheless can be certainly identified. In the Leiden system this is shown by a dot beneath the transcription symbol, but I have given reasons for objecting to this practice. I see no objection to Dickins's convention here of representing a damaged rune in italic (underlined in typescript).[42]

2. For a completely lost rune that can be supplied with certainty, either from the context (though given the vagaries of the Anglo-Saxon spelling system and our ignorance of many dialectal details, this will rarely be possible) or from reliable early drawings of the inscription. 'Ann Arbor' and Dickins put such reconstructions within square brackets, Dickins further italicizing the letter(s) supplied. I follow Dickins here.[43]

3. For a damaged rune whose position is certain, but where the remaining fragments are ambiguous and the context cannot guarantee identification. 'Ann Arbor' puts a dot for such a rune, but this will not work for English runic inscriptions. Dickins experimented, ultimately using the small open point within square brackets. The objection to this is typographical – the typewriter does not have the symbol, which also confuses the typesetter who finds it hard to distinguish from the point. I suggest here a point between square brackets, following on from 2 above.

4. For lost runes where it is impossible to say exactly how many are missing. Leiden uses square brackets here, a sensible convention to follow.] can be used alone for the loss of the beginning of an inscription, and [alone for the loss of the end;[44] for

---

[41] There are, of course, abbreviated forms in runic inscriptions, as **mkmrlawrta** (? *mik Mērila worta*) on the Etelhem brooch (Krause and Jankuhn, *Runeninschriften im älteren Futhark*, pp. 39–40), but no consistent way of indicating abbreviations.

[42] An objection raised at the Ann Arbor symposium but wisely suppressed in the discussion report is that it is confusing to represent both damaged letters and normalizations in italic. The two are, of course, easily distinguishable since representations of runes are in single quotes, normalizations not. I take it that in, say, Greek epigraphy it is not always feasible to employ a distinctive type-face for damaged letters, since not all printers have, for Greek, contrasting types like roman and italic.

[43] Dickins is more liberal in his use of the italic between square brackets. He uses the convention for 'lost characters which can reasonably be inferred' ('System of Transliteration', p. 19).

[44] The single inverted commas are useful here; otherwise it might be difficult to use [at the end of a sentence – the punctuation of the sentence might mislead the reader. A. G. Woodhead comments, in a private communication, that epigraphists should not 'leave square brackets unclosed . . . for the line

an indeterminate number of runes missing within a text, [ ]. There may be a refinement if it is possible to calculate roughly the number of characters lost: this number can be put within the brackets, as [-5-].[45] There may be cases where convention 4 should be combined with 3 above; for example, the Great Urswick ii text which Dickins gave as 'lylþi | swo . . .'. In fact the last fragmentary rune is uncertain: it is either 'o' or 'a', but too little of the lower arm remains to show which. Presumably Dickins read 'o' because of the common verbal form *worhte*. However, we know practically nothing about the Old English dialect of north Lancashire/ Cumbria, and the Mortain Casket has the (?) Anglian verb 'gewarahtæ'. Possibly, therefore, the Great Urswick fragment ended 'a'. Since this damaged rune had a clear place on the stone, it should be rendered '[.]'; it is followed by an unknown loss, '['. I would therefore transcribe Great Urswick ii 'lylþi | sw[. '.

5. A letter added by the editor because the rune-master either (a) omitted it in error, or (b) put in the wrong rune. Leiden has the convention of angled brackets, < >, here, and it is reasonable to follow this well established tradition. This sort of emendation will be rare in Old English runic texts since we know too little about them to dare emend freely. A clear example is on the Overchurch stone, where the preposition 'f o t e' must surely be 'f o <r> e'. Surprisingly Dickins makes a silent emendation at this point.

6. It may be desirable to have a convention to show when a rune-master put in a superfluous character: the Leiden hooked brackets, { }, would suit here. The only case I can think of – and we cannot be sure even of that – is again on the Overchurch stone whose first word should perhaps read 'f o l c {æ}'.[46]

7. I would also suggest a convention to show where a rune-master supplied a letter he had previously omitted in error. Here it might be convenient (and not confusing) to use the round brackets ( ) which are still available. A clear case is the Hartlepool II stone where the name form reads 'h i l d ‖ d i (g) y þ'.

8. Lineation. It is important to report how a monument divides its text into individual lines. For runic, as in Leiden, two methods can be used:

(i) The original lineation can be reproduced in the transcription. If this is done, the single inverted commas that indicate runes can be omitted from the transcript, since it is clearly runic. Using this system, the Thornhill III stone text reads:

> +*j* i l s u (i) þ : a r æ r d e : æ f t [.]
> b e r h t s u i þ e . b e k u n

came to an end *somewhere*'. However, there might be a case for a significant distinction here: closing the brackets where the inscribed surface survives though the inscription is lost, and leaving them open where the inscribed surface is broken away.

[45] Here is a case where Leiden does not produce a unified system. Some epigraphists will use [-ᶜ.⁵.-] where others use [-5-].

[46] Dickins's treatment of this inscription ('System of Transliteration', p. 19) is curious. Though he silently emends 'fote', he notes this anomalous 'æ' in a footnote. Whether 'folcæ' is anomalous or not is uncertain: see above, p. 91.

o n b e r g i g e b i d͡d a þ
þ æ r : s a u l e

It has the disadvantage of wasting space and making the general content of the inscription less accessible. Its advantage is to show at a glance how the text is laid out, and the general shape of the monument. Both qualities would be manifest if the main texts of the Ruthwell Cross were transcribed in this way. Those of the west face, for instance, would begin:

+ k r i s t w æ s o n	
[m] i	r o
þ s	d i
t r e	h w
[ʃ] u	e þ
m g	r æ
i w	þ e
u n	r f
d a d	u s [.]

This is certainly useful in showing how inefficiently the runes are set out on the cross and how hard it must always have been to understand the texts.[47] It is unhelpful to the reader interested in the material or the language of the inscriptions.

(ii) A more convenient method is to write out the text continuously, each line end indicated by a vertical stroke. By this method these Ruthwell Cross lines would appear: '+ k r i s t w æ s o n | r o | d i | h w | e þ | r æ | þ e | r f | u s [.] |' and '[m] i | þ s | t r e | [ʃ] u | m g | i w | u n | d a d |', which is marginally easier to follow.

9. The British Academy's corpus of Anglo-Saxon stone sculpture introduces a further convention which could be useful for runic inscriptions. Where an inscription is divided by, say, a band of ornamental carving, or a structural feature, the division is shown by the double vertical stroke ‖. Leiden uses this symbol to mark the beginning of each fifth line of an inscription, but that is unnecessary for English runes where the texts are seldom that long. An example of the convention in runic use is Hartlepool I, 'h i l d i ‖ þ r y þ', where the shaft of the incised cross divides the name significantly into its two elements. Another example is the mysterious legend on the Thames silver mount. This reads '] ‖ s b e͡ r æ d h t ɨ b c a i ‖ e͡ r h͡ a d͡ æ b s'. The runes were split into groups by the rivets that held the mount to whatever it was fitted to. Whether the division into groups of characters has any significance or not I do not know, since

---

[47] This lay-out helps to justify my suspicion that these runes, so clumsily arranged, are a later addition to the cross, not part of its original plan. However, U. Schwab has pointed to foreign models for this lay-out ('Das Traumgesicht vom Kreuzesbaum', *Philologische Studien: Gedenkschrift für Richard Kienast*, ed. U. Schwab and E. Stutz (Heidelberg, 1978), pp. 131–92, at 161).

Pro	amp	hed	his	out	ien	ein	eei	sag
fes	tel	oes	way	tex	t,b	ter	fot	ree
sor	lsm	not	ofs	tsi	uti	est	her	wit
R.J	eth	thi	ett	nef	twi	ing	rea	hhe
.Cr	ats	nkt	ing	fic	llb	tos	der	r.

I do not know the meaning of this inscription. But the transcript gives the reader the opportunity to consider the possibility.

10. I have found it useful to have a symbol for a character whose form can be clearly seen, but whose signification is unknown. These mysterious characters appear from time to time in runic texts (Leiden does not seem to find them), and it is convenient to represent them by an asterisk: thus, the Chessell Down scabbard mount has the text 'æ c o : * œ r i'. The asterisk warns the student that there is something amiss; he should return to the object, or to photographs or drawings, to find out what it is.

1	2	3	4	5	6	7	8:		9	10	11	12	13	14	15	16:
f	u	þ	o	r	c	g	w:		h	n	i	j	÷	p	x	s :

17	18	19	20	21	22	23	24:		25	26	27	28	29	30	31.
t	b	e	m	l	ŋ	œ	d :		a	æ	y	ea	k	k̄	ḡ .

FIG. 4   Suggested modification of the Dickins system of transliteration (cf. fig. 1)

The Leiden system, adapted as it is to Classical epigraphy, has a few more conventions which are probably too sophisticated for Anglo-Saxon purposes. To take two cases. Leiden envisages a more elegant lay-out of legend than the Anglo-Saxons achieved or even attempted; so it provides a convention to show when part of a line is left vacant. Many of the Anglo-Saxon inscriptions are execrably set out on their objects, so it would be hard to know how to use such a convention for them, or even to know if it were worth while.[48] The Great Urswick i text overran the panel that was cut to hold it, and had to be finished off in the spaces left by the sculpture beneath it. The Hartlepool II stone has its personal name divided in two by the shaft of the incised cross, but the halves are not symmetrically placed. The Kirkheaton stone has an inscription casually divided into two grossly unequal parts. Again, I suspect that Classical Greek inscriptions use a more secure set of spelling conventions, or at least provide a much larger body of linguistic material to base an opinion about spelling on. This means that for them conjectural restoration or emendation is more securely based. English runic inscriptions, perhaps inevitably, will be transcribed with less detail and precision, and the scholar will have to go back the more readily to the original. There are, of course, some English examples where no transcription will be satisfactory. An example is the Hackness stone with its variety of scripts and its cryptic texts. Another is the Dover brooch where it is hard to tell which way up to hold the inscriptions and in which direction to read them. A third is the Ash/Gilton

---

48 E. Okasha writes, in a private communication, 'In [Anglo-Saxon] non-runic texts, deliberate spaces are not infrequent and I like these to be marked'.

sword pommel where there are uncertainties about which are runes and which arbitrary marks in the metal surface. For these the student needs photographs and careful drawings. In more conventional cases I have no doubt it would be salutary – despite Thompson's demurrer here – to print the inscription in runic symbols as well as in transcription, though there will be practical and financial objections. But it would help the scholar to think in runic terms rather than in roman, and might save him from false argument.

Lastly there are two adjuncts to transliteration over which there need be little disagreement. Thompson asks (a) that linguistic normalizations of runic inscriptions be put in italics, and (b) that translations of them be set between double inverted commas. Of course, (a) is a requirement more suited to Norse than English needs, for there is a fairly standard system of writing Old Norse (usually Icelandic) which looks little like a runic transcript with its bizarre spelling, the result of the inadequacy of the sixteen-letter *fuþark*. Save for the specialist, **kurmR:kunukR** needs to be converted to *Gormr kunungr*, and **þurlibr:nhaki** to *Þorleifr hnakki*.[49] With Old English this hardly applies, perhaps because there is no standard to convert the runic spelling to. However, a normalization is sometimes useful, if only to mark proper names by capitals and divide a text into its individual words, and it is customary to put it in italics. Translations of English runic texts (as indeed of other Old English texts) I have hitherto put between single inverted commas. This worries Einar Haugen who complains that it is confusing to use 'single quotation marks to indicate both transcriptions and translations'.[50] Apparently he cannot readily distinguish between the Ruthwell cross transcript 'k r i s *t* w æ s o n | r o | d i' and its modern equivalent 'Christ was on the cross'. To save him embarrassment I am happy to begin putting translations between double inverted commas, though editors of learned journals may object that this conflicts with their conventions.

FURTHER PROBLEMS

Thompson has stressed that a system of transliteration can only be an elementary guide. Its required qualities are accuracy, consistency and simplicity. I think the Dickins system, as I have emended it, has these qualities, though of course individual scholars may interpret differently the conventions affecting damaged or lost letters. In my opinion it is an advantage to distance the English runic texts from those of Scandinavia, as does the Dickins use of roman letters within single quotes. Yet I must admit a major difficulty in using Dickins. It requires the runologist to identify a text as Old English and this cannot always be done. Obviously one cannot assume that every runic text found in England is Anglo-Saxon – there are several Norse runic monuments in the country.[51] Nor are all runic texts in English necessarily in Old

[49] K. M. Nielsen, 'Jelling Problems: a Discussion', *Medieval Scandinavia* 7 (1974), 156–79, at 156; Olsen, 'Runic Inscriptions in Great Britain', p. 193.
[50] Discussion after Thompson, 'On Transcribing Runic Inscriptions', *Michigan Germanic Stud.* 7 (1981), p. 96.
[51] See 'How Long Did the Scandinavian Language Survive in England? The Epigraphical Evidence', above pp. 181–95.

English – the Bridekirk font with its Norse runes and its (?) early Middle English inscription warns us otherwise.

On the other hand, if a runic text is found in England and includes distinctive Anglo-Frisian runes, it is natural to accept it as Anglo-Saxon. For instance, the newly-found Undley, Suffolk, bracteate has the retrograde legend 'g͡ æ g͡ o g͡ æ . m æg æ . m e d u': 'g͡ o' shows the Anglo-Frisian 'o'. This is presumably English even though the art historian links the bracteate design firmly to Denmark/Schleswig-Holstein. I would regard the find-spot as decisive here.[52] What, however, does the runologist do with the Caistor-by-Norwich inscription? In my transcript this reads 'r æ i̇ h æ n', though a Norse runologist might give it as **raihan**. The provenance is English but the context is more ambiguous since archaeologists have suggested links between the Caistor-by-Norwich cemetery and South Jutland/Fyn, while the inscription's *h*-rune shows the single-barred form typical of North Germanic. If in fact the inscription is North Germanic, it follows that any transcription which gives the fronted vowel, as 'r æ i̇ h æ n', is misleading. Hence a Dickins-type transliteration should not be given, even for this find from an Anglo-Saxon cemetery. More problematic still is a famous solidus, a copy of one of Honorius, with a runic inscription usually rendered *skanomodu* ('s c a n œ m œ d u' in my present system). The piece is unprovenanced, first recorded in the collection of George III. The most recent survey of Anglo-Saxon gold coins regards it as English, though there is a slight philological preference for Frisia.[53] On numismatic grounds it is placed in the last quarter of the sixth century. A difficulty is the significance of the rune 'œ' (*oeþil*). By virtue of its name this should represent *o. . .i*, yet on the runic solidus it appears as *o* not susceptible to *i*-mutation. Since the inscription uses the Anglo-Frisian 'a', it should also have 'o' (*os*). That it does not implies that, at this date, 'o' and 'œ' had not been conventionally distinguished. In contrast, the Chessell Down scabbard mount, which S. C. Hawkes dates to the mid sixth century,[54] shows conventional distinction in its inscription 'æ c o : * œ r i'.

Prehistoric sound-changes are, by definition, impossible to date,[55] nor is it feasible to say precisely when, in a transitional period, a rune developed a new form or a new

---

[52] B. Odenstedt comes to a different conclusion, *The Inscription on the Undley Bracteate and the Beginnings of English Runic Writing* (Umeå, 1983), p. 19. He argues that the bracteate must, on archaeological grounds, be attributed to southern Denmark or Schleswig-Holstein, and that the evidence for this is so strong that it outweighs both the presence of the Anglo-Frisian rune form 'o' and the provenance. I disagree, but I have not yet seen the full report of John Hines, on which Odenstedt relies.

[53] I. Stewart, 'Anglo-Saxon Gold Coins', *Scripta nummaria romana: Essays Presented to Humphrey Sutherland*, ed. R. A. G. Carson and C. M. Kraay (London, 1978), pp. 143–72, at 154; Page, 'The Runic Solidus of Schweindorf, Ostfriesland, and Related Runic Solidi', above p. 160.

[54] S. C. Hawkes and R. I. Page, 'Swords and Runes in South-East England', (1967), p. 17.

[55] This does not stop philologists from dating them. For instance, Luick, *Historische Grammatik*, § 291, admitting 'eine gewisse Unsicherheit', puts the first stages of the development of **ans-* to *ãs/ōs* at '1. Jahrh. vor und 1. Jahrh. nach Christi Geburt', and *i*-mutation at '6. Jahrh., wahrscheinlich erste Hälfte'. H. T. J. Miedema studied the relationship between some of these sound-changes and the Anglo-Frisian runic system, coming up with quite different dates, in 'Dialect en Runen van Britsum en de oudste Anglofriese Runeninscripties', *Taal en Tongval* 26 (1974), 101–28.

value. The distinctive Anglo-Saxon runic developments are the effect of sound-changes spread over several centuries, so there could have been no sudden change from Germanic to English runic systems. Consequently there will always be a problem about how to transliterate early or transitional runic inscriptions: a single system will not suffice to represent accurately both early and late texts. It might be more convenient, faced with the legend of the Honorius solidus, to transcribe it **skanomodu**, stressing thereby that the rune *oeþil* had its early value of *o*. Such a transliteration would underline the difference between this piece and, say, the later Anglo-Saxon rune-stones (whose legends would be transliterated in a Dickins-style system), and might predispose the reader to think the solidus was non-English. The differences of the system imply a difference of runic traditions, which may not be true. I confess I do not know the solution to this dilemma. For my part I prefer – and it is only a personal preference – to signal the distinctive tradition of the later English runes by a distinctive transliteration system, rather than to stress the common nature of the later English and non-English runes by using a common bold-face for both. Difficulties remain. From Southampton comes an inscribed bone, with no associated finds that would help precise dating. The text is clear to read, and I have transcribed it 'c a t æ', suggesting that it may be a personal name or nickname.[56] In a private communication Professor D. Hofmann has given an alternative suggestion that looks convincing, although it leaves some philological points to be disposed of. Southampton was a trading port with contacts with Frisia. One of the runes on the bone, the *a*-rune, might show a minor variant form diagnostic of Frisian. In early Frisian written texts appears the word *kāte* in a not very clear context but apparently with the meaning *Fingerknochen*.[57] Since the Southampton bone is the proximal phalange of an ox or cow, it could perhaps be called a *Fingerknochen*. Hofmann therefore suggests that the Southampton inscription could be a Frisian one. A casual visitor simply cut on the bone the word for what it was. In that case we should, I suppose, transcribe the text **katæ**. A Dickins-style transcription might be misleading in such a case.

A further problem is that the use of the two different transcription systems disguises similarities between English and non-English texts. One example is the Welbeck Hill bracteate legend, perhaps from the later sixth century. Its runes, set radially and retrograde, are 'l æ w'. I have suggested that this is a copy made, without understanding, of the well-known bracteate text **laþu**.[58] A copyist could easily have confused 'w' (*wynn*) and 'þ' (*thorn/thurs*). The similarity between 'l æ w' and **laþu** is, however, disguised by the different symbols, 'æ' and **a**, in the two transcripts. This is inevitable since any system suitable for English runes has to admit the fronting of *a* to *œ/e*; but the use of contrasting type-faces does not help. Another case is that of

---

56 Page, *Introduction*, pp. 170–1.
57 On this word see J. and W. Grimm, *Deutsches Wörterbuch* (Leipzig, 1854–1954), under *köte, kote*, and E. Verwijs and J. Verdam, *Middelnederlandsch Woordenboek* (The Hague, 1885–1941), under *cote, kote*. [Hofmann's suggestion was, in fact, published: 'Eine friesische Runeninschrift in England', *Us Wurk* 25 (1976), 73–6.]
58 Page, *Introduction*, p. 183.

the newly-found runes on a Byzantine pail from the Chessell Down cemetery.[59] The inscription is partly eroded but the ending is clear, '] e c c c æ æ æ': indeed, from what remains two e-runes could have preceded this, giving 'e c æ' in triplicate. The c-rune is not quite the usual form, but matches that of the Chessell Down scabbard mount, so it may be a local variant. The tripling of the letters shows that this is not a plain language text. A group of Scandinavian pieces, amulets, bracteates, stones, has texts containing the sequence **eka/ika** which may have magical implications.[60] It is natural to compare the roughly contemporary Chessell Down II text with these, but again the differences in transcription systems, 'e c æ'/**eka**, conceal what may be a significant similarity.

Yet another objection to the use of a distinctive system for English runes has been put to me by Professor R. Derolez, in a private communication. He argues for contacts between rune-masters east and west of the North Sea after the Anglo-Saxon settlement, and fears that 'the distinction would only serve to project back the modern idea of national (political and linguistic) unity to a period where it just did not exist'. The objection is a cogent one and the only reply to it is pragmatic. Are there not equal, indeed I suggest greater, dangers in using the same system for English and non-English? There can be no completely satisfactory answer, and I present this modified version of the Dickins system only as one that will usefully serve the later Old English runic texts with their distinctive characteristics and their particular importance for early dialectal history in England. The problem raises again the point that Thompson dismissed so cursorily, whether it is helpful to print an inscription in normalized runic type as well as in transcript. In the cases I have adduced, there are good reasons for it. Such normalized types could include the coarse variants, the mirror image 's', 'n' and 'i' forms, the variant 's' of St Cuthbert's coffin and the Thames scramasax. Whether it should include the finer variants like the Chessell Down c-rune (also found on the Honorius solidus) or the Thames scramasax 'y' (also recorded in a graffito in the Leningrad Gospels) is less sure. For single variants – which may be rune-master's errors – the reader needs a photograph and drawing.

Finally, are there any more conventions to be added to the system, bearing in mind Thompson's caution that it should 'not become overly complicated by trying to indicate too much'? I can think of two, though I do not know if they are really desirable, or if they add unnecessary complication to the transliteration system:

(1) the direction of writing. In English texts this is overwhelmingly left to right, but there are reversed legends, particularly on coins. It might be worth signalling, as Leiden does by an arrow, when a complete line is retrograde: as in the *sceat* legend ←'e p a'. Parallel is the case of inverted runes, rare but sometimes found. A similar arrow ↑ could indicate a completely inverted line, though this convention could cause

[59] C. J. Arnold, *The Anglo-Saxon Cemeteries of the Isle of Wight* (London, 1982), pp. 27, 60 and fig. 10.

[60] As on the Danish Lindholm amulet and Sjælland 2 bracteate (Jacobsen and Moltke, *Danmarks runeindskrifter*, cols 315–17 and 535–6); Noleby, Sweden, stone (Musset and Mossé, *Introduction*, pp. 361–2); and elsewhere (Krause and Jankuhn, *Runeninschriften im älteren Futhark*, pp. 210 and 215).

complications in, for instance, one of the *Æþiliræd* coin types[61] whose legend is in two lines, each retrograde but the second one also inverted.

(2) an alteration or correction on the stone or other object. This happens occasionally, a very clear example being on the Ruthwell cross where the 'œ' of the sequence 'l i m w | œ r i g | n æ' was first cut as 'g' and then emended, presumably by the original carver. For this the Leiden double square bracket [[ ]] (which in Greek epigraphy denotes letters intentionally erased) could be adapted to alert the reader to the correction: 'l i m w | [[œ]] r i g | n æ'. There may not be enough examples to make this worth providing for, but future finds might change the situation.

There remain some untidinesses in the system. For instance, the use of the superscript to distinguish 'k̄', 'ḡ' from 'k', 'g' strikes me as clumsy, and perhaps an improvement might be devised. However, there are difficulties in this particular rune range, partly in consequence of the difficulties Anglo-Saxon rune-masters themselves found in representing the various reflexes of PrOE *k, g* and *ȝ*. For convenience it is as well to retain the well-known Dickins graphs here.

I present this paper as a contribution to the discussion of the problems of transliterating English runes, not as a solution to them. The example of Leiden should be kept in mind. Though Thompson sets it out as a single, agreed system of transliteration, in fact it is not that: it is adapted to different purposes, and there is some element of personal interpretation in the way it is used. Moreover, it is worth remembering that the Leiden system is not thought suitable for rendering all early Greek epigraphical texts. To take a special case, those of the Cypro-Minoan syllabaries need a completely different system, one that is in some ways closer to those used for runes, since the original characters are transliterated into roman or italic forms of the Latin alphabet.[62] I see no reason why there should not also be different systems in use for the wide range of scripts that we call by the one term 'runic'. On the other hand it is certainly desirable that Anglo-Saxon runes have some consistent principle of transliteration. This article points out the problems: I hope it goes some way towards solving them.

I have several times implied – and I end by making the point explicit – that a system of transliteration is to be used with discretion. Different degrees of rigour are appropriate to different purposes. The epigrapher presenting a corpus of inscriptions must be rigorous, but the Anglo-Saxonist who wants to refer in passing to a runic spelling may be less so. An obvious example affects the matter of lineation. For a corpus of inscriptions it would be desirable to lay out the text of the Ruthwell cross

---

61 Page, *Introduction*, p. 126.
62 O. Masson, *Les inscriptions chypriotes syllabiques: recueil critique et commenté* (Paris, 1961), p. 91. That system of transcription is liable to infuriate the runologist, for it uses italic for undamaged letters and roman for damaged ones. Greek characters are available for normalization. Runologists might benefit from the experience of students of these syllabaries, as, for instance, in the matter of variant rune forms which occasionally crop up. Cypro-Minoan scholars have devised a system of numbering graph forms, the common ones in arabic figures, archaic ones in roman. In this way, individual graphs can be referred to by number: see E. Masson, *Cyprominoica: répertoires, documents de Ras Shamra, essais d'interprétation* (Gothenburg, 1974), pp. 11–17.

Dream of the Rood in short lines, as the rune-master did. For referring to a possible early locative form on Ruthwell a writer might be content with 'on rodi' or at the strictest 'on|ro|di' if he wanted to stress it was a runic spelling he was quoting; otherwise he might put *on rodi*. Again, in the matter of corrections, the epigrapher presenting the text formally in a corpus would presumably give it, error and all – thus the second line of the Overchurch stone would read '] *b* i d d a þ f o t e æ þ e l m u *n* ['. Later in his discussion he might prefer to emend and perhaps to divide it into individual words, '] *b* i d d a þ   f o <r> e   æ þ e l m u *n* [', particularly if he wanted to compare this rune-stone's *(ge)biddan* formula with those of other memorials. Such freedom would not be misleading within its context, since the brackets would warn a forgetful reader what the editor was up to. In this paper I have tried to define a precise system of transliteration which can be used with some flexibility. In the last instance any system of transliteration falls down if it is too complex for the printer. Only experience will show whether the average British printer can cope with this one. The appendix shows the system in operation, with varying degrees of rigour.

APPENDIX: SPECIMENS OF RUNIC TRANSLITERATION

1. Auzon (Franks) Casket, left side:
'r o m w a l u s *a n d r e u m w a l u s t w æ g e n* ‖ *g i b r o þ æ r* ‖ a f œ d d æ h i æ w y l i f i n r o m æ c æ s t r i : ‖ *o þ l œ u n n e g*', *Romwalus and Reumwalus, twægen gibroþær, afœddœ hiœ wylif in Romœcœstri, oplœ unneg,* "Romulus and Remus, two brothers, a she-wolf nourished them in Rome, far from (their) native land".

2. Auzon (Franks) Casket, front:
'f i s c . f l o d u . ‖ a h o f o n f e r g ‖ e n b e r i g ‖ ← w a r þ g a : s r i c g r o r n þ æ r h e o n g r e u t g i s w o m ‖ → h r o n æ s b a n', *fisc flodu ahof on fergenberig; warþ gasric grorn þær he on greut giswom: hronœs ban,* "The fish beat up the sea(s) on to the mountainous cliff. The king of (?) terror became sad when he swam on to the shingle. Whale's bone".[63]

3. Bramham Moor/Harewood/Sherburn-in-Elmet amulet ring:
'æ r k r i u f l t | k r i u r i þ o n | g l æ s t æ p o n̂ t o l'

4. Chester-le-Street stone:
E A D m | V n D

5. Dover stone:
'+ *j* i s l h ea r d :', *Gislheard,* masculine personal name.

---

[63] Here the transcription, normalization and translation hide a number of problems: whether in the transcript the points should be given, since they may be (and in one case certainly are) only space-fillers; whether the normalization should present the text as two lines of alliterative verse, and what is the function of the additional phrase, *hronœs ban*; what is the meaning of such compounds as *fergenberig, gasric,* and how should the first sentence be parsed.

6. Kirkheaton stone:
'e o h : w o r o | h t æ'

7. Llysfaen ring:
+ A | L H | S T | A n |

8. Mortain Casket:
    + g o o d h e l p e : æ a d a n
    þ i i o s n e c i i s m e e l g e w a r
    a h t æ[64]

    + *Good helpe Æadan þiiosne ciismeel gewarahtæ*, "+ God help Æada (who) made this (?) reliquary".

9. Mote of Mark bone:
'] a þ i l i' or '] a þ i l i ['

10. Overchurch stone:
    f o l c {æ} a r æ r d o n b e c [
    ] *b* i d d a þ f o <ꞃ> e æ þ e l m u *n* [

11. Ruthwell Cross, part of east face:
'[+ . *n d*] g e r e | d æ | h i | n æ | ḡo | d a | l m | e ɨ | t t i | g þ | a *h* | e w | a l | d e | o n
| ḡa | l g | u g | i s t | i ḡa | *m o d* | i g f | [*o r e*] | [-3-] | m e n | [*b u g*] | ['
+ *Andgerede hinæ God Almehttig þa he walde on galgu gistiga, modig fore . . . men, bug. . .*, "Almighty God bared his body as he prepared to climb the gallows, valiant in men's sight . . . bow . . .".[65]

12. Thames scramasax:
i. 'f u þ o r c g w h n i j ɨ p x (s) t b e ŋ d l m œ a æ y ea'
ii. 'b ea g n o þ'

13. Thornhill II stone:
    + ea d r e d
    * s e t e æ f t e
    ea t e ɨ n n e

---

[64] Here there is a decision to be made about the lay-out. The Mortain text is divided up by raised bands in the metal surface. Should they be represented in the transliteration? If so, the text should read:

    + g o o d h ‖ e ‖ l p e : æ a d a n
    þ i i o s n e c i i s ‖ m ‖ e e l g e w a r
    a h t æ

The bands do not divide the text into significant groups. On the other hand, putting them in the transcript stresses how unsymmetrically the inscription is cut.

[65] It is difficult to know how to normalize this text. How much should the editor change the lettering of the original to produce a text that looks like the Old English that scholars are used to? I have normalized 'a l m e ɨ t t i g' to *Almehttig*, but should I have put *Almehtig*? The double 't' is curious. On the general question of double runes in English inscriptions, see Page, 'The Use of Double Runes', particularly for the present case pp. 101–2 (above).

14. Whitby comb:

'd̑ [æ] u s m̑ æ u s ‖ g o d a l u w a l u ‖ d̑ o h e l i p æ c y ‖ [',

  Deus meus, God Aluwaludo helipæ Cy. . ., "My God, may God Almighty help Cy. . .".

ACKNOWLEDGEMENTS

I am grateful to a number of scholars who read this paper in first draft and commented upon it: Professor R. N. Bailey, Professor R. J. Cramp, Professor R. Derolez, Professor C. E. Fell, Dr M. Lapidge, Dr E. Okasha and Mr A. G. Woodhead. I have found their comments useful and stimulating, even if I have not always agreed with them.

POSTSCRIPT

As this paper makes clear, it is a pragmatic rather than a philosophical one, its purpose to define a workable and efficient system for use with English runes. The British Academy's *Corpus of Anglo-Saxon Stone Sculpture in England* has begun to appear, and readers of it may wish to check how precisely its volumes use this or a related system of transliteration.

My paper is already a little outdated as its occasional reference to 'the type-setter' reveals. The rapid development of computer-based type-setting has allowed writers to have a more direct control than before over materials published in their names. As against this there is the undoubted fact that as yet not all word processing systems in general use have access to the range of graphs needed for such a specialised purpose. In so far as a writer still depends on an intermediary to create camera-ready copy, my system runs into difficulties. It is hard to convince an operator that a slur over two letters does not instruct him to run them close together; all I want him to do is reproduce my slur that indicates a bind-rune. Similarly if I put an arrow before a text, this does not mean that I want that text shifted over in the arrow's direction. Operators are so used to following semiotic commands that they find it hard to reproduce what they see rather than follow what they interpret as their instructions. Spacing the letters of an inscription creates, as I anticipated, infelicities in these days of electronic line justification. The machine cannot distinguish between a space between words and a space between a pair of letters; and a text line may well end in the middle of a continuous inscription. These are irritations rather than major difficulties.

A fairly lengthy critique of the system defined here is included in Bengt Odenstedt's monograph, *On the Origin and Early History of the Runic Script: Typology and Graphic Variation in the Older Futhark* (Uppsala, 1990), pp. 140–2. His most important objection, it seems to me, is that a system designed specifically for Anglo-Saxon runes 'obscures the fact that the English runic script represents an unbroken tradition from its origin in Scandinavia, and that . . . it differs only in fairly trivial details from Scandinavian and continental inscriptions in the older *futhark*'. The origin of runes in Scandinavia is of course a theory rather than a fact, even though it is a plausible theory. Whether the English runic tradition is 'unbroken' is a matter of definition and also of perception. My point that at an early date the English tradition (unlike the Scandinavian and possibly unlike the Continental) became contaminated by Latin spelling and epigraphical practices remains. Using single inverted commas to enclose a transliterated text worries Odenstedt as it worried Haugen. They are, he says, 'traditionally . . . reserved for indications of *meaning*'. Which suggests that Odenstedt has little experience of the vagaries of editors of periodicals whose practices in the matter of quote marks show a generous diversity. There could, I suppose, arise ambiguities from the use of single quotes for more than one purpose (particularly for readers of somewhat stunted intelligence), though in my system it should only occur in quoting single runes since a text of more than one rune would be spaced.

My reasons for writing my article were based on problems experienced rather than on theoretical considerations: the real difficulties of using bold and the obvious reluctance of printers in the English tradition to apply it (Scandinavian printers more accustomed to runic transliterations may not share this reluctance); the need to make English runic texts more easily available to Anglo-Saxonists who are not runologists (so that, for instance, we may see fuller use of runic evidence by historical linguists); the desirability of signalling a distinct local tradition to runologists more familiar with Norse practices.

This last is something of a political point. Scandinavia has far more runic monuments than any other region, and only there has runology been recognised as a serious discipline; only there are there institutes committed exclusively to runic studies. It is inevitable that in the popular and even in the scholarly mind runes will be linked first to Scandinavia. Yet other areas have their runic monuments which may be only collaterally related to those of Norway, Denmark, Sweden and their colonies overseas. English runes have, to some degree, their own forms, practices, rules and applications, and there seems some point – and no great difficulty – in having a distinct system for transliterating them.

Finally with respect to Odenstedt's comments, a semantic observation: the implications of the word 'otherness' which, as I make clear, I borrowed from Claiborne W. Thompson, student of Swedish runes. Odenstedt comments, 'it is meaningful to talk about the "otherness" of English runes, but only if we recognise the "otherness" of continental runes and of late Scandinavian runes'. I confess that in talking of the 'otherness' of English runes, I thought I conceded the 'otherness' of other runic traditions. Else, as Charlie Brown nearly said, the epistemological implications alone are staggering.

A more serious because more assiduously worked out discussion of problems of transliterating English runes is that of Anne King.[66] Strictly speaking, it is Dickins's

---

[66] 'The Ruthwell Cross – a Linguistic Monument (Runes as Evidence for Old English)', *Folia Linguistica Historica* 7 (1986), 43–79.

system that comes in for her criticism but many of her points apply also to my adaptation of Dickins. King's concern is with 'gaining access to and presenting the linguistic evidence embodied in OE runic inscriptions, especially where this is phonological', and her 'transcription' is into the symbols of the International Phonetic Alphabet. She rejects the Dickins solution because of its 'unsatisfactory mix of different kinds of symbols'. She is unsure of Dickins's purpose in developing his system: 'are the symbols of his target script designed to convey only orthographical information . . . or are statements or suggestions also being offered about phonological values?' I cannot answer for Dickins though I think I know what his answer would have been and also how tersely he would have expressed it. My own opinion is clearly stated. I would prefer not to transliterate at all. I do it in the interests of accessibility – and that is not only to phonologists but to other students of Anglo-Saxon records too. There is no mystery about my intent – it is to make runic texts easier to read and print, easier to compare with non-runic; and as far back as 1962 (see above, pp. 87–92) I stressed the danger of treating a transliteration as an original. My system is a graph-to-graph one fulfilling Wellisch's definition that 'the graphemes of a source script are converted into graphemes of a target script', and in principle with his further proviso that this should be done 'without any regard to pronunciation'. On the other hand it seems sensible to produce forms which resemble those of written texts (King finds 'no good reason for such a practice' which suggests she is happy to restrict her readership to those who share her phonological interests: we older folk are vainer). After all, the purpose of transliteration is to make a text more rather than less accessible. To the extent that Anglo-Saxon scribal practice offers suggestions about phonological values, so does the Dickins-Page system of transliteration. (Incidentally many of King's objections would apply to the transcriptions modern editors make of the letter forms found in manuscripts; they – like many of the writers of the manuscripts themselves – use a perhaps unsatisfactory 'mix of different kinds of symbols' and by their use of certain letters offer suggestions about phonetic values.)

As becomes a younger scholar, King is bolder. By using IPA she makes statements rather than offering suggestions. She calls her method 'conversion' rather than 'transliteration', and abandons the one-for-one system, giving distinct equivalents for the palatal and velar allophones that in some runic inscriptions are both represented by the single graph *gyfu*. This is to allow interpretation to intrude into transliteration, and it restricts its usefulness. For runological work it then becomes necessary to reproduce the runes side by side with (or rather above) the transliterated forms, as indeed King does in the later part of her paper. While there is no objection to this in principle – indeed, as I say in my own paper, it may be desirable – it puts the scholar once again at the mercy of the printer handling unfamiliar forms. (The malicious reader, were there to be one, might gain a wicked delight in spotting the mistakes in the runic reproductions in King's article.) Here again modern word-processing technology may come to the aid of the struggling scholar.

The use of IPA leads to a further difficulty that King does not face. Her article transcribes a very restricted selection of runic texts. A wider range might have revealed the inadequacies of her 'system'. It would be interesting to know which two

IPA graphs are to represent the last two runes of Franks Casket 'f i s c'; or is the transcription ('conversion') to comprise one graph fewer than the original? Or, to put the question another way, what pronunciation would she reconstruct for the final consonant (? cluster) of this word? Again, which symbol is to be used to represent the final rune of the royal title 'r e x' (on some coins of Beonna of East Anglia), particularly in view of the alternative form REss, if indeed that is what it is; or rEis, if indeed that is what it is? And, mischievously, how will she convert the runes of the Thames and Brandon *fuþorcs* into IPA? Above all, what does the IPA make of the Christ title 'x p s' on the coffin of St Cuthbert?

The last example raises a clear point of principle. Not all Anglo-Saxon runic inscriptions are phonetically based. 'x p s' obviously derives from the scribal/learned/epigraphical/display form XPS of common Christian usage. Was it ever pronounced? And how, and where? This is not a solitary example, though it is a significant one. There are other Anglo-Saxon runic texts – Falstone is an obvious one – where we must suspect a background of non-runic epigraphy or at least orthography. A system of transliteration of runes must be applicable to a wide range of inscriptions if it is to be epigraphically and runologically (not just phonologically) useful. It follows that it must be descriptive rather than interpretative. King creates a system where evidence and interpretation are intermingled, an elementary error in a scientific discipline; and defends it by claiming that such a system as Dickins's, in its use of roman characters mingled with other graphs, also confuses evidence and interpretation. But it does this only in the minds of those who are confused – quite unnecessarily – about its purpose. The Dickins (Dickins-Page) system of transliteration is an attempt to produce an efficient, cheap, unambiguous and practical way of representing such runic graphs as are found in an inscription, indicating something of their layout and condition. No more than this. It is, as I said, presented as 'a contribution to the discussion of the problems of transliterating English runes, not as a solution to them'.

19

(1987)

NEW RUNIC FINDS IN ENGLAND

In a pair of publications some fifteen years ago I defined the Anglo-Saxon runic corpus as it was then known. Beginning in 1969 with the article 'Runes and Non-Runes',[1] I examined the corpus at that date, added to and subtracted from it. A few years later, in 1973, there came out the book *An Introduction to English Runes* which looked in some, though inadequate, detail at the corpus so established. There are, of course, errors and deficiencies in both works, for they were intended only to clear the way to a definitive corpus of English runes, a project that has been in hand, on and off, for many years. Since 1973 there have been new finds (and new studies of old finds), and these need to be taken into account.

Before dealing with these, I want to recapitulate a few details of and to make some comment on the published work hitherto. In particular I want to draw attention to some aspects of what I attempted years ago which may not be generally appreciated.

When I published my introductory survey I tried to provide distribution maps for the early and the late runic texts with clear provenances. It was a difficult, perhaps impossible, task since dating and provenance may be uncertain. Consequently the maps produced were crude ones and plotted only part of the English corpus.[2] The most convenient date for a boundary between early and late turned out to be *c.* 650, but I stress the word 'convenient'. Other division dates may have produced more striking results, but would have been harder to establish. In any case, the contrast between the geographical distributions of known pre-650 and known post-650 inscriptions was sharp. In the earlier map (fig. 1) I plotted ten objects that were certainly runic, and indicated five more that were possibly runic. None of them are rune-stones. The later map (fig. 2) showed over forty plots, the great majority rune-stones.

The earlier map gave two general areas of runic finds: the South and the East Midlands. There was a group in Kent and on the south coast/Isle of Wight – the so-called Jutish areas. Another scatter appeared in Lincolnshire, Nottinghamshire and East Anglia. The later map also showed inscriptions from the South and South-east (though not in general the East Midlands), but most of its inscriptions came from an area north of a line joining the Dee and the Wash, with clear local

---

[1]   Above, pp. 161–78.
[2]   *Introduction*, pp. 26–7.

FIG. 1   Pre-650 runic monuments (1973)

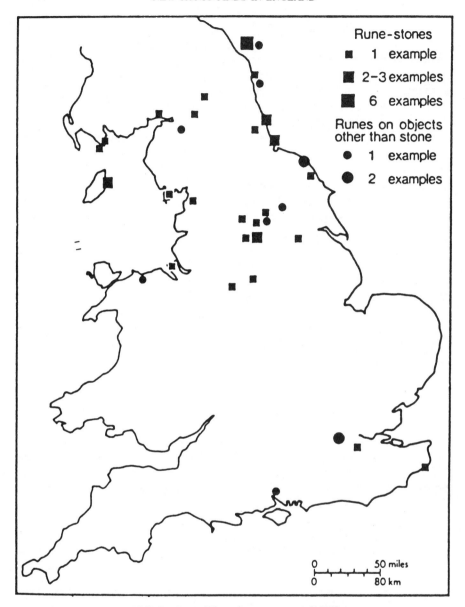

FIG. 2   Post-650 runic monuments (1973)

distributions in the West Riding of Yorkshire and along the north-east coast. Furthermore, some important inscribed objects which cannot be given an English provenance fit linguistically into the northern and later section of the distribution pattern. For instance, the Franks Casket turned up at Auzon, Haute-Loire, France, but scholars in general date it firmly to *c.* 700 and the language of its texts links it to Northumbria or North Mercia. The Mortain reliquary, from Normandy, seems from the language of its legend to be Anglian, and could well be eighth-century. If we include these, the later map shows not only a preponderance of inscriptions in the North and North Midlands, but, equally important, a preponderance of comprehensible and lengthy inscriptions in that area.[3] Compared to the flimsy texts from the South, the northern area can show the Ruthwell Cross inscriptions (some 320 runes), or, accepting its northern origin, those of the Franks Casket (over 260 runes). Compared with the baffling letter sequences of the (early) Dover brooch or the Chessell Down scabbard mount, the North has memorial stones like those of Hartlepool, Great Urswick, Thornhill and Lindisfarne whose texts can usually be read with some ease.[4]

The early inscriptions are mostly uninterpreted or uncertainly interpreted. This is partly because they are so short and because they are earlier than any substantial Old English texts, and so are likely to contain early forms and words that are hard to identify. But principally it is because we do not know the contexts of the inscriptions, what they might be expected to say and how they might say it. In contrast, the later, mainly northern, inscriptions are easier to interpret. Some are well-known personal names, while others are epitaphs in formulaic wording that presents little difficulty. This ease of access means that the later inscriptions are the more useful to philologists, particularly to the Old English scholars who are not expert runologists. Moreover, the splendour of some of the later monuments – the Ruthwell Cross, the Franks Casket, even the Bewcastle Cross despite its weatherbeaten state – has attracted the art historian and the archaeologist, and so they have become famous. It is not surprising, therefore, that the northern, later, texts are better known and more carefully studied than the earlier ones.[5] If my crude division of the English runic monuments into early and late did nothing more, at least it asserted the distinctive character and importance of the early inscriptions from the South and East, a distinction that tends to be hidden if runic monuments of all dates are plotted on the same map of Great Britain.

The find-histories of the earlier English runic texts add a further dimension. Two

[3] Further items may be added to these maps, not because they are new finds, but because their provenances become established. An example is the gold runic ring until recently only generally provenanced in Lancashire. B. J. N. Edwards ('An Anglo-Saxon Ring Provenance Narrowed', *Antiquaries Journal* 63 (1983), 132–4) now shows that this is probably a ring found in Manchester, so this adds a new plot to the later map.

[4] Details of inscriptions given no reference here will be found in Page, *Introduction*.

[5] For instance, A. Campbell (*Old English Grammar* (Oxford, 1959), pp. 357–8), listing important inscriptions, gives from Northumbria and Mercia some eighteen rune-stones as well as runic texts on other objects, but from the South only the late runes of the Thames scramasax and the Dover slab. H. Sweet (*A Second Anglo-Saxon Reader: Archaic and Dialectal*, 2nd ed. rev. T. F. Hoad (Oxford, 1978), pp. 102–4) includes a small number of texts from rune-stones, all northern, as well as the Franks Casket inscriptions.

278

of the southern ones were discovered early: the Ash/Gilton pommel and the Chessell Down scabbard mount. The Selsey gold fragments were found in the 1870s, published by George Stephens[6] and then mislaid; so they were largely unknown until I republished them in the 1960s after a hunt through the vaults of the British Museum.[7] The Sarre pommel was found in 1863/4, but its runes were not spotted until 1965. The Dover brooch turned up in 1962, when V. I. Evison's hawk-like eyes saw the faint runes at once. Of the objects that are uncertainly runic, the inlaid spearhead from Holborough, Kent, was first published in 1956, while only fairly recently has attention been drawn to rune-like symbols on objects from Faversham and, again, Gilton.

In the eastern region too the finds are predominantly recent. The Caistor-by-Norwich astragalus was first published in 1960, though it was unearthed a couple of decades earlier.[8] The Loveden Hill urns were dug up in 1955 and thereafter. The Welbeck Hill disc appeared in 1963, and the runes on the Willoughby-on-the-Wolds bowl and the Sleaford brooch were identified only recently. The symbols on the Hunstanton brooch – which may not be runes – were also noticed only in late years. Thus of the fifteen objects of the early map only two were generally known before 1955. The remapping of 1973, while not playing down the value of the northern English runes, yet emphasised the significance of the South and East in the early runic tradition of England. Those areas seemed more important in 1973 than they had done twenty years earlier.

The study of Anglo-Saxon coinage which has made such strides over the same decades, serves to develop this theme. Some of our most important inscriptions are runic coin legends, but it is doubtful if they can properly be plotted in the distribution maps. A single pair of coin dies may produce a number of coins of fairly scattered distribution, and it is at least arguable that it is the place where the dies were made and/or used that is significant, rather than where the coins are found in modern times. At the same time, if the mint-place is not named on the coin, we can only get some idea of where that mint was by studying where the coins turn up. Acting on this sort of evidence, numismatists have reattributed many of the Anglo-Saxon runic coins. The *sceattas* with the name 'p a d a' were long ascribed to Peada (or sometimes Penda) of Mercia on the basis of the name, since the coinage was assumed to be a royal one.[9] In 1960 S. E. Rigold restudied this group, and there and in subsequent and related papers he dated the 'p a d a' coins to the mid-seventh century, gave them a provenance in the south-east, in Kent, and asserted that Pada was a moneyer, not a king.[10] A similar, later, series of coins with the legend *Æthiliræd* in various spellings,

---

[6] *Old-Northern Runic Monuments* III, 463.

[7] S. C. Hawkes and R. I. Page, 'Swords and Runes in South-East England', (1967), p. 26.

[8] R. R. Clarke, *East Anglia* (London, 1960), pp. 137, 230 and pl. 43. An earlier notice, though hardly a publication, of the inscription had appeared in M. L. Samuels, 'The Study of Old English Phonology', *TPS* (1952), 15–47, at 36.

[9] For transliterating English runic texts I use the system defined in 'On the Transliteration of English Runes', above pp. 245–70.

[10] His original study of the *sceattas* was S. E. Rigold, 'The Two Primary Series of Sceattas', *BNJ* 30 (1960–1), 6–53, with addenda and corrigenda in *BNJ* 35 (1966), 1–6. He developed and adapted this

was once given to Æthelred of Mercia rather by analogy with Peada: these coins are now thought to be Kentish too. Coins with the name legends 'e p a' and its variants Rigold dated to 695–725, and showed that they had distributions in the South-east and southern East Anglia. An apparently small coinage, intermediate between *sceattas* and pennies, with forms of the name *Beonna/Benna* and the title *rex* in either runes or roman script, continues the East Anglian connection, for it has long been attributed to the little-known king Beanna/Beorna/Beorn(us) who flourished in East Anglia in the mid-eighth century. And finally, C. E. Blunt showed in 1961 that pennies of Offa of Mercia with runic legends were struck in East Anglian mints.[11] Thus the coins are seen to form a link between the early eastern English runes and the later ones of the North and North Midlands.

The danger of producing, as I did in 1973, a pair of geographical distribution maps is that new finds may soon make them out of date and even misleading. The danger of drawing conclusions from such maps is that new finds may wreck them. This paper records the new finds made since the 1973 corpus, and the impact they have on our thinking about runes in England.

Here it is convenient to continue with the runic coins, since this is a field where there have been striking results and some rethinking by the numismatists. Coins register well on metal-detecting equipment, and nowadays hoards are found with some ease. Urban excavation, as at Southampton and Ipswich, and at Continental sites such as Ribe, Denmark, has produced numbers of new *sceattas*, though most of them are non-runic. A simple example of a significant new find affects the *Æthiliræd* coinage. In 1973 I recorded nine examples of these coins, with three known provenances: Canterbury and Reculver, both in Kent, and Walcheren in the Netherlands. Hence the deduction that these *sceattas* were struck in Kent. We now have a tenth specimen, a die duplicate of the Reculver coin, found during excavation at Stone-by-Faversham, Kent, and so supplying a convenient confirmation of the theory.[12] Of the very common runic *sceattas*, the 'e p a' and 'æ p a' types, there are continuous new finds, and it is hard to keep up with them, though none of the new ones I have heard of have any special runological significance.[13] Most important, however, are developments in our knowledge of the eighth-century Beonna coinage. In my introduction I noted five examples, one using only roman characters in its legends. Since then, a large hoard at Middle Harling, Norfolk, and smaller finds from Barham, Pakenham and Burrow Hill, all in Suffolk, have increased the number of

work in 'The Principal Series of English Sceattas', *BNJ* 47 (1977), 21–30, together with S. E. Rigold and D. M. Metcalf, 'A Check-List of English Finds of Sceattas', *BNJ* 47 (1977), 31–52.
[11] C. E. Blunt, 'The Coinage of Offa', *Anglo-Saxon Coins: Studies Presented to F. M. Stenton . . .*, ed. R. H. M. Dolley (London, 1961), pp. 39–62, at 49–50.
[12] Lord Fletcher and G. W. Meates, 'The Ruined Church of Stone-by-Faversham: Second Report', *Antiquaries Journal* 57 (1977), 67–72, at 69. In contrast there is the embarrassing report of an *Æthiliræd* coin (which I have not seen) from Southampton: Rigold and Metcalf, 'Check-List', p. 48.
[13] The runic *sceattas*, however, need far more detailed treatment than I have space for here. New finds have certainly produced new runic legends, as one with a form of the name *Tilbert* from East or Middle Harling, Norfolk, recorded in *Annual Reports of the Syndicate and of the Friends of the Fitzwilliam* (Fitzwilliam Museum, Cambridge) for the year 1983, p. 23 and pl. X.

known specimens to about fifty.[14] In 1976 D. M. Metcalf claimed that Beonna's coins 'evidently belong to Suffolk, and presumably the Ipswich district';[15] it would be interesting to see if the attribution holds. In 1973 only one moneyer's name, *Efe*, was known. The newly-found examples show two more moneyers, Wilred and Werferth, who use runes for their names, differing here from Efe. There is also a new runic or pseudo-runic symbol to be seen on obverses of Wilred's coins, where the royal name, divided into two parts by pairs of crosses, reads '+ b e n + n a ⟨⟩'. All other known coins of Beonna have the royal name followed by a title, some spelling of *rex*, so it is natural to take ⟨⟩ as representing the title. It is perhaps formed from a conflation of 'r' and 'x', ᚱ + ⟨⟩. This symbol could have been invented to solve Wilred's problems of spacing and lay-out, for he needed six symbols divided by crosses into groups of three, and therefore had space only for one more character in addition to 'b e n n a'. Incidentally, Wilred also uses in his name a minor variant of the *d*-rune, ⟨⟩ instead of ᛗ.

In addition to these important discoveries of coins, there has been a good deal of rethinking of the early coinage of Anglo-Saxon England, some of it dependent upon metrology. There has been debate on the chronology of the issues, though in general this has sought only to refine the dating within the seventh and eighth centuries rather than do anything more radical. But it has important implications for royal administrative control over the coinage, and this could affect our discussion of the 'official' use of runes in the mid-seventh century.[16]

Perhaps more significant than the coins for the general history of English runic studies are nine new finds made in Great Britain since my 1973 introduction. For my present purpose I omit the important publication, by Professors Derolez and Schwab, of the English runes at Monte S. Angelo, Foggia, Italy.[17] I also omit here new manuscript runes, even those incised in manuscripts, as the part of the personal name cut on p. 128 of Corpus Christi College, Cambridge, MS 326: the runes read 'a þ i l f', presumably a name such as *Athilwulf* or *Athilferth*.[18]

Nine inscriptions may not seem very many, particularly to Scandinavian runologists, but it is to be remembered that the 1973 *Introduction* index lists only between sixty and seventy Anglo-Saxon runic monuments, together with a few more, uncer-

---

[14] Some of these coins are published in V. Fenwick, 'Insula de Burgh: Excavations at Burrow Hill, Butley, Suffolk 1978–1981', *ASSAH* 3 (1984), 35–54, at 44–50. [See also the additional note following this paper.]

[15] D. M. Metcalf, 'Twelve Notes on Sceatta Finds', *BNJ* 46 (1976), 1–18, at 18.

[16] For recent reviews of modern numismatic thought on these coins see I. Stewart, 'Anglo-Saxon Gold Coins', *Scripta nummaria romana: Essays Presented to Humphrey Sutherland*, ed. R. A. G. Carson and C. M. Kraay (London, 1978), pp. 143–72, and M. Blackburn, 'A Chronology for the Sceattas', *Sceattas in England and on the Continent*, ed. D. Hill and D. M. Metcalf, BAR British ser., 128 (Oxford, 1984), pp. 165–74, the latter unfortunately marred by several slips of dating.

[17] R. Derolez and U. Schwab, 'The Runic Inscriptions of Monte S. Angelo (Gargano)', *Academiae Analecta*, Mededelingen van de Koninklijke Academie voor Wetenschappen, Letteren en Schone Kunsten van België, Klasse der Letteren 45, 1 (1983), pp. 95–130.

[18] I omit also, by virtue of the subject, new Norse runic finds from England, as the Winchester stone (B. Kjølbye-Biddle and R. I. Page, 'A Scandinavian Rune-Stone from Winchester' (1975)) and a couple of unpublished rune-inscribed bones from eleventh-century deposits at St Albans.

tainly runic, objects. Nine is an impressive increase, and to this number there are, again, a few uncertain examples to be added. Moreover, the new finds are on portable objects, not stones, and most are from the South and East of the country (fig. 3). They are:

(a) from the south coastal region: a bronze pail from the cemetery at Chessell Down, Isle of Wight; a bone fragment from a pit at Southampton.

(b) from East Anglia: a pair of tweezers from Heacham, Norfolk, a casual find; part of a pair of tweezers from a habitation site excavated at Brandon, Suffolk; a bracteate from Undley, Suffolk, a casual find. To these should be added a group of cremation urns with impressions of a single pottery stamp of unusual, probably runic, design from a cemetery at Spong Hill, Beetley, Norfolk.

(c) from the East Midlands: a brooch from the cemetery at Wakerley, Northampton-shire. Uncertainly runic are symbols on a bronze openwork disc from the cemetery at Willoughby-on-the-Wolds, Nottinghamshire.

(d) from northern England: a brooch from the cemetery at Heslerton, North York-shire.

(e) from south-west Scotland: a bone fragment found in the Anglian phase of the fort at Mote of Mark, Kircudbrightshire. From the same site came a piece of sandstone that may have runic marks on it though little can be seen.

So far in my account, the finds have been discreetly made, in areas that correspond admirably to the 1973 distribution maps. The last of the new finds breaks this rule.

(f) from the West Country, specifically the border-land between Mercia and Wessex: a copper-alloy fitting for a case for balance and weights from an inhumation burial at Watchfield, Oxfordshire.

These finds can be classified in several ways:

1. Two are scratched on metal brooches (Wakerley, Heslerton); one is impressed in a bracteate looped for suspension as a pendant (Undley); two are on items of personal equipment (Heacham, Brandon). Presumably these are all from the up-market section of Anglo-Saxon society.

2. Four are grave-goods (Chessell Down, Wakerley, Heslerton, Watchfield); two are casual finds of metal objects (Heacham, Undley); two are from excavations of habitation sites (Brandon, Mote of Mark). There is presumably a bias here in favour of (i) metal objects, because of the use of metal detecting apparatus, (ii) personal possessions.

3. Dating. Two are unstratified and so can be dated only on the general grounds of the nature of the sites (Southampton, Mote of Mark). Some of the rest are dateable on the evidence of archaeology or art history: Undley, fifth century; Chessell Down, Wakerley, Heslerton, Watchfield, sixth century; Brandon from a site dated to the Middle Saxon period, 650–850; Heacham with parallels in the eighth and ninth centuries. Thus of the new finds, five are from the earlier period, two clearly from the later.

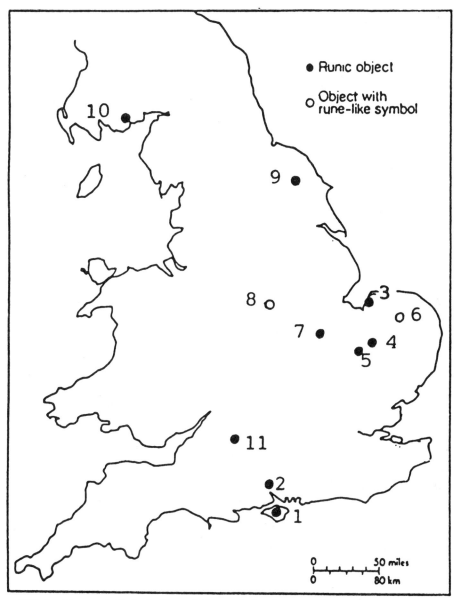

FIG. 3   New runic finds: 1, Chessell Down; 2, Southampton; 3, Heacham: 4, Brandon;
5, Undley; 6, Spong Hill; 7, Wakerley; 8, Willoughby-on-the-Wolds; 9, Heslerton;
10, Mote of Mark; 11, Watchfield

Adding the new inscriptions to the distribution maps increases significantly the weight of importance of the early/southern and eastern runes, and so continues the developments reported in 1973.

When we come to examine the contents of the inscriptions, the picture looks less exciting. Of the nine new legends only one, Brandon, is clear and unambiguous. This gives the personal name, '+ a l d r e d', presumably that of the owner of the tweezers. The letters are carefully cut and seriffed, which suggests a link with formal lettering in the roman character, and that is not surprising since the excavators have tentatively suggested that the site may be ecclesiastical.[19] The Mote of Mark bone may also have an easy interpretation, though here we are faced with the fact that the inscription may not be complete. What remains reads 'a þ i l i', which could certainly be a personal name form.[20]

Of the rest of these new inscriptions two have not been included in my count of nine, since I am a little uncertain of their runic nature. The Willoughby-on-the-Wolds disc has, on the front, a number of rune-like symbols resembling 'd' and 'n' (or 'g'). These are not very convincing as runes, but nor are they convincing as decoration, being irregularly placed on the surface. There is a resemblance here to the Hunstanton, Norfolk, openwork brooch which I also think doubtfully runic.[21] The Spong Hill urn stamp is somewhat more convincing.[22] This has the symbols ᚠ ᛏ ᛗ which are more rune-like than runic, yet Dr C. M. Hills, who has probably more experience of Anglo-Saxon pottery stamps than anyone else, regards this design as so outré that a runic explanation is likely. Peter Pieper has come up with the ingenious suggestion that these curious forms are double-sided runes representing the well-known magical word (not previously found in Anglo-Saxon England) 'a l u' written double. My own doubts about this explanation are somewhat stilled by the discovery of the two-sided w-rune of Illerup, while Pieper has adduced a number of additional examples of apparently doubled runes from various sources.[23]

Of the certainly runic legends, two present difficulties of reading and interpretation, those of Southampton and Heacham. The Southampton runes are incised on the face of a small bone fragment which is also carved with an interlace design. The runes were at one end, most of which has broken away. The only complete letter is 'd', and this is followed by three or so damaged characters whose bases are lost. It is hard to see how the poorly written staves that survive fit together, or indeed which lines are intended and which accidental. Heacham seems to have the same text cut twice, once on each side of the pair of tweezers. Corrosion of the metal renders the texts difficult to make out, and the runes are very confused, for I am not sure which

---

[19] *Medieval Archaeology* 26 (1982), p. 208.

[20] L. Laing, 'The Mote of Mark and the Origins of Celtic Interlace', *Antiquity* 49 (1975), 98–108, at 101 and pl. X.

[21] Page, *Introduction*, p. 94.

[22] C. M. Hills, 'A Runic Pot from Spong Hill, North Elmham, Norfolk', *Antiquaries Journal* 54 (1974), 87–91 and pl. XXIV. Since that article appeared Dr Hills has found other uses of the same stamp on finds from Spong Hill.

[23] I am indebted to Mr Pieper for speaking on this subject at the Sigtuna Symposium on Runes and Runic Inscriptions.

way round to read the inscription or even which way up to hold it. A composite version of the two legends, ignoring the fact that some forms appear inverted and others retrograde, is something like 'x u d f i c d', which makes no obvious sense and cannot be used as a basis for informed discussion.

In contrast the two brooch inscriptions are easy enough to record, though less so to interpret. The Heslerton text is cut or scratched on the back of the tail of a cruciform brooch. The reading is 'n e i e', or possibly though less probably, 'n e i m'. The Wakerley brooch is a square-headed one, and the inscription is incised on the back of its head. It reads 'b u h u' or, if a final vertical is a rune, 'b u h u i'. Significant is the form of 'h', which has a single cross-stave.

The new Chessell Down inscription is a curiosity. The object is a decorated bronze pail, an import into Anglo-Saxon England from some part of the Eastern Empire. This vessel is decorated with a punched design, a continuous hunting frieze depicting a hound chasing hares and a leopard pursuing a stag. Cut across this, and showing no respect for the decoration, are the runes, set between framing lines.[24] The surface is corroded and several letters are lost. What remains appears to be 'b w s [ ] e c c c æ æ æ'. The repetition at the end makes it clear that this is not plain language, and leads naturally to the supposition that it is magical, on the basis of the Second Law of Runo-Dynamics which states that anything that cannot be understood must be magic. I do not wish to go into that here, and am content to draw attention to the form of 'c', which is   as in the well-known Chessell Down scabbard-plate legend.[25]

The retrograde text of the Undley bracteate is easy enough to read. It begins with groups of bind-runes 'g͡ æ g͡ o g͡ æ'. The second pair contains the Anglo-Frisian rune 'o', a little blurred in form but certain enough. The text continues ← 'm æ g æ . m e d u'. Dr Odenstedt and I disagree over this inscription. To me the presence of the Anglo-Frisian rune, together with the find-place in East Anglia, confirms this as an English text. Odenstedt relies on art historical evidence which asserts a close link between this artefact and the Schleswig-Holstein region, so close indeed as to suggest to him that the bracteate is an import into England. From this he concludes that the so-called Anglo-Frisian runes 'were created on the continent, perhaps in the Schleswig-Holstein area, and from there brought to England'.[26]

The Watchfield inscription is excellently preserved: it reads **hariboki : wusa**. The **k**- and **s**-runes are of archaic form, and the **h**-rune is single-barred. I take the text to be two personal names, the first in an oblique case, perhaps dative.[27] The forms of the runes are sufficiently distinctive to raise enquiry, while the find-spot, near the

---

[24] The inscription is reproduced, not entirely accurately, in C. J. Arnold, *The Anglo-Saxon Cemeteries of the Isle of Wight* (London, 1982), fig. 10.

[25] See the drawing in Page, *Introduction*, p. 11.

[26] B. Odenstedt, *The Inscription on the Undley Bracteate and the Beginnings of English Runic Writing* (Umeå, 1983), p. 19; cf. my comment in R. I. Page, 'Runic Links across the North Sea in the Pre-Viking Age' (1985), pp. 37–8.

[27] This is not the only suggested reading. [See the reference in my additional note at the end of this paper. The inscription has been further discussed in C. Scull, 'Excavation and Survey at Watchfield, Oxfordshire, 1983–92', *Antiquaries Journal* 149 (1992), 124–281, at 246–51.]

Wessex-Mercia boundary, is also unusual. On these grounds I have tentatively suggested that this piece is a traveller, and have given its runes a non-English transcription.

The new finds give rise to a number of questions:

1. Does Undley require us to reconsider the status, place of origin and distribution of the Anglo-Frisian additional runes?

2. Hitherto the form of the h-rune has been thought diagnostic, with the single-barred type in the north, and the double-barred one in the south and in Anglo-Saxon England. Thus, the Caistor-by-Norwich single-barred h was one item of evidence for attributing that text to the North Germanic area.[28] We now have two more single-barred h-forms with certain English provenances, Wakerley and Watchfield, as well as several examples more doubtfully identified. Is it time now to re-examine the distribution of these two types, and following that to reconsider the relationship between early northern and Anglo-Saxon runic inscriptions?

3. Arising from 2, was the introduction of runes into England a more complex process than we formerly thought it to be?

4. Should Watchfield make us more ready to accept the possibility of early epigraphical runes in Wessex? Wessex is usually thought devoid of epigraphical runes, though I would draw attention to two neglected gold coins with runic legends, from Dorchester, Oxfordshire, and Eastleach Turville, Gloucestershire; perhaps from a West Country mint.[29]

5. Is it now possible, with the increased number of early examples, to develop a typology for early English inscriptions, so as to define their purpose and content?

There is enough here to keep runologists busy for some time.

Since this paper was written there have been several developments, which I record briefly here. Now published are: the new Beonna coins in M. M. Archibald, 'The Coinage of Beonna in the Light of the Middle Harling Hoard', *BNJ* 55 (1985), 10–54; the Watchfield fitting in C. Scull, 'A Sixth-Century Grave Containing a Balance and Weights from Watchfield, Oxfordshire, England', *Germania* 64 (1986), 105–38 (see notes 14 and 27). A most important work defining modern views of the runic coinage is P. Grierson and M. Blackburn, *Medieval European Coinage with a Catalogue of the Coins in the Fitzwilliam Museum, Cambridge: I The Early Middle Ages (5th–10th Centuries)* (Cambridge, 1986), particularly pp. 155–89. Mr Blackburn draws my attention to three hitherto unknown Æthiliræd coins, two unprovenanced in the collection of the Coin Cabinet of the State Museum, Berlin; the third is a new find from Great Bircham, Norfolk. Perhaps the most important development

[28] On this point see Page, 'Runic Links across the North Sea', pp. 39–45.
[29] C. H. V. Sutherland, *Anglo-Saxon Gold Coinage in the Light of the Crondall Hoard* (Oxford, 1948), pp. 77–8; Stewart, 'Anglo-Saxon Gold Coins', p. 149.

is the discovery by Professor Martin Biddle of runes on a bone writing tablet from Blythburgh, Suffolk: on the finding of this object see *PSAL* 2nd ser., 19 (1901–3), 40–2.[30] This gives a further East Anglian example set within the Christian period.

POSTSCRIPT

This paper, published in 1987, is the content of a lecture given two years earlier at the Second International Symposium on Runes and Runic Inscriptions, Sigtuna, September 1985. It tried to bring the English runic record up to date for the benefit of runologists working in other fields. It is now out of date again, with the appearance of runic finds from Wardley (Leicestershire), London, Cleatham (South Humberside), Harford Farm, Caistor-by-Norwich (Norfolk), Boarley (Kent), and Worcester.[31] The excavations at Brandon in Suffolk produced runes not only on the tweezers mentioned here but also on a disc-headed pin and a bone handle.[32] These new finds are plotted on updated distribution maps above pp. 14–15. In addition, runic coins proliferate at an alarming rate. Most recently, for instance, there have turned up coins from hitherto unknown dies of Beonna of East Anglia, and, perhaps most important, a silver penny of an issue attributed to the little-known Æþel-berht/Alberht of East Anglia (mid eighth-century), with runes used both for royal and moneyer's names.[33] Further discoveries of Anglo-Saxon runic graffiti in Italy might also be noted again here.[34]

[30] [On this tablet see below, p. 324, and above, p. 3].

[31] K. Gosling, 'An Anglo-Saxon Runic Inscription from Leicestershire, England', *Nytt om Runer* 3 (1988), 14; *idem*, 'Runic Finds from London', *Nytt om Runer* 4 (1989), 12–13; J. Hines, 'A New Runic Inscription from South Humberside, England', *Nytt om Runer* 4 (1989), 14; *idem*, 'A New Runic Inscription from Norfolk', *Nytt om Runer* 6 (1991), 6–7; D. Parsons, 'German Runes in Kent?', *Nytt om Runer* 7 (1992), 7–8; *Hereford and Worcester Archaeology: Newsletter of the County Archaeological Service* (September 1993), 2, and above pp. 1–2.

[32] D. Parsons, 'New Runic Finds from Brandon, Suffolk', *Nytt om Runer* 6 (1991), 8–11.

[33] See above, pp. 2, 6. Other recent numismatic developments have been recorded above, pp. 178–9 and 144.

[34] For details see above, p. 3, n. 6, and below, p. 313.

20

(1987)

A SIXTEENTH-CENTURY RUNIC MANUSCRIPT

Among the books that Archbishop Matthew Parker left to Corpus Christi College, Cambridge, in 1575 is a paper manuscript of sixty-five leaves mainly in the distinctive and undisciplined hand of the Tudor antiquary Robert Talbot (*c.* 1505–1558).[1] This manuscript, which now carries the press-mark CCCC 379, is a miscellany.[2] Part of it is made up of casual jottings, collections of proverbial lore, accounts, sententiae, etc. Part copies various writings in Latin, Greek and Old English, the latter being the preface to Ælfric's translation of the Hexateuch, taken, according to Ker,[3] from British Library MS Cotton Claudius B. IV. The most extensive material in the volume refers to the Antonine Itinerary, a text (fols 19–22) of the 'Iter Britaniar*um* a Gessoria de Gallijs' (this not in Talbot's hand), followed (fols 24–65) by 'Annotationes in eam partem Itinerarij Antonini quæ ad Britaniam pertinet' (headed 'Manus Roberti Talbot cle*r*ici') which Hearne printed in his edition of Leland's *Itinerary*.[4] It was presumably because of this section that Parker collected the volume, since its entry under the press-mark 12.4 in the Parker Inventory (MS CCCC 575, p. 76) lists it simply as 'Talbot commentaria in Itinerariu*m* Ant Augusti', while MS CCCC 101 has, among other Parkerian transcripts, one of this text and commentary.

The modern binding of CCCC 379 is very tight, and it is not possible to be certain of the collation, particularly as folios have been cut out of the book. Watermarks of the papers used give a clue to the manuscript's history. Most of the paper is from a single stock, probably originally made into quires of twelve. Here the watermark is of a common type, an open hand surmounted by a five-pointed star. This can be dated only generally to the first half of the sixteenth century, possibly 1530 ± 15.[5] At the

---

[1] There are illustrations of and comments on Talbot's hand in N. R. Ker, 'Medieval Manuscripts from Norwich Cathedral Priory', *Trans. of the Cambridge Bibliographical Soc.* 1 (1949–53), 1–28, at 3 and pl. I, and C. E. Wright, 'The Dispersal of the Monastic Libraries and the Beginnings of Anglo-Saxon Studies', *Trans. of the Cambridge Bibliographical Soc.* 1 (1949–53), 208–37, at 235–7.
[2] Fuller details of the manuscript's contents are in M. R. James, *A Descriptive Catalogue of the Manuscripts in the Library of Corpus Christi College Cambridge* (Cambridge, 1912) II, 226–7.
[3] Ker, *Catalogue*, p. 179.
[4] T. Hearne, *The Itinerary of John Leland the Antiquary*, 2nd ed. (Oxford, 1744) III, 144–64, though Hearne took his text from a Bodleian Library manuscript, apparently MS e Mus.188.
[5] I am grateful to Paul Needham of the Pierpont Morgan Library, New York, for help in identifying the watermarks of CCCC 379.

middle of the second quire of this was inserted the quire containing the *Iter Britanniarum*, written on a different paper. This has a watermark that can be identified as Briquet 12061, a Troyes mark with the paper-maker's name CPINETTE on a banderole, for which dates between 1559 and 1564 are suggested in Briquet.[6] The final verso of this quire is pasted to the neighbouring recto (leaf 7 of the second quire), covering a text. This practice, of sticking new or insert sheets over pages of text, is common enough in Matthew Parker's collection, so it seems likely that the text of the *Iter* was added at Parker's instigation to supplement Talbot's commentary. The only other date attached to the manuscript is that contained in the 'Epitaphium D. Nicolaj Hauchini' (fol. 14) which ends 'Obijt 6 Januarij Anno domini 1534', confirming a likely date for the composition of Talbot's part of this notebook as 1535–58.[7]

It is fol. 9ʳ (the verso being blank) which is of importance to the present note. Fol. 9 is an integral part of the first quire, originally one of twelve. It presents an 'Alphabetum anglicum ordine latino/nam apud anglos ordo diuersus est/vt .f. prima litera sit'.[8] A glance at this alphabet shows that it comprises a mixture of runic material, for it reproduces four rune forms and a host of rune-names derived from both English and Scandinavian traditions. It reads, as far as such an untidy text can be reduced to print:

a	ᛐ	ar reuerentia. inde ar/worth venerabilis
b		beor. beorc. bercon
c		coun. coën. cen. con
	ᚦ	thus. thorn. thors:, d simplex:. vel raphatum[9]
d		dæg daeg: .dd. dubbl.d. dagg essatum/.l. dies
e		e. vel ech
f		fe vel feh. .l. pecunia
g.		geofu vel. gyfu. .l. gratia.
.h.		hagol. hægel. hægil. .l. grando.
i		is. is. .l. glacies.
k		kaïc vel calc. nescio vtrum
l		laur. lagu. logu. loër
.m.		Monr. Mander.
n	ᚴ	Nou. ned. noð. vel noth
o		os. oſ.
p		peorð peorð peörth
q		quar. quar.

---

6 C. M. Briquet, *Les filigranes*, rev. ed. A. Stevenson (Amsterdam, 1968).

7 The text reads 'Hauchini', not 'Hanchini' as James transcribed it. In fact, this is Nicholas Hawkins, the ecclesiastical lawyer who acted as Henry VIII's ambassador to the Emperor Charles V and died on diplomatic service: see his entry in *D.N.B.*

8 James reads 'ut l(?) prima litera sit'. It is strange that the man who wrote that splendid ghost story *Casting the Runes* did not recognise the opening letter of the *fuþorc*.

9 So the text seems to say, but I cannot recognise the word nor have classical scholars to whom I have submitted it come up with any explanation.

R.		Reiðer .l. rad reð
.s.		sol. sigil. sigel.
t	↑	tiur tyr
u		ur.
x		.ilx.
y		.yr.
/diphthongs/		oe. oethel } sunt vt ab
		ae aesc .l./.l. fraxinus } breuiaturæ
		ea. ear .l. annus nonnullæ:-

The text is not all of a piece. The Latin glosses on the rune-names look like additions, as do various other comments (those on *dæg*, *oethel* and *aesc*) and the word *diphthongs*. Nevertheless, despite its diversity, most of the material on the page derives from a single source that can easily be tracked down.

Among the manuscripts that have been traced in Talbot's possession is the collection of computistical works which is now St John's College, Oxford, MS 17. Fol. 5ʳ of this codex illustrates a number of cryptic texts and alphabets, among them several rune-rows.[10] These are (a) a sixteen-letter *fuþark* of the Danish type, with roman equivalents and rune-names, the latter much corrupt: the order of the runes in the *fuþark* is incorrect, (b) a somewhat garbled twenty-eight-letter Anglo-Saxon *fuþorc* with many additional rune forms: this also has rune-names, and the first six letters have roman equivalents, *f*, *u*, *th*, *o*, *r*, *c* in a sixteenth-/seventeenth-century hand, (c) another sixteen-letter Danish-type *fuþark* with rune-names, followed by later additional Scandinavian runes with roman equivalents, (d) an extended Anglo-Saxon *fuþorc* with roman equivalents, (e) an Anglo-Saxon runic alphabet with variant rune forms, but no names or equivalents. Between them items (a), (b), (c), and (d) provide much of the substance of CCCC 379, fol. 9ʳ. So, (a) has the names *fe*, *ur*, *þurs*, *e* (wrongly for the *a/o*-rune in fourth place), *reiðer*, *coun*, *hagol*, *nou*, *is*, *tiur*, *bercon*, *sol*, *ar*, *monr*, *laur*, *reiðer*. (b) has the rune-names *feh*, *ur*, *þorn*, *os*, *rad*, *coen l cen*, *geofu l gyfu*, *is*, *sigil*, *sigel*, *peorð*, *ilx*, *tyr*, *beorc*, *mech*, *ech*, *logu* underpointed to give *lagu*, *hægel* underpointed to give *hægil*, *ned*, *ka lc* (sic), *dæg*, *oeþel*, *ac*, *aesc*, *yr*, *ear*, *quar*, *ing*, some of these repeated. (c) has *fe*, *ur*, *þors*, *os*, *reð*, *con*, *hagol*, *noð*, *is*, *ar*, *sol*, *tyr*, *beor*, *mander*, *loer*, *yr*. (d) distinguishes between the *þ*-rune with the value *d*, and the *d*-rune with the equivalent *dd*. These supply nearly all the primary runic material for Talbot's list. The omission of the rune and name *wynn* from (b) would account for the absence of *w* from Talbot's Anglo-Saxon alphabet, as the omission of the English name for the *m*-rune (*mon*) would explain why Talbot did not give that either. Talbot sometimes duplicates a rune-name, perhaps because English and Norse rune-rows have the identical name for a rune (*is*, *os*) or because *fuþorc* (b) gives variant forms of a rune, each with its name (*peorð*, *quar*). A few of

---

[10] N. R. Ker, 'Membra Disiecta', *British Museum Quarterly* 12 (1938), 130–5, at 131, and Ker, *Catalogue*, p. 435. There is a detailed account of the runes of this manuscript in Derolez, *Runica Manuscripta*, pp. 29–34 and 38–44.

Talbot's rune-name forms incorporate spelling rationalisations of his own (*daeg, noth, peörth, oethel, thurs, thorn, thors*).

From this it is fairly clear that CCCC 379's runic material was taken from St John's 17 by a man with limited runic understanding. Talbot did not distinguish between Norse and English runes, lumping all the names together and in no consistent order. His *a* is of the Scandinavian form, a letter which in Norse has the name *ár* (< **jāra*), 'year, harvest, season'. Talbot took the name *ar* from the Norse *fuþarks* of St John's 17 (ignoring the *ac* of the Anglo-Saxon rune-row there) and interpreted it as an Old English word *ar*, 'dignity, honour, respect', whence his gloss *reverentia*. In support he added the word *arworth* (a form not recorded in Old English and presumably a sixteenth-century aberration).[11] His other Latin glosses are sound enough except for *ear*, which he confused with *gear* and translated *annus*.

There only remains to be explained the name for *k*, 'kaïc vel calc', words which Talbot admitted baffled him. The rune *calc* is of course a rare one, found epigraphically only in a group of inscriptions from the North of Anglo-Saxon England: the Ruthwell and Bewcastle crosses, the Great Urswick (Cumbria) and Thornhill III (Yorkshire) memorial stones, and a pair of related amulet rings, one from the neighbourhood of Bramham Moor (Yorkshire) and the other from Kingmoor (Cumbria). Consequently it is not included in all manuscript *fuþorcs* and runic alphabets, and its name may not have been well known. Talbot's spelling *kaïc* is presumably a misreading of, or a misunderstanding of notes drawn from, *fuþorc* (b) of St John's 17, which has 'ka lc', the gap occasioned by a deleted letter, perhaps *c*. According to Healey and Venezky, *Microfiche Concordance*, the form *calc* occurs only twice in recorded Old English texts, in two British Library runic manuscripts, Cotton Domitian IX and Cotton Galba A. II. Galba A. II was completely destroyed in 1865 after severe damage during the great Cotton fire of 1731, and its runes and names survive only in the plate made from Wanley's drawing of them for Hickes's *Thesaurus*.[12] Its runes were closely related to those of St John's 17, but the rune-names often have distinctive spellings. Whether Talbot knew this manuscript or not I do not know, but the rune page of CCCC 379 shows no sign of the characteristic Galba A. II spellings of the names. The rune page of Domitian IX Talbot certainly knew, and indeed annotated,[13] so it is reasonable to assume he took the form *calc* from there, where the name occurs twice in different hands.

To Domitian IX Talbot added a group of Latin glosses on rune-names, some of which coincide with those of CCCC 379, *reuerentia, dies, pecunia, gratia, grando, fraxinus, annus*; all those, in fact, in CCCC 379 save *glacies* and that he presumably omitted because Domitian IX has *inc* for the name of the *i*-rune in place of the correct *is*. Domitian IX also has Talbot glosses that are not in CCCC 379: 'e ethel .l. patria',

---

[11] It is not in A. diPaolo Healey and R. L. Venezky, *A Microfiche Concordance to Old English* (Toronto, 1980), though that does have the forms *arworðiað* and *arworðig*.

[12] G. Hickes, *Linguarum vett. septentrionalium thesaurus grammatico-criticus et archæologicus. 3. Grammaticæ Islandicæ rudimenta* (Oxford, 1703), tabella VI. On these runes and their relationship to those of St John's 17, see Derolez, *Runica Manuscripta*, pp. 45–52.

[13] C. E. Wright, 'Robert Talbot and *Domitian A. IX*', *Medium Ævum* 6 (1937), 170–1.

'th. thorn. spina vel s[. .]tes (? *sortes*)', '.m. man .l. homo vel mann', 'st. stan .l. lapis', '.R. Rad. .l. co*n*siliu*m*', B. berc. .l. cortex', 'S. sigel .l. velu*m*', 'v.vr .l. noster', while the group 'ea. .gear .l. ann*us* vel: ear' is a variant on CCCC 379 material.[14]

It would be natural to assume that CCCC 379 was written before Talbot glossed Domitian IX. Why otherwise did he not include in CCCC 379 all the Domitian glosses, particularly since the CCCC 379 glosses are additions to the original text? However, the Domitian IX material is not so simply summed up as that, since it too was not written at a single sitting. Some glosses were added later, as *fraxinus* and *ear*, and probably the last four glosses, on *R*, *B*, *S* and *v*, that form a column of their own. Two, *vel s[..]tes* and *vel mann*, may even be in a different hand as Derolez suggests.[15]

Apparently significant is the Domitian IX gloss '.a ar .l. reue*r*entia' since that, with its Norse rune-name in place of OE *ac*, would appear to derive from CCCC 379 and ultimately from St John's 17. But even here we cannot be sure, for, as Derolez points out, the *a*-rune of the Domitian IX *fuþorc* has a name of uncertain form: 'Either it was first written *ac*, which was then altered to *ar*, or vice versa'.[16] I am not so sure of that, but the last letter of the word certainly looks odd. I suspect, however, that anyone reading it would take it as *ac* rather than *ar*, and conclude that the gloss *ar.l.reuerentia* in Domitian IX does in fact originate in CCCC 379.

Fol. 9[r] of CCCC 379 adds a footnote to the history of English runic studies, and in particular to that of the *runica manuscripta* which have been René Derolez's special concern. The manuscript is, I suppose, of no great importance in itself, though it adds somewhat to our knowledge of Talbot's interest in the script. Elsewhere I have tentatively suggested that Talbot added rune-names and additional forms to the page of Cotton MS Otho B. X that held the Old English *Runic Poem*, now known only from Hickes's printed text, and that this encourages us to trust in the integrity of the Hickes transcript.[17] His notebook in the library of Corpus Christi College, Cambridge, confirms that he was sufficiently excited by runes to have done so.

POSTSCRIPT

Mr Tim Graham, who has made a detailed study of Robert Talbot's very difficult cursive hand, has suggested a few corrections to my original paper, some of which I have incorporated into this reprint. Fol. 9[r] provides a composite text, and some of its additions were written in a very cavalier manner and are hard to make out. The form I give here as 'diphthongs' is in fact 'dighthong*es*' with a careless spelling error and, if Graham is correct, an ending which is Talbot's abbreviation for *es* rather than

---

[14] The page is dirty and the ink often faint, so details of these readings, particularly the pointing of the text, are uncertain.

[15] *Runica Manuscripta*, p. 7.

[16] *Runica Manuscripta*, p. 13.

[17] Above, pp. 204–6.

the long ʃ I took it for. The form which he takes to be 'dagg essatum' (which I originally read as 'dagg rafatum') presents us with another unidentifiable word (cf. my footnote 9). Graham thinks the form I have read as '.l.' should in fact be '.i.' (for *id est*), but here I am less convinced, for it is a simple unpointed tall vertical, unlike Talbot's usual *i* and at least as like his usual *l* (? for *vel*). Luckily these are points of detail which do not affect my general discussion.

21

(1987)

RUNEUKYNDIGE RISTERES SKRIBLERIER: THE ENGLISH EVIDENCE*

'Ja, hvad er der ikke fremsat af mærkelige og "arkaiserende" grammatiske former på grundlag af runeukyndige risteres skriblerier!', exclaims Erik Moltke in his magnificent book, *Runerne i Danmark og deres oprindelse*.[1] Or, in Peter Foote's equally vigorous translation in the revised version, *Runes and their Origin: Denmark and Elsewhere*, 'How many remarkable grammatical forms – often smoothly glossed as "archaisms" – have been presented to the world on the basis of illiterate rune-writers' slovenly habits!'[2] It is certainly true that in many of the early runic texts he examined, and in particular those on the bracteates, Moltke faced difficult, perhaps impossible, forms, and often incomplete words and clauses; he solved the problem of how to deal with these at a stroke by simply regarding them as the work of illiterates, of people who copied letter forms without understanding them, and so were likely to make more blunders than would a trained scribe working in the tradition of a monastic scriptorium.[3] The theory implies, of course, that the customers they served were also illiterate, satisfied with sub-standard work, with something that looked like an inscription, though it was a blundered and meaningless one.

Moltke sums up: 'The moral is: be wary of inscriptions, whether antique or medieval, on any kind of metal object. The craftsman who does not know his letters will make mistakes much more readily than someone who does'.[4] True indeed, as far as it goes, though Moltke uses the pretext of illiteracy to explain difficulties in texts on non-metal objects – on the Gørlev and Tirsted stones, for instance[5] – and it

---

* This paper has not been previously published. It was read at a conference on 'Literacy and Society in Early North-Western Europe, 400–1200' in May 1987.

[1] E. Moltke, *Runerne i Danmark og deres oprindelse* (Copenhagen, 1976), p. 71.

[2] E. Moltke, *Runes and their Origin: Denmark and Elsewhere*, trans. P. G. Foote (Copenhagen, 1985), p. 80.

[3] Though one should not over-estimate the accuracy of the products of the scriptorium, as any student of mediaeval manuscripts knows. On this see further, p. 309, below.

[4] Moltke, *Runes and their Origin*, p. 116. 'Morale: Vær på din post over for middelalderlige og ældre metal-indskrifter! hvis smeden ikke kender bogstaverne er det lettere for ham at begå fejl, end om han kunne læse og skrive', *Runerne i Danmark*, p. 92.

[5] Moltke, *Runes and their Origin*, pp. 239 and 299–300; *Runerne i Danmark*, pp. 192 and 250–1.

is proper to question a methodology that evades interpreting difficult letter combinations on the excuse that they are blunders.

In apparent contrast to Moltke's observations stands a comment by the Norwegian runologist, Aslak Liestøl, in an article on the cursive aspects of Norwegian runes of the Viking Age: 'I think we are bound to conclude that the majority of Viking Age Scandinavians – at least those of any standing, and those intent on making their way in life – were able to read and write (*sc.* runes). Their system of writing was in constant use, and the inscriptions extant today are merely the pitiful remains of the wealth of documents written by them'.[6] Here Liestøl was not thinking of those Viking Age monuments we prize so much, the great rune-stones that give direct information on life, conditions, social ranks and activities during that period; but of the scant remains of inscriptions on wooden sticks, in that version of the script known as *stuttruner* or short-twig runes, which he saw as a commercial script developed for business and other practical purposes.

Of course, the materials on which Moltke and Liestøl based their conflicting claims are not comparable, nor can we assume that either was typical of its date. In his discussion Liestøl was drawing on much later material than that used by Moltke. It would be unwise to derive general conclusions from the data of either scholar, whether about runic inscriptions as a whole or about the inscriptions of a particular date.

Yet different though their conclusions are, Liestøl and Moltke are in agreement on their point of departure. Both think of runes as essentially a script developed for the practical purposes of communication and record: thus runes are important as an indication of literacy. Not all runologists agree with them. Most recently the Swede, Bengt Odenstedt, has written against their view, supporting a contention of Anders Bæksted's. In his paper Odenstedt pointed to the earliest surviving runic inscriptions, noting that they hardly support the assertion that runes were a practical script. The earliest runes 'do not indicate a well-established communicative tradition', for their texts are short, primitive, often obscure or incomprehensible;[7] even if the last adjective begs a question, at least it suggests there was not a lot of overt information passing in the early runes. Thus, if you accept Odenstedt's point of view – and it has much to be said for it – whether people were widely literate in runes is not a very helpful question.

There has, then, been debate among Scandinavian scholars about the significance for literacy of the inscriptions of the early and middle periods. None of it seems to have struck the English writers on literacy in Anglo-Saxon times. Nor is that surprising, for runes play a much smaller part in early English than in Scandinavian. In the main, English writers on early mediaeval literacy derive their thinking either

---

[6] A. Liestøl, 'The Literate Vikings', *Proceedings of the Sixth Viking Congress*, ed. P. Foote and D. Strömbäck (London and Uppsala, 1971), pp. 69–78, at 76.
[7] B. Odenstedt, 'Om ursprunget till den äldre futharken', *Saga och Sed* (1984), 77–116, at 109–12 and 116.

from manuscript studies (as Dr M. B. Parkes)[8] or from the study of history (as Mr C. P. Wormald),[9] and I suppose that both would have in their minds the link between literacy and the monastic scriptorium. Other types of evidence are inevitably neglected. Perhaps the best-known statement on Anglo-Saxon literacy is that of Wormald, based on a lecture delivered in 1976. He dismisses the epigraphical texts in a few crisp phrases: 'Inscriptions in sufficient quantity and quality *may* be symptoms of a literate society . . . but they do not themselves establish its existence. Even so extended and impressive a text as the *Dream of the Rood* on the Ruthwell Cross only might have been designed to expound the Redemption to a secular public; it might just as well have been addressed to the Redeemer himself'.[10]

I confess I find the first of these sentences a commonplace, and even as such of little use without a definition of 'quantity and quality'. The second seems meaningless. The main texts of the Ruthwell Cross – now as they always were – are the verses on the crucifixion allied to the Vercelli Book poem known at the *Dream of the Rood*. Yet, as Professor Ó'Carragáin has made clear, they are significantly different from the *Dream of the Rood*. Like the neighbouring sculpture, the Ruthwell poem has close links with the liturgy; yet it is not itself liturgical.[11] It describes Christ's passion as it was experienced by the cross itself, a subject on which the Almighty might think Himself well informed. In no way is it addressed to the Deity: it implies a human readership.

Yet the lay-out of the text on the Ruthwell Cross does little to help a reading public. There are horizontal lines of runes along the top borders of east and west faces of the lower shaft stone (and there may have been similar lines along lower borders that were hacked away centuries ago). Apart from these, the poem is set out in short horizontal lines of between two and four letters. In general there are no word separators.[12] The whole inscription is very hard for the visitor, even the visiting runologist, to make out. What then is the intended audience? John Higgitt has suggested one in an important paper. Warning against the 'Fallacy of the Anticipated Audience', he shows that 'prominent or important inscriptions would sometimes be read or interpreted by those who could read to those who could not'.[13] The Ruthwell

---

[8] M. B. Parkes, 'The Literacy of the Laity', *The Mediaeval World*, ed. D. Daiches and A. Thorlby (London, 1973), pp. 555–77.

[9] C. P. Wormald, 'The Uses of Literacy in Anglo-Saxon England and its Neighbours', *TRHS* 5th ser., 27 (1977), 95–114.

[10] Wormald, 'Uses of Literacy', p. 96.

[11] É. Ó'Carragáin, 'Liturgical Innovations Associated with Pope Sergius and the Iconography of the Ruthwell and Bewcastle Crosses', *Bede and Anglo-Saxon England*, ed. R. T. Farrell, BAR British ser., 46 (Oxford, 1978), pp. 131–47.

[12] Of the several recent drawings showing the lay-out of the Ruthwell cross runes, perhaps the most readily available is in E. v. K. Dobbie, *The Anglo-Saxon Minor Poems*, ASPR 6 (New York, 1942), p. 114. See also above, p. 261. In general the runic texts of the cross include no symbols for word separation, yet it appears that there are points, probably intended, after 'a l m e ɨ t t i g' and 'k̄ y n i ŋ c', that is at the ends of these poetic lines.

[13] J. Higgitt, 'Words and Crosses: the Inscribed Stone Cross in Early Medieval Britain and Ireland', *Early Medieval Sculpture in Britain and Ireland*, ed. J. Higgitt, BAR British ser., 152 (Oxford, 1986), pp. 125–52, at 125–6.

Cross texts may have been of this sort. The public did not read them; they were taken round the monument by a local guide who expounded the texts as he explained the sculptures. Since he knew the wording virtually by heart, he was not put off by the idiosyncratic lay-out of the letters. There was a specialist reading audience, not a general one.

However, the Ruthwell Cross is a special case, and not a good one for Wormald to take as his major example. What of the more common type of rune-stone? Different, I take it, is the case of the inscription raised to someone's memory; particularly if it contains a 'Pray for the soul of NN' formula. After all, there is not much point in a text asking for prayers for someone's soul if nobody could read it. There are numbers of these prayer inscriptions from Anglo-Saxon England, both runic and non-runic, Latin and vernacular. In Old English there are the memorial stones from Great Urswick, Lancaster, Overchurch, Thornhill, apparently the main text of Bewcastle, Dewsbury and Falstone.[14] And of course there are even more examples of simpler stones, grave-markers with only a personal name on them. Perhaps at this point it is necessary to distinguish between the monuments from great ecclesiastical centres and those from more modest foundations. It is no great discovery to learn that there were literate men at Lindisfarne, Monkwearmouth and Hartlepool, or even that there were visitors enough to those places to justify having guides to show them round. It may be surprising to find in these places people literate in runes, but that is a complex matter which I cannot go into here. Presumably on this postulate there should have been a great foundation at Ruthwell for which the only evidence is the great cross, but that too is a complex matter beyond this paper. But what of, say, Thornhill, a small place in West Yorkshire, of no great distinction now or, as far as we know, then? It has three memorial rune-stones, one with a prayer formula. Surely someone was supposed to read these.

I would not press this too far, however. A simple analogy will illustrate. Many English parish churches have Elizabethan funerary monuments with fulsome epitaphs in Latin. Nobody, I take it, supposes that the average Elizabethan churchgoer understood Latin. If Archbishop Parker's certificates on the state of the clergy are anything to go by, many Elizabethan priests also were not too strong in that language.[15] I do not expect that English churches had guides to take visitors round the monuments. So it seems that these inscriptions imply a standard of literacy which was recognised even in small places, though seldom achieved.

However, runically speaking the matter is more complex than this, even in apparently straightforward cases. An example is the Hartlepool gravefield, with its name-stones, runic and non-runic. It is usually assumed that this cemetery belonged

---

14 Details of most of the inscriptions mentioned in this paper can be found in Okasha, *Hand-List*, and Page, *Introduction* (1973), supplemented by 'New Runic Finds in England', above pp. 275–87.

15 Parker's certificates, the replies to a questionnaire sent out in 1560/1561 to diocesan bishops on the state of their clergy, are now Corpus Christi College, Cambridge, MSS 97, 122 and 580. They list the various incumbents of the parishes and give, among other information, estimates of their erudition. Some are described as *doctus*, but many are *mediocriter doctus* and others *parum doctus* or *(omnino) indoctus*; occasionally *latine non intelligit*.

to the monastery of *Heruteu* mentioned by Bede.[16] Thus the stones should presuppose a literate audience. Though several of them have single names, others have a prayer formula *ora(te) pro NN*. Presumably the inmates of the house were intended to read and obey this instruction; but the find-reports of these stones, unclear though they are in sum, suggest different. They were discovered under the earth's surface in obscure connection with graves; some records imply actually in graves beneath the skulls of the dead.[17] Yet certain of the slabs are heavily weathered, showing that at some time they lay above the surface, presumably acting as grave-markers. However, one runic stone, Hartlepool I, is so excellently preserved that it has suffered virtually no weathering. Taking note of the find-reports, one might suggest that this was always inside its grave, perhaps as identification should any translation of the body be contemplated. The stone's inscription is a single personal name. For this text there may have been no living audience.

Another example, different in nature because of its different context, is the coffin-reliquary which the Lindisfarne monks made in 698 for St Cuthbert's body. This wooden box is decorated with figures of Christ, Mary, the Evangelists, Apostles and Archangels, boldly incised. Each figure has its name cut nearby, in runes, roman or a mixture of the two. The letters, in contrast to the figures, are finely cut: indeed so delicate are the incisions that many of them are now very hard to see because of the conservation treatment the wood has received.[18] But they must always have been difficult to make out, and I wonder in what circumstances they were supposed to be read. The reliquary was kept above ground to be revered by the pious pilgrim, but what lighting conditions could enable him to identify the inscribed names? Professor Kitzinger suggested that the figures on the coffin represented a sort of 'litany', 'invoking the help and protection of the saints'.[19] The names could be part of this, and again may not have been intended to be read by people.

So far I have touched on the literacy of readers; but what of the literacy of rune-masters? Of the training of Anglo-Saxon rune-carvers in general, and the extent to which they can be identified as rune-masters – the devisers as well as the cutters of texts – we know nothing. Presumably this varied with time and circumstance.

What I mean by circumstance is best defined by example. When there is an elaborate memorial stone, say Thornhill III, we may, in its inscription, be dealing with either a professional carver who copied an exemplar closely though he himself may have been illiterate; or a carver who was literate, setting out a text he understood.

---

[16] *Historia Ecclesiastica*, iii. 24, iv. 23.

[17] The stones were unearthed between 1833 and 1843 as chance finds; there was no formal excavation. For such find-reports as we have we depend on local newspapers (*Durham Advertiser* and *Gateshead Observer*), and the accounts printed in the *Gentleman's Magazine* that to some extent depend upon them. The September 1833 issue of the *Gentleman's Magazine* reported the find of skeletons, with the detail that some of the skulls rested on small flat plain stones, 'and under a few were discovered stones bearing inscriptions, and marked with the cross'. Other accounts are less precise.

[18] The most recent conservation, reported in J. M. Cronyn and C. V. Horie, *St. Cuthbert's Coffin: the History, Technology & Conservation* (Durham, 1985), has made some of the letters more legible.

[19] E. Kitzinger, 'The Coffin-Reliquary', *The Relics of Saint Cuthbert*, ed. C. F. Battiscombe (Durham, 1956), pp. 202–97, at 280.

Each would result in an accurate text, nor can I devise any test that can distinguish with certainty between the two (though I will suggest one below). On the other hand, when there is a much less formal text cut on an object of no substantial value, then it is more likely to be the autograph of a literate carver.

An example is a find made recently in eleventh-century deposits at St Albans, Hertfordshire. Among other bones was a roe-deer's scapula from a bit of butcher's meat.[20] On it was cut a text in a Scandinavian language and in Danish-type runes. It is defective because the bone is damaged, but much of the inscription is the common rune-cutter's formula *NN risti rúnar*, 'NN cut (these) runes'. Part of the name of the cutter is broken away, and moreover seems to have been the subject of some experiment or jest by the carver: it is apparently either *Thor* or one of the *Thor*-compound names. The phrase **risti runa**R is quite clear, and there are possible trial letters on the other side of the scapula. I cannot see any reason for writing such an inscription on a bone (perhaps fished casually out of the dinner pot), except to show that the carver could in fact cut runes – a bit of private boasting or advertisement. It is probable, then, that this is the cutter's own invention, and to that extent he was literate – though that may have been the full extent of his literacy.

We can point to occasional parallels to this in the English runic tradition, though they are not close nor are they many. Perhaps the most cogent is the Southampton (Hamwih) bone, the proximal phalange of a cow, with, incised on it with a sharp knife, the four runes 'c a t æ'. The piece is of no intrinsic value, so there is no reason to think its inscription anything other than a fairly casual doodle though the runes are well-shaped and neat. For the meaning of such a casual graffito it is natural to look first to a personal name, perhaps a masculine *Cat(t)* or feminine *Catte*; the name coincides with the common noun 'cat, wild-cat', and is unrecorded in Old English save in place-names,[21] but there is nothing inherently improbable in the interpretation. An alternative, no less probable, has been suggested, linking the word with early Frisian *kāte*, 'finger-bone', with the further implication that this text is the work of a Frisian visitor.[22] In either case, it looks as though the runes were cut by someone who did it as a way of passing the time; and again this is an indication that he was literate.

In a different medium and a quite different context there is the inscription on a cremation urn from the cemetery of Loveden Hill, Lincolnshire, a long legend cut in the clay before it was fired. It reads something like: 's i þ æ b æ d ‖ þ i c w ‖ h l æ [.]'. The first sequence looks like a personal name but the rest is baffling. The rune-cutter used a wedge-shaped implement, perhaps a slip of wood. His letters are badly spaced and crude, though here and there he may have tried to tidy up or sharpen an incision. For all that he did not take the opportunity his soft medium afforded him of refining his runes, improving infelicities of form and removing ambiguities, completing joins, correcting over-runs, and so on. It is as though the inscription, once incised, had achieved its object: it was important to cut the runes, not to read them.

---

[20] Since this was written, a second bone inscription has appeared from St Albans.

[21] Page, *Introduction*, pp. 170–1.

[22] See above, p. 265.

Perhaps they served some ritual function in the burial. If so, the cutter presumably had the power over the runes – he was literate. It is interesting that the excavator of the cemetery, Dr K. R. Fennell, recorded that the urn was buried slightly on its side with the inscription concealed. There was no appeal to any reader.[23]

Moltke's argument for illiteracy rests primarily on the evidence of early metal-work. Comparable material in England certainly shows early inscriptions with no obvious meaning, though that may be more a reflection on our competence of comprehension than on the metalworker's abilities. There are, for instance, two back-of-brooch inscriptions: one, from Wakerley, Northamptonshire, reads 'b u h u' (or perhaps 'b u h u i') and a second, from Heslerton, North Yorkshire, has 'n e i m' or, less likely, 'n e i e'. I do not know what these mean, while the diphthong (if that is what it is) in *neim* should cause worry to philologists looking for some sense.

There are, however, clearer supports to Moltke's scepticism. A well-known sword-pommel from Ash/Gilton, Kent, has runes/rune-like forms on it. The space available for any inscription is small, and the characters are very roughly incised. Five runes, in the centre of the inscription, are clear: 's i g i m'. Surrounding these on both sides are cruder scratches which can individually be identified as runes with greater or lesser plausibility. Some are fairly clearly arbitrary shapes, apparently put in to fill up space. Different scholars have identified different numbers of runes here, but most modern readers accept that at least some of the scratches are not real letters.[24] Being a sceptic I accept fewer than many, and regard most of the forms as attempts to give the appearance of an inscription without the reality. Perhaps they tell something of the literacy of the sword's owner. Moltke's dictum (applied in his case to the bracteates) may apply: 'their marks were meant to give the ignorant customer the impression that he had got his hands on a reliable and potent charm'.[25]

There are other cases, though they are not so decisive, of objects that have rune-like characters on them, without there being any obvious textual meaning. I think here of the openwork disc-brooches from Hunstanton, Norfolk, and Willoughby-on-the-Wolds, Nottinghamshire, where there are scattered symbols which could be runes, but which form no clearly coherent sequences. More important for the present survey is the elaborate disc-brooch found at Dover. On the brooch-back, and set some distance apart, are two inscriptions. The first, two runes set in a frame, is '← w d'/'d ← w', perhaps standing for a personal name *Wyndæg or *Dægwynn. The second text is more complex. It also is cut within a frame. There are six characters, the first

[23] I am indebted to Dr Fennell for permission to quote from his unpublished Nottingham PhD dissertation, *The Anglo-Saxon Cemetery at Loveden Hill (Hough-on-the-Hill) Lincolnshire, and its Significance in Relation to the Dark Age Settlement of the East Midlands* (1964): pp. 96, 316–17 and 364–7 deal with this urn.

[24] R. W. V. Elliott, 'Two Neglected English Runic Inscriptions: Gil<t>on and Overchurch', *Mélanges de linguistique et de philologie: Fernand Mossé in memoriam* (Paris, 1959), pp. 140–7, at 141–4; S. C. Hawkes and R. I. Page, 'Swords and Runes in South-East England' (1967), pp. 3–4; B. Odenstedt, 'Giltoninskriften: en omstridd engelsk runinskrift', *Ortnamnssällskapets i Uppsala årsskrift* (1979), 55–68.

[25] Moltke, *Runes and their Origin*, p. 239. 'De skal give den i runer ukyndige forestillingen om, at han havde fået en god og kraftig beskyttelsesformel', *Runerne i Danmark*, p. 192.

and the last being 'b', but in each case with the bows pointing inwards; that is, one is either retrograde or inverted. Thus from the beginning there is the difficulty of knowing which way round to read the letters. Whichever way they are taken, there will always be some runes of the legend that are inverted or retrograde with respect to the rest. Inverted or retrograde runes are not unknown in early inscriptions, but I do not know anything in the English tradition that is quite like this Dover text. The runes appear to be 'b c c n l b' or 'b s s n l b' though they may be intended in the reverse order, or indeed in some other, reading from each end in turn. In no case is there any meaning that I can discern, and the lack of any vowel rune in the group implies that no pronounceable word is represented. Yet the letter forms are quite neat and professional looking. They are not formed or laid out in a way to suggest that the cutter was careless or ignorant, and they may from the first have been intended to be cryptic, mysterious or mystical.[26]

That early English runes sometimes have a content that is not plain language is shown by the inscription on a copper bowl of Eastern Mediterranean workmanship found in the cemetery at Chessell Down, Isle of Wight.[27] Though the bowl has been known for many decades, its runes were noticed only comparatively recently. Their neglect over the years is the consequence of three factors. Runes were not to be expected on so clearly non-Germanic a piece. The bowl is in places corroded, and this affects the central part of the text. The bowl is decorated with a hunting scene, a hound chasing hares, and a leopard in pursuit of a stag, in punched work, and it is across this sequence that the runes are placed. Thus they are not easily spotted, and indeed may never have been intended for general view. The runes are finely scratched in a single row between framing lines. The beginning is not clear, but the first visible runes – and these may be the opening of the text – are 'b w s', which does not look reassuring. The last readable runes – and again these may be the end of the inscription – are 'c c c æ æ æ', which is also disturbing. Fairly clearly, this is not plain language; but it does not look like error either. What was engraved was deliberate, but not straightforwardly comprehensible. Any literacy it implies was literacy of a rather esoteric sort.

Compare this with the better-known text from the same cemetery, that on a silver scabbard-mount. This text looks more purposeful than its neighbour, yet it shares with it one characteristic, a rare and probably transitional form of 'c', which suggests that the two Chessell Down inscriptions belong to the same runic tradition. The scabbard-mount text has seven runes, divided into two groups by a pair of dashes in vertical line, and the letters are quite well formed. There is one rune, the fourth, which is of uncertain value. Perhaps in consequence, though there have been many attempts

---

[26] V. I. Evison, *Dover: the Buckland Anglo-Saxon Cemetery* (London, 1987), pp. 46–7. In the first inscription Evison reads *thorn* where I read *wynn*, and in that case there is no need to assume a retrograde character, though the meaning is made even more obscure. For the second inscription, Evison suggests a reading *bliss* closing with a retrograde 'b' to balance the text. This involves replacing my reading 'n' by 'i', which in turn requires the line across the stave of this rune to be rejected as unintentional.

[27] C. J. Arnold, *The Anglo-Saxon Cemeteries of the Isle of Wight* (London, 1982), pp. 27, 60 and fig. 10, where the drawing of the runes is not accurate in detail.

at explicating the meaning of this text, none has, in my opinion, succeeded. There is a further refinement of doubt. If Mrs Hawkes is to be believed – and she has made a meticulous examination of the scabbard assembly of which the mount was part – the runes are cut on a late addition to the complex, and are so little worn that they may have been added shortly before the burial.[28] Who then would have read the text? When the sword was worn, even on a corpse, the inscription would have been invisible, against the wearer's body.

Another example of an apparently meaningless runic sequence is on one of two bits of metal from an unknown object, picked up on the Sussex foreshore somewhere between Bognor and Selsey Bill. The two are thin strips of gold, broken away at each end, and corrugated into rough zigzags of five or six elements. One face of each strip has runes scratched on it. On one the sequence is inconclusive, for it is '] a n m æ [', or something like it, too fragmentary to tell anything. The other seems to have the baffling group '] b r n r n [', unlikely to be plain language. Unfortunately the context is sparse, so it is not possible to determine whether or not this is another case of Moltke's ignorant rune-smith deceiving an ignorant customer with a spurious inscription. Or if the sequence has some magical or ritual significance, now unrecoverable. Or if the individual characters are to be taken as logograms, *Begriffsrunen*, *begrepsruner*, each representing a specific word and concept.

So far I have taken examples from the early Anglo-Saxon period, an age of which we are too ignorant to be able to assess ways of thought or expression. But there are occasional cases from the later period too, and here there should be more to guide us. One such is a silver-gilt binding strip or mount taken from the River Thames near Westminster Bridge. This elaborate piece (whose purpose is unfortunately unknown and which is incomplete) has on its surviving part two groups of runes, carefully cut and seriffed. They read: 's b ē r æ d h t ɨ b c a i e͡r h͡ a d͡ æ b s'. Art historians date this piece to the eighth/ninth century, but, despite efforts by several philologists in the past, there is no way in which the legend can be interpreted as Old English of that period. Some years ago I suggested that it may be code or magical gibberish based on alphabet magic, and this may still be the most likely explanation.[29] If so, our apparent acquaintance with the historic period gives little help towards clarifying a baffling sequence of letters.

In a case like this we cannot judge of the accuracy of the rune-cutter's copying, because we have no idea what he was copying. There is, however, one Anglo-Saxon cryptic text which seems clearly to contain error, and this we can trace because we have other copies of the same sequence. One text has been attempted on three distinct objects, two agreeing against the third. The legend in question is on a group of three rings. It is cryptic because it is magical gibberish, part of which can be confirmed from manuscript charm texts.[30] One of the ring legends, from Kingmoor/Greymoor Hill, Cumbria, reads: '+ æ r k r i u f l t k r i u r i þ o n g l æ s t æ p o n | t o l'. A second, from Bramham Moor, North Yorkshire, or near it, has almost identical

---

[28] Hawkes and Page, 'Swords and Runes', pp. 16–17.
[29] R. I. Page, 'The Inscriptions' (1964), pp. 78–9.
[30] *Ibid.* pp. 73–5.

lettering, differing only in the way its sequences are divided up: 'æ r k r i u f l t ‖ k r i u r i þ o n ‖ g l æ s t æ p o n t o l'. Both these are goldsmith's work, and by Moltke's criterion ought to be suspect. Yet it is the third of these rings, an agate one of unknown provenance, that has the error. This reads: 'e r y . r i . u f . d o l . y r i . u r i . þ o l . w l e s . t e . p o t e . n o l'. There are a number of differences, but the significant one for the present discussion is the agate ring's use of 'y' where the others use 'k'. This rune, called *calc*, is one of a very localised distribution in epigraphical use. It is confined to the North and particularly the north-west of Anglo-Saxon England. 'y', *yr*, is a much more widely known rune, and its form has some, though fairly slight, resemblance to 'k'. The cutter of the agate ring, not recognising the 'k' of his exemplar, cut the closest form that he knew instead. He was unaware of this late and local subtlety and made an error of identification. It is an error of sight, not of hearing. The carver copied without understanding.

However, we must not jump too readily to Moltke's conclusion that a carver has been incompetent or deceptive to a customer. A useful warning against overhaste in this respect is given by the scramasax taken from the River Thames at Battersea. This famous ninth-century short sword has, inlaid in the blade in various metals, a set of decorative patterns, a *fuþorc*, and the runic personal name 'b ea g n o þ'. The name, though a little rough in execution, is in general without reproach, especially considering the difficult technique the smith was using – having to cut in the blade matrixes for his letters and then fill them with coloured wires.[31] The *fuþorc* is another matter. In the first place it has no obvious meaning in the context, and indeed it is often assumed that a *fuþorc* of this sort must have magical implications simply because there is no clear practical purpose. In the second there is an undeniable indication of carelessness in the smith's work, for he originally missed out one letter, 's' (no. 16), and had to squeeze it in afterwards.[32] But there are other uncertainties. The common order of letters in the *fuþorc* is dislocated at runes 20–24, 'ŋ d l m œ' instead of 'm l ŋ d œ'. The 'j' and 'œ' runes (12, 24) are rare types not commonly found in Old English inscriptions. And the 'd' rune (21) is otherwise unexampled. Is it therefore an error, and so an indication of the smith's imperfect command of the script? It is tempting to think so, but the form of the 'y' rune on the sword should give us pause. Instead of the inset small 'i' which this rune usually shows, the Thames 'y' has an inset cross. This was once thought to be the smith's aberration, again evidence of ignorance. The discovery of another example of the form, cut into the central margin of a page of the Leningrad Gospels (Leningrad, Public Library, F. v. 1. 8, fol. 213), showed it to be an acceptable, if rare, variant. Without this find we would have misjudged the smith. It rather looks as though the unusual Thames runes are types more common in manuscript accounts of the script, and perhaps the aberrant 'd' will turn out to be the same.

From all this it is clear that English runic inscriptions on metal objects can comprise (a) texts meaningless to us, (b) unpronounceable sequences, or those

---

[31] D. M. Wilson, *Anglo-Saxon Ornamental Metalwork 700–1100 in the British Museum* (London, 1964), pp. 144–5.

[32] As Professor Evison pointed out, *Antiquaries Journal* 45 (1965), p. 288.

unlikely to be plain language, (c) texts containing errors, (d) texts with apparent errors, (e) groups of pseudo-runes, characters that appear to be runes but aren't. There are also, rarely, texts that are comprehensible; as the personal names on the Llysfaen ring and the Brandon tweezers, or the maker and owner formula of the gold ring from Manchester.[33] That some of this material suggests literacy in rune-master and/or owner is clear. That there is also indication that a customer might be satisfied with something less than a formal inscription is equally clear. That runes were not always used for communication or record seems certain. We should, however, be aware of the sparsity of evidence. In 1973 I listed some seventeen metal objects with runes (not counting coins), and to this I have added seven more.[34] There are also a few uncertainly runic pieces. So there are around thirty individual pieces from a variety of dates, from the pagan period, as the fifth-century Undley bracteate or the sixth-century Wakerley and Heslerton brooches, to well into the Christian age, as the Mortain and Brunswick caskets and the Thames scramasax. Occasional examples, though strictly speaking metal, may properly belong in other groupings, as the Mortain Casket whose text is cut in the copper plating that covers the wooden reliquary. Both early and late objects preserve baffling letter combinations, as 'g͡ æ g͡ o g͡ æ' on Undley and the difficult sequences of the Thames mount. Corrosion or wear have damaged several of the objects, and their texts are hard to establish; as the Sarre pommel, the Cramond ring and the Heacham tweezers. It would be a rash scholar who drew a general conclusion from this incoherent mass of material.

To return now to the formal inscriptions, cut perhaps by professional carvers. Here I begin with the rune-stones, so maybe we should think of professional masons, trained to reproduce more than one script. When we approach a more formal, indeed public, text, how can we assess the literacy of the carver? I would suggest asking – and it would be interesting to see if this is thought a fair test – if it is significant that an inscription is divided into sensible and meaningful word units. Or if the text is set out anyhow, without regard to word or sentence division.

A first specimen is the Thornhill III memorial stone which has the inscription:

'+ j i l s u i þ : a r æ r d e : æ f t [.]
b e r h t s u i þ e . b e k u n
o n b e r g i g e b i d͡ d a þ
þ æ r : s a u l e'

'Gilswith set up a memorial on a (?) mound for Berhtswith. Pray for her soul'. This is sensibly set out, with its four lines dividing at word ends. Yet by modern standards

---

[33] The Manchester ring was formerly ascribed generally to Lancashire. For the corrected provenance, see B. J. N. Edwards, 'An Anglo-Saxon Ring Provenance Narrowed', *Antiquaries Journal* 63 (1983), 132–4.

[34] Page, 'New Runic Finds'. There are further additions to the corpus since that article, some of them on metal; as a rune-inscribed metal plate from Wardley, Leicestershire, and a possible inscription on a hanging bowl from Cleatham, Manton, South Humberside. See the postscript to 'New Runic Finds', above p. 287.

it is badly arranged.[35] The final line is only half-full (eight runes and a division symbol), leaving a blank at its end. In contrast, the other lines are cramped, having nearly twice as many characters. In the third line two *d*-runes are bound together so that they can fit in better. The reason for this discrepancy is clear enough if you follow the content of the inscription. The carver was trying to divide his text into discrete words, and to avoid breaking a word between two lines. In line 3 he had the long word *gebiddaþ* which he did not want to split; so he had to get it into either line 3 or line 4. In either case he would have had difficulty with spacing, leaving one of the lines half-full. But the recognition of the difficulty implies that the cutter carried out his task not mechanically, but with understanding.

The lay-out of the Thornhill II stone text has a different point of interest:

'+ e a d r e d
* s e t e æ f t e
e a t e i n n e'

'Eadred set up (this stone) in memory of Eadthegn'. The final word, 'e a t e i n n e' is something of a problem. I interpret it as an oblique form of *Eadþegn*, but what of the doubled 'n'? There are certainly several cases in English runic inscriptions of doubled letters for which there is no obvious philological explanation, but I suspect this is not one of them. I suggest an alternative. Again the carver was wanting to set out his text with care. He doubled the penultimate letter of his last line to fill it out. He wanted to get each of his two personal names into its own line, but the second name proved too short to fit into the space available. So he added an extra 'n' (just as a sixteenth-century compositor would add an inorganic -*e* to a word to justify a line of type). Here again is a conscious attempt to arrange a text intelligently.

In contrast stands the less successful Thornhill I:

'+ [.] þ e l b e
[.] t : s e t t æ f t e
r e þ e l w i n i : [.] r [

'Ethelberht set up (this stone) in memory of Ethelwini . . .'. The carver did not succeed in getting the whole of his first name into line 1, so he divided it. In consequence he had to split the word *æfter* and did it foolishly, so that it is not easy to read. In so doing he (perhaps intentionally) omitted the inflexional ending of *sett<e>*. This suggests a less comprehending rune-cutter, one who copied letters mechanically and without understanding.

On the rune-stones there are numbers of other cases of careless or thoughtless splitting of words; indeed, sometimes words are divided in a way so outré that it does not fit anything we would recognise as appropriate word division, nor does it

---

[35] This can clearly be seen in the drawing (taken from a rubbing) of the inscription in Page, *Introduction*, p. 155.

correspond with the sort of word division that, for instance, Dr Lutz has reconstructed.[36] There is the Kirkheaton stone's 'e o h : w o r o | h t æ', 'Eoh made (me)', or the Lancaster cross's 'g i b i d æ þ f o | r æ c y n i b a l | þ c u þ b e r e [ ]', 'Pray for Cynibalth Cuthber. . .'. But the worst example is that of the Great Urswick stone, where the setting-out is so abysmal, and the workmanship so poor that it may well be the product of an incompetent and unintelligent rune-cutter, who had not the least idea of the implications of his characters:

```
'+ t u n w i n i s e t æ
æ f t e r t o r o ɨ
t r e d æ b e k u
n æ f t e r h i s b
æ u r n æ g e b i d æ s þ e
r s        a u
         l æ'
```

'Tunwini set up in memory of Torhtred a memorial for his (?) lord. Pray for his soul'. The carver got his first two words into line 1, but thereafter he failed. For line 2 he had to split the name *Torhtred*, but did not divide at the end of the first element. Similar uncouth word divisions close lines 3 and 4, and by the end of the fifth line he still had two words to complete, so he fitted in six runes in the quadrants of a cross below the rune panel. This lamentable work then has a maker's formula cut crudely across the two relief figures at the stone base, again with little consideration for word division: 'l y l þ i | s w [', 'Lyl <made> me'. If I am right this is not the artist's signature (for then he must have been literate): it is the name of the commissioner of the piece.

The two runic inscriptions from Hartlepool form an interesting contrast, since they show such different qualities of mind. They are, it will be remembered, from the cemetery of a monastery, where literacy should be assumed, and they occur in series with other inscribed stones, two of which have Latin prayer formulae which I suppose were readable by the inhabitants. One rune-stone (Hartlepool I) is in splendid condition, apparently little exposed to weathering. The workmanship corresponds: the letters are neatly cut, provided with elegant serifs, and there is an alpha and omega in the upper quadrants of its incised cross. The text reads 'h i l d i ‖ þ r y þ', a well-known dithematic personal name, divided by the cross-shaft into its two name elements. This is altogether a good professional job. The second rune-stone (Hartlepool II) stands in contrast. Its weathered condition and damaged surface do not help; but the runes are crude in comparison with Hartlepool I. They are poorly spaced, with a distinct gap after the fourth letter. The text reads 'h i l d ‖ d i (g) y þ', the rune 'g' originally missed out and added later, underpointed to show where it fitted in. The 'd' is doubled for no obvious reason. The division of the name by its

---

[36] A. Lutz, 'The Syllabic Basis of Word Division in Old English Manuscripts', *English Studies* 67 (1986), 193–210.

incised cross-shaft does not reflect the division into name elements. Altogether this is a poor piece of work and we might conclude that it was cut by an illiterate carver who did not know about spelling or word division. Is it possible that he had, chalked on his stone, the form 'h i l d ‖ i g y þ', and that he mistook 'i g' for 'd i', being led astray by the preceding 'd'? This would indeed imply that the cutter was at best semi-literate, but presumably under some supervision since he remedied his omission.

Hartlepool II should, however, be seen also in series with the other, non-runic, stones from this gravefield. Where it is possible to get a certain reading, it appears that on them dithematic personal names divide between first and second elements, though the composition vowel may open the second part. Thus, EDIL ‖ UINI (Okasha III), ORA ‖ PRO | UER | MUND ‖ TORHT | SUID (Okasha IV), BERCHT ‖ GYD (Okasha VI),] ‖ UGUID (Okasha VIII). In the similar series from Lindisfarne (both runic and non-runic), dithematic names divide at their elements. A stone of the same general design from York appears to have LEOB ‖ DEIN (Okasha VI). The matter (like all matters of Anglo-Saxon word division) requires thorough research, but this brief survey suggests that letter-cutters in general recognised the principles of dithematic name formation. Hartlepool II, on the other hand, stands distinct in its incapacity.[37] There is clear implication of illiteracy, though it was clearly unusual.

Probably signs of carelessness rather than illiteracy are the mistakes on the Overchurch stone, and here the supervision was inadequate to correct them. This memorial text reads:

'f o l c {æ} a r æ r d o n b e c [
   [ ] b i d d a þ f o t e æ þ e l m u n ['.

'The (?) people erected (this) monument. Pray for Æthelmun<d>'. The second line has a certain error, 't' for 'r' in *fote*. Line 1 has the words *folc* and *arærdon*. Between them is a clear 'æ' which serves no obvious function, and Dickins rejected it as 'perhaps a blundered or damaged character abandoned by the carver'.[38] That is the easiest way of disposing of this difficult reading, and the error at 'f o t e' and a possible second in a miscutting of 'l' in 'æ þ e l m u n [' might justify it. Yet it is unsatisfactory. A form *folcæ* is unlikely; Elliott's tentative suggestion that it is an archaic plural needs consideration, but perhaps not a lot of time spent on it, since otherwise there is nothing noticeably archaic/archaistic about the inscription.[39] In the absence of word separation there is the theoretical possibility that the text was to be read *folc æarærdon* . . ., with a curious (?) glide vowel beginning the verb, but that again seems unlikely, a counsel of despair. Yet to regard the superfluous 'æ' as 'blundered or

[37] As does the part-runic name form (?) added to the Chester-le-Street stone, EADm | VnD. But that may be the effect of trying to fit a name form into the space available on an existing monument: R. Cramp, *The British Academy Corpus of Anglo-Saxon Stone Sculpture, I: County Durham and Northumberland* (Oxford, 1984), p. 54.

[38] Dickins, 'System of Transliteration', p. 19.

[39] Elliott, 'Two Neglected English Runic Inscriptions', pp. 145–7.

damaged' when it shows only slight sign of damage is also despairing. The error in 'f o t e' – and it can only be an error – is puzzling, for there is no similarity of form between 'r' and 't' (or between *r* and *t* in case the carver was transliterating from a roman text), nor do 'r' and 't' appear close together in the *fuþorc* (in case he was laboriously and without knowledge encoding a roman text into runes).

No single explanation covers all these cases. Moreover, before we jump to the accusation of illiteracy we must check against the work of these rune-masters the competence of some scribes of manuscripts. By definition, a scribe must possess some literacy, yet it is fascinating to see how marginal is that literacy in certain cases. Take that of MS CCCC 383, a legal miscellany of the late eleventh/early twelfth century.[40] The estate names in a list of shipmen added at the end suggest that the manuscript was the property of a major foundation, St Paul's, London. The hand responsible for the bulk of the text is a neat, competent one. Yet the writing practice is chaotic. Errors of carelessness abound. Eye-skip is common, usually producing meaningless sentences. There is frequent misreading of the exemplar, creating such nonsensical forms as *englifcne* (*engliscne*), *falfe* (*false*), *yrfer* (*yrfes*). Other mistakes are due to dittography as *on dægelæge* (*on dænelæge*), *belimbe* (*belimpe*). An initial is omitted, producing a non-word in *<B>orges mon* (in the middle of a line and with no space left for a rubricated initial). Carelessness leads to the mistake 'for "yes" read "no" ', when the negative prefix is omitted from *<un>awended*. Spelling is inconsistent so that often two or more different spellings of a word occur in successive lines, as *kingc, kyning, kyningc, cyning, cynig, cynnig, cyng* for 'king'. This manuscript also evidences some of the faults that characterise the Great Urswick inscription: notably curious misdivisions of wording, with *þanon* divided *þa non*, *gyslas* put *gys las*, the phrase *ær geypped nære* appearing as *ærge yppednære*; this sometimes occurs within lines, sometimes at line ends, as *geor/ne*, *geonwæ/tere*. And there is confusingly irregular punctuation and frequent demotic spellings, with decline in the precision of representation of unaccented vowels, and variation of initial *hr/r* and *hl/l*. The scribe of MS 383 is no more illiterate than the carver of Great Urswick, but he is not noticeably less.[41]

Nor does a comparison of runic and non-runic inscriptions suggest that *runeristere* were specially liable to produce *skriblerier*. One of the longer Anglo-Saxon non-runic inscriptions is that on the eleventh-century sundial at Kirkdale, N. Yorkshire.[42] Here the layout of the text begins quite formally, but soon degenerates:

+ORM·GAMAL·
SVNA·BOHTE.SCS
GREGORIVS·MIN
STERÐONNEHI
T.WESÆL·TOBRO

---

[40] Ker, *Catalogue*, no. 65, pp. 110–13.

[41] I have given a single example, but readers of Anglo-Saxon manuscripts will readily recall others, including manuscripts with frequent errors or non-classical forms in Latin texts, as CCCC 23 and 422.

[42] Okasha, *Hand-List*, pp. 87–8. Details of punctuation of this inscription are not always clear.

CAN·7TOFALAN·7HĒ
HIT·LET·MACAN·NE WAN·FROM
GRVNDE·XPE:7SCSGREGORI
VS·IN·EADWARD·DAGVM·CN̄G
7N·TOSTI DAGVM·EORL+

'Orm Gamal's son bought St Gregory's minster when it was quite ruinous and collapsed, and he had it restored from the foundations for Christ and St Gregory, in the days of King Eadward and Earl Tosti'. The text is in two parts in matching panels, but it is clear from the transcript that the first panel's text is more widely spaced than the second, perhaps to give greater prominence to the name of the church's owner. If he had wanted to (and had agreed its importance), the carver could have done better. Accepting that *minster* had to be divided, there was in fact space to get the whole of *hit* on its line (instead of committing the absurd HI | T) which would have helped the carver avoid dividing *tobrocan* (actually split between two panels, just as in MS 383 the scribe sometimes divides a word between adjacent pages). But it is at least likely that Anglo-Saxons had a lower respect for tidiness in a text than we have, and that this is a better explanation of the crude lay-out than illiteracy. So too we could account for the unbalanced form of the Mortain Casket's:

'+goodhelpe:æadan
þiiosneciismeelgewar
ahtæ'

'God help Æada (who) made this (?) reliquary'. Or for the Kirkheaton stone's:

'eohworo
htæ'

'Eoh made (this)'. Or the Lancaster cross's

'gibidæþfo
ræcynibal
þcuþbere['

'Pray for Cynibalth Cuthbere['. Whether such lay-outs imply illiteracy or simply unconcern is hard to say. The variation between 'war | ahtæ' and 'woro | htæ' suggests the point of division is chance rather than intent.

The most complex of Anglo-Saxon runic monuments is the Franks (Auzon) Casket.[43] In discussing it I will make a couple of assumptions, and it is important to keep in mind that they are assumptions: that the top and all four sides are by the same craftsman, and that the carver was also the rune-master. I omit from discussion the

---

[43] There is a detailed record of this object and its texts in A. Becker, *Franks Casket: zu den Bildern und Inschriften des Runenkästchens von Auzon* (Regensburg, 1973).

fourth, cryptic, side which, having a text in code, presents difficulties and problems that are, in my opinion, insuperable, and in any case may not be relevant to the purpose of this paper. Of the craftsman we can say that he knew (i) Christian and ancient history/legend, and Germanic tale, (ii) the appearance of Latin and Old English, (iii) the forms of runes and roman script. So we would expect him to be literate. Perhaps in confirmation is the careful lay-out of the texts. An artefact of such elaboration would need planning, and this is shown in the setting of the words. On the three sides (excluding the cryptic one) where longer texts are placed, the craftsman took pains to ensure that words did not overrun their panels; though each text is subdivided into several groups, there is no divided word save the long *fergenberig*, which could not be got into a single section. It is convenient in presenting this material to depart from the original and give loose transcripts with the texts set in their separate words to show the divisions between panels:

(a) 'fisc.flodu. | ahof on ferg | enberig | warþ gasric grorn þær he on greut giswom | hronæs ban'. 'The fish beat up the sea(s) on to the mountainous cliff. The king of (?) terror grew sad when he swam on to the shingle'; 'whale's bone'.

(b) 'romwalus and reum*walus twægen* | *gibroþær* | afœddæ hiæ wyli*f* in romæcæstri: | *oþlæ unneg*'. 'Romulus and Remus, two brothers, a she-wolf nourished them in the city of Rome, far from their native land'.

(c) 'her fegtaþ | titus end giuþeasu' | HIC FUGIANT HIERUSALIM | 'afitatores'. 'Here Titus and the Jews fight. Here the inhabitants flee from Jerusalem'.

There is an interesting distinction on the side, (c) above, which has part of its text in Latin. Some of the Latin is in roman script – mixed uncials and capitals, given in my transcript by capitals – and here a Classical spelling of Latin is used (apart from a palpable error in grammar, *fugiant* for *fugiunt*). But the final Latin word, in runes, shows a different spelling tradition, 'a f i t a t o r e s' for *habitatores*. There is loss of an initial *h-* and the intervocalic *-b-* is represented by the spirant rune 'f'. This is presumably a contemporary pronunciation spelling. Thus the carver (? designer) was acquainted not only with the 'standard' spelling of Latin, but also with that which represented a demotic pronunciation, and he was able to switch from one to the other in accordance with the writing system, learned or (?) demotic, that he was using. This suggests a sophisticated attitude to language. It seems too that, though there was certainly a planned lay-out, it also showed some element of improvisation. Another feature of the casket's inscriptions supports this: the solutions to the problem of how, in using a left-to-right writing system, you put texts at all four sides of a rectangle; what in effect you do with the bottom line. The carver (? designer) tried two solutions. On side (a) he wrote it retrograde so that it ran from right to left and closed the rectangle. On side (b) he achieved the same effect by writing his bottom line upside down. On side (c) he avoided a bottom line altogether, and this may be the reason why he carved many of his runes so much smaller and used a small roman script, so that he could get all his text into the top and the two side borders.

When a word did not quite occupy the space available, the rune-master used points as space fillers, as in 'r o m æ c æ s t r i :'. Whatever we may accuse the carver of, therefore, it does not seem to be lack of care. Yet there are two very difficult readings in the casket's texts which have led to considerable debate: *flodu* and *giuþeasu*. The second is usually translated as 'Jews', a nominative plural which should have the form *Giuþeas*. What then is the superfluous -*u*? The form *flodu* also has an unnecessary -*u*, since at this date (*c.* 700) that ending should be lost after a long stem syllable. Can we explain the two as space fillers added to fill up a panel where simple pointing would be inadequate? It is an uncomfortable explanation, but the best I can think up.

The point of this discussion of the Auzon Casket is to suggest that, even in texts which, as far as any practical examination can tell, are the products of a literate carver, there may yet be lexical forms which are philologically doubtful or inexplicable, even apparently archaic. In other words, we do not have to adduce illiteracy to explain hard forms.

It is not difficult to find other examples of this general point, that within a literate context there can be word forms hard to explain from philology. One case is the rune-inscribed bone comb found at Whitby, and presumably connected with the Anglo-Saxon monastery of *Streoneshalh*.[44] Across it is cut the text '$\widehat{d}$ *[æ] u* s m͡ æ u s ‖ g o d a l u w a l u ‖ d͡ o h͡ e l i p æ c y ‖ [', 'Deus meus, may God Almighty help Cy . . .'. Here there is no need to doubt that the rune-master composed his own text. The runes are incised simply in the surface of the bone with a sharp knife. The object is one of no great value, not the sort of thing one would commission specially from a craftsman, complete with legend. The carver was literate enough to know some, if elementary, Latin. Yet his Old English text, brief as it is, has an unusual convention of spelling: the occurrence of glide vowels between the liquid *l* and a neighbouring consonant, as *aluwaludo, helipæ*. It is not that such spellings are not found elsewhere outside this text. They are. But we would hardly expect three examples in a text of three words.

Something similar occurs in the Mortain Casket inscription. This is an article of church furniture, apparently a reliquary or a box for the consecrated host. The runes are crudely cut into the copper plating covering the wooden shrine. The plating has Christian decoration with Latin texts in roman script as well as the runes. The runic inscription contains the learned loan-word *ciismeel*. Again we would deduce a literate milieu. Yet there is unusual spelling, this time the doubled vowel, in *good, þiiosne, ciismeel*. Again this is not unparalleled, and again it is the number of occurrences that is significant. The implication of these examples is that inscriptions may use different patterns of spelling from manuscripts. Cutting a text is after all not the same as writing one, and it may produce formal differences in words or sound-combinations represented. Divergence from a more commonly attested practice is not necessarily a sign of illiteracy.

This discussion has ranged quite widely through time and space. Because of the sparsity of English epigraphical evidence I have brought together material from both

---

[44] From the various early find-reports it seems that this comb, a casual find, came from a site east of the River Esk, between it and the present abbey ruins. A link with the Anglo-Saxon foundation is consonant with provenance and language date.

early and late Anglo-Saxon times. But it is dangerous to assume the two have much relevance for each other; the early period knew no literate tradition outside the runic, whereas the later had a strong learned, literate culture running parallel with and sometimes interacting with that of the runes. For the same reason it is unsound to compare anything but the earliest English material with that of Dark Age Scandinavia, where too the only literacy was runic. Again I think it unsound to treat as one inscriptions of different sorts: those which suggest an educated background and those likely to be base, common and popular. Anglo-Saxon inscriptions will not of themselves demonstrate a literate society, as Wormald pointed out. But some will show runic literacy side by side with roman; some may suggest, quite strongly, the probability of limited lay literacy: some will imply that epigraphical literacy had different practices from non-epigraphical, which makes comparison of linguistic forms dangerous. Each inscription needs studying within its context, expressed as precisely as possible. And we must not assume error or illiterate practice too easily.

POSTSCRIPT

This discussion did not exploit the discovery, in early tourist centres of Italy, of runic graffiti giving Anglo-Saxon names, presumably those of travellers, perhaps pilgrims.[45] The great collection of names of various nationalities at Monte Sant' Angelo in southern Italy, includes several English ones in runes. Comparable to these is a further English runic find, a name scratched on a fresco in the Cimitero di Commodilla, Rome. All these graffiti have been given a general date between the late seventh century and the early ninth. They suggest that at any rate some English travellers of that date were literate enough in runes to cut their names in the script. They may have deliberately chosen runic rather than roman to assert their Englishness in a foreign environment. What degree of runic literacy it implies I do not know. Modern Britain has enough examples of people who can write their own names and not much else. But if these Anglo-Saxons were pilgrims, there is a suggestion of more general literacy, and perhaps of an ecclesiastical context. Something similar applies to the runic texts found at Brandon[46] where a *fuþorc* and a name on a metal implement were found in proximity to an apparently meaningful runic inscription on a bone handle at a high-status settlement site with likely ecclesiastical implications. These are all cases where at least limited runic literacy must obtain.

Perhaps from an earlier period the back-of-brooch inscription from Harford Farm, Caistor-by-Norwich, with its minimal word separation, suggests a workman with again some runic literacy. His text reads 'l u d a : g i b œ t æ s i g i l æ', 'Luda repaired the brooch'. John Hines dates the brooch *c.* 610–50, but of course this does not date the repair. On the other hand, there is the occasional new inscription that suggests a

---

[45] See above, p. 3, n. 6.
[46] For references to these and the following inscriptions see above, p. 287.

more limited control of runes: for example, the text on the seventh-century hanging-bowl found at Cleatham.

Finally, I draw attention to R. Derolez's important article, which approaches the subject from a completely different angle from mine, 'Runic Literacy among the Anglo-Saxons'.[47] But to discuss that would need a whole new article of my own.

[47] *Britain 400–600*, ed. Bammesberger and Wollmann, pp. 397–436.

22
(1989)

ROMAN AND RUNIC ON ST CUTHBERT'S COFFIN

Among the contents of the new runic periodical *Nytt om Runer* is a running bibliography, its final section headed *Fantas(t)isk litteratur*.[1] This lists writings that show runes as an occult script, one suited to oracular pronouncement in modern as well as medieval life. The recent past has seen a good deal of this sort of writing, and occult bookshops can usually be expected to have a shelf or two of books on runes. They have no scholarly value, and serve only to document that fascination with fantasy, that flight from reason that is such a sad feature of the modern world.

Occasionally, however, a book in this field has claims to scholarship, and therefore merits more formal consideration. One such book is *The Way of Wyrd* which its author, in the preface, describes as 'a report of a major research project'.[2] Though written in narrative form as a series of connected 'tales of an Anglo-Saxon sorcerer', the material is 'reconstructed from research evidence', and each episode has been subjected to 'a process of rigorous analysis'. The events are set in the later seventh century, the principal episode in 674. The hero, a young man with the slightly unusual Anglo-Saxon name of Wat Brand, is a Christian who learns the practices and beliefs of paganism, and in the course of this makes acquaintance with runes, 'the mysterious writings of the pagans'. The author comments on the Christian attitude to this script:

> In Mercia runes were now officially outlawed, though peasants still unlaw-fully carved them on sticks and threw them as lotteries, foretelling the future. Brother Eappa knew how to read and write runic inscriptions, but they were forbidden to initiates in the scriptorium for they were sacriligious (*sic*).[3]

Weird though this is, it nevertheless calls for comment. It has often been asserted even in scholarly works that the runic script was intimately linked with paganism, with the implication that its employment conflicted with Christian teaching and so was unacceptable in Christian times. In fact there is, as far as I know, nothing from Anglo-Saxon England to support this contention. Some twenty years ago I summed up the English evidence for the magical or cult use of runes, and concluded that it was unconvincing.[4] I have seen no reason to change my opinion.

---

[1] *Nytt om Runer: meldingsblad om runeforskning* 1 (1986), 30.
[2] B. Bates, *The Way of Wyrd: Tales of an Anglo-Saxon Sorcerer* (London, 1983, repr. 1984), p. 9.
[3] *Ibid.* p. 78.
[4] 'Anglo-Saxon Runes and Magic', above pp. 105–25.

It is particularly difficult to support any assertion about runes in seventh-century Mercia, for there is little known directly from that time and place. Nor is there, to my knowledge, any survival anywhere in England of wooden stick charms or lotteries such as the author of *The Way of Wyrd* predicates. From its text and decoration the copper-coated wooden shrine now at Mortain, département Manche, France, may have been made in Mercia *c.* 700, though the evidence is not at all conclusive.[5] The shrine is decorated with figures of Christ and the archangels Michael and Gabriel, yet its maker formula is in runes. By the second half of the eighth century runes were certainly acceptable for formal use in Mercia since Offa allowed them on some of his coins.[6] The later Anglo-Saxon period shows runes used for a Christian memorial inscription on a carved stone from Overchurch in the Wirral.[7] So whatever sacrilegious content officials found in the script in late seventh-century Mercia does not seem to have lasted long.

Nor is there any general reason to believe that runes were kept out of the scriptorium. Indeed, by the eighth century two runic graphs, *thorn* and *wynn*, had penetrated English bookhand, and would presumably be taught to initiates.[8] In more sophisticated work, as Michelle Brown has reminded me, occasional runic forms were used in display scripts. A clear case is in the Chad Gospels (Lichfield Cathedral Library), tentatively ascribed to the West Midlands and the early eighth century.[9] Its formal scripts show runic influence, and even the borrowing of individual runic graphs, sometimes correctly used, sometimes not. Examples are on the openings of the Gospels of Mark (in XpI, using runic 'p') and Luke (in QUONIAm, the 'm' runic).[10]

Runica manuscripta, English manuscript accounts of the runic script, are quite common in the later Anglo-Saxon period, but none of them, to my knowledge, comments that runes are pagan or sacrilegious.[11] Indeed, some scribes put the Anglo-Saxon rune-row alongside Hebrew, Greek and other esoteric alphabets, so they seem to have thought there was nothing specially sacrilegious about it. Earlier than these manuscripts is a bit of concrete evidence direct from the scriptorium, though it is neither Mercian nor seventh century. This is the (?) eighth-century writing

---

[5] The first monograph on this piece, M. Cahen and M. Olsen, *L'inscription runique du coffret de Mortain* (Paris, 1930), gives a date '660–700 (725), vraisemblablement vers 680' (p. 50), but more recently the casket has been put rather later; Dahl, for instance, suggests '8th–9th c.', *Substantival Inflexion*, p. 28. I agree with Dahl in finding the only clear evidence of dialect to be the stem vowel of the verb *gewarahtæ*, which suggests the West Midlands.

[6] C. E. Blunt, 'The Coinage of Offa', *Anglo-Saxon Coins: Studies Presented to F. M. Stenton . . .*, ed. R. H. M. Dolley (London, 1961), pp. 39–62, at 49.

[7] For the Anglo-Saxon runic inscriptions cited in this article see Page, *Introduction* (1973).

[8] Campbell, *Old English Grammar*, § 57 (6) and n. 1.

[9] G. Henderson, *From Durrow to Kells: the Insular Gospel-Books 650–800* (London, 1987), pp. 126–9.

[10] Illustrated in J. J. G. Alexander, *Insular Manuscripts 6th to 9th Century* (London, 1978), plates 50 and 78. In fact, the Mark page has an unusual form of 'p', doubled as in the *fuþark* of the Breza, Jugoslavia, stone. In the word *scriptum* on the same page, *p* is given by the rune 'm' (or 'd'). The doubled 'p' represents *m* in *multi* on the Luke page.

[11] Derolez, *Runica Manuscripta*.

tablet of bone found at Blythburgh, Suffolk, early this century (British Museum accession no. 1902, 3–15, 1).[12] Though the tablet has been known for decades, its runes were spotted only recently, by Professor Martin Biddle. On the recessed surface, which in use would be covered by a wax layer, there are irregular lines of engraved marks which, under the binocular microscope, reveal themselves as runes. Parts of three lines can be traced, though in general they make no sense and are perhaps the epigraphical equivalent of *probationes pennae*: 1, '[ ] o g (or should this be read 'n'?) u a t [-2-] þ [ ]'; 2, '[ ] s u n t [ ]' (is this intended as the Latin word?); 3, '[ ] m a m æ m æ m [ ]'. In case anyone should argue that these, being ordinarily covered by wax, were secret or surreptitious letters which would escape the critical eye of the writing master, I point to a fragment of a runic text on the raised rim, just by a break in the surface, 'u n þ ['.[13]

I have dwelt on this point because the function of the runes on the coffin of St Cuthbert is at first sight puzzling. If runes were essentially pagan/cultic/magical/ sacrilegious, it is hard to explain why the monks of Lindisfarne used them on a public piece of tomb furniture for their revered saint in 698, a couple of decades only after Wat Brand's adventures with the mystical. Clearly at Lindisfarne at the end of the seventh century runes were not 'officially outlawed', nor were they thought unsuited to professional Christian or learned use. There could be a geographical distinction, with Northumbria showing – as was to be expected – a more balanced and sensible view of the script than regions further south. But I think it more likely that this reflects a general attitude in Anglo-Saxon England, that runes were a script as any other; if they had been employed for pagan practices, all the more reason for applying them to Christianity, so that people accustomed to using them might be reconciled to a new religion. Whatever else the later history of Anglo-Saxon runes shows, it makes clear that the church, far from discouraging writing in runes, exploited the script.

The inscriptions on St Cuthbert's coffin, and in particular the runes, are poorly preserved. This is partly because of the condition of the wood, attacked as it is by a fungoid infection that has made it crack both in the line of the grain and at right angles to it. But the carvers of the runes must take some responsibility for the difficulty in reading them. Runes were originally devised for cutting on wood, and their shapes are such as can properly be made in a grained material. The forms are made up of straight lines, vertical and sloping; the verticals cut the grain at right angles, while the sloping lines cut it at oblique angles. Thus the staves stand clear of the grain. The Lindisfarne rune-cutters did not observe these rules. On the coffin the rune stems run parallel to the grain and can easily be lost in it. And it may be this

---

[12] J. G. Waller in *PSAL* 2nd ser., 19 (1901–3), 40–2.

[13] For Anglo-Saxon runes I use the system of transliteration defined in 'On the Transliteration of English Runes', above pp. 245–70. It is interesting to note that runic parallels to the Blythburgh tablet – though rather later – have come to light in Scandinavia in recent years: so, a rune-inscribed wooden tablet from Bergen (A. Liestøl, *Runer frå Bryggen* [Særtrykk av *Viking* 1963] (Bergen, 1964), pp. 11–12) and a similar though less well preserved example from Trondheim (J. R. Hagland, *Runefunna: ei kjelde til handelen si historie* (Trondheim, 1986), pp. 7–10). More distant is a rune-inscribed stylus from Lödöse, Västergötland, Sweden (E. Svärdström, *Runfynden i Gamla Lödöse* (Stockholm, 1982), pp. 30–3).

that renders parts of, for instance, the name *Iohannis* and the Jesus form *ihs* illegible. From this we might deduce that the Lindisfarne carvers were unused to cutting the characters, at any rate in their traditional way on wood. Even though Lindisfarne had other saints to honour, it is likely that St Cuthbert's coffin was a unique piece. There was no direct model to copy, and the rune carvers were left to their own devices.

Because of the difficulties in reading the texts on the coffin, it is advisable to make use of early drawings that show the inscriptions when they were more accessible. There are, I think, only two publications that give first-hand information on the inscriptions before the work that led to Battiscombe's 1956 volume on the relics. These are the ones of James Raine (1828) and William Greenwell (1899). Other drawings before 1947 derive, I think, from these. Bruce Dickins saw the coffin in the 1920s and made notes on it which unfortunately do not survive. By 1956 he was already able to say that the inscriptions 'have become decidedly more difficult to read' because of the effect of the preservatives applied. It is this condition that McIntyre's 1947 drawings record. Presumably Dickins's readings for the 1956 volume depend to some degree on his earlier notes, so they have independent importance. My own detailed examination of the coffin was in 1967, since when it experienced, in 1978, further conservation and cleaning, the then condition recorded in the Dickinson drawings published in 1985.[14] A brief recent examination suggests to me that the inscriptions are now slightly easier to see than in 1967. Moreover, there are a few newly identified pieces of the coffin with fragments of inscriptions on them which will fill out, though not significantly change, the present readings. Clearly there is need for yet another detailed examination of the inscriptions.

Raine's drawings reproduce the inscriptions: ANDREAS, THOMAS, 'x p s',]PVS, MATHEAS (Raine's pl. II), PETRVS, LVCAS, RAR[, SMICH[(pl. III). Greenwell shows: on the lid, 'm͡a t h e u s' ('t' inverted), 'm͡a r c u s', LVCAS, 'i o h a n n i s' (Greenwell's pl. 9); on the archangel side *RAP*[*h*]AEL, SCS VRIA[, SCS and]VmIA[(pl. 10); on the apostle side PETRVS, IACOBVS, IOHANNIS, AN-DREAS,]PVS, BAR[, THOMAS, PA[and MATHEÆS (which Greenwell read as MATHEAS) (pls 11 and 12); on the Christ and Mary end]AR[and 'i h s x p s'; on the other end]CSmICHÆL and]ABRIÆL (pl. 13).

Dickins has:

(i) '*m/atheus*', '*m/arcus*', LVCAS, '*iohann*[*i*]s'.[15] Of these I would comment on: (a) the ending of the Matthew name, for I can see only three stave bases between '*h*' and '*s*'; which could imply that '*e*' and '*u*' here formed a bind-rune. Greenwell confirms

[14] J. Raine, *St Cuthbert, with an Account of the State in which his Remains were found . . .* (Durham, 1828), plates II and III; F. J. Haverfield and W. Greenwell, *A Catalogue of the Sculptured and Inscribed Stones in the Cathedral Library, Durham* (Durham, 1899), plates 9–13, supported by plates 1–5; B. Dickins, 'The Inscriptions upon the Coffin', *The Relics of Saint Cuthbert*, ed. C. F. Battiscombe (Oxford, 1956), pp. 305–7, together with the McIntyre (D. McIntyre and E. Kitzinger, *The Coffin of St Cuthbert* (Durham and Oxford, 1950) plates VII–X; J. M. Cronyn and C. V. Horie, *St Cuthbert's Coffin: the History, Technology and Conservation* (Durham, 1985), pp. 92–100.
[15] For convenience I reproduce Dickins's transliteration here though it differs in some details from my own. He does not space runes, uses the form 'm/a' to indicate a bind of the two runes, and a distinctive symbol to represent the unusual *s*-rune of the coffin; I do not follow him in this last.

the three bases as does Dickinson, while McIntyre is obscure here. (b) the Mark name shows some damage in the drawings from McIntyre onwards. Greenwell gives it intact. (c) LVCAS is clear and generally accepted. (d) the John name. Greenwell has this complete save that his second rune looks nearer 'æ' than 'o'. Dickins remarks that 'the short verticals that rise from the ends of the main twigs of the second character are just discernible', and both McIntyre and Dickinson show them, though I could not see them. Nor could I see either of the 'i' runes – both McIntyre and Dickinson had difficulty with these – and only the centres of the 'n' runes.

(ii) defective names of two archangels at the head end. Dickins reads [S]CS MICH[Æ]L. The final letter is on a separate fragment absent from Greenwell's drawing of the coffin end, though implied in his transcript of the name (which, it will be noted, contains a runic 'm' for which there is no justification, and which is not on the general drawing). Raine misses the end of this name, so the fragment probably appeared in the 1899 excavation. The vowel preceding L cannot be supplied from what survives now or from any known drawing. Dickins must be conjecturing here. He reads the second name [SCS G]ABR[I]ÆL. McIntyre does not show the two vowels before L. Dickinson shows only the top of the second vowel, which is all that I could see. Greenwell records clearly IÆ, the second vowel having a shape divergent from that of the apostle name MATHEÆ̂S.

(iii) at the foot end Mary and Christ. For Mary, Dickins gives [M]AR. McIntyre shows only A and a stave of R, while Dickinson shows nothing on his main drawing, but A on the smaller version. I saw the final stave of M (or this could be the rune 'm'), A and the top of R. Greenwell, Dickins, McIntyre and Dickinson coincide in giving the Christ name and title entire: 'i h s x p s'. Of 'h' and 's' I could see only staves, but 'x p s' remains clear. Raine did not note 'i h s' at all.

(iv) on the archangel side are parts of three names and forms of *sanctus*. Though not listed at all by Raine, all are confirmed by Greenwell, McIntyre and Dickinson. Dickins reads (a) RAPHAEL. I cannot see the letter H, nor could Greenwell, for he supplies it as the runic form 'h'. McIntyre and Dickinson confirm that the letter is almost completely lost, as indeed is the preceding P. The name is to the right of the archangel's halo; to its left I thought I saw very faint traces which might have been [S]CS, not recorded by anyone else. (b) SCS VRIA[EL]. Greenwell confirms that the last two letters are entirely Dickins's conjecture. (c) SCS, which Dickins combines with an otherwise unplaced [R]VmIA[EL]. Again it is clear from Greenwell that what is visible of the name now,]VmIA[, was all that remained in 1899.

(v) on the apostle side names and fragments of ten of the twelve apostles. Raine has six of the names. Greenwell, McIntyre and Dickinson agree in what survives, and Dickins completes some of the names. I give the order reading in pairs from right to left, and Kitzinger points out that this represents the litany of the canon of the mass.[16] (a) PETRVS. (b) PA[, which Dickins completes as *Paulus*. Greenwell shows the A

---

[16] E. Kitzinger, 'The Coffin-Reliquary', *The Relics*, ed. Battiscombe, pp. 202–97, at 269.

entire in his transcript, though not in his general drawing of the side. (c) ANDREAS. (d) Here should be a form of *Iacobus*, which indeed Dickins supplies, and see now Cronyn and Horie, 'The Anglo-Saxon Coffin: Further Investigations', *St Cuthbert, his Cult and his Community*, ed. G. Bonner *et al.* (Woodbridge and Wolfeboro, NH, 1989), pp. 247–56, at 253 and figs 18–19. (e) IOHANNIS. (f) THOMAS. (g) Dickins reads IA[*CO*]*B*VS, corresponding to Greenwell. There is no trace of the *CO* in modern times. (h)]*P*VS. Greenwell omits. Raine suggests the bow of a preceding P. Dickins reads [*PHILIP*]*P*VS. (i) BAR[, as Greenwell, corresponding to Raine's RAR. In this case Dickins does not complete the name, perhaps being uncertain whether it was *Bartholomaeus* or *Barnabas*. (j) MATHEA͡ES. This used to be read MATHEÆ, which Kitzinger took to be a vocative appropriate to a litany form. Dickins drew attention to the base line of the last letter (which Raine had tentatively, and Greenwell confidently recorded) which converts Æ to Æ͡S, but accepted that the form is an odd one, presumably for *Matheus*. Yet the evangelist's name (in (i) above) also has some sort of ambiguity in its ending. (k)]*NV*S, apparently what Greenwell meant by his angular P + VS. Dickins leaves the name incomplete. Kitzinger notes that Simon Cananaeus fills the litany at this point, and suggests a form *Simonus* if not an irregular spelling of *Cananaeus*. (l) a lost name, which should be *Thaddaeus*, which Dickins does not supply.

Though there are these minor uncertainties (as well as the additions that must be made from the newly found fragments), the inscriptions show no serious problem of meaning, only of form. Epigraphically they are of some interest. The roman characters are what Dr Okasha calls, rather uninformatively, 'AS capitals',[17] but which perhaps should be called mixed Insular 'display' letter forms. They are mainly angular, but here and there, in O, P, the carver condescended to curves. There are variant forms of some of the letters used, A, H, for instance. Whether this points to more than one carver I do not know.

The runes are neatly and carefully incised, and though there are a couple of rare forms, the only unorthodox usage is the inverted 't' of *Matheus*. For this there may be an artistic rather than an epigraphical explanation: the desire to set an arm of 't' neatly beneath those of the preceding 'a'. The 'o', if that is what it is, of *Iohannis* has its side staves set unusually far apart, but not unrecognizably so. The rune 'x' is rare in inscriptions, simply because Old English does not need the character. The only other epigraphical example with the certain value 'x' is on a group of related coins of Beonna of East Anglia, where it occurs in the title 'r e x'.[18] Otherwise it appears in an uncertain context on the York spoon, and in its proper place in the *fuþorc* of the ninth-century Thames (Battersea) scramasax, where it has no ascertainable value.[19] However, 'x' is a standard equivalent for this character in Anglo-

17 Okasha, *Hand-List*, p. 68.
18 M. M. Archibald, 'The Coinage of Beonna in the Light of the Middle Harling Hoard', *BNJ* 55 (1985), 10–54, at 39.
19 In 1932 Dickins suggested that this rune was 'a fossil in Old English', and placed its transcription in brackets to signal the fact: as '(x)' (B. Dickins, 'System of Transliteration', pp. 16–17). Presumably

Saxon manuscript accounts of runes.[20] The 's' form of St Cuthbert's coffin is Ⴤ, for which Dickins here uses the distinctive transliteration 'ʃ', deriving it from the Insular minuscule character.[21] It is not common elsewhere in inscriptions, though it appears on the Thames scramasax, and on an amulet ring from Kingmoor, Cumbria, where the related ring from Bramham Moor, Yorkshire, has the more common *s*-rune. It is also recorded in a pair of manuscript rune-rows. Besides its 's', the Thames scramasax has a couple of other runic forms which suggest manuscript inspiration for its *fuþorc* – 'œ', and perhaps 'j' and 'y'. There is a suggestion here, then, that the St Cuthbert's coffin runes derive directly from manuscript tradition rather than epigraphical, but I admit it remains unproven.

The intrusive 'm' in]VmIA[is to be noted. There are several epigraphical examples of this rune in otherwise roman contexts, probably because of its similarity to the roman letter. So, the memorial stone at Chester-le-Street has the name EADm | VnD, while 'm' occurs in legends in roman characters on Anglo-Saxon coins, as mONE (for *moneta*), DAIEmOND for the moneyer's name *Dægmund*, and often in the royal name on the St Edmund memorial coinage.[22]

I cannot discern any pattern behind the differential employment of runes and roman script on the coffin. Why Matthew, Mark and John are runic, but Luke roman. Why Christ's monogram is runic but, as far as it survives, Mary's name is roman. I classify this piece alongside such an object as the Franks Casket, which has on one of its sides the description of the scene carved nearby, part in roman, HIC FUGIANT HIERUSALIM, and the rest in runes, 'a f i t a t o r e s': 'here the inhabitants flee from Jerusalem'. There is, however, a significant difference. In the case of the Franks casket, words in roman script are also classical in form, more or less. The word in runes uses a different form, with the spelling based on contemporary pronunciation. On the coffin of St Cuthbert, the runes give texts in classical form, more or less. Particularly important is the sequence 'i h s x p s', for that is a straight transliteration from roman, with no basis in pronunciation at all. It could not exist without a precedent roman form: that is, the runes are secondary, dependent on a pre-existent roman. This tends to confirm the general impression that the coffin runes are learned letters, deriving perhaps from manuscript sources. The carvers were not at home in the script; hence its peculiarities.

This poses a further question: why are there runes on the coffin at all? And to this there is the supplementary question: who was supposed to read them? To take the supplementary first. It is a proper question for all runic texts, but particularly cogent for St Cuthbert's coffin. The coffin-reliquary stood above ground as an object of veneration. From some early date unknown, it was swathed in linen cloth covering the whole surface and obscuring the carving. Even in its earliest days the faint inscriptions would have been hard to see in a dimly lit church, for their incisions are

---

he changed his mind for in 1956 he abandoned the brackets for his transliteration of the coffin text. See on this pp. 257–8 above.

[20] As in Derolez, *Runica Manuscripta*, pp. 9 and 59.

[21] This derivation is not at all certain: see above, p. 257.

[22] Keary, *Catalogue*, pp. 91–2 and 114.

slight, considerably thinner than those of the decoration.[23] Theoretically this could have meant that the inscriptions preceded the figures, and were intended to direct the carvers as to the designs to be cut. But this cannot be so in one case – if my observations are correct – for the figure of *Scs Raphael* has precedence over the text, with the two parts of its inscription falling one on each side of the saint.

Moreover, I have shown that the runes are a secondary script at Lindisfarne, and it is odd that directions to carvers should arbitrarily employ two scripts, one of them a specialist one. Professor R. W. V. Elliott suggested that Christians used runes on their tomb furniture because an old belief survived of their efficacy 'for the dead man's salvation or against his haunting his survivors';[24] but it seems unlikely that the Lindisfarne monks who honoured their great saint had so little faith in him as to have recourse to such adventitious aids.

A casual mixture of the two scripts is not all that uncommon in Anglo-Saxon England: witness the legends on the rings from Manchester (Lancashire) and Llysfaen: + æDRED MEC AH EAnRED MEC agROf, 'Ædred owns me, Eanred engraved me', and + ALHSTAn, a personal name. The St Cuthbert's coffin case is something different. Yet there is also, in the east of Northumbria, an extended tradition of the use of the two scripts side by side but distinct. Examples can be found elsewhere at Lindisfarne, at Monkwearmouth and at Falstone. Lindisfarne I, a name stone, has *Osgyth* written twice on it, once in runes in the quadrants above an incised cross, once in roman below (fig. 1). A similar stone, Lindisfarne V, seems to have two names, both with the second element *-wini*: '[.] a m | w i n i' and]*A*[*D*] | WINI. There are other cases, though the names are damaged on other Lindisfarne stones. The second Monkwearmouth stone is only a fragment, but it preserves two name openings, 'e o [' and *ALD*[, giving two distinct first elements of personal names. Most revealing is the Falstone stone which has a double inscription, virtually the same text in both roman and runes. The stone is in a poor condition, but enough of the two inscriptions survives to show it is a memorial to one *Hroethberht*. The name form in the two cases is significant. In roman it is HROETHBERHTÆ with the vowel of the first element – which represents the *i*-mutation of *ō* – given by the two graphs OE. The runic form is badly damaged, but it has the first element vowel represented by two runes 'oe'. This is clearly copied from the roman. The self-evident way of representing the vowel *ō* . . . *i* in runes is to use the single rune 'œ' which, by virtue of its name *oeþil*, must give this sound. Here again, then, there is runic and roman on the same object with the roman predominant. To these examples we may add – though they are not so convincing – the groups of stones of related design, some of which have runic and some roman legends; as the name stones from Hartlepool. Here there is a further refinement. Hartlepool I has a runic text 'h i l d i | þ r y þ', but the letters are carefully seriffed, as though roman (fig. 2). Again a link between the

---

[23] The same problem affects dry-point glosses in Anglo-Saxon manuscripts, which are, at any rate now, almost illegible save with careful side lighting, but presumably were readable in Anglo-Saxon lighting conditions.
[24] Elliott, *Runes: an Introduction*, p. 71.

FIG. 1   Name stone from Lindisfarne, with feminine name Osgyth

scripts, with roman convention imposed upon the runic. As if to stress the learned background, Hartlepool I also has the letters *alpha* and *omega* cut in the quadrants above its incised cross.

Thus, while I can give no reason for the mixture of runic and roman on St Cuthbert's coffin, I can at least set its inscriptions into a context that is both local and learned. It seems there was a north country practice – and one which the Christian church approved – of using runic script in the company of roman, either mixed in with it or side by side with it. The coffin shows this was in operation by the end of the seventh century, some two generations after Edwin accepted Christianity at his

FIG. 2   Name stone from Hartlepool, with feminine name Hildithryth

council held near York. Already runes had lost any sinister associations they may have had. They had become an esoteric script, regarded perhaps with antiquarian affection by the learned and religious.

POSTSCRIPT

The general subject of this paper – links between runic and roman script – has been much discussed in the last years. I give some of my latest thoughts on the subject in the introductory essay to this volume, together with references to recent work. Significant is the site at Brandon, Suffolk, a high status one from the Middle Saxon period (600–900) whose finds, including three runic and one roman-inscribed object, have prompted the suggestion of a monastic community. David Parsons, who was able to examine the Blythburgh, Suffolk, writing tablet in more detail than I could, concludes that the runes visible on the recessed surface are what remains of marks made on the wax that covered it.

The 'additions that must be made from the newly found fragments' of St Cuthbert's coffin (p. 320) are detailed by J. M. Cronyn and C. V. Horie.[25] They consist of, on the apostle side, (v, b) additions to the name fragment P*AVLV*[S] and (v, d) the otherwise lost name [*I*]*ACOB*[*VS*], and on the archangel side, (iv), a group of fragments that may contain *A*[.]*VRI*[.]*IA*.

[25] 'The Anglo-Saxon Coffin: Further Investigations', pp. 249–53.

23

(1990)

DATING OLD ENGLISH INSCRIPTIONS:
THE LIMITS OF INFERENCE

For decades epigraphists have tried to establish principles for the linguistic dating of Old English texts, though without much success. The topic is raised again by the proposed republication of the great runic crosses of Bewcastle (Cumbria) and Ruthwell (Dumfries and Galloway). Those concerned with the art historical aspects of the project are properly eager to find out what support they can get from linguistic techniques of dating, and indeed a comparison of the conclusions of the two disciplines may produce useful confirmation of the methodologies of each. On the whole I think it doubtful if any very firm conclusions will come from my reconsideration of the problem. I can point to difficulties, but I doubt if I can overcome them. At least, however, I may save other scholars from oversimplification.

There are few Anglo-Saxon inscriptions that can be dated precisely from their historical reference. The only runic example is, I think, St Cuthbert's coffin, presumably made by the monks of Lindisfarne for the translation of the saint's body in 698. But its texts are of very limited interest to the student of Old English, consisting only of the names of evangelists, archangels, apostles and of Christ and Mary.[1]

Non-runic inscriptions of historical significance are slightly more plentiful, though hardly abundant. In her *Hand-List* Dr Okasha lists several Latin inscriptions (which may incorporate Old English personal name forms): there are individual examples from Deerhurst and Jarrow, there is St Cuthbert's portable altar, the Sherburn ring of Queen Eaðelswið and the Laverstock ring of King Ethelwulf and so on. But, if we except the Alfred jewel on the grounds that it is uncertainly attributed to the great king, the only inscription of any length in Old English firmly datable on historical grounds is the famous text of the Kirkdale (N. Yorkshire) sundial (inscriptions studied here are transliterated in the Appendix). This has referent points that put it between 1055 and 1065. Otherwise there are only coin legends, which have distinctive characteristics and problems, and in any case produce texts that consist largely of personal or place-names. Clearly there is nothing here on which a pattern of dating can be built up on historical evidence alone, to compare with the epigraphical evidence.

---

[1] B. Dickins, 'The Inscriptions upon the Coffin', *The Relics of Saint Cuthbert*, ed. C. F. Battiscombe (Durham, 1956), pp. 305–7.

There are, of course, inscriptions whose dates can be inferred from the limiting dates of the institutions they derive from. Grave-markers, if they can be ascribed to a particular ecclesiastical house, are not likely to pre-date its foundation or post-date its destruction. On such grounds we can give general dating limits to, for instance, the grave-markers at Lindisfarne, Monkwearmouth and probably Hartlepool, though even in these cases we should not be too confident that we have determined the absolute outer limits of Christian occupation of the sites. In any case, such dating can be only within a couple of centuries or so, and is a very blunt instrument indeed.

Art historians and archaeologists are often eager to help by adding their dating of monuments. Unfortunately there is equal imprecision in their methods. For sculptured stones, for instance, Professor Cramp has shown how much the scholar must rely for dating on the uncertain tools of typology and style.[2] Here again there are too few examples clearly datable on external grounds to provide a matrix into which others can be fitted. The effects can be disconcerting. For instance, when I first wrote about the Great Urswick memorial cross I dated it on linguistic grounds to 750–850. To my surprise I found that art historians put it rather later, in the tenth century.[3] I was happy to find that the new Cumbria volume of the corpus of Anglo-Saxon sculptured stones brought it into the ninth century.[4] Here, I thought, was a support to my own dating. It was something of a blow to learn that the art historians had moved the cross back into the ninth century in part because that is where the philologist had said it should be. What seemed to be an independent confirmation turned out to conceal a circular argument.

Dating by archaeologists may equally be tentative. The excavation report put into the fourth century the cremation urn that held the Caistor-by-Norwich runic bone.[5] Dr Catherine Hills, whose knowledge of East Anglian cremation pottery is unrivalled, tells me that there is no reason why this urn should not be fifth-century. The linguist can say only that the Caistor-by-Norwich inscription is very early, but has no means of deciding how early. Again, while an archaeologist or art historian may be able tentatively to date an object, he may not be able to date its inscription. Sonia Chadwick Hawkes pointed out, in a meticulous examination, that the inscription on the Chessell Down (Isle of Wight) scabbard mount was a late addition, probably shortly before burial, to a sword assembly which was already of some age.[6] The Chester-le-Street (Durham) stone has been assigned to the late ninth century;[7] the inscription does not look part of the original design, and may have been added to an existing stone at some later date.

---

[2] R. Cramp, *The British Academy Corpus of Anglo-Saxon Stone Sculpture, I: County Durham and Northumberland* (Oxford, 1984), pp. xlvii–xlviii.

[3] W. G. Collingwood, *Northumbrian Crosses of the Pre-Norman Age* (London, 1927), pp. 53 and 63.

[4] R. N. Bailey and R. Cramp, *The British Academy Corpus of Anglo-Saxon Stone Sculpture, II: Cumberland, Westmorland and Lancashire North-of-the-Sands* (Oxford and New York, 1988), p. 150.

[5] J. N. L. Myres and B. Green, *The Anglo-Saxon Cemeteries of Caistor-by-Norwich and Markshall, Norfolk* (London, 1973), p. 46.

[6] S. C. Hawkes and R. I. Page, 'Swords and Runes in South-East England' (1967), pp. 17–18.

[7] Cramp, *Durham and Northumberland*, p. 54.

Occasionally there is real coincidence of evidence. An example is the Franks Casket. Art historians assure me that their dating for this piece is *c*. 700. The evidence of philology and runology suggests 700–750. Dr T. A. M. Bishop, on consultation, observed that the few non-runic letters of the texts suggest a date *c*. 700. Here is an almost perfect case of three different types of evidence agreeing.

However, in general the philologist who enters upon epigraphy must beware. The physical context of an inscription must always be taken into account, for it may affect the linguistic form. In a recent oral discussion of the early runic inscriptions of the Germanic world, a distinguished Danish scholar averred that what we needed was a full transliteration of all the available material from different parts of Europe, so that it could be examined dispassionately and as a purely linguistic exercise. To this I demurred for I was aware that a linguistic study alone could not allow for peculiarities that can only be understood if the texts are examined within their physical context. A simple example is the text cut in a censer-cover from Pershore: +GOD-RICMEWVORHT, 'Godric made me'. This is how it would appear in a transcript, divorced from its object. There appears to be loss of final -*e* in the verb, surely very early if this is, as the art historians assure us, a tenth-century piece.[8] But of course, this is not evidence of loss of the unstressed vowel. The explanation is that the carver did not lay out his inscription competently, and reached the end of his space before he completed his word (perhaps because he had added a superfluous V); so he had no option but to omit the final letter, whatever it was. So far so good. But the observation gives rise to further questions. Did the carver omit the vowel knowing that it was not required for the understanding of the text? Or was he only semi-literate (as Moltke has argued in parallel cases from Denmark[9])? If he had been literate, might he not have tried to ligature a final -E with his T – which would be both possible and easy to understand? Or was the unstressed -*e* at this date so imprecisely pronounced that a loss of the graph would be acceptable in a demotic written text? Our assessment of the inscription's language depends to some extent on the answer to questions like these.

In contrast there is the Great Edstone (N. Yorkshire) sundial's maker inscription: +LOÐAN | MEWRO | HTEA, 'Loðan made me'.[10] As it is thus given, the ending of the verb looks very odd indeed. When you see the text on the stone, however, you realise that though the carver provided a large panel for his wording, he cut on only a small part of it, and the text is almost certainly unfinished. Presumably it was to continue WROHTE A(ND) . . . – there are no clear gaps between words – but was never completed.

In the case of the Kirkdale sundial we are fortunate in having a historical dating. It would be interesting to see what conclusions about date can be drawn from the language of the text alone. It is clear from a first glance that this inscription shows deviations from Standard Old English. There is decline in precision of inflexional

---

[8] D. M. Wilson, *Anglo-Saxon Ornamental Metalwork 700–1100 in the British Museum* (London, 1964), p. 158.
[9] E. Moltke, *Runes and their Origin: Denmark and Elsewhere* (Copenhagen, 1985), pp. 95 and 114.
[10] Okasha, *Hand-List*, p. 73.

endings in *svna, tofalan, tobrocan*: loss of the distinctive 2nd weak infinitive ending in *macan*: an irregular ending to *newan* if *minster* is neuter, and to *ilcvm* if *tid* is feminine. On the other hand, the weakening of the dative (singular or plural) ending (often regarded as a later development) is not evidenced in *dagvm* (2x), *ilcvm*. Since there are some clearly latish features, what conclusion can properly be drawn from the uninflected genitives *Eadward dagvm cng* and *Tosti dagvm eorl*? The two panels holding the two sections of the main text are roughly the same size, yet they hold vastly different numbers of letters, fifty-four to the left (not counting punctuation symbols) and ninety to the right. Presumably what happened, and it is clearer from a photograph than a transcript, is that the carver found he had used up half his space when he had reached only a third of the way through the text. He may have spread out the beginning deliberately to give greater prominence to the name of the owner and to his patronymic. When he found himself pressed for space he began to squeeze his words together, letters became thinner, some were missed out (or perhaps we should say ligatured), CNG for *cing*, 7N for *and in*. Can we argue then that the genitive endings were omitted towards the end of the inscription to save space? It was clear what was meant and so the grammatical indication was superfluous. This could be the explanation, but there is a slightly embarrassing feature: the text ends with a cross, and what is more, with a rather elaborate cross which occupies a good deal of room.[11] If the carver were really pressed for space, he could have omitted it and found room for at least one genitive ending. So the uninflected genitive may be a genuine local feature of either dialect, or date, or both. Such a genitive is well-known from the later Middle English period,[12] and this may be a very early example of it. In that case the Kirkdale examples should point to a date late in the Old English period at the earliest. However, Kirkdale may be a special case. Since this is an Anglo-Norse region, we may have here an early case of the decline of inflexional endings in a bilingual community.

We know nothing of the training of the carvers who produced the inscriptions of Anglo-Saxon England, how carefully they were taught and their epigraphical work supervised. Who wrote the text – the mason himself or his master, who handed to him writings written on, say, a wax tablet which the craftsman, rather slavishly, put on his object? Is there a single answer to this question, or does it have different answers for different circumstances? A runic graffito cut casually on a bit of bone could well be the composer's autograph, as that from Hamwih/Southampton.[13] A text incised in a sword-blade might be the work of a semi-literate smith, producing work to order, but perhaps not closely supervised, and that may explain some of the aberrations of the Thames (Battersea) scramasax.[14] The carver who cut the Crucifixion poem on the Ruthwell Cross[15] must have been literate, or following a carefully

---

[11] I suspect, however, that this cross was intended to act as a signe de renvoie, keying the main text to the maker formula on the dial, for the latter begins with a similar form of cross.

[12] T. F. Mustanoja, *A Middle English Syntax. I: Parts of Speech* (Helsinki, 1960), p. 71.

[13] R. I. Page, *Introduction* (1973), pp. 170–1.

[14] Wilson, *Catalogue*, pp. 144–6.

[15] Page, *Introduction*, pp. 150–1.

arranged plan of carving, for otherwise he would have had trouble accommodating his lengthy material. Some runic carvers were cognisant of non-runic as well as runic scripts. For instance, the craftsman who cut the carefully seriffed runes on a pair of tweezers found at Brandon (Suffolk) was presumably used to engraving roman capitals, and it is not surprising that the excavators suggested that the site was ecclesiastical. The man who cut four runic words of Old English on a bone comb from Whitby could also manage a bit of simple Latin, so he was not entirely untrained in scholarly pursuits.[16]

From this survey I conclude that there was a good deal of literacy – or of careful copying of exemplars – among Anglo-Saxon carvers. Yet there also seems to be a high incidence of irregular, or slightly unusual spellings in the epigraphical texts. There is inorganic doubling of consonants and common doubling of vowels, as in 'a l m e ï t t i g', 'æ þ þ i l æ', 'g i s t o d d u n' and 'r i i c n æ' on the Ruthwell Cross, 'g o o d', 'þ i i o s n e', 'c i i s m e e l' on the Mortain Casket. There is an unusually large number of examples of the glide vowel between liquids and consonants: 'g e w a r a h t æ', Mortain, 'a l u w a l u d o', 'h e l i p æ', Whitby comb, 't o r o ï t r e d æ', Great Urswick stone, 'w o r o h t æ', Kirkheaton stone, as well as a number of cases of the element -bereht on name-stones and WYRICAN, BEROÞOR (2x) on the Brussels cross.[17] There are comparable examples to all of these in scribal texts, but what is striking in the inscriptions is the large proportion of cases, with the implication that the carvers are to some degree working in a different spelling tradition. As some have pointed out, producing an engraved text is a more laborious process than writing a manuscript, and this may influence spelling practice.[18] Further, as I suggested many years ago, it may be misleading to compare, in transliteration, different writing systems, runic and roman.[19]

The process of carving commits the writer more completely than that of writing on parchment. It is relatively easy to scratch out a writing error, as any reader of mediaeval manuscripts knows. Once a letter has been cut, either in relief or in intaglio, it is hard to get rid of; so errors may remain more extensively in engraved than in written texts. There are, of course, cases of epigraphical error corrected. The Ruthwell Cross has examples. Its texts are long ones and laid out in a curious way, in short lines containing between two and four letters. It is not easy to read this, but it obviously needed a good deal of planning in advance. It seems that the letters were cut in lightly at first, then checked and cut more deeply with a punch. Thus an error could be corrected in the second carving, provided there were space for it. In '[b] i s m æ r æ d u' the final letter was originally cut with two full verticals, and in 'l i m w œ r i g n æ' the rune 'œ' with two full cross-staves (as 'g'). Both errors were

[16] R. I. Page, 'The Whitby Runic Comb' (1966), p. 12.
[17] Okasha, Hand-List, p. 57.
[18] S. T. R. O. D'Ardenne, 'The Old English Inscription on the Brussels Cross', English Studies 21 (1939), 145–64 and 271–2, at 151; E. G. Stanley, A Collection of Papers with Emphasis on Old English Literature (Toronto, 1987), pp. 392–3.
[19] 'A Note on the Transliteration of Old English Runic Inscriptions', above pp. 87–92.

corrected in the second cutting. On the other hand, the form *bismærædu* may be an uncorrected error for *bismæradu*, though there is some dispute over the reading.[20]

A related problem is that we have no idea how far the present state of an inscription represents what an Anglo-Saxon was supposed to see. The main shaft-stone of the Ruthwell Cross has certainly been under cover for much of its long history, but we do not know whether it was sheltered from the first. There may have been colouring on the stone, outlining the cut letters, which would allow corrections to be incorporated at a late date. No colouring remains, I think, but that may be because it weathered away. There are certainly faint traces of paint on other Anglo-Saxon inscribed stones (and it is not uncommon on Scandinavian rune-stones too[21]) and in some cases suggestions of a skim of plaster on which the colour could be laid.

There are occasional inscriptions which reveal uncorrected errors that look too gross for correction. A clear example is the memorial stone from Overchurch (Cheshire). This has two lines of runes, partly defective, but those that remain are in general clear and deeply cut. The first line has the group 'f o l c æ a r æ r d o n', with a curious intrusive 'æ' which Dickins thought 'perhaps a blundered or damaged character abandoned by the carver'.[22] The second line has a form of the verb *(ge)biddan* with the sequence 'f o t e' following: there is no doubt that this is an error for the preposition *fore*. The cutting is so deep that it is unlikely that colouring could disguise it unless there was a thick covering of plaster.

The condition of many of our inscribed monuments makes any detailed examination of their language perilous. The Kirkdale inscription is well preserved because it is under cover and has probably been so for much of its life (though it is undoubtedly odd that a sundial should be inside a building).[23] Consequently, the only difficulty

---

[20] D. R. Howlett, 'Three Forms in the Ruthwell Text of The Dream of the Rood', *English Studies* 55 (1974), 1–5, at 1–2. Dr Howlett suggests that in fact the error is not in the cross text, but in the work of scholars who have read 'b i s m æ r æ d u' here. He bases his argument on (1) the correct verbal form, (2) his own reading 'a' rather than 'æ' for the seventh rune, (3) the, as he thinks it, consistent reporting of 'a' by early recorders of the inscription. My own note-book shows that I read the rune as 'æ', but queried a possible alternative 'a'. In my dissertation I preferred 'æ' (R. I. Page, 'The Inscriptions of the Anglo-Saxon Rune-Stones' (unpubl. PhD dissertation, Nottingham Univ., 1959), p. 121), but when, a few years later, I came to write this entry up for the projected corpus of runic inscriptions, I changed my mind. I wrote the revised version some years before I saw Howlett's 1974 article, and it is worth repeating what I put then since in some degree it acts as independent confirmation of Howlett's position: 'This (i.e. the disputed rune) is faint but seems to be 'æ', presenting the reader with the embarrassing verbal form *bismærædu* which most editors emend to *bismæradu*. The difficulty is that the early drawings are unanimous in reading 'a' here: so, clearly, Gordon, Cardonnel and Ridell; Nicolson, though uncertain about the form, shows something a little nearer 'a' than 'æ', and Duncan too. Modern scholars commonly read 'æ' and what appears on the cross makes it tempting to do so. Vietor implies that the rune may have been 'a' weathered to look like 'æ'. In view of the unanimity of early readings I prefer to put 'a' here, though I do it with some hesitation'. However, I suspect that neither Howlett nor I have given full consideration to all the early drawings of this passage – there are several by Nicolson which do not always coincide – so the matter remains in some doubt.

[21] S. B. F. Jansson, *The Runes of Sweden* (London, 1962), pp. 147–55.

[22] Dickins, 'System of Transliteration', p. 19.

[23] The sundial is set over the south door of the church, but now protected by a porch. Whether the sundial is in situ or not is a matter of uncertainty (H. M. and J. Taylor, *Anglo-Saxon Architecture*

in reading it results from the fact that it has been painted over at some time or other, and it is not clear how much that can be read is in the painting rather than the engraving, while the position of the stone, above the doorway into the church nave, makes it difficult of access. The Brussels cross, a treasure kept in a treasury, is also in splendid condition. But these are exceptions. Thus the Bewcastle Cross inscriptions, of vital importance as they are, are impossible to read in detail. The stone has been in the open for some 1300 years, suffering the attack of Cumbrian fell weather. When you see the main face from some distance, the first impression is that it is not so worn after all. Surely this time you will read it. But the nearer you get the less optimistic you are, and when you stand directly in front of the main inscribed face, you realise that, as usual, you are going to read only a few of the badly weathered runes.

Ruthwell, on the other hand, has been generally under shelter, and what remains of its main text is relatively easily read. But its shaft was much hacked about and battered in the storms of the Scottish Reformation, and bits of the edges (with some of the runes) are irretrievably lost. Even here, then, a good deal needs supplying, while occasional letter groups in incomplete sequences are ambiguous.

Clearly there is often difficulty in establishing a text. Even in unquestioned texts interpretation of the spelling may be a problem. For instance, the last line of the Thornhill II (W. Yorkshire) memorial stone is 'ea t e ᛁ n n e'. I take this to be the oblique personal name form *Eadþegne*, but why the doubled 'n'? This could be a case of the inorganic doubling of consonants that I discussed above as a possible indication of a divergent spelling tradition in inscriptions. But there is another explanation. The carver of this monument, fairly unusually for an Anglo-Saxon, set out his text carefully so as to avoid splitting words at line ends and to give each of the two personal names its own line. Thus 'ea t e ᛁ n n e' had to occupy a whole line and the cutter may have added a superfluous 'n' to spread it out more acceptably, as a sixteenth-century compositor would happily add an inorganic -*e* to a word to justify a line of type. If that is the case, the doubling of the consonant has no linguistic significance; only an artistic one.

A more complex pair of examples of the same sort of thing occurs on the Franks Casket, which has two difficult forms, 'f i s c . f l o d u .' and 'g i u þ e a s u'. The first of these is particularly important since it has been taken as a significant form for dating the piece.[24] In both texts involved there are problems of translation which I cannot go into here. The word *giuþeasu* has usually been interpreted as a nominative plural 'Jews', but then has a superfluous -*u*. *Flodu* may be either nominative or accusative, either singular or plural (I prefer accusative plural), but then also has an unnecessary -*u*, or very late retention of -*u* after a long stem syllable. Save on the

(Cambridge, 1965–78), p. 740). For what it is worth, the earliest drawing of this dial that I know describes it as 'over the South Door on the outside of Kirkdale Church' (British Library MS, Stowe 1024, fol. 199, which, from its connection with John Anstis, must antedate that of Brooke: Okasha, *Hand-List*, p. 87).
[24] A. C. Amos, *Linguistic Means of Determining the Dates of Old English Literary Texts* (Cambridge, Massachusetts, 1980), pp. 23–4.

cryptic side of the casket (which presents its own difficulties), the rune-master, in setting out his material, was scrupulous not to divide a word between two successive panels, except in the case of the long *fergenberig*, where he had no alternative. Can we explain these two superfluous -*u* endings as space fillers, put in because he had come to the end of a word without filling his panel, and did not want to begin another word which would have to be completed elsewhere? If we can take it thus, we should then note the occasional other runic case where -*u* is something of an embarrassment, as on the *skanomodu* solidus (if that is English[25]).

It is the difficulty of establishing and assessing the linguistic significance of a text that provides the first obstacle to dating an inscription. A second is the amount of linguistic material an inscription is likely to contain, compared with even a short written text. One of our shortest Old English poems with significant dating features is *Bede's Death Song*, which consists of 25 words. *Caedmon's Hymn* has 42 words, the *Leiden Riddle* 88. Few inscriptions are as long. The Crucifixion poem of the Ruthwell Cross, the longest of our runic inscriptions, has about 320 characters, some 72 words or fragments. The Kirkdale sundial has, in its three texts, a total of 49 words, the Brussels cross has 32 (plus 2 Latin), the Sutton, Isle of Ely, brooch 20. But these are long inscriptions. To take more common-sized ones: the Thornhill III memorial has 54 runes, 10 words; the Great Urswick cross 67 runes, 14 words, while several inscribed stones carry nothing but a single personal name. It is likely that in many cases there will be too few significant forms to give statistically valid results. Hence the tentative nature of much of our linguistic dating of monuments; as 'it can reasonably be claimed that the indications favour the seventh and eighth centuries, are not so favourable towards the ninth, and still less so towards the tenth'.[26]

To date an inscription we need control texts, datable written texts that can properly be compared with the epigraphical one. Of course, linguistic development varies according to local dialect. A sound change may take place earlier in one dialect than another, so that the control text must come from the same region as the inscription. This is a problem, for it may not be possible to find such a control. Up-to-date local distribution maps of the Anglo-Saxon inscriptions are not available, and of course some important examples are not provenanced in England at all – the Franks, Mortain and Brunswick caskets are cases in point. Moreover, in the case of portable objects the find-place is not necessarily the place of manufacture. Any distribution map must then be tentative: there are helpful preliminary ones in Okasha, *Hand-List of Anglo-Saxon Non-Runic Inscriptions*, pp. 140–1 and Page, *An Introduction to English Runes*, pp. 26–7. These show intriguing patterns.

Taking the distribution of inscribed stones (and we regard this as more significant than that of the portable objects simply because they are in general less easily movable from the place they were made in), we can note clear concentrations in the North and

[25] See above, pp. 154–5, 159, but cf. I. Stewart, 'Anglo-Saxon Gold Coins', *Scripta nummaria romana: Essays presented to Humphrey Sutherland*, ed. R. A. G. Carson and C. M. Kraay (London, 1978), pp. 143–72, at 154.

[26] F. S. Scott, 'The Hildithryth Stone and the other Hartlepool Name-Stones', *Archæologia Æliana* 4th ser., 34 (1956), 196–212, at 205.

North Midlands. Elsewhere, taking the evidence of all the available maps, there is a general scatter of inscriptions over southern and eastern England, with gaps noticeable only in the central and West Midlands. Unfortunately, this distribution does not coincide with that known for the Old English written records. We know practically nothing of the Old English of East Anglia, so there is no control material for the inscriptions from Norfolk, Suffolk, Cambridgeshire or Essex. Though there are certainly Old English manuscripts from the North and North Midlands, they are limited in content and there is a limited range of provenances. For the middle and later period there are texts from Lindisfarne (*Liber Vitæ* of Durham), Chester-le-Street (Lindisfarne Gospels gloss and Durham Ritual), as well as minor materials from Durham and elsewhere, together with the Rushworth₂ Gospels gloss from some place further to the south. For the earlier period we have a small number of lesser works, but none whose extant form can be localised precisely; though the early linguistic material from the *Historia Ecclesiastica* must derive ultimately from Monkwearmouth/Jarrow.[27] Thus there is nothing that we can certainly localise on the west coast of Northumbria; nothing therefore which is appropriate for comparison with the Ruthwell Cross, the Great Urswick stone, the two rune-stones from Maughold, Isle of Man, and the Carlisle cross-fragments.

To compare with the considerable numbers of inscriptions from the old West Riding of Yorkshire, there are no written texts closely localisable, except perhaps for Rushworth₂ in the tenth century. Whether that is a suitable control for the Thornhill and Dewsbury cross inscriptions, I do not know.

Yet there are more difficulties than I have outlined so far. For instance, I have assumed that the west coast inscriptions at Urswick and Ruthwell share the same local dialect; but the places are some ninety kilometres apart, separated by the fells of the Lake District and the waters of the Solway Firth. Campbell may describe Ruthwell as 'a spot in the heart of Northumbrian territory',[28] but the heart is an organ notoriously off centre, and the main region for surviving written Northumbrian is likely to have been a good deal further east. I have asserted that the find-spots of inscribed stones ought to be significant because stones are unlikely to be moved about much (which is true in general, if not in particular).[29] But though stones may be fixed, stone-carvers may travel, and it is possible, as Professor Cramp has suggested,[30] that the Ruthwell sculptors came from a distant part of Northumbria. What dialect they recorded on their cross can only be conjecture. There may, after all, have been a prestige sub-dialect within early Northumbrian which stone-carvers tended to use, whatever their own speech was. If so, we do not know about it.

So far I have assumed the integrity of an inscription: that its language does not

---

[27] Dahl, *Substantival Inflexion*, pp. 1–21 gives an account of these early Northumbrian texts.

[28] A. Campbell, *Old English Grammar* (Oxford, 1959), p. 4.

[29] It is something of a commonplace that stone monuments were not transported over distances in the Anglo-Saxon period despite the well-recorded case of the stone cross carried from Lindisfarne by the community of St Cuthbert (R. N. Bailey, *Viking Age Sculpture in Northern England* (London, 1980), pp. 22–3). We tend to think of such monuments as huge and heavy chunks of material, forgetting such tiny pieces as the Hartlepool name-stones, which would fit easily into a brief case.

[30] R. Cramp, *Early Northumbrian Sculpture* (Jarrow, 1965), pp. 10–12.

intentionally deceive, but represents a genuine form of Old English roughly appropriate to the date the text was cut. However, some scholars have suggested that inscriptions are likely to be archaic in language. C. L. Wrenn argued this in the specific case of the Ruthwell cross.[31] I do not believe his thesis myself,[32] but Professor Stanley has recently reinterpreted Wrenn's position in much modified and more acceptable form.[33] It is certainly evident that inscriptions containing fixed formulae, as *gibidæþ foræ NN* or *NN worohtæ*, may also contain fixed grammatical forms which remain unaffected by sound-changes in the current tongue. If an inscription contains such archaic – or even archaistic – spellings, it is liable to mislead the linguistic dater.

Finally, closely linked to linguistic but essentially distinct from it is palaeographical dating, dating by reference to the forms of letters used. It is tempting to assume that letter forms found in inscriptions have their counterparts in manuscripts, and that it is feasible to date the one from the other. The occurrence of Gothic script on Victorian memorials should give us pause, for it is evident that display scripts may make use of archaic or unusual forms. Dr Okasha has presented a preliminary survey of the scripts of the non-runic monuments of Anglo-Saxon England,[34] to which she has added, in a personal communication, the query 'whether it is legitimate to argue a direct dating link . . . from manuscripts to inscriptions'. Runic inscriptions give even less comfort, for inevitably there are few manuscript parallels and no adequate typology can be built up from the epigraphical material alone. There is the occasional clearly early form, as the variant *cen*-rune of the two Chessell Down inscriptions and the *skanomodu* solidus; while there is the occasional latish and local graph such as the *calc*-rune which seems restricted to the north-west and is not recorded before, say, 700. These distinctions are too blunt to base dating points on.

When a philologist suggests a date on linguistic grounds for an inscription, then, the non-philologist will do well to bear in mind the type of difficulty I have sketched in this paper, and be suitably cautious. Dating on the linguistic evidence alone will be barely even approximate. For dating an inscribed piece, it is important for the various experts, archaeologist, historian, technologist, palaeographer, philologist and art historian, each to reach an independent conclusion, and only thereafter to see if any harmony of opinion can be struck, Even if it can, it is unlikely that dating will be other than approximate until a lot more primary material comes to light.

[31] C. L. Wrenn, 'The Value of Spelling as Evidence', *TPS* (1943), 14–39, at 19–22.
[32] See 'Language and Dating in Old English Inscriptions', above pp. 29–43.
[33] Stanley, *Collection of Papers*, pp. 391–5.
[34] E. Okasha, 'The Non-Runic Scripts of Anglo-Saxon Inscriptions', *Trans. of the Cambridge Bibliographical Soc.* 4 (1964–8), 321–38.

APPENDIX

The following transcripts are not necessarily complete, and are given here only to clarify my argument. Other useful transcripts are in Okasha, *Hand-List* and Page, *Introduction*. Inscriptions in versions of the roman alphabet are given in CAPITALS. Runic inscriptions are transliterated according to the system defined in Page, 'On the Transliteration of English Runes' (pp. 245–70 above).

1. Auzon (Franks) Casket, front:
'f i s c . f l o d u. ‖ a h o f o n f e r g ‖ e n b e r i g ‖
← w a r þ g a : s r i c g r o r n þ æ r h e o n g r e u t g i s w o m ‖ → h r o n æ s b a n'

2. Auzon (Franks) Casket, back:
'h e r f e g t a þ ‖ t i t u s e n d g i u þ e a s u' ‖ HICFUGIANTHIERUSALIM ‖ 'a f
i t a t o r e s'

3. Caitor-by-Norwich astragalus:
r a ᛁ h a n

4. Kirkdale sundial (I am uncertain of the punctuation in these transcripts):

left panel:
+ORM·GAMAL·
SVNA·BO HTE.SCS
GREGORIVS·MIN
STERÐONNEHI
T.WESÆL·TOBRO

right panel:
CAN·7TOFALAN·7H̅E̅
HIT·LET·MACAN·NE WAN·FROM
GRVNDE·XPE:7SCSGREGORI̲
VS·IN·EADWARD·DAGVM·C̅N̅G
7N·TOSTI DAGVM·EORL+

dial panel:
+7HAWARÐ·MEWROHTE·7BRA N D | P̅R̅S
+ÞISIS·DÆGES·SOLMERCA+ ‖ ÆTILCVMTIDE+

4. Mortain Casket:
'+ g o o d h e l p e : æ a d a n
þ i i o s n e c i i s m e e l g e w a r
a h t æ'

5. Overchurch stone:
'f o l c {æ} a r æ r d o n b e c [
] *b* i d d a þ f o <r> e æ þ e l m u *n* ['

6. Ruthwell Cross:

parts of the east face:
'[+ . *n d*] g e r e | d æ | h i | n æ | g̅o | d a | l m | e i̇ | t t i | g'
'[.] | i c r | i i c n | æ k̅ y | *n* i ŋ | c'

parts of the west face:
'h w | e þ | r æ | þ e | r f | *u* s [*æ*] | f e a r | r a n | k w [*o*] | m u [*æ*] | þ þ i l | æ t i l | a n u | m'
'a l e | g d u | n h i æ | *h* i n æ | l i m w | œ r i g | n æ g i | s t o | d d u | [*n*]'

7. Southampton/Hamwih bone:
'c a t æ'

8. Thames (Battersea) scramasax:
'f u þ o r c g w h n i j i̇ p x (s) t b e ŋ d l m œ a æ y ea'
'b ea g n o þ'

9. Thornhill II memorial stone:
'+ ea d r e d
* s e t e æ f t e
ea t e i̇ n n e'

10. Whitby comb:
'd̅[*æ*] u s m̅ æ u s ‖ g o d a l u w a l u ‖ d̅o h̅e l i p æ c y ‖ ['

THE PUBLISHED WRITINGS OF R.I. PAGE
TO 1994

1957
'Drauma-Jóns Saga', *Nottingham Mediaeval Studies* 1, 22–56

1958
* 'Northumbrian *æfter* (= in memory of) + Accusative', *Studia Neophilologica* 30, 145–53

1959
* 'An Early Drawing of the Ruthwell Cross', *Medieval Archaeology* 3, 285–8
* 'Language and Dating in OE Inscriptions', *Anglia* 77, 385–406

1960
Gibbons Saga, Editiones Arnamagnæanæ B 2 (Copenhagen: Munksgaard)
* 'The Bewcastle Cross', *Nottingham Mediaeval Studies* 4, 36–57
'William Nicolson, F.R.S., and the Runes of the Bewcastle Cross', *Royal Society Notes and Records* 14, 184–90

1961
* 'The Old English Rune *ear*', *Medium Ævum* 30, 65–79

1962
'The Finding of the "Bramham Moor" Runic Ring', *Notes and Queries* 9, 450–2
* 'A Note on the Transliteration of Old English Runic Inscriptions', *English Studies* 43, 484–90
* 'The Use of Double Runes in Old English Inscriptions', *Journal of English and Germanic Philology* 61, 897–907

1963
Review of Peter Hallberg, *The Icelandic Saga* (Lincoln, NE, 1962), *Scandinavica* 2, 68–9

1964
* 'Anglo-Saxon Runes and Magic', *Journal of the British Archaeological Association* 3rd ser., 27, 14–31
'The Inscriptions', in David M. Wilson, *Anglo-Saxon Ornamental Metalwork 700–1100 in the British Museum* (London: British Museum), pp. 67–90
'Lapland Sorcerers', *Saga-Book of the Viking Society* 16 (1962–5), 215–32
Review of Arthur Brown and Peter Foote, eds, *Early English and Norse Studies Presented to Hugh Smith* (London, 1963), *Saga-Book of the Viking Society* 16 (1962–5), 94–5

Review of Peter Hallberg, *Den fornisländska poesien* (Stockholm, 1962), *Scandinavica* 3, 62–3

Review of Sven B.F. Jansson, *The Runes of Sweden*, trans. Peter G. Foote (London, 1962), *Saga-Book of the Viking Society* 16 (1962–5), 101–2

Review of Gwyn Jones, *The Norse Atlantic Saga* (London and New York, 1964), *Notes and Queries* 11, 349–50

Review of E.O.G. Turville-Petre, *Myth and Religion of the North* (London, 1964), *Notes and Queries* 11, 391–2

1965

'Anglo-Saxon Episcopal Lists, Parts I and II', *Nottingham Mediaeval Studies* 9, 71–95

'A Note on the Text of MS CCCC 422 (*Solomon and Saturn*)', *Medium Ævum* 34, 36–9

* 'Ralph Thoresby's Runic Coins', *British Numismatic Journal* 34, 28–31

Review of Theodore M. Andersson, *The Problem of Icelandic Saga Origins* (New Haven and London, 1964), *Notes and Queries* 12, 320

Review of Hans Bekker-Nielsen and Thorkil Damsgaard Olsen, eds, *Bibliography of Old Norse-Icelandic Studies, 1963* (Copenhagen, 1964), *Medium Ævum* 34, 82

Review of Hans Bekker-Nielsen and Ole Widding, *Arne Magnusson, den store håndskriftsamler* (Copenhagen, 1963), *Scandinavica* 4, 70–1

Review of Wilfrid Bonser, *The Medical Background of Anglo-Saxon England* (London, 1963), *Journal of the British Archaeological Association* 3rd ser., 28, 135–7

Review of Tryggvi J. Oleson, *Early Voyages and Northern Approaches, 1000–1632* (London, 1964), *Notes and Queries* 12, 34–5

Review of Viggo Starcke, *Denmark in World History* (Philadelphia and London, 1963), *Medium Ævum* 34, 81–2

1966

Anglo-Saxon & Other Manuscripts: Catalogue of an Exhibition in the Library of Corpus Christi College, Cambridge (Cambridge: Corpus Christi College)

'Anglo-Saxon Episcopal Lists, Part III', *Nottingham Mediaeval Studies* 10, 12–24

'The Whitby Runic Comb', *Whitby Literary and Philosophical Society, Annual Report*, pp. 10–15

Review of Hans Bekker-Nielsen and Thorkil Damsgaard Olsen, eds, *Bibliography of Old Norse-Icelandic Studies, 1964* (Copenhagen, 1965), *Medium Ævum* 35, 176–7

Review of Bruce Mitchell, *A Guide to Old English* (Oxford, 1965), *Medium Ævum* 35, 175–6

1967

'Saxon Sundial in the Parish Church of All Saints, Orpington: Note on the Inscription', *Archæologia Cantiana* 81, 289–91

With Sonia Chadwick Hawkes, 'Swords and Runes in South-East England', *Antiquaries Journal* 47, 1–26

Review of Peter Berghaus and Karl Schneider, *Anglo-friesische Runensolidi im*

Lichte des Neufundes von Schweindorf (Cologne and Opladen, 1967), *Numismatic Chronicle* 7th ser., 7, 304–6

Review of R.G. Finch, ed. and trans., *The Saga of the Volsungs* (London, 1965), *Notes and Queries* 14, 280

1968
* 'The Old English Rune *eoh, ih,* "yew-tree" ', *Medium Ævum* 37, 125–36
* 'The Runic Solidus of Schweindorf, Ostfriesland, and Related Runic Solidi', *Medieval Archaeology* 12, 12–25

Review of Hans Bekker-Nielsen, *Old Norse-Icelandic Studies: a Select Bibliography* (Toronto, 1967), *Notes and Queries* 15, 469–70

Review of Barthi Guthmundsson, *The Origin of the Icelanders*, trans. Lee M. Hollander (Lincoln, NE, 1967), *Scandinavica* 7, 80–1

Review of Alf Mongé and O.G. Landsverk, *Norse Medieval Cryptography in Runic Carvings* (Glendale, CA, 1967), *Scandinavica* 7, 70–1

1969
'Note on the *Hamwih* Inscription in "Saxon Southampton, II" ', *Proceedings of the Hampshire Field Club* 27, 86–7

'Old English *cyningstan*', *Leeds Studies in English* n.s. 3, 1–5
* 'Runes and Non-Runes', *Medieval Literature and Civilization: Studies in Memory of G.N. Garmonsway*, ed. D.A. Pearsall and R.A. Waldron (London), pp. 28–54

Review of Theodore C. Blegen, *The Kensington Rune Stone, New Light on an Old Riddle* (St Paul, MN, 1968), *Journal of American Studies* 3, 281

Review of Wolfgang Krause, *Die Runeninschriften im älteren Futhark* (Göttingen, 1966), *Medieval Archaeology* 12, 217–18

1970
Life in Anglo-Saxon England (London: Batsford; New York: Putnam's)

Review of Niels Åge Nielsen, *Runestudier* (Odense, 1968), *Mediaeval Scandinavia* 3, 202–4

1971
* 'How Long Did the Scandinavian Language Survive in England? The Epigraphical Evidence', *England before the Conquest: Studies in Primary Sources Presented to Dorothy Whitelock*, ed. Peter Clemoes and Kathleen Hughes (Cambridge), pp. 165–81

1972
Review of Richard F. Allen, *Fire and Iron: Critical Approaches to 'Njáls Saga'* (Pittsburgh, 1971), *Scandinavica* 11, 149–51

Review of Peter Foote and David M. Wilson, *The Viking Achievement* (London, 1970), *Medium Ævum* 41, 89–94

Review of Gwyn Jones, *A History of the Vikings* (London, 1968), *Medium Ævum* 41, 89–94

1973
An Introduction to English Runes (London: Methuen)

'Anglo-Saxon Scratched Glosses in a Corpus Christi College, Cambridge, Manuscript', *Otium et Negotium: Studies in Onomatology and Library Science Presented to Olof von Feilitzen*, ed. Folke Sandgren (Stockholm), pp. 209–15

* 'Anglo-Saxon Texts in Early Modern Transcripts', *Transactions of the Cambridge Bibliographical Society* 6, 69–85

'The Runic Inscription from N59', in J.N.L. Myres and Barbara Green, *The Anglo-Saxon Cemeteries of Caistor-by-Norwich and Markshall, Norfolk* (London), pp. 114–17

1974

'The Lost Leaf of MS. C.C.C.C. 196', *Notes and Queries* 21, 472–3

'The Revd John Duncombe, M.A., 1729–86', *Letter of the Corpus Association* 53, 13–21 [Commemoration Address, 1973]

'Runic Script', *The New Cambridge Bibliography of English Literature* I, ed. George Watson (Cambridge), pp. 220–6

Review of William Morris and Eiríkr Magnússon, *The Story of Kormak the Son of Ogmund* (London, 1971), *Scandinavica* 13, 63–4

Review of Klaus von See, *Die Gestalt der Hávamál* (Frankfurt am Main, 1972), *Scandinavica* 13, 61–3

1975

With G.H.S. Bushnell, *Matthew Parker's Legacy: Books and Plate* (Cambridge: Corpus Christi College)

'A Canterbury Tale', *Letter of the Corpus Association* 54, 33–5

'Matthew Parker and His Treasures', *Letter of the Corpus Association* 54, 32–3

'More Aldhelm Glosses from CCCC 326', *English Studies* 56, 481–90

' "The Proper Toil of Artless Industry": Toronto's Plan for an Old English Dictionary', *Notes and Queries* 22, 146–55

With Birthe Kjølbye-Biddle, 'A Scandinavian Rune-Stone from Winchester', *Antiquaries Journal* 55, 389–94

Review of Alistair Campbell, *Enlarged Addenda and Corrigenda to the Supplement, by T. Northcote Toller, to 'An Anglo-Saxon Dictionary'* (Oxford, 1972), *Medium Ævum* 44, 65–8

1977

'Christopher Marlowe and the Library of Matthew Parker', *Notes and Queries* 24, 510–14

'A Corpus Record?', *Letter of the Corpus Association* 56, 30–1

With Martin Biddle *et al.*, 'Sutton Hoo Published: a Review', *Anglo-Saxon England* 6, 249–65

1978

'Bruce Dickins 1889–1978', *Cambridge Review* 100, 76–8

'Doing Research at the Parker Library', *Old English Newsletter* 11.2, 7–11

'Old English Liturgical Rubrics in Corpus Christi College, Cambridge, MS 422', *Anglia* 96, 149–58

1979

'Bruce Dickins', *Saga-Book of the Viking Society* 20 (1978–9), 4–5
'Dumézil Revisited', *Saga-Book of the Viking Society* 20 (1978–9), 49–69
'More Old English Scratched Glosses', *Anglia* 97, 27–45
'OE. *fealh,* "harrow" ', *Notes and Queries* 26, 389–93
Review of Régis Boyer, *Les Vikings et leur civilisation* (Paris and The Hague, 1976), *Saga-Book of the Viking Society* 20 (1978–9), 152–4
Review of J.D. Pheifer, ed., *Old English Glosses in the Épinal-Erfurt Glossary* (Oxford, 1974), *Studia Neophilologica* 51, 161–3
Review of Barbara C. Raw, *The Art and Background of Old English Poetry* (London, 1978), *Book Auction Records* 76 (1978–9), x–xi

1980

'Bruce Dickins, 1889–1978', *Proceedings of the British Academy* 64 (1980 for 1978), 341–57
'Rune-Masters and Skalds', *The Viking World*, ed. James Graham-Campbell (London), pp. 155–71
* 'Some Thoughts on Manx Runes', *Saga-Book of the Viking Society* 20, 179–99

1981

'The Audience of *Beowulf* and the Vikings', *The Dating of 'Beowulf'*, ed. Colin Chase (Toronto, Buffalo and London), pp. 113–22
'More Thoughts on Manx Runes', *Michigan Germanic Studies* 7, 129–37
'New Work on Old English Scratched Glosses', *Studies in English Language and Early Literature in Honour of Paul Christophersen*, ed. P.M. Tilling (Coleraine), pp. 105–15
'The Parker Register and Matthew Parker's Anglo-Saxon Manuscripts', *Transactions of the Cambridge Bibliographical Society* 8, 1–17
'Two Marlowe First Editions', *Letter of the Corpus Association* 60, 48–50
Review of Richard N. Bailey, *Viking Sculpture in Northern England* (London, 1980), *Antiquity* 55, 150–1

1982

'Archbishops, Bishops and Gospels', *Letter of the Corpus Association* 61, 62–4
'The Study of Latin Texts in Late Anglo-Saxon England: the Evidence of English Glosses', *Latin and the Vernacular Languages in Early Medieval Britain*, ed. Nicholas Brooks (Leicester and Atlantic Highlands, NJ), pp. 141–65
'A Tale of Two Cities', *Peritia* 1, 335–51
Review of David Yerkes, *The Two Versions of Waerferth's Translation of Gregory's Dialogues* (Toronto, Buffalo and London, 1979), *Medium Ævum* 51, 115–19

1983

'Four Rare Old English Words', *Notes and Queries* 30, 2–8
* 'The Manx Rune-Stones', *The Viking Age in the Isle of Man*, ed. Christine E. Fell *et al.* (London), pp. 133–46
'Matthew Parker's Copy of *Prosper His Meditation with His Wife*', *Transactions of the Cambridge Bibliographical Society* 8, 342–9

Review of Carl T. Berkhout and Milton McC. Gatch, eds, *Anglo-Saxon Scholarship: the First Three Centuries* (Boston, 1982), *Notes and Queries* 30, 443–6
Review of Robert A. Hall Jr, *The Kensington Rune-Stone Is Genuine* (Columbia, SC, 1982), *Speculum* 58, 748–51

1984
* 'On the Transliteration of English Runes', *Medieval Archaeology* 28, 22–45
'Toki Learns the Runes', in Chris Fell, *Toki in Jorvik* (York), pp. 14–15
Appendix on Runes, in Christine E. Fell, *Jorvikinga Saga: the Saga of the Jorvik Vikings* (York), pp. 23–4
With Catherine M. Hills, review of C.R. Dodwell, *Anglo-Saxon Art* (Manchester and Ithaca, NY), *Antiquity* 58, 72–4

1985
Anglo-Saxon Aptitudes (Cambridge: Cambridge University Press) [Inaugural Lecture]
'Codicological Note', *Dægboc anes Nathwæs and The Werkes of Umffrey*, ed. Walter Nash [Nottingham], pp. 6–9
'*Gerefa*: Some Problems of Meaning', *Problems of Old English Lexicography: Studies in Memory of Angus Cameron*, ed. Alfred Bammesberger (Regensburg), pp. 211–28
'The Legends on the Coins', in M.M. Archibald, 'The Coinage of Beonna in the Light of the Middle Harling Hoard', *British Numismatic Journal* 55, 10–54, at 37–40
'Runic Links across the North Sea in the Pre-Viking Age', *Beretning fra Fjerde tværfaglige Vikingesymposium*, ed. Hans Bekker-Nielsen and Hans Frede Nielsen (Moesgård), pp. 31–49
'Two Problematic Old English Words', *Sources and Relations: Studies in Honour of J.E. Cross*, ed. Marie Collins *et al.*, Leeds Studies in English, n.s. 16 (Leeds), pp. 198–207
Review of Carol J. Clover, *The Medieval Saga* (Ithaca, NY, and London, 1982), *Saga-Book of the Viking Society* 21, 299–303
Review of Robert T. Farrell, ed., *The Vikings* (London and Chichester, 1982), *Saga-Book of the Viking Society* 21, 308–11

1986
'A Conservation Devoutly to Be Wish'd', *Letter of the Corpus Association* 65, 28–33
With Bengt Odenstedt, 'The Runic Inscription', in Christopher Scull, 'A Sixth-Century Grave Containing a Balance and Weights from Watchfield, Oxfordshire, England', *Germania* 64, 123–6
Review of D.M. Wilson, *The Bayeux Tapestry* (London, 1985), *Antiquity* 60, 156–7

1987
Runes, Reading the Past (London: British Museum)
'A Most Vile People': Early English Historians on the Vikings, Dorothea Coke Memorial Lecture 1986 (London)
* 'New Runic Finds in England', *Runor och runinskrifter: föredrag vid Riksantikvarieämbetets och Vitterhetsakademiens symposium 8–11 september 1985* (Stockholm), pp. 185–97

'Scandinavian Runes in the British Isles', *Popular Archaeology* 8.6, 35–9
* 'A Sixteenth-Century Runic Manuscript', *Studies in Honour of René Derolez*, ed. A.M. Simon-Vandenbergen (Gent), pp. 384–90
'Yet Another Note on Alfred's *æstel*', *Leeds Studies in English* n.s. 18, 9–18
Review of Erik Moltke, *Runes and Their Origin*, trans. Peter G. Foote (Copenhagen, 1985), *Antiquity* 61, 149–50

1988
'Bewcastle' and 'Urswick', in Richard N. Bailey and Rosemary Cramp, *Corpus of Anglo-Saxon Stone Sculpture, II: Cumberland, Westmorland and Lancashire North-of-the-Sands* (Oxford and New York), pp. 61–5 and 172–3
'A Little Liberal, Or Else a Little Conservator?', *Old English Newsletter* 22.1, 20–8

1989
* 'Roman and Runic on St Cuthbert's Coffin', *St Cuthbert, His Cult and His Community*, ed. Gerald Bonner *et al.* (Woodbridge and Wolfeboro, NH), pp. 257–65

1990
Norse Myths, The Legendary Past (London: British Museum)
* 'Dating Old English Inscriptions: the Limits of Inference', *Papers from the 5th International Conference on English Historical Linguistics*, ed. Sylvia Adamson *et al.*, Current Issues in Linguistic Theory 65 (Amsterdam and Philadelphia), pp. 357–77

1991
Martin Bucer in Cambridge: an Exhibition in the Parker Library (Cambridge: Corpus Christi College)
'Anglo-Saxon Runic Studies: The Way Ahead?', *Old English Runes and Their Continental Background*, ed. Alfred Bammesberger, Anglistische Forschungen 217 (Heidelberg), pp. 15–39
'Audits and Replacements in the Parker Library: 1590–1650', *Transactions of the Cambridge Bibliographical Society* 10 (1991), 17–39
'A New Runic Find from Cumbria, England', *Nytt om Runer* 5 (1991 for 1990), 13
'New Runic Fragment from the Isle of Man', *Nytt om Runer* 6, 6
'The Title of the Old English *Apollonius of Tyre*', *American Notes and Queries* n.s. 4, 171–2
Notes on Runic Inscriptions, in James T. Lang, *Corpus of Anglo-Saxon Stone Sculpture, III: York and Eastern Yorkshire* (Oxford), *passim*

1992
'Celtic and Norse on the Manx Rune-stones', *Medialität und mittelalterliche insulare Literatur*, ed. Hildegard L.C. Tristram, ScriptOralia 43 (Tübingen), pp. 131–47
'The Sixteenth-Century Reception of Alfred the Great's Letter to His Bishops', *Anglia* 110, 36–64
'Comment on "The Runic Inscription by Bengt Odenstedt" ' in Christopher Scull, 'Excavation and Survey at Watchfield, Oxfordshire, 1983–92', *Archaeological Journal* 149, 249–51

1993

Matthew Parker and His Books, Sandars Lectures 1990 (Kalamazoo: Medieval Institute Publications; Cambridge: Research Group of Manuscript Evidence)

'On the Feasibility of a Corpus of Old English Glosses: the View from the Library', *Anglo-Saxon Glossography. Papers Read at the International Conference Held in . . . Brussels, 8 and 9 September 1986*, ed. R. Derolez (Brussels, 1992 [1993]), pp. 77–95

'Runes and Rune-like Marks', in A.G. Kinsley, *Broughton Lodge: Excavations on the Romano-British Settlement and Anglo-Saxon Cemetery at Broughton Lodge, Willoughby-on-the-Wolds, Nottinghamshire 1964–8*, Nottingham Archaeological Monographs 3 (Nottingham), p. 65

'Runes in Two Anglo-Saxon Manuscripts', *Nytt om Runer* 8, 15–19

'Scandinavian Society, 800–1200: the Contribution of Runic Studies', *Viking Revaluations. Viking Society Centenary Symposium 14–15 May 1992*, ed. Anthony Faulkes and Richard Perkins (London), pp. 145–59

Review of Ian Wood and Niels Lund, eds, *People and Places in Northern Europe 500–1600. Essays in Honour of Peter Hayes Sawyer* (Woodbridge, 1991), *Saga-Book of the Viking Society* 23, 529–35

1994

'English Runes Imported into the Continent', *Runische Schriftkultur in kontinental-skandinavischer und -angelsächsischer Wechselbeziehung* (Berlin and New York), ed. Klaus Düwel, pp. 176–94

'The Parker Library and its Collections Today', *Conservation and Preservation in Small Libraries*, ed. Nicholas Hadgraft and Katherine Swift (Cambridge), pp. 8–13

'The Conservator and the Scholar', *ibid.*, pp. 15–19

'Runes in East Anglia', *Proceedings of the Third International Symposium on Runes and Runic Inscriptions*, ed. James E. Knirk, Runrön 9 (Uppsala), pp. 105–17